DUE DATE

AUG 3 0			
JAN 3 0 1996			
10-28-15			
11-4-15			

Books by Edith Schaeffer

Commonsense Christian Living
Lifelines
The Tapestry
L'Abri
Hidden Art
Christianity Is Jewish
What Is a Family?
A Way of Seeing
Affliction
Everybody Can Know (with Francis Schaeffer)

Books by Francis Schaeffer

The Great Evangelical Disaster
A Christian Manifesto
The God Who Is There
Escape from Reason
He Is There and He Is Not Silent
Death in the City
Pollution and the Death of Man
The Church at the End of the 20th Century
The Mark of the Christian
The Church before the Watching World
True Spirituality
Basic Bible Studies
Genesis in Space and Time
The New Super-Spirituality
Back to Freedom and Dignity
Art and the Bible
No Little People
Two Contents, Two Realities
Joshua and the Flow of Biblical History
No Final Conflict
How Should We Then Live?
Whatever Happened to the Human Race? (with C. Everett Koop, M.D.)
Everybody Can Know (with Edith Schaeffer)

EDITH SCHAEFFER

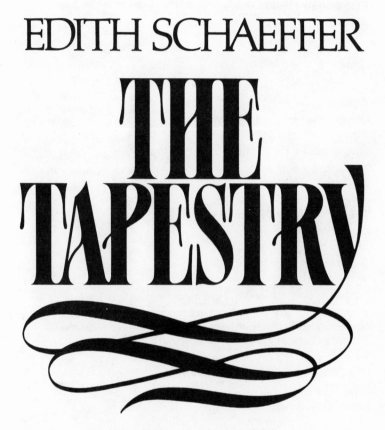

THE TAPESTRY

The Life and Times
of Francis and
Edith Schaeffer

SPECIAL MEMORIAL EDITION

WORD BOOKS
PUBLISHER
WACO, TEXAS

A DIVISION OF
WORD, INCORPORATED

To all the threads in The Tapestry who have been so amazingly woven into a pattern in history, affecting each other's existence in the flow of history. This book is dedicated to the threads whose names are mentioned but also to many "in the wings." Particularly it is dedicated to some of the "twigs" who are on our branch of the larger family tree:

John and Priscilla Sandri	Ranald and Susan Macaulay
Lisby	Margaret
Becky and Rodman	Kirsty
Giandy	Fiona
	Ranald John
Udo and Debby Middelmann	Franky and Genie Schaeffer
Natasha	Jessica
Samantha	Francis VI
Naomi	John Lewis
Hannah	

And lastly to any future "twigs"!

First printing, October 1981
First printing, Special Memorial Edition, November 1984

THE TAPESTRY: THE LIFE AND TIMES OF FRANCIS AND EDITH SCHAEFFER.
Copyright © 1981, 1984 by Edith Schaeffer.
Printed in the United States of America

Library of Congress catalog card number: 81–51009
ISBN 0–8499–0284–3 (hardback)

Library of Congress Cataloging in Publication Data

Schaeffer, Edith.
  The tapestry.

  1. Schaeffer, Francis A. (Francis August)
2. Schaeffer, Edith. 3. Christian biography.
I. Title.
BR1725.S355S3 1984   267'.13'0922[B]   84–22229
ISBN 0–8499–3016–2 (pbk.)

All Scripture quotations unless otherwise identified are from the *The Holy Bible, New International Version*, copyright © 1978 by New York International Bible Society. Used by permission of Zondervan Bible Publishers.

Grateful acknowledgment is made to *The Hampden-Sydney Record*, Hampden-Sydney College, Virginia, for the use of the quotation on page 119.

CONTENTS

A NOTE FROM THE PUBLISHER

The Christian community has been saddened by the loss of the physical presence of Dr. Francis A. Schaeffer. At the same time it is sustained and gladdened in knowing that he has gone to the place prepared for him by his Lord. All who knew him, heard him, read or saw him have been blessed by the gifts he shared so generously, even almost to his last breath. We owe a tremendous debt to this Christian disciple who so truly exemplified what it means to know that God is here with us and that He responds to us in every facet of our lives if we acknowledge His Truth.

We at Word Books are honored to have been chosen to publish *The Tapestry,* the Gold Medallion Award-winning book in which Dr. Schaeffer's beloved wife, Edith, has so candidly, vividly, and meaningfully written of his life and times—and of hers also, as they are inextricably interwoven. In gratitude we offer this Memorial Edition. It is our hope that all who read this intimate record of how Francis Schaeffer became who he was, touching and giving the impetus that has changed so many lives, will be newly enriched or reinspired.

November 1984

ERNEST E. OWEN
Vice President/Editorial Director
WORD BOOKS, Publisher

FOREWORD TO THE
SPECIAL MEMORIAL EDITION

Dear Reader:

It seems appropriate that I am sitting by a window looking out at Lac Leman through a variety of trees, to watch the gulls swooping around a sailboat as the morning lake boat approaches from Geneva. I wrote this book close to this place, as you will find when you begin the first chapter. I think it is no accident that my *eyes* can be filled with the same beauty of mountains, sky, lake, and trees while my *mind* is filled with memories of living through the years, and especially the months of recording something of those years. This foreword—or as I think of it, this short talk with you—could not be the same if written elsewhere. Fran and I spent half of our lives living and working in Switzerland. That is a precise amount!—not carelessly speaking. Now that Fran's life on earth is finished and his dates will always be carved on stone as 1912–1984, it can also be remembered that we lived together in Switzerland from 1948 to 1984. He was seventy-two years old when he died, and he lived in Switzerland thirty-six years. You see why it is so appropriate that I am in Switzerland as I write this to you.

My habit of writing notes of thanks or requests to the Lord as I pray and then fastening them around the margins of my Bible, means that I have another precise amount of time to be

7

keenly aware of. One of those notes tells me that it was exactly three years ago that I finished this book, on the very day the Schaeffer Family Reunion of 1981 was beginning. In fact, I had to miss the first lunch together with all the family because I was typing away, literally finishing the last chapter. That first night of our reunion, our granddaughter Becky wore her wedding dress, and Rodman the suit in which he married her; the wedding flowers were duplicated, and we sat and listened to Av's wedding sermon. (As you read the book you will find out why Fran chose the word *Av*, Hebrew for "father," rather than "grandfather," as his name for the grandchildren to call him.) After the wedding sermon, I read chapter 6 of the manuscript to the whole family so that they would hear at least a part of *The Tapestry*, privately read to them, as from me.

Yes, that was three years ago . . . and as I write this, we have just had our Family Reunion for 1984, the first one without our dear husband, father, grandfather. Av is the first one of this family of three generations to be waiting for the reunion in heaven. So . . . he was not here to meet granddaughter Margaret Macaulay's husband, Doug Curry, nor to look at their wedding pictures, eat their cake, and look at pictures of Nepal where they expect to be going as missionaries. Perhaps those in heaven surround us as witnesses, in some way. It will be interesting to find that out some day. Also, the next generation is on the way, as Becky and Rodman, whose wedding was three years ago, will be having our first great-grandchild just before Christmas. One day "the root and offspring of David, the bright and morning star," will return, and the resurrection will take place, and perfection will be known to us. Meantime, the generations will go on, as a continuity with the past.

I will be always grateful to Franky, our son, for pushing me to write this biography, and to Fran for agreeing that it must be written during a time when we could talk together day after day. Fran, as you will find I have told you in the book, was a "magpie" or "squirrel," saving endless papers and documents in banana boxes under the eaves of the attic. As I prepared to begin writing, he pulled out boxes of stuff and arranged things into years, with signs on top of piles, and a rock on each to keep it from scattering. We talked together as to what would be important to the book. Then, in spite of putting things aside, so *much* had to be condensed . . . yet the "flavor" of the weeks, months, and years was kept.

You see, Fran made an agreement . . . which was also a request. "Edith, any time you finish a chapter, I want to lie down with a cup of tea and have you read it to me from beginning to end, undisturbed!" That agreement was *kept*, precisely! No matter what time of the day or night I finished a chapter, he would lie down on the chaise longue, and I'd fix tea and toast, sit at his feet (in a chair with my feet up against his), and read. I love to read aloud, so it was no chore. I was always anxious to know his reaction, or response. Those times of day differed. For instance, once it was four o'clock in the morning when the last paragraph of a chapter was finished. Fran was awake because this was during the yearly Members' Meeting of L'Abri, and the meeting had lasted until after three. So . . . I read! "Are you sure, dear? Don't you want to wait?" "No, *now!* Tomorrow morning we have to go on with the Members' Meeting business, and you have to start the next chapter of the book . . . so, now."

Time is unrepeatable! The precious moments of life cannot be put off. I will always treasure the reading of those chapters to him. There was nothing he wanted changed. He wept over so many parts of the book. He could scarcely speak after I read the chapter about his own salvation—his walking down German-town Avenue in Philadelphia on that hot August day and wandering into the tent, his working for RCA and almost going on to be a labor agitator. As he wept, he said, "Oh, Edith, you have given me a reliving of my life. This is such a gift. I am able to relive our lives so *vividly*. I don't know how you have done it, but you have caught it perfectly—my mother and dad, college days, those Bible schools and camps, our churches in St. Louis, Grove City, and Chester. It is all there . . . and I am living it all over again. Thank you!"

It was a reliving for me, too, as I wrote. I was being given a new perspective, a perspective of history, of fitting into a stream of history with a precise place and a need to fulfill my own bit. Each of us has a period of time, and that time is not endless. The relay of truth from one generation to another, from one's sharpness of perception that is meant to be passed on as a brightly burning torch to another, is not to be carelessly handled for selfish reasons. How often Satan tempts us, each of us, to put self first instead of the Lord and His truth, or to put self first, instead of each other first, or children and other family members first (there are degrees of first—God is to be first of all). The selfishness of Cain led multiple generations away from truth. It is not exaggerated, but true, that not only could I not have written this book without Fran being alive to talk things over with, and then to have the joy of reading to—but that the reliving I did in writing gave me a fresh perspective. It was done *in* time.

The book has been "out" now long enough for me to have received many, many letters from an amazing cross section of men and women who have told me how the fresh perspective they have received, the understanding they have been given, in reading, has changed the direction of their lives. One man, a musician and conductor, said it had meant more to him than any other book he had ever read . . . and had given him courage to go forward in a fresh music project that is developing excellence.

My strong feeling is that this book could *not* have been written "later" . . . that this book as it is could *only* have been written when it was, three years before Fran's death, as a special review of his own life, which he could enjoy and for which he could give thanks to God. Really, it is a book that was *for* him, not just about him . . . and it is therefore a very special sharing of something that was written as a personal and honest account of life.

Sincerely,

Edith Schaeffer

A THANK YOU NOTE

Sometimes private thank-yous should be made public to widely acknowledge special help that has been noticed and truly appreciated. First I want to thank God for the reality of His help given in a diversity of ways in the midst of the often overwhelming task of completing this work. Without the literal response to prayer for His strength to be given time after time in my weakness, I couldn't have done it. I thank God, but also thank all who so faithfully prayed for me, day after day, believing that prayer brings real response and changes a portion of history, and believing that as they prayed something would actually take place in the content of the book, as well as in my physical strength to keep on. The many who prayed included L'Abri Workers, and our children, as well as Fran, who so often stopped to pray with me, as well as for me. It's a startling demonstration of the centrality of God's existence that when one says "thank you" to Him, immediately that thanks is so naturally woven together with a thank-you to human friends who have called on Him for help.

Thank you, Elsa, for carefully searching through father's things and sending me our parents' and grandparents' precious old documents. For encouragement so needed time after time, thank you, Prisca and John, Sue and Ran, Debby and Udo, Franky and Genie. Encouragement is a terrific antidote for discouragement, so thank you for cheering from the sidelines. Thank you, Gail Ingram, for sorting out the banana boxes into the ten-year periods in preface to Fran's sorting. Thank you, Greg Grooms, for responding to sudden calls for researching historic facts stored in your encyclopedic memory, and for double-checking in books I didn't have—at many odd moments! Thank you, Mike Sugimoto, for your long hours of caring for the telephone, the front-door arrivals, the meals and teas to be prepared and served to Fran and me, and to the various people Fran talked with, throughout the weeks of writing. Without Mike's taking my place in soup-making, noodle-making, ice-cream-making and a great variety of cooking and serving, it wouldn't have been possible for me to stay in a little sunroom-office at the typewriter for fifteen to eighteen hours a day, day after day, shut away from life, in order to write about life. Thank you to everyone who did things I would otherwise have been doing in L'Abri too, from caring for people to going to Members' Meetings, and leading days of prayer. Thank you for being understanding when I couldn't see you fellow Workers, and for not making me feel guilty!

With love to all you threads,
From another thread,

WHAT IS *THE TAPESTRY* SUPPOSED TO MEAN?

How can anyone else know really what happened in your lives and work, when they didn't live through it? Why don't you write a biography while you are both living and can talk things over, as well as search all through the collection of letters and papers you've saved?" This came from our children, in one context or another, at one time or another, and was constantly shoved aside with, "I don't want to write a biography. The thing that fascinates me really is the weaving of lives together, the fabulous way God works in history, while at the same time people's choices cause changes in history, for good or bad." As time went on and thoughts whirled around in my mind or became more concrete in discussion, an idea emerged: "Why not write a book that weaves something of history together with glimpses of people's lives and the glimpses of God's plan, recognized in often short flashes of understanding, along with glimpses of crucial choices made which changed the direction of life for one—then for thousands of other people affected by that one?"

The Tapestry seemed a concise title for such a book—the idea being that each of our lives is a thread. You are a thread, and I am a thread. As we affect each other's ideas, physical beings, spiritual understanding, or material possessions, or as we influence each other's attitudes—creativity, courage, determination to keep on, moods, priorities, understanding spiritually, intellectually, emotionally—we are at the same time affecting history. History is different because you have lived, and because I have lived. We have each caused ripples that will never end, and we continue to cause ripples. In the picture brought to our minds by *The Tapestry*, we are being woven together, threads that are important to a pattern, the pattern of the history of our lifetimes, but also the pattern we affect in the future of history.

Do I think of each thread as having a predetermined rigid place in a fatalistic view of history? Absolutely not. The title *The Tapestry*, and the thought of threads woven into that Tapestry, are not meant to convey any thought of solving the problem of how God has made us as human beings in His image, to have true, valid choice affecting creativity, love, communication, ideas, which in turn have an impact or influence on each other, and on history. As soon as we think we have a pat answer, or can do away with the distance between the parallel lines of God being truly God, and human beings having true choice, we then have done away with the distance between finiteness and infiniteness.

There is a huge gap—a gap that must always remain—between being finite, and being infinite. Only God is infinite! There is a mystery that remains. Our deep awe and worship continue.

The title *The Tapestry* applies to the togetherness of many lives woven together affecting each other. "God has no chance behind Him" is a statement my husband often makes. Of course we are to realize God has a plan. The Bible frequently tells us of the fact that God will guide us, not just temporarily in a tough spot, but "to the end." God is our "counselor," "guide," as well as "father" and "friend." As we look back at what we can see of *The Tapestry* behind us, we thrill over some of the wonder of how God has woven people together, woven their lives together, woven their talents together, and of how He has brought them into contact to be woven side by side in a pattern that has continuity with other parts of the pattern!

No illustration of any kind is all-inclusive of the total reality being illustrated. *The Tapestry* speaks immediately of a Designer, an Artist, a Weaver, and of threads being held in his or her hands. We know very well from Adam and Eve and The Fall, that their individual choice brought about the abnormal events that are still happening as a result. Their effect on history was pretty devastating. So the *threads* need to *ask* The Designer, The Weaver, The Artist, time after time to be used in the pattern where He would have them be. It is not automatic. Mystery? Yes, a mystery that is without solution for the finite mind but completely understood by our Infinite God.

This book will not only follow the immediate families whose threads are being traced and looked at under a microscope, but will bring into your imagination a far wider thing of parallel history, parallel threads having an effect at the same period of time, and often crossing the same geographic space. In a way, the book has no beginning and no ending because it is only a tiny bit out of the middle of history, and none of us have yet seen the full picture, not even in "outline form."

There are many many many people, threads, who have come in and out of our personal lives and in and out of L'Abri who have not been able to be included. If you are one of the threads whose place was not pointed out as you were woven in with us, please forgive me for not being able to get you in. It has not been without sorrow! A list of names and a list of events would make dull reading and would remove the atmosphere of wonder concerning all that God has let us see of His creativity. It would be like reading the index of a zoology or botany book rather than a description of nature's wonders.

It has been an "impossible" task to go back through all the banana boxes full of papers and letters, memorandums and diaries and to select what to include. It has been an emotional experience to live again various parts of our own lives, and to try to live with our ancestors, and with other people included in the story. As I have read the whole book to Fran, and as he has helped with the sorting of all the papers, he too has relived the years and shared the emotions. At times during this writing we felt as if we were looking through the wrong end of a telescope and seeing a miniature of the whole picture, *The Tapestry,* or the portion of it that had been real to us. We felt that suddenly we saw it all in a new way as we saw more of what God had done, and of the wonder of it fitting into history. When I put a period at the end, it seemed almost like folding up our lives together, to put it all in a box again, along with the papers going back into the banana boxes!!

One thing is certain out of it all, one thing is valuable in having put together what I have seen take shape in the writing, and that is the exciting greatness and kindness and creative imagination of our marvelous God, Whom we now know only slightly, and need an eternity to appreciate.

THE MYSTERY OF BEING 1

Another summer has become a part of the past. Autumn's slowly changing leaves and golden sun-warmed chrysanthemums have been rudely blotted out by a covering of snow, an unwelcome winter storm having arrived before it was expected. On whitecap-ruffled Lac Léman (Lake Geneva), duck families are bobbing bravely along, close to the walls of Castle Chillon, with dignified swans gliding behind them. Standing on shore near the castle, I find myself wondering, "How many generations of ducks and swans have given life and beauty to this lake scene? . . . How far back do their ancestors go? . . . and when did they first arrive on this lake?" Scarcely aware of the wind's buffeting, I turn my thoughts to the parade of human beings whose lives centered in Castle Chillon through the ages.

How temporary and insignificant our short lifetimes seem as I think of the centuries of people who have been born, married, imprisoned or lived princely lives there. If the castle walls could communicate, what fascinating tales they could tell of the stream of inhabitants—their individual hopes and fears, their ambitions and schemes, their noble desires and the wicked plots in which many were involved. Tourists from Japan or Germany, Australia or America visit this castle daily. To think that in 1150 it was being taken over by the dynasty of Savoy rather boggles the mind. This castle has been an arsenal, as well as a place where taxes were paid in grain, hay, wine, and fish, and where the defense of the countryside was carried out. Remembering all that impresses me with the impossibility of recounting the complete history of one such piece of ground on the earth's surface, let alone of tracing the history of the human beings brought together in such "impossible" ways from so many geographical spots— human beings whose very "being" is dependent on so many other people's lives and choices.

I interrupt my reverie to walk to the dock and board a lake boat with my husband. As we sway and pitch in the storm, I resume my look backwards in time, blotting out the highway, the railroad, the paved roads, and the apartment houses, homes, and buildings of Veytaux and Montreux. "Seeing" the rounded promontory of rockbased land jutting out into the lake, providing a place between the lake and the sharp rise of dark mountains to hold off marching armies, I imagine enemies attacking the castle from a fleet of boats on the lake, or from the narrow lake road, their assaults thwarted by arrows flying from the holes built in the castle walls.

What vivid parallels we can draw from history to show how things that stand out as "central" to us, went unnoticed by the people who were living the events! Visitors to Castle Chillon— whether you, or our family during our reunions nearby—always spend time walking around the pillar where François Bonivard was chained by the Duke of Savoy from 1530 to 1536. What impression did Calvin, twenty-one years old in 1530, have of Castle Chillon? Do we think of how close Geneva is to Castle Chillon, and that Calvin was writing his Institutes there and Erasmus was dying as the prisoner Bonivard spent his sixth awful fettered year? In that same period Luther was waging his courageous war for truth in Germany. With Vienna under the shadow of a Turkish assault, he was writing the hymn we sing so lustily . . . "A mighty fortress is our God."* Michelangelo was also alive, painting and sculpting the works we marvel over. But how many of his contemporaries were really conscious of what fantastic fruits his incessant labors were producing? Right in the nearby

---

* As Jeremy Jackson says on page 135 of *No Other Foundation*, "The enemies against whom Luther invokes God's protection are more Moslem than Roman."

church at Aigle, Guillaume Farel, whose dates parallel the prisoner's, was preaching the truth of salvation by faith in Christ without works. He preached the same message in the eleventh-century church in Ollon where our four children (and now one of our grandchildren) have all had their weddings. When Farel traveled to Geneva, by foot or horseback, he had to pass Castle Chillon, and look at it with *some* thoughts in his head. We know that in 1536 he was in the midst of persuading Calvin to stay in Geneva rather than to go back to Strasbourg. In March of the same year, two big boats and a few other vessels under the Bernese, aided by Geneva, attacked and took over Castle Chillon, the Bernese bear taking the place of the arms of the House of Savoy on the facades. I wonder when Farel first noticed the Bernese bear on the castle?

A parade of years, a parade of people . . . passing by, living in, being imprisoned in, being fought in, being entertained in Castle Chillon. Can we *feel* the impossibility of thinking of these people, of imagining their feelings, with true understanding? Chillon saw many trials for witchcraft in the seventeenth century, as well as other trials during the time it was a court of justice. It became a prison again in the eighteenth century. On August 31, 1792, Fernand-Antoine Rosset and Georges Albert Muller de la Mothe, two Vaudois accused of taking part in a revolutionary banquet of the "Jordiles," were condemned to imprisonment in Chillon. Their sailboat left Ouchy the same day; they arrived at the castle the next morning and remained there until January of the following year. . . . But if *you* have taken a lake boat from Ouchy at Lausanne to Castle Chillon you have had a ride of about an hour and twenty minutes, after which you have strolled happily around the castle watching the ducks, or taking pictures!

The prisoner Rosset described, in his memoirs, the cell in which he was confined: "This cell was number 12. It was vaulted. When they had closed the three doors, I figured out that it was 12 feet long and 8 feet broad. The furniture consisted of a bed and a wooden chair. The daylight could hardly penetrate and in order to read I had to climb on my chair and raise myself up to the grill through which dim rays reached me. . . ."

Did the people in Chillon know about what was taking place in Germany, one wonders? Johann Sebastian Bach (1685–1750) had lived, written his music (which is as alive today as it has ever been), and died before the last prisoners spent their sentences in Chillon. In the twentieth century, Bach's music is played during music festivals in a romantic great hall in the castle, and some of our own grandchildren had the experience of hearing it one very special moonlit night. But . . . how many people living in Germany at the time Bach was composing heard the sheer wonder of that gorgeous music with their ears, or felt it flow through their whole beings? Only those of Leipzig's St. Thomas Lutheran Church, which had a new composition of his every Sunday of the year as an expected part of their worship service, and very few others. Were they filled with awe and thankfulness for being the ones to worship God with such fabulous waterfalls of praise splashing over them? Many of us would like to be able to slip back through the years and sit in a pew in that Lutheran church to listen to Bach play week after week. Would we have been conscious of what really was taking place in that service? How astonished Bach himself would have been to know how widely appreciated his music would be one day. During his own lifetime only a few compositions were ever published. Faithfully he continued what he was doing, believing God was sufficient audience.

Two really opposite things astonish me at the same time: First is the fact that people living at the same period of history—working, agonizing, discovering, creating, slogging on in mundane work, suffering, pressing on toward defined goals or muddling in confusion—have *not* discovered each other, whether across the street, in another end of the same city, or across the borders of countries. How unlikely it is that John Bunyan would have sung his hymn knowing that the prisoner in Chillon was being a faithful pilgrim when he, Bunyan was eight years old!

> He who would valiant be
> 'Gainst all disaster,
> Let him in constancy
>   Follow the Master.
> There's no discouragement
> Shall make him once relent
> His first avowed intent
>   To be a pilgrim.
>   After John Bunyan (1628–88)

Yet—there is also the fact that people who were limited in the number of people they could communicate with in their lifetime, or whom they could come to know, were, without then realizing it, to be a priceless help to generations to come. What encouragement has come to each of us—to Fran and me—as well as to myriad others, through the sheer courage, the comfort, the inspiration and determination to carry on, that is given by the lives of people "unknown" to their contemporaries, yet closer to us than some of our neighbors! What a surprising phenomenon this is!

To write about one person at any point in history, no matter how interesting that one person is to you, and to attempt to give some true picture of that personality or life, without giving a setting of the whole family and the people involved with him or her, would be like taking a tiny hook and trying to pick out one strand of yarn from the middle of a gigantic tapestry. One could perhaps unravel that thread from the others for a bit of time before it would break, but what would one have? A limp thread to place under a magnifying glass.

In my picture, all history is The Tapestry. Does God have a plan? I believe He has. He Himself has told us in His careful Word that there is that which spoiled His original creation, and that we have to wait until a final victory takes place to discover what perfection is like. However, although a battle continues, and the consequences of "the Fall" affect each of our lives, and the world's history, yet God has not removed Himself from the present portion of that battle. God is at work in history. Kings rise and fall. Dictators come and go . . . and end up hung upside down from lamp posts. In *How Should We Then Live?* Francis Schaeffer says, "There is a flow to history and to culture." He goes on to speak in that book of the wellspring that is in the thoughts of people. People matter; people's ideas and actions matter. The Tapestry of History is made up of people. The Tapestry is not a pattern predetermined by God, or by the Devil. The Tapestry is woven, blended, filled with events, ideas, devastating wars, catastrophic destruction, positive rebuilding, creative works and practical inventions. History is going somewhere—The Tapestry will have a moment of being completed and taken off the loom altogether!

Is *The Tapestry*, this book, going to be an attempt to sketch all history? No, a million times no. Nor will it be an attempt to take a piece of geography, or a piece of time, and to give a complete picture of that. It tries, however, to put a small magnifying glass on one tiny, minuscule bit of The Tapestry to see something of the way threads of lives are woven together, affecting each other and bringing forth creativity or events which otherwise might not have taken place.

Can we unravel the mystery of our being, of our place in the Tapestry? I think not. The very existence of each one of us involves the powerful reality of God's sovereignty. And at the same time the very existence of each one of us involves the reality of an amazing number of choices made by an uncountable number of people in the centuries preceding our birth . . . your birth, my birth. God can say, "I knew you before the foundation of the world," and we can be comforted. We cannot demand to be given total understanding of the fact that choice is involved in the birth of each human being. "Trust" is a word that implies a scope of having trust in a person without knowing all the details of the situation in which the trust is needed. Really to exhibit confidence in a person, we need to have situations following situations in which there is an element of the unknown. Believing without seeing, for which we are to be blessed, is not only believing in the existence of God, in His love and compassion, and in the truth of His promises, but it is actively and repeatedly showing confidence and trust in calling upon Him in our times of need, and expecting something to be different because we called. To be able to dissect and analyze and make a mathematical formula of what happens when we call for God's help is *not* what we are promised. God is God, and He remains God. We are human beings and we remain human beings. We can have a relationship with, be children of, be friends of, come to know in a very real way the living God, Creator of the Universe, but our relationship, our friendship, our communication with Him does not lift us out of the finite and make us a little bit infinite. A mystery of being remains. The mystery of existence remains. The mystery of life and death remains.

This book is not an attempt to clear up the mysteries, any more than it is to sketch all history. Rather, in this "detail" of the larger work we may glimpse some of the weaving of people, time, and space; of choices and God's intervention; of hard work and answers to prayer; of mistakes and of amazing supplies of needs; of sickness and of health; of better and of worse! It also lets us see how God has taken weak things to "confound the mighty," of how He can use even a stick of wood put into His hands. But most of all it attempts to show that there is simply no human explanation for what we ourselves have observed and lived through in the last thirty-two years of our lives since the beginning of L'Abri. Nor, for that matter, is there one for what has happened to bring any of us into existence at our moment of history. The fact that Johann Sebastian Bach and John Bunyan have had more effect on *us* than they did on their contemporaries is all a part of the kind of understanding that may come from looking at one small bit of The Tapestry and watching the threads form into design.

* * *

When Franz August Schaeffer (Fran's grandfather) was born in Berlin, the last prisoners in Castle Chillon were experiencing better conditions than their predecessors, and Bach's grandson Wilhelm Friedrich Ernst Bach was composing and performing his music right there in Berlin! Did either of these facts matter to Franz August Schaeffer? We can't know, but it seems unlikely, although he was Lutheran and probably attended church in Berlin.

Family tradition has it that Franz August Schaeffer was at least "the second," that is, he was named for his father. We know that he married Carolina Wilhelmina Muller from the Black Forest region. How did he meet her? We can only imagine the scene. (Do you know the gentle rolling hills, the dark pine forest regions, the beautiful villages that seem to "grow" naturally in their setting of fields in the Black Forest area?) Perhaps when he was young he had come to work on a farm or in a blacksmith's shop with the thought of settling there. Whether he took Carolina back to Berlin and found work in factories in the growing Industrial Revolution or whether he became discouraged with the famine which came after the wars, we again can only imagine. Wherever his wife and little girl were at the time, young Franz August went off to fight in the Franco-Prussian War. Soon after that, in 1869, he turned his back on the possibility of fighting again and looked with whatever dreams and hopes filled his mind and emotions to a different kind of life in the new country—America—with all the promises it held out in his imagination. History tells us that steamboats were plying the Atlantic by the mid-1800s, and the little Schaeffer family may very well have crossed in one of the new steamers. After tossing in those ocean waves, how glad they must have been to get on solid ground, even if their crossing took less time than the Mayflower's sixty-six days! Emigrating from Germany to Germantown, Philadelphia, Franz August Schaeffer and his family had only the Iron Cross award to remind them of his honorable discharge from the army.

The new opportunities and door to a new world didn't last long for this "Grandfather Schaeffer"; in fact, he never lived to see his family grow up, let alone to know about a grandson. On November 28, 1879, Franz August Schaeffer was killed in an accident as he was working on the railroad in Philadelphia, leaving a little boy, Francis August Schaeffer III, just three years old.

When this child was being put into his mother's arms in a house in Germantown one mid-June day, with the maple trees in full leaf and the wisteria in bloom, another baby boy, born on a blustery day in March, was in his cradle in Pittsburgh, being hovered over by a bevy of admiring sisters. In two towns three hundred or so miles apart, two baby boys born three months or so apart were one day to be grandfathers of the same children! The utter mystery of being causes us to be in awe at our own existence—yours and mine—as we consider the enormity of possibilities that would have prevented our existence, and the extreme unlikelihood of any of our parents ever meeting each other in the first place.

George Hugh Seville, my father, will be introduced more completely later on. But added to the fact that he was born just three months before Fran's father, Francis August Schaeffer III, geographically so close, and the fact that Franz August Schaeffer II could so easily have been killed in the Franco-Prussian war (and was indeed killed so early in his son's life), is the fact that my father was the seventh child of his mother, born when she was forty. What an amazing list of factors that could have prevented the next generation from ever having come into existence!

What I am pointing out is not unique to us in our family story, nor unique to our being in existence. It is simply a portion of the force which should strike us all when we put a magnifying glass on the circumstances surrounding our conception and birth. How fantastic that the forty-six chromosomes which are you, or me, or each one I'll be telling about, ever got together, ever survived nine months of life before birth, ever survived life after birth. How amazing! What a thrill that the sovereign God exists and knows the answers about our existence, which we can leave in His wise possession without fretting about it. And how exciting to know that does not conflict with the choice our parents made, upon which our existence depends.

The mystery of being, or existence, is paralleled by the mystery of the diversity among human beings—the diversity within any one family, as well as the diversity of people across all history and all portions of the earth's geography. Add the diversity of environment and opportunity to the diversity of talents and energy, mix these with the place choice has and "the battle" has, and you have enough unknowns—known only to God—to take a lifetime of trying to figure out the "whys" of the difference between one life and another. "What would so and so [or I] have been like if only this factor or that factor had been different?"

For little fatherless Francis August Schaeffer scuffing his toes in the dirt roads as he walked in the woods by the mill stream, we can know—though he couldn't—that the lives of a lot of people were going to be affected by his courage just to keep on living and pursuing the hard course of work that was ahead of him—so often seemingly insignificant drudgery.

Not far from where the Schaeffer family lived, was a place called Fisher's Hollow. The fast-flowing Wingohocking Creek ran through this hollow, and along its banks a half dozen thriving mills had grown up during the early 1800s. In 1857, before the Schaeffers had left Germany, and twenty years before Frank was born, a Sunday School building was finished on Fisher's Lane (later called Lindley Avenue). That Sunday School building was to turn into a public primary school where Frank (as *this* Francis was called) was to have his short years of learning to read and

write and do arithmetic. The sound of the rushing stream and
of millwheels turning probably came in the open windows of
that little school and filled the children's minds with thoughts
of throwing sticks and stones into the water as soon as school
would be out. Memories of playing near that Wingohocking Creek
still brought a flicker of a mischievous smile to Frank Schaeffer's
lips years later when, as he recovered from his first stroke, he
was able to be driven many times to see that area. Although
the creek had long since dried up and dirt roads had been covered
with paving, the memories were alive—a small package of memories, tied up in his mind with a special ribbon. You see, the school
days were a precious, short-lived period.

Sometime before he was eleven years old, the home situation
had become insurmountably difficult for Frank's mother. She was
now married to her deceased husband's brother, but he was not
providing enough to care for the basic needs of daily life, and
young Frank had to join the ranks of the many child laborers
in that time of the Industrial Revolution. In one of the coal-sorting
buildings, Frank, along with many other children, bent over moving belts of coal, culling unwanted stones, putting pieces into
size categories, all by hand—human drudgery in preface to mecha-
nization yet to come.

What a childhood. No tender moments of being read to before
a fireplace. No days of running free in the woods, or playing
games or competing in sports. Yet here was an amazing sense
of responsibility—one felt in talking to Frank in later years—
that had produced not bitterness, but a thankfulness for having
done his best to provide for the needs of his mother. A perfect
person? No, far from it. But here was a lad who had fiercely
determined to fulfill his place as the oldest son of a mother who
needed him to work. Small wonder that when he spoke of going
to the Lutheran church as a boy, he had little feeling of its being
anything he could share in: "They were all rich kids, and the
pastor didn't know what work was; he just stood up there and
talked." By comparison most people in the parish lived in a world
of ease, totally ignorant of what it meant to struggle to bring
home enough money for the week's food. The money Frank
earned was handed over to his mother. This continued when he
changed from sorting coal to working in one of those mills close

to his school. Can't you imagine his feelings at times as he trudged past his old school, his hands dug deep into his pockets, his lips tightened at the thought that those walls were there to keep him out, not to shut out the noises that would disturb the reading lessons!

In his early teens young Frank ran away from home, but not from his determination to provide for his mother's needs. Adjusting his age to meet the requirements, he joined the navy and went off to sea to learn the lessons of adjusting to the waves of seasickness, as well as to conquer any squeamishness about climbing up the masts. His training ship was the old *Constellation,* sister ship to the *Constitution*—sailing vessels that were to the sea what bucking broncos are to riding horseback! In later years Frank would tell tales to his son of fighting a hurricane halfway across the Atlantic on his first trip across that ocean, with the waves at times above him as he swayed in his position up on the rigging. Whenever payday came around, the largest portion of his pay was sent home to his mother.

Fran and I have among our papers his two honorable discharges from the United States Navy, one showing service on the steamship *San Francisco* for a number of years, and one certifying that Frank Schaeffer served on the steamship *Puritan* during the Spanish American War, "declared by Congress to have begun April twenty-first, 1898." In addition to that is a yellowed old scrap of paper with penciled writing telling of how he was paid off in Provincetown, Massachusetts, and then went to Miami, Florida, paying his own fare, to sign up for service in the war, "on the Puritan, a monitor for a period of one year at Key West, Florida."

The sea had given Frank Schaeffer a love for daring to work in precarious places, with no fear of heights—places where, feet fixed on small surfaces, he would work away with his hands as if he were on the ground. For a length of time he worked as a rigger in the Midvale Steel Works in Germantown, high on the steel girders, laughing at the idea of fear. Then one day his feet slipped. Falling from a height that should have killed him instantly, he reached out for a guy wire as he was falling past, grasped it, ripped open his hands, but broke his fall in a way that saved his life. Had he not caught that thin "connection" to life, there would be no story to write!

Frank continued to be a working man all of his life. He studied fat books on practical subjects concerning stationary engineering, so he knew endless things—and passed exams too—about repairing elevators, working on stationary steam engines, and so on. He was the sort of person who could do anything with his hands, whether finding out how to wire a house when gas gave over to electricity for home lighting, or making his own radio. . . . But this comes in during Fran's childhood, later in our story.

No one opened any door to Frank Schaeffer in any academic, philosophic, or cultural area. He was to have nothing to pass down to his son in these areas, nor in the area of spiritual understanding. However, always frugal as well as resourceful, he saved enough money to buy a house—one equipped with gas lights, completely furnished, including both a gas stove and an old-fashioned coal range—before he asked Bessie Williamson to marry him. He made certain she would be financially provided for before asking her to share his life. And—he was still giving a certain amount of money to his mother week by week!

A CONSTANTLY REPEATED PATTERN 2

ver since the direct creation of Adam and Eve, a woman has been essential in the mystery of "being." Without a woman there would be no next generation. Although the Bible's genealogies name the succession of men, it does not leave out the importance of the women. Women are not relegated to second-class status by the fact of their bodies providing "homes" for both men and women during their lives. Women and men need this place of protection for the first nine months no matter where life takes them later. It is the first home of kings and peasants alike.

The Book of Ruth ends with a genealogy, a careful list of fathers and sons. It is the genealogy of David, and therefore a part of the genealogy of Christ. I find a wonder of balance in its placement at the end of a book about two women—Naomi and Ruth. Listen to the crescendo of the story which is like a beautiful song: "So Boaz took Ruth and she became his wife. And the Lord enabled her to conceive, and she gave birth to a son. The women said to Naomi: 'Praise be to the Lord, who this day has not left you without a kinsman-redeemer. May he become famous throughout Israel! He will renew your life and sustain you in your old age. For your daughter-in-law, who loves you and who is better to you than seven sons, has given him birth' " (Ruth 4:13–15, NIV).

What a gorgeous gift—the gift of birth—placed within the realm of woman's possibilities. Think of it. Bach's mother gave him the gift of birth. Luther's mother gave him the gift of birth. Michelangelo's mother gave him the gift of birth. Beethoven's mother gave him the gift of birth. Farel's mother gave him the gift of birth. The Prisoner of Chillon's mother gave him the gift of birth. Robert Fulton's mother gave him the gift of birth. Without the conscious choice to make this often costly gift of birth (which today so many mothers' choices have turned into the gift of death), the gifts individual people have brought into the stream of history could not have been given. Scientists, inventors, artists, musicians, explorers, those who have handed down the flag of true truth generation after generation—the gift of birth was essential to each of them.

Let us turn again to The Tapestry. Focusing in with our magnifying glass, we can trace the threads needed to bring to life another woman who gave the gift of birth—Bessie Williamson, Fran's mother.

In 1816, just nine years after Robert Fulton had invented the steamboat in America, and just twelve years after the first steam locomotive had been made in Great Britain, Fran's great-grandfather William Joyce was born in Nottingham, England. Britain had been plunged into the Industrial Revolution in the late 1700s as a result of Watts's invention of the steam engine in the 1760s. Each of us, I'm sure, has thrilled over the exciting picture of a little boy watching the steam come pouring forth from his mother's kettle. Imagine that bright little mind suddenly recognizing the power that had never been harnessed, captured, used, as he watched that so very common sight—the kettle coming to a boil for the pot of tea he would soon be sharing. But little Watts was not dreaming thoughts of tea with milk put into the cup first, and a dash of sugar to satisfy his hunger; rather, he was imagining the potentialities of steam. What a change was to result in the lives of individuals because of this teatime "birth" of invention! And what change was to take place not only in travel, but in trade between nations because of the steamships and steam locomotives!

Roads were so bad, so bumpy and full of holes and ruts, that in William Joyce's growing years the means of travel was limited to horsedrawn wagons and pack horses. Stagecoach travel came later when a Scotsman began to make improvements on roads. How welcome the steam locomotives must have been in spite of the smoke and cinders. But when William Joyce chose to travel, for some reason he set off to sail the ocean to America, rather than to travel by land to continue his trade as a weaver in his native country. He came to Philadelphia, Pennsylvania, to Germantown in 1846. The town consisted then of little more than the Main Street (Germantown Avenue), and all its roads were of the most primitive sort. Newspaper articles at the time of Great-grandfather Joyce's 94th, 95th, and 96th birthdays tell us that he first worked in America in those same Germantown mills. Later he became a shoemaker, and still later, a postman. Amazingly, for many years he walked twenty-five miles a day delivering mail, yet on his "day off" enjoyed long walks! The paper says he was known to many as "Uncle Billy" and always gave strong opinions on politics and the conditions in the world! His grand-daughter (Fran's mother) frequently used to tell of his walks on Sunday afternoons into the woods of the Wissahickon (still a wooded park area), when he would bring home truffles he had gathered, which they would cook and eat with scrambled eggs, tea and homemade bread, as the Sunday evening treat. He knew mushrooms well enough to gather edible ones for other times of treat. (Amazing though it may seem, truffles *did* grow in the moist darkness of the leaf-covered soil of the Wissahickon woods.)

Great-grandfather Joyce married early in his time in America and had two little girls, one of whom, Mary, was to be Fran's grandmother. His wife died when she was thirty-five, and little is known about her. William Joyce must have cared for his girls until Mary married, and after that he lived with this married daughter until his death at ninety-six.

Fran and I have a fascinating old document, the naturalization papers of William Joyce. With lettering as flowery as its language, this document makes it known that on the third day of October, 1848, William Joyce declared it was his "bonafide intention to become a citizen of the United States, and to renounce forever all allegiance and fidelity to every foreign prince, potentate, state, and sovereignty whatsoever, and particularly to the Queen of Great Britain and Ireland of whom he was before a Subject."

Fantastic to think of it! Here he was renouncing allegiance to Queen Victoria, and happily trudging the streets, or dirt roads rather, delivering mail in Germantown.

I think it is important here for us to get a feel of what was being woven in other portions of The Tapestry of that time of history. In the mid-1800s, Reginald Heber's hymn "Holy, Holy, Holy, Lord God Almighty! Early in the morning, our song shall rise to thee," was being set to the music of John B. Dykes, and being sung in church after church, one day to be familiar to me, and to you, wherever we first heard it. Not too many years after that, in the village of Champéry, Switzerland, Frances Havergal was walking along paths, resting and writing some of her hymns . . . and nearby, the last prisoner was not yet out of Castle Chillon. While "Uncle Billy," or Great-grandfather Joyce, was so proudly declaring that he was "attached to the principles of the Constitution of the United States, and well disposed to the good order and happiness of the same, and having declared on his solemn oath before the said Court, that he would support the Constitution of the United States . . ." in his native England, probably in London, two men were engaged in writing something that would change much of future history, and the lives of myriad individuals. The men were Karl Marx and his friend Engels, the year was 1848, and the book was *The Communist Party Manifesto.* The date on Uncle Billy's document was 1848.

What small glimpses we get of the preparation of the ground for the planting of evil seeds, leading to despair, and the preparation of ground for the planting of the seeds of truth and true hope. What had any of these people living in William Joyce's day to do with him? Yet how astonished he could have been if someone had handed him a paper to be written one hundred years later, to read of the influence Marx and Engels had had upon young Americans through many years! And how surprised he would have been to know that the great-grandson, placed in his arms as a baby, during each visit of his granddaughter, was to cross the same ocean with *his* family just one hundred years after his own signing of his solemn pledges. It was in 1948 the Schaeffers' ship was to be ploughing across the Atlantic, and before too long they would be walking the same Champéry paths as Frances Havergal and singing her hymns in their own family times of worship. But I am getting ahead of my story.

Great-grandfather Joyce's daughter Mary had married Wallace Williamson in 1877. One of their two daughters was Bessie Williamson, who was one day to meet and marry Frank Schaeffer and become the mother of Francis August Schaeffer—the fourth to have the same name. Mary was twenty-five when she married twenty-six-year-old Wallace, and ten years later she was left a widow with four children and her retired father to take care of. There seemed no other way to supplement their tiny income than by taking in washing. So it was that Fran's mother, who had her diploma from Germantown Grammar School in 1897 at the age of seventeen, had found life such a grind of hard work. Getting up before light to help her mother start the washing, helping with the ironing after school, and doing studies by gaslight at night, she became bitter about hardships and blamed "having children" for some of her own unhappy existence. Her resolve that she would "never be a slave to bringing up children," must have been fiercely made during those years.

In understanding Bessie Schaeffer, it is necessary to remember that her father died when she was eight, and from then on her home seemed more a laundry than a home. Other people's dirty clothing had to be hand-rubbed on boards, with the homemade soap rubbed on dirty spots, and knuckles getting raw from the washboard's ribs. Bacon fat drippings and any other fats or grease, from whatever sources they could gather it, had to be kept in jars until there was enough for the soap-making, mixing it with lye and cooking it up in a pot. Long years after that Mother Schaeffer continued making her own soap "to rub the spots" and shaving it with a knife into "flakes"—more coarse than Ivory Flakes, but in that general form. I can still remember the odor of that homemade soap being melted in hot water and stirred on the stove as she prepared it for "Monday wash days." Familiar too, and a homey part of washday, was the odor of laundry starch mixed with cold water and then stirred as it came to a boil, a bowl of thicker starch being set aside for cuffs and collars of men's shirts and a thinner batch to dip the tablecloths, napkins, dresses and aprons in.

Although Bessie had finished enough education to teach in a primary school, it seems she continued to help her mother cook, clean house, market, make clothing and do the mending for the household of six people. Even after sisters and brothers left home, she was the one who remained to help. Her life included church attendance in the Evangelical Free Church and in Christian Endeavor Society with its big choir practices leading to concerts. For Bessie, who loved to sing, these practices were favorite times. In later life she told of hayrides, sleigh rides, and various outings of young people in the Wissahickon—so her life wasn't all work. But something through it all gave her a bitterness that colored her personality with an unsympathetic selfishness, and a resolve that was a forerunner of the "rights" emphasis of today's drives to protect oneself. "Take care of number one; nobody else will" was a saying she would repeat with a tight-lipped anger. Or was it hurt more than anger?

In spite of the Lutheran church exposure Frank Schaeffer had in his childhood and the regular church attendance on the part of Bessie Williamson, the knowledge of the riches of the Word of God and its marvelous truth—which would have given a different "base" for life and an understanding of not only life eternal, but the moment by moment help the Lord can give now—was lacking to these two. They met, became engaged, waited primly until there were material things enough to furnish a house, to set a table with everyday dishes and a sprigged rosebud English china set for Sundays. In months of industrious preparation for marriage, Bessie had made a "hope chest" full of tablecloths, runners, and doilies, to put on every available surface, heavily embroidered and trimmed with handmade crochet and tatting, along with sheets and pillowcases also properly embroidered and hemmed, dishtowels, tea clothes, and the inevitable pile of linen guest towels. They never knew of any other kind of preparation, spiritually, or in the area of human relationships. Questions concerning the purpose of life didn't seem to be verbalized, if indeed they floated about in their minds. They were going to marry and establish a new home. That home would be, for both of them, as much as they could make it, without the poverty that had spoiled their own childhoods, in different forms.

Frank's idea of being a good husband was to earn enough money for food, clothing, and all the daily expenses. He began immediately to bring home his paycheck, hand the bulk of it over to his wife to apportion in proper balance for their needs and to put in the bank proudly when she could save enough of it; and a small amount he put in a tin box on his special shelf in the cellar, his own spending money!

Bessie's idea of being a good wife was to have the house always spotlessly clean and tidy. Monday was washday, with her home-made soap prepared ahead of time, her clothesline properly rubbed with a clean wet old face cloth before hanging out the wash and her tubs out and ready to be filled by 4:00 A.M. Frank felt that a good husband should fill the tubs for his wife, and "work" the hand-powered washing machine, running two loads through before leaving for work!

Tuesday, ironing day, the kitchen table of good oak wood was fixed with blanket padding and topped with sheets to make a wide ironing board. Here piles of clean shirts, dresses, hand towels, tablecloths and sheets came into a crisp and beautifully ironed state, drying on a rack (the old English method) before being folded and put away.

Wednesday was mending day. Any buttons that were off, any hems coming out, any socks with holes waited in the basket where they had been gathered. Bessie would sit in the kitchen rocking chair and mend, then turn to other sewing after her morning's "everyday" work was done.

Thursday was the marketing day. Off to Germantown Avenue—or "the main street" as she always called it—would go Bessie with her market basket over her arm. It was so exactly like the child's game and song, "Here we go round the mulberry bush . . ." with each day having its special job.

Friday, cleaning day, meant tying up one's hair in a kerchief and dusting walls and woodwork, window sills and baseboards, as well as polishing all the furniture and brushing the rugs (later with a Bissell sweeper, electric vacuum cleaners not having come into existence). Windows had their regular weeks to be washed, and as for spring and fall housecleaning—!—that meant taking everything out of its place, and airing mattresses as well as pillows and blankets out in the garden. It was an amazing ritual. Every rug had to be thrown over a line outdoors to be beaten with a wicker rug beater.

There was church to attend, and the ladies' societies, in order to do the proper good works for the church, rolling rolls of bandages and folding single ones and making nightgowns or aprons or children's clothes to send to needy countries through the Red Cross or church missionary societies. There was Fourth of July with fireworks to set off while neighbors were setting off theirs, and other holidays with their parades to attend. On hot nights there was the treat of getting ice cream in a pail at the corner store and eating it outside where the air was "moving a bit," or the watermelon to put on a cake of ice in the icebox until it was cool enough to split and cut into huge wedges.

It was into this kind of a home that a baby was to be born. Bessie had resolved she would never have more than one, "because I'm not going to be a slave to children." And she never did.

There hadn't been any natural childbirth classes or any explanation of what was going on, but "It's time to call the doctor" was positive enough a statement to send Frank Schaeffer on the run out into the night. He found the doctor all right, and they came back in his buggy, but the hindrance to the night's proceedings was that the doctor was rip-roaringly drunk. He was quite in control of the situation in that he tied a sheet to the footpost of the bed, told Bessie to pull on the sheet with all her might and main, and . . . "push." It must have been just the right moment of transition, and she must have had an easy time, because she always told me in retrospect of that night, "It was easy. I just pulled on the sheet and pushed, and the baby was there on the bed!"

The doctor automatically did all the right things about tying off the cord and getting the baby washed, but as he left, his fuzzy brain and overwhelming sleepiness wiped all remembrance out of his mind the next morning of his need to register that birth at the proper office. So . . . years and years later, when Fran went to get his passport to make the 1947 trip for a survey the mission board was sending him to do, he found he had no birth certificate. Fortunately his mother was still alive and could swear in front of a notary to the fact that her son had been born on January 30, 1912, and that his name was Francis August Schaeffer.

It fascinates me to consider that as Fran was born, C. S. Lewis was a boy of thirteen in his miserable boarding school, Salvador

Dali was an eight-year-old. Jean-Paul Sartre was a seven-year-old, and Picasso had already painted his "Demoiselles d'Avignon." (Look at page 188 in *How Should We Then Live?* to see Fran sitting in front of this painting talking about it. Note, on the very next page, Duchamps' "Nude Descending a Staircase," painted in that very same year of 1912.) Timing of "being" and "existence" is overwhelming when we consider the influence events, ideas (other people's and our own), and historic situations have on each of us, and the people with whom we come in contact in the span of history our own short lives cover. For Christians, there is special meaning in being responsible for "handing on the flag" in the relay of truth from generation to generation.

Individual people matter. Choice matters. However, we are meant to take comfort from being informed very carefully by God in His communication, the Bible, that He has kept a remnant alive in each moment of history. Noah and Abraham encourage us no matter what "minority" means in our own struggle. But the fact we must always remember is that the Bible has condensed history for us, and although genealogies show how much each individual mattered, yet great jumps left out generations for the sake of a readable-sized volume. Think of the myriad people whose names have never been mentioned, not only in the Bible but in any book of any sort, yet who are going to be among the ones to be "honored" and chosen to have the "high places" because of being faithful in "little things." The word to each of us comes as a sweet trumpet note heard through a storm: "Keep on." . . . Keep on, because you don't have any idea what fantastic importance your words or your actions or just your being has in the midst of history. . . . "Keep on." . . . Keep on because you have no idea of the enormity of difference your prayers for some *one* person is going to have in the midst of history.

In a very real way Picasso's "Demoiselles d'Avignon" was the "watershed" into the modern world. The Armory Show in New York in 1913 was where Marcel Duchamps' "Nude Descending the Staircase" was the central piece. (If you don't know this painting, let me explain that it is so "fragmented" that you see no nude, and no staircase.) It was this Armory Show that brought the twentieth century world into the attention of American newspapers, and therefore to the general population. Albert Camus was born in 1913, so he was unaffected at that moment!

Was it "by chance" that this newborn baby in the tiny Pastoria Street house in Germantown—Francis August Schaeffer, lying in a cradle in that humble house where neither philosophical things nor basic Christian teaching, or even books, art and classical music would be introduced to him—would one day be able to speak to the modern world in understandable terms? Was it to be "by chance" that, in 1947, while French writer Albert Camus was writing "The Plague," Francis Schaeffer would be sent on a survey trip to Europe, to be introduced at the same time to the wonders of art museums in thirteen countries between appointments in his impossibly heavy schedule of meeting the men with whom he had to talk? How are people prepared and educated for whatever God means them to have as a preparation for what He had for them to do, when they themselves have no idea of their place in the battle?

I'm not suggesting history is only a chess game, with the devil's pieces placed in brilliantly planned moves and God's greater plan always prepared to checkmate the victory. But, however it is, God does continue to put the "salt" or the "warriors" or the preservatives and the soldiers for His side of the battle, in the right place at the right time, for the constantly continuing war.

Old photographs, old bits of paper with diary-like notations, old certificates (Baptismal Certificate, Cradle Roll, Beginner's Sunday School, etc.), and memories stirred give us some of the flavor of the life in that little house before school days started in 1918. As the baby began to walk, his only play space was always tiny and hedged in by an iron gate in the iron fence, tied with a rope that was never to be touched by Francis. A pocket-handkerchief-sized grass plot was bordered by flowers, and a lilac bush in one corner had a small space where the dirt could be spooned into a little pail. "Don't get your white stockings dirty" was the constant admonition. To Bessie, who certainly hadn't read anything about rearing children, keeping the white stockings clean seemed a key to good upbringing, and one of Fran's earliest memories revolves around the stockings. He had a "piece" to recite in a Christmas program for the church, "Where did the hole go?" all about a hole in the stocking of a child who had fallen down. On his way he trotted ahead of his mother, fell down and tore a huge hole in the knee of his own stocking. Instead of finding this tickled her "sense of humor," he was dragged back home by a stern and tight-lipped mother, who spanked her erring son and re-dressed him in another pair of little white stockings. With the tears rubbed away and clear voice ringing out loudly, he recited the poem with no one being aware of the illustration it might have had!

There were no reading times when the world of books was introduced to young Francis; there were no picnics, no pets, and few playmates were ever allowed to come in. The breaks in monotony were the visits of his aunt's dog or the delivery wagon's coming to a stop, or even going past the gate. Everything was delivered by horse and wagon in those days—fish, vegetables, and waffles! The waffle man was the most exciting, as he served hot waffles from his cart, liberally buttered and sprinkled with powdered sugar. A scissors grinder rang a bell, stopping to sharpen scissors and knives right there, spreading his work out on the sidewalk. In the twilight the lamplighter came to light each gas lamp on the street individually, setting his little ladder in place, climbing up, and putting his lighter in as the gas was turned on to give just the right flame.

There were the visits to Fran's grandmother's house, where each time until he was six months old he was put into the arms of great-grandfather Joyce. After his death, Bessie continued to go to help her mother with her housework, taking her little boy with her. And once a year in winter there was the Mummer's Parade, and in summer the yearly trip to Atlantic City. A trolley car was the first piece of transportation; it took a bit over an hour to get to the Delaware river. Then came the ferry across the Delaware (no bridge in those days). The waiting train at the other side took passengers right in to Atlantic City for a day on the beach and boardwalk—wearing the modest bathing suits of the day (snapshots showing the wool suits coming down to the knees and elbows). At day's end, it was back home again by train, ferry, and trolley car, full of wonder about the sea, the sand, and the unfamiliar food sold on the boardwalk.

"Helping Pop" became a primary part of life, starting before schooldays and continuing right on through high school. Frank taught his boy to hold a piece of wood as he sawed. Although the small finger got too close and had a deep cut once, that didn't deter the father or the son in going on. Before his mother thought

he was big enough to climb a ladder, little Francis was given a brush and told where to paint from his place so precarious on that ladder, as he and his father painted the outside of the house together. There wasn't much discussion going on, but there was a teaching of hard work well done, and of keeping tenaciously at a job until it was finished.

A razor strap was kept in the cellar way, in reach of the kitchen doorway, and whenever mother Bessie thought punishment was needed she reached for that and a chase ensued . . . round and round the kitchen table until, as Fran still remembers, his mother was out of breath. He thought it would be a silly idea to stand still. His father never punished him. His stern tone, "Francis," was enough to stop Fran in his tracks, whatever he was doing wrong.

School was a rough tournament of little boy's fights . . . but so often this has been children's first experiences of what the world is like. Who doesn't have scars like Fran's from a tin pea-blower another boy stabbed his cheek with? The walk was over a mile each way, and as his grandmother's house was only half a block from the school, it was there he went for lunch, remembering always the generous amount of sugar grandmother put on his buttered bread, in contrast to the thin layer left when his mother shook it off back into the sugar bowl!

What Fran remembers most of these early years of school are incidents such as a teacher's marching back with fist doubled up to punch him and his ducking his head and feeling glee when her punch missed him and landed on the back of the bench— bringing a howl of pain from the teacher, rather than from him! And another time when pupils were "showering" the teacher with apples (each one rolling an apple up the aisle to supposedly arrive at the teacher's desk), Francis mischievously hauled off and threw one at the blackboard when the teacher's face was averted. "Now, now, children, not so hard," was her remark. Later this teacher was to become a very good friend of Fran's.

Something he never knew about was discovered when we were going over papers together—old report cards from the very first grade up. Among them we found a blank check, faded blue, with a pencil note from his mother stating that Francis had been tested in school and found to have the second highest intelligence that they had recorded in twenty years. No one shared this test result with him at any time.

His first big wagon was not just for having rides on the sidewalk, but was to be used to pull home mother's purchases at the market each week, and Fran remembers being sent, while still very young, to purchase the weekly blocks of ice. The downhill ride was a gloriously dangerous one of careening around bends in the road to the icehouse a mile away—but that was more than matched by the perspiring uphill pull to get the ice home. With all these economies, Bessie insisted on getting her little boy's clothing from the best boys' store in Philadelphia, and we have evidence that his parents seriously thought of sending him to a private school, Germantown Academy, but then put that idea aside.

The excitement of the first airplane that could be heard and seen flying over their house is still a remembered wonder, while an introduction to the marvels of radio was an affair of watching Pop make one. Pop took a round cardboard Quaker Oats box, wound it as a coil, used a "cat's whisker" (as this was before the day of vacuum tubes), and worked away with a homemade aerial. At two o'clock one morning, Bessie and young Francis were wakened by a shout from the kitchen: "Bess, BESS, Francis, FRANCIS, come, COME . . . I've got something." Shaking their heads in unbelief, and rubbing sleep from their eyes, they ran down to be rewarded with the sound of squeaks and squawks but also an unmistakable human voice soaring in jerky warbles as someone was singing an operatic aria. The radio was working . . . and Pop had made it himself!

When Francis August Schaeffer was two years old, in 1914, two significant things happened that he knew nothing about: In Europe, which was one day going to mean so much to him, World War One started. In China, his wife was being born. We'll go into the story of that second item later. As for the war, all that survives of it in Fran's personal experience is the indelible and vivid memory of being taken at about the age of four to a crowded park where people were lustily singing. "Over there . . . over there . . . over there. . . . We're going over there . . . and we won't be back till it's over, over there." The fierce patriotic fervor of all those people and their attitudes is a memory that he has never lost.

What the countries "over there" were going to mean to Fran in his lifetime—and what that baby being born in China as he tried to keep his white stockings clean was going to mean to him—those things were as totally hidden from his imagination, as well as knowledge, as your future, and mine, are hidden from us now. The future ahead of this little boy was most unlikely.

DOORS AND THE DOOR 3

In Switzerland and other European countries, when a child is eleven, a very special set of school examinations is taken, the results of which determine a direction—whether the child is going to go on to enter a *collège classique* or a secondary school course of study. Each of these leads to a very different set of possibilities for the future.

Without any such formal examinations, and without any realization that a period of preparation was now being entered, Fran's eleventh birthday ushered in a special period. However, all that could have been observed by anyone looking on at the time would have been Fran's change of schools, from the grammar school to Roosevelt Junior High School. Two important things took place the first day: First, Fran entered the "home room" of Mrs. Lidie C. Bell, who was to be the first person to open doors to him—just a crack, but doors into another world, nevertheless—as she taught art appreciation and drawing. This wasn't anything cataclysmic, but it was an introduction to another world of whose existence he hadn't known before. Second, Fran took steps to make sure he would *not* be going to college, lining up subjects that would please his parents—mechanical drawing, woodwork, electrical construction, and metal work (at a forge). This emphasis of subjects carried through high school, in an ironic turn away from academics just as a new interest was opened in fresh areas.

His grades were up and down as incentive was very sketchy, although in general the average was above normal. That same year he joined the Boy Scouts, a year ahead of the age for joining. Representing his troop, he entered a Scout speech contest, and won. I have his cup here to copy: "Pyramid Club Cup Four Minute Speech Contest Won by Francis A. Schaeffer, Troop 38, 1923." That was the year his father had told him to "choose a new church, any one you want to go to," and he had chosen the First Presbyterian Church of Germantown because of the Scout troop! In working for various merit badges, Fran learned things about trails and woods which stood him in good stead later in the Alpine hiking he did, and gave him summer camp as well to look forward to right then. A YMCA membership from his father opened the way for him to learn to swim and do a certain amount of gymnastics. Music lessons, started this same year, turned out to be a fiasco, as Fran had a "total incompatibility" with the piano teacher, and he gave up. His playing the cymbals in the Scout band also had a swift ending, as he got the idea all mixed up, so it seems, whanging away in a manner that flattened the cymbals . . . as well as coming in at the wrong time. Music, at least as a performer, was clearly *not* his talent.

In the winter there was sledding down hills where today you would find thickly populated suburbia. Do you remember the old Flexible Flyer sleds with runners divided to allow steering? The front half was hitched to the bar which our hands grasped when we went "belly-flopping," as we used to call lying flat on one's tummy while flying down the hill. Woe be to anyone who went straight into a wall in such a position! Sledding straight towards a frozen little pond one frosty winter's day, Fran flew merrily out over the ice, when—crrrrack—the ice broke. Into the icy water he fell as the jagged edges lowered him and his sled through the too-thin ice. It was not tragic, as he was able to climb out, and get his sled out too, but the walk home was a not-to-be-forgotten time of misery.

Another misery experienced by Fran—a very severe case of scarlet fever—dates back to that period. In those days any contagious disease had to be reported to the city health officer by

the physician in attendance. In very short order a man would appear at the front door, make an announcement to anyone who opened the door that he had been sent to "place the quarantine," and with no more discussion he would get out his hammer, four nails, and a white cardboard placard, which measured, as I remember it, about sixteen inches square. This placard would have in very heavy letters the information needed by all passersby . . . so that they could keep passing by. Quarantine! Under that ominous word would be even larger letters elucidating the nature of the quarantine. "MUMPS" or "MEASLES" or "CHICKENPOX" or "WHOOPING COUGH," the placards would announce. One of the most dreaded signs was placed on the door of that little house, "SCARLET FEVER." Below this enormous word would come smaller print telling of the fine that would be levied upon any person or persons removing the sign. The only person permitted to take out those tacks and remove the solemn warning was the health officer officially designated for the task.

It was a serious thing to be under quarantine, but for Fran it was an even more serious time, because he really was dangerously ill. His fever soared, and delirious dreams continued for three or four days and nights. To this day he remembers the dreams vividly, and he says the only way he could know that the monsters in them were not reality would be the sight of his mother's blue dust cap floating into view as she came to give him a sip of some cool drink.

Sometimes people forget what diseases were like before sulfa and then penicillin and other antibiotics were discovered. Survival was not taken for granted, and the hush of an approaching crisis in days of soaring fever meant a tiptoe situation in the house, with anxious inquiries by neighbors staying a respectful distance from any germs that might float out the doorway! Fran remembers his father coming to the window once a day. Recovery time was longer too. Viruses may be fighting back today, but there are differences younger people can't have a feeling about, because of being unaware of what the "before" was like, in a variety of areas in life.

"Before electricity" is a meaningless phrase, to anyone who has always lived with a nearby switch for light, or an outlet into which to plug such a diversity of equipment. Gas lamps and gas stoves may still be chosen and appreciated, and even thought of as a luxury, but there are not many Americans, English, Europeans, Australians, or people in a variety of electricity-oriented places, who can appreciate the excitement of the switch from gas lights to electric lights with the kind of thrill people had "back there when. . . ."

Picture a slim boy wiggling through places in the attic too small for Pop to crawl through, fishing the wires through, and helping to get the whole house ready for the change from gas to electricity. This of course fit in with what he was learning in school about electricity, giving him a base for feeling kinetically with his hands, all through life, that which workmen were doing. As the next years went on, Fran was to do every kind of work with his dad—laying floors, building a garage, bricklaying, mending gutters on the roof, remaking a coal bin in the cellar, plumbing work, cement work, etc. And as the first little house was sold, the new larger house on Ross Street needed fixing up. By the time this move took place, Fran was in Germantown High School.

It was not until the junior year of high school, when Fran was seventeen, that the "big" things happened to him which led him to Christianity. His life before he became a Christian, in retrospect, seems to him something like a film being seen through a mist—something almost outside of himself. "The new birth" was a vivid reality to him, with no relationship to emotion, but to the very substance of life. He says the years of junior high and high school were a period separated from childhood, as well as from the reality of the next steps. There were no "drop-outs" in those days, but inwardly Fran had "dropped out." What was the use? There seemed no reason to push on. So he simply did, in a machinelike sort of way, the series of things which seemed to come along, without a great interest in any of it.

Outwardly what would you have seen? A growing boy going to school, joining the Rifle Club, leading Cub Scouts, playing basketball once a week at the church, roller skating at the rinks, designing and making forged iron things like candlesticks or wall brackets, and working on Saturdays. He took a job on a fish wagon, shouting "Fish—FRESH FISH" with such fervor that he feels it must have been his training for public speaking. Housewives would hear that voice through closed doors, and come running with their baskets. Finally he quit the job because the man was so cruel to his horse that Fran couldn't stand it.

The next Saturday job consisted of working for a meat market at Reading Terminal, an hour's trolley ride into town. After enduring freezing hands to unpack meat in the ice cold room, he helped deliver it—the day's work was from 5:00 A.M. to 5:00 P.M. Another job entailed scaling a steam boiler, using a hammer and chisel to scrape sedimentation from the inside until Fran thought his lungs would burst! A different experience was delivering ice, which included "tossing" 200-pound cakes of ice in the icehouse for loading purposes. He then turned to making beaded flowers that were popular at the time as pins. He taught his mother and some of her friends to make them for him, developing a small "factory" situation for which he became the salesman, and sold them by the dozens to Wanamaker's Department Store and some other stores.

When he joined Sigma Delta Kappa fraternity, the initiation consisted of the old members taking their new pledges out into a vacant lot, covering them with molasses and bird seed, amid much hooting, and demanding, "Whistle like birds now . . . go on!" The hitch in this performance came when police ran in. Thinking the boys were covered with blood, they hustled them into a paddy wagon and let the explanations come in the station house. Although Fran was the youngest and not the leader, he was chosen as the official spokesman, and evidently told such a plausible account of it all, through his birdseed-covered lips, that they were sent away with simply a warning, "Don't do it again!"

The "crack in the wall" concerning the existence of art, filled in with moss, so to speak, in this period of time, but another such "crack" came unexpectedly. One day Fran went with the Scout Troop to an electrical show held at the City Auditorium (now very near Doctor Chick Koop's hospital, Children's Hospital of Philadelphia, where so recently we were all together for filming). The most spectacular part of that electrical show was the playing of Tchaikovsky's *1812 Overture*—with stage props simulating buildings, castles, etc. Cannons boomed, houses fell, drums rolled, and the music played to its crashing finale. This was the first piece of classical music that broke into Fran's ears and understanding. A few days later when he turned on the radio, out poured the *1812 Overture,* his "friend." In joyous recognition he pressed his ear against the speaker so as not to miss any of it, and a love for classical music was born which was to grow as soon as opportunity came to hear more.

At Sunday school, a teacher who was not much help in biblical things was, however, the next person to "open a door," when he got Fran to helping a White Russian count to learn to read English. The count's idea of a beginning book to read was the uncensored account of the life of Catherine the Great. After a few weeks of this, Fran said, "You are never going to learn English this way." The count was ready to agree, and that week Fran took a trolley in to Philadelphia's famous bookstore—Leary's— and asked for a beginner's English reading book. Fran has always been a bit overwhelmed by the "providence of God" that sent him home with the wrong book—a book on Greek philosophy.

As he began to read, he felt as if he had come home! From this time on his interest flared like a fire that has had gasoline poured on it, and he read everything he could get his hands on. He would wait until his parents were asleep, then turn on his light again and read on into the night. It was exciting to be stimulated into thinking in the basic philosophic areas, but as time went on he felt that all he was getting was defined questions— with no answers.

As Fran considered what he was hearing at church every Sunday, he felt there was a parallel; the preaching was just as devoid of answers. "I wonder," he mused to himself, "whether, to be honest, I should just stop calling myself a Christian, and discard the Bible?" (What he had really become was an agnostic.) Then he reconsidered, and faced the fact that he had never read the whole Bible in his life. Since at this time he was reading Ovid, he decided that before discarding the Bible, he'd read some of Ovid and some of the Bible night by night. Gradually he put aside Ovid altogether (not to finish it until he read it in the original Greek in college) and spent all the time he had to read, on reading the Bible.

How did he read it? Who helped him to understand? No one gave him any suggestions. He wouldn't have known who to ask, and in any case, he had no idea there was any way to read it other than to read it in the same way as any other book. He started at the beginning of Genesis and read to the end. If you want to know why Fran has such a high regard for the Bible and feels it is adequate in answering the questions of life, the answer is right here. As a seventeen-year-old boy with a thirst for the answers to life's questions, he began to discover for himself the existence of adequate and complete answers right in the Bible.

Have you ever read Christina Rossetti's "Sunshine Country," the story of a little shepherd boy who finds the Gospel of Mark in a cave in the hills and goes back every day to read more of the story? Remember his excitement and sheer wonder in finding what he thought no one else had ever discovered before? This was the same way in which Fran discovered truth as he read. As we talked about it today, he said with deep emotion at the clear memory of that time, "What rang the bell for me was the answers in Genesis, and that with these you had answers—real answers—and without these there were no answers either in philosophies or in the religion I had heard preached."

Sometime in the next six months Francis Schaeffer became a Christian. He believed and bowed before God, accepting Christ as his Savior, having come to an understanding directly from the Word of God itself. He thought he had discovered something no one else knew about. He thought what he had found was unique, and that he alone had found it. If what he had discovered was being a Christian, then he thought he was the only one. But—he didn't call himself that. It was a transforming reality that changed his whole outlook; it began to change his marks at school and the way he looked at the woods. But, for a time, he did not know there was anyone else who shared this truth he felt he had discovered. You see, he thought Christianity was what he had heard preached by an old-fashioned liberal who gave ethical talks and who did not preach Biblical truth. At that time Fran was totally ignorant of the fact that there *was* any other kind of preaching.

An obstetrician will tell you that births are very unpredictable. Diversity is something that is demonstrated by the difference in human beings lying in the tiny cribs in a hospital nursery, even though they may all be the same age! The individuality of each human being is in terrific contrast to the boring exactness of machine-made objects!

The spiritual new birth is also a very individual matter. Each person enters the family of the Lord, or becomes one of God's people, through the blood of Christ, or on the basis of Christ's finished work on the cross. Yet each new child of God is an individual and is significant, important, personal to God, who receives them one by one into His family. As we focus on one part of The Tapestry—and our short lives can't enable us to focus on more than a minimal proportion of the whole—we can look forward with expectancy to having all eternity to discover something of the fantastic variety of not only how people have found truth and come to believe, but of how God then wove them into history. There isn't any person, including ourselves (I believe), who won't be surprised to see how it all fits together, and just what our part was after all! I think that "seeing through a glass darkly," or "seeing in part," means this, as well as other things.

There was no set of blueprints suddenly dropped into Fran's lap. He saw no handwriting on the wall. He heard no voice in his ear telling him that there would be a change in direction. He simply went on to high school, and the themes he wrote for English not only began to have more content to them, but the writing improved drastically. He was the Treasurer of the Senior Class Washington Trip, which gave him his first view of "the world" outside of Philadelphia and Atlantic City, was the Secretary of the class (or co-secretary, perhaps it should be called, as they had one boy and one girl secretary!), and graduated in June 1930, but with no expectation of going on to college, heading toward Drexel Institute to study engineering.

Fran's father had given him a new Model A Ford for graduation. The cost was $567.00! His diary notations (he started to keep a diary at this time) tell of his driving lessons, then of going to the art museum for the first time, and also of a continuous series of trips to a library in the city to supply his increasing activity in reading. He began to look for a job, but with the big depression well under way, it wasn't easy to find anything. House-painting jobs, thoughts on Carl Sandburg, movies that he had seen, jobs he was doing for his dad in fixing up the new house, purchase of his first razor and suit—these and a like assortment of things filled his diary, for a time. Then came one of the "crisis" notations, one of the milestones to be recorded.

August was a hot month. Philadelphia heat and humidity brought people out to sit on their "stoops" or porches, or big screened-in verandahs, depending on where they lived. Ice cream vendors did a big business from their carts, in spite of the depression. A nickel cone was a big dip, and lasted long enough to be worthwhile. Walking down the main street (Germantown Avenue), Fran felt depressed and lonely. He hadn't found anyone who cared much about his discoveries in the Bible, and he was wishing he could find a job for the summer, as well as wondering about the next year. As he walked further and further down in the direction of Wayne Junction, he came to a tent pitched on an empty lot on the corner of Ashmead Place. Now, Ashmead Place was going to mean a lot to him in the next few years, because that was to be the street my parents were going to move to when they would leave Canada . . . but that was in the future, and he had no idea that this corner would be one he would be hastening to impatiently through the next years. Right now it was the sound of a piano and hymns being sung that piqued his curiosity. "What on earth is going on in there?" he wondered.

Pushing the tent flap open, he walked in to find benches placed in rows, a sawdust aisle between them, a small number of people singing, and a man standing in front leading them. Before long, a sermon followed the lusty gospel hymns, and it poured forth in earnest simplicity verse after verse of the basic gospel. Fran listened with wonder to the speaking of this man, an Italian-American, who told of his conversion out of crime and drugs and of his being freed not only from his cell sixty-six in prison, but from his sin.

The sermon did not deal with philosophical answers to the questions of life, nor did it point out a line of demarcation between liberalism and true biblical Christianity. But one thing became clear as crystal through the fiery speaking in an Italian accent— this man was talking about the same Christianity Fran had found for himself; this man believed what Fran believed. There *were* others! It broke out like a blast of a trumpet into Fran's consciousness, and he hurried to the front, up the "sawdust trail" (as evangelists have called the aisle) in response to the "invitation." When the evangelist asked, "Young man, what are you here for, salvation or reconsecration?" Fran was confused and didn't know how to explain the wonder of what he was declaring as he had come to take his place among the believers.

As the evangelist turned away, probably thinking this young man was a bit foolish, Fran went out into the night, with a singing heart, with a formulated decision as to how he would then live. If the curtain into the future could have been pulled back, not only would Fran have caught a glimpse of Ashmead Place as the locality where he would one day make another decision— asking me to marry him—but he would also have been able to stand amazed that, at a more distant date (in some forty-five years), the young evangelist's son and his own son would meet to make a film together called "How Should We Then Live?" You see, the evangelist was Anthony Zeoli, and his son was to be Billy Zeoli! However, the Lord does not pull curtains back, and we each need to go on, one step into the next hour.

Fran's next hour that night was spent in rushing home and writing down in his diary, which is yellowed but still readable, beside me now: "August 19, 1930—Tent Meeting, Anthony Zeoli—have decided to give my whole life to Christ unconditionally." You see, his decision that night was a basic one of how he intended to live from that time on. He felt if this which he had previously discovered was indeed the truth, then he wanted to give his life to making that truth known. Dramatic? It is only God who writes this kind of script!

Fran's diary notes that he went back to the tent meetings to hear Zeoli again on August 22. Then he carefully puts down the fact that he "cursed twice" on August 23, evidently resolving from then on that he will keep a check on himself, asking God to help him break this habit. August 26: "Went to the tent meeting again and took some others along." It didn't take long for him to want other people to hear this very different kind of preaching!

How does the Lord lead? Is there a standard formula, identical for each person, a "key" that opens an easy way of finding out just what to do? It cannot be said too many times, we are individuals, and our God is a Person who deals with us personally. The succession of things that took place in the next year was not of things that fall into a category of "how to know the Lord's will in changing the direction of your life." Nevertheless it was a year filled with struggle, and agony, along with an unmistakable leading of the Lord. God is very gentle with His children as they ask with a measure of honesty and desire to do His will.

Remember now, that Fran's father wanted him to work with his hands, and that he felt all ministers were drones who did not work, but were parasites of some kind! Remember that both his parents wanted him *not* to go to college, but to go on with mechanical engineering in Drexel Institute, a path chosen in his very studies for the past six years.

The easiest way to relive some of that year with Fran is to read bits of his diary.

September 2 [this is exactly two weeks after his first time in the tent meeting, and his decision that night]: "Registered at Drexel Insitute for night school in Mechanical Engineering."
September 3: "Decided all truth is from the Bible."
September 14: "Talked with Mr. Moore and Mr. Sam Osborne about Hampden-Sydney College." (Mr. Moore was the Sunday School teacher. Mr. Osborne was the Headmaster of Germantown Academy, and a Hampden-Sydney alumnus himself. He was eager to have Fran go to his old school and suggested it as a preparation for theological school later on. Evidently Fran had sought these two men, both members of the First Presbyterian Church, for advice about education—if indeed he were to make a change in order to prepare to use his life to make truth known.)

It is not yet a month since the tent meeting, yet a practical battle is now raging inside—whether to please parents and go on in engineering, or to turn toward an academic preparation which had now become a burning in his bones!

September 15: "Started night school at Drexel."
September 25: "Went to RCA Victor, stood in long line, got job for 32¢ an hour. Worked at Victor's. Rough place but hope with God's help to affect the environment, rather than sinking to its level."

September 27: "Hope I may please God in my use of leisure time."

Just when this "leisure time" existed is not clear, as he had to get up at 5:00 A.M. to get out in time for an early trolley car to the river, then cross on a ferry to Camden and put in a full day's work at the RCA factory. He would have supper at night in the Horn and Hardart's Cafeteria. (In a few years I was to experience the blast of aroma that hits the nostrils there—the stewed tomato with a bit of onion and green peppers cooked in it, the fresh pumpkin pies with one dark spot slightly burned on purpose to give it the extra homemade look, and the mashed potatoes and gravy that accompanied the slab of slightly grey beef—for that was where I stopped for lunch day after day when Fran was in the hospital for an appendectomy and we were in seminary and I was pregnant! But I need to tell it all in proper order.) After supper he went directly to Drexel for a full evening course and got home late at night to study at the kitchen table.

September 29: "Worked, school at night, supper at Horn and Hardart's doesn't sound exciting, but it is, for I feel my new motto is being helped by God."
October 7: "Someone stole my coat and my lunch at work."
October 8: "Sam Chestnut asked if I would come and drive the grocery truck for deliveries."
October 11: "Quit Victor's [after the strike] and worked at Chestnut's grocery."

An explanation is needed here. The work at RCA Victor was assembly line work, and Fran was just a bus boy. Women worked on the belts, doing their individual "thing" to the parts as they passed them. In that one area of the enormous barnlike room, with all the noise and confusion of the machinery, there were five drill presses, feeding parts of amplification units for assembly by the women. Five men worked the drill presses, and some days a special thing happened. At about half an hour before closing time, a "big boss" (with the always present cigar hanging out of the corner of his mouth) would come in waving a fistful of five-dollar bills. There were only five fives, and the promise of encouragement he shouted to the five men ran like this: "If you guys at the presses will turn out more parts, double it in the next half hour, there'll be a fiver for each of you." Faster and faster the drill presses would run, and in a frenzy the conveyer belt would be supplied with double work for the women. No extra money for the women—only extra work at the moment they were ready to drop with fatigue. By the end of the half hour some would be weeping, but a person couldn't quit in the days of depression because there was always someone to take your job if you dropped out.

On this particular day in early October, one woman got to a point of rebellion at the unfairness and stood up yelling, "STRIKE . . . S T R I K E." Gradually a few others took their hands away from their frantic work and joined in the same shout. Some began to pull others up by their hair. Fran at that point jumped up on a counter and yelled in his loudest voice, "STRIKE . . . S T R I K E," and almost every woman stood up and let the parts go sliding by unfinished.

As Fran looks back at that moment and remembers the emotion and indignation within him, he realizes that at that point of history, under different circumstances, he could easily have gone on to become a labor organizer.

As it was, we see by his diary that an amazing offer came—when offers were not being made for jobs—for him to work with the father of a school friend, and he took a place delivering groceries for the next months. Of course choice was involved. Of course Fran was the one who said "yes" to that change that particular day. But, looking back, the wonder of it is the realization that God was answering prayer for direction, not with big supernatural signs, but quiet and definite leading.

November 29: "Swore once today."
December 1: "Took exam at Drexel on Steam Power."
December 5: "Got a B in Algebra—Drexel."
December 10: "Prayed with Sam Chestnut today. Now my mind is fully made up, I shall give my life for God's service." (It is significant that he is personally talking about Christianity and praying with Sam now quite naturally.)
December 11: "Had dinner at Dr. Finney's apartment [he was the assistant pastor]; have fully made up my mind to prepare

for the ministry." (In that time the term "the ministry" did not carry as wide a meaning as today, and it designated preparing to be a minister or pastor.)

December 13: "May I always be in God's keeping especially in social functions." "Have found real joy of living in trying to serve God and others."

December 14: "Mother and dad still hostile to my plan. I hope guidance comes strongly and surely."

December 15: "Worried all day over mother and dad's *not* being back of me for my life's work. Decided to leave all to God."

December 16: "Talked to dad alone, he said to go ahead and that mother would get over it."

December 31: "Spent this New Year's Eve day taking stock 'til midnight at Sam Chestnut's grocery store! Another year gone— may all the future years bring as much development as this one." January 1, 1931, New Year's Day. "May this year bring joy to the world, and guidance to me."

January 30: 19th birthday: "Switched today from Drexel to Central High School, evening school. Taking Latin and German, now definitely preparing for Hampden-Sydney College—as per arrangement by Sam Osborne. Also having extra tutoring in German. Still working in grocery store."

February 8: "Read Grace Livingston Hill's *The Witness* and it shook me to the core." (Remember that Fran's own Bible reading, the tent meetings, and the continued preaching at his church were all he'd ever had thus far.)

The notations for the rest of that spring and summer were in the same direction. Hard work in German and Latin brought marks in the 90s, and by the end of summer 1931 he was all set for Hampden-Sydney College. His acceptance had come through— but there was no one at home to share his excitement. No brothers and sisters, no cousins, no close friends. He had dated a girl out at Beaver College for a time, but there had been no great exchange of ideas in the areas that interested him most. Sam Chestnut was the only one with whom he could pray. At home the idea of his leaving for college was ignored.

Early in September, the day came when packing for college could no longer be put off. Fran had taken a wooden box his father brought home one day (strongly made to hold two office typewriters) and had put it on newspapers in the cellar and painted it a battleship grey with a half-can of paint left over from painting the kitchen floor. No new clothes had been provided, no sports equipment, no matched towels and sheets and pillow cases—a grim-faced mother turned her back as if no packing were going on.

Fran had no idea how he was going to pay for college (in those days that total amounted to about $600 a year), but he started to pack. As he folded his clothing from his bureau drawers and took things from his cupboard, he decided to wear his one suit with long trousers and pack his grey tweed knickers. (Yes, though Swiss Alpine climbing or cross-country skiing knickers which he feels so comfortable in now, were *not* anything he knew about, he had never felt a need to change from the knickers of his high school days, to become more sophisticated!) There were a bathing suit, a raincoat, and his gym clothes; and then his mother, with tightly pressed lips and no comment, threw a few old towels and a cake of soap on top. With his Bible, a few books, toothbrush, and shaving brush and soap, along with the razor and blades, the box was ready for its top. In Pop's nail and screw box, neatly in categories, Fran found four big long screws, and proceeded to carefully screw the top down at the four corners. College packing was finished!

Before he went to bed, Pop said, "Get up in time to see me before I go to work . . . 5:30 . . ." When Fran came down in the morning, Pop was standing by the front door. Turning to give Fran a long hard look, he said, "I don't want a son who is a minister, and—I don't want you to go." It was the end of his dreams for his son—dreams of a son who would work with his hands and be a "good honest worker," dreams of a son who might be a little farther along in education but who would continue to "work around with him," and maybe live on the same street. Dreams of a son he would be proud of by *his* standards, were being destroyed by a harsh daylight of reality.

How many fathers and mothers have stood by a door like that one, figuratively if not literally, and said, "I don't want a son whose life is going to be made up of putting God first." "I don't want a son (or daughter) whose ambition for—" and a variety

of things would be inserted—fame, power, success, affluence, leadership, "is being put aside for anything so ridiculous as 'following
God.' " "I don't want a religious son," or, "I don't want a religious
daughter." So very, very many people can identify with Fran in
that moment, as they also have stood, one by one, with a father
or mother or both confronting them with a choice. "Who are
you going to choose to follow?" We can go back and place the
picture of Joshua as a kind of transparency on top of this scene:
"Whom will you serve?" Go back and read Joshua 24:14a, 15:
"Now fear the Lord and serve him with all faithfulness. . . .
But if serving the Lord seems undesirable to you, then choose
for yourselves this day whom you will serve, whether the gods
your forefathers served beyond the River. . . . But as for me
and my household, we will serve the Lord" (NIV).

Century after century sons and daughters have stood with two
ways before them, making a choice that might seem too trivial
to parallel Joshua's plea for choice, but which is really a central
choice. There comes a time, a moment, a choice, that is stripped
of all other factors and becomes a basic thing of truly putting
the Lord first. It isn't recognized as central sometimes, and often
people think they can make the choice later on, not recognizing
how much more difficult that is going to be. Century after century
we could follow the stories of the Calvins and Luthers, of the
Prisoners of Chillon and others—finding places where they made
central choices that turned the direction of not only their own
lives, but the lives of many, many other people.

So very often when we stand in the place of Joshua, there is
no troupe of people in sight. Our declaration "as for me and
my house" seems a feeble little commitment, because there is
no one else in sight. Yet, a choice is being made in a very real
way for all the unborn sons and daughters of another generation!
Will the choice to serve the Lord, and to obey Him first of all,
push away a mother and father eventually? I believe the answer
is no; it will not make it harder eventually for them to come to
truth. But the mother and father are not all of our "household"
there are to consider. Whether we are to have physical children
and grandchildren or not, there are to be spiritual children and
grandchildren to be considered. The choice we stand and make,
in early daylight, or twilight, with "no one watching," is not

unwatched at all, but eagerly viewed, I believe, by angels and demons who know that our choice is going to have a tremendous effect in The Tapestry.

In the dim light of 5:30 A.M., the milkmen were not yet rattling their bottles in their baskets, and silence stood like a pillar between Fran and his father—an agony of silence. Then Fran asked in a strained voice, "Pop, give me a few minutes to go down in the cellar and pray." In a fear of uncertainty as to what to do, he went down and wept and wept hot tears of sorrow for his father. He knew there was a choice that must be made in minutes, and he wanted to make it exactly as God would have him make it. But how to know what that will of God was?

In an act of desperate and simple faith, he did what he wouldn't advise anyone else to do, but what he felt was the only right thing for him to do then. He prayed (if anyone every prayed sincerely, he did then), "Oh, *please*, God show me. . . ." Then he took out a coin—"Heads I'll go in spite of dad's desires"— and he tossed it. It was heads. Still weeping, he cried out, "God, be patient with me. If it comes up tails this time . . . I'll go." He flipped it again, and it was tails. A third time he pleaded, "Once more, God . . . I don't want to make a mistake with Dad upstairs. Please now, let it be heads again," and it was heads. So he went upstairs and walked to his dad and said, "Dad, I've *got* to go. . . ."

His dad looked hard at him, then went out to slam the door. But just before the door hit the frame, his voice came through, "I'll pay for the first half year. . . ." It was many years later that Pop became a Christian, but Fran thinks this moment was the basis of his salvation.

Full of a mixture of emotions, Fran went up to his room to get last-minute things ready, and what hit his eyes was a text he'd stuck up on his wall some time before: "But as for me and my house, we will serve the Lord." It seemed an added underlining of his choice.

Driving his own car, with the grey box in the back, and accompanied by Charlie Hoffman (a family friend) to drive the car back and put it away for the school term, Fran was soon putting miles between himself and Philadelphia on his first trip to Hampden-Sydney, Virginia.

When Fran arrived at Hampden-Sydney, the first person he met was "Greek Wilson," who was to be his Greek professor, and, in today's language, "the vibes were bad"! This professor was assigning dorm rooms, and noticing that Fran had stated that he was a "pre-ministerial student," put him on "Fourth Passage of Cushing Hall." Now this Fourth Passage was a place of sophisticated fellows who would be so antagonistic toward ministerial students that he would be *sure* to have a hard time. It didn't take long for Fran to know he was being looked at as an alien. He was a Northerner in a place full of Southern aristocrats, so he was "the Yankee," and having given his name as "Schaeffer from Philly," he ended up being nicknamed "Philly," which lasted through the four years. His grey box looked as out of place as it could look among the shiny trunks and matched luggage, and his own clothing was about as strange among the white flannels, blazers, and brown-and-white shoes of the self-assured young men, many of whom were following their fathers in this school that had been started in 1776.

Where was the excitement of arrival at the "goal"? How could scorn and antagonism be an atmosphere for a new life of study and preparation on the background of the choice so recently made?

Fran lugged his grey box up the stairway of an incredibly beaten-up building. Outside, the dorm buildings fit in perfectly with the marvelous red-brick, white-columned Southern architecture . . . beautiful in the quiet setting of clipped lawns, woods inching up to the campus, wonderful rambling fences, autumn roses and red-berried shrubs. But inside, the dorms were the domain of the students, where rooms were never repainted, and mice could be shot with .22 rifles as an evening's pastime! As a matter of principle, professors never entered the building.

In a later chapter, we'll come back to life in Fourth Passage and to the four years of college which are now history, but that day it was all an unknown future, and Fran entered his room with one big determination—that he was going to "make it" here, "with God's help," and have a place of respect before he graduated.

ANCESTORS—AN INDISPUTABLE FACT OF LIFE! 4

It was in the late 1950s that our "English trip" took Fran and me to the North of Ireland. For so very long I had heard my father talk about County Down and the town of Saintfield, where his mother's people had come from. Now at last I was going to be in the location of some of my ancestors. As Fran and I peered together from the window of the plane, we saw what seemed to be waves of sand, rising, falling, streaming out over a green beach! The colors seemed all wrong. No green-blue waves with white froth against a sandy beach—rather, with a strange pulsating movement, as though sucked by a strong undertow, sand-colored waves were pulling back in great curves to reveal a green beach. As the plane swooped down to skim the runway and land at Belfast airport, we saw that the waves of sand were wild, beige-colored jackrabbits, scurrying away in fear from the noise and wind of the landing plane, clustered so closely together in their mass exodus that the bright Irish green grass was seen in bare curves as the waves of rabbits receded into the safety of distance.

And what was happening a hundred years before that? And a hundred years before that? And a hundred years before that? As we pull out bits of paper with penciled lines and tiny printed names spraying out from the lines, we are likely to feel we have all multiplied like rabbits and are equally as hard to trace back into the fields or woods. What is the difference? Well, we may have brown eyes, be small-boned and given to not growing very tall or we may be Viking-like blue-eyed blonds swinging through our lives with seven league boots . . . but we are *not* rabbits, nor peas in a pod, and there has been a lot more to our genes than the brown or blue eyes; the red, brown, black or blond hair. We are human beings, and being human is something we need to spend time and attention on, since a lot of people are making it their life work to try to teach us to be *in*human, especially about other human beings, and to treat them like rabbits, or peas in a pod!

Continuity is a part of who I am, and who you are. Recognizing something of what our ancestors had to suffer, as well as to enjoy, during their numbered years of life, is important in understanding what the human being that is me, or you, has to be or do . . . whether we are carrying on "unfinished business," "picking up the dropped stitches," or "building on a foundation." And none of us is the last man on the totem pole. Or, that is, we can't say that until after Jesus has come back, because we don't know how many generations may come after us. We have something to do for the next generation too, something to pass on, something to start which they can go on with, something to prepare that they may complete. "Ah," you say, "that lets me out because I am not going to have a child." But—that really isn't an excuse. Just look at the importance of single aunts and single uncles in the line or on the family tree or in The Tapestry. We do not stand alone touching no one. We cannot slide into the water and cause no ripple. We are human beings, even if we are not being human. Other people have made a difference to us, whether we can point it out or not, and we are making a difference to other people right now. However, the people who have made the most difference to us are the ones without whose existence we would not "be."

If it hadn't been for a line of people—couples and their sets of chromosomes—that had met, made choices, passed something on to the next generation, made more choices, started in the North of Ireland, or Scotland, or Wales, or Manchester, and ended up in American and then China . . . there wouldn't have been any "me," that is certain!

Except for God's intervention in bringing forth the unique,

once-in-all-history virgin birth of Jesus Christ, *every* human being has come into existence because of the meeting of twenty-three chromosomes with twenty-three other chromosomes—both sets coming from distinct human beings, one a male, one a female. God's creation of perfect human beings was spoiled when the Fall took place—when Adam and Eve both became "sinners" and handed down a new image, or put their stamp, so to speak, on the next generation. They produced with their "spoiled genes," "spoiled human beings" . . . which soon became evident in Cain's behavior. We are made in the image of God all right, but we have a long line of genes behind us (each one of us), which have given us a lot of imperfections, physically, psychologically, emotionally, and spiritually. There is no perfect human being.

When scientists talk of making clones . . . what "perfect" human being would they want two of?

In looking back over my "line," I'll be tracing first the portion of my genes that came from the North of Ireland, and I am going to come to my grandmother through the women of the family. Back in the 1700s, Lord Stirling in Scotland had a daughter named Mary Stirling. Mary Stirling married a Montgomery and named her daughter Mary. Mary Montgomery married General Monroe and named her daughter Mary. Mary Monroe married Hugh McMillan and had a daughter she named Ann. Ann McMillan married Hugh Boyd. Then came Rachel Boyd who married Samuel Crooks, and they had a son—Jacob Crooks—who was my great-grandfather.

The generations covered in that paragraph bring us to 1820, and we have been looking in the records which tell of County Down and Saintfield in the North of Ireland, with a line back into Stirling Castle in Scotland. One wonders about the love stories connected with all these names listed so primly on lines making a family tree, with brothers and sisters branching off into other fresh lines of their own. What ambitions and expectations were lived through? What excitements and disappointments? What appreciation of the heather and rocks, the fields of sheep, or the patches of potatoes? What wonder did they have about the wool which could be cut, cleaned, carded, spun into yarn, and then knit into marvelous afghans, blankets, hundreds of stockings, sweaters, mittens, and caps . . . while other yarn was spun to be woven on great looms into Irish tweed, or Scottish tartans? Who lived in a castle and had her children in a castle? And what girl said, "I care nothing about the kind of a dwelling place; I love *him,* and any small cottage with him in it will be better than a palace without him"?

In 1741 Handel was living in a little stone house in London. He was fifty-six that year, and the greatest work of his life was to be done during a three-week period of that same year. We are told he wrote the *Messiah* in twenty-three days, while shut into one room of that little house and eating the food a servant brought him, without much thought of what it was. His head must have been full of all the music you and I hear when we shut all else out and listen to the *Messiah* on some good disc we have of it. The wind can be blowing a gale, the rain or snow hissing against the windows, and the music seems *our* music, our *own* praise of God, something sent straight from God to give us a vehicle rich enough to express what *we* feel. The difference is that Handel composed it. It is reported that he wrote in great exultation, that the inspiration which filled him as the notes poured out shook his whole being, and that after completing the second part of the oratorio with the "Hallelujah Chorus" in it, he exclaimed with his face streaming with tears, "I did think I saw all Heaven before me—and the great God Himself a Light shining in the darkness." His work has brought truth in a rich way to the ears of the world.

The *Messiah* was first performed in Dublin, Ireland, 1742. I wonder how many people alive at that time in Ireland and Scotland and throughout Britain heard it, and how soon it reached their ears and minds and attention in the following weeks, months, and years.

Had Jacob Crooks's ancestors been among those who heard the early performances of Handel? We don't know, but we do know that my great-grandfather Jacob Crooks and great-grandmother Nancy McRoberts Crooks of Saintfield, County Downs, North Ireland, with their two small children, Eliza Jane, born in 1841 (100 years after the *Messiah* was written), and her little brother David, sailed to America in 1844. The family set forth on a sailing vessel that required the passengers to bring their own food, which in their case consisted of a few sacks of potatoes!

A long, far cry from Lord Stirling and from any semblance of a castle or a mansion. This tiny family that so bravely set off to a new land with so little material goods, in New York City sold the leftover potatoes for a number of shillings. But shillings in American coins were worth only half of the English shilling, so that handful of coin meant Grandfather Jacob had been cheated, and there was no way to make it right.

I wonder how they got to Pittsburgh? There were railroads, the B&O line having started in 1830, and the first locomotive express from Boston to New York had begun in 1839. It is stated that in 1835 there were 200 chartered railroad lines in the country; however, all these were short runs. Probably Jacob and Nancy and Eliza Jane and David boarded a stagecoach. It must have seemed a long way, but somehow they got settled in Pittsburgh. Their small house was very close to the Allegheny River (now the North Side area) which overflowed its banks yearly. One Saturday afternoon the family had to come back home by boat from the preparatory service for communion the next day. I wonder what happened to the loom? Grandfather, who was a weaver, continued in that trade, and his loom was set up in the front room of their house.

These two were my father's grandparents. They had nine children, and in the records, beside the name of five of them (two were twins), is a small *d.,* meaning that child died in early infancy or during the first year. What sorrow and heartache this emigrant mother must have had, with no telephone to ever make possible the comfort of hearing *her* mother's voice from Ireland.

There are two pages of "grandmother's sayings" written by Cousin Marion, who well remembered them as often repeated by the whole family—"sayings" which revealed a sense of humor and something of her character. She spoke of a housekeeper so efficient that "she made up all the beds in the house before anybody was up." When Grandfather Crooks complained about the flour barrel becoming empty so soon, she said, "Aren't you glad you lived to see the last of it?" In speaking of things printed in newspapers (whether true or not), she remarked "Paper and ink never refuse anything."

But we can't linger in this generation. It is two of the children of this family who have affected me the most: Eliza Jane, who became my father's mother, and her younger sister Rachel who was not only to become my father's first teacher, but whose name Rachel was to be given to me. However, before we can have Eliza Jane married, we need to bring the Sevilles to America.

John Seville was born in Manchester, England, and lived there until he was eleven years old. It must have been at the turn of the century that he came to America in a sailing vessel with his parents and located in Philadelphia. We have the fact that in 1819 he moved from Philadelphia to Pittsburgh where he followed his trade, that of tailor, later engaging in furniture dealing. He continued to move further west, and in Ohio he "embarked in the grocery business and purchased an interest in a line of canal boats." At the outbreak of the Civil War he was one of the first to volunteer. I quote from Western Pennsylvania records: "He required no government document to discharge him from the perils and dangers of war, freedom from such further duty having come to him at the battle of Fredericksburg where he met his death." His wife was Hannah Williams Seville, and of their nine children, three sons died while fighting in the Union Army in the Civil War, and two daughters were "deceased."

What tragic news came in the lifetime of this dear Hannah as she had to have the news of her husband's death, and, one at a time, the news of the deaths of three sons in the war. What nursing did *she* do, what nights of worry and fear did she endure as she cared for two baby daughters who died? She was my great-grandmother. Someday I'll meet her in heaven and hear the whole story . . . but with the fullness that only heaven can bring. Right now, records from archives can give only stark, almost mathematical facts. "Born." "Died." And in between? The whole reality of purpose and meaning, and the handing down of a "flag" so that it might not be lost. Threads in The Tapestry, each one important, each one a part of the pattern—yet in our limited vision, with eyes that get strained and blurred at times, we have to narrow things down.

John Franklin Seville was a son of Hannah and John who did not die in the Civil War, and who did not die at birth. Because he lived, I am here to tell you the story. John Franklin Seville was born in Pittsburgh, Allegheny county, Pennsylvania, October 21, 1836. I'll just quote the account in the genealogical and personal history of Western Pennsylvania to give you the flavor. "He was there reared and educated, in early life learning the plumber's and gasfitter's trade, which he followed until 1868. In that year he moved to Ross township, where he purchased land, set out many orchards, and became a fruit grower, in which he prospered. . . . Both he and his wife hold membership in the United Presbyterian Church, of which he is a trustee."

And who is the wife? None other than little Eliza Jane Crooks who had come over with her mother and father and the sack of potatoes on that sailing ship. It was on her eighteenth birthday that Eliza Jane was to be married—March 9, 1859. She was four feet, ten inches tall, with long, thick brown hair and dark brown eyes, a slim bit of a North of Ireland girl, with lots of spunk and a determined will. Can't you just hear someone say that she must wait until she was eighteen? And her arranging the wedding on her birthday to wait not one day longer! It was her mother who had all those famous sayings, one of which was "She'll be sorry for that, once, and that'll be all her life." She is said to have made that remark concerning someone who was marrying "too young." However often she said it, Eliza Jane wasn't frightened off from marrying her beloved John Franklin Seville on her eighteenth birthday and becoming Mrs. Seville with a twenty-three-year-old husband.

It is a breathtaking thing to hold the magnifying glass on this bit of The Tapestry and follow the pattern from the vantage point of about a hundred and thirty years later. We can see what they couldn't see. Eliza Jane had a younger sister Rachel, born in America, who looked so much like her, people would have thought they were twins. Also four feet, ten inches; also with dark brown sparkling eyes and long brown wavy hair, Rachel was to become a very good schoolteacher and then to marry George Paden, who would become an official in the Union National Bank of Pittsburgh. John Seville's ten-acre fruit farm was to be next to the Padens' property. Great Aunt Rachel started a "Dame's School" for primary education, to which not only my father would go, but also some of his brothers and sisters, Aunt Rachel's own daughter Marion Paden, and later some of the grandchildren of the family, as well as "outside children." In this school Rachel must have given a fantastically good foundation, for the children she taught were later to be the highest in their classes in university, and still later, leading doctors and missionaries as well as leaders in other professions.

Eliza Jane and John Seville were to have eight children—my Aunt Edith, for whom I was named, and Aunts Bess, Jennie, and Alice, as well as my doctor uncle Dade, Uncle Frank, Herbert who died in infancy, and my father George Hugh Seville, born 1876 to live until 1977, dying when he was one hundred and one years and three days old!

Before going on to my father, let me say that Aunt Rachel and Uncle George Paden's threads, as well as Cousin Marion's, can be followed right up into L'Abri in Huémoz, Switzerland. Aunt Rachel gave her own daughter a good foundation in her Dame's School, and as language was one of her best subjects, it is not surprising that she went on to be extremely good in Arabic, speaking as well as reading the language. Cousin Marion went to Egypt under the United Presbyterian Board, and continued in girls' school teaching for forty years. Her father felt that she was his gift to the Lord. "I am sending my daughter to Egypt as my gift to God's work, and therefore I want to support her and her work completely as far as financial expense goes, as well as to pray for her." His only other child had died, and he was able to care for Marion's needs all through his life and to leave her enough to go on with through her life.

When Cousin Marion retired from the work in Egypt, she came to live with my mother and father for a time. By that time the Family Letters for L'Abri were being sent out once every two months, and with my mother she helped fold them, taking part as well in the Monday days of prayer, and days of fasting and prayer called for any special reason for L'Abri. When Cousin Marion died, much to the surprise of the entire family her frugal living had enabled her to leave a sum of $20,000, and it was given to L'Abri Fellowship Foundation. It came just as we were praying for the needs of Farel House. That money not only purchased the first tape recorders for Farel House study, but also finished the building (that is, the Farel House underneath the chapel) and purchased a piece of land for L'Abri as well. In those days a dollar was worth 4.36 Swiss francs.

So, as Uncle George Paden worked faithfully away in the bank, (and here beside me, still telling good time, I have the watch that was given him the year before I was born, for "forty years of faithful service in the bank . . .") he was not only working in Egypt for the Lord, but in L'Abri. Such are the patterns of The Tapestry! Also the little rocking chair you have seen in pictures at the foot of our bed in Chalet les Mélèzes, where Fran sat to dictate all his letters, to carry on conversations, and to write his first books, was Aunt Rachel's rocking chair in which *she* sat to teach my father.

Continuity? Only God can give that kind of continuity in His pattern and design of weaving threads.

I'm way ahead of my story, but I simply have to pause to say that if you think Eliza Jane was any worse off for having eight children and living on a fruit farm, and that her seventh child, George, was not extremely important as a part of her life's work to raise and to prepare for all that was ahead of him, as well as the other people her life influenced; and if you think Rachel was "downtrodden" because her brilliance was limited to offering a very thorough education to a small number of children whom she gave a foundation that is rare in this day—then, as grandmother would say, "You have another think coming."

Certainly there have been things worth fighting for, and limitations that have been unfair for women, but it is not all "black and white." If there were women for whom life was "hell" in those days of many children, there are also women for whom life is "hell" today in their places of "freedom," as they walk in and out of marriages with multiple divorces, and as they face untold disappointments and discouragements in offices and careers of a diversity of kinds. I'm not saying women aren't supposed to have careers; Cousin Marion had a very satisfactory and fulfilling career in her forty years of outstanding work in Alexandria, Egypt. But the diversity of the career that the artwork of raising children and creating a continuity of family holds forth, is something that mustn't be forgotten as we look at The Tapestry of history. If gold medals aren't being handed out, or Nobel Prizes, then at least in our own understanding we need to shift some of our twisted ideas as to what "outstanding achievement" consists of—twisted only by some of the monolithic thought of today.

It is the understanding of the *whole* of history that is limited, and the understanding of the *whole* person that is limited.

Little George Hugh Seville used to recoil when other children sang out in sing-song mimic, "Georgie Porgie, pudding and pie . . ." as children have found ways of teasing each other through the ages. When he was ninety-seven, Susan Macaulay (our second daughter) made a tape of his talking about various portions of his life. I have just been listening to this for four hours. It is a rather fantastic experience to hear the voice and personality of your father, still there at ninety-seven, and now in heaven for over three years! He remembered so vividly, almost smacking his lips, the flavors of the "Bartlett pears, Seckel pears, Flemish Beauty, apples of a great variety, sour cherries, black and white cherries . . . mmmmm . . . and all those berries, black raspberries, red raspberries, strawberries, currants. . . ." He goes on to say with such strong feeling: "I had to pick gooseberries and currants, because they couldn't be spoiled! It took years to graduate to the blackberries, then the red raspberries which were considered the most delicate." He wasn't allowed to take the reins and drive the horses when they went out in the carriage either, as his father or older brothers always preceded him. "And when mother would take me for the long walk to the train to Pittsburgh, people passing us would lean over and say, 'Oh, you have your mother's eyes.' I felt so annoyed; I knew I had my own eyes, and as a six-year-old it made me resentful to hear this silly remark."

While little Frank Schaeffer was sorting coal and thinking about running off to sea, George Seville was picking berries on the fruit farm and forging ahead in Aunt Rachel's school, not only reading and writing and doing arithmetic, but starting the languages he was to love so much—Latin, Greek, and German. What a difference in their childhoods. German was a language George loved to learn from a cousin of Aunt Rachel's, on her mother's side of the house. McRoberts was an artist who came to live with the Padens, with his wife for a time, and to paint there. McRoberts's wife (Grandfather Seville still remembered at ninety-seven) taught him the differences between Northern German and Southern German— *"Ich"* or *"Isch,"* and so on!

Until George was twelve years old, the Sevilles lived on the farm. Then John Seville bought a property, with three other families in the family buying adjoining lots, so that what my father called "a family compound" came into existence. His older brother, Dr. Dade Seville, with his wife and children, lived on one corner. It was here that he had his offices and became a well-known and respected doctor in Pittsburgh. His sister Bess and her husband, Mr. Dade Wills, a banker who later became President of the Federal Reserve Bank in Cleveland, Ohio, lived on another corner, and Aunt Rachel and Uncle George Paden on another, with the Sevilles on the fourth. What a close family life—with onenesses and differences of opinions—there was for some years there.

By the time he was sixteen, George went from Aunt Rachel's school to Shadyside Academy, where he was a classmate of Andrew Mellon—not that that made any difference to his life. As far as we know they had no more effect on each other in school days than Handel and the Prisoner of Chillon had on people they studied with in their teenage years. The *lack* of effect on people with whom we are thrown in history, and the amazing weaving together of threads in totally impossible or unexpected ways, are equally a mystery. We know "choice" is *not* all that is involved. And we know that this is *not* a "deterministic" universe, nor a fatalistic history. What we are looking at is *reality*— not a fairy story spun out of human imagination. If I were spinning a yarn or writing a romantic novel, I could rush ahead here and imagine Andrew Mellon spending half his great earnings in days ahead to further the work of the China Inland Mission in which George Seville, sitting in the next desk, would one day be involved. But he didn't. That is *not* what happened.

All was not idyllic in that family-compound growing-up situation for George. There was his eldest sister Jennie's "bad marriage," which gave her some agonizing years of waiting for an alcoholic husband to come home from his wanderings, at which time he would gather up some of her possessions and whatever money he could find and disappear again for indefinite periods of time. One day Jennie asked if she could live with her sister's family, the Wills, on one of the "corners" of the land, and she became a quiet little person, cooking marvelous food, serving it beautifully, caring for the house, and seeing that all the mending was done. "You, Bess, need to be with the children, or by your husband's side as he advances in banking; just let me do this," she would say. At one time she said of her passion for the man she married, "It was like a disease that I had caught. I wish someone had locked me up until it was over!"

A lesser yet puzzling difference in the families' ways of looking at things took place at Christmas time. The doctor's wife, who was Episcopalian, loved to have a gorgeous big Christmas tree with piles of presents under it, arranging that it would suddenly "appear" on the morning of the 25th of December, having been "brought by Father Christmas during the night." Not one hint of trimmings, pine, gift wrappings, or tinsel could be found anywhere ahead of time. It all "happened" sometime between midnight and early morning. But just across the lawn on the other corner, strict Scotch United Presbyterian grandparents frowned on Christmas trees, no matter who prepared them, and on piles of gifts or any other "heathenish decorations." At their breakfast table on the 25th of December modest little piles of gifts, clearly marked with the names of the givers, were placed beside the plates of oatmeal. Just what the official explanations were I've never been sure, but many were the lively discussions among the cousins, young aunts and uncles and their nieces and nephews as to these and other "differences" among them. By the way— in case you are wondering—the Christmas tree and all the decorations disappeared, leaving no traces, sometime in the middle of the night between New Year's Eve and New Year's morning.

When Father (at ninety-seven) talked with Susan, his warmest memories of Shadyside Academy were his times of "reading Greek with Professor Crabb, the Headmaster. He and I read three books of Anathemus together, and it was a great experience, really putting me ahead of the others in Westminster College when I got there. I remember there were two girls doing Greek at that time in college, and since they were congenial to me, we read Greek together every day." I guess they were more than "congenial," as my father broke the rules and went "buggy riding with the girls," for which he was called up on the carpet and warned, "Once more and you will be expelled!" His big brown eyes and thick, curly dark hair must have done more than protect his head from accidents playing football. He was the quarterback on the team. Small and wiry, a good player, he shone in that position. He excelled also in tennis, his other good sport. When boys began to grow their hair long in recent years, he said, "Why, the very idea; they have no reason. You see, *we* grew our hair long because we needed more hair to protect our heads for football, since we wore no helmets!" He went to Westminster College, New Wilmington, Pennsylvania, from 1895 to 1898, earning an A.B. with high honors. Sports and studying were not all that filled his time, as he played a guitar and was in a quartet; and with a sense of humor and skill at mimicking, he was often called on for skits, often with his own jingles or rhymes about some current subject.

For two years after college, father taught Latin and Greek in a boys' prep school. Then, having heard of the China Inland Mission and the need of China for more people to be willing to make the gospel known, he began to find out all he could about Hudson Taylor's work—past history and present need. He prayed, then felt that the next step God was leading him to make was to prepare with a theological education. Thus it was that he entered the Allegheny Theological Seminary of the United Presbyterian Church in Pittsburgh, to study for the years of 1900, 1901, and 1902. Now he was studying Hebrew as well as Biblical Greek and all the other subjects. His averages for each of the three years are here before me on his report: 97 and 1/8th, 97 and 19/22nds and 98 and 2/15ths. I'm not sure how they got all those fine fractions, but it was an impressive record!

George Hugh Seville, five feet three inches in those days (he got shorter in his old age, before he reached 101!), with his curly black hair and mustache and twinkling dark eyes, must have made quite a picture setting off by steamship, the *Maru* (a Japanese boat), from Vancouver about November 3, 1902, with blond, blue-eyed Will Hanna, about six feet one inch. Father had left Pittsburgh by train on October 28, so I've given him long enough to get out there at the train speed of those days, and—perhaps romantically—have dated his sailing on my birthday! No one knew there would be a special November 3 to come!

How can anyone be *blasé* about his or her existence? How much faith it takes to believe in "chance"! Father was setting sail (oh, yes, I know it was a trembling sooty steamship—noisy, not gliding out on sails—but the expression is beautiful) into the beauty of a sunlit sea, expecting all kinds of sacrifices, but not knowing that in China there was to be starting another set of lines on the family tree and not thinking about The Tapestry and wondering where his thread would be woven in. At least I don't think that was in his mind.

Father laughed with his funny chuckle as he told, at ninety-seven, of how seasick Will Hanna was. "You see, I didn't get seasick, and I think it was because I stayed up on deck all day, while Will wouldn't get out of his bunk. Why, the very idea—that was foolish. You see, I walked, and I enjoyed the wind and waves. When we were at the Aleutian Islands west of Alaska, there was a snowstorm, with a good thickness of snow, which stayed on the deck. I had a great time throwing snowballs! I'm sure that's why I never got seasick. You need to stay in the open air." When the ship got to Japan they stayed a week "and looked around" before going on to Shanghai. Arriving on December 2, 1900, Father received his introduction to the mission home of the China Inland Mission at the end of his first ride in a rickshaw pulled by a coolie. The first man he met in the compound of the China Inland Mission was "Guiness of Honan." This came as quite an amazing circumstance to me, since later on in my own life not only was I to be a dressmaker for a time for Geraldine Guiness Taylor, but Os Guiness would some day be a L'Abri Worker.

I must, however, pull the magnifying glass back to 1900. After the proper time of language study, the time came for both father and Will Hanna to be assigned to their stations. This is where the seasickness came in. One assignment was to be far inland, in "the Switzerland of China," a journey by oxcart. The other assignment was to be in Wenchow, Chekiang Province, entailing a boat trip down the coast and then up a river into the city of Wenchow. Will Hanna never wanted another boat ride, not if he could help it, which affected the choice of assignment—mercy being shown! Had the assignment been switched . . . there never would have been a Janet, an Elsa, a John Eldridge, or an Edith Rachel Seville. So you might say seasickness had something to do with my existence, if you were looking for a line for a play.

Down a river on a Chinese riverboat sailed father, watching with interest as his meals were cooked on deck, over coals, and getting his first glimpse of Ningpo as they stopped there. The journey continued out to sea, around the coast, and up the Wenchow river to Wenchow itself. Father had a pigtail by this time, as this was a requirement that Hudson Taylor made of his missionary men. If a man could not grow his own, then one could be fastened to his round black silk pillbox hat, but a pigtail he must have—or a queue, as it was called. Hudson Taylor felt it was imperative for missionaries to dress exactly like the people among whom they were working, so that they would not look or seem strange.

My father scorned tacking a queue onto his hat, so began to grow one as rapidly as possible. He had his head shaved in a circle around the crown so that what was growing came from an inner circle, covering the top of his head. The black silk pillbox hat had a hole in it, out of which the well-braided queue was to hang. Around the outside of the pillbox the head was to be shiny and hairless, giving a neat appearance by these standards. Father's curly black hair grew rapidly, and braided into a very fine thick queue indeed, one he was proud of . . . and all his own! Wearing a mandarin gown of brocaded silk with sleeves that were not only wide, but longer than his arms, to properly hide his hands; the proper kind of trousers that peeped out of the bottom of the gown; and hand-made cloth shoes; father looked *very* Chinese. In time his manner of using his hands, along with his good pronunciation of Chinese, made him fit in well. It is said that often the Chinese who did not know who he was, thinking he really must *be* Chinese, would say of him, "Look at that Chinese; he looks like a Westerner."

Boy meets girl? The "boy" in this case, now twenty-eight years old, looks quite Chinese as he reaches his station of work after such a long preparation. The "girl" he meets is a young widow of thirty years old, who has been in China far longer than he, having arrived in 1899. Jessie Maude Merritt Greene was also dressed in Chinese fashion, wearing the customary women's trousers under a side-buttoned tunic with its high mandarin collar. She was trying hard to look Chinese, but with her light auburn hair and blue, blue eyes, she didn't succeed very well. But the "girl" had no interest in this George in spite of his extensive repertoire for making himself noticed! In any case, she had long ago resolved that she was never going to marry again and that her life in China was to be that of a single missionary with a single purpose.

George plunged into his assigned work, teaching and preaching in good Chinese, and learning the Wenchowese as well as the Mandarin he already knew. In his time off he played tennis not only better than his opponents, but he did it while cutting up, performing antics such as judging when the ball would arrive where he was, then jumping up and twirling one full turn before he hit it, winning the game nonetheless. He also wrote skits, and "took off Shakespeare" with such adaptations as "To shave or not to shave, that is the question," accompanied by appropriate actions. Since George could play the piano as well as the guitar his take-offs included musical ones like imitating Paderewski, or an outstanding orchestral conductor directing Tchaikovsky's *Nutcracker Suite.*

Charlie Chaplin was becoming well known at that time, and as father had a small mustache and looked a lot like the comedian, the missionaries nicknamed him Charlie Chaplin. "Clown" is a good term to describe him, at least one part of him. A sense of humor was one of his basic characteristics. Yet father was a person who all his life hated any kind of impudent or facetious reference to the Bible, or of anything related to Christianity or marriage— the things he felt were a part of God's law, not to be made fun of, or treated as a joke. Father's "acts" as a comedian had amazing scope and diversity. His was a special talent, but with all his skit-writing and his clowning, he never found a need to use anything he would call questionable. This self-imposed standard simply made him use his imagination in a most versatile way.

Jessie Greene may have laughed with the others, but she remained cool. Of course, with the mission rules of that time, there wasn't much opportunity for face-to-face communication among unmarried people of opposite sex. They were rarely left alone together, as it was thought that this would be misinterpreted in the China of that day. When they went out for a walk, a married man would walk with my father yards ahead of my mother and the other man's wife! An occasional remark could be tossed over the shoulder, but as you can imagine, it wasn't exactly conducive to "getting to know one another." Fifty paces, or about fifteen meters, was the accepted distance to give the proper appearance in public places of the modest behavior of men and women. Naturally "the Westerners" were under observation, and the rules were made by those who felt this was the only way to let it be known that proper behavior was being observed and Chinese sensibilities considered.

George Hugh Seville was falling madly in love with Jessie Maude, and he was using every bit of his imaginative mind to make this known to her without upsetting the proprieties of the Chinese or the rules of the Mission Board. I came across a diary of his, written in his tiny handwriting with a fine pen, at just this period of his life. He was pleading with the Lord to show him how to make Jessie love him. The diary entry also stated that he was going to write and ask his brother Dade (the doctor) in Pittsburgh to select a diamond ring and have it sent to him so that it would be ready, "in case she says yes."

You'll have to wait until you have had the background of how Jessie Maude Merritt came to be in the world—where her genes came from, what amazing impossibilities might have prevented her "being"—and read the story of how she got to China in the first place to be where she was, before it is time to tell you what tactics George thought up to make a proposal possible!

WARS AND RUMORS OF WARS 5

I f anyone doubts the Fall and the resultant abnormality of the universe; if anyone doubts that the War was a reality which started in the heavenlies, directly attacked Adam and Eve, continues through the ages, and infects as well as affects all human beings—it seems to me a small look at history and a glance at today's newspapers should be enough to emphasize the truth. Even pacificists use such warlike vocabulary in their defense of peace that it becomes an offensive attack as frequently as a defensive one. War is woven in and out of The Tapestry of history from the very beginning. And God tells us clearly there will be wars and rumors of wars until the fantastic moment when the last war will be fought and peace will reign forever. Real peace, not a facsimile.

So many of us have seen little boys lying on their tummies, fighting a battle with their tin or lead or plastic soldiers, or perhaps with wooden spools and toothpicks, if toy soldiers are denied them. Many of us have watched little boys pick up sticks and shout "bang-bang" if they are not allowed toy guns, or we have seen them charge the enemy with fluttering bits of paper ammunition. Space wars and armies arriving from other planets capture today's imaginations, and all too soon the little boys are the men making decisions, whether in airplanes, or warships, or behind

desks in a diversity of the world's capitols. The Fall was a design
of Satan's in his war against God. Fallen human beings have never
since stopped being involved in some kind of war. The Bible
tells us that we are meant to be fighting against evil and against
the evil one. The whole Christian life is a battle, as Ephesians 6
puts it.

This is not going to be any attempt to sort out the wars we
need to mention in the history reported in this chapter, but only
to relate what is glimpsed as the magnifying glass moves to look
at some of the threads coming from my mother's background.

Little girls have just as fiercely attacked or defended in their
own way—or in whatever way has been opened up to them—
whatever they think, or believe, is worth attacking, or defending.
It is not necessary to go into the stories of Joan of Arc or other
leading figures in history to remind ourselves of women who
have affected history in their own particular wars for what they
thought was right.

Can't you imagine the passion that burned in the breast of a
twelve-year-old, William Hargill, as he heard of the Boston Tea
Party and determined that he was going to *do* something to insure
freedom from unfair taxation and tyranny of various sorts? The
burning desire to "make the world better" is in essence a good
thing. It is sad to look back on the high hopes and expectations
so often dashed to pieces in one lifetime, or in subsequent years.
Yet always we can think, "What would have happened if *no one*
had ever stood up against oppression? . . . if *no one* had ever
fought for freedom? . . . if *no one* had cared about equal opportunity and better conditions and the possibility of a fresh start
for a young country?" The Boston Tea Party was in December
1773.

William meant to *do* something, and he finagled his way into
the navy far too young. Still, "powder monkeys" had to be young
and small enough to slip into the small spaces required for their
dangerous job. In this time of the Revolutionary War, America
had very small ships which could not at all stand up against
the large British Navy, but which nevertheless harassed the British
merchant ships. Against tremendous odds, the little ships bravely
charged out into their diverse attacks, three men manning each
cannon. After firing, one of the men had to swab out the cannon

with a kind of giant Q-Tip—rags wrapped around a long stick. If he in any way did a careless job and left traces of sparks in the cannon, the powder monkey would be blown up! Now as a teenaged powder monkey, my great-great-grandfather William Hargill also had as his job to carry the powder bags to the cannon at the proper moment, jam the cannon full of the powder, and then step away to let a man do the finishing touches before the firing. Powder monkeys slept under the cannon and had to be ready at any time. No soft bed, no books or good food . . . this was *war!*

William was captured and thrown into the prison of a British ship twice in his war experiences. He had had manacles on his wrists which cut so deeply into his arms that many years later his little girl Abigail used to sit on his lap and put her fingers into the deep hollow places on his wrists left by the deep scars. He told of the cruelty of the British seamen on that particular ship (the cruelty of human being to human being must always hit us, whatever part of history we are reviewing). The conditions in "the hole" at the bottom of the ship where the prisoners were kept were indescribable—overpowering stench, inadequate food, water, or air space. (If ever you have seen the old warship in Portsmouth Harbor which tourists may inspect—Lord Nelson's flagship, H.M.S. *Victory*—you will have some idea of what William lived in in "the hole.") Each night a shot would be fired indiscriminately down into the dark, and in the morning two men would come to drag away the body of whoever had been hit and toss him overboard. William had such a hatred of "the British," whom he blamed, that I am afraid he never got over it in a lifetime!

As you know, the Declaration of Independence was signed in 1776. As all this was going on, however, it is startling—even flabbergasting—to think that George Whitfield, the great revivalist preacher, had crossed the Atlantic Ocean no less than thirteen times, had preached to great crowds on both sides of the Atlantic in the open air with his powerful voice and even more powerful message, and had died in 1769 in Newburyport, Massachusetts, so few years before the Boston Tea Party. Whitfield is buried in the Presbyterian Meetinghouse in Newburyport, so close to places where the Revolutionary War would be raging; yet his own "war" for the truth of the Word of God and its consequences in life was blended all through that part of history, and affected lives then, and now. When you sing, "Hark, the herald angels sing,/Glory to the new-born King,/ Peace on earth, and mercy mild;/God and sinners reconciled!/Joyful, all ye nations, rise,/ Join the triumph of the skies," please remember that the words of that hymn are attributed to a combination of George Whitfield (1714–70), Charles Wesley (1707–88), and Martin Madan (1726–90), and that the music is Mendelssohn's. What a beautiful blend of talents and of the understanding of the One who was "born that man no more may die,/Born to raise the sons of earth,/Born to give them second birth."

That same year of 1776, Hampden-Sydney College was officially started, and among other men on its board of directors was Patrick Henry. Of course, in 1776, no one down there had ever heard of my great-great-grandfather William! . . . nor did anyone know that Jane Stuart Smith, who would some day be at L'Abri would be the daughter of another board member of Hampden-Sydney College in later years . . . and surely no one knew Francis Schaeffer would one day be graduating from Hampden-Sydney. The Tapestry's threads are amazingly woven, bringing lives into contact, and not "out of nowhere."

William Hargill did not die of a powder blast, nor did any of the bullets hit him in the dungeon. He lived to have his wedding day on April 5, 1794 in New London, Connecticut, when he married Elizabeth Blackley. Had he been killed, the rest of the story would have been wiped out.

We have a document from the National Archives in Washington, D.C., which although hard to read, has been deciphered in part by my sister Elsa. "State of New Jersey, sixth day of November, 1848 . . . Elizabeth Hargill, a resident of the Township of Hackensack, aged 74 years, doth on her oath make the following declaration in order to obtain benefit of the pension made by the act of Congress passed July 7, 1838, entitled. . . ."

" . . . That she is the widow of William Hargill who was a seaman and 'Captain of the Maintop,' on board of some one of the United States ships or vessels during the Revolutionary war, that in frequent conversation with her said husband from the time of her marriage until his death, she learned from him, and had always understood, and believed the facts to be, that her said husband first shipped as 'powder monkey' on board of the United States Ship *Providence* in the year 1778 and that he was subsequently in other U.S. ships or vessels in the character of seaman, and was appointed Captain of the Maintop, and that he was wounded on the top of his head, and also on his arm and wrist, in an engagement with the enemy, and that he carried the scars left by these wounds to his grave . . . that he was twiced imprisoned on board of the Jersey Prison Ship, once for a period of three months, and once for six months—that he continued in the Service until he was discharged after the peace was proclaimed. Dependent cannot state the precise time. . . ."

The next page is blurred, having an additional story about the taking of the Jamaica Fleet, and ends with the time of death of Wm. Hargill as August 21, 1817. So their marriage lasted only twenty-three years, and Elizabeth was a widow by the time she was forty-three.

That marriage brought into the world Abigail Hargill, who was to marry John Allen in New York City and who would become my great-grandmother. Their daughter was named Elizabeth for *her* grandmother, and so it was that my grandmother—my mother's mother, Elizabeth Hargill Allen—was wooed and won by John Wesley Merritt. He was to be the only grandparent I would meet in the "land of the living"!

I'll take just two sentences to cover a lot of history in saying that John Wesley Merritt came from a long line of Americans. His "tree" branches from one Captain Michael Pierce who is said to have been captain of the second trip of *a Mayflower*, but who did not stay in America that trip. Patty Patience Pierce married a Welshman, John Eighmy; their daughter, Fanny Eighmy, married a Gilbert Merritt, and it was their son, born near Acre Point in the Catskills, who married my grandmother, and brought into existence my own mother.

It may make you dizzy, but don't skip the reality that, whether in biblical genealogies or in your own family tree, you didn't come out of nowhere, nor did any of us. (Whether anyone has kept a family tree for you or not, you have one in reality.) The basic dash of ice water that hits you or me in the face is that history is going somewhere, that it has always been going somewhere and that if only we could see the total pattern, we would see how it hangs together. Yes, there is an ongoing war (and I don't mean just all the wars between nations, and within nations) in which we *are* on the winning side, and God has told us clearly there will be a final victory. But our lives are not to consist of a shrug of the shoulder and a copping out and a saying of the equivalent of "I don't matter to anybody, so I'm not going to fight any longer." Life could easily have seemed "too much" to my mother, and she could have just settled down to doing the easiest thing at hand in Newburgh, New York, instead of persisting in answering what she felt was God's call to her to go to China. It took a lot of persistence, and the making of hard choices, however.

John Wesley Merritt and Elizabeth Hargill Allen were married and lived on a farm near Newburgh, New York. Jessie Maude Merritt was born October 15, 1874, the fifth of six children. She was to be teased by older brothers so frequently that she felt she was ugly. "Cow eyes, cow eyes; your eyes are so big you look like a cow and your hair is like carrots," they repeated and repeated. In actual fact she had wonderful big blue eyes and auburn hair and was a beautiful girl . . . but she really didn't ever believe that.

The Merritts were Baptists—in spite of the name Wesley!—and were what is known as pillars in the church. Stories of the farm were favorites of ours as children. Perhaps the one most repeated was about the young boy who had come straight from Scotland to help on the farm. When the large serving bowl of oatmeal, which was intended to serve the whole family, was passed to the new boy, he placed it in front of him, put sugar and cream on it, and proceeded to eat through the entire bowl. Mother's blue eyes grew bigger and bigger, in astonishment that anyone could eat that much oatmeal. It seems that was a normal-sized bowl where he came from!

Jessie Maude was especially good in mathematics, and when she finished high school she got a job in the Sweet Orr Overall Company, doing accounts in the office. She was called an accountant, but I am sure that title didn't mean what it means today, as she probably added, subtracted, multiplied, and divided—in other words, did what a computer would be doing today. But computers don't have big blue eyes, auburn hair, a lovely sympathetic smile, and a compassionate interest in other human beings. Nor can computers add other tasks to their mathematical job, or talk the work over, training younger office girls.

Another thing computers don't do is fall in love, make a decision, and get married. Walter Greene was mother's first love, and a truly fine Christian he must have been. She never talked about him to me until I was fourteen, and we had one of those rare evenings alone together when she didn't have any appointment, and no one else was home. I hadn't even known until then that she had been married before. I'm not sure why, but I never saw any records with the name Jessie Greene on them. "Edith, he was a wonderful person, and I loved him very much. We planned to go to China together. I resolved that I would never never marry again when he died."

Let me tell the story in her words, as I heard it that night, full of fourteen-year-old sorrow for my dear mother's young agony and suffering so many years ago . . . my young, young mother, whom I had never known, as she was forty when I was born.

"We were married when I was just twenty [that would be 1894], and I kept on working at Sweet Orr offices as long as possible, because we were saving up our money to go to Toronto Bible College in preparation for going to China. We had read about Hudson Taylor's work in China, and felt strongly called to go with the China Inland Mission to make the gospel known where so few had ever heard. Then—our first baby was born at the end of that year—a beautiful, perfectly formed, healthy, normal baby boy. The tragedy was that the cord had strangled him during birth; he was strangled to death on his own cord coming into the world."

You can imagine that at this point I got up and hugged mother so tightly I might have cracked a rib! Words didn't seem to come, but tears flowed, and it was an attempt at comforting a sorrow that was beyond my understanding, yet a sorrow that hurt. Dear mother. What an empty night that must have been.

"And then, Edith, three weeks later Walter came home from his work with his blue eyes burning with fever, his cheeks a high pink and his lips just too red. He looked handsome, but too bright—like a lamp that flares up just before it burns out.

It was frightening. The doctor pronounced it 'galloping consumption,' a rapidly progressing kind of tuberculosis which in those days had no cure. 'No hope,' was what the doctor said."

They had three weeks, those two, to end their one year of marriage and to say good-by. Mother was a widow, having lost her first baby, with two graves side by side in a Newburgh cemetery the only tangible evidence of having her hopes and expectations ended, by the time she was twenty-one years old!

This was the year 1895. The China Inland Mission had been founded in the year 1865. Hudson Taylor was an Englishman. He had started a very new kind of mission, not a denominational mission, but interdenominational. It was a mission that he wanted to have as a work based on prayer, particularly prayer for needed funds to carry on the work and to send forth new missionaries. Prayer meetings had been established all over England to pray for the work in China, and such prayer meetings were also beginning to be started in Canada, Switzerland, Sweden, Germany, and America. Mother had been involved in praying for China, and had resolved before the Lord to go with Walter. Now that Walter had died, she did *not* change her direction. Her certainty was unflagging. She would not give up because of being alone, nor because of having lived through sorrow. She would save up money as she continued to work, then go to Toronto Bible College in Toronto, Canada, and prepare for China.

Who says women were frightened rabbits, scared to do anything different, or anything on their own?

From Newburgh, New York, to Toronto, Canada, was not as short a distance in 1895 as it is now. But off went Jessie Maude Merritt Greene to take her three years of Bible College, make her application to the China Inland Mission, finally go through her trial time as a candidate, receive her acceptance, and sail off from Vancouver to Shanghai in 1899—all before her twenty-fifth birthday.

She arrived in China the year Adolph Hitler was ten years old somewhere in Germany, the year C. S. Lewis was born in England, and the year Ernst Haeckel wrote *The Riddle of the Universe at the Close of the Nineteenth Century,* saying that matter and energy are eternal. But, unaware of the various ingredients of the battle that were being launched in other parts of the world; unaware

of the war for men's minds, as the explanation of materialism
was being given; unaware of the war that would one day take
place in the ten-year-old boy's surging to a time of power in
Germany—Jessie Maude was to be plunged into an immediate
war situation of which she was indeed to be *very* aware! You
see, Jessie was to arrive in China just in time to be thrown into
the dangers and complications of life that the Boxer Rebellion
would soon make vivid. No artifical "testing time" faced the new
young missionary, but a war as real as the one her great-grandfather had been involved in . . . although it would be shorter, and
she would not be a powder monkey nor would she carry a gun!

You see, it was in this same year of 1899 that the Empress
Dowager gave private encouragement to a secret society called
"the Boxers." This name meant in literal translation, "Society
of Harmonious Fists." The "harmonious" part about it was that
they all struck out at once at the foreigners, and at the Chinese
Christians who had embraced the "foreign religion." Although
the *World Book Encyclopedia* will tell you that 230 foreigners were
murdered and that Roman Catholic and Protestant missionaries
were among them, you'll be interested to know that in the China
Inland Mission 58 adult missionaries were brutally murdered (with
knives and machetes, etc.) and 21 of the missionaries' children.
Hudson Taylor himself was not a well man at the time, and was
unable to "rush to the aid"—which would have had to have been
in various directions at once—because of physical weakness which
made him unable even to cross a room. It is said that he was in
such anguish of soul for his missionaries who were being martyred
that he himself nearly died at the time. All he could do was to
pray fervently day and night for each one of them.

The missionaries were praying fervently also for the Chinese
Christians who were in danger, but before it was all over several
thousand Chinese Christians had been murdered. Mother has told
me of how, covered with a blanket, she hid beneath a window
sill, along with others who were hiding too. Outside that house
where they hid, some were killed in plain sight of those very
windows. It was during the dark of a night that mother, and
others, were carefully dressed and hidden in some conveyance
and slipped into boats. Of course the Wenchow River went out
to sea, but so did other rivers. I am not sure really whether she

was in language school at the time, in Shanghai, or in Wenchow, but she told of being successfully taken, along with others, to escape to Japan for a period of months. They stayed in Japan until the Boxer Rebellion was over and it was safe to return.

It was August 14, 1900, before the Boxer madness (as it was called) began to die down, but the return from Japan was a bit after that. It must have been with a terrific seriousness and re-evaluation of the "cost" of saying, "Anything, Lord—I'll serve you in China no matter what" on the part of these missionaries, my own mother included, that they returned and plunged into language study in earnest. When it came time to be assigned to a station, my mother was sent to Wenchow, Chekiang Province, where, as you already know, she had been teaching in the girls' school for quite some time when my father arrived in 1904.

Teaching in the girls' school meant first of all that Chinese had been mastered to a fair extent. The first language learned for our district of China was Mandarin, and then the Wenchowese dialect. The million people who lived in Wenchow claimed that Wenchowese was actually the oldest and purest Chinese, and they were very proud of their language indeed! Not only did mother teach in Wenchowese, but she had other duties connected with the school. For instance, each Saturday—or was it Friday?— she had to carefully comb the girls' hair, one head at a time, with a fine-toothed comb, looking for lice, then apply "the remedy" to get rid of any lice that were there, ending by shampooing the hair with a special medical shampoo. Quite a different portion of her responsibility was to arrange marriages for the girls. You see, the Chinese custom of arranged marriages threw the Chinese Christians into a quandary—if they sent their daughters to school, and did not bind their feet . . . who on earth would marry them? An educated girl with big feet was most "undesirable." The old custom of preparing girls to be ladies and not peasants consisted of bending the toes under (during the growing period) and binding them to prevent further growth. Tiny, hurting feet resulted, causing the thus "beautified" girls to hobble with short, mincing steps. The C.I.M. had a requirement (you may call it trying to westernize, if you like) that any girls being admitted to the girls' school had to have their feet unbound so that they could have a possibility of growing normal feet for a more comfortable walk through life!

There was a boys' school also in the compound, and boys would shyly come to mother and indicate some girl they felt would be a very special one to marry. In fact, both the boys and the girls had something to say about these decisions. The "arrangement" was not without their "asking" nor without the girl being allowed to say "yes." Mother in fact was a go-between. Many were the hilarious stories she could tell about the funny reasons or the strange descriptions as to which girl would be "first choice" and which "second choice" . . . and also the definite responses both in the strong negative, or the strong affirmative.

The mission compound consisted of a large piece of land, with the mission house built on it, a two-story house surrounded by a verandah, with a garden of grass and bamboo trees where I first played. The girls' school and the boys' school, both of which had dormitories, and a Chinese church were also in the compound. Services were attended not only by people living in the compound, but those coming from all over Wenchow on Sundays and other times of meetings. In addition there were the Chinese pastor's house, the cook's house, Amah's house, and the houses of others who worked on the compound, including dear old Adgipah, the gatekeeper. Yes, there was a gate in the high wall surrounding the entire compound—a stone wall, needed to keep out bandits and thieves. The locked gates were of solid wood, with a lattice-work window across them, through which Adgipah looked to see who might be wanting to come in and made certain it was someone whom he could trust to be honest.

The living room of the mission house had windows out onto the verandah so that anyone sitting in there could see not only the garden, but whoever was walking along the verandah. Of course, whoever was walking along the verandah could also see into the living room..

George Hugh Seville hit upon a plan whereby he could bypass the rules to "have a word alone" with Jessie Maude Merritt Greene. One day Jessie was embroidering, sitting close to the window for better light on her work. Up and down the verandah George walked, trying to catch the attention of his beloved person.

With daisies he had picked from the garden (extras stuffed in his pocket, no doubt), he walked jauntily along, daisy in left hand held as obviously as possible, right hand plucking petals— "She loves me, she loves me not, she loves me, she loves me not, *she loves me, she loves me not.*" Was she deaf and blind? "She loves me, she loves me not." I don't know how many daisies he demolished before Jessie looked up with as stern a look as she could muster, and said, "The answer is—no." As far as she was concerned it was definite, and final. She told me in that one time of sharing confidences, "I thought he was a cheeky extrovert, breaking rules surreptitiously, and trying to be so clever. I wasn't the least impressed, and I meant 'no.'"

However, George was in love. And—George was a persistent person with much imagination. In the following days not only did he write to his brother to send a diamond ring, but he prayed a lot about Jessie's changing her mind. He had no intention of taking "no" as the final answer. Time after time he had asked her the same question, finding moments, finding opportunities to ask again, and again. Had he stopped . . . there would be no story to tell. Had she been stubborn forever and stuck to her resolution never to marry again, no matter how she felt about anyone . . . there would be no story to tell. In that same moment of telling me about it, mother had said, "Really, I still dreamt in my sleep about Walter . . . and although I was growing fond of George, I felt as if I would be a bigamist."

There are a few things that are important to say right here. First, it is important not to have standards lower than the Bible, but also not to have standards higher than the Bible. God who made us, knows our needs and did say that "until death do us part" is to be the length of oneness. It is not that it is necessary to marry again, but one must realize one is not lower on some spiritual measuring stick if one marries again after becoming a widow or widower. Second, there is more to marriage than happiness or personal fulfillment or even companionship. Marriage is also a oneness which brings forth something into history which would not have been there otherwise! Never forget that in the midst of the foggy, mistaken ideas of marriage that drift around in the twentieth century. History would be different in so many ways had not there been the impact on other people of the "two," as well as the bringing forth of whatever children result from the "oneness." The mystery of being is all bound up in this, and so is the on-going War . . . intellectually, spiritually, and in every area where the enemy attacks. A far too trivial idea of marriage prevails today—without the astonishing and frightening reality of what may or may not happen a hundred years from now . . . "if—" and "if not—." Your existence has significance.

The tenth time the question was asked . . . the answer was "yes." So in Shanghai, on March 29, 1905, a wedding was held in the Mission Headquarters of the China Inland Mission. The bride and groom were dressed in Chinese dress—George with his own pigtail hanging proudly down his back, and Jessie not looking a bit Chinese but very demure in her brocaded gown over the trousers, the mandarin collar setting off her auburn hair, her blue eyes, and the pink-and-white complexion that went with it. Five years after her death almost fifty-five years later, George was to write to his son-in-law Ralph Bragdon: "This is the sixtieth anniversary of our marriage in Shanghai—1905—the beginning of fifty-five years (within two months and a few days) of a wonderful life together. I realize now more than I ever did before what a talented, tactful, and true wife 'Mother Seville' was, what a help she was to others (e.g., the wives of students and teachers in Faith Seminary, as well as the girls in the girls' school in Wenchow and the Bible women and members of the Wenchow church). Her own daughters, too, owe their mother a lot for their skills and for certain of their traits and character."

That was written after fifty-five years of living together and having much experience of what "for better and for worse" had been all about in their own "piece of history."

When father was reminiscing to Susan when he was ninety-seven, he laughed as he told of Janet's birth. "The other missionary couples in Wenchow had no children, and the local Chinese church people were a bit curious about Westerners because of that. When Jessie and I had a child we realized our 'stock had gone up'; we were considered to be really normal human beings." Janet Elizabeth was born January 13, 1906. Then on November 7, 1907, a boy was born—named John for his two grandfathers. You can imagine the rejoicing on both sides of the Pacific Ocean at the

news of his birth. His was a short life, and his death was a deep sorrow mother and father never got over.

Does one ever "get over" death? How clearly the Lord tells us that "the last enemy to be destroyed is death. . . ." Death is an enemy, and is a result of the Fall. Bodies and souls were made to be together, not to be torn apart. Thank God for the final restoration we look forward to at the time of the resurrection, of which Christ's resurrection was the "first fruits."

I have John Eldridge Seville's baby book here, and on a page next to the one with a sweet picture of mother holding her five-month-old son, are the notations of his life: "Began to roll all the way over May 25. Began to creep July 1. Began to pull himself up by crib rail July 10. Walked the length of his crib two days later. Took him to Chefoo, North China, the beginning of July—where he died July 25. Buried in the new cemetery, Chefoo." The doctor's certificate is still clear: "July 25, 1908. I hereby certify that John E. Seville of Wenchow, aged 8 months, died in my presence at Chefoo and the cause of death was gastroenteritis and diarrhea, (signed) Albert Hogg, M.D." I also have the official document "Report of the Death of an American Citizen" from the American Consular Service in Shanghai. "This American Citizen being 8 months and 18 days old, a native-born American citizen residing in Wenchow, in this Consular District."

What possible difference to history could that short life have had? Yet it would be unfair to go on without making it emphatic that not only is John in heaven, now having been with his parents and grandparents for a long time, but also that his birth, short life, and death have made a difference. His life and death gave a sweetness and sympathetic understanding to Jessie Seville which helped many young mothers and other people in the midst of their sorrows. Not even a wee baby "slips into the water and causes no ripple." The Tapestry is different because of the existence of that person.

My sister Elsa Ruth was born October 24, 1909, in Wenchow. She was there as a loving "big sister" to welcome me at my birth, although Janet was off in Chefoo School (the C.I.M. boarding school) and had the rather "flat" experience of being called into the headmistress's room to be told, "You have a new baby sister" . . . with no previous warning!

In 1814, a hundred years before I was born, the war of 1812 was still going on, and Washington, D.C., was being burned. It is recorded that both the White House and the Capitol Building were burned, and their red brick exteriors were hopelessly stained. To cover the damage, the bricks were painted white after that disaster, and they remain glistening white to this day. In 1914 the First World War broke forth—the war that was to "end all wars, and make the world safe for democracy"! This great proclamation reminds one of a sentence from Augustine's *City of God:* "Even wars, then, are waged with peace as their object, even when they are waged by those who are concerned to exercise their warlike prowess, either in command or in the actual fighting. Hence it is an established fact that peace is the desired end of war." If you have read Volume 2 of Malcolm Muggeridge's *Chronicles of Wasted Time,* you have had a fascinating view in the second section, "A Grinning Honor," of the Second World War as seen from his astute and humorous accounts of life at the GHQ Home Forces. Francis Schaeffer was just two years and eight months old, so he was having no personal "viewpoints" of the First World War, humorous or otherwise, when it broke out—nor did he know that half the world away, a "war baby" was being born who would affect his life!

I used to resent the label I was given in casual conversation when I was little, "Oh, yes, Edith was a war baby." The label was given, evidently, to babies born in 1914! The official "Report of Birth of Children born to American Parents—American Consular Service" states that: "Edith Rachel Merritt Seville—Sex, Female; Date of birth, November 3, 1914, 9 A.M." . . . was born at Flower Garden Lane, Wenchow, China, . . . and that the doctor was Dr. E. T. A. Stedeford, United Methodist Mission, Wenchow, China.

Although I was born at nine o'clock in the morning of November 3, this official cablegram, registering my birth in Washington, D.C., as was necessary, arrived in Washington on November 2 (due to the time difference) . . . which has always given me some delight in knowing that, in a sense, my grandparents and relatives knew about it a day ahead of time—or, that I might feel I could celebrate two days!

The ages of my parents given on this official report are: George

Hugh Seville, age 38; Jessie Merritt Seville, age 40. Remembering that mother could have been killed during the Boxer Rebellion, as were fifty-eight of her fellow missionary friends, and that she had said "no" to my father nine times, and had meant not to change her mind—along with all the other "impossibilities" add this, that today doctors are advising women to abort if they are as old as forty. The likelihood of my existence having come about by chance is very slim. The hope that I would be a boy was strong in my parents, I know. When Elsa was told I was a girl, she stood looking at me, and then sighed a deep five-year-old's sigh of disappointment, asking with a shred of hope, "Don't boys *sometimes* have brown hair?" My "welcome" was not an ecstatic one, although love and acceptance were there. The day was going to come when not only a little boy would be glad that I had been a girl, but others whose lives and existence would be dependent on that which had brought disappointment to my immediate family.

Meantime the war raged in Europe . . . but in China, German, British, American, and Swiss missionaries worked side by side against a common enemy, working in togetherness in the same army the Lord is speaking about when He says, "Fight the good fight." Here were individuals whose passports were from countries at war with each other, and from a neutral country; they were getting letters from relatives telling of tragic deaths, lost properties, uprooted family lives and lands. Can't you imagine the strained, uncomfortable moments when the mail arrived and was being opened? Can't you imagine reading conflicting news in whatever newspapers trickled through? War casualties bringing tears to be comforted by Christian brothers and sisters whose earthly blood relatives were divided by sharp lines on the maps! As history flows on, time puts a distance between us and our ancestors who were on different sides, so often we are blended in one physical family.

Wars, and rumors of wars. . . . So often the Lord's people, "the sheep of His pasture," are strangely caught on battlefields, or waiting for fearful news from half the world away, about cities, towns, villages, land, and the people comprising all that the word "home" includes.

The marvel is that actually heaven is our home country and

our citizenship there is not an airy-fairy kind of spiritual fable, but more real than anything on earth. The miracle is that there *is* a oneness that needs no earthly papers to prove, no earthly passport to identify—a oneness of the people of God, the Lord's family, the Bride of Christ, which *exists.* This oneness can cross all barriers at any point of history, whether they be barriers of civil or global war, or the barriers in the sad "wars" dividing people in heated theological discussion. God Himself knows "who is on the Lord's side," and His army is united in the reality of what will count all through eternity.

The China Inland Mission did not fall apart during the First World War, nor did the Revolutionary War stop missionaries from America (descendants of soldiers) from coming into the work of British Hudson Taylor, nor will Satan's devices to assail the true oneness of God and His people ever prevail. Thank God.

MISSING BIRTH RECORDS! 6

What do you mean, "missing birth records"? Didn't you have all sorts of proper papers in the American Consulate in Shanghai, and the right office in Washington, and the correct cablegrams arriving at the required time to establish without a doubt American citizenship for a lifetime? Yes, yes, all was in order. It was Fran who had had a doctor who was inebriated when he assisted at his birth; it was Fran's birth records that were missing. What's that got to do with this chapter?

As I start to go back over my own growing-up years, trying to be fair in choosing what would give an accurate account, trying to pull out of the dust of years the facts that would be helpful to someone wrestling with a variety of things in his or her own life, one reality hits me as important to relate. That is that in contrast to Fran, who had vivid assurance of a before and after concerning his discovery of truth, and his new birth—a period of time that can be pointed to, remembered, recorded, comprising a birth record for that most important entering into the family of the Lord—I had no idea of when I became a Christian. Now, we know that a Book exists, and names are faithfully written there, so a record *is* in heaven right now, and the promise is that the names will be read one day, and we will probably know *then* the moment we were actually born into that family. From

99

Revelation 21, as we thrill with the description of the Heavenly City so brilliantly lighted by the glory of God, and "the Lamb is its lamp," where on no day the gates are to be shut, we also read that the people who will be there are described as "only those whose names are written in the Lamb's book of life." There *is* a permanent record, an indestructible record.

My problem at each stage of childhood was a longing that I could point to a moment when I had suddenly discovered truth; or had passed out of a dark circle of wickedness into a changed life; or had, like Pilgrim in *Pilgrim's Progress,* felt a heavy burden of sin like a bag of rocks on my back, and had come to the "foot of the cross" bowed, and felt it slip off, rolling on down the hill behind me. I wanted a before-and-after story, and a clear birth record to point to—and it was missing! You see, the trouble was that when I was honest with myself, I couldn't remember a time when I had not believed the truth of the Bible and when I had not, at least in some imperfect way, loyally trusted and loved the wonderful God of the Bible to the level of my understanding. Somehow this didn't seem to fit in with what other people talked about, and in a variety of circumstances I would privately tremble as to whether my apparently missing birth records after all meant I hadn't been born!

That comes later in the story. At this point I've just been physically born, the war is raging in Europe, and my grandparents are soon to die natural deaths, in the sense that they were in their eighties. Grandmother Eliza Jane Seville died before I was two months old, and Grandfather John Seville died seven months later. I didn't know about it at the time, naturally, but today as I write, I have before me the typed copy of the funeral sermon for Grandfather Seville, preached in Pittsburgh by a Rev. Milligan. "Precious in the sight of Jehovah is the death of his saints" was his theme, and he presented the joy of mothers and fathers when their children come home, as a picture of the Heavenly Father welcoming *His* children. It is a short sermon, giving the other side of death, that is, the aspect of being present with the Lord and together with those who have gone before. Seven months were all these two had been separated, which the pastor found special, since they had been so many years together—from her eighteenth birthday. During the same period of time my grandmother Elizabeth Merritt also died, so while they were all meeting each other in heaven, I was never to have a living grandparent, except Grandfather John Merritt! Generations are amazing measures of time—overlapping, merging, each new one dependent on the past ones for very existence; affecting each other, passing genes to the next ones, influencing coming ones both during a lifetime and after the lifetime is over.

There is a terrific responsibility we each have during our lifetime: "The living, the living—they praise you, as I am doing today; fathers tell their children about your faithfulness" (Isa. 38:19). How many generations are being talked about? Children become fathers for century following century: "He is the Lord our God. . . . He remembers his covenant forever, the word he commanded, for a thousand generations . . ." (Ps. 105:7–8). With which generation will the responsibility stop? Certainly not the one we are in today . . . unless "today" is the day Jesus will return. Until that moment, until that "twinkling of the eye," we are to "walk around the reality of God's Word and His Works" in a way which seems to me described in Psalm 48:12–14: "Walk about Zion, go around her, count her towers, consider well her ramparts, view her citadels, that you may tell of them to the next generation. For this God is our God for ever and ever; he will be our guide even to the end." (All three quotations are NIV.)

Today, as I am writing this, it is November 3, 1980. It is my sixty-sixth birthday, so an appropriate time to be "living" in these verses I have just quoted! It is an appropriate time to be facing the reality of generations, when I have already lived through, or observed, several of them! You and I are a part of the total Tapestry, whether we examine our bit with a magnifying glass or not!

I was starting to stand up in my "gatse"—a smaller-than-a-playpen little movable enclosure made of bamboo in which to keep a baby safe—when, in another China Inland Mission house, in another compound much like ours, in the city of Chungking, Szechuan Province, a new baby was being born to the Bird family. I was to meet "Birdie" one day in dancer Linette's Chelsea apartment in London, when Fran was answering questions during a "L'Abri evening" there. Birdie, who was later to become a very special part of L'Abri in Huémoz, is still living and being used

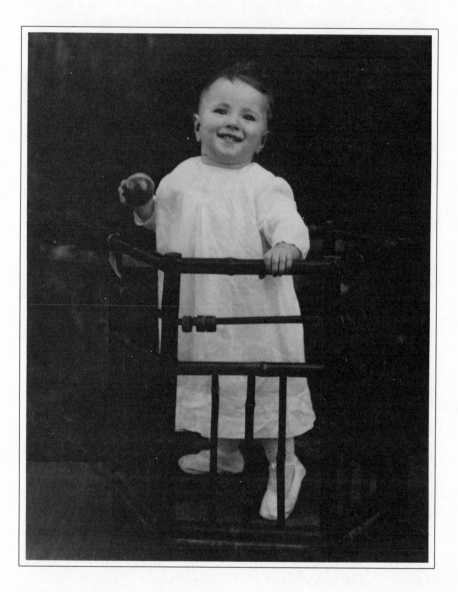

by the Lord in her tiny music-box chalet "The Nest" perched above the sloping fields at the lower side of Huémoz. She may have had her birth on August 17, 1915, registered in New Zealand, but my birthplace and hers, as we write it on any papers to be filled out, must always be the same—China.

Two threads in The Tapestry were put on the loom very close together, both geographically and in time, but only the Lord knew there was to be a time of much greater closeness! Birdie's grandfather Doctor Herbert Parry was one of the medical doctors in the famous group of seventy new missionaries Hudson Taylor had prayed for, who went to China during the 1870s, so early in the China Inland Mission. Birdie's mother was born in that same mission house where Birdie was born. In fact, Birdie's mother was one of the first pupils ever to go to Chefoo School, and Birdie was in Chefoo right after both of my sisters were there. The only reason I wasn't sent to Chefoo was that we returned to America before I was old enough! Not one of us has a "history" isolated from the *flow* of history.

My early memories are very vivid, but I can't put dates to them, except that all these things happened before I was five years old. One of my earliest experiences of affliction and pain came when I had the dread disease trachoma, which then was supposed inevitably to result in blindness. I still remember the feel of Dr. Stedeford's knees pressed tightly against my ears, holding my head as if in a vise so that I couldn't twist it, or move even a fraction, as he turned back my eyelids and rubbed bluestone against my pupils. He must have been extremely skillful, or the Lord answered prayer directly to use the doctor's treatment to make me better, because I was completely cured of this "incurable" disease from which my eyes should have been permanently damaged. Another of my early "afflictions" came when Amah, preparing my bath, had brought a pail of boiling water up to the bedroom and set it next to the door. The big tin bathtub stood on a grass mat in the middle of the floor. She had gone out to get the cold water, when I pulled at the pail and tipped the boiling water over on my legs, resulting in second degree burns on both of them.

For days (how many I can't tell you) I sat swathed in bandages, with burning pain that remains in memory, and with a succession of gifts brought to distract me, lovingly presented by Chinese friends on the compound. There were two white rabbits and a very young white kid. The wee kid was to be my favorite companion when I got well enough to run around again, and got hauled in and out of the old rowboat in the garden. This was my favorite "travel game." "All aboard for Shanghai," I'd call out in Chinese, and if the kid didn't oblige, I'd drag it in with its four legs resisting! The day came, however, that brought this companionship to a swift close. One of our favorite games used to be my pretending to be a kid too, and, with lowered heads, we'd run full speed ahead, charging into each other. Then, as if from one day to the next, the kid's horns, still invisible under the hairy forehead, sprouted and banged into my head with such force that two blue "horns" appeared on my forehead. With no further ado, my playmate disappeared to spend his life in the manner of ordinary goats sprouting horns.

Having a "working mother" whose days were occupied with her duties in the girls' school, I was cared for by my Chinese amah, who ate with me, gave me many of my first answers to a diversity of questions, and taught me Chinese. In later years, father disclosed that I picked up not always the best vocabulary, as she would say "fichaw" ("shut up") instead of the more polite "fichi" ("keep quiet"). I learned a lot of Chinese too from all the people in their own houses, as, being a very willful child, I didn't heed my parents' wishes that I should eat Chinese food only once a week. Their idea of a proper supper was scrambled eggs and toast or milk toast, and they felt Chinese food was "too rich for little girls." I don't think Amah agreed with that idea at all; in fact, she probably aided me in my daily trek to each of the houses. Later, people told mother that it was uncanny the way I seemed to know exactly when they had the meal ready, as at just that moment I would appear at the doorway, always to receive a warm welcome.

I not only learned to speak Chinese in these visits, but how to manage chopsticks, and how to stuff the left side of my mouth with rice and drink tea down the right side, not disturbing the rice. I remember faces bent over my small stature, anxiously inspecting to see if indeed the rice was still there after the tea was safely down the throat. An achievement!

I learned more vocabulary, tones of voice, and gestures from cook, as he taught me to bargain with tradespeople. Evidently I became expert, and since I was so tiny, the Chinese must have felt it was great to have me deal with the tradespeople selling vegetables, fish, meat, fruit, and so on, and actually get the prices down to where they were correct. My Chinese was sufficient also to tell about the need of believing in Jesus in order to be ready for heaven. I remember being very earnest about the messages I'd "preach" when playing church with my Chinese playmates. We'd sing away, and then I'd say, "Do *you* want to preach? No? Well, then, I'll preach." Or I'd say, "Do you want to pray? No? Well, then, I'll pray." It was more than a game, I know, as I felt a strong sense of responsibility to make it all understandable. I asked questions, and made strong statements of "doubts" at a very early age. I remember listening to the story of Peter walking on the water, and declaring, "I don't believe it. No one can walk on water." I then received careful explanation as to the fact that God is the Creator, and that Jesus could do anything at all. It was He who had made the water. Once convinced, I fiercely believed it was unshakable fact. "Fiercely" is the only word for it.

My sister Elsa went off to boarding school at six, but as she was a precocious reader, and spent vacations at home, I'm sure she was the first one to read *Pilgrim's Progress* to me, and I know she must have been the one to "play Pilgrim's Progress" with me. That game consisted of climbing laboriously up the stairs with a pillowcase stuffed with the pillow and a few heavier things slung on one's back. Then, at the top, with all seriousness, one bowed where the imaginary cross stood (the drawing in the old copy of the book as our model), suddenly letting the pillowcase slide out of one's hands, watching it go tumbling down the stair. The "burden of sin" had rolled off! Just what it consisted of I might not have known, but I wasn't ignorant of the fact that I was naughty and there was forgiveness. It was more than a game. John Bunyan had an effect on me, and the vivid pictures of that journey that flowed in the words of his imagination were woven into my feelings, as well as into my thought world, with a growing measure of understanding.

As you move the microscope or magnifying glass—however

you think of looking back 250 years—marvel over the effect on thousands upon thousands of unborn people of this one man's faithfulness to God and willingness to "slog on!" Born in 1628, John Bunyan was an earnest, fiery preacher, who as a dissenter was thrown into Bedford Jail in 1660 to stop him from preaching. The conditions were horrible, but rather than make a promise to stop preaching, which would have effected his release, he declared he'd preach within a day, whenever he could get out. The book *Pilgrim's Progress*, started in that prison, was to be used to bring many generations of people out of a worse prison—the prison of darkness and ignorance of truth. Little would he have dreamed when it was printed in 1678 that people would still be reading it in the 1980s! Yet in his own lifetime, misery was the lot or "reward" of Bunyan and his family in exchange for his faithfulness. The books are not balanced in "the land of the living"; we look in confidence to the time and the place where indeed they will be balanced and the martyrs will be rewarded in ways beyond our imagination.

I was to learn something of the wickedness as well as cruelty of human beings to human beings in the midst of my childhood in Wenchow. At times I was taken in a rickshaw to a compound across the city to play with my friend Nina. Her father was in the French consulate, and her mother was Chinese. As we were making one of those trips one day, the coolie was running along at an even jog, bumpety-bump across the cobblestones, when suddenly a little one-year-old toddled out into his path. The coolie just kept right on, knocking him to one side as if he were a movable bush in his path to be kicked aside. I cried and clung to mother's hand and nearly fell out of the rickshaw trying to see if the baby was all right.

The reassurance I was given never blotted out the deep impression that that man had considered the child as nothing but a hindrance in his path. To me it was a demonstration of the disregard for human beings among people who had only idols to worship. An even more vivid impression of disregard for human life came during my frequent walks with Amah. We would often pass a pagoda along the Wenchow city wall, which was the place for unwanted newborn baby girls to be thrown away. Whimpers could be heard at times. It takes a newborn baby *time* to starve to death!

My question "Why?" had mingled with it the realization that I myself was a third girl, and I wanted the comforting reassurance of the answer that came: "Meifuh . . . Meifuh [my Chinese name], these people don't know about God, or about Jesus His Son. That is why your parents came to China." I felt certain that of course it wouldn't be long until people would know about God, and that then all baby girls would be as much wanted as the baby boys! Some day no more baby girls would be thrown away, if we could just let people know the wonder of the truth.

I had a third kind of personal contact with disturbing results of "heathenism"—the sad loss of my beloved kites. Chinese kites are fantastically complicated and beautiful, and I had been given some box kites with amazing designs. As Amah and Adgipah, and maybe a kitchen boy too, helped me get mine flying high and I ran proudly along the garden holding the string, suddenly my kite pulled at my hand. Before I could really see what was happening, it seemed tangled with another in the air, and, swish, it was whipped out of my hand and . . . gone! It was explained to me that kite thieves were adroit at whipping kites out of unsuspecting people's hands, and that this could be very successfully done from the *other* side of high walls.

My false picture of America was that *there* everyone knew about God, and that therefore there would be no bandits, thieves, or unkind men who could knock toddlers down; and of course no person in America would ever throw a baby away to die. I had much to learn about the world, America included. It was to be a long time, however, before the shock would come in realizing that people could easily throw away their babies, boys as well as girls, in hospitals where science had perfected ways of helping babies to *live!* Recently I've remembered that pagoda of my childhood walks, and have felt some hospitals where abortions take place ought to have roofs of a different shape.

The fact that life begins at conception was a matter-of-fact part of life in China—so it seems to me—as the nine months before birth were counted in one's age. On Chinese New Year's Day, all the newborn babies became one year old, and this continued to be the day through life when another year would be added to one's age.

When the fabulously weird, beautiful, ugly, amazing, intricate, terrible and wonderful New Year's Day parades went by our gate,

someone would always lift me up to watch the floats and the frighteningly masked individuals go by to the tune of Chinese music. People walked on stilts hidden under super-long trousers, skillfully balancing without sticks, supporting enormous heads, dragon bodies and faces, or other imaginative animals and creatures, all made from colorful paper and fashioned in astounding original ways. There were other occasions for parades, but none quite so elaborate as New Year's Day.

Watching all this with a mixture of fascination and revulsion, I was given an unanalyzed but very real and permanent understanding of what the worship of idols consisted of. As I read the word "idol" in the Bible, so woven into the admonition to have no other gods except the true living Creator of the Universe, it is with the background of recognizing something of what was being demonstrated in these parades, as well as in seeing other idols during my walks with Amah. The word has never been an academic one to me. I can see them being carried by on floats, having "eyes that see not" and "ears that hear not"!

Titanic changes come in life with little real preparation. One goes to bed for the last time in a room, in a house, in a garden, in a city, and wakens the next morning to leave that location and the people there . . . "forever"? Continuity is a precious thing to human beings that needs caring for with thought and imagination. At times, however, there is no way of preserving continuity, and, without our knowing it, a day begins which is the ending of a complete chapter of life, as well as the beginning of a totally new one.

All the Chinese were gathered to say good-by. Now was the time to ask my mother, "Don't you think Meifuh is healthy?" and then to let it be known that she had had Chinese food every day, with good rather than harmful results! My official Chinese name, Meifuh ("beautiful happiness"), so familiar to me daily, was no longer going to be my basic name. But the changes were not announced, because as far as anyone in the circle of warm farewells knew, these good-bys were for a period of furlough in America—at the most a year—and then we would all be back again for at least another seven years. As far as my limited understanding went, we were just changing compounds for a year. I imagined being in a compound called America which would be full of relatives. I didn't know anything about "cultural shock" as the old boat *The China* set forth from Shanghai at the end of the summer of 1919. And my father and mother didn't know that this farewell to their beloved work and home and people in China was for a lifetime.

The trip was to take a full month and was to be full of unforgettable experiences of a great variety. There was a curved stairway with wonderful dark wood banisters to slide down. There were decks to run on in the sunshine. There were services for Sunday with a chance to choose my favorite hymns—"When all my troubles and trials are o'er, and I am safe on that beautiful shore . . . that will be glory for me!" and "One Day . . ."—and to sing them at the top of my lungs with my sisters and the other children in that community. A boat voyage like that is a world all its own, rather than simply "travel." The skirting of a typhoon gave drama, and the stop at Honolulu, where we could feast on the panorama of white houses under red tile roofs seeming to grow naturally among the palm trees backed by green hills, filled me with determination that *I'd* live there some day.

One strong memory will let you know I was far from being "good" all the time. A little boy and I decided on our own to do an "inspection" of the cabins. In tiptoeing around one woman's cabin, we discovered a tall, round, shiny enamel box with lovely pictures of sweets on it. We tugged at the cover together, got it open and found beautiful smooth pastel sticks—blue, lavender, turquoise, pink, white—which when tentatively sucked to "inspect" the contents, were found to be covered chocolate sticks. We "inspected" and digested a few of them, put the lid back on the box, and ran off. When I told mother about this foraging we had just done, she sternly told me it had been stealing, and that I was to go immediately to the owner of those chocolate straws and confess what we had done.

I'll never forget the fast heartbeats and the heat that fear brought to my cheeks as I went hand in hand with the boy to "confess." The owner's reply was so surprisingly comforting that we ran back in the greatest of joy to tell mother, "*She* says it was all *her* fault for being so *selfish*, and that she should have passed it around to us long ago!" I'm not sure mother was satisfied with the result of my confession, but it was not all a lost lesson to me. Perhaps the memory of *not* being selfish to other people's detriment had a value beyond measure. To not steal was a by-product.

America! What an impression it made on me: My first elevator in San Francisco which I wanted to ride all day. My first train ride—five days across the United States peering out of dark windows at night to see station platforms from my bed. My first relatives—aunts and uncles and cousins in Pittsburgh, Cleveland, Newburgh, New York—bewilderingly far apart, and unexpectedly short visits. My first mission compound—the C.I.M. Headquarters on West School Lane in Germantown. My first American school experience in kindergarten in Stevens' School for Girls in Chestnut Hill. Not only did I not have any idea my own girls would have two very separate years of going to that school far off in the future, but I had no idea that my future husband was trudging to school daily in Germantown at the very same time! Two of The Tapestry's threads were close . . . but unaware of future weaving, unaware of the existence of any plan involving each other!

Before the year was over my mother was to be told she could not have the needed medical OK for going back to China, and we moved to California for a two-year period. At Orange Avenue School in Monrovia I was to experience the feelings of being in a minority as the children pointed their fingers at me during recess and chanted, "Chinky, chinky Chinaman, sitting on a fence; trying to make a dollar out of fifteen cents! . . . Ya, ya, ya!" In furious retort I drew my small six-year-old frame up to its height. "And they *can* too, and that's more than you can do," I declared as I stood up for the country and people of my birthplace. In California I was to have dysentery, pneumonia, and a series of such things as measles and so on, and my sister Elsa invented wonderful games to be played as she stood on the other side of the screen of my "room," which was a sleeping porch.

My father went to the East Coast to take a year of further study in Gordon College in the Boston area (1921–22), so we were to feel a homesickness for him, yet to have the one period of time of having a grandfather live with us. Grandfather Merritt in his eighties was still painting houses, and I trotted off through orange groves to take him his lunch pail many days. I remember the pride I felt when, as he was painting the house across the street, the ladder slipped and fell, and he hung onto the gutter until someone came running to right the ladder . . . and grandfather's joy was that he had *not spilled any paint!* It was a very different period of my childhood—almost like borrowing someone else's life.

Continuity? As far as houses and lands and even countries were concerned, let alone states or towns and schools, I had none. Churches? In China there was the C.I.M., and I knew nothing about the existence of denominations, not as a five-year-old. In California we went to a Baptist Church. Mother had been brought up a Baptist in Newburgh. Father was a United Presbyterian. The China Inland Mission was interdenominational, so the differences had never been central. What mattered was a firm belief in the truth of the whole Bible. When I was seven, I asked to meet with the board of deacons and to be baptized by immersion so that I could take communion, which seemed so important to me. I remember sitting on a chair, swinging my feet far from the floor, answering questions with great vigor. Yes, I *was* certain I had believed that Jesus is God and that He had taken my punishment. It wasn't only the memory of my "sins" rolling down those stairs in the house in China. I wanted to be a part of the people who were obeying Jesus' command "this do ye in remembrance of me . . . until I come." I wanted to be identified with the family of the Lord, and I really understood enough to make this decision.

Following that period in California, we lived in New Wilmington, Pennsylvania, for a year while my father "candidated" for a church. We lived in one side of a mission house, the other half of it being occupied by Doctor Tom Lambie of Abyssinia, and his wife and children. He inspired me with his colorful stories, and I resolved to grow up and gallop all over Abyssinia on a horse, doing missionary exploits like his medical exploits!

We moved after a year to Newburgh, New York, where father had been called to be pastor of the Westminster Independent Presbyterian Church. Once again I was an outsider going to a school where everyone else knew each other. However, we were to stay in Newburgh for seven years, so my good friend Emily, with whom I started to play at eight, continued to be my friend until we left when I was fourteen. I never lived that long in any one place again until we came to Switzerland, now thirty-two years ago.

Newburgh was the place where I joined the Girl Scouts (while Fran was doing his scouting stint in Germantown) and where at the "Y" I became a tumbler along with acquiring other gym skills, and I learned to swim at the "Y" camp. My sisters had been brilliant in Latin and Greek, to the satisfaction of my father. But I was a disappointment to him, because although I shone in geometry and algebra, English, and sciences, I was a flop in Latin and only suffered through four years of it because of the requirements at that time. And I'm afraid I looked off into the distance thinking of other things when Father was trying to help me with my homework.

My father's salary was very small, so there were economies of every kind. Mother had learned to sew by a Singer Sewing Machine Company correspondence course, and she did ingenious things with fabric bought on sale—remnants—and with clothing that she ripped the seams out of, washed, and made into amazing "new" garments. Her cooking of necessity had to be simple, but she gave things a twist as to flavor and beauty. When I wanted to earn money by starting a candy business, many long hours she helped me to make fudge and penuche and coconut bars, until she got neuritis in her shoulder from doing so much handbeating. We made the magnificent sum of seventy dollars from our combined efforts. I was the salesperson peddling the five-cent "bars" wrapped in wax paper. What a bargain people got!

Church consisted of morning and evening services on Sunday, a prayer meeting which my father began on Wednesday evenings—when people repeated Scripture verses, and one or two prayed short prayers, and Father gave a Bible study. And then there were the socials. There was the "waistline social" when each person's waist was measured and one penny per inch was paid per person . . . and the "covered dish social" when each person brought a "covered dish" (surprise!) of food and also paid something to come, to meet the need of whatever fund was being collected. There was a fair where the women brought all their knitted and crocheted things to display, along with patchwork quilts and jams and jellies to sell, with the proceeds going to the church. Father and mother disapproved of this way of raising money but felt that the idea of "giving directly to the Lord" or tithing needed to be taught gradually. Understanding would come in time.

My personal discussions with Emily, who was a Christian Scientist, were in the realm of whether or not "matter" existed, as she held firmly to the presupposition that "mind is all and all is mind." Many were the long conversations we would have, with various reference books dragged out.

My parents had taught me that in addition to "modernism" (which we discussed in detail at meals), which was a doctrinal turning away from the truth of the Bible, there was also "worldliness," which consisted of such things as dancing, playing cards, going to see movies, smoking, and drinking anything alcoholic. This was during prohibition, so the sale of alcoholic beverages was against the law, and speakeasies and bootleggers were the ones connected with such sales! Women in the churches belonged to the Women's Christian Temperance Union and wore pins made to look like white ribbons. It was a different era. I remember being taken to a meeting of this organization, and feeling a bit strange at the football cheer kind of thing as pledges were made and everyone shouted, "White ribbon!" Yet I was convinced that alcoholism had wrecked a lot of lives and homes, and I thought maybe something needed to be done about it. I must say for mother that she never gave the impression she would want to make this the center of her life's work.

During the time Fran was reading his Greek philosophy and starting to read the Bible, plunging into the period when he was going to discover the truth, I was living in what I felt was a bracket . . . like that [ ] . . . a bracket separated from the rest of my life. Between the ages of fourteen and seventeen—when I met Fran—I didn't rebel in the way children of Christian parents rebel, at times, against the truth of the Bible, against Christianity as such. I was convinced that Christianity was true. I fought in biology classes and zoology classes, arguing with my professors against evolution, using my own feeling that I couldn't possibly have faith enough to believe what they were teaching me in class or in the books. I talked to people—if and when I found anyone who was interested in discussing these things—but found only a limited number who cared about what might be "true" in giving answers to life.

Why the bracket? This was a period of time before any of the Christian youth organizations had started, and I really didn't know any young person anywhere near my own age who had certainty about Christianity being true, or who cared to talk about it. My conclusion was that if I wanted to "do anything normal," such as go to the basketball games, football games, and school functions, then I'd better simply put off what my parents would have called a "Christian life," and live in a [bracket]. Although I had been forbidden to go to dances or movies, I had their OK to go to the sports events. My dates were for games, but often a dance in the gym followed a game, and I was a natural-born dancer who didn't need to learn. What I am saying is that I deceived my parents, by simply going to school parties, which did have bobbing for apples etc., going on in various parts of the building, but where I spent the evening dancing. I also went to an occasional movie. And in these times, I must say, having been taught as I had been, I *felt* very suspended from being the person I intended to be. Sometimes I'd say to a boy, "You really don't know me, because I'm not really being me. I'm really a very serious person, and I intend to spend my life making truth known." To say that I had struggles and frustrations would be correct, because, however foolish and ridiculous I am describing myself to have been, one thing is true—I was feeling an artificial quality about my words and actions and choices of people to be with and talk to, as well as about the subject matters of conversation and inflections of voice, that made me feel as if I were someone acting in an ongoing play, rather than being myself. That is the best job I can do of describing that period which extended through a year of high school in Newburgh, New York, two years in Toronto (where my father had gone to be Assistant Editor of C.I.M.'s monthly magazine *China's Millions*) where I went to the North Toronto Collegiate, and my senior year in Germantown, Philadelphia.

My greatest release and times of reality came in the midst of reading. I loved to curl up in a tree, on a couch, in bed, on a stone, daytime or night, and read. Living in another period of history, in other geographic locations, inside other personalities, in the midst of the working of other people's minds, gave reality to a diversity. What I lived through in the books, and the friends I had within them, are as much a part of my past life as the people I knew in school. I've never been in Prince Edward Island, but in all of L. M. Montgomery's books (the *Anne* books, the *Emily* books, and others) the people and places seem to be a part of my own background. The very trees and meadows, the shoreline and special rocks seem a part of my own growing-up years. This is one reason it became such a joy to me to share my own books in reading aloud to my children. Happily, in life we are not limited to only the people we are able to meet, to talk to, to discuss with, to think with; books give a wider possibility of a communication that really isn't as one-sided as some people might think! Books do give real continuity from generation to generation—as well as to those who have to live in so many places that the usual roots have no time to grow. Reading and studying Shakespeare and old English poetry and literature in school is another kind of bridge back into another generation, another moment of history, another set of roots.

Just before I was to have my last year at Toronto Collegiate, my father was asked to come to Germantown, Philadelphia, because *China's Millions* was going to be printed in Philadelphia rather than Toronto from that time on. House-hunting turned up "just the right place for us," on a street named Ashmead Place South, and once more mother went to work to make a home out of another set of walls and windows. The house had a brick fireplace and bay windows, and though I didn't know it, it would be the background for real discussion, long and satisfying conversation, courting, and eventually a wedding reception. But for the moment it was the new home for George and Jessie Seville and their six-teen-year-old daughter Edith, soon to enter her third high school.

To plunge into the last year of high school with people who have been together for three years, is as much of an outsider situation as you can imagine. As I walked by the vacant lot on the corner of Ashmead Place day after day, going up Germantown Avenue to Germantown High School, I didn't see any "ghosts" of an evangelist's tent, nor of any of the people who had been in it. Nor did I have any idea my feet were tracing the footsteps of Francis Schaeffer, who had walked out onto that same sidewalk with a firm resolution that was going to affect my whole life. All I saw was a dusty lot and the beginning of the building of a new gas station, and all I felt was discouragement about my feelings of once more being an "alien"—this time with a Canadian accent.

The Tapestry? Threads being brought to the same place geographically? Threads being untwisted in the hands of a weaver to be threaded into the position for a new section of the pattern? Writing about Ashmead Place South gives me the feeling right now of being in an empty theater, with the artist painting a central backdrop for a play no one but the script writer has yet read, and no one has yet heard but the artist to whom he has read it. Thirty Ashmead Place South . . . one year after Zeoli's Tent Meetings . . . and one year before a totally other kind of "meeting" is to take place. The scene is set.

THE MERGER 7

May 31, 1980. Hampden-Sydney College Campus is almost deserted. Francis and Edith Schaeffer are sitting on the old fence, made of beautiful iron rods, held by white posts at regular intervals. Perched on the top rail, feet on the second rail, they look out over the lawns of the campus, bordered by deep woods. A gorgeous pink rosebush, spilling petals on the ground, makes it look carpeted in pale pink, while fresh blossoms are still opening to fill the bush. "Amazing tranquility," she muses. "Just think of all the hubbub of city campuses, and this fantastic beauty and quietness the Lord gave you for four years." "I know, it doesn't seem possible, but it just hasn't changed in almost half a century," he says. "Let's walk over to my old home, 'Fourth Passage,' and look in. Surely the inside will be all spruced up and changed . . . but that wonderful Southern architecture of red bricks and white columns never changes, does it?"

Exactly forty-five years after Fran's graduation day and forty-nine years from his entering the freshman class, we are back at Hampden-Sydney by invitation. No one has been knowingly clever in arranging to honor Fran on this precise date by asking him to come back to his Alma Mater to be presented with a Phi Beta Kappa key, of which the college did not have a chapter when he was a student.

Let me quote from the Summer-Fall 1980 issue of *The Hampden Sydney Record:*

Elected earlier in the spring but not initiated until May 30, because he had to fly in from Switzerland to receive the honor, was Dr. Francis A. Schaeffer, '35, named to Phi Beta Kappa as an alumnus member on the strength of his contributions to human knowledge. These consist of twenty-one books and two series of films, in which, as the leading evangelical Christian apologist of the age, he has exemplified the Hampden-Sydney spirit of devotion to the logical pursuit of truth by insisting with Plato, that "the only viable approach to an honest expression of faith is the well-examined one," as President Bunting remarked in introducing Schaeffer and his wife Edith—an authoress in her own right—to the Board of Trustees of the College. "Schaeffer has achieved world-wide prominence for his rigorous arguments that belief in the infallibility of the Bible as the Word of God is rationally credible and defensible, requiring no existential 'leap of faith.'

'His home, L'Abri, near Geneva, has become the hub of international discussions about the intellectual defense of Christianity, and Schaeffer's arguments have received global attention through his books and filmed treatments of the roots of modern despair and the origins of our attitudes toward abortion and the value of life.

Dr. Graves H. Thompson, '27, who served as acting president of the Phi Beta Kappa meeting at which Schaeffer was initiated on May 30 in the Jones Rare Book Room, delivered this charge to the new member: "Dr. Schaeffer, any charge on my part would be superfluous; you have already received your charge from a higher source. Suffice it to say that as an undergraduate at Hampden-Sydney College you would have become a member of Phi Beta Kappa on the basis of your scholastic record, if the College had had a chapter at that time. Your promise then has been borne out since by your many scholarly achievements. Election to Phi Beta Kappa is generally considered an honor; may I say, however, that in accepting our invitation to membership, you also do us an honor."

The initiation had been followed by a tea given by Dr. and Mrs. William C. Holbrook in their lovely home on the campus, where such a variety of old college friends, and people newly friends because of Fran's books, or L'Abri, were gathered. Almost a half century of life squashed into focus in a strange way, like looking out of the wrong end of a telescope! All so very small!

What is any of it worth? How short is time, after all? The only value is to be found *not* in honors given by men, nor in recognition for work accomplished at any point in the years. If that is what anyone is working for, it is less than the value of the rose petals that have fallen after their moment of glory! For a Christian, the value is that whatever our "work" (yours and ours) has been, is today, or will be—as we are in some measure faithful in doing what we have been given by the Lord to do—it will end with the welcome word: "Well done, thou good and faithful servant"— a word of lasting value.

We sat on the fence that idyllic, sunny May morning, talking over the hours we had spent in the previous two days—being so warmly welcomed and having the special delight of an annual trustees' dinner in the beauty of the old library building with its long, curved clear glass windows outlined in the colonial white woodwork, and its tables set with gleaming crystal, silver candle-sticks, and bowls of garden roses. We talked about the strange feeling of sleeping in the "V.I.P." bedroom of "Miss Lacey's house," which had been a boarding place for the "favored few" in Fran's college days. We sat amazed at the drama of being in that place welcomed by President Josiah Bunting III right after graduation—such a precise block of time after Fran's graduation, so much behind us, Fran's cancer ongoing, yet work still ahead. We remarked at the strangeness of finding the chair Fran had reupholstered when he was President of the Literary Society sit-ting regally in the museum of the historic objects of the college. To be in Hampden-Sydney with empty buildings, students all gone, crickets singing, leaves blowing, grass unchanged in color, well-tended gardens but no gardener in sight, forty-five years having lapsed—it was almost like coming back after one had left the world!

We slipped off the fence and walked over to "Fourth Passage." As we opened the door, we saw with a gasp that it was *not* modern-ized inside. With the unreality of silence and emptiness of human movement in the familiar old barren hall, there came a wave of emotion at discovering that the broken old stair railings and sag-ging steps were still there, unchanged. But the people whose feet had taken those stairs two at a time, where indeed were they? People—more fragile than "things" . . . people—more temporary than wooden steps and old baseboards, let alone marble, or even brick! Yet, people—significant in history . . . and people—with a capacity for eternal life! Some of the people, the boys who had taken the steps two at a time, are already in heaven. This is a fact we know.

If this were a movie—right as we are musing these thoughts in that dusty, deserted building, emptied of students for the summer, suddenly a fade-out would begin to take place. The present view of the two of us in 1980 would begin to blur . . . the May trees and flowers of the campus would merge into autumn colors . . . the silence allowing soft sounds to be heard would shift and with a change of music would come a hum of voices . . . boys with short haircuts and the clothing of forty-five years ago would fill the walks, jump over the fence, clamber up the stairway of Fourth Passage, Cushing Hall . . . and a short-haired, very young-looking nineteen-year-old Francis Schaeffer would appear, standing determinedly beside his grey-painted box, with screwdriver in hand. He would be seen to start removing the four long screws holding on the lid before unpacking, and we would be ready to look back into September of 1931.

The antagonism for ministerial students in Fourth Passage showed up rapidly, and things were made hard for Fran. Hard? There were a variety of ways. First of all, his roommate, Snerp, beat him regularly. Hazing was a regular part of a freshman's life in those days, and it consisted of being beaten with a paddle or a stick, for any one of a list of things (there was an official list), such as sitting on the fence, being outside anywhere without a "dink cap" on, not producing matches or anything else asked for by an upperclassman rapidly enough to suit, and so on. Snerp beat Fran with a coat hanger. One day, after some weeks of this treatment, Fran felt he'd had enough of it; he was tired of it. So, he went against the *un*official rules, and when Snerp started after him he grabbed Snerp and fought him, ending on top of him. Another upperclassman, Pat, was standing in the doorway watching. As "top dog" or "ruler" of Fourth Passage, Pat said in his slow drawl, "You're the biggest little man I've ever seen, Philly." From that moment on, Fran's hazing stopped.

It was soon after this that Fran started a "prayer meeting" in Fourth Passage. Now, the school had a Student Christian Association which had prayer meetings in each of the dorms, but there had not been one in Fourth Passage. The "Christian memory" made things different in that moment of history; nevertheless, it was a phenomenon that anyone came at all. Some did come. And . . . the numbers grew. Fran kept it short, as everyone needed to study, or go on with what they were doing. He would read a short passage of Scripture, make a comment or two, and then ask if anyone wanted to pray. One or two or even three would pray, and then Fran prayed. That was it! But it was one way he felt he could make truth known.

At times Fran's persistence in inviting someone would stir up a hornet's nest. Chisel, being asked one too many times, threw his talcum powder (in the can) at Fran's face and hit him just above the eye. Bleeding profusely, Fran stood there, and Chisel waited to see what he would say. The persistent question came again, "How about coming to prayer meeting?" Chisel's answer was, "O.K., I will if you can carry me." Brushing the blood out of his eye, Fran strode over and, standing five feet six inches beside Chisel's six feet two inches, took a fireman's hold, slung him over his shoulder, and staggered down the dark stairway with him to the floor below. (The boys shot at mice that ran along their baseboards with .22 rifles, so the baseboards were full of more than mice holes! But rifle practice also did away with any semblance of light bulbs, so the halls and stairways were always pitch dark.)

Although this was in the middle of Prohibition, there was a lot of liquor flowing; in fact some was distilled very near by. The sophisticated aristocrats of Fourth Passage also could put away a lot of liquor—especially Saturday nights. As the weeks went on, Fran began to be someone the boys yelled for when they couldn't find their way in the midst of those black halls and stairways. As one after another came home drunk, they'd hit the front door and yell, "PHILLY . . ." and Fran would go down, undress whoever it was, stick him under a cold shower, and help him up to bed. He made a bargain with them: "If I take care of you and put you to bed Saturday nights, then I'll expect to wake you up and take you to church with me on Sunday morning!" Quite often Fran would go to church with a line of big athletes tagging a bit sheepishly behind.

Now, if anyone asks you what Francis Schaeffer's apologetics were in college, I'd say the reply should be that "he had such a sense of the lostness of people that he did what he felt would help them to be shaken or startled to the point of listening when he would give them the truth in some manner." Caring for the boys who needed this care on Saturday nights was first of all the kind of thing Fran considered being a Christian was all about. Secondly, he felt it to be the best kind of "apologetics" for the people with whom he was face to face at that moment of their need. Saturday nights Fran got a lot of studying done. He always determined he wouldn't go to bed until the last one got in, so he'd be on hand to help whoever that might be! And, of course, he had lots of time to study in between.

By January 10, 1932, Fran had started to make a trek through the woods and across cornfields by little footpaths to go to a small, simple wooden building where there was a Sunday school for blacks. He loved teaching there, and during the entire four years never missed a Sunday, unless he was really sick. The children he taught were from eight to thirteen years old, and there'd be from eight to a dozen or so of them. One girl—Martha—wrote to him for years as she went on to become a nurse in Richmond. He had contact always with the blacks, and visited in the little shacks scattered through those fields, to find out why Mary, or Joe, hadn't come to Sunday school, and to talk with the parents. When an epidemic of mumps hit this little settlement, Fran was the one who visited Five Points. Johnny Morton, an old black man who cleaned the rooms at the college, became ill and had a long time of being in bed. Fran's diary reads over and over, "Visited Johnny M.," until the notation about visiting Johnny Morton's grave at "Mercy Seat" (the name of the black church).

A part of each visit consisted of reading the Bible and praying with Johnny. His concern was that there would be understanding given, as well as comfort—and the setting was a little cabin in a cornfield with an old man as important to the Lord as any king!

That first year at Hampden-Sydney, Fran was pledged to Theta Kappa Nu fraternity, elected to the Cabinet of the Student Christian Association, which was the governing council, and became a member of the Ministerial Association. He joined the Literary

Society and began to take part in debates. The only sports he took part in were "touch football" and running the low hurdles in track meets. He always says wryly, "With a few rare exceptions I chased everyone else around the track!" However, he was on the track team. Climbing the water tower was an exercise he enjoyed doing alone, and he remembers with pleasure the surprise on a professor's face when he looked up and saw him on the top peering over. "Good morning, Professor," said Fran looking down, and a hurried "Good morning, Mr. Schaeffer" floated up!

Leafing through the diaries of this time, one finds, "April 9, 1932. Finished reading Borden of Yale. May I be like him." And again, "Not my will but thine" appears from place to place, and on the flyleaf of each of his Bibles.

Was it on Saturday nights in between boys needing the ice cold shower and Fran's help putting them to bed, or was it on Sunday evenings after being out in the settlement in the cornfields, that bits of poetry came to mind and had to be written down? It isn't good poetry, but it is a window into some of the development, some of the struggles, some of the groping and growing in understanding of the Christian life. As we read these penciled scribbles, we may recognize some of our own longings and aspirations, as well as understand something of who Francis Schaeffer was at twenty.

> Cause and reason,
>   love must be.
> But how shallow ours
>   compared to that of Thee.

> A bug crossed a learned paper.
> Might not we too be crossing things
> We cannot read?

> May I never be
>   too big
>   or too small.

> Oh, God, not
> only for a time,
> but for eternity
> may I serve thee.

Not only in
the dim future
of some eternal space,
but right here
and now, may I
know thee.

O God, I thank Thee
for thy loving kindness to one
who has sinned grievously
against Thee. Amen

O God I thank Thee, that You
use me to win souls
for Thee.
O give me strength
to speak the words
Thou wouldst have me
speak to them. Amen.

Fill my heart, O God.
With true love for thee, and
the people you have made.
May I serve, but
   first I want to
     learn to
keep my eyes on
     Thee. Amen.

May I be
   foursquare,
but the corner
   stone must be,
     my love for Thee.

"O God, I thank Thee for the year,
   that has come and gone. Bless it
     to thy use, I pray . . . and guide me on, and upward,
                             Amen.

In constant penciled scribbles, with words misspelled, these
prayers go on page after page and day after day. Whatever of
poetry it is—struggles for a close walk and a deepening under-

standing, praise written concerning beauty of creation, aspirations poured out—it is written only to God. And to the comfort of each one of us, we may know that in private communication, in whatever form *we* reach out to talk to the Lord, it doesn't have to reach Him in perfect manuscript form. He has read our yellowed penciled pages, as well as our minds and hearts. He reads our written prayers on the back of envelopes, on the margins of our Bibles, on the back of weekly memo calendars or in the unwritten whispers in the middle of the night. We have a Person to whom we may communicate, and our cries and requests do make a difference in history.

To help out with expenses, Fran washed dishes at the dining hall daily. He remembers that a new glass was recognizable because, if held up, you could see through it, while looking through the ones that had been washed a few times was like trying to see through a cloud. Tales of the wonderful food at Miss Lacey's didn't make it any easier for those eating in the dining hall to stand the awful diet and poorly cooked food. One night, in the dignified beauty of a colonial dining hall, someone started to throw the watery yams in sheer rebellion. Soon everyone was tossing yams that splashed against the walls and chairs and some heads. Things were a mess. Fran remembers taking part in this with a degree of satisfaction that still brings a grin to his face. No terrible results came. A lecture about not doing it again was all he remembers.

However, Fran wasn't one to think up or perform practical jokes. The usual sort of 1931 "jokes" went on there that took place in other colleges. The bell clapper was stolen so that there could be no signals given for a time. The bell itself was "kidnapped" once, and buried. Another time several fellows hauled a cow up a winding staircase and got her arranged, after a manner, in "Snapper" Massey's classroom. Now, Snapper was the fine Bible expositor who taught Fran his basic foundation in Bible, one of the people who indeed "opened a door" that was exciting, and helpful for a lifetime. Fran looked forward to his class with eagerness because of all he was learning.

This day a stench like a barnful of cows filled Snapper's nostrils as he followed the students in. The black janitors had evidently managed to get the cow back down the stairway, although at some points they thought they'd have to kill and butcher her and take the pieces down! Standing a bit uncertainly, the boys looked at their seats, rows of chairs with the wide arm for writing, all fastened to their precise spots on the floor. Fresh wet cow dung had turned them into something a bit worse than a barn floor. Snapper stood at his desk on a raised bit of platform, and looked dignified and as if he saw nothing unusual in front of him. "Gentlemen, be seated," he demanded. Squish, squish—the young gentlemen sat down and began to take notes for an hour.

In that first year Fran's grades hit a high level, a standard he maintained throughout his years as a student. After the first term a letter was sent home from the Dean's office.

February 1, 1932
Dear Mr. Schaeffer:
   We are very much pleased with your boy's conduct and excellent work. His high average for the first term entitles him to a place on the first honor roll. We hope that he continues as he has begun and that he is as well satisfied with the College as we are with him.
                                        Sincerely yours,
                                        Macon Reed
                                        Dean

He had studied hard. In fact, all through life Fran's best quality has also been his worst feature: such severe concentration on what he is doing, come wind or come weather, that nothing stops him. As for girls or social life, the extent of time he gave to amusement was a trip over to the nearby village of Farmville for a movie, or an occasional date with one of the girls at the Teacher's College. He didn't find conversation very interesting with any of them, he says, so felt it was a waste of time. He ended the year being welcomed back to Fourth Passage with real acceptance. The boys admired "his guts" for keeping on in spite of being an outsider and a Yankee. He fought them back. And— he could be counted on to take care of them on Saturday nights! He had proved himself to be a very different sort of ministerial student, not at all what they expected.

*   *   *

Autumn of 1931 brought a special abundance of color to Germantown, as yellow, gold, copper and red leaves first flamed on the trees and then blew swirling in the wind to drift on the sidewalks. For a time ordinary walking to school became a wonderfully satisfying scuffing through piles of drying leaves. Whether it was enjoyment of leaves, or of the first excitingly soft mornings of silent snowfalls, my mind was full of a diversity of things as I traipsed off to school day by day that year. The change from Newburgh to the Canadian system of taking a "pass course" or an "honors course" in preparation for the University of Toronto had been hard two years before. Now all that had to be more or less scrapped to tidy up the credits for graduating from American high school, which presented almost no challenge at all. Finding it impossible to really meet people in the enormous school with its noisy halls and large classes, I asked about where a certain tall, dark and handsome boy went to church, then proceeded to go early Sunday evenings to that Christian Endeavor Society. On Sunday mornings I went with my parents who were driven a distance to Bala Cynwyd to hear a fine Bible expositor preach, but that was too far for me to return in the evenings.

My background had by now made me well aware of the need of "discernment." I had had positive teaching at home and, with a variety of Christian pastors, theological professors and others having meals with us from time to time, I had been exposed to considerable negative discussion about "modernism." Often I read books, pencil in hand, to "detect" and underline grossly liberal— or "modernist" as we then termed it—statements, such as some by E. Stanley Jones in *The Christ of the Indian Road.*

My older sister, Janet, in college had ceased to believe that God exists, and had become convinced that the Bible was not true; talks with her had given me a strong desire to be *so* well informed that professors, such as her psychology and sociology professor in a "Christian college," would not shake my certainty in what I really believed to be *true.* I expected to fight for truth all my life. I was already extremely interested in the beginning of Westminster Seminary, and in lectures and books by the Greek scholar Dr. Machen and the Hebrew scholar Dr. Robert Dick Wilson and in their defense of the New and Old Testaments. All this gave me knowledge I could aptly use in discussions. But

I had a conflict for which I judged myself, and that was a desire for a warm, lively gathering of people to be with, which the stiff atmosphere at lectures did not fill.

As I went off on Sunday evenings to the First Presbyterian Church of Germantown, I discovered that this was *not* the church of that boy I had wanted to meet, as after all he was an Episcopalian. But I did meet Sally, the niece of Dr. Elizabeth Taylor, who in later years was going to be my obstetrician and deliver my first baby! Sally was living for a year with her aunt, and Dr. Taylor felt she needed to meet young people, so opened the doors of her attractive apartment each Sunday night for as many as Sally would invite. There were steaming cups of hot chocolate, homemade cookies, popcorn, music on the record player, and conversation, though much of it was trivial. Often I tried to discuss, or refute, the point of view given in the meeting we had all just come from, but few cared to get into a discussion at all. My [bracket] was wearing a bit thin! I really could not have given a proper reason to anyone who might ask, or to the Lord, as to why I was continuing to go to these Sunday night meetings. However, to my credit, I did pray very earnestly that my going might be used in some way to help someone hear and believe the content of the Bible. I even arranged for a speaker from the China Inland Mission once, in high hopes that that would "do it"!

Before graduation I had been taken to the senior prom at the high school by the tall, dark, handsome boy—who brought me an orchid to wear on my shoulder. Even though she knew this was a dance, mother made me a lovely green lace dress from a Vogue pattern. (The material was bought on South Fourth Street in South Philadelphia from a shop that sold remnants, a place to get amazing bargains if you could detect good material. In fact, for the next six years anything I wore came from bits and pieces from that little "hole in the wall," including my wedding dress material!) When I was dressed, ready for my date, she simply said, "You look lovely," and then whispered in my ear, "Remember whose you are and whom you serve."

Dear mother. I loved her, and really admired her. You know, I wondered if she might be right, and that I shouldn't be going . . . but I did love to dance and I danced well, and although I had been told that "no one can talk about Christianity on a dance floor," I had found conversation about serious things was not at *all* impossible. On the other hand, it wasn't the "perfect" evening I had thought it might be, and although my dress and the flower and the handsome escort certainly "made a picture," it was all more like acting in a play. Somehow I was being an actress and not *me*—not really.

Let me stop to say right here that Fran and I in recent years have not made a list of rules that, if kept, signify one is a "spiritual Christian." And we feel that some "rules" are artificial to the degree of blurring the *real* struggle for reality, and that the positive search to find a closeness to the Lord does not consist in what is *not* done, but in what *is* done in communication with Him and in discovering the wonder of Himself and His Word. We would not be bringing up our children in exactly the same way we did if we were starting today. At the time of history in which I was living my teen years, Keswick had started but not any of the "movements" for young people, though they soon would. The basic admonition and distinction was to be a "separated Christian" in contrast to being a "worldy Christian." There is a danger in each age; there is a danger today. We are all too likely to try to define a growing relationship with the Lord in terms of carbon copies. God is a Person, and He treats us as individual persons. Of course we can learn things from each other. However, it is dangerous and unfair to discourage people by presenting them with a pattern which they are meant to try on for size to see if indeed they "measure up"!

I certainly didn't measure up. I was five feet two and weighed a hundred and two pounds and wore very well-made clothes that looked as if they had come out of the best shops. (Mother made them, or as time went on I did, always from Vogue patterns.) My feet were a "sample size" so my shoes came in wonderful finds on sales along that same South Fourth Street of our remnant shop. I loved the jazz of that time and ballet music as well. Movement seemed to me to be an expression, whether it was gymnastics and dancing for a May day program, or whatever. I was afraid that I wasn't measuring up to being a "spiritual Christian" or a "separated Christian" . . . and as for my clothes fitting me and looking "too elegant," as a very young child I had said, "I may be a missionary when I grow up, but I'm not going to look like one." That part didn't hurt my conscience, but the "non-separated" finger pointed at me gave me some nights of weeping into a pillow, wondering if after all—since I couldn't point to a *time* of becoming a Christian—there was something wrong with my certainty. How important it is to search the Word of God and to take our patterns from Him Who made us, and Who alone knows what is needed in order to be fulfilling His commands both positively, and negatively. There are things which *do* need to separate us from the world in every age.

It was June 26, 1932, after graduation, that I went to the Young People's meeting as usual on Sunday night. The topic for the night had been selected by the "leader," Ed Broom. The fact that he had formerly been a member of the Presbyterian Church and of this society but had left to join the Unitarian Church seemed to make no difference to anyone as to his being the leader. His topic was "How I know that Jesus is not the Son of God, and how I know that the Bible is *not* the Word of God." I sat down and began to fume inside. As I listened, my reaction was to jot down things in my head to use in a rebuttal—things I had gathered from lectures about the original manuscripts that I felt might help people who were listening, even if they did nothing to convince Ed Broom. As soon as he had finished I jumped up to my feet and started to open my mouth . . . when I heard another voice, a boy's voice, quietly began to talk. I slid back into my seat and listened, startled.

"You all may think what I am going to say is influenced by my having sat all this year under a Bible teacher at Hampden-Sydney College whom you would term 'old-fashioned.' He has taught the Bible to be the Word of God, and I do believe that too. I want to say that I know Jesus is the Son of God, and He is also my Savior, and has changed my life. I've been away all year, and this is the first time any of you has seen me since college, but although I can't answer all the things Ed has said, I want you to know just where I stand."

"Who is that?" I whispered to Ellie Fell beside me. "I didn't know there was a real believing Christian in this church. . . ." "That," said Ellie in a hoarse whisper, "is Fran Schaeffer, and his parents have been real mean to him because they don't want him to be a pastor." My mind resolved to somehow comfort "the poor boy," but I then jumped up to say what I had been going to say.

My "say" was made up of some quotes from Dr. Machen and Dr. Robert D. Wilson, and it gave that type of apologetic for the truth of the Bible which I had heard in lectures and read. Then I sat down. While I was speaking, Fran whispered to Dick, the fellow sitting next to him, "Who on earth is that girl? I didn't know anyone in this church knew that kind of thing." Dick's reply was, "That is Edith Seville, and she has just moved here from Toronto, Canada. Her parents used to be missionaries in China."

As the last hymn was sung, and the benediction "May the Lord watch between me and thee while we are absent one from another" was mumbled, the usual hubbub occurred of everyone trying to get out quickly to the "real" evening, at someone's home. I saw Dick and Fran Schaeffer pushing through people, coming in my direction. Suddenly Dick was saying, "Edith, I want to introduce you to Fran Schaeffer. Fran, this is Edith Seville." (People introduced people in those days!) Fran's next words were, "May I take you home?" I replied, "I'm sorry, but I already have a date." Where upon Fran flatly urged, "Break it." Desire to communicate to someone who really believed and had courage to say so overcame my natural inclination *not* to break a promised date, although it was only to go to Ellie's house. So I said, "Well . . . yes, I guess I will." We walked out to the sidewalk followed by Dick and a couple of others who were giving instructions as to how to get to Ellie's and making fun of Fran for not being able to find his keys. (To this day he has a sudden panic about finding a key at the time he needs it!) And soon we were off.

Our conversation was about serious things of Christianity— not just its defense, but the wonder of all we believe. However, we had met "on the battlefield," and now forty-nine years later, we are still fighting together on two sides of the room, so to speak, but on the same side of the issues in a diversity of places and in the midst of an ongoing history. The threads which had started in Germany; in Nottingham, County Down, Scotland; in Wales; which so easily could never have existed—were now being merged, without our being conscious of it yet, to *do* something and *be* something which neither thread (Fran or I) would have been or done, alone or with two other threads (people). Never will you, or I, or anyone get to the end of the mystery of "guidance" or of being "led by the Lord." Choices are so very important. Yet we know God is God. Fran so often puts it this way: "You recognize you have made significant choices, and then you stand still and look back and you see you are on an escalator."

As I look through Fran's diaries and our letters to each other, our year books from college, the piles of papers and magazines and guest books and "Family Letters" and so on that are piled on the floor in little piles around me as I write this . . . I see what he means. You look back, and you see you have been on an escalator, not in a vacuum or in an uncharted bit of outer space. Thank God for the clear promise, "I will never leave thee nor forsake thee"—even when the wind is shrill, the waves are high, the hail is slashing, and the boat seems to be sinking. It is not just at times of the provision of being fed at a "table in the wilderness" that we can look back and be conscious of the escalator, but also when the "presence of the enemies" is *all* we are aware of.

When Fran had come home from college he had signed up for a job selling Real Silk Hosiery from door to door! That Wednesday night, as his diary says, he "called on Edith" after he had finished working. My family left that week for the missionary cottages in Ventnor, New Jersey, for a two-week vacation, and as Fran wrote his first letter to me there, evidently the reply was an invitation from my parents to come for the weekend. We had so much to discover as to what we thought about such a variety of things, and as to what we were reading, and studying—to say nothing of remarks about the froth of white waves, the moon, and the special beauty of the New Jersey seaside— that we walked the length of the Boardwalk to Atlantic City and back (the entire walk is seven miles long) and never stopped talking. We went swimming together, and I discovered that he could swim well and do several kinds of dives impressively.

In Fran's careful diary he has every date marked, so we can clearly see that we were together a great deal that summer. August 6 we went to our first Robin Hood Dell concert together and sat in the outdoor amphitheater, and on August 6 he read Machen's *Christianity and Liberalism*. On August 7 he spent the entire

day at our house, with much discussion! He played tennis with my father a few times, and we went to the movies to see *As You Desire Me*, to another Robin Hood Dell concert, and to the Philadelphia Museum of Art.

With August rapidly approaching the date when it would be time for Fran to go back to Hampden-Sydney, he drove me sixty miles one night, to a particular spot he had chosen, on a bridge, which carries a canal, over a river. It is an amazing spot, and on this full moon night, he wanted to show me the beauty, and had decided he was going to kiss me. I had worn a big floppy hat of fine straw, in the fashion of that time, and was conscious of how well that went with the whole scene! As we looked out over the canal, over the river, he very romantically kissed me. Then, getting back into the car, he said, "I'm sorry, I shouldn't have done that" . . . which made me become sarcastic because I felt rebuffed! However, he piqued my curiosity, and my interest was increased rather than blotted out. I didn't see what he wrote in his diary that night, until we hauled out all these papers to write this book—forty-eight years later!

> It would be an easy matter,
> to let my passions run riot.
> Easy that is, if it were not for Thee,
> guiding us, keeping us strong.
> May we find our happiness in Thy way.

Up to that time, and for some time after, he hadn't said anything to me about "us," and of course I couldn't read what had been written! It remained hidden in a drawer for forty-eight years.

As Fran headed back down to Virginia and Hampden-Sydney, I entered Beaver College for Women, which had a divided campus at that time, in Jenkintown and Glenside. My father simply didn't have money to send me away to school, and it was decided that by going as a day student, by way of trolley car on Germantown Avenue, and then train from Wayne Junction in Jenkintown, I could have an unglamorous but satisfactory place in college. Not living on campus put me at a disadvantage, but I was nevertheless a very real part of the total life there.

There existed, at that time, a course of study called Home Eco-

nomics that included an amazing amount of diversity. This led
to a Bachelor of Science degree because of the inclusion of four
years of chemistry, microbiology, along with general psychology,
abnormal psychology, educational psychology, child psychology,
philosophy of education, etc. The degree program led to the possibility of teaching chemistry, as well as opening the way for what
we called "Heinz's 57 varieties" (Heinz pickles and other products
were advertised with a big number 57, and it seemed this course
offered that kind of diversity!), the four years of English and a
philosophy and ethics course providing a general base. I thought
of all this as "cream." In our program we had thirty-two clock
hours of class and lab time per week compared to sixteen hours
for the Arts program, but I felt this was a gift. You see, we had
courses in foods, dietetics, dressmaking (which gave scope for
designing), interior decorating, art appreciation, and so on—an
amazing preparation for both practical and creative development,
that is, if one added one's own spark and imagination to the
assortment of courses taught. Quite frankly, I had every expectation of being married, and I wanted my talents developed and
at my fingertips for doing a lot with a little.

If I had any foolish daydreams in my teenage years, quite apart
from my desire to "do" something for the need in the world as
a Christian, they revolved around an imaginary art student's garret
in Paris, where I pictured myself making a fantastically charming
place, with atmosphere, out of "nothing," and producing marvelously tasteful meals in one pot on a small flame, under the sky-
light! It seemed to me that practical talents for cooking, sewing
(involving interior decorating as well as clothing), or producing
an atmosphere in whatever tent, house, attic, or cabin I might
end up, *had* to be developed along with whatever other knowledge
I might get in college—which, after all, could be added to by
reading and by listening for the rest of my life. It was a pretty
sensible idea, but one which seems to be totally foreign to many
today. So much of life, whether one is married or single, is spent
in the environment one has created oneself. Why people think
that spending all their available time, energy, ideas, and originality
in life on a career, is all that is needed to ensure them of an
interesting environment in which to live, I cannot understand.
The need of a "shelter" (a place to be which somehow brings

refreshment because it does not clash with one's tastes in sound, texture, color or whatever) is basic to each one of us. A "home" where one or two individuals, or a family of a dozen, can eat, sleep, listen to music, and be creative; can read, think, pray, get ideas, be inspired—can have a base—is worth preparing for and working on.

As Fran plunged back into his studies, the black Sunday School, his track team practice, and the growing number of organizations, he added a new factor—writing letters. Our correspondence the next three years filled more than a bushel basket. At first we wrote twice a week; then it became three times, and after Christmas we agreed on a letter every day, with a special delivery for Sundays. A special delivery stamp cost ten cents in those days, and the service was so excellent that every Sunday without fail the boy arrived and rang the bell, bringing the gift of an eagerly awaited letter. To put it in two words, we communicated!

We were exchanging our ideas and thoughts, as well as reporting what we were learning and being involved in in our colleges. I'm sitting on the floor now, surrounded by yellowing paper with two distinct handwritings amazing me in the record these letters give of our aspirations as well as the growth of our love for each other . . . and for the Lord. The letters were written not for you, nor even to be read by us forty-five years later, but for the moment—the very private moment of unfolding what we were really thinking and feeling about realities.

Before copying any of the letters for you, so that you may recognize for yourself how many of the seeds that would become full-grown plants later in life were being unconsciously sown then, it is necessary to finish the outline of those three years after we met.

Strange, the mixture of the trivial and the important, isn't it? How do you know a person and discover anything basic about him or her? A college yearbook shows a very young picture of a man with no lines on the face, and declares—? That he was on the Student Christian Association cabinet, became its treasurer his third year and its president his senior year. That he was in the Union Philanthropic Literary Society and in successive years became secretary, vice president and president. That he was not only in the Ministerial Association but was secretary one year, treasurer another; and he was treasurer of the Finance Board his senior year. Track (1, 2, 3, 4) is a short and sweet statement of exercise. He was a member of Theta Kappa Nu fraternity and of Epsilon Chi Epsilon, the language fraternity. He was elected to the Honor Society (founded at Washington and Lee University in 1914) Omicron Delta Kappa, on the basis of his marks and so forth. And a letter from the Dean at the last semester tells of not only Honor Council status, but of being second in the Senior Class.

If you were to ask the question "Who had the greatest influence on you in the college?" probably Fran would answer with names in two categories. Spiritually he would say Twyman Williams, the pastor of the college church, and "Prexie," or President Joseph Dupuy Eggleston, who had led the college as one who really believed, but especially his Bible professor, "Snapper," or Professor James Buckner Massey. As for "opening doors" intellectually, it would always be Dr. Maurice Allen whom Fran would speak about first. I'll quote what he recently said to a reporter asking that question: "I had a philosophy professor in college, Dr. Allen, who was brilliant. I was his favorite student, because I think I was the only student in the class who understood him and stimulated him. He used to invite me down at night to sit around his potbellied stove and discuss. He and I ended up in two very different camps: he became committed to neo-orthodox thinking, but he was very important in stimulating my intellectual processes. Theologically my basic outlook was developed all the way before I went to seminary. The Bible professor, the college president, and the college chaplain were outstanding Christians."

It will take a handing over to you of some of our private letters, however, to see how we were influencing each other, and what development was going on which had nothing to do with exam papers or with leadership in organizations. Perhaps in those letters you will get glimpses of the fact that Fran was marking Spanish papers as Spanish assistant to earn money, as well as taking hours to make me an original Valentine each winter, and that he often wrote about some cake or box of other food I'd sent him. Perhaps you will get glimpses also of the fact that I was president of the Honor Council (the student government council dealing with cases of cheating and so on) in my junior year, and being glad because that gave me a senior year office before I "gave up" my senior year to marry Fran! You will see something of the fact that Fran cut classes (being on the dean's honor list gave him unlimited cuts) to hitchhike up to see me so frequently one wonders how he kept up all his work! So I'll leave all those things to be glimpsed from whatever letters there'll be space for. The letters have reminded *me* what we were like then—forty-eight, forty-seven, forty-six, and forty-five years ago!

Funny how you forget what you were thinking. It's like being in one of those plays where there are constant flashbacks . . . except that you suddenly remember all the emotions that went with it, all the yearning for perfection in a naive way, and all the deep and earnest expectations as to what would be the results if one would honestly want God's will. Weird, reading those letters and having the "in-between forty-five years" spread out on the floor in boxes, as well as spread out in memory! Weird, writing about it. There is a merging of past and present that seems to make it all a kind of plateau in time.

We'll end this chapter forty-five years before the beginning of the chapter, but in the same location. It is graduation time, and the dates given on the engraved invitation I so excitedly opened were:

The Faculty
and Senior Class
of
Hampden-Sydney College
request the honor of your presence
at the
One hundred and fifity-ninth Commencement
June ninth to twelfth
nineteen hundred and thirty-five

Graduation came earlier in 1980, hence the empty campus at the end of May, but June 9 to 12 in 1935 had the same atmosphere of pink roses, green grass, gardens overflowing with flowers, and strawberries brimming over cut glass dishes. And Fourth Passage Cushing Hall was just as patiently waiting for boys and luggage to leave and finally give the mice peace and space to run in and

out of the bullet holes! As always, three days had to go by before
the parents, girl friends, and relatives stopped adding to the confusion with all the squeals of surprise, and profuse southern greetings stopped and all the formal and informal festivities were over.

The beauty of the chapel surrounded the silently involved audience as the graduates filed in, each one to be the sole attention
of the few who really cared: human beings—so in need of appreciation and attention on the part of family or friends—human beings
not made to be alone. Polite attention was given to all the class
by everyone, but caring with breathless centeredness can only
take place where there is love in some measure, love of some
category: each one a son, a grandson, a nephew, a brother, a
fiancé, a friend to someone; each one with someone in the audience
who cared as he reached out for that piece of paper. Four years—
minus the summer months—from the first day that each had come!
And now the speeches, the prizes, the awards, and the diplomas:
a graduation from and a commencement of . . . ! . . . an ending
and a beginning! How incredible it is that Christianity gives us
that to look forward to. We don't have to watch the sand run
out of the sandglass of life's time for ourselves or for our loved
ones without realizing that really, truly, actually, without any
vestige of doubt, cruel though separation is, and hard though
the contemplation of change is, we are moving toward a graduation which is also a commencement.

There we all sat, waiting for the actual moment of graduation
to take place. "What's all that pile of white rolls tied up in ribbon?"
Pop was sitting beside me, all stiff in his three-piece suit and
white shirt and tie. He was whispering. "They're the diplomas,
Pop. They prove they have their degrees." Pop looked at the
programs and found Fran's name. "He's got three of those names
beside his. That's better than two, isn't it?" Pop's whisper again.
"Yes, Pop, Fran's getting his Bachelor of Arts *magna cum laude,*
and that is great. He has done so well," I assured him, right into
his ear so as not to disturb the prim and proper people around
us. Pop squeezed my hand with pleasure. Whatever Fran had
done here for four years with all that studying, he was glad he
had done better than most of them; that showed he'd not been
lazy. He had worked and won out! He guessed it wasn't a waste
of that money.

Now, as the diplomas were given one by one, the degrees con-
ferred, and the honors read, the clapping came—a spatter after
each one smilingly held out his hand and took the white parch-
ment, rolled and tied in the good old fashion! And then special
prizes and honors were given. Pop reached over for my hand
again because a voice was slowly announcing a name: "Francis
August Schaeffer." As Fran stepped forward, a copper-framed
plaque was held out to him, but before it exchanged hands, President Eggleston read the plaque, prefacing the reading by announcing, "This is awarded to the outstanding Christian on the campus
during his four years."

ALGERNON SYDNEY SULLIVAN MEDALLION

Established by The New York Southern Society 1925

"As one lamp lights another nor grows less, so nobleness
enkindleth nobleness."—Lowell

"He reached out both hands in constant helpfulness to his
fellow men."—Sullivan Memorial Fountain, N.Y.

"And never yet was anything seen so beautiful or so
artistic as a beautiful life."—A. S. Sullivan

"I must not consider how much they love me but rather
how much I love them."—A. S. Sullivan

Awarded by Hampden-Sydney College

to

Francis August Schaeffer

A graduation from the four years started with that old grey
box! A graduation from four years of teaching at the black Sunday
School right up to the last Sunday. A graduation from four years
of not only studying, but learning so very much, and discovering
the key to go on learning more. A graduation from the circle of
woods and fields and colonial buildings and history as well as
the protection and separation from the buzz of cities and progress
that this rare spot had given for four years. A commencement
of the merging of two lives to go on together to be prepared as
a unit, a merger, a new pattern in The Tapestry.

With Fran holding the diploma and the medallion out behind my back, and the tassel from his cap tickling my nose and cheek, we kissed, in the middle of the hubbub, on our way to the southern fried chicken and home-cured ham dinner . . . kissed good-by to being apart much longer, kissed a welcome to the merging of the next step of life!

ANIMAL? VEGETABLE? MINERAL? OR—HUMAN BEINGS? 8

There is nothing that quite points out the gap between human beings and all else as does verbalized communication. And there is no verbalized communication that underlines that gap more thoroughly than correspondence or letters, the printed page, the handwritten manuscript, or clay tablet that preserves ideas that were first in someone else's mind before appearing there for us to read. Relaying the past through the spoken word that depends on keen memory is a possible thing, but how fantastic it is that people were made in God's image in being able to communicate and to be communicated *to* through the diverse possibilities of the written word. It is staggering—if you now have time to look out at the mountains or the waves of the sea, at the distant shore of a lake or bay or just a tree—just to contemplate what a human being can do with a pen, brush, chisel, pencil, typewriter, printing press, Telex, or computer in enabling someone miles away, or years away, to communicate what were, are, or have been the impressions generated in that human mind!

What a marvel it is that human beings are not only capable of *having* ideas, but of verbalizing them, and preserving them. Never mind whether the masses of written ideas are *worth* preserving through the centuries; it's just that those ducks, swans, and sea gulls out there today on Lac Léman in the fog and mist could not only not tell me how many generations it has been since their ancestors lived on this lake, but they have no way of preserving their abstract ideas, even if they have had them! Being human is an awesome thing. Human beings are different!

Fran and I met in June, 1932. It was New Year's Eve afternoon at the end of that year, that Fran said "good-by" to me. He had decided he was growing too fond of me, and that we'd better break up the relationship because probably the Lord wanted him to go where no woman could follow. (I'm not sure just what he visualized that place to be like, nor where it might be; nor does he!) We seriously parted . . . "forever"? And with promise to pray for each other, we parted before supper and he went off to his home.

My tomato soup had extra salt water in it that night, and my father gruffly remarked, "Of course, no one would tell me what this is all about," and mother patted my shoulder! As they went off for a New Year's Eve meeting at the Bala Cynwyd Church, the phone rang for me, and it was a *Saturday Evening Post* cover artist wanting me to go with him to some girl's home with a group of others to listen to records "while the New Year comes in." Since I had still been dating all through that first semester of school, and since I was not going to ever see Fran again, I thought I might as well be sorrowful in the midst of people, rather than all alone. However, as I was getting dressed, the phone rang again, and this time it was Fran. "I've been so miserable since I left you. I know now I can't live without you. Please can I come down for a half hour?" . . . He had been gone a total of two hours! I said, "Yes, of course," and felt relieved that it would only be a half hour, since that wouldn't make too embarrassing a change in the evening! It was during that half hour that Fran asked if I would "wait" for him. It wasn't exactly a proposal, but of course it was! He sealed my answer with a kiss, and then went off to see the New Year in with his parents because he had promised them he'd be right back.

When the artist came and we started to drive off, I announced, "Oh, by the way, in between your call and now, I've just more or less gotten engaged. I thought I should tell you!" It sounded pretty ridiculous, but that was exactly the way it was. This was my last date with anyone else. I became a curiosity to the girls at school, not going to the school dances, always being "alone" and in their eyes, "wasting" my freedom and my youth and my college life. I was doing an unheard-of thing . . . even if I had had a big diamond to flash at them, which I didn't.

Just before coming to Europe in 1948, to try to diminish our number of trunks and boxes, we burned our bushel basket of letters, saving out a few handfuls without really making choices. Now we have fourteen grandchildren, and three of them are ages that correspond to the age I was when I wrote to Fran in those years of not-so-patient "waiting," often in agony of what seemed the "slow" passage of time. There wouldn't have been these letters, if Fran's college had allowed married students. But a rule was passed just before he entered Hampden-Sydney that any student who got married would be expelled, and after his graduation that rule was removed! Because of that waiting these letters exist and we can discover something of what was going on in our thinking when I was Lisby's, Margaret's, and Becky's age, and when Fran was twenty-one, twenty-two, and twenty-three successively.

Fran's very orderly way of doing things in every department of his living is evident now in the exact dates he always put at the heading of his letters. Evidently I felt it was more "personal" or "cozy" just to put "Sunday afternoon" or "Monday night," but after reading through the handful of letters we saved, I can sort out fairly well the general period of time.

In the following letter, written sometime late in 1933, I'm replying to a letter in which Fran has told me of how boys at school jumped all over him for something he had done which he had then apologized for.

Sunday afternoon

Franz dear—

We humans fall so far short of our ideals at times that it is discouraging. But we wouldn't want to preach that side of it—I mean we wouldn't want to say—"Well—once a month it's a fine thing to break through and do something entirely opposite to what you believe is right"—just because all of us do do things like that. We don't want to sanction it—just for the sake of "preaching what you practice"! We want to really preach the Christian life—and then we want to live it so far as is possible—but because we are human—we can't be perfect. That's where forgiveness comes into the picture—forgiveness for our mistakes. I don't know whether you can read into this what I am trying to say or not. Anyway—I think the fellows are all wrong in picking on one small slip—when there is so *much* in your life that is parallel to your "preaching." In fact I think it might help your influence for them to know that a Christian is just as human as anyone else—the difference is that he has someone to go to with his mistakes—and difficulties—to get them smoothed out—and that instead of pulling him down . . . he goes on again—a bit more prayerfully—and a bit stronger for having found his feet and climbed up the hill he slid down. See???—That's what I think anyway. And—furthermore I think you're splendid—I *know* it—and I admire the way you straightened it out. I admire your courage to do it immediately, and I love you all the more for it.

How's your spring—we've been having snow. Last night the trees were covered with ice and a thin coating of snow on top made them really beautiful—however I'd rather see red buds this time of the year. . . .

I'm going out for Grecian Dancing for May day—practices start soon—won't be that "the nerts" gliding around the grass in my bare feet! . . .

I've just been listening—with one ear—to a conference in protest of Hitler's treatment of the Jews—stirring times, eh!!?

Two weeks from Thursday—I'll be seeing you!

Sweet dreams . . . Ede

This is another Sunday afternoon in March, 1933:

Franz—

Every word of your letter struck a responsive chord in me—it was so marvelously alive—not just words. Since then I have had feelings—emotions I never knew I possessed—I don't know how to describe it . . . but I've wanted to weep—that sounds contradictory—but it's true. . . . It's not just love, it is bigger than that—it's big enough to include my love for you—but it is something more. That I should be wanted—to help someone—who in my mind is, and will be, one of the greatest servants of God—that I might share everything with him. . . .

Other people will know "the wonderful man of God"—the "splendid person"—the "peach of a guy"—but I will be the only one who will know him perfectly—at all times—and be his companion—through everything—! Why Franz, it seems such a perfect life to be going to live when I have done nothing to deserve it—that all I can say is—"God is good to allow it," perhaps even to plan it—life is short—but there is an eternity ahead of that, and to think that through it all—you will be there— Young man, have you any faults? I think, "Now everyone has faults—what are Franz's"—and I say now—"forget that you love him—look at it impersonally" but no matter how much I pucker my brow—nary a one can I conjure up— It wouldn't make any difference if you did have—but you *don't.* Being late—or running the car into sand doesn't count—they are virtues that make life interesting!—an adventure you know!

Yesterday I studied. I had one class to go to, at 8:30, then came home and made penuche fudge, packed a box for you and monogrammed a handkerchief to go in it—then off to do Psychology work all afternoon—time out for dinner—and then Chemistry experiments to write up, and a notebook to do from 7:00 P.M. until midnight-thirty. This morning I was dead, and still had writer's cramps and a pain in my back from sitting in one position all those hours afternoon and evening. I *made* myself get up and go to church nevertheless and was amply rewarded by a really good sermon by Dr. Bieber. As usual I was wishing every moment that you were there, so that you could hear him too. Everything from a good piece of cake—to beautiful scenes and lovely music I'm enjoying—"I wish Franz were here to enjoy it too."

There is a new moon, a tiny sliver of a moon—have you seen it yet? . . . I think I'd better end here—I want to do some reading—an English play if I can find it on our shelves. I'll try to write a note in the middle of the week—but I promise you a fat one when exams are over!!

Ede

Page 9 of the "fat one":

". . . It's a windy windy day—with snow on the ground and cars making crunchy sounds as they go by. Little stray flakes of snow that forgot to come down last night are being spilled out now, and sort of dancing around, reluctant to settle down with the rest of them. It's a nice sort of day for talking, for sitting cozily by the fire—while the wind rattles the shutters and makes weird sounds around the corners of the house and moans in the trees. It's a nice day to stay by the fire, and when evening comes to pull a little table before the fireplace, and eat baked apples from amber plates—with just the firelight and a twinkly candle in a carved brass holder—to throw lights and shadows on the face of the one you love—to stay there through the evening talking, and perhaps reading a bit—out loud—a bit of favorite verse—or prose—and then dreaming—and feeling your hand clasped tight, as the embers die out. It makes me feel all shiny inside just to think of it. Somehow today I feel very peaceful, and you seem very near—if I speak you'll answer. I could touch you if I put out my finger—I shut my eyes and I'm sure you were there—but no—

I've been reading some of John Galsworthy's plays this weekend—Have you read his "Justice"?

This feeling I have for you . . . I can't conceive of it ending . . . before I couldn't see how anything couldn't end—at least after millions of years . . . now . . . do you understand?

Your Ede

Jumping to February 2, 1934, and a letter from Fran:

Hampden-Sydney College

Baby:

Greetings m'love, I love you. I wanted to be with you the last couple of days. We have had a holiday since Tuesday one o'clock and it is bad to have time with nothing to do. Wednesday we were supposed to have off, but then good old Dr. Bagby died and so we had two more days off. I am glad I had his full course last year. He was a great man but if he had had love in his life he would have been greater.

How were the last of your exams? I hope you came through
with colors flying and general satisfaction. Old dear, I love you.
I did better than I expected, and got first honor roll again.
Unlimited cuts! My average was 91 2/3, I heard it was the best
in the junior class, but I'm not sure. Greek 86. Fair lady, I lay
my laurels at your feet. They are yours.

So my folks gave you some of my "boy" pictures. I'm glad
you like him. He is an odd fellow, but sometimes I think I like
him better than the older boy he grew into. Still the older boy
has one joy in his life that supersedes all the minor traits he
has lost, or rather I guess there are two—an increased
understanding, and the second is what I thought of first—your
love.

I hope we shall have such a boy, but one who will be very
very much better because of your share in his personality. I would
liked to have seen you blush when Dad called you Mrs. Schaeffer
Jr. I will be glad to see you write it for the first time after we
are married. I love you, dearest person. . . .

Cake, cake, who has the cake? I am waiting in suspense for
the arrival of your all-afternoon cake. I shall take small bites to
get more kisses. I shall make the others take large bites. Dearest,
wonderful person, I adore you. You are my love. I need you.
Now if this is to reach you I must mail it right away, to reach
you in New Jersey . . . Happy Holiday!

Franz

February 2, 1934 H.S.C.

Edith dearest:

Speaking of a letter every day, here are two in one day! Did
you get my Special? Anyway this one will say, "welcome home."
I hope you enjoyed yourself and feel all pepped up for your
exams. I have tasted the fruits of success or something, and have
had a good time being important on the strength of my grades
for the last couple of days. But alas and alack, what goes up
must come down, and I feel a siege of the "blues" coming
on. With all your Home Ec do you know a long distance cure
for such an illness? Possibly the cake, if it arrives tomorrow,
will help, but the kisses brought by the cake may make me

want a few of the real thing—woe is me! I love you.

There is still hope for the 16th—Art took his car in and by some miracle they can weld the block—cost $15. I never heard of welding an engine block, but they guarantee it, and so I expect we will be seeing you. Of course there is the minor question of his dad paying for it and buying new N.Y. license plates which are due. Still—hope is high in my breast.

I'm sorry the Special had to be rushed—I didn't get nearly all that I wanted to say in it. This morning they told me I didn't have any mail. I went to the shop after dinner—and there was your letter with your address in New Jersey in it. One hour to write and two hours worth to say. I missed the mail but caught Mac going to town and he mailed it to you. How did you like the change to "baby" on the special? You see how you have me wrapped around your finger? One word from you and I hasten to obey, do I not, old woman? Ha, ha. I love you.

Did I tell you I was elected vice-president of the lit society, and secretary of the Ministerial Association? If I did I'm not trying to make a little seem a lot by repeating—but if not I don't want to keep any secrets from my wife! Now goodnight and I wish I were kissing you. . . .

Franz

Plainfield, New Jersey, Saturday night . . .

Dearest . . .

There are so many things I want to kiss you about!! First— you're special. When the mail came at home this morning, and there was no familiar scrawl for me, my heart sank to my toes for I had wanted terribly to hear. All the way on the train to Plainfield, I thought of you . . . wished you were beside me. . . .

The fields were dazzling in whiteness—and soft piles of snow snuggled in the branches. Well . . . when I arrived Ellen was there all beaming to meet me. We went shopping, then to a cute tea room paneled in dark wood, for lunch, after which we shopped for things for dinner tonight, and came home laden with bulky parcels. The apartment house is swanky!!—As we opened the door—the first thing we saw was *your special* on the floor! And

my heart went hippity hop—right up 'til it was soaring in the
sky. Oh I love you. Then I read it—retiring to the bathroom
to do so. It is a lovely bathroom tiled in the most heavenly
shade of pale green. The letter was exactly what I needed. Thanks,
darling, for coming to the rescue. My weekend is complete
now.

Second, your marks—they are splendid—I'm so very very proud
of you, husband—and I am thrilled to the core to be presented
with such laurels . . . no Greek maiden was ever more so. I love
you.

Then we started the dinner in the oven, and went to see "Dinner
at Eight"—I was disappointed in it. After which we rushed home
to get dinner for the four girls she had invited to meet me.

Monday night . . . back at Ashmead Place.

As you know your letter came in Plainfield, and then this
morning I wakened and bounded down the stairs and got the
other letter! Then got back in bed to read the Special, and the
new letter together. More congratulations! You deserve a telegram,
but the budget won't allow it so my congratulations this way
and a kiss later! Vice-president—secretary—very fine. But don't
let them overwork you. There's another association you are going
to be "president" of you know, and that company wants you—
un-worn-out! I left my pen in Plainfield, isn't that dumb? So
I'm using mother's. Sunday night I came home just because I
love to ride a train at night. I love to hear it shriek—and feel it
rushing through the blackness. I gave other reasons, but that was
the real one. School again today. . . . Sociology and History of
Education are going to require heaps of reading. I see myself
spending hours in the library this spring. I'm still thinking in
terms of spring—even though it is bitterly cold. . . .

This is Tuesday and I haven't heard yet whether the cake came.
I have visions of the postmaster eating it surreptitiously behind
a newspaper . . . or something. I love you. . . . All of a sudden
I don't want to waste any more time away from you. . . . No
use talking about that thought. . . .

War, war, war. . . . There's so much talk about it—or maybe
I've been listening to the wrong programs. The international air
seems full of it. Then Austria—France—Germany are getting

tangled up. The good old U. S. A. is even getting wise enough
to enlarge their Navy and Air fleets—it all gives me the queerest
cold chills inside.

> I love you—dearest dearest,
> Ede

Hampden-Sydney
September 4, 1934

Dearest Edith:

Nothing special in the letter old dear, but I couldn't write
yesterday and I wanted to be sure this reached you Friday . . . so
Special Delivery.

Yesterday was the last day of rushing and rush was right. I
began at three in the afternoon and did not stop until three last
night. . . . I had everything pulling for us except Prexy and the
bell-tower! Now as a parting gift to the frat I want to give it
the best trained group of goats that it has had since I've been
in the school. I am goat master, and I'm going to do my best to
help these new men and thus the fraternity. If I do that, and
this rushing is successful, then I will feel I have redeemed myself
for three years of nonchalance towards the frat. The hardest part
is over, and then I can get down to more important things and
activities.

Dear Edith, here is something I want you to do for me when
we are married; if I am ever slightly mad, and want to join some
secular organization, remind me of the fraternity and read this
letter to me. Then do your best to keep me out of whatever I
want to join! Even if it apparently would widen my influence,
still shout this to me: No matter how good the organization is,
if it is not primarily Christian, do not give allegiance to it. In a
long run its lines will cross your Christian lines and it will also
take time and energy for a lesser cause when the Greatest Cause
needs all you have got to put into it. . . . They are sure to throw
things into your face that are contrary to your Christian life,
and this can separate you from other men on a plane that is
not worthy of you. You cannot be altogether faithful to your
Christian work and life—if you are united into brotherhoods with

elaborate oaths and rituals. Sweets please put this letter where you can always get to it and have me read it if I am thinking of joining a society—then we can talk it over and pray over it and decide together what is best.

. . . I enjoyed your Sunday letter very much. It helped me— muchly. Your drawings, and the smell of flowers brought me your overflowing love of life. Edith, you are magnificent. How I won your love I do not know, but of the fact I am glad. . . . You said about your not being brave, my last letter shows just how steady I am! We are non-brave when separated, but I am not afraid of our courage when we stand together. I hope my last letter wasn't too hard on you . . . it helped me no end to pour it out to you. . . .

Now to a class. I haven't even opened a book but I don't expect to be caught for it is a lecture course (Abnormal Psy.) —Later—OK. It was on hypnosis, and as I am studying the subject in my parallel reading for Philo IV I know more about it than the fellows who had read over the lesson.

The material [a sample scrap] looks interesting, but it is that and nothing more until you make it up and wear it . . . then . . . ooo la la. I hope the eggshell satin of the silk dress overshadows the green. I don't know why, but greens do not seem to suit you (that is as far as I am concerned). I see you remembered that by carefully explaining that there would be more eggshell than green in the dress. I adore you dearest. You treat me well, and I do appreciate your thoughtfulness, you know. I love you.

I expect to get back to you for the Hampden-Sydney Swarthmore game. I have a ride, and unless something unforeseen comes up, I'll be there. If my ride peters out, I'll bum up. I must see you then, the only trouble is that it is so far away. . . . I don't see how I can wait. If you can get down before, I do want you to come here. Sweets, I want to see you as soon as possible, or the fact is sooner than possible. Tomorrow would be too long!

No matter what my mood, the letter that arrives each day is a constant source of strength and joy. Please do as much as you can on them. I need them . . . the things you do, events around you, and most of all the things and words that retell me how much you love me. I am quite dependent on you. I find more all the time that this is so. Do you like that? I hope so, for I'll be more and more dependent on you all the rest of my life. I'll try to get radio WCAU on Fridays from 10:00 P.M. on. I think it will be easy. I need my other half to make this half work well! I love you.

Franz

Tuesday, 5:45 P.M. . . . waiting for dinner

Darling old person,

How goes it at the end of another day, I wonder?—and so they pass—one after another in parade—each one nearer the end of the line—and one day Franz they'll have gone—and we'll be together truly forever!! . . . And, these days of waiting should be ones of living in faith happily . . . IF the Lord should suddenly give us all we want so much—how ashamed we'd be of the impatience. I mean, we *should,* knowing He can and will make it possible at the right time, be satisfied to leave it in wiser hands than ours believing it to be for our utmost happiness. I love you dearest Franz of mine, love you more than ever.

I finished up that Honor Council case today. . . . Wrote the penalty—talked to Dr. Greenway, and he thought we had done the right thing. So—that's that until the next case!

I got a package from one of the Westminster Church ladies in Newburgh today. Her husband works in the bleachery and can get ends of material free. She said to tell her what of the cottons she has that we could use. I think we can get enough for window curtains for our rooms. 'Twas nice of her. Mrs. Simpson told her that I sewed, so she thought I could use these cottons. Soooo we'll have material for curtains . . . and I'll make them as soon as we have windows! Won't that be fun! It's going to be glorious to fix up a place together for our own home, isn't it? . . . I adore you. Oh I forgot to tell you that Cherry said she and Dot could drive me down to Hampden-Sydney sometime this year.

Be good to yourself for me—
my own love . . .

your Ede

Tuesday 10:30 A.M.

Franz dear:

First of all—I want you to know that I am *glad*!! To have you
in God's will—to have you live the life He has planned for you—
whether it be with me or not—to have Him come *first*—to have
your love for Him Supreme—to have your love fully
consecrated—is what I would rather have for you than anything
else in the universe—even tho' it may leave me entirely out. It's
because I love you so—because I truly love you—and don't only
love you to fill my needs for companionship, etc. that I want
the very best for you. There is nothing more glorious than the
position you have taken—that of putting Christ first, really first.
And—Franz—I feel that I have come to the same point. I thought
I had before, but I never really considered laying *you* on the altar—
because I felt God had given you to me, that He really meant
us to be together. And now—I see— Not that I feel we are *not*
meant to work together, but that He must know our love for
Him comes first—that we would be *willing* to give up the most
precious things . . . so that we put no "ifs" in our surrender.
And—I believe I have done this today, if never before. I am willing
to go wherever He wants me—even alone— All my life since I
have been tiny I have wanted His will for my life—but in little
things I have clung—not willing to give them up. But I have
one by one given up things. Yet . . . as I've prayed for His will
saying I would be willing to go anywhere—to the ends of the
earth—I have also asked that He would give me a helpmate. When
I loved and was loved by one who had the same purpose in
life, I thought it was a direct answer to this prayer, and I really
never faced the question of giving *you* up.

When I got your letter this morning, I must confess I wept—
Why? I wasn't sure . . . I knew I was glad for your decisions
yet the thing bewildered me since I had been thanking Him for
giving us this "most perfect" human love. There was no school
this morning as we are snowed in, and I'm glad for I could not
have gone to classes until I settled this in my heart, soul and
mind . . . nor could I have gone weeping! I had a stormy siege.
I read my Bible, prayed, read your letter again—and prayed some
more. Then on my knees I gave up all for Him . . . and told

Him that if it were His will—I would work alone—and as He gave Isaac back to Abraham—so I feel we will be given back to each other. But understand Franz—it's not because I knew He would do so that I came to that point, but because I was truly willing to leave everything. If it is to be separately—we will be much more fruitful for having come to this point—knowing it is the right thing. If it is to be together—our lives will be much more fruitful for having come to this point—we will know that He *does* come first—and that what we tell others is not merely "words" but something we have known ourselves. We will know the true meaning of the word "first" as we could not otherwise have known.

As for winning souls—that has always been my main desire in going into Christian work—and I'm trying now in my preparation—to do a bit. But how much more I *could* do! I'm going to pray harder—both for souls—and for courage to speak to people—and for wisdom in selecting the right words to say.

And now Franz, I cannot say that I feel any definite call to work alone—my heart and mind are open—but I still feel God has brought us together—that He has given us this good thing. God is a *loving* Father and His goodness is wonderful. I feel He can use us together to glorify His Kingdom. I feel a praise in my heart for Him—who gives His children the best. But if you ever feel definitely called to work alone, know—that I have left our love in His hands. God doesn't have two right ways for us— if He did bring us together—if He does mean us to marry—then— He has a work for us, that can *only* be done together.

I love you
Edith

(That struggle occurred after Fran had heard Dr. Howard Taylor speak, and had given his life in a fresh way for "anything Lord" . . . and my letter was a reply to his question as to whether I felt the same way. . . . You can read between the lines. As letters go on it is plain to be seen we agreed that the Lord was calling us "together.")

December 10, 1934
Monday, just before dinner.

Darling,

I was glad to get your happy letter today. I'm so glad you
are feeling better. That makes me feel better than anything could.
I am still interested to know just what that "medicine" of Good's
is. Please drink plenty of orange juice and tomato juice whenever
you get a chance. I'm studying vitamins in dietetics—and it is
surprising the things that result from the lack of them—from
ulcers—to sterility! I'd like to experiment with rats and see some
things for myself.

I'm trying to get in touch with the research department of some
magazine that deals with food (right now the Ladies Home
Journal)—through Betsy Poor. If I could get an interview—I'd
like a job there better than anything. Of course it would have
to be wherever you will be for seminary.

You remember the letter telling about Betty Scott and John
Stam's wedding?—and of their having a baby? Well *bad* news
came in a cablegram today. Their station has been looted by the
communists—and it is "rumored" (so it said) that they have been
captured and carried off by the communists. Of course we don't
know whether they were captured or whether they are hiding.
At any rate their home was looted, and they're missing. It didn't
mention the baby—but oh Franz, it is so *cold* in that district of
China—and those communists are so ruthless. They need our
prayers.

I think your petition is very logical. It should go through. I
hope it may. You're a splendid old person with fine ideas. I love
you for them . . . your ideas and your splendidity. I love you
dearest heart—more all the time, and for so many reasons, and
in so many ways. I'll be interested—and more than interested—
to see your "Philosophy of Life" article—when does it come out?

My pet pain hovers around in the background. Today I've had
a dreadful headache, all around my eyes. That's most annoying—
when one has to be looking at professors, or books, or boards,
or writing, all day—and studying and sewing the rest of the time.
But—don't worry about me, after Christmas is over and presents
all made, I'd like a couple of days of complete rest for my eyes

and see what that does. Someday I'll have a honeymoon when I won't have to look at a thing but you—and then my eyes will have a rest!

Here I am studying History, or trying to, with witchhazel soaked rags tied around my head. I look like the battle of Bunker Hill!! The Schlichters are downstairs talking with mother and dad about their going back to China. I'm not concentrating on History very well. Oh for the quiet of our apartment—some future day!

> Goodnight sweetheart . . .
> get lots of sleep . . .
> I adore you,

> Edith

(News of the Stams being beheaded came soon after.)

January 18, 1935, Hampden-Sydney

Dearest Edith:

I'm in bed, but in my own room and not so sick. I just feel better in bed.

I got through the exam in a certain fashion. Incidentally your letter helped very much. I had seven characteristics of God's decrees to think of, and all that would come was one. I had saved your letter, and opened it to read and clear my mind. I got down to the part on the Stams' and then my mind blazed wide open and awake. Not on the decrees, but on their experiences. You see we both can understand what that meant for them, because we know what it would mean for us. It horrified me, yet not so much as that it set me afire. I talked to Snapper about it; then sat down and remembered five of the other six decrees. No, this weekend does not mean we are heading for China, but if God will use us, we are heading somewhere, at home or abroad, more definitely than ever. There is so much to be fought in the world, and my prayer shall increasingly be that we may be used to fight it in some small way.

Take Communism, for instance. I feel that Christianity must meet that within our lifetime. It is a glorious time to live, and a time worth death for, worth even what the Stams went through to combat that consummating force of rationalism that is undermining and overflowing Christ's work.

The Church is asleep, but Christianity is not—it is rushing on, it cannot ultimately be defeated. I feel we are on the right side—I know we are, not only by being on the side of Christ, but by being on the side of the awake Church, instead of the asleep one. Or I wonder if those two are not the same thing—Christ and the awake Church; yes and the dead Church and adversaries of Christ also matched?

Sweets, I have a verse I found today, in fact three verses: I Corinthians 3:21, 22, 23, "Therefore let no man glory in men. For all things are yours; whether Paul, or Apollos, or Cephas, or the world or life, or death, or things present, or things to come, all are yours; and you are Christ's; and Christ is God's."

"All things, all things." Does that make your heart sing? Both life and death, and the present, and the future, all things are for us, in Christ, for we are Christ's and Christ is God's. The Stams died, but death was already theirs. And who knows the extent of the influence of their death in awakening the awake Church to the increasing peril?

Edith, a point blank question: You and I and our children may face what the Stams faced . . . are you with me even to that? Our call may take us anywhere, and our future may be anything from a dull life in a backwoods village, to the stark horror of the other—if we go together—it may be either. I want you, and I think that even if you knew our life was to be the Stams' replayed, you would come down the way with me, is that not right?

Supper, and my temperature is up. I hope I don't have to go to the infirmary, that would be tragic with exams on the way. The above is something of an outburst—but not just that. Exams, flu, and all the rest of it, but I feel close. There is so much to be done, and I hope we will soon be on our way to do some of it.

When your Dad gets done with the North China Herald with the Stams details in it, I would like you to send it to me. I'd like to read it and the fellows would too.

I think of you and your exam preparations often and long. You take up much of my thoughts in all directions . . . among which the physical is not slighted. I hope our time may be this June . . . just so we are sure it is right.

Sweet woman of mine, my adoration grows by leaps and bounds in all directions. It is constantly up.

Franz

Morning . . . I've been to see the doctor, and I have to go to the infirmary. I don't like that . . . but if I must I must. This will wreck my grades, but I can't help that either. I realize what your constant presence would mean even more than ever at times like this. Edith, Edith, I love you.

Franz

February 11, 1935

Hello!

How are you, old squeedunk? I've been in bed all day . . . knitting and painting and coughing and blowing and feeling pretty punk generally, but I'm going to school tomorrow.

Wish I had a million dollars—and I'd build a seminary—and get all good professors—and good students without any "chips" when they graduated. I'd have them fight when necessary and shut up and be sweet when it was necessary. I'd have it unmixed in the conflict—standing for the right but not talking about it! . . . being very positive—believing thoroughly—but presenting all sides fairly—unprejudiced, never finding fault. I'd have it all rosy doing good to church and community, but making everybody feel comfortable and not sticking pins in any one . . . yet accomplishing the work of seeing that people had the chance to find the true Word of God. . . .

Franz, Franz maybe I'm a fighting person but isn't the desire to test the message of a man—by the only yardstick we have, a desire to save people? . . . I didn't mean to end up here. I started out to be "funny-sarcastic," and ended up in a tangle. But Franz don't judge a Seminary by comparing the conversation of fresh graduates with that of older Christians who have been softened and have grown through years of Christian work. Probably those fellows aren't all fight either, but they're young and they naturally feel like measuring up everyone because they know of the modernism, and they are interested in the outcome in their own church. . . . The Lord may be leading you to look into Bible

Schools thru this dissatisfaction with Westminster. I feel I'll always be in sympathy with Westminster, tho' don't worry I won't harp on it. I know you want the Lord's will and so do I. If His will for you lies in some other place of preparation, you will have my wholehearted support of your decision (thru His guidance). I adore you sweetheart—I'll be praying much about this thing—pray for me too Franz—that I may lose whatever is wrong with me. I mean—I know I'm too rigid, or whatever the word is that would describe it—pray that the hot insistent feeling inside me may go, and that I may look at things more as you do. I reckon I'm not fair enough Franz. I wish I were different— it would be a lot more comfortable. I mean I shouldn't be so decided in my opinions—W. W. Whites for instance— If that's to be your solution, pray that I may see it as right. Pray please that I may never spoil things for us by being too dogged in stubbornness. I am afraid I can be nasty, like "cherry cider," you know—and I don't want to be.

[Then come pages on W. W. Whites in New York and the pros and cons of that school, indicating Fran's varied search for the right place to prepare.]

What do you think of Abyssinia? Or have you seen the papers? Mussolini is wanting to annex Abyssinia to Italy! He has mobilized the Italian troops. Poor Lambies. You have heard me speak of Dr. Tom Lambie? He is in Abyssinia now. I wonder what this will mean to the mission work. I always had a dream of going to Abyssinia—ever since we lived with the Lambies once in New Wilmington when I was eight years old.

Why can't I *trust* more for the future? Oh Franz . . . Franz I love you . . . goodnight dearest,

Edith

(In the midst of the pile of work on studies, and in the organizations at school, the petitions that seemed so urgent to be made, and the agony of soul about choosing the right seminary . . . Fran was busy preparing a Valentine for me! He took a college catalog, grey cover, many pages describing courses, etc. and on every page pasted a red construction paper heart—which he cut laboriously himself—and an arrow on the opposite page . . . with a four-lined original verse on each heart! It was an enormous work, proudly finished to send off special delivery for the 14th of February, 1935. Just twenty years later in Champéry on the 14th of February, 1955, Fran was going to be walking into our chalet with another set of papers introducing another chapter of life. But in 1935 we didn't know about the twenty-years-ahead event! God knows the timing of all His individual threads He is weaving, and of all the choices His threads, human beings, are making . . . and the total of The Tapestry is seen by Him even now.)

February 15, 1935   Thursday morning

Sweetheart

I'm in the Wayne Junction station once more. Missed my 8:16 by a fraction of a minute, and have to wait for the 8:59!!! Be rather late for class. But it doesn't bother me much for I want a chance to write to you. Yesterday was so full, and I didn't get home until eleven P.M. . . . hence no chance to write. Your *perfect* valentine—left nothing to be desired—it was perfect Dearheart. I love you. I got it late, when I came home last night . . . read it over and over again—and finally went to sleep with it in my arms. Yes, 'twas literally in my arms clutched tightly all night, and I woke up with it that way! Incidentally I was careful of it even in my sleep, as not even a corner of it got bent!! The words you wrote were alive and vibrant . . . I love you, consider yourself kissed.

My beloved . . . I love you . . . I can't stop telling you I love you, tho' I started this paragraph to tell you about last night. The tea yesterday lasted until six. I floated around offering the faculty mints, nuts, and candied grapefruit peel, and snuck a cookie at times on the sly! As teas go it was fun. We had *made* everything, and the cookies were delightful. Would you like a Chinese Chew? I'll send you some as soon as I get time to make more. Then Betsy and I ate dinner together in the tea room and went to chapel. Wonder of wonders, Betsy has agreed to come with me to hear Bieber preach sometime. You know she doesn't believe in the existence of God . . . and she says she'll come to our Wednesday meetings sometime too. [Meeting of The League of Evangelical Students which I started at Beaver.] I think maybe I'll start a Bible Class with Daddy teaching. Betsy and Dot said they'd come. Betsy hasn't an idea as to why she is here . . . and doesn't believe there is any future life. I am hoping that her listening and showing interest will lead to something more than just the satisfying of a curiosity. . . . Then I got hold of Chardy after our Y Cabinet meeting (at which we voted to have a real week of prayer and study groups, with some "big man" coming to speak this Spring. . . . I've been trying to get that over—now for the higher authorities!)—and I took her over to our League prayer meeting. We had a pretty good meeting . . . discussed predestination which was bothering some of them, and the Second Coming. Pretty good discussion.

The valentine is so exquisite—you can hardly imagine the thrill it gives me. This sweet pea blossom and fern will bring you a kiss from me. [After forty-six years it is still intact in its dried state!] It is the loveliest Valentine anyone ever got—and it's mine. I'll keep reading it over and over. . . .

"Because you come to me with lofty love . . .
. . . .
Because God made you mine."

Yes . . . I'd like to start being with you forever tonight—as friend—lover—companion—co-worker—wife. My dear dear, I love you . . .

Edith S.

(The S. stood for Seville-Schaeffer.)

Tuesday night . . . (February)

Dearest man,

Now you're hard at work on Biology. I hope you're not feeling woozy after your flu. . . . Well—the change has begun! Dad got a letter from ——— yesterday saying that after the middle of February he could be relieved from the office, and would be put on the retired list. That means both dad and Schlichter are out in four weeks. Schlichter is waiting for final word from Shanghai to find out whether he is to come out. . . . As for us we will be on retired remittance which means less for house rent, $35 to be exact, and nothing for coal, light, gas, telephone, which has been paid for, and less actual money to eat and do the additional things.

You know Daily Light today was good for all of us. . . . What does all this mean for us? It would seem that College for me would be out next year, and of course underneath it all is the undercurrent of . . . "I wonder if this is the beginning of the indication that it is right for this June." Mother said tonight, that if we do marry in June—and have an apartment next winter— we can have a few things, such as the green chiffonier and dressing table. We can scrape them and paint them to suit us. So now all we need for our bedroom is a bed. Would you love me without a B.A.? . . . This of my family's seems to feed the fire of wanting to be wholly dependent on the Lord, and to find out how it is to be trusting entirely on Him, in the darkness to be led one step at a time. I feel ready for something . . . and surer than ever before of His faithfulness and of the fact that I not only "want" His will, but that we are going to have it. This is rather jumbly—but Franz sweetheart you understand the feelings so strong, yet elusive when it comes to putting them in words.

. . . Sunday night . . . (five days later)

Dearest:

I've been jittery all day—excited—my heart goes pit-a-pat and I can't keep still. "He's coming soon . . . only two more days . . . he is coming soooooooon." It's been a long time, seven weeks, and I'm thrilled to be seeing you again.

Mother didn't feel well today—funny heartbeat and headache (she worked too hard yesterday scrubbing) so I tucked her up on the couch, and we had a sermon on the radio—and I got dinner and made beds, etc. Then this afternoon I went up to see your folks, listened to Machen on the radio, talked with them, and had a fine time. I read your Special Delivery . . . but longed for a P.S. to see how you were feeling now! . . . I'm anxious to get tomorrow's letter but I have to stay at school until late at night for a joint Honor Council and Student Council meeting to discuss changing the honor system. So that means another whole day of not hearing from you . . . a day of feeling not quite right inside! I've loved you more than ever all day today.

Dad stopped working in the office, and though they've both known it for a time—the actual laying down of work and facing idleness is a blow to them. Mother is misty-eyed and wistful and it hurts to know that they are hurt. Last night I tried to make things cheerful by bringing home flowers to mother, and chocolate peppermints for Dad—with my first paycheck from Saturday work. [I worked at Lit's Department Store for a time. Pay was $2.50 for eight-hour day, plus two fifty-minute trolley rides there and back!] And we celebrated! Then today Dad was asked to preach morning and evening in the Wayne Avenue U.P. Church, and as we were sitting over dinner a phone call came inviting him to preach March 3 at the 12th U.P. Church. So we pray the Lord will work the rest out the way He has these first two weeks of "idleness."

I am praying that you will be definitely sure of the Lord's will for you in Seminaries this weekend as a result of the conference. It will be nice when that is settled, and we can make other plans accordingly. I'm sure that only one place is right for you, and that the Lord will show which that is. . . . Dearest, I'm thinking much about your "petition." I hope it goes through. Remember this, and don't let your knees knock together . . . "All God's giants have been weak men, who did great things for God because they reckoned on His being with them" (Hudson Taylor). We don't need to fear men, old sweets. Know that I am with you in thought and spirit, and what is more He is with you. And after it is all over hurry home to tell me all about it. I'll be waiting, and will expect you Wednesday evening. Here's a kiss on this rose petal! I suppose we'll all be eating in town at the conference [a Conference of the League of Evangelical Students with Machen as chief speaker] at Tenth Pres. . . . How about getting a gang to go over to the Chinese restaurant for one meal?

Goodnight wonderful,
Edith S.

March 3, 1935

Dearest Edith:

Hello dearest most wonderful woman, another short letter. It is 1:40 A.M. and the old eyes are a bit heavy. I just finished my letter of application to Professor Paul Wooley of Westminster Seminary, and as soon as I hear from you about the scholarship, I'll send all the necessary stuff to him. I have written to Mr. Finney and asked him to send a letter of recommendation for me. To make doubly sure I'm going to ask Snapper also to send one. That with my grades should sew the matter up.

Tomorrow I'll see Dr. Eggleston about our job—and I'll also see Dr. Williams and Dr. Massey, and write to Page. You write to Mrs. Lathem.

My work is fairly well in order and now I can get along to our problems, parallel reading, track, and the drinking question. The latter is getting terrible, really so, worse than ever. We are all praying that something will break on it during the Harry Rhimmer meetings. Please pray earnestly about this; humanly it looks like the last chance to do anything about it for some time.

I read a good book yesterday for abnormal psychology parallel—"Fear" by Oliver. It is the first book I have read by an eminent psychologist that takes not only a religious but a Christian viewpoint. The theology that creeps in is "High Church English" but it is Christian and what a relief that is! I started to read a bit of it yesterday afternoon and lo and behold I only took time out for supper and finished it at 2:00 A.M. A real book. It will be easy to write a long report on anything as good as that.

I hope you got up to see my folks today. They will want to know how you liked the cedar hope chest. . . .

'I found out something today in Psych book. Men have a change of life as well as women, only purely psychological. It is characterized by a "lust for change." This may come about in interests, business, location, or relationship to his wife. That explains some of the things I have observed in aging men. I guess we both will have to help each other over a bad period up there ahead somewhere! But I know we can do it with the strength of our love, and our ever increasing common interests and service. . . . A Christian's love for God ought to fill up all the gaps, shouldn't it? I know the way you feel about your school turning down your choice for Christian speakers, not surprising tho. Keep the little determined chin up, and remember things work out for Christians even if it is not in the way we want. I love you for your stand and determination, little Christian helper of mine.

Congratulations on the May Queen's Court. I'm glad for you. Remember you may be in the Queen's court to everyone else, but you are the Queen to me.

Goodnight again, and know how I adore you and how much I want you for my wife this June,

Your man,
Franz

H.S.C. April 26, 1935

Dearest Edith:

Good afternoon dearest Sweets. It is sunshiny and a fine Spring day. I wish you were here to go for a walk. I took an hour or so off this afternoon and went to the first baseball game I've been to in a couple years. Not much school spirit I'm afraid, but I did enjoy this one. We beat St. Johns six to three. The History test was a queer—the other class (of two sections) flunked theirs to a man. I'll tell you my grade when it comes thru. I have so much to do I don't know where to start, yet I'm too lazy to get going. The Spanish Prof must think I have nothing to do except mark his papers, from the amount of them he is giving me. Spring fever is here! I love you and do wish you were here with me. I know it will be soon, but I'll be glad when you are my wife . . . and that no matter what happens you are my wife. Have you written Mrs. Lathem? [about a summer camp job together] I would like to get the date settled for keeps.

I've been thinking about your new Honor Council case a lot. I hope it clears up and does not have to be dropped. I admire your stick-to-it-ness, something is sure to turn up to show just who did it . . . the cheating. One can never be too sure about judgment of people. Thanks for the clipping. . . . Let's put these men on our prayer list as they come to trial—Machen and

McIntire. The latter one especially as he is so young, and in such a position he should have our prayer help.

I walked through the woods on my way back from the library and picked this dogwood for you. Find a kiss at its heart. Now—down to work.

1:00 A.M. . . . a lot of work done. Gee sweets I wish you were here, I'm lonely for you tonight. Mac just came in with my history mark and I got a 94. Now on to Biology test on Tuesday, and the Bible paper. Both will be stiff.

Goodnight . . . the kiss in the dogwood will tell you of my love,

Your Franz

(The waiting time is coming to a count-down. "Fleece" have been put out as to choice of a wedding date—dependent on a summer job. Acceptance into Westminster Seminary brought with it a scholarship, and the married student's allowance of $22.50 a month for an apartment. The summer would have to be cared for, and then food money earned for Seminary years. It was the depression—and jobs were thought of as an impossibility.)

April 28, 1935

Dearest Edith,

I'm lonely for you tonite, very much so. A lot of things have come up I wish I could talk and pray over with you. . . . It has been a warm day but not clear. I think dust clouds from the West have more to do with the cloudiness than rain. The dust came in light *waves* this afternoon, enough to make it look like rain. I worked all day on my Bible parallel reading. The table by the window facilitated my reading in the day, and as I now have a big light, the nite work runs easy too. Have read two books this week, and have two more full ones to read and additional notes to take on other books, and then I'll be ready to write the paper. The History Prof is going to assign an extra 400 page book to read before end of term. Big fun—it's a good thing we decided I'd better not try for the prize. Don't see how I could do more.

Here is a clipping I thought you'd be interested in. It seems

that more than just Russia is anti-Christian. I wonder what the
outcome is going to be. It will be either a new surge ahead through
a great revival, a change in the basic beliefs of Christianity, or
the Second Coming. The basic beliefs have always been the same
and held to by the *real* church, the other two, either one, mean
watchfulness and prayer. We must be on our toes and
waiting. . . . I have begun reading Genesis again. . . . I'd
forgotten how inspiring and interesting the old Bible stories are.
Bill Junkin was talking in the mission today about how thankful
we should be for the Bible. How true!

Think what it would be not to have the Bible, especially in
this age. We would have no standard to measure all this
controversy of theories against. As it is I forget what is in the
Bible between readings—we would be overwhelmed in no time
if we could not take constant strength from it. It is truly a gift
to give thanks for. Christianity is of the BOOK, and when that
Book is struck against we can be sure something is wrong—
whether the one striking is a sweet sounding philosophical
scientist, or the German government.

I have realized that I am lacking in that sweetness of action
that shows the man who really keeps Christ's two great
commandments. I also know that that sweetness is based on a
love of God and man I have never attained. In its place I feel I
have to a large extent its antitheses of pride and passion. I know
I can never witness as I should with this true. It is the strong
but sweet Christian who really shows the Christian way of life.
Of course I realize that this develops with age in real Christians,
but I feel I should have more of it than I do. The last couple of
days I've been reading the "love chapter," the 13th chapter of
I Corinthians, over a couple of times a day, and when I feel my
ire rising over little things, or catch myself fishing for compliments,
or being hurt over my pride being walked on—I quote myself
part of that. It has helped, and I hope it will continue until I
have those qualities I now so definitely lack.

It is the wonderful sweetness, yet staunch standing for the
uncompromising truth of belief and action than can best lead
men to Christ. I mean the Howard Taylor types, or your mother,
and not the milk-sop variety. Another thing, I don't believe we
can attain to keeping the advice Dr. Howard Taylor gave us,

till we get it this way. [That advice was—in marriage put the Lord first, each other second, and self last.] Try it, and see if it doesn't make your days run smoother. I hope I don't go on and forget this, for it would make life a lot happier and smoother to really love God and man continually and wholeheartedly, and not have pride getting continually underfoot.

The modernists have talked Christian love into the ground, . . . but the only trouble is that what they mean by "Christian love" and what the Bible means are two different things. They mean love as doing away with the other Bible truths—and people like your mother have found it possible to live a life based on love because of the other Bible truths being true. Like the Social Gospel and stressing the Sermon on the Mount—there is nothing wrong in this, for all this is a part of the Biblical truth—but they cannot be taken to exclude all other truths or the truth of Christ and the Gospels.

[This letter goes on for eight more pages, talking about his black Sunday School children having mumps, etc.; talking about possibilities for summer jobs; discussing my making my wedding dress . . . and then . . .]

Your dress, your ring, it all seems so unbelievably close now. You are dear and sweet, and may our years together be one long melody of happiness, joy and service. I will try to love you as your perfectness should be loved. . . . Two weeks of cramming . . . and college will be finished for both of us.

Tuesday

Darling—I love you—I'm in Bible Class and I've just had an argument about creation. He's so wobbly—it's no fun talking to him—I like strong *positiveness!!* I love you forever and a day, and if I do nothing else all my life—I'll be your chief helper— through prayer—and acts—and words—and love. I'll always be behind you in prayer, and beside you in any work—and if anyone ever felt called to anything—I feel called to help you in every way possible. If you should ever fall short of the plan in store for you—'twould be my fault—and it won't happen if your silent partner can help it.

Later. . . . I'm studying for a Chem exam now . . . who cares about nucleoproteins and albuminoids!!—If there is anything I *don't* feel like doing, studying is all six of them!!! I'm tired of school and feel horribly impatient today—I'm sick about learning this and that—I'd rather put it all into practice! Oh dear, I must study Chem again. . . . I sit here and write a line to you, look off into the distance, chew my pen—and feel like chewing rusty nails! I have 75 pages of History of Lit. to read for English, besides Noah's flood and this horrible, hideous Chemistry. . . . Wish I were lying on hot sand, digging my toes in it and letting it slip through my fingers, kissing your sandy arm and getting ready to dash into the ocean! . . . You'd better put this letter in the minus column! I love you which after all is all that matters, isn't it?

Edith

May 18, 1935   Hampden-Sydney

Dearest wonderful sweetheart,

We do have a glorious future to look forward to and should find joy in it even now. Enough joy to blot out the things which are hard and unpleasant now. . . . Things are better now, and the end of the pre-examination preparation is at hand. A few more Spanish papers to mark—and then exams! My activities are about closed, or will be after tomorrow. I'll be thinking of your May Day today—how I would like to be with you. I miss you so and want your companionship. Today I would like to talk over our plans together. I'm glad you did not find "move up night" too hard [move up into the Senior class, when I was going to leave school]. . . .

I'm sorry about mother last Sunday. I know how that must have hurt, I have felt that hurt in the past and so can understand. However, I am glad you are going to the play with her on Friday night, that should help. I'll be glad when this is all over and arguments done, so we can stand together from then on in all decisions with no one else to be accountable to. I appreciate the way your folks have taken our plans, and have helped us. I do hope mother breaks over and comes to the wedding. . . .

Something to be happy about, Good asked about wedding presents tonight, and I told him "sheets" were a problem, and he said we could count on him for help there. Knowing Good I think a portion of that problem will be well solved. We will find out how soon the rent is paid, so we can arrange for that in our summer plans. . . .

No one else can fulfill any side of mine, or even be totally sympathetic to any side, and here you are who can completely fulfill all parts of me, and you soon will be my wife. Think dear, actually my wife! You are what I could sit down and coldly figure out that I wanted in a woman. But, how in the world, you so gloriously perfect for a Christian's wife have come to me I do not understand. But you have, and I give thanks for you. I do not understand why you have come to me anymore than I do not understand why *I* was called into the ministry, but I know both are true, and I am glad for both—great are the mysteries—but how much better we are cared for, than we could care for ourselves. How fine it will be to know that we will be responsible to each other and for each other and that everyone will expect us to put each other first. How I hope we may have many many years of service together, and finally entrance together into eternity. Perhaps Christ will return in our lifetime, and then it will be for sure together—I hope He does!

Now sweets, goodnight I adore you,

Your person, Franz

*   *   *

A bushel basket of letters, tossed with some hurt and sadness into a furnace fire. . . . three years of waiting, writing, struggling with a desire to be honest . . . three years of a special kind of preparation, recorded in two kinds of handwriting . . . all in smoke and ashes!

Yet the "chance handful" out of it all, as you have discovered, has had an amazing sequence, and covers an almost "selected" variety of subjects, or passing thoughts, or incidents, which give a glimpse that no "memory" could have conjured up by trying to remember that particular spot in The Tapestry. To me the sorting out of this handful of yellowed, dry, brittle bits of paper has been one more important incident in my own life that causes me to look back and realize I have been on Fran's imaginary escalator.

No one but God knew that I would be praying forty-eight, forty-seven, forty-six years after those letters were written, for His help in giving me what I needed to show a true picture of eighteen-, nineteen-, twenty-year-old Edith, and twenty-one-, twenty-two-, twenty-three-year-old Fran, without being fanciful about it! The prayer has been answered in making this chapter possible without having to rely on imperfect memory.

In fact, we—Fran and I—are reading this chapter together with wet eyes, being reminded of how faithful God has been (in spite of our many failures and the times of unfaithfulness to Him); of how He has answered our prayers of that time, and unfolded that which He had started to give in understanding then . . . into a much more mature understanding. We didn't know much about the deep afflictions of life by experience then, nor how short *time* is. Writing all this is like looking at life through the wrong end of a telescope.

FUTURE BECOMES PRESENT 9

There are so many periods of "waiting" in life that make time seem long, while the rest of life flies! There is waiting to finish school, waiting for exam results, waiting for the wedding day to arrive, and waiting for the baby to take nine months to grow; there is waiting for a long illness to "break" and signs of recovery to be real; there is the waiting for that event all Christians most urgently desire (at least in most periods of their lives)—for Christ to return and restore the fallen world, giving us our new bodies to be His Bride, with only glory ahead and no waiting left. That will be a fulfillment with no shadow of disappointment to which the word "perfection" really applies!

If you are all ready to be envious of perfection in our lives—Fran's and mine—you can stop holding your breath, because there are no perfect people, no perfect relationships, no perfect marriages, no perfect work, no perfect children, no perfect families, no perfect periods of time, and there is no perfect formula for how to have perfection! "But," you may say, "he wrote and told you how perfect you were, and you wrote and told him he had no faults, and you went on and on about it for all that time. . . ." Yes. And we felt very strongly that we could find no flaw in each other. But we were to come to discover what those flaws were and that we were going to live with the flaws, which would become a part of our history, day by day. Unhappily, no one stressed to us what we are stressing to others—that if you expect, or demand, perfection or nothing, you will have nothing! So we were going to have some "bumps" discovering realities and sorting out values through the years. Perhaps no one told us what continuity means in life, but, happily, we were going to recognize that in time, time after time.

My friends at Beaver—Dot and Lou, Chardy and Carol, Cherry and others—had prepared a surprise shower for me that was a real surprise I hadn't guessed. Stopping with Lou for "a book I left here at Dot's house," we were led casually around to the back garden, and I was handed a clothesbasket. "Will you help me take down the wash?" As I looked down at the basket and took a few more steps, suddenly a chorus of voices shouted, "Surprise, surprise!" as girls rushed out from behind the bushes and I saw that packages, wrapped and tied with ribbons, were fastened to the clotheslines with clothespins! When all the packages had been put into the clothesbasket, refreshments were passed around and I sat on the living room floor opening packages amid a hubbub of exclamations over the contents. Those dear friends had really stocked our kitchen! To this day I am using a lot of those things— the frying pan, the pitcher with a cat for the handle, the tea cloth, etc. My cedar chest filled up that night, and a bridge was made between college and that unknown new home where seminary life would begin. And I'd be a perpetual senior!

Fran had come home after graduation to look up the head of the bakery in which he had worked the summer before. He landed a job for the time left before the wedding—three weeks—which would enable him to earn the wedding cake, complete with lovely white roses in icing sugar, and a little more. While he was earning the wedding cake, I was making a white lace peplum blouse to turn the white crepe evening gown into a wedding dress. That white gown had been my last clothing class project, but it needed a bit of change. There were also bridesmaids' dresses to be made, and mother and I worked on those together. My two sisters, Janet and Elsa, were to be bridesmaids—the only time our family would ever be together in that way, a very special time that we enjoyed without knowing it was to be an "only." Life often has its moments like that, which need to be not wasted.

I'd be working away sewing on the cotton dimity materials (one sprigged with tiny pink roses, the other with blue) for the bridesmaids when Fran would come to spend the evening and talk about all our plans. One evening he stood at the door and asked, "Please get me a good sharp kitchen knife—a big one. I've found a torn-up old couch on the lot at the corner, and I want to rip the springs out of it to make a back for our couch." Right where Zeoli's tent had stood there was a filling station, and behind it someone had thrown this couch. Our first piece of furniture for our living room, it consisted of the pull-out bit of a bed (one that can become bigger by pulling a twin bit out). It had only two legs, so Fran improvised two back legs and then made a back out of the loose springs. This was not exactly pink-and-blue-dimity-in-the-living-room kind of handwork, so he hauled it down to the cellar to work on.

We had found an apartment—a third-floor rear on Greene Street near the Philadelphia Art Museum. The neighborhood may be "restored" now, but in those days it was pretty much a slum area. The apartment consisted of a tiny living-dining room, an even tinier bedroom, a bathroom, and a small kitchen—with the redeeming feature of opening onto a tin roof, giving us an "outdoor" vista that overlooked ugly backyards and sides of buildings but afforded us a bit of sunshine each day. The landlady's name was Mrs. White, and she said we could have it from September on. The rent would not start until then—$23.00 a month. As Westminster Seminary then was located on Pine Street, it was just far enough for the walk to be good exercise for Fran.

With this apartment in mind, we were "decorating" in our imaginations, as much as possible finding what we needed before the wedding, since afterwards we'd be leaving for our summer job. Our answer to prayer which gave us the guidance we had prayed for—to get married in July—was a summer job. We were to be summer camp counselors at Camp Michidune in Michigan, a Christian camp run by Rev. and Mrs. Lance Latham. The job was to be divided. Fran would be kitchen help while I was counselor during the girls' camp; then he would be a counselor and I would too (teaching leather work) for the boys' camp. We were to have board and room and $30 for the two of us, for the two months—total. And gas for the Model A Ford there and back again. We had prayed for something that would take care of us for the summer. This was exactly that. The timing was also right for the piece of summer we had free before seminary started. So we joyously thanked the Lord for that final piece of guidance, along with the apartment, the old springs, and the various essentials for starting housekeeping. It marked the end of our waiting, and we were appreciative.

My father was going to marry us in the Wayne Avenue United Presbyterian Church (that is the old U.P. before the merger). He didn't want to walk down the aisle with me and then change places, so he suggested that his good friend Paul Wooley take his place as my father in giving me away. So the Professor of Church History of Westminster gave me away! I knew the Wooley family, and especially enjoyed a friendship with Lennie Wooley, his wife, a Russian baroness whom he had met in Germany. In fact, I had baby-sat for them a number of times. They had expected to go to China as missionaries under the C.I.M. and through that common interest had come to know my parents well.

Fran's best man was another Westminster man, Richard Gaffin, who, with his wife, decorated the church with wild flowers. As all this was going on, Fran had no idea whether his mother was going to change her mind and come to the wedding or not— not until the last minute when he realized she was dressed up and waiting for him to go to the car. As for me, I was in our cellar making the flower wreath of white rosebuds for my hair and the twists of blue cornflowers for Janet and little pink rosebuds for Elsa as well as arranging their bridesmaids' bouquets. My bridal bouquet came ready-made as a gift from the Christian florist, Miller. A surprise! How I got myself into all that last-minute work, I'm not sure, but I managed to be in the cellar doing flowers when the cars came . . . and I was not dressed yet!!

Finally we were all collected and in our right places at the right time. The organ was playing and the girls were walking up the aisles, and there stood Fran looking at me as if no one else existed in the room, almost as if he wished they'd leave.

What about weddings? They belong to the parents . . . then after that to memory for later years. The day itself—it seems to me—would be rather flat without *some* sort of notice on the part

of family and friends, in some sort of festive setting. It is a waited-for day, a looked-back-to day, and it needs to be marked by music, flowers, and some kind of pleasant food, and by people who need to be a part of that time for their own sakes.

There is also the making of one's vows loud and clear, specific and definite before God, and before God's people. "Till death do us part" is a big and important promise; "for better or for worse" is a fantastically realistic promise. A lot of time is being vowed, and a lot of situations are being suggested. This is a set of promises for imperfect people to make to imperfect people in an abnormal world where everything has been spoiled since the Fall! "For richer or for poorer" is a reminder of Paul's declaration that he is able to be abased or to abound. This is what we are meant to vow to the Lord as our willingness in serving Him; we will serve Him no matter what—in palaces or in huts, in distressing situations and in beautiful ones, which if *He* gives we need not be ashamed. So in our marriage declarations we need not whisper but speak so that people can hear us say that we are stepping into a "togetherness," facing an unknown future which neither one can know about ahead of time.

The Model A Ford was packed and ready for us to go. After the reception all we needed to add was my suitcase. The two boxes of food were in. Food? Oh, yes. We had a romantic idea about what were then called "overnight cabins"—cost, $1.00 a night, or, with hot shower, $1.50—and we were going to take a one-burner electric plate, a small pot and a frying pan, dishes, and groceries. You see, this honeymoon was going to cost zilch! I had stupidly filled a little glass jar with butter. (It was July 6, with the temperature in the nineties and the humidity nearly as high.) The other ridiculous side of my preparation was that I had made a trousseau with little hand-tucked blouses, a white "going-away suit," and dainty things that would have been fine in a luxury hotel and resort. The first thing we did after waving to the rice-throwing guests was to head toward the country and stop at a drug store on the outskirts of town to cool off with a milk shake. In my elegant white suit I sat on a high stool at the counter sipping my chocolate milk shake; then when swirling around to get off, I found that someone else's milk shake had been spilled on the stool. My skirt was hopelessly stained with chocolate milk, ruined.

"Nothing mattered" . . . but that stained skirt kept going through my mind's eye, with all the carefully hand-whipped seams and Paris-couturier type of work I'd done on it . . . just to sit on a drug store stool? It was a vivid first lesson (though I didn't analyze it or even recognize it as that) of the basic fact of relationships—that *people* matter more than things! Fran remembers clearly that he felt sorry, but that he felt the magic moment of starting out together was more important than the spoiled skirt. He also remembers that I had started to make a fuss about it, but that I stopped short and didn't mention it again. Stopped in mid-air, so to speak, I had made a decision that was *not* perfectly kept in our lives together, but which *was* made time after time. The decision was to stop, try to recognize the total value of what was happening, and make a deliberate choice that the broken, torn, spilled, crushed, burned, scratched, smashed, spoiled *thing* was not as important as the person, or the moment of history, or the memory.

Fran lugged our wooden boxes and hot plate into the little room, then looked around for a spot for his suitcase and for the new big one father had so proudly bought me. Not much floor or hanging space. The jar of butter was leaking its liquefied fat. The cabbages sat on the little table, along with lettuce and tomatoes. . . . Where to put the hamburger? This was one of the more "expensive" cabins and had a shower . . . but where was I going to "glide glamorously" in my hand-made satin nightgown? . . . from where to where? There wasn't an inch of floor space!

The next noon, as the hamburger cooled and the corn and then the cabbage had their turns to cook, the cabin filled with a mixture of fragrances not exactly resembling subtle French perfumes. I'm afraid I must confess that tears of a sudden wave of homesickness engulfed me. Just about now, I thought, mother and dad would be sitting down to their lovely Sunday dinner discussing the wedding, and the morning sermon. It hit me that I had severed myself completely from my former home, and as yet I couldn't see at all what that word was going to mean—"home." Human beings and their emotions are unpredictable, and no one has a carbon copy of anyone else's experiences, but I would say that Fran and I have been very careful to see that our own children, and now our grandchildren and also the "spiritual children" close to us, have at least a few days of special luxury to start their honeymoons. So we feel the odor of cabbages and of dirty dishes being washed in the wash basin have helped a lot of other people get started a bit differently.

However, don't feel too sorry for us. We went on from cabin to cabin with a variety of menus, in spite of Fran's reaction to what he was handed when he asked for "butter, please." We had only three hundred and fifty miles to drive, and we were trying to take two weeks to do it. (You see, we hadn't any more gas money.) We stayed near Altoona, Pennsylvania, for two nights because of finding a good and cheap swimming pool, and a place where we could get chocolate ice cream sodas for five cents. Cheap even in those days. And we found another place near a quarry where there was a deep pool of mysteriously icy cold water we dove in, to find out later that it was "bottomless and very dangerous." We have fun memories and a host of funny stories to tell.

Our time at Aunt Bess's home in Cleveland introduced Fran to my father's sisters—Bess, Jennie, and Edith—and to Cousin Marion. They had made a gorgeous meal for us of fried chicken and hot biscuits, fresh peas, and piles of wonderful salad. Aunt Bess was famous for her varieties of home-made jams and perfect jellies. "Real butter," I whispered to Fran. "Take some . . . we won't see that for a long time. Ours will be margarine." "No," Fran stubbornly refused, "I'll ask for margarine, because I don't want to get used to the butter when we can't have it." I *still* feel frustrated by that which was his form of "sleeping-on-the-floor-to-train-for-China" training of Hudson Taylor . . . because I can still taste those gorgeously tender hot biscuits with real butter, jam, or honey and feel my intense distress that Fran was not tasting that same flavor. I must say that my desire to have Fran share the same flavors, sound of music, beauty of sunsets, wonder of museums—whatever—has extended now to a desire for each of my children and their spouses and children also to see, hear, smell, discover, and have the variety of things it *hurts* to have alone!

We arrived at Camp Michidune on the shores of Lake Michigan to discover to our dismay that camp consisted of log cabins with wide screened windows, rows of beds in each, and a counselor assigned to each eight or ten children—men for the boy's camp, girls for the girl's camp, with the "odd" counselors sharing another space depending on which period of time it was. Fran and I looked at each other, and then he spoke courageously, for having this job had been our "sign that it was right to marry in July," and we had no other way to live until September. "Edith and I have just been married, and we really do want to sleep together, so please could you make another arrangement for us, and we'll work as hard as necessary to make up for it in other ways."

The "arrangement" consisted of their finding an attic room in a big old wooden Summer Bible Conference building about a quarter of a mile away. The attic had a tiny window with a screen keeping it up, and two canvas cots narrower than anything we had ever seen. A "mattress"—a sort of one-inch thick pad—was on each one, along with a thin pillow, case, and sheets. There were two straight chairs and a thin cupboard with a few wire hangers. Period. And heat pulsating from the non-insulated roof. This was our "first home."

It was in this room I was to make the nail keg stool—covered with leather bought for twenty-five cents a pound—which was to look really stunning, and to last a lifetime. It was in this room I was to make another stool of a wooden cheese box covered with laced pieces of brown and white leather, which Priscilla would love to sit on as a one-year-old. It was in this room I was to practice cutting Fran's hair (a bit ragged the first time) to save the fifty cents for a haircut . . . and to start that which never stopped, as I became his official barber for life. And it was in this room we were to put two mattresses on one cot for a bit more softness, and to sleep as pretzels, with my declaring I didn't mind sleeping with one hand braced on the floor to keep from falling out. After all, we were so relieved to be given a place together that it all seemed sheer luxury by contrast to being treated as "single" camp counselors. (I'd just like to say here that the attitude of Christian groups toward their responsibility to *help* togetherness or coupleness, rather than their ignoring the need, is an appalling prelude to helping the opposite thing happen.)

Fran peeled potatoes, chopped wood, and hauled in groceries during the girls' camp . . . and among other things I nearly drowned. The girl whom I "rescued" during that period of time, wrote me only a number of months ago, telling of her appreciation, forty-five years later. You see, I really had been pushed into life-saving though I didn't have the proper knowledge. As I swam holding to her shoulder and trying to keep from being pulled under, I called out to the Lord, "Help me save her, Lord," but forgot the fact that I would have drowned too. Had I drowned, needless to say, *The Tapestry* would not have been written, nor this story lived.

During the boys' camp, Fran swam, dove, played tennis, hiked, and taught the boys, while I concentrated on leather handwork. I bought a couple of leather punches, some sharp scissors, and leather at a factory nearby that supplied it to shoe factories. The pile that I got for twenty-five cents a pound for ourselves to take back to Philadelphia had some rather large pieces in it that had been discarded, as well as masses of smaller ones. I stuck to browns, blacks, yellows, whites, and beiges. I didn't know it, but that was to be part of my "career" to make money for our food and basic expenses through seminary years. As I taught the boys, using *original* ideas—actually I had never learned anything about leather work, and didn't know a thing—it burst forth as an untaught natural talent. I figured there wasn't a "right" way; if other people had invented things, I could too.

We had learned things about working with children, both young boys and girls, that would be used the next year, and the next, and the next. And washing Fran's white shirts and starching them in a pail was to make the next stage of laundry seem efficient by contrast, just as our little apartment in the slums was going to seem spacious by contrast to the attic room.

As we were going back, our route took us through Grand Rapids, Michigan, on a Saturday night. That was to be the last of my personal driving career. Since I had passed my driver's test in Philadelphia under a tough policeman and had been congratulated, Fran had let me take the wheel during this five-mile-an-hour Saturday night traffic. As we crawled along, I suddenly called out, "Oh, Fran, look at the pretty fountain . . . colored lights . . ." And c r u n c h—we had locked bumpers with the car ahead. Fran went out in his stocking feet, jumped on the bumper, unlocked it, said something to the man, and got in—to berate me for being an idiot incapable of driving anything! I made a strong and never-to-be-broken resolve that I would never drive again. It seemed to me that that was one strain it would be better to keep out of our marriage altogether. Right, or wrong, I've stuck to it. However, that was only for thirteen years, because after coming to Europe we did away with having a car for many years and together have enjoyed buses and trains with a "driver."

Settled down in our apartment, we made our own furniture out of a variety of old things, but the place was so small it didn't need much. Fran scraped the old paint from the dressing table, the chest of drawers, and the three-quarter size iron bed that had been his at home. Repainted in a cream color and given new drawer handles fashioned of London tan leather, those pieces of furniture, along with the new curtains and bedspread of brown and white, transformed the tiny room into a really lovely looking place. It didn't matter that a card table for study had no room; it could rest on the bed, with two feet on the floor, and Fran was all set for night-after-night seminary "swatting." I set up the sewing machine and my leather work in the tiny living room. There were brown, white, and yellow laced-together leather covers on the couch which Fran had made from the old springs, and the cedar chest was covered with turquoise piqué I had "picked up" in South Fourth Street, along with the material for the curtains, bedspread, and pillows. It was all uncomfortable but elegant, with mother and dad's old straight chairs of no "period" sanded and covered (that is, the seats) with more of the cream-colored leather.

We had chosen a White's Domestic cabinet sewing machine rather than the similar Singer, simply to save $13.95 . . . which was enough to buy the gate-leg table, which when pulled out would serve our seminary dinner guests! That sewing machine, along with the leather and two punches, was to provide our living during the depression's lack of jobs. Yes, I was a working wife. It didn't seem to be a subject of conversation or of question. It seemed the perfectly normal thing to do when one's husband was working on studies essential to whatever the future would be for both of us. My creativity was having an opening, and ingenuity was also, but these reasons didn't have to be given. The topic wasn't on people's lips. Anyway, my mother had been a working mother as a China Inland missionary, along with all the other mothers and wives.

It seemed to me that a woman's "place" was to share the life and the work of the man she had made a choice to say "yes" to in whatever way the moment of history required, with the possibilities and diversities being endless. Farmers and their wives share the haying or the freezing of corn. The scope of going through life shoulder to shoulder in work, home, and vacation, includes a variety of changing "roles"—if you want to use that word, which I don't like. So I did dressmaking, and I designed, made and sold leather belts and buttons. The proceeds went to purchase our food and gas and so on—just enough to squeak through.

Fran shared in a weekly thorough housecleaning in which we polished everything, washed windows, shook out our little rag rugs, washed and waxed floors, and so on. We had no vacuum cleaner, or even rugs to vacuum. He also helped with the washing, plunging a contraption on the end of a broomstick into the sheets and towels and other items as they soaked in a soapy water in the bathtub. Long wringing and rinsing followed, and we hauled the various items out to the tin roof to hang them up on the inevitable lines out there. A homey feeling. Fran had taken two butter tubs and filled them with wonderful dirt from the Wissahickon woods, and by the next spring we were growing a lush crop of heavenly blue morning glories as well as petunias, ivy, and some ageratum. Our garden turned that ugly roof into a penthouse roof garden as far as we were concerned.

A daily pattern developed as seminary started. I made "packed lunches" identical for both of us. Where was I going? Nowhere outside of the apartment, but I wanted *not* to eat more or less than Fran, so that we could taste the same lunch, and feel the same degree of hunger by suppertime! I had no calorie problems, and I felt so strongly that we must be together in this. My idea was that then I'd know just what he would feel like for dinner. The lunches were very diverse, with walnut sandwiches as well as cheese ones, different each day, and little packets of carrot sticks, celery sticks, raisins, lettuce, and so on. The challenge was to do it all on five dollars a week and keep it interesting. My romantic ideas may have been a bit much, but looking back on it, that was preferable to not making any kind of an attempt. The mind-set or attitude of working at "feeling together when apart," whether eating the same food, or reading the same book at a certain hour, or whatever it is, is not just a worthless, mechanical, meaningless "trick," but a practical fulfillment of that mind-set or attitude.

As Fran continued studying until 2:00 or 3:00 A.M., I did my sewing or leather work that late too. I tried to use the machine when he wasn't home (to keep the noise from bothering Hebrew vocabulary), but I did mountains of the hand-sewing. "You know what MacRae said today?" "Mmmmmmmm . . ." I'd take pins out of my mouth . . . "What?" . . . and the account would start a discussion for minutes . . . or an hour.

In many areas, thinking developed together, as Fran studied, stopped to talk, and I could listen or respond, although my hands were busy. It helped him also to think out loud as he outlined ideas and compared different viewpoints. However, it would be unfair to give a picture of smooth communication at all times. Many many times in those seminary days, Hebrew "cards" (with the Hebrew on one side and English on the other) would take my place as Fran's constant companion, and as we were on a walk I had to be completely silent and clap my hand over my mouth to stop exclaiming over a bird or a fern. "Don't *talk*. Can't you see I'm learning Hebrew? When I've finished seminary there will be plenty of time to talk." "Plenty of time" . . . somehow that is always in the future, with a few rare and precious exceptions.

The professors at Westminster at that time were Dr. Machen, Dr. Stonehouse, Dr. Allis, Dr. Van Til, Dr. Kuiper, Professor MacRae, Professor Wooley, and Professor Murray. Professor MacRae, Hebrew and Old Testament scholar, gave Fran what he feels to have been the most excellent teaching on Old Testament prophets and essential stability to Fran's exegesis. As in college it had been Dr. Maurice Allan who opened the door for Fran to a wider area intellectually in philosophy, so it was Dr. Van Til at Westminster who opened another door, not so much in details, but in wider sweeps of thinking. Laird Harris (later to be Dr. Harris and not only to teach at Covenant Seminary but to have a large part in translation work on the *New International Version* of the Bible) was registrar of Westminster at that time, and we came to know him and his wife, Libby, well.

Our closest friends at seminary were Doug and Snook Young. Doug and his brother John both were at seminary at the same time as we were, sons of missionaries in Japan. Doug and his wife, Snook, rented an apartment similar to ours, accessible by going down one flight of the fire escape and knocking on the kitchen door. We had a great relationship with them—talking over everything from biblical and theological questions, to food, international affairs, my dressmaking, and Hebrew! Dr. Douglas Young was one day in the future to begin the Institute of Holy Land Studies in Jerusalem, about the same time as we would be starting L'Abri, and we were to have a meal together and talk over "old seminary days" in their home in Jerusalem the day after we had filmed the Abraham scene in episode 5 of *Whatever Happened to the Human Race?*. . . .

But all that was unknown to us—behind a curtain, in a cloud— and we gazed together at a map of the world, or maps of countries, with equal curiosity as to where God would be leading us. On the wall beside our small kitchen table Fran and I had the map of China that Dr. Howard Taylor had autographed, with "Serve the Lord with gladness" on it in Fran's handwriting. Often in thanking the Lord for our food, we told Him we were ready to go anywhere on that map, or the world map. The future was a total mystery to us—and of course it remains so.

Sundays we divided between our two families—after church, one place for lunch and afternoon; the other, for supper and evening. The same thing was done for Christmas and New Year's as 1936 was ushered in.

Casual decisions? . . . to go for a long walk in the woods alone, or to divide the day with parents? No, but changing decisions which cannot be listed for other people, which cannot bind the conscience of others. Individual history is diverse. Life is not frozen for any of us into one unchanging pattern. If a longer sweep of history is behind us, the thing that is learned, it seems to me, is the fleetness of "time." We mustn't get panicked, because we have eternity that is really real. We mustn't agonize endlessly over use of time in the past—the "If only I'd realized" sort of agony—but be aware that proximity of loved ones is not an endless situation. We are glad for the use of those Sundays, and not just for the cans of baked beans and Campbell's Soup, or the fruit that our parents slipped into a bag when we left. We can't wait for the piece of time suddenly to arrive, marked "time to care for parents and exhibit love in a practical way." That time comes and goes.

Our answer to prayer for a job to care for the summer of 1936 came with a letter. We were to be in charge of Camp Richard Webber Oliver in Rumney, New Hampshire, in the White Mountain area. Our great love for the mountains and our first mountain climbing were to begin that summer. The camp was a part of the work of the New England Fellowship, a thoroughly evangelical organization, which also had conference grounds there, and whose central work was the opening of closed churches. We cared for a range of little boys—taught them, hiked with them, read them stories at night, tucked them in, prayed with them, led them to the Lord with a measure of real understanding, tied their shoes, put mercurochrome on their cuts and ice on their bruises, scolded them and loved them. We grew to love New England, and we prayed for the whole of that group of states with the dream and hope of going back to indeed open one of those closed churches and start a work there. We thought that the Lord was preparing us for that.

Now so many years later (we really have prayed for New England with some degree of faithfulness), L'Abri has a branch in Southborough, Massachusetts, but that is ahead of the story! A succession of people came from New England to Switzerland through the years, and in some ways we felt the Lord was using us *for* New England in Switzerland, more effectively than if we had been in New England. We believe that is true of other parts of the United States and of other countries. People came, asked their questions, listened, struggled with the truth, came to believe—people who wouldn't have come to a similar place near their own homes. So often answers to prayers for places, people, problems, or even material things, come in very roundabout ways, and there is a danger of not recognizing the answer, or saying "thank you." Our fervent prayer in the White Mountains brought very real answers in the Swiss Alps.

While we were working at the camp, word came that Dr.

Machen had been "defrocked" because of having started the Independent Board for Presbyterian Foreign Missions in order to send out the believing graduates of Westminster Seminary, who were being refused by the church boards. Carl McIntire also had been put out. Fran felt he should immediately resign by letter from the Northern Presbyterian Church, and he went under care of the newly formed Presbyterian Church of America; that is, as a seminary student he went under care of the new presbytery. The fire of battling for the truth burned within us, and we talked together long into the night that night.

Dr. Machen had not begun by wanting to form a new church, but to reform from within, to "feed back" staunch, well-educated Bible-believing pastors into the "old church" to stand against the wave of liberalism. Now came the new church for which we had such enthusiastic high hopes. As we went back for the second year of Westminster, it was with determination to "get on with it"!

That autumn I became pregnant. Continuing the dressmaking (my customers bought the material, of course), I made fully lined and tailored winter coats for $8 and dresses, even long ones with hand-whipped rolled-hem ruffles, for $5! Our late nights of sewing and studying were interspersed with *much* discussion about the things which bothered us.

We had been troubled in college, and it was still in our conversation—how *could* people stand for God's holiness and the purity of doctrine in the church, and in one's personal life, yet not have it turn out to be harsh and ugly? Now when you read Fran's books, written after years of growth in living and understanding, you can hear him speak of this as a "simultaneous exhibition of the holiness of God and the love of God." But then we didn't have his books to read, nor did we have those years of "life" behind us.

The second thing that bothered us was what Fran today would call "a deterministic view of the Reformed Faith." This was more present then in Westminster than it is now, and the way some of the professors taught these things greatly troubled Fran. I too felt it keenly, especially in a seminary wives' prayer meeting when one professor's wife chided me for praying for something specific. God is sovereign, she said, and therefore we should only ask for blessing and for spiritual requests, but never for anything material. "It isn't fitting to bother God anyway" was the gist of the admonition; and her idea was that it was disrespectful! It seemed to me that real prayer, prayer that can change history, was being ruled out. So our discussions, accompanied by the "click click" of the leather punch as belts were made, came from various areas in the midst of the same issue—a deterministic view of the Reformed Faith.

Early in my pregnancy, Fran had to have an emergency appendectomy. As Dr. Lee, a Christian surgeon, arranged for a little room that was considered an annex to a big ward, Fran had privacy for study, and the possibility of having my visits last all day. In those days, after such an operation, the patient could not swing his feet over the side of the bed for the first seven days, and the hospital stay was two weeks. I vomited daily when I went to eat in Horn and Hardart's Cafeteria, the overwhelming odors of cooking food sending me to the ladies room before I could push my tray through the line. That also was my time to spend late nights copying all of Doug and John Young's notes from seminary classes, so that Fran wouldn't get behind. (Recovery time included six weeks before classes could be resumed, so my note-copying went on.)

Thanks to Doug and John's good notes and to Fran's determined, nonstop studying, his extremely high marks—a 1.26 average (equivalent to an A+)—continued without a break. Quite amazingly, the exam Dr. Machen set for Fran because of his being in the hospital, and which had Dr. Machen's personal scribble on it, was the last he would set. It was at that time Dr. Machen went to the Dakotas to speak in a series of tiny churches. Though he became ill with pneumonia, he continued to speak, and he died very suddenly. His death was such a loss to us all. His last words, reported by someone at his bedside in that far-off hospital, were, "I am so thankful for the active obedience of Christ." And his favorite hymn, sung at the funeral, was the simple, yet profound "There is a green hill far away." His was a deep and simple faith in the Lord whom he loved so well. Scholarly expression and fighting for the early manuscripts in the original Greek did not dim his simple love and praise for the Lord.

When it came time for Fran to leave, we realized that whatever the hospital bill would be, it would take the small amount of money we had in the bank to pay for the baby's birth. Praying a lot about it together, we explained to the Lord that we could use that money, but that we would like to ask Him to provide something so that it could remain untouched for the baby. I went trembling to the proper hospital office to ask for help from their special services for "worthy" people who were not paupers! To the dignified man sitting at his big desk, I explained all about our being seminary students, about my sewing not bringing in more than we needed each week, and about my being pregnant. He spoke quietly about the purpose of his hospital fund but said it was administered month by month, and could not be touched for anything that was not within the *time.* "I will see what is left in the fund for *this* month. It may be all gone. Come again tomorrow."

I went the next day with the hospital bill clutched in my hand, a bit breathless but *trying* to "trust quietly" as we had been praying so very much: "Please, Lord, we know You can answer . . . but also we want Your will." When the man asked first, "Now, what does the total bill amount to?" I took out the bill and read him the enormous amount (or so it seemed to me), "It is seventy-five dollars." (Remember, with five dollars for making a dress, that would be fifteen dresses' worth!) The man smiled a beautiful smile and responded with pleasure in his voice, "Well, now, that is remarkable, as we have exactly seventy-five dollars left in our fund." Dr. Lee charged nothing for his surgery, saying it was his work for the Lord. . . . The Lord had given us encouragement to keep on "bothering Him."

In May a synod meeting was held which brought about another "split." Differences flared up in hot discussion, and accusation was leveled, "You're not Reformed. . . ." However, two other factors entered in. The majority of men at Westminster held a view called "Christian liberty," while others felt strongly there was a list of things which the "separated Christian" could not do. Differences in the views of prophecy also came into the taking of sides. Fran got involved. We both had strong opinions and positions. Fran would come home to the apartment from these meetings and scarcely taste the beautifully cooked end-of-the-day "bargains" I had scrounged in the market to find. He was all steamed up, and I would listen and get all steamed up too. We might as well have been eating sawdust! There was a cause to be fought for, and the decks had to be cleared to get on with it. We felt that any sacrifice would not be too much to do the "right thing" in the midst of all this.

After having lived on through the history of our lives to 1981 we now think back to that summer of 1937 with mixed thoughts and feelings. This is true of so many things in the fallen world! Perhaps it is always easier to understand in retrospect. A new church *was* formed, and every person wanted it to be his "perfect church." With that in mind, it is easier to be more understanding. Other things entered in too. Dr. Machen had died and there was a struggle for leadership. We still think the first two things that had troubled us at that time are crucial. The issues of "Christian liberty" and differing views of prophecy should have been settled in patience over a number of years within the denomination.

Looking back on that time, we wish we could have been less intense, less steamed up. Certainly we would not now say some of the things we said then. We would be glad if we could erase them!

As years have gone by, we have said to the men involved that we were sorry. So often in differences among Christians it is not the issues themselves that continue tensions years later. With such differences, whether in the relationships within families, between husband and wife, or in the church, it is the things said with harshness or in anger in the midst of speaking of "issues" that stick in the memory and still hurt years later. Often the sharpness of the issues has softened, yet sitting and quietly talking still is put off.

As you know from Fran's letters from college, he had been troubled by the "chip-on-the-shoulder" attitude then, as he was trying to choose a seminary. That factor did not change his realization that we must struggle against liberalism when it enters a church or a denomination. As we look back over life now, realizing how brief time is, we are extremely thankful that we have not used all our time to struggle against liberalism within our own denomination but have been freed to go on with a positive work.

Having said all that, we are troubled by the lack of love at that time, and we realize that we got caught up in "the cause" so passionately that we ourselves did not show the balance we would struggle for if we could live that section of history over again. There was still another eighteen years, however, during which we had much *much* more to learn in the struggle for balance.

You know, there is a sad thing about history! As we learn things, grow, discover mistakes, recognize where we took a detour or failed to clean up weeds, and then try to direct others into the cleared-up path, the climbers who are slogging up the mountain behind us insist on blazing their own trail. Then in not heeding any warnings or markings, and in leaving the traveled path, along which more progress could be made, for their new rough one, so their distance in the end is not added to in the way it might have been! Pity. Yet how patient God is with us, dealing so gently with us and working through us—each of us—with whatever few "fish and bread" bits we hand over to Him in our eagerness to give our all to Him, with some measure of understanding in the face of some measure of sacrifice.

So . . . there were to be a "new church" and a "new seminary," both of which would fulfill all the dreams and have all the right balances and emphasis! "This time we are *really* on the way. . . ."

Practically, what happened was that a board was formed to commence Faith Theological Seminary, and Dr. Samuel Laird invited this seminary to hold its classes in the Sunday School rooms of his church building, right across the street from the Baltimore and Ohio Railroad Station in Wilmington, Delaware. What difference did the B&O make? Well, any man who was a student at that time, or who taught there then, will know what a pivot of interest was the swift passage of the "Royal Blue Express" from New York to Washington, D.C. Whether the subject being taught at the time was Hebrew verbs or church history, there was a general rush to the window. Doug and John Young, Francis Schaeffer, John Sanderson, Art Glasser, Delbert Jorgensen, James Lipscomb, Walter Cross, Homer Emerson, Vernon Grounds, Robert Hastings, Norman Jerome, Jack Murray, Philip Stutsman and others (all dignified older men by now!) made a general exodus from their seats while MacRae was shouting, "Sit DOWN!" or some other professor was having his own brand of catfits. And they would stay at the window until the Royal Blue disappeared.

Many years later, my father was to go with my mother to

meet that train during its two-minute stop at the Wilmington Station. My niece Lydia had gone with them to point out Jane Stuart Smith, whom she had known at L'Abri, so that they could rush to the spot where Jane would lean dramatically out of the window to drop a diamond pin into their upstretched hands. The pin had been brought from England, a gift to L'Abri for "the English trips," given by a lady in Ireland. But that is away in the future, and now the Royal Blue is no more! However, it was to figure in the lives of all of us through a number of years, in diverse and amazing ways.

After Dr. Laird's invitation was accepted by the Board, they dispersed for the summer, and Dr. MacRae, who was to be president of the new seminary, began to work on details, along with Fran, who worked for him that summer. Into all this, Priscilla was born on June 18. Our first baby. Did the world stop moving for our so titanic event? Fran had rushed me to the hospital with a police "escort" getting into the scene (first to arrest him for fast driving, then to go along to "protect mother and child")! After a night of what we then called labor pains (which have turned into contractions now) these turned out to be "false labor." Fran, arriving anxiously in the morning with a 99-cent drug store electric fan to "cool you off during labor," was disgusted and even angry that I had gone backwards in this whole process! It was an embarrassing thing to him, and he wasn't a bit sympathetic. A week later we were to come again at exactly 7:00 P.M., my water having burst during supper with mother and dad, and Priscilla was born at 11:20 P.M.

Now, had natural childbirth been practiced then, I would have been an excellent subject. But it wasn't. No one had given me any exercises or breathing help, so I did all the wrong things, like clutching the bed and tensing all my muscles. Ether was given rectally, which burned like fire and seemed to add to the general "discomfort." Then, as the baby was coming more rapidly than anyone had anticipated, I was rushed into the delivery room and a mask of ether placed over my twisting-away-from and trying-not-to-take face!

As Priscilla entered the world, it was to not breathe for a half hour. The nurse there, a daughter of Dr. McQuilken, knew we were Christians and rushed out past Fran in the hall, weeping, certain there would soon be tragic news for us. Oxygen was given the baby—no go. Then Dr. Taylor gave her mouth-to-mouth resuscitation and started her breathing. No cry came, but she was living. Why isn't Priscilla a hopelessly brain-damaged person? The Lord had another pattern for her life, is all I can say.

The "why" comes in both directions in life, and again we have to say—there is the reality of God in answering prayer. There is the reality of a young father praying in the hall, terrified by the silence of the delivery room. And—there is the reality of the sovereignty of God. The "whys" of life, and of death, are not to be understood until we finally are where we can see more of The Tapestry than we can see today. Priscilla, however, her husband, her three children, and later another generation, will hold their breath as they read this, over *her* first breath, realizing how many people's breathing was tied in with that sudden intake of air into that baby's lungs.

The mystery of being? We never get to the end of it.

Visiting hours were afternoon and evening. "Mother, please don't let anyone come in the evening hour, from eight to nine, as that is the only time Fran can come." Everyone complied. But—Fran was working with MacRae in a downtown office on all the details of the new seminary, outlining what had to be done in Wilmington before the opening date in September. And MacRae, a bachelor at that time, was not exactly in tune with my eager waiting in the hospital. I would carefully get a basin of water brought to me—remember, in those days it was a two-week stay, and the whole thing of *not* being allowed to get up and walk was a part of that era, now past—and wash, brush my hair and braid it, tie blue or pink or black velvet ribbons on the ends of the two braids, put on a fresh nightgown with a bedjacket, and arrange myself into what I thought would be a fetching picture of a young mother awaiting her husband. The minutes would go, and go, and go . . . and the precious hour would be almost up . . . only five or ten minutes left.

By the time Fran would rush into the room with "Oh, I'm so sorry, MacRae asked me to—" I'd be brushing away my tears, determined not to let the only time we had be spoiled, and all too soon the nurse would appear at the door with a bundle. "Time to go," she would say. "Babies are being fed—" (No father's germs allowed in those days!) "Oh, please . . . my husband just came from work . . . please take all the others first, and bring mine a little bit later!" A few minutes to squeeze in all that was to be said . . . about the beginning pains of preparing a new seminary, and our loneliness for each other, and the ins and outs of my varied troubles, needing molasses-and-milk enemas and the baby's X-ray treatment for an enlarged thymus gland . . . and whish . . . the time was over.

So very, *very* often, life's preciously awaited "centrally important" times, "to-be-undisturbed" times, "one-in-a-lifetime" times are mélanged with the battle of trying to live in a balance of first things first. No one can know when he or she is having the most priceless alabaster box of perfume to pour on the Lord's feet, saying, "This, Lord, *You* are worthy of receiving," even if it seems too much from a human viewpoint of evaluating importance. No one knows when he or she is having a rare opportunity to say to the Lord, "Thank you for saying 'a cup of cold water given in My name' has value, is accepted, is remembered, is worthwhile to *You*." My "cup of cold water" in those two weeks was the giving of precious time with my husband to the new seminary . . . but really to the Lord. Some days the gift was annulled by my feeling resentments.

A month later we were given the commission of going to Wilmington and looking for, finding, selecting . . . ? . . . houses "suitable for students, and, oh, yes, quarters for married students, and a house for faculty apartments, for beginning seminary in September." So it was that one hot July morning we left Priscilla with her adoring Grandmother Seville and drove off on a "wild goose chase" . . . which turned into an afternoon of being amazed at the answer to prayer the Lord gave us.

The only cash we had was forty dollars which belonged to Priscilla's first piggy bank. Three ten-dollar gifts and two five-dollar gifts had been sent to us with "welcome baby" cards, and we took all this along, "just in case." After being told, "We have nothing," by several real estate dealers, Fran started to drive within a small radius of the church where classes would be held. And with breathless astonishment we found on one block of 14th Street, just a two-block walk from the church, four houses with big "FOR RENT" signs on them, three with a different real estate company's name, and one with the owner's name and phone number. Within an incredibly short time, we had put a ten-dollar down payment on each of the four houses.

One was to be the students' house with a living room for the students' general use. One was to be apartments for some of the professors (others would rent elsewhere), and two were to be made into apartments for married students. They were three-story houses, and although the one for students was bigger, the others were three rooms deep, or four rooms deep, so that they could be broken up into an apartment on each floor.

The check handed Fran to "get the necessary things to make those houses ready to live in" was woefully small. So Fran began charging around Philadelphia to all the junk yards, piling through the chaos to find sinks, stoves, toilet bowls, bathroom wash basins, making sure they had no cracks or chipped places. The average price he paid was five dollars apiece. By going to widely separated places, he found enough to "do it"! Excelsior! Now for secondhand stores to find "good furniture" for the student lounges and enough student beds to start with; the others would have to furnish their own places. For extremely low prices, we found enough decent pieces, and also, for us, a couch and chair that were in good condition and comfortable, at ten dollars for the two as a set.

Leaving the baby with mother again, we went to Wilmington, this time for Fran to look up plumbers and electricians and get promises from them to do the work, "in time." Our next trek was to the Bancroft Mills to look for mill ends and marked-down bolts of cotton materials, to make curtains and slipcovers for the student living room, and curtains and slipcovers for ours. Again, the most expensive stuff we got was 35 cents a yard for 50-inch-wide material! (The "good old days," eh?) We were now ready to move!

Moving day was one of the worst days in our lives, yet a day which Fran looks back to as one of the most important in his life. He thinks of it as a day when he learned one of the most valuable lessons spiritually that he ever learned—one of those never-to-be-forgotten times of reality in the Christian life.

Try to picture it, if you have a good imagination. The usual packing had taken place—books in boxes, newspaper-wrapped dishes in bushel baskets, lamps standing hopefully ready, the bed taken apart, medicines and soaps and groceries all in shoe-boxes or grocery boxes—the usual chaos, plus the "things to be ready to use right away" like the diapers, oil for baby's bottom, damp facecloth at hand . . . and, "Oh, yes, we'll have to feed her on the way."

A big complication, however, loomed on the horizon like a black cloud. Are we ready? "Mmmmmmm. . . ." "Then," says Fran, "I'll go with the truck and get the junk." What junk? you may well ask. You see, all the sinks, stoves, toilet bowls and so on, plus the second-hand furniture—about six stops in varying places—had to be picked up with Fran guiding the truck driver as a starter. All our "moving" was to be put on *top* of this charming load of stuff.

A most irate Fran returned a couple of hours later. "They tried to cheat me at a couple of places. I had to try all that stuff again and look for cracks and leaks. . . . It wasn't all the same junk I had so carefully chosen." Then—"WHAT have you been doing? Why isn't the baby dressed? . . . HURRY . . ." And as the man helped Fran carry all the lumpy, awkward stuff down the narrow stairs, and things bumped and fell and became heavier on the way down, the irateness grew. "Broken . . . that infuriates me . . . no sense to it . . ." and so on. Finally our Model A Ford was packed with the more "precious" things, and mother had squeezed herself into the back seat in the few inches of space left. I got into the front seat with a very recently fed baby.

The rain poured down, and fog misted up from the hot streets. The truck got out of sight, a red light blinked on at the wrong time, a wrong turn was taken. . . . One thing after another happened, and Fran got angrier with each thing. Suddenly the sweetly dressed pink-and-white baby, looking like a rosebud, emitted from both ends at once. A gush of so recently swallowed food came up over my shoulder, down my back and splashed over the seat back, while simultaneously a rush of what could have been mustard leaked forth from both sides of the beautiful white knitted soakers with diapers carefully pinned under them, and covered my lap, my legs, and my shoes. "Can't you even take care of that baby? . . . Don't you know how to put on diapers? WHAT IS THE MATTER WITH YOU?"

Suddenly another thing happened. Within seconds Fran had

skidded, and our car had slid into another car on the slippery street. It might have been a bad accident, but it wasn't. My instant thought was, "Oh, now he'll really be mad." But the reaction was entirely different. Fran said he instantly felt as if God had spoken to him. He didn't hear a voice, but he was very vividly conscious of Hebrews 12:11, and he said aloud so that mother and I both heard him, "All right, Lord, I'm sorry; it's enough."

He felt a great calm and peace, recognizing something he never forgot again. It was not that he never got angry again—that wasn't it—but it *was* that he saw something very profound concerning chastening. He was sure for himself that one thing after another had been allowed by the Lord, in a cumulative way, to bring him up short . . . to bring him to a place of saying to the Lord, "I'm sorry," and of discovering just what is meant by chastening producing "the peaceable fruit of righteousness" in those who are really "exercised thereby," in those who come to a point of saying, "Okay, Lord, I do get the message. I'm sorry." This was one of those times of a "nail in the wall" being put up in Fran's own Christian life, and he felt it was the thing which took him to Wilmington to face all that was ahead in a better state of understanding and quietness.

Ladies who are still living and who were in Dr. Laird's Faith Bible Presbyterian Church at that time remember taking care of Priscilla as a two-month-old baby during their missionary meeting the day we moved in. I soon "set up shop" for a kind of sewing different from what I'd been used to, as I turned the lengths of cloth into curtains and slipcovers for the student lounge and for our own living room. Our summer days lasted from early morning till late night, as the plumbers and electricians added their work to ours. By the opening date, the "students, faculty, board, and friends of the seminary" came to an "opening tea" served in the room we had just finished. Decorations consisted of arrangements made from flowers some of the ladies brought from their gardens—beginning of "hidden art" training for us! People arrived— Doug and Snook, Laird and Libby Harris, and John Sanderson (now Dr. Sanderson of Covenant Seminary)—asking, "Where is the campus?" We explained to each new student that the house across the street, plus the other houses on that ordinary, American, tree-lined street, and the church around the corner, were "it."

Fran had prepared a dossier of my father's credentials for teaching beginning Greek, and missions, and mother and father were installed very soon in the bottom apartment of the faculty house, with the Harrises above them. It became an unforgettable year for me, a never-to-be-repeated year of living across the street from my parents, to say nothing of the fact that with mother leading them, the wives' prayer meetings were something so warm and special that many people look back to her as their "spiritual mother" in many areas of understanding. Father taught at Faith for seventeen years before he retired to be "home secretary," so to speak, of L'Abri in 1955, the year L'Abri started. He was eighty years old at that time!

Graduation day came, with Fran having been the first student to register at Faith. He also had kept his record of top marks as he had straight "ones" in all his subjects. He also was the first pastor to be ordained in the Bible Presbyterian Church, as he graduated in the first graduating class. The outstanding moment of Faith graduation ceremonies, as far as I was concerned, was the singing of "Give Tongues of Fire to Preach Thy Word" by the whole student body as they stood on the platform together. My eyes sting with tears just writing about it. What a plea to the Lord! What a longing in hearts of young men! Yet . . . how easy it is for something to get in the way of its becoming a reality, especially with an enemy trying to put hindrances in the way of doing just that, or even the reality of *caring* to do that.

During the year we were to be in the United States just before L'Abri was to start, Fran was to preach in many places a sermon which he called "Give Tongues of Fire to Preach Thy Word," subtitled "The Lord's Work in the Lord's Way." Do read that sermon in his book *No Little People*. That sermon was to be preached *before* L'Abri had ever been dreamed of . . . and it was to be preached fifteen years *after* his graduation! But as we walked out into the warm May night, along tree-lined 14th Street, we were filled with emotion . . . looking back over the stormy, yet so fulfilling year . . . looking forward to . . . ? . . . an unknown future. My silent plea to the Lord was made with a strong rush of fervency: "Please, Lord, give Fran a tongue of fire to preach your Word. Never let the fire cool off."

THE REVEREND AND MRS. SCHAEFFER 10

We were packing again. It had only been nine months since we had moved to Wilmington with two-month-old Priscilla. Now seminary graduation was over; it was still May; Priscilla was eleven months old and walking, to our great excitement; and the apartment was being dismantled, with newspapers coming into their own once more for wrapping dishes, protecting the clock, bunching in around pots and pans, and padding boxes for books. The map came off the wall with a few pangs of regret, for instead of going to some exotic-sounding place halfway around the world, we were soon going to be driving about 350 miles to Grove City, Pennsylvania. It was to be across the street, in a sense, rather than across the sea. But we had said, "Anywhere, Lord," and as far as we could know, this seemed His clear direction.

Two of our new elders were coming to drive our furniture and all our other belongings. We would follow in the Model A Ford which had lived an active life for seven years now. A coffee delivery truck drew up in front of the house, announcing Howe's Coffee Company, and Mr. Howe and Mr. Hall solemnly greeted us, "How do you do, Reverend and Mrs. Schaeffer." It didn't sound a bit like us, and I was tempted to look over my shoulder to see who might be standing behind us. We were to plunge into a new category which somehow drew an invisible, uncomfortable, separating line around us—"The Reverend and Mrs. Schaeffer." Ouch!

The Covenant Presbyterian Church consisted of eighteen people who had left the "big liberal Presbyterian Church" and were meeting in the American Legion Hall. Next door to this lodge hall was a square brick apartment building, with eight small apartments. The first-floor apartment (turn right when entering the front door) was to be ours. We had a living room, a dining room which became our bedroom, and one bedroom that we decided would be for Priscilla. It was dark, but at least off to one side the kitchen opened into what then was our bedroom, and we managed to eat in there most of the time. Our salary was to be exactly $100 a month. The rent of the apartment was $36 plus $1 per month for the incinerator, and with insurance at $18 a month, you can see there wasn't much leeway for unspecified spending. We allotted $5 a week for food, so the shopping had to coincide with the moment when prices came down on Saturdays for wilted vegetables, day-old bread, and so on. As we unpacked the boxes our now-walking eleven-month-old found one that had been parked on the bathroom floor, full of such things as Vicks Vapo-Rub, aspirin, toothbrushes and toothpaste, nail brush, and other such items. Quick as a flash she delightedly threw them all into the toilet and pulled the handle . . . flush . . . down . . . overflow flood! The apartment belonged to one of the other elders of the church whom we were yet to meet—and the circumstance of meeting was not exactly what we had planned. We had the added pleasure of meeting the local plumber that same day.

Sunday morning found us next door in the Legion Hall. Here we were discovering what had to be moved around and put in place to turn the upstairs hall, which had had a lodge meeting in it until late the night before, into a "church." The eighteen people did not bring their children because of feeling they should still have the benefit of a larger Sunday School and their old friends. I sat a bit nervously with Priscilla—trying silently to amuse her without distracting "Reverend Schaeffer" as he preached his first sermon after being ordained! Hopes, dreams, aspirations, desire to be willing to walk through fire and water

with love for the Lord, a burning message of important truth in the heart and mind to impart—no matter whether in China, Korea, Africa, South America, Europe, North America, Australia, wherever you are, the ingredients have to be the willingness, the message, the call, and then—the people!

And what about the pastor's wife? For me, I felt my very big responsibility (along with caring for Priscilla) was never to stop praying for Fran as he preached. I felt keenly that it was up to me to pray for the power of the Holy Spirit, for the Lord's words to be given, for the message to really touch not only others but the speaker himself. "Speak to him, and through him" was not just a formula of prayer; it became the cry of my heart. This was to continue through the years, and it was very, very possible and practical (I know because now I have forty-five years behind me) for me to continue no matter what, even if we had just had a "fight" of some sort before he spoke . . . very possible and practical for me to "sit under the word of God" really forgetting *anything* personal, to listen to what was coming forth, and to be thankful that Fran was "hearing this," as well as to "hear it" myself. In the hope of helping some new, young, pastor's wife, I would say that it is imperative *never* to sit thinking, "How can he say that when he has just been so unreasonable?" It is imperative really to believe God is able to speak through the one for whom we pray and able to speak through us ourselves when we ask Him to, and at the same time to know that the speaker is being spoken to too. To feel that no one can preach who has not been perfect in the area in which he is preaching about, is to miss the reality of the truth of what fallen human beings are like, and what the word of God is like. To grow, to strive for reality, to call out to the Lord for forgiveness, and to seek to live in the light of His word are of course important. But perfection is not to be reached in the land of the living, though we are called to teach a "perfect message" which has come from the perfect God.

Fran's first thought was to start reaching children in the town, but he hadn't one child to start with, let alone a nucleus. He discovered that Grove City Park had a section, formerly strip-mined, that had wonderfully been planted. Stepping into it, one might as well have been hundreds of miles away in a wilderness.

Fran chose a lovely spot in this, and prepared things for a hot dog roast. The church gave him a small fund to buy hot dogs and rolls and marshmallows and a few other things, and he set forth to find boys! "Hey, there—how would you like to come to a hot dog roast?" he called out to two boys playing marbles on a sidewalk. "Oh boy . . . sure . . ." "Well, hop in and take me to some of your friends." By the time the Model A Ford was full to the brim and its ample running boards were full also with ecstatic boys hanging onto the window frames or seat backs through the open windows, he had a good seventeen. The whole scene looked like one of those circus tricks where impossible numbers of people pour out of a phone booth or out of a Volkswagen Beetle. Eventually Fran was to pile in a record number of twenty-one!

The hot dog roasts were just that, and when tummies were full and the fire was dying down, Fran would talk about the wonders of creation, and what had happened to bring us all into the state the world is in now. The boys, really interested, wanted a "next time," and affectionately called Fran "Rev." "Rev" he was from that time on in Grove City. After Rev's hot dog roasts had continued for a few weeks, Fran and I asked the church people if they would help with a Summer Bible School. We would fix up the Legion Hall for two weeks of morning Bible School and share the teaching. As my mother had said she would come out and help, there would be the two of us, and several other ladies said they would give their time. However, with no children in Sunday School, everyone was extremely skeptical as to any attendance. Who would come?

But there were the hot dog roast boys now. Fran gathered them into a "visiting team" with him, and, car filled with boys, Fran drove up one street and down another. Wherever anyone knew a child, Fran would stop the car, walk up to the house, introduce himself and the fact of a free two-week Summer Bible School for all ages, and leave a small paper telling of times, etc. Having learned to operate a printing press, he employed his skill with the machine available at Mr. Howe's coffee and nut factory to prepare a variety of leaflets and posters in the work. I painted a big poster to put up in a prominent place . . . and the advertising was launched.

At most of the front doors, Fran would stand on the doorstep and assure the mother of the marvels of this coming Bible school, but at some places he went inside and had a really good conversation about Christianity with whoever was there. Actually, pastoral calling was one of Fran's talents to be drawn into immediate use, as he not only called on the congregational members and their relatives but on other "needy" people and the parents of children with whom we were working. Much of his time was spent in calling.

When the morning dawned for the Bible School to begin, we were an apprehensive little group who stood in front of the Legion Hall. Would there be any children? The notices had said, "Bring your Bibles." We had song sheets for them, catechism booklets, and material to illustrate Bible stories, and so on. Emptiness. Quiet, cool early morning air, and an empty street. Then suddenly they began to come—a trickle of children with assorted sizes of Bibles under their arms. Then more, and more, and more—five-year-olds clinging to the hands of ten- or eleven-year-olds, boys and girls. There were even teenagers. Tears were not far from spilling, just somewhere behind our eyelids. Eighteen in church, no child in Sunday School; yet here they were—seventy-nine that first morning, and before the time was over it grew to more than one hundred children.

The closing exercises of songs, Bible verses (even whole Psalms) recited by heart, answers to questions, the repeating of the names of books of the Bible as if they were a football cheer provided an evening filled with excitement, as most of the children had brought at least one parent, or an aunt or uncle or grandparent. Two teenage girls, Bea and Leatha, were saved during that Bible School, in my mother's class, as were others. We still keep in touch with them and their children as they have gone on through the years. In fact, Bea and her husband Eddie were to have their twenty-fifth wedding anniversary in L'Abri in the Swiss Alps, many years later. But at that time we only knew the present, and it was 1938!

After the Bible School, there was no influx into the church services. A few did come to Sunday School and church, but this was a trickle. Late Sunday afternoons I'd try to casually meet someone as I'd walk up the alley behind us, praying I could get at least one more person for the evening service. I felt so sorry for Fran having to preach to so many empty seats. Grove City College was right there in town, but in spite of our having a very well-attended party for the students, complete with refreshments of home-made cookies and punch, almost none of them came to the young people's evenings we had started in our home.

Fran had spoken that summer in a conference on Lake Erie where we met Mrs. Eleanor McCluskey of Atlanta, Georgia, who had started "The Miracle Book Club," an organization for home Bible study with high school young people. This group came before *any* of the other national high school young people's organizations were started. We became friends with Mrs. McCluskey and have been friends for a lifetime. We also started a chapter of the Miracle Book Club in our home. This was the beginning of our work with young people that later grew into L'Abri, even as the Bible School was our beginning work with children that was going to include our "Children for Christ" work later. Many seeds were planted in Grove City.

We moved from the apartment to an old beaten-up house out on the main road, which was also a highway and therefore dangerous for a two-year-old. Howe's coffee and nut factory was nearby, next to a garage where cars were repaired, which was next to us. We had a rambling, bumpy lawn, and dug up a patch of it to make our very first vegetable garden. One of the farmers in our church gave us a load of manure, and since the garden was so small, we had about ten inches of manure all over it. We were ahead of time! It was like going by the new principle of planting closer together in over-fertilized ground. We had masses of harvest from our little plot, and I "put up" twenty-two quarts of tomatoes we had grown, plus twenty-two each of peaches and pears given us by farmers.

The house was old and falling apart, but we camouflaged it, blotting out the view of ugly broken cars and busy highway by getting Japanese bamboo roll-up curtains wide enough to cover a whole wall, then curtained the sides with drapes. Fran got some old front seats from cars, for nothing, and built a frame for them to sit on out of the wood he took out of an old coal bin in the cellar, and I made slipcovers for them. Not that we didn't have a coal bin—we had to "tend the furnace" during long winters, finding out how to coax it along to keep it going through the nights. We added other furniture for a dining room now, with chairs that were real antiques but had been thrown away! Fran spent fourteen hours each on sanding them before we could give them an oil and turpentine finish.

Fran's pastoral calls included taking a chair along to sand while he talked to a farmer milking a cow. He felt that working together provided a better atmosphere for conversation, something real rather than just "polite." In one barn he spied a little table that was being used to put milk cans on. When he asked how much it would cost to buy it, the reply was, "Oh nothing . . . that old thing." The top was cracked all the way across, so it isn't valuable, but it is mahogany, and, after twenty hours of sanding, with a cloth on top and glass on that, we have used it for a coffee table all through the years. An old butterbox lid, round, became a tray, which I burned with a design to match the fruit on our drapes. Gradually we had a very attractive place for our young people's Miracle Book Club, the session dinner meetings, and other entertaining we did, as well as for our family life with one child, growing.

Priscilla went along with her daddy on calls a lot of the time, but one day Fran returned alone. "Where is Janet Priscilla?" I asked a bit agitatedly. "Oh . . . I forgot I had her." He had to retrace his steps, asking a bit embarrassedly at each home if he had left Priscilla there. He found her half-way through the list—playing happily, confident that she would be picked up sometime.

Mrs. Armour, wife of one of our elders, had a very advanced case of multiple sclerosis and could sit up only if propped up, and she could not eat anything but Jello or liquids. "I do get so tired of sweet things, and wish I could taste meats or fish," she would say. I used to invent all kinds of broths, using cooked, ground-up, and put-through-sieve meats such as chicken and veal, along with onion and celery, to get a delicate blend of flavors to make into a mousse with gelatin. This was something she could hold in her mouth and taste before it slid down. The same thing was possible with finely ground up salmon or white tuna fish. Fran felt that Mrs. Armour was one of his most important helpers in the church. This was *not* just making a category to make her feel needed; because he could trust her with problems in the church, or in individual lives, and know that she would seriously take time to pray as her very specific work, he really felt that her prayers made a tremendous difference in very real situations and had a very real part in our ministry's success.

As time went on, our little church grew, and the congregation felt they needed a building. Fran, with some of the men, discovered an idyllic little white clapboard church in a valley that was going to be flooded to make a lake. The session bought this building, which had four stained glass windows, very cheaply, and then proceeded to have it taken down, board by board, to be rebuilt on a lot in town. As the church went up, Fran was to help in practical ways. Finally he and another elder, Mr. Clarke, were the only two who had "heads that would take heights"— and who had the courage to climb up the ladders to paint the steeple!

The ceiling was to be of natural colored plaster board, that is, a natural linen shade. Squares of this were to be the ceiling, but the committee felt there should be a centerpiece that would somehow fit in with the windows. Who would attempt to paint such a piece? It seemed to me it was a job that needed to be done. So, with no experience in using oils, and nothing but a brash sort of feeling that if a human being was needed I was a human being and could attempt anything, I prayed for help, and then offered . . . "I'll try it!" Taking four squares of the plaster board, I designed a "coming together of the four windows" which formed an arch, bringing them together as four arches meeting at the center of the large square of four squares. By this time I was pregnant again, and I found that I needed to stand up and bend over a table in order to keep my rounded smock out of the paint while doing this large piece of work. I knew nothing about dryers for the paint, but that work is dry by now. My system worked! The finished effect was one of small patterns of varied colors of leaded stained glass, as I had used thin black lines of paint to separate the patterns. As Fran was painting the steeple and I was painting the ceiling, we had a tremendous feel of a different area of working together.

Many, many years later we were to go back to Grove City to speak in the College, which had never opened up to us when we lived there. Fran was to be warmly welcomed by the president and faculty. The gymnasium was full to capacity, and people had come in buses as well as cars from all over that part of Pennsylvania. By this time some of the books had come out, but as yet not the films. I remembered as I stood up there so exposed on the makeshift platform with so many mikes, feeling so "at home" with over two thousand people, how trembly my voice and how shaky my knees had been when I had *first* spoken as "the minister's wife" to about a dozen women at our missionary society! How amazingly the Lord works *in* His children, as well as through them. It was with special nostalgia that I went into the auditorium of our old church the next afternoon to meet with some of the dear people for whom I had been "the minister's wife" at the beginning of the path the Lord had for us to walk. There was the ceiling piece looking almost the same as the day it had been happily put up, and as we walked outside, there was the steeple.

It's a bit overwhelming each time we are hit by the fact that "things" people make last longer than the people who make them! True of every "thing"—every work of art, every piece of architecture, or anything made by human beings, but—oh glorious reality of truth—this is not true of the Creator and His works. He lasts forever and forever and forever to create new works of art, according to His own will, and He has said we are to be given "everlasting life" through the provision He has made through the death of His Son Jesus Christ, if indeed we choose to believe and bow, accepting that provision.

Lasting things? or lasting people? We are given the possibility of having a part in both categories of results as we work day by day in the areas that are unfolded to us.

Just about that time, as Pop Schaeffer was shaving himself one morning at work, he saw his mouth drop at one corner, and felt a strange feeling go through his body. He suspected the worst . . . and called a taxi. When had Pop ever called a taxi? As he got in, he gave his address on Ross Street in Germantown—forty-five minutes' to an hour's drive. As he went up the front steps, his foot was dragging, and as a worried "Bess" opened the front door, he staggered in, saying, "Bess, I'm finished, call a doctor." We got the phone call soon after that, "Pop's had a stroke, come quick." When Fran walked into his father's bedroom, the greeting was . . . "Boy, tell me about that Jesus of yours."

The preparation for this moment had been when Fran had put the Lord first and really trusted Him for his father. Years of faithful prayer and using any opening to speak had followed. Now there was an eager listening to all the explanation Fran had to give as he made clear, in a way he felt his father would understand, what it meant to believe in the existence of God, to come to Him seeking with honesty and sincerity, and to accept Christ as his personal Savior. Pop became a Christian, a child of the living God, a brother in Christ to his own son, that day. His prayer might have sounded a bit awkward, mixed up with some repeating of Lutheran creeds he had learned as a child, but I'm sure it was precious to God.

Now, added to the finishing of the church building, the young people's clubs in our home, the boy's work, the growing Sunday school and church, the endless pastoral calls, the missionary society, the special meetings for which we had arranged Dr. Howard Taylor as speaker, the coming conference we were preparing, my pregnancy, the daily care of growing Priscilla, the housework, the dressmaking (mother-and-daughter outfits now!) . . . we were to have a prolonged visit of Grandmother and Grandfather Schaeffer. As we only had two bedrooms, we gave them ours. We made a "bed" on the living room floor each night, and whisked it away in the morning. Pop was appreciative to the extent of seeing that our two main lacks were provided. We were given an early Christmas present, a stupendous gift of a washing machine (our first) and an electric refrigerator! A big difference to daily work—I can really vouch for that, remembering five years of before and all the years of after. So much is taken for granted.

The whole story might have come to an abrupt end one bitterly cold winter morning when our glasses of water had frozen in the bedroom. Fran, Priscilla, and I were dressing in the bathroom where the kerosene stove gave some heat. I was unable to see my feet by that time because of the size of my abdomen, and I also could not see the hem of my skirt as I was putting on my smock—as close to the stove as I could get. Suddenly a flame leapt up nearly to my chin, and my right thigh began to burn like searing meat. My skirt was on fire! My only reaction was to tug at the burning cloth and back away against the door, frantic with pain. As quick as a breath, Fran shoved Priscilla to the other side of the room, grabbed a bath towel, and beat downward strokes against the flame, putting it out. In the stupidity of my own reaction, it wouldn't have taken long for me to breathe in the right amount of smoke or flame to have killed both mother and child.

One might ask "why?" again. Why do we ask "why?" concerning tragedies and not concerning the fact that we survive so many dangerous moments? The Lord, it seems to me, has shown some of the "why" in the small glimpses we will have in the rest of this book, to say nothing of the hints we have of the reality of His weaving together the things of history for the good of His children and for His glory, in patterns we cannot even imagine in our wildest flights of imagination. We survive for a purpose, even as our very existence has purpose, for whatever short or long period we are to have in the land of the living. We are significant in a significant history.

The new church building was to be dedicated, every seat full, one very special moment of time. There were 110 members and new people constantly coming to services by then. In some ways it seemed we were ready to begin. Yet one of the elders had remarked to Fran that he felt any minister had said all he was ever going to say in three years, and should go and say it somewhere else, where it would be new! So when Fran was asked to come and preach as a "candidate" in Chester, Pennsylvania, that remark made him feel that perhaps it was the right thing to do, as we had been in Grove City three years.

I clung to the sink for a moment as a sweep of pain came, a very real contraction, and then went on getting supper. As the evening went on, I determined I wasn't going to repeat the false rush to the hospital we had had when Priscilla was born. It was 2:00 A.M. when we decided it would be foolish to wait longer, and Fran rushed out to the home of a girl who had been "saved" in our Summer Bible School and was now a member of the congregation—Louise Bowie, a capable teenager. He was to throw pebbles at her window as a signal . . . and it worked! In half a minute she flew out of the front door, excitedly ready to go to be with Priscilla while we went off to Grove City Hospital, where a veteran missionary doctor from China, Dr. E. Lewis, awaited me. Wearing a pink housedress, she was talking about Chinese mothers having babies in the field and then going on working.

She didn't believe in ether, and though I'd had no breathing instructions to help this birth process, still I was wide awake and saw Susan the moment she was born, 6:20 A.M. on May 28, 1941.

Louise made the announcement to Priscilla the next morning; "You have a little sister, Susan," to be answered with, "But I wanted a little brother." History is so full of people who are important because of a "purpose" that is personalized to fit that particular *one*. Think today of the aborted girls who are thrown away because a boy is wanted by parents who think that is the path of *choice!* I shudder to think of the mothers who would never have had a chance to be born, and of their sons, and their daughters, and their sons—generation after generation. I'm so glad the Lord sent Susan! So is Priscilla.

The rumbles of the Second World War were going on by that time. It was September 1, 1939, that the Germans and Russia attacked Poland, and Britain declared war on Germany soon after. Germany invaded France in May, 1940. These were newspaper headlines, but in Grove City, in our tiny church, three boys were having military training, one a tall handsome young man, son of the pianist Mrs. Knotts. I remember his tossing four-year-old Priscilla into the air, and sighing as he caught her. She looked so sweet, in a pink dress with a brown velvet gilet and brown velvet ribbons on her hair, that he remarked as she fell laughing back into his arms, "I can't wait until I can have a little girl like this." We were to move to Chester before any of these boys would go off to war, but two of them never came home, and this lad was one of the first to die at the front. Tragedies come in all sorts of packages.

There is something particularly horrible about graduating from college to die in war. But, death is never convenient to the surviving loved ones, nor is it ever timed so that it can be lightly called a good exchange for life. We were created to be complete body and soul—forever. How ugly the Fall was, and what a flow of ugliness has followed in the abnormalities of the history we know, and don't know. Thorns, thirst, sickness, war, accidents, sorrows multiplied! Yet the victory is ahead over all that the Fall brought forth, and that victory will be complete. Thank God we will see those boys who didn't come home, because they have gone to the eternal home, and we are all on our way! The time gap shrinks.

As Fran preached through these years, he preached into the reality of that present history, year by year—not off on cloud nine, separated from reality. There were wedding sermons to be preached and funeral sermons to be preached, as well as sermons in the midst of the newspaper headlines, and the congregation's telegrams!

Now there was a farewell sermon to be preached, titled "And They Saw No Man Save Jesus Only," as Fran sought to turn each person's mind to the Lord Himself, rather than to a departing pastor, or a search for a new one. It was a moving sermon for both of us too—a strong call to remember that Jesus was to be always the center of our lives, whatever lay ahead of us.

Newspaper clipping, Grove City newspaper:

COVENANT PASTOR TO PREACH LAST SERMON SUNDAY
Rev. Schaeffer Accepts Call to Chester

Rev. F. A. Schaeffer, Covenant Presbyterian Church pastor, has been called to associate pastor of the Bible Presbyterian Church of Chester, Pa., unaffiliated, and has accepted the call. The Chester Church has as its pastor Dr. A. L. Lathem, 76-year-old founder of the Summer Bible School . . . Rev. Schaeffer is moderator of the Great Lakes Presbytery of the Bible Presbyterian Church, a member of the Home Mission Committee of that denomination, and is on the Board of Directors of the Summer Bible School Association. He is the first regular called pastor of the Covenant Church and has been in Grove City since June 1938. This was his first charge. He says he regrets leaving Grove City, the many friends he has made here, and especially those who have labored so faithfully with him to establish this testimony. . . . At the farewell party the congregation presented Rev. Schaeffer with a gold Elgin watch and Mrs. Schaeffer with a beaten aluminum bowl and platter. [This bowl and platter have been used to serve orange rolls and High Tea sandwiches, or for flower arrangements in L'Abri, and are still being used!] The Enterprise Sunday School where Mr. Schaeffer preached monthly, gave him a money gift of ten dollars. Refreshments were served prepared by the ladies of the church. . . .

That summer we had been asked to stay for our vacation in Wilmington in the lovely home of Dr. and Mrs. Laird, so it was that we were very near Chester to househunt after Fran had accepted the call. We found a house being built in a suburb, only halfway along, but to be ready when we needed it. We could choose wallpaper as the sample books were spread out that very day on the floor when we went through the house! I even designed white ships for the blue shutters. It was Pop who loaned money to put with the mortgage so that we could buy with monthly payments which were less than rent. With an acre of land, this house was exactly $3400. Yes, times have changed! For that, we had four bedrooms—one for us, one for Priscilla, a tiny one for baby Susan, and the other to use as a "study for the pastor."

We had a moving van this time, and arrived in our "new car" which the Grove City elders had insisted Fran buy. His Ford had begun to lean over to one side, and they thought it didn't look dignified! The new car, a second-hand Chevy, was full, with the baby in her basket and with Priscilla, now four years old, and ourselves, plus all the necessary things that have to be right where you can reach them for baby, picnic, and emergencies. We were getting to be old hands at this business of moving.

The church consisted of about five hundred people who had been led out of the big Presbyterian Church by Dr. Lathem as he stood against modernism. They met in an old mill building. Fran, as associate pastor, preached on Sunday nights, did a great deal of pastoral calling, worked with the young people, and visited saloons to talk to men about Christianity or to take someone home to a waiting wife before all the Saturday pay was spent. Now he was finding that he could talk to shipyard workers just as well as farmers, and that he could get along with neglected children who were sent to the movies along with a bag containing two doughnuts to "wait until mom comes" as well as he did with small-town children from better homes. There was a wide cross-section of people, and the diversity of needs, hopes, fears, sorrows, and problems seemed endless. Fran's preaching was loved by such a variety of people who would be amazed if they had known that there would be a day when some would say, "Schaeffer reaches only intellectuals." As far as they were concerned— these dear laboring men, shopgirls, policemen, truck drivers, as well as schoolteachers, college young people, businessmen and so on—any one of them would contend: "Boy, I love hearing

Rev preach. You can always understand him, and, gosh, you learn so much each time."

We learned a very strong lesson about vegetable gardening the next summer, which applies to the Lord's story about seed-sowing too. We were going to have a huge garden, not a tiny one like the Grove City one, so we prepared a very large plot of ground. We planted rows and rows and rows of carefully marked seeds, patting them lovingly into the ground, our mouths watering from the seed catalog descriptions. We also happily put long sticks someone had pruned from some forsythia bushes into pails of water to root so that we could plant an embryo hedge. Then it was time for Summer Bible School, after which we were going to have a Summer Camp in the Blue Ridge Mountains of Virginia "for all ages." For three weeks we would leave every morning for Summer Bible School with the two children. By the time those hours were over and the mill cleaned up, there was a late lunch, after which, with Fran off "visiting" homes of children, I tried to cope with piles of washing, ironing, housework, dinner to cook, endless phone calls, and preparation for the next day's teaching.

The garden grew alone. But—so did weeds. We discovered that weeds grow more profusely and with sturdier roots than the good plants, and that ground, when not frequently hoed so that air and water can freely blend with soil to keep it moist and soft for growth, becomes like cement instead. By the time three weeks was over, to our agonized dismay we had already lost our garden, though we frantically tried to repair some of the damage. The camp preparations and departure were suddenly upon us, and when we returned, the vegetable garden looked like an unkempt jungle of weeds. Now we never sow seed of the more lasting sort—that which the Lord has give us to sow—without remembering the mess of that garden. We need to take care of tender plants, or pray for others to do the gardening and weed-pulling that is crucial to growth and production of a fruitful harvest.

We had our camp program very carefully worked out, with the speakers (for older people and young college and high school age) and special leaders for children all lined up, as well as the campers signed up, complete with medical examinations! Dr. Mac-Rae, Dr. and Mrs. Seville (my parents), and Dr. Buswell were coming as speakers, and there were a whole list of people to teach, lead games, and cook! Fran had organized it to a "T." There were two last-minute slip-ups, however. First, news arrived that the cook, a very capable man who had experience, could not come. So although I didn't have any experience in cooking for 118 people on two wood stoves, nor of having six church ladies working under my direction, I said, "Oh, don't look so worried; I'll do it. Sure—I'll just multiply recipes and work it all out."

The second slip-up came as we stood—all 118 people from one-year-old Susan and five-year-old Janet Priscilla to my parents in their sixties—on the railroad platform. Fran had a reserved car on the B&O which was making a special stop for our party. Whoo-o-o-o-o-sh . . . the train whizzed by the station and we all were blown a bit backwards by the gust of wind, our lovely reserved car with stickers in the window right in the middle of it. A wave of "ooooohs" and "uuuuuuhs" and groans went up from 118 throats! Fran rushed immediately to a telephone, had a quick reply from the B&O, "Yes, it is our mistake. Call the Pennsylvania line, and we'll make it right."

Front Royal, Virginia, received the excited contents of that railroad car later that day. A lot of children who had never been out in the country before, children who had never had a properly balanced meal in their lives, sat down with a cross-section of others of all ages and all kinds of backgrounds, to become a camp family for two weeks and to eagerly eat not only a lot of good physical food, but also spiritual food. And they also tasted of the wonder of beauty of woods and streams, of fun games, and of music, by moonlight, campfire light, and sunlight. The cost was seven dollars a week, and some had come on scholarships. The rent was not too much, so a lot of that could go for food. I had a great time serving three-course meals. I made piping hot muffins, hot biscuits, cakes, and homemade cookies to accompany vegetable soups, roast beef dinners, quarters of a chicken apiece, with cantaloupe with a scoop of ice cream as a finale . . . *and* I excitedly found that my "budget" allowed me enough to buy vitamins, so that each one had an all-purpose vitamin pill a day! I was determined with the fresh fruit, vegetables, salads, baked potatoes, and whole-grain cereals, eggs and good breads and milk to add another touch of nutrition for my most malnourished among the campers. You can imagine that the changes were not only in the spiritual area of lives as it came time to go home, rosier and healthier.

Fran was camp leader, and had worked out a point system which everyone enjoyed, with points for everything from cleaning up cabins, doing KP duty well, and winning tournaments, to taking part in Stunt Night skits (by cabins), etc. The days were organized from 6:45 A.M. rising time to the cabin prayer meeting just before 10:00 P.M., following the camp fire. There were swimming, hiking, softball games, treasure hunts, and a special overnight hike. Fran was the one who stayed in the thick of all this, not only teaching, but playing with the boys, hiking, and talking to individuals as well as to groups. There were lectures and Bible study times for adults who were not going off on overnight hikes or similar activities, but a lot of the time the stress was on togetherness in what I later would call "integration of ages."

Susan walked around the big kitchen and under tables, her head just missing the tabletops, while Priscilla went off with the campers, feeling quite old enough to join in! I found it was a full-time job in the kitchen, learning how to bake, roast, and boil food on the two wood stoves for so many people. Chickens arrived plucked, but with long necks dragging feathered heads, and needed to be cut up into frying pieces. Each of the older women disclaimed having any notion of how to do this, so I flourished a butcher knife, took an ax and hit the knife as I placed it at the spots I thought division should take place. This amazing system worked, and I was quite proud of my achievement, under the admiring gaze of the women clucking their tongues appreciatively. But pride went before a fall. As I rinsed the knife, I was still talking a mile a minute about how to accomplish this great feat. Holding the dishtowel in my left hand, I dried the knife swiftly . . . and fell to my knees. I hadn't looked to see which side of the knife I had slid with such force between by first finger and thumb, and I had cut myself to the bone! Blood was gushing out, and for a few minutes someone else had to take over for me. For years the nerve I had almost severed behaved strangely but finally the injury became past history and normal usage returned. There are all sorts of lessons!

The final Saturday evening of camp we had a "Christmas party," during which people trimmed a tree, exchanged ten-cent presents, sang carols, and had a lovely candle-lit supper, ending with a campfire. The Sunday night service was the time for not only the final message and any kind of commitment people wanted to silently make, but for the handing out of awards and telling of the camp reunion which would be held in the winter back in Chester. Some of those children, and young people too, felt they *never* wanted to leave, that they wanted to stay "forever" . . . but the reunion made it easier to say good-by until next year. All this was a long way from L'Abri, yet there was an amazingly real family atmosphere which supplied something people had been hungry for, though they hadn't known it. Christianity was taught, the Bible was explained, questions were answered, all in the context of the wonder of God's creation, and also in the context of day-by-day living which somehow did *not* turn out to be institutional. Perhaps one of the important things was that "mother was in the kitchen"?

There may have been something in the fact that Rev had a five-year-old enthusiastically joining in and asking questions he answered along with the rest. Perhaps it helped that the cook was his wife who mothered not only her one-year-old running around under foot in the kitchen, but her five-year-old, and who seemed to care about the color scheme and beauty of the plates, as well as the surprise treats for the taste buds. It did seem that there was in the camp a subtle feeling of home that included everyone, though nothing had been organized as a model or pointed out at all! There are a lot of things you can't teach from a platform, and a lot of things you can't schedule or buy for atmosphere!

That autumn, 1942, was the one when air raid practices began to take place regularly, and the big part of that was the enforced blackouts of towns. It had been Sunday morning December 7, 1941, that the Pearl Harbor surprise attack had found Americans asleep. When the news came on our little radio, I was playing with seven-and-a-half-month old Susan on the floor, and Priscilla was helping me to build toy block houses for Susan to knock down. That news seemed as unreal as the easy crumbling of the houses. It didn't seem possible that *real* attack had swooped down on the unsuspecting "protectors of our nation." The suddenness seemed almost a tale being told to awaken people to danger, rather that a *fait accompli.* "Boom!" . . . "See, the house fell down, didn't it? Build it up again!" But Pearl Harbor had not been a child's game, and Congress had declared war on Japan, right then. Now, a few months ahead, the next fall, America was in the midst of preparing not to be surprised at anything.

Fran, being a pastor, was allowed to have his headlights painted black, with a one-inch-wide slit for light so that he could make necessary visits. Otherwise, when the sirens blew, all cars had to be off the streets, and the street lights were put out. Everyone had to have their blackout equipment inspected—black plastic to cover windows, or makeshift covering of blankets, whatever would do the job. The acid test came, however, during the blackout. If even a tiny streak of light pierced the darkness, the air wardens, with their tin hats and happy though attempting-to-be-serious smiles, would come and knock, calling "Lights out now . . . your blackout isn't properly done . . . it's no good."

There was a lot of camaraderie about the darkened towns, no cars, and people all sitting out on their steps feeling neighborly. Mugging hadn't become as common then. Fran used to enjoy visiting in the evenings with his mysterious-looking headlights, but it wasn't all easy to live through.

That was the fall and winter that our two little girls had chicken pox, whooping cough, and then mumps—very severe cases—one after the other. We had only one little hall, and that was upstairs. With a set of blackout curtains over the opening to the stairway, we were allowed to have light there, but nowhere else. At its worst, Susan's whooping cough reached spells of coughing and whooping for twenty-five minutes, every half-hour! I'd rush to pick her up, hold her in the hall, rock and care for her, give her a little orange juice to have something in her tummy before she would get the next spell and vomit it all up. It was no joke. One illness followed another, and one blackout followed another, and the girls got very thin and pale. But—there were no bombs! This was just practice, and little girls and boys too were having whooping cough and mumps and chicken pox where the war was really going on.

Priscilla went to visit her Schaeffer grandparents while she still had the mumps. She still remembers Pop letting her do things she wasn't supposed to do, and is still appreciating his awkward way of showing her kindness. It was June 1943 when Pop had his last birthday, and a call came telling us that he had had another stroke. Fran and I and Mother Schaeffer spent three days and nights by Pop's bedside as he never regained consciousness. Fran and I read the Bible, talked to him, prayed with him, and were comforted by a trace of smile that would cross his face. It is so important when anyone is in a coma to disregard the "cold" medical advice that is sometimes given, as when one is told, "It is no use, he (or she) can't hear you." There is evidence that people sometimes *do* hear, and even if they do not, it doesn't hurt to keep singing hymns, reading the Bible, and talking with a real desire to communicate love and comfort. Pop died in the middle of the night, about 3:00 A.M. during a blackout. The hospital did not have blackout curtains on that room, and insisted we could have no light, nothing but the pinpoint flashlight of the nurse looking at her watch. We stood by the light of that flashlight for hours (this was what we called a "double blackout," double normal length), vividly conscious of the contrast between light and darkness, and thankful for all the promises telling us that ". . . there'll be no night there. . . . "

From the time we came to Chester there had been a building program, and Fran was the one to work with the Philadelphia contractor on plans. Here his mechanical drawing stood him in good stead, as did all his past experience in building. However, this was a stone church, very different from the little wooden one in Grove City. When the basement was finished, the services moved into it from the mill, though problems of a leaking ceiling called for emergency all-night work putting on tar paper before the next time for a meeting! Many were the nights Fran would work with the men of the church who gave their after-supper time to working on the building as their gift to the new church. Rev got right up on the scaffolding with them, and they liked that, opening up in conversation in a way they wouldn't have during a prim and proper pastoral call. He was "one of us" in their minds and hearts. When the day came for a dedication of this building, Fran felt it was a good enough building for many years ahead. However, Dr. Lathem wanted to go right on, building a larger auditorium, at which time this structure would be the

Sunday School. Now Fran began to feel very uncomfortable about more money being raised and poured into brick or stone when it didn't seem essential.

It was after Pop's funeral, Summer Bible School was over, and another camp time had rolled around when a "call" came to Fran from the Bible Presbyterian Church in St. Louis, Missouri. We loved the people in Chester and felt their sorrows as well as joys, longing in many ways to keep on being a part of their lives. For some time Fran and I prayed about making a change and struggled over how it would be possible to know the Lord's will. It had been only a little over two years that we had lived in our new home, and the forsythia hedge had just really taken root—to say nothing of our own "roots."

During this time, Fran hurried in one day in the midst of his calling and said, "Edith, fix me a little bottle of sweet oil, will you? There is a little girl who has an incurable tongue disease. They say the doctor doesn't give any hope for her life, and the mother has asked if I would come and pray with her and anoint her with oil. I've called some of the elders, so several of them are going to come with me now." I found a clean little bottle, poured some ordinary sweet oil in it, corked it, and gave it to Fran. He told me later he read the passage from James 5:13–18 at the child's bedside, anointed her head with oil, and as the elders placed their hands on her too, he prayed very simply and earnestly, asking the Lord to give this child back to her parents. He felt he was simply taking literally the admonition so clearly given in James, to come quietly with the elders at the request of someone in the church who had needed this help in the midst of trouble. The doctors could not explain the change which took place, as the little girl's tongue was better each day from that time on until she was completely well again.

Now, did Fran then feel he had any "special gift"? I would say "no," and he would say the same thing. He felt that this was a quiet and literal "doing" of the Word, and praying for an extreme need in answer to the request of the family. Has he ever done this same thing again? Yes, a number of times. Has the result always been the same? No. There have been other times when someone has been healed of a disease pronounced incurable, but there also have been times when no change came at all. Why?

Ah, that is the "why" that has its parallel in asking "why" any of us have survived the close shaves with death that we have had.

The "why" is the same in both directions. We simply can*not* insist on knowing all the factors involved in the history of an individual life, and the timing of an individual death, and the effect that that life and that death are to have on other people and on history as a whole. We are not meant to consider prayer as a magic button to touch whenever we want anything. Nor are we to ever stop praying, as if we were lacking trust in God, just because we think He may not give exactly what we ask. We are to come with total faith and total trust, believing that He exists, and that He *does* "reward them that diligently seek Him." We must believe that something specific takes place in history as His answer, something as a result of our asking, because He says this is so. Faith is believing even when we don't recognize or "see" the answer.

The diversity of the things Fran did during those two years included speaking at street meetings and in rescue missions as well as at hospital bedsides, giving himself to the needs of people's problems and afflictions, questions, and misunderstandings as he visited in their homes, or wherever they were, with his Bible under his arm. People were individuals to him, and they mattered. He didn't just "preach" or "lecture" or even give "Bible studies" as compositions, but cared about the variety of individuals with personal attention. Fitting into this was the time he spent with Ralphie, a child with Down's syndrome, whose parents could not afford to give him special education. Fran went twice a week with colored blocks in a variety of shapes and patiently taught Ralphie. As time went on, a girl who had the same kind of problem joined the "class," and Fran had two children. He was as excited about the progress they made as if they had been working on a Ph.D. It was real progress; the children were opening up and being prepared to have wider possibilities, and the parents were encouraged. To Fran this was as important a part of his work as talking to any university student about his intellectual problems. Being finite, each of us has the problem of time, and we need guidance as to how to use the hours and minutes today, during this moment of history. Choice to do one thing with an hour is also choice *not* to do several other things with the same hour!

As the choice for St. Louis became final and Fran felt certain that God was leading him to say "yes," many things came crashing into my mind to cause sleepless nights and sinking feelings as I went about my housework and care of the children. It wasn't mainly that Janet Priscilla was so happy in her school two blocks away, nor that she was looking forward to "graduating" from kindergarten to first grade as "head of the class," nor that I had put all my little inheritance from Aunt Jennie ($75) into making a play-yard enclosed within a white picket fence, with swing and sandbox in it. The Lord could supply another school and garden. Rather it was the burden of the *people*. There was the Bethel Missionary Band, filled with ladies who were dear to us, and growing so in their prayer lives (later these were among the nucleus who began "The Praying Family" for L'Abri—Jane Mitchell, Ann Puhlen, Mrs. Bigger and her daughters, the Duckworth sisters and others). There were our two favorite "clowns," as funny in their skits and general "cutting up" at camp as the Marx brothers—Ray Dameron (now a professor in Covenant College) and "Mitch," who is retired but who drove dangerous truckloads of explosives for many years! These two and others among the young people, as well as children and older people, didn't help any with their pleading for us to stay. Ray brought Priscilla a little quilted dressing gown as a going-away gift . . . but with hope that we'd change our minds.

Fran was very methodically visiting every family, every single person, every home in the congregation before leaving . . . simply because he loved the people and wanted to assure them of continued prayer and to answer any last-minute questions.

One afternoon, just after an older and very deeply committed Christian woman had visited me to try to persuade us to stay, and Fran was out "calling," I knelt down beside our big old chair and buried my face in the depths of the natural-linen-covered cushion, making a damp spot with my very real tears. "Oh, Lord, I don't even know how to pray . . . but how can we be sure that we are right? What about all these people? Please, please make Your will clear. . . ." Suddenly I sat back on my heels,

and began to sing. The weeping had stopped and the words began
to flow to the familiar tune.

> My will made known to thee,
>   As thou dost wait on me.
> The future now thou canst not see,
>   But I will work for thee.
> My will, My will made known to thee,
>   As thou dost wait on me.
> My will, My will made known to thee,
>   As thou dost wait on Me.

"How special," I said out loud to myself. "I'm going to look
up that hymn. I didn't remember there were any words like that."
Hurriedly, I looked up Frances Havergal's hymn, set to the tune
I had sung so often, the first verse ending,

> Thy life, Thy life was given for me,
>   What have I given to Thee?
> Thy life, Thy life was given for me,
>   What have I given to Thee?

I read all six verses. Sure enough, there was *not* the verse I
had just been singing so fervently, with such awe and amazement.
Where had it come from? I had not heard a voice, but the words
had suddenly started to spill forth, set to the tune, without falter-
ing. There had been no time for thought, or composition; I was
simply hearing my own voice sing words that fitted my need of
the moment. It became clear to me that God put the words and
tune into my mind to encourage me to keep on "waiting" upon
Him in prayer. I was convinced that the immediate decision had
been led by Him, but also that as the future choices would loom
up time after time, I could be comforted by the expectation that
He would make His will known one way or another. This "extra
verse" for that hymn has frequently been sung by me when I
have been alone in my own prayer times, reminding me of twenty-
eight-year-old me, with tear-streaked face and such fears within,
being given a warm glow of assurance that indeed the need was
to *keep on* "waiting" upon the Lord with faith and trust in His

responding, in space and time in the midst of changing history.

Remember in chapter nine when I told about Fran's "nail in the wall" experience concerning the Lord's chastening in order to bring about a change? The same kind of a never-to-be-forgotten lesson was to be learned by me next! As we discussed going to St. Louis, and the invitation to live the first weeks with a member of the congregation until we found a house, my very strong declaration burst forth. "Oh, *no*, I'd never do that! Not with Priscilla and Susan, and all the ups and downs of family life. That would be a ridiculous way to start out in a new pastorate."

After Susan and Priscilla had finished their bout with chicken pox, whooping cough, and mumps, eighteen-month-old Susan had started a pattern of not sleeping in the middle of the night, but bursting forth with "ideas unlimited" and boundless energy to climb out of her crib and set forth to have adventures! She went through the dark house to the refrigerator, pushed a stool over, climbed up on it, hit the handle opening the door, pushed back the stool until it opened fully and the light came on, pushed it against the fridge again . . . and feasted upon whatever contents looked attractive to her! She hit Priscilla with her bottle, waking her from a deep sleep, and demanded, "Wake up play wif me."

Trotting into our dark room, she stood in the middle of the rugless hardwood floor and emptied her block bag—crash . . . clatter . . . bang—which awakened us with a rude shock! We had tried every idea we could think of, including spankings— which caused her the next night to awaken, turn on her light, get her doll and start spanking it with, "You bad bad bad baby you go to sleep," at the top of her eighteen-month-old voice! Now, Dr. Byram (a missionary doctor who with her doctor husband had recently been released from a prison in Manchuria) had been visiting us, and she suggested carefully wrapping Susan in a sheet, as a restraint, hands across her chest, some cotton between the ankles, not to hurt, but to keep her from jumping up: "She'll cry a few minutes at first, but you'll see, she'll sleep quietly all night." It worked! But how could I take this "system," plus all of Susan's other unceasing series of bright new ideas, and six-year-old Priscilla, into someone else's home, to eat someone else's cooking, to be disciplined by someone else's ideas for an undetermined length of time?

My answer was . . . I couldn't, we couldn't, and, what was more, I and we wouldn't. Furthermore, I had an "idea." Where was my glorious verse? The Lord had led us to St. Louis, I was certain, and the comfort of that hymn verse was still with me. Right now I was simply working out the details! Stubbornness and pride were quite unrecognized. I simply had a bright idea, and I was sure it would work. I maneuvered my plan to get Bea Turner (the teenager from Grove City who had become a Christian there) to come take care of the children and cook for Fran during my absence. Then I obtained a round-trip railroad ticket to St. Louis and found a place to stay for a week while I went househunting. My suitcase was packed with not only clothing in which to meet people for the first time without the hassle of children and moving—neatly!—but also with tape measure and notebook to measure windows for curtains (when I found the house!) so that I could make use of the cotton mill's low prices in nearby Wilmington. It was a very efficient, clever plan. And it was all mine.

If you want an illustration of "lighting your own sparks" . . . this is it!

The train was the all-night one and would leave in the evening, but by midafternoon I had had my bath, washed my hair, and was completely dressed except for my suit, made in dark brown wool from a Vogue pattern, with a peplum in the current style, and a blouse with a soft bow-tied neckline, the hem of which I had carefully hand-rolled. The ironing board was up in the dining room, and with my steam iron spraying forth a mist, I was doing an entirely unnecessary piece of work in *re*pressing my blouse and suit before putting it on to wear all night. The phone rang. I left my ironing, and talked too long, trying to reach the plug to disconnect the iron but not succeeding. By the time I got back to it, the steam had stopped misting out of the holes.

I'd had this new invention only a short time, and out of curiosity I placed it flat on the sink drainboard and undid the black screw-top plug which stopped up the hole where the water went in. (Happily, steam irons have improved since them.) Foolishly I held my face directly over the hole, to peer in and see how much water was left. An explosion was heard upstairs and brought Bea running. Scalding steam and pieces of calcium from the inside of the iron had flown up into my face, and all around my left eye. The pain was blindingly excruciating. "Tea," I gasped to Bea. Poor frightened Bea was trying to scatter dry tea leaves from the box onto my face when Fran came in.

He took one look, told Bea to get my bathrobe, and bundled a very protesting me out to the car. "The hospital—" he was saying. "I'm going to St. Louis. I've got to go—" I was wailing! I will never forget that ride. My stubbornness was louder than my pain! "What time is it? When does the train go?" were my questions, and my determination grew stronger all the time. In the emergency room, I climbed obediently up on the table and soon two doctors and two nurses were consulting and working on my face. A thick (about half an inch) covering of ointment impregnated with sulfa powder was spread on my whole face (second-degree burns had been the pronouncement) and then a pressure bandage was applied, so that in the end I had a head double the normal size, totally covered in thick white, with slits cut for my eyes, and a slit to allow a straw to go through into my mouth.

At some moment on that table, a change had come in me, and I had said meekly and with confession of my sinful stubborn will which had not even asked for the Lord's will: "I'm sorry, Lord. I'll stop my struggling against your will, whatever it is. I see now that this has been all my scheme, and I give up. I won't go until we all go. I'll stay at whoever's home you want us to stay." What, you may say, do you believe the Lord burned your face? No, I know the steam built up because I had stupidly put the holes on a flat surface. I can trace the history of all that. But I do know, without a shadow of a doubt, that the Lord used that to stop me from going on with my plan. I accept it as a chastening, as I did at the time.

In my book *Affliction* I talked about many many aspects of affliction, but it is important to let it be known that both Fran and I have accepted, and recognized, and have been thankful for chastening at certain specific moments. It is not for someone else to say to anyone else, "Aha and aha . . . see . . . you are being chastened." I did not say that to Fran when we had the car accident that day in the succession of things when he was getting angrier and angrier. And he did not say that to me although he knew I was being very determined and stubborn about my plan or scheme. We each have recognized our own moments of chastening, and we have stood alone before the Lord to tell Him so, and have personally been "exercised thereby" and have noted some of the "peaceable fruits" that have resulted. Being chastened is a very private thing. Communication between the Heavenly Father and His children, and their recognition of what He is saying and their responding to it, is diverse. It is not always the exciting positive answer to prayer which other people can envy!

ACROSS THE STREET AND ACROSS THE SEA 11

St. Louis—with its Forest Park—a wonderful park with rolling ground, trees, a lake, an art museum on top of a hill, a complete zoo, and a marvelous and constantly changing greenhouse where large trees and basic plants remained, but where flower displays were a kind of succession of "shows" fitting the season—was to be our home city. St. Louis—with its Kiel Auditorium and emphasis on symphony concerts, with its lovely big downtown stores (before shopping malls began), when errands could be done so efficiently and one could have special luncheons or a refreshing "bite" (a salad and an iced coffee) when meeting someone for conversation—was to open new doors for us. St. Louis—where "city homes" were solid red brick or stone, on tree-lined streets, some of the more affluent "private streets" with their magnificent old wrought-iron gates taking one back to another period of history (before the move to "the county" had taken place). St. Louis—a city with two universities, medical colleges, and especially good private schools, enormous hospital complexes, some very successful businesses, as well as Roman Catholic seminaries, and the Lutheran Concordia Seminary; a city with a wide cross-section of people from the country-club set to the underprivileged—was to be an education to us, in some new ways, as well as a challenge! St. Louis—called in travel guides "Gateway to the West" as it stands on the Mississippi River, which connects a fantastic range of places from Minneapolis to New Orleans— was to be our home city, and, as far as we knew, it was to be for a lifetime. As our transplanted roots took hold, new shoots not only began to come out from underground, but appeared also on our stems—new leaves and buds showing a reality of transplanted life.

"This could be the place," I thought to myself, "where we are to have a family homestead, the things I've wanted ever since coming to America from China." Our househunting took place with a special kind of interest. The answer to prayer for "just the right house, Lord"—what would it be like? And for how long?

We lived with the Blair family in Webster Groves for those first weeks, a continuation of my lesson in accepting the Lord's path instead of following my own fancy plan of what my imagination had pictured as ideal. We had a good relationship with the Blairs, and a time of entering into the family's needs of prayer, as well as of having them really care about our househunting and moving. There are a lot of such in-between periods in a lifetime—practical times of seeing how the Lord cares for us in a variety of patterns, as well as important experiences of deepening our understanding of other people's imperfect situations. There certainly were a lot of disrupted individuals and families at that parallel time of history—September 9, 1943, was the date that the first American troops were sent to Italy, and troops are made up of individuals who have some sort of home or family they are *not* with, whom they have left lonely.

Fran had plunged into the full schedule of preaching two sermons each Sunday, morning and evening, and of giving a Bible study at the Wednesday evening prayer meetings. In addition, he had a full calendar of committee meetings, Session meetings, Sunday School Board meetings, and meetings with smaller groups to see what we could do for the yet untouched young people and children of the city. The church building was at the corner of Union and Enright, not far from the park and near what used to be the very best residential portion of the city. It was red brick, with a high arched ceiling, arched stained glass windows, dark paneled walls and huge beams, dark wood pews, a pipe organ and choir loft—all of which seemed really elegant to me.

In fact, we loved it. We loved the people too—who of course *are* the church, the church who meet in the building! People had us for Sunday dinner—a lovely old-fashioned American custom, where against the backdrop of a well-set table, wonderful food, and a warmth of welcome, there was always a time of really discussing the morning sermon, before going to the living room to sit in front of the fire while the children played with a game on the floor or went to the basement game room. Fran would excuse himself to prepare for the evening, and those first weeks before we had a home, he would be given a room. Then we'd have a "bite" before going off again to the young people's meeting and the evening church service.

The househunting brought us to a lovely old house at 5248 Waterman Boulevard, near enough the park to hear the lions roar at night when the wind was right and to walk to on our "afternoon off," which was Mondays. Located on one of those old St. Louis streets, it was a three-story, thirteen-room house with a big basement. A garage and a brick pit where trash could be burned were on the alley. The house had bay windows, some with built-in window seats, a brick fireplace with bookcases built in on two sides, a sun room which made a wonderful sewing room, a good big study on the third floor where Fran could be quiet, and a staircase with a romantic landing which looked quite perfect for a bride to descend. All sorts of features like these gave it "possibilities" in many directions—for having a growing family, guest meals, children's Bible classes, and adult committee meetings, classes, or whatever! We proceeded to fall in love with it . . . and the church session decided that it was a very good buy for a parsonage. It was not too far from the church, and centrally located as far as the city was concerned.

Our moving was supposed to come whenever we let them know that the house was ready, but there was delay. We had prayed that we could get into our own home before Christmas, but it was Christmas Eve before the huge van turned into Waterman Boulevard and stopped in front of our house. We had been waiting, with all our groceries in and some bits of "new secondhand" furniture to fill out missing essentials—so with a kitchen table to work on, we had cookies made and a turkey stuffed. We also had stockings ready to stuff, and a Christmas tree decorated. The

children were sitting by the fireplace, basking in the warmth of
the fire and enjoying the tree, as the movers carried things in . . .
not finishing until midnight!

Any of you who have moved don't need to be told what it is
like, with everything in boxes, to try to find sheets to make beds,
or the essentials to have a well-set Christmas dinner table, along
with all sorts of other things, *after* midnight on Christmas Eve!
It is no wonder that after Fran signed the releases, we discovered
that some things were missing—such as two calfskins we had
been given, which we had hoped to put in front of the fireplace!
But at least we were home—together—and it was Christmas—
so the mood was one of rejoicing in spite of the short "night"
of sleep. We had been given a wonderful new set of dishes—
San Francisco pottery, patterned with purple grapes and dark green
leaves on an off-white background. Set on a lace tablecloth, over
the dark mahogany wood of the amazing find we had bought
in the secondhand store (an oval dining room table with plenty
of leaves to elongate it), those dishes caused us to feel festive
indeed, without the boxes getting unpacked. The dishes were
the "welcome to St. Louis" gifts of the Barkers and the Edwards,
and the memory of that welcome is stirred each time we use
the dishes, as a portion of them are still intact.

It is extremely important for us to be aware not only that the
Lord accepts the things we do for each other, the gifts we give,
the thoughtfulnesses that prompt actions, as having been done
for Him, but also that we have done something lasting *for* each
other.

Priscilla started walking to Hamilton School, where in three
years Susan would also be going. Meantime, Susan played with
a couple of little girls in the neighborhood. With Priscilla and
Susan's small friends, we soon started a children's class in our
basement, with children from a diversity of backgrounds coming—Jewish, Roman Catholic, Lutheran, Episcopalian, and those
who had never been in any religious group. Simultaneously with
my starting this class, Fran invited women of our church to come
once a week to prepare to teach children's Bible classes in their
own homes. Soon twenty such classes were started. We gave a
weekly lesson as if to children, and the ladies took notes. Using
the Ping-Pong table in the basement for a working surface, they

cut out pictures for lesson illustrations and pasted flannel on the backs, so that the individual classes were prepared for, together. We then prayed for the children of our various neighborhoods, compared notes, exchanged ideas, and drank hot chocolate or tea. These very practical evenings were really the beginning of the work we were soon to call "Children for Christ."

Our thought at first was simply to help our own church reach out to the children of St. Louis. We called the program "Seven Points How," suggesting seven possible activities which could be connected under the work entitled "Children for Christ." The home Bible classes were point one. Point two, "Released Time Classes," included ideas on how to take advantage of a program being allowed by some states in which pupils were released or dismissed from school for voluntary religious teaching an hour a week. Point three was a program for "open air work" with children, informal gatherings allowed in some states in parks or on beaches to give Bible stories and have hymn sings, and other activities. Point four we called "Empire Builder Clubs" for boys and girls. Fran prepared manuals similar to Boy and Girl Scout manuals but with Christian teaching going along with the scouting activities. Point five consisted of a yearly Summer Bible School. Point six was a camp program suggested for after the Summer Bible School, and point seven was a large, once-a-year children's rally. Its purpose was to gather a sizable number of children together so that they could see that as Christians they were not as much in the minority as they might think from their small weekly gatherings in home classes.

We prepared a "Camp Program," a "Children for Christ Certificate," and the "Empire Builder's Manuals," using on all these, as well as on posters for the rallies, a picture of three-year-old Susan and seven-year-old Nicky Barker. Each child is carrying a Bible and looking intently at something in the distance, as they are holding hands, apparently walking somewhere. The printing was superimposed over a grey soft fadeout in the background. We designed pins—fish with the word *Ichthus* in Greek letters on them, for identification—and a host of other things.

As time went on, classes increased, and various of the "Seven Points" became realities, we had our first rally. I drew huge silhouette pictures to illustrate the story of Noah and the Ark, then cut these characters and objects out of cardboard (later they were cut of plywood), and attached supporting sticks to them. For a screen I arranged a frame with a bed sheet stretched on it, with dark flannel reaching from the bottom of the frame to the floor. Behind this frame there was enough room for adults to crouch and manipulate the cardboard figures. With brilliant lights behind the illustrations and lights all out in the church, we had a "shadowgraph" picture with moving parts as the story was narrated by someone standing in the dark beside the screen. Over 700 children came, stuffing our church to the doors. The *St. Louis Post Dispatch* put a spread of pictures from that event in a Sunday paper, calling it an original way to illustrate Bible stories, and showing how we crouched to move the animals, etc. The next year I prepared the Jonah story in the same way (in fact, we have in our attic in Europe a set of Jonah figures I brought with us, but have never used), and again the rally filled the church to the doors.

Children for Christ not only was used in our own church in St. Louis, but it spread also to churches in other denominations and in other geographic locations. However, I must say very frankly that at that time Fran was in the American Council for Christian Churches, and our Children for Christ was made available only to churches in this "separatist circle." History must be told with some semblance of chronological order, and this is where we were right then. What is the difference now? We still believe in the need of caring for the "purity of the church." However, there is a great difference between a negative thrust which attacks *people* avidly, and that which deals with the false teaching they may be involved in. It is not an easy balance to strive for, but at that time we were not aware of how to strive for that balance, only aware of a vague uneasiness.

Actually, Children for Christ was going to be one factor in our coming to Europe, but that is ahead of the story. Right now it was a portion of our work *in* St. Louis, and *had* it been the Lord's plan for our "life work," it could have been developed to take our full time in diverse places. As we look back at the "escalator" aspect of the Lord's carrying us along, we are very certain that this was *not* His pattern for our part of The Tapestry in the next thirty-seven years. We couldn't know that then.

At our rallies and Summer Bible School, Jane Andrews played the piano with skilled vim and vigor, and I led the singing. A variety of choruses and an enthusiastic, eager crowd of children lustily joining in "When the Saints Come Marching In" produced goosebumps in many, making them conscious of the thrill of expectation of that great day ahead when Jesus will stand up and return—a very tiptoe expectation! When we listen to our old record pressed at that time (no tapes or cassettes then), we are reminded of the closing exercises, with parents from all over the city coming to hear their children give them that which we prayed would speak to their own "ears of understanding." We hear Fran call out the names on this record for the awards of red ribbons or blue ribbons: "Hurvey Woodson . . . Will Barker . . . Karl Woodson . . . Nicky Barker . . . Bob Woodson . . . Gibs Edwards . . . Ben Edwards . . . Gail Kern . . . Sandy Gale" . . . and we visualize these "children." They, along with so many many others, became Christians, or grew in the reality of their Christian lives during those years, and now are helping many others. Hurvey will be back in this book, along with Karl, as part of L'Abri's history. Will is President of Covenant Seminary and, with Gail Kern, whom he married, is in St. Louis, teaching among others, students who have come *there* to study after becoming convinced of the existence of God and the truth of His Word, *here* in L'Abri. Nicky and Sandy are in Covenant College where he is also "Dr. Barker," teaching history to some L'Abri students, among others.

It is an absorbing study to follow "under the microscope" the interweaving of the threads that are introduced into The Tapestry together in one geographic spot and then leave each other to appear elsewhere in the pattern. No one but God knows just how much we are really "used together" to affect each other personally or to affect other people in succession. The real oneness of Christian work is not made up of organizations, nor of committees laying out clever plans and choosing "qualified workers." God astoundingly chooses those who are to plant seeds, water them, cultivate them, and pull weeds, and He lets us know without question that it is *He* who gives the increase.

We had many warm friendships and good relationships among the people in St. Louis. There were Granny Fisher, and Mr. and

Mrs. Iaggi, Mildred Kern, and Connie and Mary Grier; there were Virginia Edwards and Nan Barker and of course others too many to name—dear people with whom we laughed, worked, discussed, agonized, wept, shared a variety of hopes and fears and longings—for the church, for the young people, for our moment of history! Fran enjoyed the session and the various boards in the church as times of good conversation, as well as for business. Fran's work was taking him also to city gatherings of Bible-believing pastors in a Council of Churches he started for those who "stood fast" on the essentials, and to national gatherings as he was a part of the leadership of the American Council of Churches. Life was getting busier and busier . . . and days were long. Whether ironing the seven white shirts a week and little girls' dresses, or sewing for the children and myself as well as making slip covers and drapes, etc., or doing housework, or making huge posters for illustrating Bible verses or for advertising special meetings or rallies—whatever I was doing—my day continued nonstop until Fran got home, often after midnight. We counted once that he had *one* free night in a month of engagements!

Our "evening alone" started at midnight, or one o'clock, or whenever he got home. I would prepare some very special sandwich and a milk shake, and in the summer we would eat together outdoors on the bush-surrounded patio, and in the winter, beside a fire in the fireplace. That meal was our most important, because it was our time to talk about whatever was uppermost in our thoughts. For a growing relationship, we believe such a planned time is important, at some regular moment of the day. As years have gone on, whether we are in L'Abri or traveling, whether the food is a dish of cereal with fruit and a glass of milk, or whatever, we always have taken a period, no matter how short, when we have an undisturbed time of sharing food, or a cup of tea, before calling the day finished. If we have any secret to share . . . it is this. Perfect? Not a bit of it, but we try to keep this from being a time to have a "controversy." We look forward to it as a time of separating ourselves from the problems and work that overwhelm us.

In more recent years, since our children have grown and I no longer read aloud to them, I have read a chapter or so of a book to Fran which simply cuts all the immediate flow of both problems and joys from our thoughts, and gives us sheer recreation together, shutting out all other topics of conversation—such books as Helen MacInnes spy stories, or Agatha Christie, Dorothy Sayers, Ngaio Marsh mystery stories, or old children's stories such as *Penrod and Sam*. Reading aloud is a together-enjoyment. Try it.

In St. Louis I was reading aloud to Priscilla and Susan—separately at that time, as Priscilla was growing by leaps and bounds in her level of interest in books, and of course Susan was going from two to three to four and needed to have many rereadings of the early books Priscilla had finished with. However, Priscilla was also reading to younger Susan, and playing games, including "playing school,"during which she instructed Susan in the way she thought she should "go." Which brought about education that was great at times, and rebellion that was noisy at others! Both of them took part in the children's classes, and set me right if they thought my teaching could be improved.

Our day-off periods on Monday afternoons after school were avidly welcomed by all four of us. Fran would drive us to the Art Museum, and we'd walk slowly around, seeing first the current exhibit and then whatever we wanted to review. The girls were given art paper and proper pencils, charcoal, and some pastel crayons. Fran would tell them to select a painting, or sketch, and to copy it, or to try to do an original of some other thing that interested them, for instance, the wonderful alabaster fountain that splashed in a courtyard in an inner room. Later in the afternoon, we'd go to the "Jewel Box" to breathe the fragrance of the ferns and flowers and tropical trees, as we would walk through exclaiming over the current display—Christmas red and white poinsettias, November chrysanthemums, and so on. In warm weather we might have a picnic, or at other times a supper by the fireplace or a "treasure hunt" meal. Clues might lead to a piece of melon for first course (to be eaten together in the spot where the tray was found hidden) and then on to a pot of beans and hot dogs and a big salad, all in the clothesbasket in the laundry, or in the cellar, to be eaten on the Ping Pong table. Then it would be on to a bottle of ginger ale and a gingerbread and bowl of whipped cream in a box behind the couch, to be eaten while a book, found in the same box, was read. Even if daddy had a meeting to go off to, the "day off" had a pattern which was special.

When Hitler was still hopeful of winning his goal, Fran in St. Louis was writing a little leaflet which was to be printed and handed out by the thousands, "The Bible-believing Christian and the Jew." The leaflet had the name of our church on it, as the session stood with him in this thrust against anti-Semitism. His ending lines were: "Not long ago an influential Jew in New York City, the Labor Editor of one of the New York papers, quoted to me a little poem which he said was widely repeated among the Jews of that city. As I have considered this rhyme, I have found it more than an interesting jingle. It speaks wisdom concerning the man who bears the name of Christian and yet is anti-Semitic in his thinking. 'How odd of God to choose the Jew,/ But not so odd as those who choose/The Jewish God and hate the Jew.'"

Many years later I was to use this jingle in my book *Christianity Is Jewish,* and also to start the book with conversations held in that very neighborhood in which we lived, around Waterman Boulevard! But at the time we are talking about, I had no idea of ever writing a book, and the conversations with my Jewish neighbors were in the middle of taking place. Fran's little leaflet pleased me no end because it was so clear and strong. "See what my husband wrote?" I'd say proudly.

Two members of our congregation, Joyce and Matt, were to be married, and it seemed our house was just the right size for their wedding. The stairway would be perfect for the bride to descend to her bridegroom waiting by the fireplace, and our big dining room table with its extra leaves in would be lovely for the reception. I offered to take the place of mother of the bride in making the preparations, including the food for the reception. There were two factors involved: One, I was pregnant and the baby was due in three weeks! Two, I was too perfectionist and felt I must houseclean every room from the third floor down, and make a gourmet buffet for the reception. I managed to safely climb stepladders and to wash walls and windows, with some help; to wax and polish and clean all the candlesticks and silver, as well as furniture and floors. Then I made "ribbon sandwiches" with pale green-colored cream cheese with nuts in it, and pale pink with ginger in it. I also made tiny cream puff shells and filled them with chicken salad . . . and so forth and so on!

When the wedding guests filled the rooms, and the ceremony started, I felt too unready as well as too big and awkward to appear and "hid" behind a door along with my lively baby "hiding in me." Somehow this stress on producing the perfect reception and beauty of background for the wedding, without having time for a proper bath and getting ready myself, and that feeling like hiding, are things I always connect with my dear baby Deborah growing to be a perfectionist. I know prenatal influence doesn't work that way, but many are the weddings Debby has helped to prepare for others, with that same kind of insistence on details!

After a night of counting contractions while trying to let Fran get his needed sleep, early on the morning of May 3, 1945, we went off to St. Luke's hospital for me to be admitted to the maternity section. At noon Dr. Roblee said he thought it was going to still be a long time, so he went off to play golf! But early in the afternoon there was no doubt that things had changed. Again, I was born too soon to have the advantage of natural childbirth training. This third baby was to be born in the era when "twilight sleep" was the accepted method, so I was to have the "advantage" of another comparison!

When I was wheeled off to the delivery room, the nurses said to Fran, "Go eat some supper. It will be quite a long while yet." And he obeyed them, believing their positive statement. The twilight sleep knocked me "out," but it was not a thing which really put a person out; rather, it simply knocked or blocked memory, so I was simply out of control! A rather stupid situation, as I look at how things go with today's mothers. I awakened afterwards with bites on my hands and arms and bumps on my head, from being out of control and thrashing around.

Oh, well . . . such was that period of history, and here I am to tell the tale, that Deborah Ann was born at 6:21 P.M., weighing eight pounds and four ounces, measuring 19¾ inches long, with light brown hair and an "easy disposition." What a welcomed and dearly beloved third daughter was put into my arms hours later in my room—the third daughter of a third daughter! Two excited big sisters came to visit the next day—an eight-year-old and a four-year-old, pushing their noses against the glass to get first glimpses of the next member of our family.

Another future member of our family—a blond, eager, bright

little five-year-old German boy, full of questions and curiosity about all that comprised his varied experiences—was quite unaware that his wife had just been born across the sea in the middle of America! He was remembering his own fifth birthday party which his mother had so lovingly and wisely had in a field out in the country. When American bombers had shrilly swooped past and bright flashes streaked the sky, he had fallen flat on his face, obeying his mother's instructions for safety. He was also remembering the awesome sight of his father smashing the furniture and cutting it up for firewood as warmth became more essential than the beautiful old furniture. Values change in a devastating way when all wood must be looked upon as the difference between freezing or being able to remain alive!

Werner Middelmann and his dear wife had three boys—Raoul, Udo, and Egon—to raise in the midst of the Nazi regime. Yet neither for the boys' sake nor for personal safety had they put aside their strong principles. Mr. Middelmann, called "friend of the Jews" and "enemy of the Reich" because of his many Jewish friends, had courageously stood his ground during that twelve-year period. On the Führer's birthday, when every house, every apartment hung out the Nazi flag, the Middelmanns' apartment window was the only one that did *not* have the flag. "Over my dead body," said Mrs. Middelmann fearlessly, "will that flag be put out!"

Baby Debby was five days old in St. Luke's Hospital nursery, and Udo was five years old in Bruchsal (near Heidelberg) when Germany surrendered. Debby's only concern was to go on sucking milk until her tummy felt comfortable. Her mother might be exclaiming over the news as her daddy brought the newspaper to the hospital, but none of the world's problems, big or little, meant anything to her. What a scale of understanding differentiates us— five days old, five years old, fifty years old! . . . Yet how minimal and partial is all our understanding of immediate history, compared to our God's perspective as He sees "the end from the beginning" in the whole Tapestry.

May 8—the day of Germany's surrender—meant a new life of great responsibility for the Middelmanns. Mr. Middelmann was picked out by the military government as being one who had stood out against the Nazi rule for twelve years. Now he

was to be trusted and chosen to be mayor, head of the fire department, chief of police, as well as to work for the settling of the
refugees who needed places to live as they streamed out of destroyed cities, and out of East Germany. (Mr. Middelmann was
to do such an outstanding job that he was later to be comptroller
of UNICEF in caring for world children's relief, but that is another
story.) Whatever five-year-old Udo was thinking about in the
midst of the big change, it was certainly not about a five-day-
old baby across the sea!

Summer Bible School took place as usual, in June. While I was
in the hospital, Fran had already started visiting homes—eventually over five hundred of them—inviting children to and explaining to parents about the three-week Summer Bible School. Over
four hundred children came! I taught as usual, taking Debby in
her carry-basket and feeding her at recess. (By the time she was
two years old, she was a "student" of Bible School and had learned
twenty choruses which she could sing in perfect tune. Priscilla
and Susan were very proud of their little sister's progress.) Summer
vacation in July Fran and Priscilla went to Wisconsin to be at
the Edwards' cabin on a lake, while I stayed with four-year-old
Susan, who wasn't well, and new baby Debby. My "vacation"
consisted of trying daily to find the Zoo and Art Museum (!!)
as I laboriously pushed the carriage with Susan trotting along
asking, "Will it be around the next bend, mommie?" "I hope
so," said poor lost me. At times we found our goal, and when
we didn't, we had lovely picnics anyway. It *is* a big park to wander
around on foot.

To gather up some of the threads of life in those St. Louis
years into one little bunch under the microscope, it is necessary
to see that "work" and "daily life" are always woven together.
To say, "Fran preached a series of sermons on Joshua," or, "Fran
started a study on Prophecy," or "Fran took — months to go
through a series on The Bible" is to give a lopsided view of reality
unless one intertwines such statements with other things taking
place at the time. Fran was elected a member of the Independent
Board for Presbyterian Foreign Missions and had to go to Philadelphia for board meetings. He also was given a membership in
the Missouri Athletic Club by Pres, so tried to get some exercise
playing handball or doing gymnastics, as well as to meet men

for lunch and conversation there. To state such isolated facts without remembering that Priscilla had the worst case of measles anyone could remember, with a high fever and hallucinations for a couple of days, and a long time of needing careful nursing in a darkened room, is to have no picture of "life."

"Life" also consisted of Susan's series of bouts with croup, a frightening sickness which brings its victims close to choking to death. This meant I stayed up all night during the most dangerous period, steaming her, singing her back to sleep, and being there to help when the coughing and choking spells came. It was Susan who discovered "the baby is awful sick, mommy, come hear her breathe," and alerted me to calling a doctor. Debby's pneumonia was recognized at an extremely early stage, and an immediate shot of sulfa was prescribed. We lived through the early stages of the use of sulfa and penicillin, which were a great help in army hospitals "at the front" too.

That summer America was still at war. Although Germany had surrendered, there was still fighting in the East, and Americans and others were still dying. The first atomic bomb was dropped on August 6, and the second on August 9. You can imagine the newspaper headlines and the strained voices of the radio announcers. On August 14, 1945, the Japanese surrendered, and the loud cry from the housetops that concerned each person in a different way was: "The war is over, the war is over." It was a hot St. Louis summer night, and I felt the baby should stay safely in her bed, sleeping calmly, as Fran decided to take the girls downtown to experience the "Victory Parade." He was right in that it was "history" . . . but their memories of that night are not exactly cheerful ones. As they returned it was to have the story tumble out in three voices at once: "The soldiers were all drunk and shouting, and—" "Masses of people and utter chaos, but it was something that had to be seen to be believed." "Mommy, a soldier burned me on the arm . . . here, see? . . . with his cigarette, on purpose. It was on purpose." Susan had been holding her daddy's hand when *that* shock came. It shook her trust in human beings!

Meantime, in Pietermaritzburg, South Africa, Ranald Macaulay, who was one day to be Susan's husband and "protector," was having a great surge of joy in welcoming his father back from the war, with a nine-year-old's enthusiasm. Ranald had been six years old when his father left his legal profession to volunteer for service in the South African Army, which was helping Britain before America entered the war. He had stood at the foot of Ranald's bed, gazing down at him as he said "good-by"—a traumatic moment, during which the father had much more understanding than the little boy of what might be the last good-by. Then John Macaulay had gone off to fight in Egypt along the Suez Canal. Ranald's mother had to go through a most difficult period of time, sharing a house with other people because of the war situation, and also needing to work as a teacher in order to supplement the low pay of a soldier. At times Mother Macaulay traipsed off with her two little boys to visit their father at the army camp in the African bush, never knowing whether he was dead or alive. After a year of boarding school, Ranald lived at home, attending the same school as a day student, earaches and other troubles making home a better place for him to be. In Egypt, Ran's father narrowly missed being captured when the rest of his regiment was taken prisoner, and after that he was to be fighting in Italy, in and near Florence.

It had been a long and disruptive break in home life. Whatever Ranald's joy consisted of, he certainly had no idea that in years ahead, off in the Swiss Alps, he would be leading his brother-in-law-to-be, the grown-up little German boy Udo Middelmann, to an understanding of the truth of the Word of God. These two "threads" in The Tapestry were about as far apart in many ways as they could be—the nine-year-old and the five-year-old.

Priscilla's vivid imagination and story-telling ability, which were way beyond her eight years that August night when the war had ended, did not project what kind of thoughts and feelings her future husband was having as he shared the same news from the Scarsdale papers! John Sandri was nine years old, and had a keen interest as a Swiss-American to discover that there would be freedom to cross the ocean and visit aunts and uncles, grandmothers and cousins—all sorts of relatives and old friends back in Switzerland and Italy. Did he say "bravo!" or "hurrah!"? Whatever it was, something was shouted in glee, and joined in by the family.

Maybe his father and mother "said it in music" since their

violin and piano are communication in a very real sense! In any case, the ending of the war meant to them great excitement about going to Switzerland after years of worry about Grandmother Sandri and Aunt Tita, who had lived in German-occupied Italy all through the war, with news almost impossible to get. (Those two were safe, and Priscilla and John now eat with the set of silver that, along with other things, had been buried under the stable floor in Turino to prevent its being stolen.) Mr. Sandri represented a Swiss company in America, and, although John had been born in Belgium, he had lived in Scarsdale from the time he was a year old. In fact, the Sandris had been visiting family in Europe when the war broke out and were on the last boat to cross the sea before the hostilities stopped travel. Who could write fiction with a less likely "meeting" of two people than the meeting of Priscilla and John ten years after that Armistice night in an Alpine chalet which had the unlikely function of being "a shelter"—*"un abri"?*

These threads in The Tapestry were separated by miles of sea, land, thought forms . . . and what about words such as *possibility, probability, likelihood, chance?* Again the mystery of being has to be mulled over, contemplated, thought about; and the marvel has to be recognized of the chromosomes and genes that have to come together in order for the next specific generation to exist. I don't know how you feel about this, but I am so thankful for the knowledge of the existence of God the Creator. I am glad He has the complete answers to the mysteries—answers I don't need to have. I can enjoy the human beings who do exist and who do have significance!

We loved our work, home, friends, and were challenged by all the possibilities ahead of us in St. Louis. The people loved us, and wanted us to stay indefinitely. It is difficult to be completely certain as to the first "stirrings" that lifted our eyes to the horizons. Our bedroom wallpaper was grey with pleasant patterned stripes of pale yellow and white. In the garage Fran had found a big mahogany frame (the mirror it contained was broken) and had polished it and backed it with cardboard covered with this wallpaper. In this frame we had placed black and white prints from the old *Asia* magazine—a fisherman casting his nets, tall dignified-looking women carrying loads on their heads, Asian beauty of fields and boats. I had printed with white tempera paint the words, "Go ye into all the world. . . ." It was a balanced poster on our bedroom wall which we enjoyed from our bed and which also stirred our praying, and reminded us of the map on our kitchen wall during seminary days. We reminded the Lord of our willingness . . . from time to time, praying day by day.

Standing one autumn day in a park in St. Charles, Missouri, overlooking the Mississippi River, as the children played in the leaves, Fran said to me, "Edith, if the Lord opened the way for me to study further—say in Edinburgh, Scotland—would you be willing for all the difficulties that would bring, with three children and the changes involved?" "Yes, of course . . . if the Lord makes it clear. All I want is what the Lord wants for your life, and if more preparation comes next . . . of course." We stood quietly, each with our own thoughts racing, watched the river, listened to the children, and then prayed, not for anything specific . . . just for "whatever" . . . "across the street, or across the sea."

At the Board meeting of the Independent Board of Presbyterian Foreign Missions held in the spring of 1947, the matter of Europe after the war was discussed. "It seems to me," Fran said, "that we should find out just what the situation is in the churches. So many have been isolated in those countries during the war—isolated from the new sweep of danger, theologically—and are sending their theological students to study in America without any knowledge of what is being taught. We also ought to find out how children can be given Bible teaching, apart from the churches—something like the Children for Christ work." Discussion went on for a long time, and the conclusion was, "Yes, we agree that someone should go and do a kind of survey and bring us back a report. . . . But Schaeffer, we also agree that you are the one to go." So it was that Fran was asked to go to Europe for ninety days—three months—that summer, to visit thirteen countries and bring back a report. He was to go as a board member of the Independent Board for Presbyterian Foreign Missions, and also as "The American Secretary, Foreign Relations Department, of The American Council of Christian Churches."

The session of our church kindly gave Fran a leave of absence, which meant that another pastor was needed for that summer.

So it was that Elmer and Jane Smick (who are now Dr. and Mrs. Smick of Gordon Theological Seminary) came to live in our house and take over our work. Needing to find a place to live for the summer, I did househunting by proxy on Cape Cod and found an old schoolhouse in Brewster which my sister and I could live in together with our children and divide the rent. We left St. Louis by train, our three little girls in red and white striped seersucker dresses I had made, with three dolls dressed in matching seersucker dresses, our suitcases packed for our summer on two sides of the sea and adventure of totally different kinds ahead. I saw Fran off in New York, while the girls stayed with my parents in Wilmington. That was Fran's first round-trip flight across the ocean . . . with absolutely no idea that he might ever cross it again!

A few days later I trundled an old baby carriage with Debby and her cousin Jonathan in it, along dirt roads to the beach, with changes of clothes and our food for the day. My sister and the other children carried an assortment of pails and shovels, balls and towels. As I enjoyed the old cemetery, the old cranberry bogs, and the marvelous view of *this* side of the Atlantic Ocean, I was thinking . . . I would probably *never* see the other side!

STEPPING STONES 12

I t was our twelfth wedding anniversary when Fran arrived in Paris, and my sister Janet and I arrived in Brewster with her two boys and my three girls. *Our* adventure started with settling into the strange rambling upstairs of the abandoned schoolhouse. The makeshift kitchen had a door that opened into an enormous barren room with a splintery old barnlike floor, full of school desks but forlorn in its emptiness of children or voices. There were facilities for cooking, beds enough, plus a crib for Debby; and a small room with dining room furniture where I spent half the nights. That room became the place where I copied Fran's letters carefully, "for publication," and faithfully wrote to him, when the others were asleep. My solitude was enlivened by the mice scampering fearlessly around baseboards and also on the top of the old blackboards! I am not the kind of person who feeds mice, like Beatrix Potter, but whose reaction is to squeal. However, one can't keep on squealing all the time when there is work to be done, and the mice take over. I valiantly kept my eyes open, my mouth shut, and accomplished my duty night after night.

Janet and I had no transportation but our own two feet (and the feet of all the children plus that baby carriage). Our two-mile walk to the beach and back gave us a healthy bit of exercise,

plus all the swimming, a bit farther each day. We couldn't afford
the clambakes and all the other touristy "summer on Cape Cod"
attractions, but we loved our beach at high tide, and also when
the tide went so far out that we could walk almost a mile on
the bottom, watching carefully for signs of the rapidly changing
tide so that we could run back in time. Never again have I spent
time of *that* sort, with my own children, or my sister and nephews.
The sudden precious moments in life need to be recognized for
the unique periods they are, not wasted by wishing for something
else.

Of course, Fran and I missed each other, and the children had
times of being swept by homesickness for their daddy. "Why
did he have to go? What's he *doing?* I want my daddy," they'd
wail. Then I'd try to explain that it seemed clear to him, and
that I had agreed, that the Lord was the One who had opened
the way for him to take this survey trip to Europe, and that
none of us could know just *why,* but maybe some day we would
see why. "Let's pray for him to do all the Lord has taken him
to do, and to come back safely to us in October when we'll all
be back in our home in St. Louis." They'd each pray with great
earnestness, and we'd also pray that whatever we were on Cape
Cod for—for the present or future—would be fulfilled.

Life always consists of grocery shopping, cooking, washing
clothes, ironing, cleaning the house (moving dirt from one location
to another), as well as whatever communication is mingled in.
My specialized "work" was at night when everyone was sleeping,
but the "living" of that summer included a lot of very real togetherness. My sister Elsa came for a couple of weeks with Lucinda
and Lydia, ages three and six. With our Debby, two; Susan, six;
Priscilla, ten; and Janet's David, eight; and Jonathan, two and a
half, there were both a variety of squabbles and idyllic times
on the beach. We also had family prayers together—on Sunday
afternoons using as our setting the fantastic old New England
cemetery with its sea captains' headstones full of interesting facts
about their lives and deaths. There we read the inscriptions, as
well as Bible stories and other stories. We also brought sketch
books for drawing "quietly," and we enjoyed talking over the
history of Cape Cod. This togetherness that came before a scattering was a gift that meant something different for each of us,

though it didn't have a label on it to tell of the value. (We need often in life to recognize value without a price tag, or without a lecture about the rarity of a gift.)

We had prayed for guidance back there in the St. Charles Park, on the Mississippi River. Now here we were in a strange period of three months without any blueprint for the future, and with no idea that the time was later going to be seen as a time of being on "stepping stones" between two sections of life—two sections as different from each other as can be two differing sides of a stream, a river, or a sea. When you are *on* one stepping stone, you may not even know you have started out to cross anything; it may seem as if you were still on the shore. There is often a mist covering both shores, and any stones ahead too. Sufficient unto the day . . . is the one stone! It is not just that the troubles of each day are enough without thinking ahead, but the guidance for one day, for one period of time, is enough without fussing to see God's blueprint before stepping ahead. That is where *trust* is meant to be demonstrated.

July, August, September of 1947 found both Fran and me completely absorbed in what God had unfolded for us to do on that immediate stepping stone in the area of time, as well as geographic space. My stone covered Brewster and its environs; Fran's covered thirteen countries, with astonishing difficulties to overcome in travel so soon after the war. My stone gave me my sisters, the children, and a few other people to talk to directly, and Fran's letters to digest and "distribute." Fran's stone gave him approximately two sets of appointments each day for ninety days (one hundred eighty appointments but some of them with several people) plus some speaking engagements, most of his meetings being with key Christian leaders. Fran's stone opened his eyes to a brand new world of understanding as the walls of provinciality were pushed down in a variety of ways. My stone gave me time to read, think about, copy, and see through Fran's eyes the things he was seeing. In a very real way we were together on this stone, crossing it in preparation for another ahead, which neither of us were aware of at all.

"A letter from daddy; the postman's got a letter from daddy!" Priscilla would announce, waving the envelope with its interesting stamp and postmark to be inspected all around the circle before

the letter was opened. If it was a rainy day, we'd gather with a cup of hot chocolate and some home-baked cookies, and I'd read aloud. The younger children would have crayons or a game to play quietly, within earshot, so we'd all be sharing the "story of what happened next." If the sun was shining, we'd carefully put the letter in a safe folder, and promise it would be read on the beach while fantastic castles, villages, or motorways were being built in the sand, or while someone was being "buried" in it up to the neck. The letters were running stories, day-by-day detailed accounts, in diary fashion, of all that happened. We had already had the letters covering Fran's time in Paris, Bordeaux, and Nîmes; now came letter number four.

Marseilles, France—Started July 15, 1947
Dearest Edith, Priscilla, Susan and Debby . . .
    I love you all very much and I'm missing you. I hope you are having fun on the beach with Jonathan and David. There are so many things I wish you could see, but the trip would be too hard for you.
    After mailing the last letter to you here I walked to the home of Mr. Max Anges. Although he was away, his wife talked to me through a young Swiss who knows English. Then I went to see René Bloche who also works with James Stewart and has a rest home for missionaries. From him I learned that there is a large conference in Beatenberg. Lord willing I'll be there in time for it.
    I phoned Aix-en-Provence from the hotel. Mr. Lamorte was away at the Beatenberg Conference, but I expect to see the professor of Church History at Aix tomorrow.

Wednesday July 16 . . .
    I took the early morning train to Aix-en-Provence, a one-hour ride. There were terrible crowds at the station. Campers are everywhere, girls, boys, women. Many in undershirts and shorts. Most of the clothing is in very poor condition. Everyone carries water, as there is none on the trains. . . . I had lunch and supper with Professor and Mrs. Ferr, and Mrs. Lamorte. Lord willing I will see Mr. Lamorte at Beatenberg. . . . I felt ill at the end of

the day, but certainly the time was well spent. All of them thanked me earnestly for the facts I had brought them. . . .

I came back to Marseilles by train and caught the midnight train for Geneva. I could not get a sleeper, so sat up all night, first class. The train did not start in Marseilles and the crowds were terrible. In second class many stood up all night, even little children. Our compartment was crowded but I did get some sleep. I arrived in Geneva early in the morning and went to the American Express. After much trying they got me a tiny room in a small hotel, with no bath. I shaved and washed and went back to the American Express to plan my trip on further. I also went to the American Consulate and found that I do have permission to enter Austria, but that I have to go to Berne to have my passport validated for it. It takes long hours to get details accomplished and to keep moving. Between government restrictions, and travel plans, it is a workout! No time left except for the necessary contacts and a bit of sleep.

I put on old clothes and in the pouring rain went looking for the pastor whose address had been given me in France. The address was incomplete and I didn't find him. However, as I was up in the old city I saw the site where Calvin had died. I also saw the great cathedral, St. Peter's, the church were Knox had preached, old Calvin College, and the Reformation monument— I found it all so thrilling! We have a great heritage and I am glad for whatever part I have in carrying it on. Soaking wet I walked along the rushing blue river in the rain. . . . Supper was the best meal I've had in Europe. Switzerland is much better off than France, and things are much cheaper. I miss being there, but there is no question in my mind but that the Lord has brought me here at this time.

Friday July 18 . . .

I feel much better after a day of Swiss food, and a really good night's sleep. Pastor Champendal came to see me at the hotel, along with his sister from India who translated for us. We got along very well. He is a pastor in the State Church but very sound. Of about sixty or so of the pastors in the Geneva State Church (comprising about 95 percent of Protestants) only two or three are Bible-believing. I then rushed out to get my tickets fixed up for Beatenberg and from Basel to Paris, changed some money and ate lunch . . . then back to the hotel to pack. At 1:30 Pastor Welti came to my room, and Pastor Champendal's sister came back to translate. Mr. Welti was the man I couldn't find yesterday! At 2:42 I was on the train to Lausanne and arrived at 3:30 to take a taxi to Emmaus Institute where I had a good talk with the superintendent René Pache. The school is about twenty years old. In the summer they have camps. Today everyone was out on a hike.

At six the train left for Berne. The ride was the most beautiful I have ever had. The towering mountains on the other side of the wide blue lake just do not seem possible, even when looking at them. After leaving Lausanne the railroad is beside the lake for a little while, then goes away from it. I arrived at Berne at 7:15 and left again at 7:23. In that time I not only changed trains but had left my hat and had to go back for it! At 7:50 we changed to three yellow "street cars" hitched together. The "street cars" went through village after village along the lake that stretched all the way to Interlaken. This was the most beautiful part of the Alps. German is spoken and I can understand some and read more. We arrived at Beatenbuch at 8:45 . . . out again and this time into a cable car that went up the mountain side. The lights of the villages were like a thousand stars. We arrived at Beatenberg at 9:10. A boy pulled my suitcase in a wagon to the Bible School. I had supper of bread, cheese and marmalade.

At breakfast Mrs. Wasserzug arranged a schedule for me to see people here. I talked to Mrs. Neighbor, widow of Dr. Neighbor of the U.S. She is representing Good News tracts and I feel she will be helpful to us as she feels we must be separated from the ecumenical movement and Karl Barth. After lunch I talked with the director of Emmaus Bible Institute—Dr. de Benoit. He knew Karl Barth as a boy. He sees the need of separation clearly. . . . I also talked at length with Dr. Wasserzug. The situation is very different in France than in Switzerland. There, there are Bible-believing churches; here with the exception of the Brethren, the Bible-believing groups are not denominations, but groups as here in Beatenberg. She gave me other contacts in Switzerland and other places. Everyone here seems to think doors are wonderfully open now in Europe, but no one knows how long it will continue.

In the afternoon Lamorte spoke on the school at Aix—a good talk. Dr. Wasserzug then spoke on their hope to develop a German-speaking faculty, similar to the French one at Aix. I then spoke on the American Council of Christian Churches and our hope of developing an International Council. Each sentence had to be translated into German and French. When we were done we sang "Ein Feste Burg" in German.

I then phoned Dr. Hugh Alexander of Geneva who has a camp near here. He couldn't arrange to see me Sunday so I just talked to him on the phone. If I get to Geneva again, I am going to try to see him. Conversations continued with the people there, including Miss Ruth Paxton who is speaking here. At 9:30 I talked to the group of leaders on the whole situation in Switzerland, France, and Europe in general, and possible fellowship together. I then talked with Miss Christoffersen of Paris. She gave me a number of contacts in Scandinavian countries.

I awakened in time to see the sunrise over the mountains, and went by boat to the next place. In Berne I went to the Allied Military office for final permission for Austria. I had a cable signed by General Marshall which I got in Geneva, but still they told me to "come back tomorrow." Finally I got in to see the Captain who gave it to me. I then went to ask about the British Zone. They say it will take a month, and I'd have to come back to Berne. I am glad the Lord is in all these things. If I were traveling for pleasure, I would give up! I don't know if I can get back to Berne at all, but if so, it would have to be after Greece.

After going to the dentist in the morning, I saw a real chimney sweep—tall hat, brush, soot and all, on my way to San Chrischona, by trolley, bus, then a two-mile walk up the mountain. There I talked with the Professor of Church History, and English. This school is also against the ecumenical movement, and the teachings of Barth. He gave me names of other people I should meet, and took me to the old church built during the Middle Ages. About a hundred years ago the Protestants cleaned out the bones, and started the present school in poverty, but hundreds of preachers

and missionaries have been trained here. It thrilled my soul. I
took pictures from its tower of the Black Forest of Germany.
Tea in the dining room with Director Professor Staub, other
professors, and a German pastor who had been in a German
concentration camp for two years. Talked with Director Dr. Veiel,
in his eighties, but he is keen of mind. I had supper with the
teachers and students—everything served on one tin plate, but
food good. I talked more with Professor Zimmerman, then walked
back through the forest with a student, and on two miles further
where I caught the train back to town where I am waiting for a
train to Paris.

We'll leave Fran there in Berne waiting for the train to Paris
while we pull our things back from an ocean wave. Debby is
being chased by Jonathan, who is wielding a dead crab by its
tail and shouting, "Watch out, it's goin' to bite you . . . it's dead,
I'm goin' to kill it," satisfied at the effect all this brave claim is
having on Debby. "Don't kick up sand now; we're spreading
out our blanket for lunch." And as the food is spread out, we
sit with our minds whirling (we older ones at least) with a variety
of things as to dangers, difficulties, results, and preparation for
whatever is to be done in the future. What a variety of wars
there are, and what varied forms of devastation. Inadequate and
watered-down food depletes physical bodies, but inadequate, watered-down, and even poisoned spiritual food endangers spiritual
life. We bow, asking blessing before we eat our sandwiches, milk,
and fruit . . . remembering to pray for "daddy," or "Uncle Fran,"
who is over there "fighting" in his particular portion of "*the* battle"
which has historic importance.

At any moment of feeling the weakness of minority, there is
no better piece of history to reread than the story of Gideon
(Judges 6 and 7) and there is no better place than a sandy beach
to pile up hills of sand and to dig out a valley in the sand to
illustrate the story, with little sticks for men. A minority truly
led by the Lord can win fabulous victories! With this in mind,
we can take courage and pray for each other to "keep on," as
we did that day. "Help Fran not to give up, and may he complete
whatever You want him to do over there."

From Paris, Fran went to Oslo, and the next letter is dated:

Oslo, Norway, July 25, 1947
Oslo Young People's Conference of The World Council of
Churches

. . . The food here is good. The halibut last night was wonderful
and guess what for breakfast? Smorgasbord! Apparently just for
breakfast, but I liked the food. After France and Switzerland the
people seem more reserved. Oslo is small but really cosmopolitan.
It is 8:15 P.M. and the sun is high in the sky, about where it
would be at 5:00 P.M. in July at home. . . .

I attended a meeting of all the Presbyterian groups this
afternoon and found it most unhappy. Dr. Visser't Hooft and a
pastor from Paris spoke. The emphasis was to urge younger people
to take the leadership and "drive the greyheads out" to have
more join the World Council. . . . It was sad to me. . . . I took
three pictures of the Conference meeting places, had supper or
lunch, whichever it is, at 6:00 P.M., took a walk, ate a sandwich
at 11:00 P.M., met two Oxford men and talked to them of Christian
things until 1:00 A.M. One was a Roman Catholic from Austria,
the other an Anglican from Britain. I hope the Lord will bless
my talk with them.

At 1:00 A.M. daylight was well on its way. There is little or
no time when there is not light in the sky, and the sun sets
and rises again less than a quarter of the way around the horizon.
In the winter it is the other way . . . with only a glow on the
horizon in the daytime!

July 26
. . . Went to early press conference, then heard Reinhold
Niebuhr speak. Niebuhr is the thinker for this group. His
interpretation of Barth provides the bridge for a socialistic
conception of Christianity, but keeping some of the religious
context. Fosdick is considered to belong to the Dark Ages. I took
a walk with the representative of the Assemblies of God from
the U.S. Perhaps my time with him will bear some fruit. Then
took a walk and saw various buildings including the royal palace.
Then I got a haircut. The barbers here hang out a metal plate
instead of a striped pole. In the afternoon I walked to locate
the addresses of the groups I want to contact. Everything is closed
all day Saturday, but now I know where places are for next week.

I returned to the hotel tired and lonely. The loneliness was more than personal. The whole Conference makes me desperately lonely for some Christian contact.

At 6:00 P.M. I took my bathing suit and went by boat to a bathing beach. I was determined to see nothing more of the Conference for a little while anyway. The ride over the fjord was lovely. The wind drove some of the bleakness of the Conference from my mind. It was a short ride but the beach was closing, so I walked about two miles to find another they told me about. The water was fine, very salty. It was a relief to see the mountains, the moon and the sun . . . and to hear wind instead of what I have had to listen to the latter part of this week!

Sunday July 27 . . .

I had breakfast and then walked to the Baptist Church which I located yesterday. It was good for my soul. I could have wept. I understood them better in Norwegian than the World Council people at the conference in English! The pastor spoke English and I spoke for ten minutes in the service as he translated for me. The General Secretary of the Baptist Union of Norway was there, and I talked with him afterwards. These men do not seem to be in the ecumenical movement, and much can be done. Boy and Girl Scouts from Arctic Norway were there on their way to an International Scout Jamboree. I came out feeling that I knew better what a meeting of saints in heaven is going to be like. Afterwards a young man who is a student in Spurgeon's College in London came out to speak to me and said he is interested in what I had to say about a Bible-believing International Council.

July 28:

After breakfast I went to the Greek service at the cathedral. It was one of the greatest emotional experiences I have ever had. To see those hundreds of Protestant young people from all over the world in the Greek service with its adoration of the Host (communion), Mary worship, prayers for the dead, and all the rest of it, was bad enough. But far worse was the fact that even this was nearer to my heart than what the Protestant men have been giving here! At least the liturgy had Christian elements in it. I could have wept, and I guess I was weeping but it was out of the depth of soul for more power to speak with a tongue of gold and fire for the cause of Christ in this age. Never have I realized more that nothing is worth the lessening of that power. I prayed for the filling of the Holy Spirit as I have never prayed before. I took no part in the worship, as you can guess, but God certainly spoke to my heart. How I praise God for the simplicity of the Gospel story.

I then went back for the new press releases. Then I went to the office of the Free Lutheran Church. I had a good time with them, and do not think it impossible that the Lord may use my visit to keep them out of the World Council. They are small compared to the State Church, but the second largest group in Norway.

In the discussion period one girl spoke of a certain program as "good but not Christian" and at once one of the representatives said strenuously, "*Anything* that is good is Christian." The leader never said a word. The statement that liberalism is changing is a grim joke. It has only another face, and the string slips badly at times. . . . The chill grows worse each day instead of less. . . .

July 29

After breakfast I went to the Travel Bureau and picked up my tickets for Oslo to Stockholm, and on to Copenhagen. At 9:00 A.M. I was at the press conference for Niemöller. A group in Germany has just made another attack on him as friendly to the Nazis. He explained at length and the World Council backed him all the way. I do not have enough facts to make a judgment. Perhaps I will learn more in Germany. At a certain point he spoke about the Communist press giving him a good write-up. I questioned him further on that, and he said he has no complaint about the Communist press. I have never known any Communist press to give anyone a break if it did not fit the party line.

I went to the Free Church office and Modalsi took me to see their church here in Oslo. They are a true evangelical church—example—no altar. He then took me by bus and train to go out to see his brother-in-law who is a teacher in their school. It certainly seems the Lord has prepared the hearts of these men. Their church is small but has the confidence of the Lutherans in Scandinavia. We talked for several hours, and had lunch together (dessert was sour cream and sugar!) They heat the place with really lovely tile stoves.

They were so enthusiastic that they insisted that I see Professor Hallesby at once. He is the foremost theologian in Norway and has led the fight against liberalism since 1908. He is in the State Church but his young people's group, for example, which is larger than any other in Norway, did *not* take part in this international Young People's Conference, because of the liberalism. They phoned him, borrowed a car, and drove me, starting at 6:00 P.M., seventy-five miles each way over terrible roads! Professor Hallesby received us cordially. He says he did not start a Free church, but he sees the need of a group to oppose the ecumenical movement, but that the antagonists are very strong. However, he said that if such a group were started, his young people's group and Inner Mission of which he is President and which is the "low church group" within the State Church, might cooperate in any conferences if we had them. I was encouraged to find that his view of Barth is the same as ours. We had supper there, in their lovely old farm house with a three-cornered fireplace. They brought me back to my hotel at 2:00 A.M. and I didn't feel well. The daybreak was well along by that time.

Wednesday July 30 . . .

I awakened about 9:00 A.M. and felt very tired, but went to the press office to pick up the last releases, and then went in to hear Niemöller. He was just following press releases word for word, so I left and went back to bed in the hotel, feeling far from well. I slept fitfully until 5:00 P.M. and awakened feeling worse. I asked the elevator boy to feel my head and he said it was hot. They drove me to a clinic where they found my temperature was 104. By this time my throat was in bad shape. They took me to a hospital because I was alone. I never thought a hospital would look so good to me. It was the university hospital and very modern and pleasant. They have been lovely to me.

Thursday July 31 . . .

The doctor says that I will be able to fly to Copenhagen by Saturday night, so early this morning I phoned Pastor Lirk of the Free Lutheran Church and he came over at once. I am learning what oneness in Christ means as I have never learned before. He took my tickets and went to the Travel Agency to try to get them redeemed. I know I can get the tickets from Stockholm to Copenhagen redeemed, but there is a question about the tickets to Stockholm—plane. There is about eighteen dollars involved. I'll miss Sweden, but that is not so bad as the best Lutheran man is now in Copenhagen at a conference to which I am going if I get there by Sunday. My fever is coming down. They are giving me penicillin by injection. I am in a large room with one boy and three men. I think and pray each day for you all, and for the church people at home. Often in the midst of other things, one or another person comes to my mind, and I pray immediately for that one then.

August 1, Friday . . .
They have given me penicillin injections every three hours, day and night (very painful), and my temperature is almost normal. [Remember penicillin at that time stung like fire, and had to be given around the clock.] Pastor Lirk came and told me I will get my money back on my tickets. How good the Lord is! When he has my flight definitely secured he will phone his brother-in-law in Copenhagen to meet me. I am glad for I will be weak. He is there in Copenhagen for the Lutheran Conference of Scandinavian men which I want to attend. Our God is a God of details! It is also of interest that all the hotels in Copenhagen are full, but I will be able to stay with the Lutherans at the school where they are meeting.

This hospital beats anything I have ever seen. I came in with a sore throat and fever, and they have given me every kind of test, blood tests, cardiogram, throat smears, etc., and I have been treated as a human being. They explain what they are doing and why. The place is spotless and cheerful. The doctors and nurses are matter-of-fact about punching holes in me, but not impersonal. If I had to be sick, I am glad I am here. I have always heard the Scandinavian hospitals praised, and now I know why. Pastor Lirk came back. Tickets are all arranged.

2:00 P.M. Friday still. A most amazing thing! A beautiful bouquet of gladioli arrived with this card: "Mr. Minister Schaeffer, Rikshospitalet. Dear Sir: With best wishes for a speedy recovery, yours faithfully, Hotel Astoria." Needless to say I was touched.

5:00 P.M. I have just finished writing an article. It was hard going in bed with still some fever, but now it is done. They tell me it is safe to travel tomorrow with all the penicillin they are shooting into me. The man in the bed across from me is reading a Norwegian translation of *A Tree Grows in Brooklyn*.

August 2 . . . During the night and this morning my temperature was below normal, and although I feel weak my sore throat is almost gone. If it were not for the Lutheran Conference and the men I want to see there, I would wait another day, but I feel the Lord wants me there. Last night I had a chance for a little testimony to the two men. I sang some hymns! I am sure they did not understand much—maybe only the word *Jesus*—but both looked thoughtful and said, "Yah!" Before liberalism came, this was very much a Christian country. Don't grieve about my being sick here; I know the Lord has something for His glory and my good in all of this. The doctor says now I am OK. Truly my experience in this hospital has been a revelation to me. Penicillin now stops. . . . Have had 21 shots of 20,000 units each. I'm ready to go on now."

Who was Fran writing to?
First of all . . . to me. These were his letters, written to enable me to "see and hear" as much as possible of what he was experiencing. (Later my "Family Letters" were to be for the same purpose for my mother and dad.) This was a fantastic period of education which no one but God could have planned. A period of—how long?—of further study leading to a degree could not have given Fran anything like what he was "seeing," "hearing," and "understanding" in ninety days. The education was a spiritual, intellectual, and artistic springboard into all that was to come in the following years. But remember—it *was* a "stepping stone." No one had said to Fran, "This is your opportunity; whatever you make of it will later be multiplied a hundredfold."
As far as Fran knew, this time was basically one of studying the situation in European churches, and of searching out any who represented Bible-believing groups in order to invite them to join in an international council of mutual helpfulness. He had gone to Europe with practically *no* names, and *no* contacts, and one had led to another. Much, *much* later we were to "pray for the

people of God's choice" to *come to us* on an Alpine slope in an unknown village. We didn't know about that, but at this time we had prayed that Fran might be *taken to the people* the Lord would have him meet. In addition to the "human impossibility" of such a thing taking place was the disrupted condition of Europe after the war, and the fact that Christians had been almost entirely cut off from each other, with very little news trickling through the borders. Also, extensive travel was "impossible" in such a short period of time, since it had to be planned and arranged day by day. As you read the bits from the letters, you must add that in every city Fran squeezed in visits to art museums, historic sites or ruins, and other museums as well. This was when he became enthralled with the marvels of painting and sculpture as he saw the originals of the old masters. No one was walking around instructing him; no one had given him help ahead of time as to what to look for. It was a case of love at first sight. Art appreciation was born.

How did that little boy who had been taught to work hard with his hands, and to ignore cultural things by their very absence, have at thirty-five such an instinctive response and recognition of the difference between the breathtakingly great works of Michelangelo, Rembrandt, and other masters, and the works of people with lesser talents? Works seen in the original, brought forth by hands diligently producing top-quality art to stand through ages in so many fields, touched off something like a pile of fireworks when a match is thrown in—a sudden, enormous blaze of response. Starting right then, a light of understanding was to develop across many so-called disciplines. In a way, the seeds of the film *How Should We Then Live?*, to be made by father and son years later, were being dropped into fertile soil that summer. The "how" of it is unexplainable, in the same way the mystery of being is unexplainable. God's amazing creation? Choice of individuals? The mystery continues throughout the history of the total Tapestry.

As Fran arrived in Paris from Copenhagen, it was to revisit the Louvre in all his spare moments, as well as the Jeu de Paume, standing long in front of his recently discovered favorite paintings. The "work" in Paris consisted of trying to get a way of going to Frankfurt worked out. The only way he could go was to get American military papers. In Frankfurt it was Chaplain Maddox, head chaplain at that time, who picked up a "red line to Berlin" to get American military papers for travel on the military trains. In Germany the regular trains at times did not come for days, and when they did arrive, people swarmed on, climbing through windows as well as doors. While waiting for his train, Fran helped some get into windows—people desperate to go wherever they needed to go. Some climbed onto the roof, in determination.

As he was going out of Munich, Fran saw lying by the tracks bodies of three who had fallen off the tops of trains. He felt sickened by the ruins of war bombing as front walls were all that remained of some buildings, with windows and lace curtains still fluttering in a breeze. In Nuremberg he stood in Hitler's stadium in its raw 1947 condition. He would have been flabbergasted if he had known that more than a quarter of a century later, he would be filmed for an episode of *How Should We Then Live?* as he spoke from Hitler's podium there, looking out over cement seats, cracked with a growth of grass lending a vivid reality to the thought that the world's leaders rise and fall! You might imagine his conversations with men in the State Church, in Inner Missions, and in Brethren groups, then in 1947.

Prague was the only city he visited in Czechoslovakia, just before the Communist takeover. A pastor with whom he was talking took him to see the little flowers stuck in the walls at points all over the city. "These are places where our people were killed as they tried to resist German takeover, waiting for the Americans to come and free us." As an American, Fran felt sick that the Americans had held back to let the Russians come in and take over. This sad arrangement was made by Roosevelt, Churchill, Stalin, and De Gaulle. The Russians were to be allowed to take Prague, Vienna, and Berlin, although the Americans could have taken any of these. As Fran and the pastor walked around the city, they saw enormous posters everywhere, announcing the "World Conference for Democratic Youth" . . . which of course was communistic, and a preparation of the youth for the takeover.

Vienna was Fran's next place in which to "look up Christian leaders," to see as much art as possible, and to prepare for the next leg of travel. A visit to the British Military Center to get British papers to travel to Venice, Italy, brought a "no." But Fran kept on pestering them (like the importunate widow pestered the judge!), so he finally did travel as a British military man. In the middle of the night everyone was made to stand in the corridor of the train, to be checked for the next section of the journey to come after a change of trains. The Russians were asking each one two questions: Are you on duty? or, Are you on leave? Noticing that those on duty could go on, while the others had to wait for another day, Fran decided that he was on duty for the Lord's work, and had his answer all ready—"On duty." The British had not given him meal tickets—maybe on purpose—but anyway the cooks kindly dished out a portion for him, which he appreciated!

When he arrived at Venice, he was horrified by the marks of war damage. A freight car pulled up in the station and, as doors opened, people poured out like grain pouring out of a sack! There were very few passengers trains in Italy at that time, and this was the only way some people could travel from one point to another. In Venice, as he looked for the Waldensian pastor he was to visit, who was one of the ones who really had stood firm on the Bible, Fran walked along little streets and over the tiny bridges, savoring marvelous glimpses of wrought iron lamps and of boats being poled along. As he stood in the Piazza San Marco, it was to see it for the first time, without tourists, without cafes on the cobblestones, without violinists—to see it alone, and almost as a ghost town, or a theater backdrop. He couldn't see the centuries of people who had lived, worked, run across that square— the boy artists apprenticed to established sculptors, Petrucci printing music with movable type in 1501.

These "ghosts of Venice past" were no more in his view than was the future. How surprised he would have been to know that his ten-year-old daughter Priscilla and John Sandri would in another ten years be having their honeymoon and sipping tea in that square . . . or that later that same summer he would be sitting with me, Susan, Debby, and Franky having tea and listening to a small orchestra, suddenly losing five-year-old Franky and to our astonishment discovering him standing with the violin under his chin as the violinist was playing it with Franky's hands! No, future and past were not there . . . and emptiness gave emphasis to the gorgeous beauty of the buildings, without distraction.

Dewey Moore was the senior Baptist missionary in Rome at

that time. Fran was to spend five days in Rome, and to drive to Naples one day for contacts there. To see the Capitoline Museum in Rome and the National Museum in Naples (which at that time also had the "finds" from Pompeii there) was to discover new amazement at what men's hands could create in sculpture— men, women, created in the image of God! The overwhelming experience of walking through the Accadèmia in Florence for the first time came in that period too. Fran looked with eyes intense with the desire of never forgetting, lest he could never return!

From August 28 to September 5, Fran was in Athens, and in Salonika, Greece. The war was still going on against the Communists there, and the home he stayed in in Athens had fresh bullet holes where, two weeks before, British soldiers had been fighting in all the rooms, driving out Communists! The dear Christian woman who had lived through all this and more gave Fran a bookmark she had embroidered, which he kept and used to remind him to pray for the Christians in Athens. Salonika was a great thrill to him, because of the wonder of seeing the ruins Paul would have seen when he preached there to the church at Thessalonica. Of course, Mars Hill and the Acropolis were an equal thrill in Athens.

Eight days in Holland gave Fran time in Amsterdam, the Hague, Rotterdam, and Kampen, where he was to meet men he would later be knowing much better. He had a fine talk with Professor Van der Schuit in Appeldoorn, not knowing that in years to come he (Fran) would be lecturing in the school there. The same was true in the Kampen Theological Seminary, where he met and talked with professors and would be speaking much later. In fact, he met at this time almost all the men who would later be working together for the commencement of the International Council of Churches in 1948. He also had a very long talk with Professor Berkouwer. Naturally, in addition to the people he talked to, he spent time in the wonderful Dutch museums. Actually Berkouwer lived very near the Rijksmuseum. The fine park, opposite his house, was still dug up for a potato garden, which it had been all during the war. Most food in Holland was rationed, and the people still had the "taste," so to speak, of tulip bulbs they had had to eat when nothing else was available!

Excerpts from Letter #15, September 25, 1947, London

Visited General Secretary of the Bible Churchman's Missionary Society—Dr. Houghton. Had a fine talk. He clearly sees the need for a Bible-believing council for the work of missions. Then I rushed off to Victoria Station. There was a long queue waiting for taxis but if I waited I couldn't have caught my train, so I went around the corner and wildly waved at a taxi, which stopped, and soon I had stopped to get my bags at the hotel, and was driving past Buckingham Palace, Trafalgar Square, the British Museum, and London University and arrived at St. Pancras Station just in time to catch the 11:50 to Nottingham. Train went through lovely rolling English countryside.

The country has a beauty about it that surpasses any other in Europe, except Switzerland, and maybe Holland. We passed many brick villages, built in the last two years. Ate in the third-class diner, and had sausages. Asked men at the table what they had in them, and a fine old gentleman said, "some meat" at which the whole table broke out in gales of laughter. As a matter of fact, the sausages are 100 percent soybean. The men said that monotony is the worst danger of food in England now, and they find they eat so little that their energy is gradually growing less. Mothers and children get special rations, and for this reason the poor children are better fed than before the war, but food shortage is really cutting down on energy of English people as a whole. Passed a large telephone factory which has a huge sign "1000 men and women needed, skilled and unskilled." These signs appear all over England.

It was a moving experience to visit the Cathedral in Nottingham where my ancestors worshiped. They are celebrating the six hundredth centenary of the present building; . . . its north wall is eight hundred years old. All this land was originally a part of Sherwood Forest.

Spent the night in a little cottage over one hundred years old, belonging to mother's relative, . . . and the next twenty-four hours being shown off as "the gentlemen from America." Went to visit Nottingham Castle—really a mansion built in 1647—and seeing the exhibit of Wedgewood pottery. They have the Black Basalt, the Etruscan Ware, and Jasperware. Also they had sketches and paintings of Richard Bonington of Arnold.

Caught the train for Edinburgh—had a third-class sleeper. In these there are four bunks to a compartment with blankets and pillows but no sheets. No one changes clothes . . . just a case of lying down and sleeping.

September 27

. . . Woke up at 7:30 and we were in Scotland. Farms clinging to these miniature mountains show the strength of the men raised on this land. There is fog in the valleys and there are sheep wandering over the fields. With all the limitations of third-class cars, tea is not lacking; everyone has a cup at six pence apiece. In Edinburgh the wind was blowing a gale . . . happy for the buttons on my coat. Went to hotel, shaved and cleaned up so that I would feel more myself again after night on third-class sleeper, and then went immediately to The Mound to the offices of the Free Church in Scotland. The next three days must be very full ones if I am to accomplish all I have come here to do. . . . [He tells of two immediate appointments and good conversations.] . . . Next I had a long talk with Dr. Miller, principal of the school, and talked until past noon. Having had no breakfast, I was quite hungry when the conversation ended. Went off to eat at a "P.T.," a restaurant in a large department store near here. Food is better in Scotland than in England. Went to St. Giles' Cathedral and looked at the graves of two martyrs. One was James Graham, Marquis of Montrose. . . . On his tomb is written:

> Scatter my ashes—strew them in the air;—
> Lord! since Thou know'st where all these atoms are,
> I'm hopeful Thou'lt recover once my dust,
> And confident Thou'lt raise me with the just.

The second is Archibald Campbell, Marquess of Argyll, beheaded near the Cathedral in 1661. His famous saying immediately before his death:

> I set the crown on the king's head.
> He hastens me to a better crown than his own.

These men are our spiritual heritage, and, standing there, I knew with renewed force that these men belonged to us and we to

them in the unity of the true Church of Christ through space
and time. Then walked to the Free Church of Scotland office
for next appointment with Professor McKenzie. His present
classroom is situated where Hume's house was. It is appropriate
that he is Professor in Apologetics. We had a fine talk together.

[Here Fran describes Edinburgh Castle, the Shrine of the
Unknown Soldier, and other things in Edinburgh, as well as an
art exhibit he went to, and talks of having "High Tea" because
his next appointments would cut out dinner.] Took a double-
decked tram to the home of the Rev. Mackay, who is the brother
of Dr. Mackay of Princeton Theological Seminary. This man was
a chaplain in the army for years, and is a real preacher of the
Word. We had a fine talk but did not want to impose on his
time, as he was preparing for the Lord's Day.

September 28

The train left at 11:00 A.M. for Glasgow. Gradually we came
to the mining country, arriving at 12:25. Although it was past
lunchtime I went straight to the Bible Training Institute of
Glasgow. As has so often been the case in the Lord's providence
during this trip, the very man I wanted to see was in and I had
an interview with the Reverend Francis Davidson, Principal of
the School, which is interdenominational.

Late that afternoon I walked to the River Clyde. The wind
was blowing and it felt like the open sea. I went on to a museum
which had everything in it from Egyptian remains and zoological
exhibits to old golf clubs and armor . . . and a collection of
Scottish paintings.

September 29

[Fran tells of three more men he spoke to for periods of time—
Rev. Findlater, and Dr. James Scott of the Baptist Union of
Scotland, and then the Rev. W. J. Moffett, a leader in the Reformed
Presbyterian Church of Scotland . . . where he ends his time in
Scotland in front of a pleasant fire, with tea! That night he travels
by train back to London, again in a third-class car.]

September 30

Talked to Dr. Martyn Lloyd Jones, and to a Spanish man whose
parents had been killed during the war that led to Franco's

government. [By afternoon Fran's plane was flying out to Paris on the first leg back home. The next paragraphs go into detail about the terrible "hassle" of getting a place on the flight to New York . . . which took a great deal of returning to the TWA offices to "pester" them. Also, because of uncertainty of flight, he had lost his room in the hotel, and was given a bathroom with a cot in it!]

Eventually, by October 2 at 10:00 A.M., his flight is starting out over the English Channel. Quoting from the last account:

As we started across the ocean, the Northern Lights stretched like a great bow on our right. Halfway, almost to the minute, between Shannon and Gander, both motors on my side of the plane stopped at once. We fell about 3000 feet in a very few minutes, and we were told to put on our life belts. I fully expected to spend the night on the wing of the plane! My chief concern was my notebook, which had grown thick and heavy during the ninety days, and I was glad I had lost so much weight so that I could stuff it under my belt into my pants. I assured a woman with two children that I would take one of them. We were dropping rapidly toward the dark ocean, as close as possible to a ship the pilot could be sure was somewhere below . . . as SOS signals were being sent out constantly. . . .

Leaving Fran hovering over that dark ocean . . . let me take you quickly to St. Louis where the girls and I were installed back in our home, eagerly awaiting a call from New York. The phone rang and I ran to it. "Edith, this is Carl Straub. Isn't Fran flying the ocean?" "Yes, yes, he is, right now somewhere!" "Well, I'm a ham radio fan, you know, and I've just picked up an SOS from a plane that is falling in the Atlantic." I stopped talking as quickly as possible and called the children into the living room and we prayed very fervently, you can imagine: "O Lord, whatever has happened to the plane, please make it all right and bring Fran, daddy, safely back. Don't let the plane drop in the ocean."

Fran was praying as the plane dropped and twisted, so that he saw stars that seemed to be below him. . . . And though he didn't know it, we were praying at the same time.

When the plane motors started humming again, Fran thanked

the Lord for answered prayer, but didn't know the full story until later. At Gander airfield the pilots said they had no idea why the motors started again . . . they couldn't understand it. We believe that God is able to start motors, as well as to do other things in space and time and history in answer to prayer.

The flight took a total of twenty-six hours (with the stops at Shannon and Gander) from Paris to New York! Happily, three students from the New York Bible Institute came to meet Fran— Ruth Gabeline, Spiros Zodhiates, and Blanche Imes—and to take him to dinner where he remembers the three glasses of milk as his greatest excitement! The trip was over, and he was on the other side of the sea again. His ending of his last letter came as he wrote on the train:

The trip is ended. This has been the great spiritual experience of my life, second only to my conversion. It has been wonderful to realize the unity of the church of Christ, and I have realized anew how right we have been in separating ourselves from the modern unbelief which is the new paganism. I have never felt more sure that our stand in the last twenty years has been the right one. Daily I have felt the Lord's hand upon my shoulder.

*   *   *

Is that the place to end this chapter?

Let me tell you that the reading of Christian biographies often has filled me with discouragement because of the tendency to write as if the discouragements, struggles, frailties and weaknesses didn't exist during a time of walking along the path, or stepping out on the stepping stone, where the *Lord* had clearly led. The criterion of being in the Lord's will, and doing what He has unfolded, so often seemed to be spelled out as "sailing through." The crescendo of this account, the close brush with death in the ocean, the honest excitement of what Fran called his greatest spiritual experience (that is, the finding of true Christians in so many places), the very real answers to prayer, the safekeeping of the children and myself on the other side of that ocean, and now, a glorious "reunion"!—wouldn't this be just as discouraging, if I stopped there, as anything I have ever read? Isn't it true? Yes, it is true. But it isn't complete.

It is ridiculous for Christian boards, committees, directors to commission men and women to do tasks alone, ignoring the fact that the Bible loudly states that sexual relationship, physical oneness in marriage, is meant to be an ongoing daily thing of fulfillment, as important to life in its own way as a balanced diet is to physical well-being, and sleep is to overcoming fatigue. That ninety days for Fran was a devastating time. He had real problems and struggles, and his "victories" were real too, not something to be taken for granted. It is not "spiritual" to *ignore* the scope of temptations, and never speak of them in considering a piece of work someone is being asked to do. The putting aside of our physical oneness, as well as of our talking everything over together day by day, was extremely hard on him. Added to that, the food was not only very often poor, but he very often skipped meals, he lost weight, and he had bouts of diarrhea as well as his strep throat illness in Oslo. His body was depleted. Added to that, he had not had enough sleep at any point along the way, and sleeping in fifty-six different places in ninety days didn't help much! Travel, far more tiring than travel today, took a toll on him physically so that he came home not only exhausted, but in the condition many of us have faced after a terrific day-and-night push of work has used up all our nervous energy. He collapsed.

He needed long hours of sleep, his favorite food, fireside times of talking and reading together, and privacy with me. Yet—someone needs to "take over" when exhaustion is so complete. Things don't just "fall into place" naturally. Ingenious ideas for caring for the children—without neglecting them, yet keeping the house "quiet for daddy to rest"—have to be thought of and put into practice. Phone calls have to be diverted: "Sorry, but can I take care of you?" And as much as possible the "demands" coming to "daddy so long away," "pastor so missed," "board member who is needed," "moderator who must come," must be sorted out, and shoved a little farther off into the future.

Never forget this . . . at any point in life, in a thousand different kinds of situations, the *answer* to prayer, "Use me, Lord, I want to be greatly used of Thee," can be the hardest thing you have ever faced. It is the *answer* to prayer that brings exhaustion of a variety of kinds, and that brings a cost to be paid that almost smashes you, and me. There is always a cost to being "used might-

ily for the Lord" and there always was. Whether that cost is
dying in concentration camp, as Dr. Hoste did in China, or having
a physical or nervous breakdown, the *reality* of having been used
is not wiped out by the resultant cost. We are in battle, and
winning a skirmish brings scars and sometimes deep wounds.

If you are raising your eyebrows in doubt of this, go back
and read Paul's list of the difficulties he went through. His prison
epistles were not a "breeze" for him to write, chained and without
nourishing food, let alone any that tasted good! Paul did not
hide his difficulties but rather says, "We do not want you to be
uninformed, brothers, about the hardships we suffered in the
province of Asia" (2 Cor. 1:8a, NIV). If he was under pressures far
beyond his ability to endure, why are we so loath to mention
pressures, whatever sort they may be? We do each other a terrible
disservice if we end on a crescendo of glory and never mention
the cost God's servants have always had woven into their piece
of the battle or their section of The Tapestry.

Fran was in such a nervous state for awhile that, when he
was asked to come to Philadelphia, he pled, "*You* talk to them
on the phone, Edith. Just say I *can't* come without you, and you
have to take care of the travel and everything." He felt he could
never buy another railroad ticket, never pay a taxi, never handle
even ordinary travel plans again.

We did go together, with my relieving him of all the details.
He showed his slides at the banquet and gave a powerful message
in his report . . . but my part of praying in the background, of
caring for the arrangements and just being with him, was essential.
He didn't have a breakdown, but if there had been *no one* to understand and take care of him, recognizing the needs, he could have.
Does that erase the marvel of all that had happened? Not at
all. But it is unrealistic to forget that until Jesus comes back again,
not one of us will arrive at a place where we are no longer to
be assailed from within and without.

Stepping stones? Yes, we had been on a stepping stone that
three-month period, and our lives were never going to be the
same again. The next stone was soon to be put into view, and
our feet were to be poised to jump over the rushing water to it
. . . but for the moment we didn't realize it. With a sigh of relief,
we thought that now we had come home, to live a normal life.

CLEAR AS A FOG! 13

ur first flush of excitement in beginning a regular schedule with the children in school—Susan in first grade, Priscilla in fifth—daddy going to the church office to dictate letters, services, children's work, committee meetings, session meetings, some dinner and luncheon engagements, was one of feeling settled in a security of the familiar.

My ladies' Bible class was a special joy to me. It had started when one of the five-year-old little girls of my Children for Christ class, had shown *so* much knowledge about the Bible that her aunt had asked me to speak . . . "Please give us a book review of the Bible at our *literary* club." My reply had been that I didn't think they would want me, as I believed the Bible to be true, and not just a book. To which she eagerly insisted, "Oh, we want something *vital;* please do come." A luncheon meeting of the literary club held at Stix Baer and Fuller's Department Store restaurant, became a most unusual affair as I hesitantly started on a Bird's Eye View of the Bible, asking at the end of a half hour if they wanted me to stop. Being urged to go on, I kept on for an hour, and then, egged on again, spoke a total of one and a half hours. The club voted to change its name and character, and to meet weekly to have me continue! It became a Bible class meeting in a library!

The "fruitful ministry," as some would have called it, was added to by warm welcome and pleasure in our return on the part of a great variety of people. It was like coming back to a garden that has been missed, and that an avid gardener longs to get his or her fingers back into.

Fran had been satisfied as to the reception of his report on the European trip by both the Independent Board and the men of the American Council of Christian Churches. For a time it seemed something that was behind him, and he plunged into preparing sermons, conducting Bible studies, visiting the sick, doing his regular pastoral calling, discussing with the young people, as well as giving some special talks with slides he had taken in Europe. He had learned a great deal, but at the time it seemed that which would enrich all that he had to say and give and be, right there.

Then—several things happened. First, letters began to come from all over Europe, from the men he had had conversations with, and from other people who had missed seeing him and had questions to ask. The gist of some of them seemed to be, "Come over and help us." Some were invitations to speak, while others were expressions of desire for fellowship, using that word in its truest and richest sense. Second, invitations began to come from pastors who were in the American Council of Christian Churches in different parts of America and in different denominations: "Please will you come and speak on such and such a date, telling us of what you heard and found in Europe." Third, after a meeting of the Independent Board, Fran was presented with a direct request that could have no neutral answer, and that could not be ignored: "We find from what you have given us in your report that we feel strongly that we should send someone to Europe to help strengthen the things that remain, and the consensus is that the only ones we would send would be you and Edith."

The first thing demanded an enormous increase of letter writing, which obviously would be too much to add to the already full work of the church secretary, Vivian Musterman. The second thing demanded letters of regret (more correspondence) or acceptance of speaking engagements. The third thing demanded an answer in the negative, or the affirmative. The one thing that could *not* be done was *nothing*. Something had to be done in each of the three things, and, before a negative answer could be given three times in a row, there had to be the agonizing and soul-searching that must precede such decisions.

What was the Lord's will? How would we be certain? Whenever a similar need for decision arises in life, the sequence is always the same—a period of time during which the need is to wait for the Lord to show, to make clear, to lead, whether a negative or positive answer is going to be given. There is no such thing as "no decision." I am impressed by the constantly repeated opportunity in life to trust the Lord in a fog, or to go from a secure place in what seems a sunny garden into a fog-covered path leading to the unknown!

We knew what living in our beloved home on Waterman Boulevard meant, and just what the work in the church consisted of, with what seemed endless possibilities accompanying that. We had a clearly defined work. I thought I could picture it down through the years, even to imagining the girls throwing their wedding bouquets from that landing on the stairway, over the lovely rail! There was a continuity that seemed within reach, a comfortable sharing of the changing years of life with friends, and our children with their children. Familiar language consists of more than simply vocabulary to be translated; the unknown is shrouded in a dictionary with blank pages somehow. All this is to say that the general feeling was one of approaching a diving board without knowing the temperature or depth of the water.

As Fran talked to the session, together and individually, there emerged a certainty that either we had to go to take care of all three points, or to put all three things aside and give ourselves to the work of the church. That seemed fair as well as definite. Before Christmas the decision had been made, and Fran had written a letter of application to the Independent Board (the correct procedure) and had been accepted. We were to be sent on a double mission, to represent the Independent Board anywhere in Europe the Lord would lead us, and to go in time for Fran to help set up meetings for the formation of the International Council of Christian Churches which would be held in August 1948 in Amsterdam. The water was icy in the first plunge.

There was a dense fog ahead. We had no idea what we were going to do in Europe past the preparation for the meetings in

Amsterdam. The only thing that was clear at that moment was what we were leaving! That Christmas was painfully beautiful—for us and for the children. Fran had been out caroling from house to house with the church young people, and it was about 1:00 A.M. when he burst in the front door. The tree was trimmed and shiny with lights; a fire was blazing in the brick fireplace; some gifts were already under the tree, although I still had my wrapping to do and the stockings to fill. I was working on the turkey stuffing, and the smell of date bars baking was filling the house. Suddenly another fragrance blotted out everything else. "Fran, what have you there? Where on earth did you get them?" In his arms were dozens of dark red roses with an amazingly strong rose odor, and it permeated everything, creating an exciting mixture of rose and pine. "I came past a florist's as he was closing up, and he had all these left over in buckets. He gave them to me for an unbelievable price, as he said they'd be ruined when he opens again." The house had never looked lovelier and the roses seemed tantalizingly to enhance it all—like an especially well-prepared and lighted setting for a drama.

Vividly portrayed in the next scenes were what we were leaving by accepting the Board's mission—a wonderful antique doll house had been given to the children (too large to take with us), and Priscilla's gift had been prepared in November—a redecorated room with new wallpaper, paint, and curtains and bedspread I had made. At long last the kitchen linoleum had been changed—no more holes, but a warm brick pattern instead—provided for by a special personal gift. And—we'd found a solid cherry corner cupboard (secondhand) that perfectly finished off the dining room. On Christmas Day a lonely nurse joined us for the day, and her pleasure in being included in the family hurt us somehow, because of a desire to do this for more people! She had brought us a dark Dutch chocolate apple, and when it fell apart in perfect slices the bittersweet odor of chocolate mingled with the roses as we ate and enjoyed the end-of-the-meal coffee. That moment is still excruciatingly clear. The beauty of the present—the fog of the future!

We were to leave early in February for a six-months period during which Fran would be traveling and speaking concerning the European trip and the next steps of his work. I was to learn to do shorthand and typing in order to be his next secretary! Bernice Killam had been his secretary after the December wedding of Vivian. Now after so short a time, he was to have a new, inexperienced secretary—me!

The final Sunday came, and of all times, the church furnace broke, so the services had to be held in a theater next door. I will never forget weeping so uncontrollably that I had to retreat to the cellar and hide there so that I wouldn't have to say good-by to each one! I almost got locked in, but someone missed me and came looking. I was weeping because Fran's sermon was so good, and I was sure he would never be preaching any more, *ever*, and that his talent of being a pastor who cared about people and answered their questions and visited them individually would be a buried talent. What did I think he would do? I had no idea, but the commission being given him in going to Europe hinted far more at some sort of administrative involvement in helping existing works, even if we did start children's work in various countries.

You see, I hadn't read the *L'Abri* story!

No one could give me a hint of what was ahead . . . a full seven years in the future.

We left on the midnight train to Philadelphia, after a farewell party at the church on Wednesday night. The children all had sore throats and fever, but Dr. Parke White had given them penicillin and said it would be safe to travel. Under their winter coats and boots they wore new pajamas with feet in them, and they looked really cheery and beautiful with corsages of pink roses some of the ladies had pinned on them, pink cheeks matching perfectly. Priscilla, ten; Susan, six; and Debby, two—here they were leaving their home and their special "own rooms," with their own toys, books, and many other things packed, not to be "found" again for over a year . . . but their favorite dolls in their arms. No time was lost in getting out of their wraps as they were ready to climb into their bunks on the sleeper, swallow the next dose, have nose drops, and listen to the story with a few interruptions to scramble around and look out the window! Our nomadic life had started. As the train shrieked its way through the dark, we rapidly moved toward the unknown . . . but with the comfort that it was not only known to God, but that we could know that He was going *with* us, that His promise "I will never leave thee nor forsake thee" was true, and not a nonsense rhyme.

The next six months were a vivid example of what it means to be willing to serve the Lord, in following His leading. Nothing could have been less glamorous. We could have rented a furnished apartment, but instead we paid the rent to Fran's mother to live with her, so that she could get to know the children before we went so far away. Although she had insisted on the arrangement, her attitude was one of being imposed upon. She was furious that we were going to Europe, and took it out on the children. As my "job" was supposed to be taking a secretarial course, I asked the mission if I might take the money for my school and use it to give the children a pleasant atmosphere in Stevens' School for Girls. They could be there all day, and I would work hard on an inexpensive correspondence course for myself.

The headmistress had just been saying, "Yes, we do have a special price for missionaries' children, so that would be enough, but we don't take any children under four" . . . when Debby piped up, "May I see my classroom, please?" With a startled little jump, the headmistress turned to her and asked, "What did you say?" "I was just asking if I could see my classroom— please." After a bit more conversation with two-and-a-half-year-old Debby, the conclusion was given, "We are going to make an exception in this case. The bus will stop for all three children." Debby took her place among four-year-olds with no problem except for her tiredness at naptime when she went soundly to sleep for longer than the others.

My stretch of time, with the children gone for lunch, did *not* mean free time to study my shorthand and typing unhindered. It meant that Grandmother Schaeffer would not be annoyed with the children, and that I could zip through housework, trying to please her perfectionism as far as dusting and polishing went. I did the grocery shopping, planned the meals, cooked, tried to cheer her up with making cream puffs when her friends came for an evening or afternoon, did the dishes, and so on. Yet—I never felt I had succeeded. My studying was not understood, and when I did go off behind a shut door with my typewriter and my "beginner's book"—laboriously doing my "ships, sails," etc.—many were the grim, tight-lipped looks I'd be given for this "nonsense." When the Lord leads, do all the surrounding circumstances turn into smooth, unbumpy, comfortable ways along which to follow Him? We can't remind each other too often of the reality of a person trying to stop us, a personal enemy, as well as The Person helping us, and giving us strength to go on.

Fran came home frequently, but was away speaking a great deal, so being the "buffer" between grandmother and the children, and the dealing with her ideas and Fran's certainty of the Lord's call, had to be my portion! It was one of the hardest stretches of time I have lived through, with loss of weight giving outward evidence of the strain. Yet what kind of limits, what kind of fences do we put around our serving the Lord when we tell Him we're willing to wash feet or to "take a low seat"? How in the world can we "define" the actual composition of the ingredients of "serving the Lord with gladness"?

It is thrilling to know that the Lord really knows who is loving Him and truly serving Him and delighting himself or herself in Him, and that some of the shiniest rewards and gorgeous surprises are ahead. That day will come when people who think they have never been seen—in dingy sordid little "holes" of history, whether in prison or caves, in wars or in unemployment, in factories or on farms—will discover that their serving was recognized all the time, by the One who matters. So often human beings have false measuring sticks or warped scales!

How do you pack for an unknown place for an unknown length of time? You don't travel light, because travel isn't what it is all about. What is happening is a transfer of your children's childhood, and of family life from one side of the ocean to the other. As much continuity as possible needs to be packed into the trunks, suitcases, and boxes. For me, that ended up being a job which took all the last forty-eight hours, non-stop! Books, dishes, some bits of furniture (such as Fran's father's old wooden chair, Aunt Rachel's rocking chair, and our nail-keg stool!) as well as blankets, towels, sheets, etc., had already been packed in St. Louis and not unpacked. But whether you are "in oil," diplomatic service, the military, Pepsi Cola, or a host of other kinds of work, including being a missionary, you know what this kind of packing involves, and how important some things are to continuity if it is possible to take them along. Books, files, notebooks of addresses, old sermon notes—these were as important to Fran's continuity of study and thought. In the tapestry of our lives, broken threads are no help in continuing the design, even if the pattern is fresh.

The last week of being in Philadelphia, Priscilla had been in the Philadelphia Children's Hospital having her appendix out. For months she had had a problem of waves of nausea and stomach ache. The pediatrician had not found any cause for this and was having "one last test" taken before insisting that we take her to a psychiatrist. Nothing is more frustrating to a child—or to parents—than being told that the source of violent vomiting cannot be found, and "it must be a reaction against going to Europe" (or wherever you are going), when the child is particularly eager about the "thing" ahead. Shivering in the white cotton hospital gown tied in back, Priscilla looked thin and wan sitting on the bench waiting for her turn to have a barium X-ray. A tall, fine-looking doctor was walking by with our pediatrician, when he glanced at Pris, and make a remark. We hadn't heard it, but what he had said was, "There's a child that has something definitely wrong with her." "Oh, do you think so?" asked our doctor. "I can't find anything." "No doubt about it; send her up to me."

Within minutes we had had an elevator ride, and Priscilla was lying down on this doctor's examining table with his skillful fingers playing over her tummy. "It's mesenteric adenitis—something I am especially studying—and I find that if the appendix is removed the glands go down, and everything is OK. Bring her to the hospital tonight, and I'll operate tomorrow morning." "Oh, but we are leaving for Europe in a week," I wailed. "What for?" And when I explained something of why we were going, the doctor exclaimed, "Oh, you are Christians! . . . I just became a Christian a couple of weeks ago."

Whereupon an amazing conversation took place with Dr. C. Everett Koop. This was the way we met, and we are sure it was no "chance happening" that the Lord used his care of Priscilla to send her off a well child, ready to gain weight and energy quickly . . . and used us in Chick Koop's life too. When he pushed Priscilla's cart to the operating table (a thing the surgeon-in-chief does *not* do), a telegram was handed to him, and he read it aloud to her (the only time he had ever read a telegram to a child before an operation): "Dear Priscilla, Remember underneath are the everlasting arms. Love, Daddy." "Wow," thought Chick Koop, "Christians really do live this way; God is real to them in the things of life." It was his first "brush" with Christian living.

No playwright could create a script as dramatic as God's. In God's "script" He had just brought together for the first time characters who would be woven in and out for years. God already could see the unborn, unconceived Franky Schaeffer who would be sitting up half the night, many years from that date, to conceive in his imagination another script which would involve this very hospital, one of the operating rooms, the intensive care unit for premature babies, and especially Dr. Koop! But in God's script the next steps would take place slowly, over years of development, while He prepared the characters to fit into the moment of history where they alone could be used in the way He wanted them to be used.

The Tapestry? Yes, each thread with a significance . . . but we can mix our metaphors and use the characters in a script interchangeably with the threads in a weaving. Just as each of us is woven into a diversity of the patterns in The Tapestry, so we enter the script with a diversity of parts to play, so to speak. Fran was away in Nashville, Tennessee, as Moderator of the Bible Presbyterian Church up to the last minute before we were to sail. As all he wanted was to let Priscilla know he was praying and thinking of her, he had no idea what his telegram was to mean to the doctor who was to be his friend and with whom he would be making a film, *Whatever Happened to the Human Race?*, so many years in the future.

If you are not excited about the mystery of valid choice being *valid*, and chance not being behind God, then you must live a dull life indeed. This is where feelings of delight about the wonder of God and His creation surge ahead, as well as where trusting Him in the dark becomes practical.

That same week, as I left the hospital after a visit, I had to make another of a series of visits to the Swiss embassy. It was necessary to apply for a visa to live in Switzerland at that time, and when I made my first inquiry, the two young men at the embassy told me our application had to be for a particular city in a particular canton. "Geneva is the best place; put Geneva in this blank space," said one emphatically, while the tall, dark, smiling one said, "Oh *no*, you must put Lausanne. That is really Swiss, and so much better for the children." When I heard the reasons given by each of them for their own hometown, Lausanne appealed far more, and so Lausanne went into the formal application.

Choice? Yes, it had been a choice; my pen had written the letters. Then M. Ochsenbein, who had advised Lausanne, said a surprising thing: "I'm going to be flying home to see my mother who is ill, and I'll look for a pension for you—a place that will be the best I can find for the children." It was the Swiss consulate then who chose Madame Turrian's pension on Rue de la Foret in La Rosiaz, sending us word that it would be ready with a crib for Debby, and we would be expected! . . . in September.

Our cabin on the *Nieu Amsterdam* was full of people seeing us off, and everyone seemed to be talking at once. As time drew close for the call "All ashore that's going ashore," Fran silenced us, and we had a short prayer meeting for all that stretched ahead in time and space. We didn't know anything about L'Abri—and wouldn't for years—yet the basic core of what would one day be known as "The Praying Family" were gathered in that boat cabin. Praying for the Lord to guide us in all that He had in His plan for our lives, we started across the sea, to the next stepping stones. We had been joined together for a work, but no one knew what the work was going to be, nor even that we had been joined together for anything more than a farewell.

Before we left St. Louis, Mildren Kern had helped me with dressmaking for the children, and I had done more sewing in Philadelphia. So the three girls were easy to find, as each day they had matching clothes—navy and white striped dresses with white linen pilgrim collars; or black taffeta jumpers for formal dinners, with pink organdy blouses; and navy blue wool coats for chilly winds at sea. Their toys, games, crayons and pads, jacks and balls, and doll clothes were all in turquoise piqué bags. These could not only be easily carried around but, whether the girls were playing on deck, in another cabin, or in a lounge, their things could quickly be put away in a marked bag and as quickly found again. It made living in a pension in Holland in two small bedrooms easier, and, later in the year, in Lausanne, where there were no bureau drawers. Going away for a vacation is one thing, but uprooting a home with no place to be transplanted for an indefinite time, is another.

The *Nieu Amsterdam* docked at Rotterdam harbor, and one had graphic reminder that the whole center of the city had been flattened by bombs such a short time before. Wide flat spaces were to be rebuilt, but the restoration was still ahead. At the docks, as trunks and boxes were placed under the *S* pile, where we were to look for ours, three little girls were soon perched on boxes, dolls carefully being cared for, and provisions for any stretch of boredom at their sides in the turquoise piqué bags. A bit forlorn-looking, yet also making that spot "home," much as circus children would. Holland, here we are! "Uncle Harllee Bordeaux," who was on his way to the International Council too, said a final good-by, with a promise of balloons (which he has kept for thirty-two years, sending big balloons for our children in every letter he ever wrote Fran, and then sending them for the grandchildren!), and the girls and I seemed to be left alone on an empty dock. "Daddy has gone to arrange for all this to go on by train to be stored in Lausanne until we go at the end of the summer."

Scheveningen by the seashore and sand dunes was the spot Fran had picked as better for the children than Amsterdam for those two months. Long stretches of beach and windswept rolling sand dunes gave an outdoor life for the girls. Priscilla and Susan soon learned their way around town on their bikes. When Fran was there, he would ride with a seat on the back of his bike for Debby, and of course I rode too. We had sold our car in St. Louis and had bought four bicycles with the money. Those brick-paved bicycle paths along the sand dunes made that exchange an appreciated one.

Food in our inexpensive pension was really pretty awful. It would be hard to find a more polite adjective. Rationing was rigid, and the allotment of meat was less than a square inch, and I don't mean a cube. Except for potatoes and cabbage, we had few vegetables at all; bread was made of very poor flour; and although some fish was served often it was a variety served raw, which we didn't have a taste for. We knew we were having the same kind of diet as most Dutch people, for a few times we ate at the home of some pastors for Sunday dinner, and they

served the same austere assortment. So we also had the same
emotions about the American tourists when we heard people who
had come to the Conference in Amsterdam complaining about
their chicken dinners, or about the steaks in the big hotels. We
knew what it felt like to hear such remarks when we hadn't
tasted a chicken for two months, and the bits of boiled meat
had all been unidentifiable. Deprivation educates appreciation in
many areas of life.

Fran spent his time in Amsterdam, and then commuted to us
whenever possible. He had to "get things set up," involving uncountable boring details, and then was to serve as the recording
secretary for all the meetings. Arie Kok, who had been the Dutch
Chancellor to Peking and with his wife had lived in house intern-
ment in Peking through the war, was the one with whom Fran
worked in the organizational things. We appreciated these two
as dear friends for years.

The meetings were held in the *Kloosterkerk,* which was built in
1400, and was the place where the Pilgrim Fathers worshiped
when they came for haven to Holland before going to the Boston
area. Leaning against this historic wall, a young art critic for two
Dutch newspapers, who was still taking his studies for his doctor-
ate, chewed on his pipe and thoughtfully began to talk to Fran
about art. They talked about art and history, art and philosophy,
art and art, and the time went by and the recording secretary
was missing from his meeting . . . a small blaze had started as
two minds set each other on fire! It was Hans Rookmaaker's and
Francis Schaeffer's first conversation, and Hans in student brash-
ness had remarked, "These people in here," pointing with his
pipe, "don't understand anything. But you and I, we can talk
and understand each other."

That week the children and I met Hans Rookmaaker too, and
his fiancée, Anky. Because of the Dutch rationing stamps, she
was having a difficult time getting enough stamps to buy sheets
and towels and other linens for the house. So I sent to America
for the needed things, not realizing we were going to become
very great friends and also to be working together closely throughout all the years ahead. After the skimpy Dutch sheets, dear Anky
was so amazed at the generous amount of material in American
ones that she cut a wide enough strip off the sides to make table

napkins and doilies, frugally using every bit of material to best advantage. As people undergo war, famine, floods, earthquakes, volcanos, fires, hurricanes, their standards as to what is "adequate," "too little," or "too much" undergo changes.

Our last week in Holland was full of packing, sightseeing (the art museums primarily, but also the streets decorated for the new queen's coronation) and typing (for me, as by now I was Fran's secretary!). We didn't try to see the parades, as people were taking blankets and seats, and were staying out all night to be on the route. On the coronation day I was washing a last batch of clothes in the washbasin in our bedroom, as the sound of the solemn ceremony filtered through the floor. Priscilla was with the Mager family below—listening and running upstairs in between goings-on to excitedly report it all to us. As the people sang their impressive hymns and Juliana became queen, the rinse water dripped off my elbows and tears off my nose. I was filled with emotion for so Christian a ceremony in a nation slipping so rapidly away from the true faith.

The hotel at the end of the street, the front of which could be seen from our window, housed the Queen Mother of Belgium, an Indonesian prince, and many other royalty who had come for the festivities. Each time they went out or came in, a long line of grey limousines accompanied by motorcycle police slowly passed our door, much to the enjoyment of the children. Two guards in full dress marched up and down all night, making their quarter turns and clicking their heels. Priscilla, Susan, Debby, and some Dutch children sat lined up in a row for an hour, staring and memorizing their actions. From that time on a new game was added—"playing guards."

Life is such an unending mixture of intense events—whether wars, fires, earthquakes, avalanches, floods, or deadlines in work, all mingled with children's hour by hour needs for eating, sleeping, brushing teeth and having clean clothing—whether peasants or queens!

We left by train for ten days of vacation. First in Brussels for two days, then in Paris for eight days, we nearly walked our feet off. Fran's method was to go everywhere by foot—to see the city "properly" and of course to see each museum properly. Naturally the Louvre was too vast to even begin to see fully in that time, but we were thrilled with the thrills of each of the children. Even three-year-old Debby pointed out original paintings excitedly from prints she had seen before. Fran also took the children to sail boats in the Tuileries Gardens—tiny sailboats, plus a stick to poke and turn them with, to be rented from an old lady, all for three American cents an hour. The children loved the donkey rides, as well as the funny little merry-go-round pushed by a little old man and a little old woman, and then later cranked by hand after it got started. The biggest excitement of all was riding in a carriage, which the children called "the golden chariot" because of its yellow spokes in the wheels. As the man clacked away at the horse and we trotted through the avenue, the children bowed from side to side pretending to be the queen.

Since milk was too expensive to buy, and was canned milk at that, I had foolishly mixed powdered milk with water so that we might all have some to drink. What a mistake that was. Our final night will take away any envy you might have of our "idyllic" experience in Paris! Susan was the first to waken in the middle of the night, to have a long spell of vomiting. Suffice it to say, the rest of us had been affected too. By 5:30 A.M. we had to get up to dress in time to make the early morning train. In spite of all the difficulties and in spite of the soot that covered us all during that train trip, we fell in love with our first sight of the French countryside's rolling hills and little villages, finally blending into mountains piled upon mountains as we approached Switzerland. We all rushed from one side of the train to the other, exclaiming exaggeratedly, running out of adjectives to let each other know our enthusiasm. As we pulled into Lausanne, we told each other we were going to have our first look at our new hometown. The taxi climbed up the hill from Lausanne toward La Rosiaz, and soon we were piling out, along with our suitcases, to be met by the Philadelphia Swiss consul's mother and sister and friend (having come two miles to meet us), along with Mme. Turrian and her Swiss German *"au pair"* girls who helped her as they learned French.

Just what we expected when we trudged up the stone stairway, holding on to the wrought iron railing, I don't know . . . but as we stood at the doorways of the two rooms, our hearts sank.

Our total space was to consist of these two small bedrooms. The one for Fran and me had twin beds, a washbasin, a big wooden armoire (hanging space plus four shelves), small bedside tables, a small bookcase, one chair and a medium-sized table . . . and practically no space to walk in between these things. The redeeming feature was three little steps to a French door that opened out to a tiny balcony—no room to sit out there but room for two people to stand and look at the sunset, or the lights across the lake at Évian at night! The other room, identical in size, held a single bed, a smaller day bed, a wooden crib (freshly painted pink for Debby!), a chest of drawers, a table and chair, and two hanging cupboards. Not any floor space to play! "Well . . . welllll . . . welllllllll . . . it looks impossible . . . but . . ." Where were we going to put the contents of the suitcases, the projector, the typewriter, files, books, toys, and—? Where were we going to live, do office work—?

One room was definitely the children's, and we discovered that the box that had been Fran's when he was little and later covered with cloth for our children just fit under the washbasin. It made a step for Debby to stand on to brush her teeth, and it would also hold the toys. More boxes would need to go under the bed to store other things. Books could go over here on the table, or—? And the jigsaw puzzle game of finding a place for things began. Our room was to be our bedroom and our office, our Sunday school and church on Sundays, a living room after supper at night—and so on. You can imagine that each one of us might be thinking of our own room left behind in St. Louis . . . but Fran was reminding me of our mahogany-framed poster opposite our St. Louis bed: "Go ye into all the world. . . ." There was no specification as to kind of living quarters in that!

Lausanne was different then from today, and La Rosiaz was still "country." Do listen to my description written to my family at that time:

"The price is cheaper than other pensions, and the house is scrupulously clean. Mme. Turrian is very kind and pleasant and the view is a gift of the Lord. The trolley line ends two houses away, so transportation is close. We are in the highest part of Lausanne, just outside of the city limits. We have country sounds and smells all around us, the smell of hay and pine trees, and

the constant music of tinkling cowbells. Priscilla, Susan, and Debby have very little indoor space, but the front garden goes downhill to a wall and has some lovely spots under the trees to play. The backyard goes straight up, and has a rabbit and chicken house in it. Priscilla is allowed to gather the two or three eggs that appear each day. The Lord is filling our needs in one way if not another!"

The children were dropped into a French-speaking school to sink or swim. Priscilla had to get on with French before she could take other subjects *in* French, except for mathematics, which she attempted right away. Susan began first grade again, and soon learned to pronounce French in her reading, but not to understand what it meant, so came home wailing, "I can't understand the children, I can't understand the teacher, and *now* I can't even understand myself." Debby at kindergarten level was happy, and began learning her French from the old ladies in the pension with us—two in their nineties, two in their eighties, and one in her seventies, with whom she visited day by day. Homesickness came in waves, but not constantly, and there were compensations.

Fran felt very responsible to preach for us, a series of sermons through the Bible, Old and New Testament, as faithfully as if he had a large congregation. We lined up four chairs on one side of our beds, and we had "church." We prayed for others to join us, and soon a little Irish lady at the pension came, as well as a divorcée from Boston with her two children (whom we had met on the street). We had "young people's meeting" on Sunday nights and the children took turns "leading." They also planned "Empire Builders' Meetings" for Saturday afternoons, which consisted of bicycle rides and the big treat of a stop in a tearoom for Ovalmaltine. The money for the pension took almost all of our monthly salary, so although Switzerland had marvelous-looking things in the *patisserie* (bakery) windows, as well as in the fruit stores, we could only give the children five cents allowance (twenty centimes) a week. Usually they chose a *ballon* as the biggest thing for the money—that is, a big crusty roll, without butter.

What were we *doing?* First of all, Fran was keeping in contact with all the men and groups he had visited in 1947, and I was taking dictation and typing letters. Then we were speaking in some parts of Switzerland, with our children going along to sing children's songs in order to start Children for Christ classes. The André family in Lausanne had not only invited us for a day so that our children could play with theirs, but one evening they invited a number of people from their Brethren Assembly to hear of the children's work, and to watch a sample lesson being illustrated with the flannelgraph. Lessons were translated into French and used in their camps. Also Mr. Hugh Alexander invited us to their Bible School at Le Roc, above Geneva, to speak and tell there of the children's work. After that M. Wutrich of *Action Biblique* drove us from one place to another to have evening meetings and to explain how to have children's classes. Since Debby was so little and didn't need to be in school, she went along and sang the songs with me. In addition, she had an interesting time playing with a variety of toys that would be brought out at each home in which we stayed, as well as having stories as she and I sat on the back seat of the tiny car together.

For a three-week period we all went to Holland, going from place to place, having meetings with Dutch dominies (pastors), and other open meetings with Christians. Fran spoke of the fact that with liberalism and Barthianism dominating the teaching in churches, many little children would never hear the Bible taught from the viewpoint that it is true truth unless they heard it somewhere outside of the church. I gave a talk about teaching children, along with a sample lesson, and the children sang various children's songs which at that time were very new in Holland. Among others who actually started children's classes in their own homes and began to translate the lessons into Dutch, were the Rookmaakers. They faithfully went on with their own class, and then interested other people in doing this too. Naturally Fran and Hans Rookmaaker also visited museums together, and our children had the advantage of seeing the Rijksmuseum with an unusual "guided tour"—a preview of later years when Rookmaaker and Schaeffer would be speaking at L'Abri conferences on various aspects of art! Previews of that sort are not labeled, however. What actually happened was that each one of us added something to our education.

If our work were to be categorized, it would have been labeled "Strengthening the Things That Remain." This was being accomplished through Fran's lectures on church history and just where the church is today and also through his doing his continued work in connection with the International Council of Christian Churches. Another heading would be "Starting Children for Christ in Europe." Looking back now, we can see that there were no stiff outlines and that so much more was being done in laying a foundation for ourselves and others, for a future work, that only God could sort out what was happening!

When our trunks and boxes had arrived, Mme. Turrian was flabbergasted! In the end she gave us a section of the cellar to store things, and the boxed furniture we stored at Lavanchy's warehouse. Three things were convenient about having trunk space in the cellar. One, we were able to take *everything* of ours out of our rooms and store all of it in the cellar when we went to Holland, so that she could rent the rooms to other people for that time.

The second was that, when Thanksgiving came and I was allowed to cook a little dinner "for the American *fête*," I could fish out of a trunk a tablecloth that my mother had embroidered and also our brass candlesticks, so that the celebration had "continuity" for us. Our menu—two tiny 1-1/2 pound chickens, stuffed (substitute for turkey), mashed potatoes, brussels sprouts, and vanilla cookies I had managed to produce with Mme. Turrian bustling around and the old ladies beaming in the background!

The third was that the day before Christmas we were able to find our old strings of lights and the transformer, and to discover to our delight that they all worked. Off we went on our Christmas shopping trip, to Schaefer's Sports store. We took one girl in at a time, leaving the other two to stand and watch the crowds walk down the steep hill under the Christmas trimmings. Fran explained to the salesgirl that we wanted to buy a Christmas surprise, and she and a salesman were pleased to try ski boots on blindfolded little girls, one after the other. They might have guessed, but they weren't allowed to feel with their hands, or to peek! Next we went to UNIP, a five-and-ten-cent type of store, where the girls figured out what they could buy for each other and for us. We put Priscilla in charge of taking the other two girls back home on the tram to wrap gifts, while we went on to buy a tiny tree, a plant for Mme. Turrian, and a few other things.

We trimmed our tree that night, standing it on the little steps leading to the balcony. We felt very much at home with our familiar lights and Christmas ornaments, even though we were so many miles from our old home! At supper we shared red and green Jello with the old ladies, who tasted it gingerly, nodding their heads. We had stockings to fill, but that came later after the girls were asleep. First we all went to Lausanne to the service at the cathedral, and came home to sing "Silent Night" at midnight with Mme. Turrian and Trudy as they trimmed their tree.

Our room seemed too small for Christmas exuberance, but Fran tried to help out by reclining in bed! Much was the excitement over the boxes from America, as well as the fun of the ski boots. The Swiss custom then was to "have the tree" at a specific hour, and Mme. Turrian's downstairs was at 8:00 o'clock after supper. Real candles were the accepted lighting, added to by sparklers (like the old-fashioned American Fourth of July sparklers). What a blaze of glory when sixty candles and twenty sparklers were on all at one moment—a burst of stars raining down, but then darkness. Susan was afraid and whispered, "I like looking at it, but I don't like being here when it is going on." Priscilla had a big surprise for us, reciting a French Christmas poem she had memorized (with a spatter of clapping as the old ladies and the ninety-year-old man showed their approval). Then the girls sang a French Christmas carol. The dinner was very good, with a six-pound turkey that Mme. Turrian thought was extremely large. Divided among fifteen people, it didn't give very generous portions, but it was delicious. Fran got out his projector and slides and showed everyone slides of America, and other places. Although the eighty-year-olds thought it was too late and too exciting for the ninety-year-olds, everyone stayed till the end.

On Sunday we had an increased congregation, as the woman from Boston brought a German boy whose parents were in Hong Kong, and who came with his Austrian nurse. As Fran preached, and later I gave a Christmas flannelgraph story for the children, it was a shadow of things to come—such a mixture of nationalities and ages. At the time it was something we were deeply thankful for—for that day and for those individual people. A constant straining to see what is coming next can be like pulling up roots to see what is growing. Tender loving care of the tiny beginnings has importance right *then*.

We didn't know enough about life in Switzerland then to know that it was the proper thing to go to a ski resort for part of the Christmas vacation. When a believing Jewish fellow, formerly German but with a British passport, wrote asking Fran to come and bring his family to a "Christian hotel" in Adelboden for a week "to speak in the evenings, just a short Christian message," we were excited. It was a surprise, however, that Mme. Turrian took it as a matter of course, and said she would remove something each day from our bill. Her reduced rate, plus a Christmas gift, paid our railroad fare, and our time was free.

What a special thing the Lord had planned for us as we were introduced to the hot sparkling sun, powdery snow, and wonderful refreshment of learning to ski under good conditions. We rented skis, and with the Christmas boots, we were all set. An English Christian toy merchant from London had brought a group of boys to ski and to join in the evening meetings, so he invited us to have group ski lessons with them. Completely unplanned by us, we had had what people plan and prepare for with a great deal of know-how in ski vacations. It was good to see Fran with a bunch of boys around him again, listening intently as he told them of many things.

Fran really distinguished himself the first day of skiing. The instructor said he could hardly believe it was his first time on skis. He pointed him out to the boys: "That gentleman has just the proper ease and suppleness; try to do it as he does." Debby had no fear and flew down the hill until she fell in a heap of sticks and skis and was picked up by the daughter of the hotel manager, Mr. Hari. This was constantly repeated, while the older two followed instructions and progressed rapidly with snowplowing and stem turning, loving every minute of that week. We were all sorry to leave Adelboden. Of course, we had no idea where we would be by the next Christmas.

It was in February that the pension became like a hospital, with everyone having flu, and some pneumonia. I helped out some with cooking, as Mme. Turrian was very ill. We felt the Lord perfectly timed two packages which had taken two months to get to us. One contained crayons, coloring books, and games; the other, fruit juices and bouillon cubes. It was perfect for our needs with three sick little girls. After this illness our French teacher, Mme. Wildermuth, talked to us about the need of getting to the mountains for the summer. "It is necessary for the children's health," she insisted. She set a day for househunting, saying she would go ahead and find two or three to chose from.

"I don't want to go househunting. You go, and I'll take care of Debby today," said Fran, so I started out on my first adventure alone in Switzerland! I marvel now at the remembrance of going up the mountainside with my nose plastered against the train window! I simply couldn't get enough of the wonder of what I was seeing as we wound up that valley so slowly. I described the Monthey hospital to my mother in a letter, never missing a heartbeat, because I had no idea of the night of fear I was to have there five years later when Franky as a two-year-old would be having his second attack of polio, with his life on a thin tightrope. I was now just describing a fascinating building perched on a sharp mountainside. It would be uncomfortable to be able to see some of the things ahead of us, and it would be too exciting to see other things.

My letter home goes on to give a detailed description of walking up a snowy path to Chalet Bon Accueil, the only chalet not yet rented for the summer. As I met M. and Mme. Marclay, they eagerly took me around into the garden where we could look down the steep hillside at the village spread out below and at the top of the steeple of the Protestant chapel directly under us. I had no idea then that for thirty-two years we would be having a Christmas Eve service in that chapel and that for years M. and Mme. Marclay would be bringing tea to us as we trimmed the chapel with pine trees. I wasn't even sure then that we would be coming for one summer! To see Champéry, surrounded on all sides by towering alpine peaks, was almost like turning the page of a book of breathtaking Swiss photographs, without knowing that we would be stopping on that one page for five years.

The little chalet was exciting as I pictured the family moving out of two rooms into a real house. There was a tiny kitchen, a bathroom with a boiler providing thirty liters of hot water a day (we had to be limited to two inches of water for our once-a-week bath, with one towel to be shared among us all, at the pension!). The view was something I would never see without thanking God for it . . . even though this was every day. Mme. Wildermuth took me to a meat store, the *laiterie* (dairy store), and grocery store to add up prices of a week's groceries so that I could see if we would have enough to pay the rent and have food and electricity! It seemed to be just right, so I signed the papers. My trip back down the mountainside and along the lake to Lausanne was in the dark, but with news to bring squeals of joy from the girls. We now had five months to dream of having a home "with mommy in the kitchen" . . . and choices as to what we would eat, and how much noise we might make . . . for July and August!

The next five months in the two rooms brought a variety of scenes played in the same small bits of space, with no added props. Our room was a busy office, with Fran dictating, me typing, and Priscilla filing, as well as taking the letters to mail and reporting on the cost of the stamps. It also was our church, with the very lively and original young people's meetings led by the children. It was the scene of surprise parties planned by Susan or Priscilla for us, and of family times of reading books. It became a hospital when Debby's sudden fever developed into pneumonia. We moved her crib into our room, taking out the chair and putting her crib between our bed and the washbasin, so that I could care for her through the night. As she grew visibly worse, we took Mme. Wildermuth's advice to change doctors and had *her* doctor—a Russian woman, Doctor Kousmine—who announced, "She wants to have pneumonia and I shall give her penicillin." Mixing the dose with Fran's blood, she gave Debby a shot, and returned at the proper intervals to continue them. An old method of relieving chest congestion was also used—that of putting on the chest small bottles holding a flaming piece of cotton which burned up in the air and formed a vacuum as the bottle hit the chest and the air was cut off. The fire immediately went out but flesh was sucked up into the vacuum. Five bottles were placed on Debby's chest; then later five on her back! After that affair, Susan determinedly marched in and gave us an ultimatum: "I love you very much and I wouldn't like to leave you. But if EVER anyone does that to me . . . I'll leave home!"

As Debby was recovering, although she still had fever, she grew lively and climbed up on the railing of her crib, fell, and cut her chin on the washbasin on her way down. Fran was ashamed to have to call a doctor to put four stitches in the chin of a child with pneumonia! Whether nursing children when they are sick, or teaching them arithmetic or skiing or checkers, bringing them up is not a matter of having a schedule that fits into predictable slots. Personalities are so very diverse and little people don't behave like machines, nor according to some of the expectations given by the psychologists. Susan, for instance, was usually so good it hurt, but at times so bad that it was necessary to hurt her with some punishment or other. She had worked out a Bible study course for Debby and had instructed her carefully in secret, then invited us to "parents' night" in their bedroom. We were amazed at the verses Debby recited and the answers she gave to questions—at the age of four. But another day Susan was egging on a little boy to walk on the rails of the crib as his act in the "circus" by saying, "Poooooh . . . scaredy cat . . . I could jump rope up there . . ." and, "Oh, I'm just training Debby to carry books on her head, because, you see, mommy, she might have to live in a country where ladies carry heavy bottles on their heads." Yes, the rooms were small, but "life" was being lived, and life does not consist of simply "tidy behavior."

We had taken the children to Holland with us, but when it came time to go to Paris for Fran's speaking on the situation in theological areas, and for our speaking about how to commence Children for Christ classes, they seemed ready to continue their lives for two weeks without us. Susan was going to stay in the home of a couple who had the school, and she was looking forward to having a room alone for that time. Priscilla and Debby were going to have the luxury of using our two rooms to spread out for study and play. Of course, Mme. Turrian would not only provide meals and care of the rooms, but would "hover over them."

A whole chapter could be written about that time in Paris, about talking with Pastor Guiton and speaking for his group. The smell of his musty book-lined office with its little kerosene stove—"The books keep the room warm," he said—and the ascent up the narrow stairway to the humble dining room where we had tea while looking out over all of Paris are still vivid in our memory. The rich time of communication in Mme. Blochet's Baptist School where many French young people received their training for that church group would make another story.

What was most important during that five months? Letters being written to those who wanted to ask questions, or to have us come to speak, from the diverse countries of Western Europe? Or the trips themselves and the speaking in Switzerland? Or were the individual conversations the most significant use of time? Our first contact with Israel came not only with a visit to the international stamp exhibition in Paris—where for the *first* time Israeli stamps were officially marking Israel as a nation—but with long, long conversations into the wee hours of the morning with a German Jewish woman who stayed at our pension. A refugee to Israel from Germany, she told us of all that had been going on in those early days of Israel's becoming a nation.

Were we *doing* what we had come for? Were we *being prepared* for something ahead? Were we teaching other people, imparting knowledge of truth in our conversations? Or were we learning more than we could in any course of study by *listening?* Could we tell just what point history itself had come to? Could we tell anything about the point we had arrived in our own history?

Finally the day arrived to puff up and down the stairs with boxes of stuff packed to store at the Wildermuths, and suitcases and boxes to take with us to Champéry for our anticipated home life. As we piled into the little truck that would take us there, it was with the expectation of two months in an Alpine chalet, away from people and alone together! The thrill of that drive grew even as we bumped along the unpaved bits of the road, mounting steadily to a higher altitude. Going from the lake level up to Champéry's altitude of about 3100 feet, the climbing, twisting old road (now a much wider paved road) took us past waterfalls and very old chalets into a different world, tucked away from any view of the Rhone Valley. Even the sky was reduced to a comfortable ceiling of blue across which we could watch the drifting clouds, pink at sunset time, moving to reveal the new moon a bit later, as if we were watching a large screen wrapped around a curving ceiling, with a hidden projector putting everything into a different scale.

Champéry at last—Valaisian chalet roof after chalet roof almost meeting over the village street; cows and goats scattered on the slopes, energetically filling the air with the varied tones of their bells. We felt this was really Heidi's Switzerland with the clarity of the air, the multitude of inviting paths waiting to be explored, the peasant life which seemed to have gone on for a century unchanged. We were filled with a certainty as to what we had come for. This was to be part vacation and "unwinding." This was to be time to enjoy each other in an easier situation and to *be* a family. This was to be a time of writing letters and preparing talks in an atmosphere more conducive to composing, as well as a time to study and think in a place where one's mind might breathe something as fresh as the air that was being breathed into one's lungs.

But were we clear as to what we were here for in this mountain spot? Had we an unobstructed view of the path ahead, of the next stepping stone? Were the reasons for which we had left St. Louis and our fruitful work there all falling into place now?

Have you been in the mountains when the morning gave the most brilliantly clear view you felt you had ever seen, and when you felt as though you must be looking through some sort of giant magnifying glass? And then, only an hour later, the fog drifted up and a cloud drifted down and you were enveloped in such a thick mist you couldn't see the tree across the road?

Clear as a fog. We were sitting in a fog, needing once more to trust the Lord to take us safely to the next stepping stone. In the fog we could have stepped into a rushing stream instead, as easily as anything. Clear as a fog! That was our position, with no wisdom to make the next choice.

ONE DAY AT A TIME 14

The refreshing wet face cloth, hot or cold, which is handed to us in a Hong Kong restaurant, or at the end of a SwissAir flight, to help us get on with the next few minutes at the end of a tiring day, or a long voyage, accomplishes the same kind of physical wake-up jolt that we so often need intellectually, emotionally, psychologically, and spiritually. The Bible frequently hands us the refreshing wet face cloth to awaken us for *today* and remind us of the importance of what is at hand. It tells us first not to worry about the tomorrows, because the day, each day, has enough troubles of its own. It tells us also not to declare what we are going to *do* on all the tomorrows of our calendar plans without prefacing such verbalization with, "Lord willing," somewhere deep inside our understanding, not just as a slogan.

Today is important. Today's tasks, humdrum or exciting, are important in history. Today might be a part of preparation for many tomorrows, but only God knows what the tomorrows will contain—internationally, nationally, in our community, or in any one individual life. Today is the day that has to be lived with reality of asking for the needed strength "for the day."

The problem with giving a true account, or an accurate picture of history, is the impossibility of describing one day at a time, 365 days a year, all the years one is attempting to cover. The ending of the Book of John, in the New Testament, is a comfort when we are faced with the problem of condensing the account of events, development of a work, or of lives of individuals, the growth of children, or the growth of ideas. John writes: "This is the disciple who testifies to these things, and who wrote them down. We know that his testimony is true. Jesus did many other things as well. If every one of them were written down, I suppose that even the whole world would not have room for the books that would be written" (21:24–25, NIV). The wonder of the Bible is that, as we are told in 2 Timothy 3, *all* scripture is given by inspiration of God, or is "God-breathed" . . . which says to me that the condensation of all that happened day by day is a condensation which is balanced for our need of knowledge of history, as well as for our need of being corrected and trained. Human writers trying to give a balanced glimpse of a portion of history, or of The Tapestry, need to ask of God's help, which He does give. No human writing, however, can ever be perfectly balanced to include everything that needs to be included to give proper understanding of the period of history covered, nor to exclude all that could be left out. The Bible is unique in this marvel of selection. Thank God for it.

Champéry! Our expectation was of being there for sixty days, one day at a time. We reveled in having space enough to choose places for such things as the typewriter and office materials, our clothing, food supplies, toys, and books. The luxury of having a bathroom in which to put toothpaste and medicines and soap, as well as in which to take a bath at any time on any day, vied with the luxury of having a tiny kitchen in which to cook the food we could choose. We had no refrigerator, but learned the value of a "cave," a dirt-floored room in the cellar where things could be kept cool. There were no frozen foods in Switzerland then, and no pasteurized milk. Fruit and vegetables were sold according to what was in season, and the milk was a mixture from all the cows wandering around the pastures on the mountainsides above the village.

As a part of their education, the children each had jobs to do each day, helping make their beds, setting table for meals, dish-drying and cooking. The favorite job was the carrying of a milk pail down the path to the village *laiterie* before breakfast each

morning to bring back three liters of milk dipped from the huge containers. Priscilla took over sole possession of the job after the morning Susan fell flat on her face hurrying back up the path and landed at home with very little milk in the pail, plus an assortment of dirt, sticks, and even a good-sized stone!

Fran made a rule that we all had to speak French from breakfast until we sat down for supper. Added to that there was an hour of study for the children, not all made up of concentrated work, however. Every five minutes Susan would shout out, *"Quelle heure est-il?* . . . Mama, Papa, *combien de temps maintenant?"* ("What time is it . . . how much time now?") The end of that hour was a relief! Fran was methodically using vocabulary cards (just as he had done with Hebrew in seminary)—little cardboard squares he had cut, with a French word on one side and the English equivalent on the other. He was never without bunches of these cards, held together with elastic bands, in his pockets. While he was keeping an eye on Priscilla as she learned to swim, back and forth across the deep end of the pool in the village, he kept his other eye on his cards—perhaps a pack of adjectives, or nouns! As he went with me to help carry groceries back up the steep path in his backpack, while I shopped he would sit outside the store on the bench (one of the wonderful benches sprinkled everywhere in Switzerland) studying his vocabulary cards. Even when we hiked, he doggedly continued adding words, except when climbing used his hands as well as his feet.

Priscilla was twelve, Susan eight, and Debby four that summer. As one day followed another we were doing what God had brought us to Champéry to do—growing in a diversity of ways, all of us. There was a togetherness in concern and understanding, a sense of ongoing purpose—not spelled out in words, or repeated together in slogans, but being lived. Perfect? Far from it, but a measure of reality that brought excitement day after day. There was excitement bubbling forth as Priscilla and Susan came back from the swimming pool (having hurried through their studies to get a swim in before lunch) to report to us that there were English schoolgirls who had come on a chaperoned excursion from Bournemouth. There was excitement on the part of all three children as Priscilla and I met these girls in the village when we were grocery shopping together and our chance conversation brought about an interest in learning what we were teaching our Children for Christ classes. There was excitement concerning the preparations for an afternoon of my showing the children's flannelgraph materials, and explaining some of the content of the lessons we were writing, to four of the girls and a teacher who were coming. That preparation included making a cake with fudge icing for tea, together with hot biscuits to serve with honey, as well as gathering some wild flowers to make the table look festive.

The girls ranged in age from fourteen to eighteen and had lived under strict food rationing for ten years. Nonetheless, their excitement over eating food such as they had only seen in magazines was matched by their keen and a bit bewildered interest in what was being said. Their Scripture classes in that English school had *not* been taught by a teacher who believed the Bible to be true in all the areas in which it gives accounts of history and the cosmos. In my answers, was I giving a preview of what Fran would be giving years later in L'Abri? No, not at all, really. I was giving a positive teaching of the central thread of teaching throughout the Bible, with a desire that the way of salvation might be remembered and tucked away in the minds of these girls, never to be forgotten.

When more of them came again for an evening, Fran showed them slides of pictures he had taken all over Europe in 1947, and he talked about the Oslo World Council Youth Conference, which fit in with their own experience of being taught what "Christianity" was all about. Was he going into a discussion of the "personal and impersonal universe"? Was he at that time talking about relativism? No—again, no. As I'll attempt to show from articles he was writing—and I was typing for him as secretary in those days—the groundwork or base for all he was to develop later was, in fact, being laid then. But—please do remember he was also growing and developing day by day, and also remember that this was the end of the '40s! Ten years of the '50s were to follow before the '60s were to begin.

History proceeds in blocks of time. The needs, the atmosphere, the climate change. It would be as bad to be too far ahead with answers to questions that have never come up as to be so far behind that one is answering the great-grandfather's questions instead of those of the present generation. Even if one *could* know everything past and future—which no one does—people to whom we are speaking need to be helped to understand the "climate" in which they live, and there is also our need to have a one-day-at-a-time preparation of *living*. I can't say too many times, we had no idea there was ever going to be a work called "L'Abri" nor did we have any blueprint as to what kind of answers were going to be given to an international stream of people. We had no "dream," "vision," or even desire or determination to have an open home. We were simply living a day at a time, together as a family, eagerly sharing a desire to make known to these English schoolgirls, and to other people we were going to meet on those little mountain paths, the truth we felt was a matter of life and death importance . . . one day at a time!

It was in the butcher's shop that I said good-by to the English girls. One had gasped, "I can't believe you can buy meat and things without a ration book, that all you need is money." It made me feel greedy to simply ask for ground beef! But the deeper sadness was knowing that they would be going back to Scripture classes and to churches where they said they had never heard anything like the things we had taught them—simply the free provision God has set forth, unrationed, for all to have without money and without price—when He has made it clear that the promised Lamb, His Son, did come, and that whosoever believes on Him may have everlasting life. It seems too easy until one realizes the titanic price that has already been paid by the Lamb Himself in behalf of all who come believing.

August 3, a few days after that, we had a letter from Mme. A., asking us to come to their camp at Ballaigue in the Jura Mountains to speak to girls there about Children for Christ. Fran was leaving the following Monday for Amsterdam, having received a special invitation to attend the Reformed Ecumenical Synod for two weeks. Mr. Arie Kok strongly urged him to attend and to give a recommendation as to whether it was a body to be joined or not. So Fran asked me to go to Ballaigue, while he stayed with the girls. Two hours later, having put a dinner in the oven, having left instructions with twelve-year-old Priscilla for other meals, and having packed a suitcase mostly with Children for Christ materials, I was on the little train, winding down the mountain. It was a most worthwhile twenty-four hours! I was back in time to take dictation of letters and an article that Fran wanted to have sent off before he left.

Let me copy a paragraph from my Family Letter of September 1949: "We miss Fran these days, but aren't a bit afraid to be in the chalet alone. The town lights twinkle down below us, and the stars twinkle above the silhouettes of the mountains, and all seems very protected. One afternoon the children and I were invited for tea by an American girl who rents a chalet with another American girl here in Champéry. Priscilla, again, had got acquainted with them! This American—Ann—is the daughter of a man in the Treasury Department in Washington; she came over for a government job and didn't want to leave! The other girl is the daughter of a naval officer. As we entered Chalet Bijou, we discovered that they had about a dozen house guests—people coming and going all the time. There was an elderly baroness who lived in Egypt forty years and lost everything during the war. There were a Swedish girl, a French girl, a Norwegian girl, and a German girl who lives in Lausanne. Several Canadian girls and an American mother of one of our diplomats in Belgium completed the picture at the tea table—all but four lived in the chalet! It was all very interesting, but the most worthwhile part of the afternoon came when I had a talk alone with a German girl who is marrying an Austrian and expects to live in Britain."

Two years later we were going to be living in that Chalet Bijou. Two years later we would be having an endless stream of international girls coming for tea and discussion, one evening after another. But that afternoon, with no knowledge that the chalet would mean anything to us personally, and no recognition of any pattern revolving around tea and discussion, Priscilla, Susan, Debby, and I were all involved in conversation with some measure of caring about the people. "I hope, mother, that we can talk to that Mme. Dumericher again, the baroness. She seems so sad."

Fran came back from the Reformed Ecumenical Synod in Amsterdam disappointed in the lack of a clearcut stand against the World Council and its apostasy. He felt he could not recommend that the Bible Presbyterian Church become a part of this synod and sent a report to be mailed out from St. Louis to all the churches and ministers in the B.P. denomination.

One day after Fran came back, he took Priscilla, Susan, and

an English boy (who had both Swiss and English nationality) for a hike to the pass in the mountains between Switzerland and France near Champéry. They took the wide, well-used path on the way, but decided to try a different route back. The path was well marked with orange paint splashed on stones—at the beginning. Suddenly it ended in a precipice. Each way they tried from that point on also ended at the edge of a precipice. As evening approached, it began to get grey and Fran wondered if they would have to spend the night there. They stopped to have prayer together, each one praying and asking the Lord to show them the way back to Champéry. Immediately after praying together, they discovered a dry stream bed—steep, but a possible way down the mountain. Sliding and crawling, they helped each other down, Fran leading the way.

It was pitch dark and raining hard when a well-soaked muddy three returned a full three hours after I had expected them. Hot baths, clean pajamas, and a hot dinner soon had them feeling comfortable. As I put Susan to bed, we discussed the object lesson of the hike. "Those orange splashes looked like the markings of a fine path, but they led to only a precipice. Just so, many people are following what look like well-marked paths to heaven, only to find that they end up on the brink of hell! As we climb mountains, it is important to follow only paths we know about from maps—and even more for people to recognize that the Bible (as the only reliable map for the most essential information in life) says there is only *one* path to heaven." "Why, mother, I see," said eight-year-old Susan, "some *people* are being the orange splashings on the wrong path, making *other* people get mixed up like we were." That night Susan's prayer was sweet with new understanding. It seemed very important to her that people would somehow be warned of the danger of following other people who were the "wrong markings."

One day at a time, that summer was lived with a terrific diversity of living full days of immediate importance. At the same time, foundations and bases were subtly being laid for each one's personal future, as well as for the future work we would be involved in together. As the summer drew to a close and the cows came down from the high pastures, filling the village air with the sound of bells, and as the tourists began to disappear and villagers came back into their own chalets (rented for the summer), the children began to plead to stay on. "Why can't we just live in Champéry?" We wanted to fulfill our promises to Mme. Turrian and return the first of September, but after giving two months' notice we would be free . . . and why not indeed? The rate for a chalet would be less by the year than for summer or winter months, and the added work of housework and cooking carried with it so many advantages, that staying up later at night to type seemed a small cost to add. We didn't really need to be in a city, since our little train would connect with trains in the valley for any direction we might be needing to go. Added time was the only factor. So we began to pray for guidance, asking the Lord to show us the right house before we had to leave, if indeed He meant us to make Champéry our home.

The answer came on the last day we were to be in Champéry. We met Mme. W.'s sister on the village street, and she asked us if we would like to see the chalet she took care of for an English woman—Chalet des Frênes. It turned out to be an amazingly beautiful and unusual chalet, completely furnished even to sheets and dishes, and at a low price. We didn't know it would only be for one year . . . but it was a gift in memory for many years, as well as a special provision for us and for all that was going to take place there in that time. A wonderful fireplace faced a marvelous picture window that framed an incredible view. It was around this fireplace we would be having our first "question-and-answer" evenings with girls from finishing schools. It was around this dining room table we would be feeding a stream of people coming from many countries to the International Council Congress the next summer. It was the front lawn of this chalet that we would be turning into our first vegetable garden in Switzerland. It was in this chalet I would be typing the "Basic Bible Studies" one at a time, one a week, as Fran would be preparing them for our medical doctor. It was in this chalet bedroom I would be having a sad miscarriage, traumatic for the whole family, as we were to lose an expected baby. All this was unknown to us— and so very much more of that next year's happenings—as we said, "Yes, we'll take this from the first of November on," and signed the agreement . . . for a year!

Back at Mme. Turrian's in our two rooms, we began two months that would take the rest of the book if we were to describe it a day at a time. In between taking dictation and typing letters to Holland (where a number of Children for Christ classes had now started and where a young art critic and his wife—no other than Hans and Anky Rookmaaker—were having an exciting class which was growing week by week) and other countries, we were making trips to Ballaigue, or visiting Baroness D., who listened to our answers to her questions with her old-fashioned ear trumpet. In between talking to individuals who were seeking us out for one kind of help or another, we were writing Luke Lessons (a simple form of study for teaching children with the flannelgraph, now totally revised and written into book form, *Everybody Can Know*, available in English and French) which Mme. André wanted to translate into French. In between riding bikes with the children on our afternoon off, they were accompanying me as I tried to teach some ladies how to teach children's classes. Mme. Depersinge met us with a bit of a worried frown the second time we came, explaining that her six-year-old boy had invited six of his friends and was excitedly standing on his head in anticipation of the first "real class." So our three girls, her three children, and the six invited neighbor children sang heartily together and sat for a translated lesson, opening a "new work" for the mother with a bang. Instead of a class to teach a few teachers, it had turned into a class for children, immediately!

In between all other things came a cable: "PREPARE GO LONDON APPEAL KENYA CASE SENDING FULL INFORMATION." This threw us into a rush of work . . . "All this must be done today, might have to go to London tomorrow." An article had to be finished (by Fran, typed by me), as did countless letters, a yearly report for the Children for Christ Board meeting, etc. What was the London trip all about? Fran and Mr. Kok had been asked to go to the British Colonial Office to interview the Colonial Secretary and explain why the missionaries of our mission in Africa were not in the World Council of Churches. This had to do with permission for purchase of land for the mission houses and so on. Fran let me know from London of the gracious reception they had had in the Colonial Office by the head of the West Africa division and of his careful listening. Fran went on to say that he had also had a meeting with a group of children whom we had spoken to in Ballaigue at the camp. They had come quite long distances to see him again, and it was the intention of the leader of that particular mission to begin Children for Christ classes. The trip turned out to have multiple results.

The multiple variety of demands upon time in that two-month period did not cease; yet somehow packing was accomplished in time for the arrival of the moving men, who hoisted heavy boxes and trunks on their backs and walked down flights of stairs inside and flights again on the outside, until they reached the street level, where things disappeared into the yawning black hole of the back of the truck. Fran supervised the departure of things stored in the cellar, while I stayed upstairs to see that Mme. Turrian's belongings didn't get carted off by mistake. When all was in, we ran for a tram to follow them to the customhouse, where all our other things had been held until we could produce a year's lease on a house or apartment. These included our refrigerator which Pop had bought us, a barrel of dishes, a box of kitchen utensils, a few lamps, pictures and knick-knacks, boxes of books, and the children's double-decker beds. All these had been packed in St. Louis almost two years before, and as they rolled out, marked with the black crayon markings, we realized they had at last reached their destination and that we were no longer in transit! We began to feel really at home.

We had the weekend still in Lausanne—to have Priscilla's eyes tested, to measure the girls for skis for Christmas, to visit Baroness D. and pray and read the Bible with her, to have a final "church service" in our bedroom, and then a lovely Sunday dinner with the André family. It was a lovely warm farewell to have one family give us a plant for our new home and another take us to the station to wave us off. Debby pressed her face to the train window, saying, "Good-by lake, good-by lake, we're going to live in the mountains."

Champéry's street was deserted, but one of the children of Mme. W. met us with an enthusiastic cocker spaniel, and also a man her aunt had sent to carry our bags on a cart down the street. Susan ran ahead, leading the trio in turning in at our own gate. What squeals of excitement followed in the girls' inspection of the inside of the chalet, in the discovery of their own rooms, and of the fact that beds were made and everything in readiness for us. Monday morning the movers put a swift end to the tidiness. We were soon knee-deep in shredded paper, but also in an atmosphere of delight as shrieks of joy greeted old books which immediately "had" to be read. "Listen to this; oh, just listen to this!" Priscilla would shout out, and soon a story reading time was begun with the remark "I love books" and the eager question "Aren't books wonderful?" Indeed, books are "home roots" of life that *can* be transplanted!

Fourteen days later we were packing suitcases again. Yes, we were home, but our lives were to consist of travel for Children for Christ work, and for various things connected with the International Council of Christian Churches, those first years, as well as of all that would take place in the chalet itself. This time we were on our way first to Geneva to meet with a group of men about the Congress to be held the next summer, and then to Paris to show the Children for Christ materials, and to lecture at Pastor Guiton's church and in some other places. Any in-between minutes we had, we visited the Louvre, or went to a concert instead of having supper. When the girls met us happily at the Champéry station that first returning time, each one was full of news. "I can knit now" . . . "Guess what the teacher said" . . . and when I said we had seen amazing things in the archaeology rooms at the Louvre, Susan said quickly, "Oh, I just love the dummies." "What," piped in Debby, "are dummies?" Before anyone else could inject an answer, Susan rapidly replied, "Oh, dummies are dead Egyptians with their arms folded like this!" Whereupon Fran corrected the false impression . . . and went on to give a short explanation of Egyptian mummies and other artifacts found in the tombs.

It's possible to enjoy the amusing mistakes children make, without laughing *at* them and making them sick with embarrassment. To take time to explain and set things right in the area of understanding, and then to use that starting place to go on talking in these areas to widen interest and knowledge, is to educate your children beyond the limits of school. One thing Fran has always been good about has been to take time and thought in conversations with his children, handling their questions or interest seriously at various stages of life. Perfect? Far from it, but these are the moments during which friendship with one's children begins.

A day at a time, life was being lived; a day at a time, a work was in progress; and a day at a time, a foundation was being laid in the area of ideas as well as attitudes and atmosphere. If anyone had asked us right then, "What have you come over here for? What are you preparing for in the future?" we would probably have said, "We are doing it." We had no plans for the future, no visions of anything different. Opening the door for someone who is on the other side, knocking, was a natural thing in a very literal way.

Our first Christmas in Champéry found us decorating a tree that was brought to us from the woods by Vic, a woman who lived far up the mountain and who came to help out. We were going to have a "family Christmas" a couple of days early, alone, as a family of four were coming from Holland, and a young missionary from France, Lorraine (now Winston), was coming from Paris, so we would be nine for a Christmas dinner after the service. The service? An unexpected excitement was a request from a Protestant pastor for Fran to preach and conduct a Christmas Eve service for English-speaking skiers who would be coming for the holidays. We had no idea that that candlelight service, with the small logs split in half and made into candleholders (the work of a South African woman who pitched in to help decorate the chapel) for a hundred candles, would be repeated year after year. We weren't "planning for the future" when we excitedly walked down the snowy street to that service.

Afterwards, we pulled the luge, loaded with cardboard boxes containing the burned-down red candles and wax-stained log holders, down the village street to store in the chalet for "another year." We didn't dream that thirty-two years later those same logs would be being brought over from Huémoz to Champéry for the Christmas Eve service, continuing in an unbroken line even after our having been put out of the village twenty-six years before. We couldn't have imagined that at that time, any more than the woman who built the chapel in 1916 in a Roman Catholic village—so that there could be services for Protestants—could have imagined what the chapel would be used for! She was English. Had she known that Frances Havergal had lived and written hymns in Champéry long before that? Whose prayers were being answered when? And how does prayer affect the pattern of the weaving of the "threads" in The Tapestry? So much is mystery, yet mystery filled with trust—trust of our God who does not tell us everything, yet gives us enough glimpses into His word, and in history, to excite us about knowing him. We don't need to know everything to be able to trust him, one day at a time. In fact it seems to us that is what trust is all about . . . trusting in a fog.

The day after Christmas, while our children and our visitors the Pols and their children were up at Planachaux at the top of the *téléphérique,* watching the ski schools begin their lessons, we were working on an article. That is, Fran was dictating and I was typing, as his secretary. Article? Gradually Fran's ideas were developing in directions which continued. I have been literally digging in dusty boxes of old papers to write this, and it has amazed me to see the continuity of his thinking as I look back over the direction of these early articles. It may interest you to look over my shoulder at the yellowed old papers here so neatly under a rubber band.

So often people have asked me, "When did your husband start thinking this way?" or, "Where did your husband get these ideas?" My answer is usually, "It's been a day at a time, over a long period of time, often in the context of answering real people's real questions. He attempts to be honest with people and to try to think of the question behind the question." But, in reading the dates and the content of a few articles, I've been startled at realizing the "seeds" have been there for many years. Because of his methodical "keeping things in case they might be needed sometime," I can give you this look, a look into the past where you will see the embryo of books to be born many years later. You will also see embryo of "answers" that were to grow and take shape during countless discussions with a diversity of people, who stimulated his thinking, and some of whom taught him far more than lectures at university would have, in their areas of science, history, art, music, during the discussions. You see, Fran has listened as well as talked to people, and with an analytical mind has seen between disciplines cross-connections which have excited him. He also has been struggling, growing. Life is *not* an act with a memorized script handed to us for our part in the play! But back now to the articles.

In the paper, *The Bible Today,* May 1948 issue, Dr. J. Oliver Buswell reviewed a book by E. J. Carnell called *An Introduction to Christian Apologetics.* In the October 1948 issue of *The Bible Today* you would read on the cover that Dr. Allan A. MacRae was writing a series on Isaiah, that Dr. George H. Seville was writing on "Men We Should Know," and that his son-in-law, Rev. Francis A. Schaeffer, had written "A Review of a Review." This review, although short, amazingly enough was to give all the basic ideas which years ahead were to help him first in his own struggles concerning truth, and which, later still, were to be formed into an enlarged study to be called by some people "Schaeffer's Apologetics." In Fran's review of Buswell's review, the framework of what would come later can be recognized immediately. Now thirty-three years later, the climax of this flow of thinking has just been prepared for the new appendix of *The God Who Is There,* coming out soon in revised edition, as are all of F.A.S.'s first twenty-two books. The striking thing is that everything that is distinctive and all that has made it possible for Fran to talk to thousands of individuals in a *living* way, everything that lifted what he had to say out of the dry dust of theoretical, sloganlike words . . . was there in 1948 in embryo!

In August of 1950 Fran gave a talk at the Second Plenary Congress of the International Council of Christian Churches in Geneva, Switzerland. The title was "The New Modernism (Neo-orthodoxy) and the Bible." This talk contained material which really has been the basis of all he has said since on the "existential methodology" showing the destructiveness of Karl Barth's teaching. (This was translated into French and Portuguese at that time.) Prior to giving this lecture, Fran had visited Karl Barth in his summer home above Lake Zurich. He had gone, along with Dr. Douglas Young and others, for an afternoon's conversation, and Fran had asked him, "Did God create the world?" Barth answered, "God created the world in the first century A.D." Fran, waving his arms out over the beauty in front of them, pointing to the tree-covered hills sweeping down to the lake, asked, "This world?" Barth answered, "This world does not matter." This was a perfect example of what Fran has called "the upper and lower story" in his explanation of the division in truth made by the existential manner of thinking. This is what Fran is still fighting, as some evangelicals adopt this same division in their thinking as well as in their way of teaching or Bible exegesis.

In March 1951 *The Bible Today* carried an article of Fran's on "The Christian and Modern Art." It gave the basic material he later developed in conversations, in thinking, and in lectures on Modern Art, including, years after that, the very much more full development in the book and film *How Should We Then Live?* in the portions concerning art. The first article was later published in *His* magazine, November 1955. As you will realize, a great deal of the history of our own lives takes place during these prim-looking dates. For instance, the article on art was first written in Champéry, before there was any idea that there would ever be a work called L'Abri, and the reprint in November 1955 came after L'Abri was about six months old!

Fran's first writing on "The Balance of the Simultaneous Exhibition of God's Holiness and Love" appeared in *The Christian Beacon* in an article dated February 2, 1950. In this he spoke of the "danger within and the danger from without," speaking of course of "the Separated Movement." The danger from without was that we would grow discouraged and compromise or withdraw from the battle. The danger from within, he said, was equally as great, but he spent more time on this second aspect. Among other things, he said, "We must say and mean with David Brainerd, 'Oh that my soul might never offer any dead, cold service to my God!' . . . Soul-winning should mean self-denying and sacrificial work. . . . The work of soul-building should mean the turning out of scholarly material and warm devotional material as well. . . . The second danger from within . . . is the danger of losing the love God means us to have one for the other. Christ has commanded us to love one another. . . . There is a danger of developing in our age of necessary contending, a will to win, rather than a will to be right. . . . Our daily prayer should be that our loving Lord will keep His arms so about us that we will neither waver in the fight nor allow the Devil to destroy us from within."

This was written five years before we resigned from "The Movement"! It also was written just before (or perhaps it actually was the beginning of) Fran's period of time described in the Preface of *True Spirituality* when he himself questioned the reality of the truth of Christianity, because of the lack of reality he

felt he observed in the lives of so many Christians, and a dissatisfaction with himself. I will quote from his Preface: "During this
time [he is describing 1948, 1949, 1950] I felt a strong burden
to stand for the historical Christian position, and for the purity
of the visible Church. Gradually however, a problem came to
me—the problem of reality. This had two parts: first, it seemed
to me that among many of those who held the orthodox position
one saw little reality in the things that the Bible so clearly said
should be the result of Christianity. Second, it gradually grew
on me that my own reality was less than it had been in the
early days after I had become a Christian. I realized that in honesty
I had to go back and rethink my whole position."

Now that you have "lived through" those "early days" with
him in this book, in his diaries and letters of that period of time,
you can feel something more of what he means in this Preface.
The development of a base for future work and life, taking place
in these articles, was not a matter of searching for something to
write about, but a matter of writing about what was actually
taking place in considering the real inconsistencies, and about
the solution.

The Sunday School Times of June 18, 1951, carried an article by
Fran entitled "The Secret of Power and the Enjoyment of the
Lord." Born out of those walks up and down in the hayloft,
this was the first thing stating in a strong positive way the conclusions that not only was Christianity true truth, but that results
are meant to be coming forth, including an enjoyment of the
Lord.

In 1953 a booklet called "Righteousness and Peace" was published, containing the above article and four others. This booklet
and a series of talks given in a conference in Dakota in July
1953 were a growing result of a continued striving for reality in
both personal life, and in teaching.

In 1954 the Third Plenary Congress of the International Council
of Christian Churches met in Elkins Park. They published "Reformation and Revival," an article by Fran which shows the unchanging direction of his struggle for a more balanced living and
speaking with more reality.

In April 1954 there appeared in *Reformation Review,* the official
publication of the International Council of Christian Churches

published in Amsterdam, an article of Fran's written earlier in Champéry: "If Our Task Is To Be Accomplished." In this he pleads that if we are to differ with true Christians, we must differ with genuine regret and tears, showing forth loving restraint in our words, seeking a solution of differences rather than seeking to win. He goes on in the vein that the world has a right to expect that grace will be displayed among Christians, even when differing.

As I sit here among these dusty faded and yellowed pages and booklets, I feel I am seeing a path that was cleared through underbrush and woods by an invisible hand—a path for many people to walk one day in reading what would come forth in *The Church Before the Watching World*. Fran would be writing this book much, much later, after our own break with that which seemed too harsh, and after years of an unfolding of reality in L'Abri. Perfection? Far from it. But day by day, one day at a time, certain scales were dropping that hindered the "seeing" and following of a path of reality. A cleared path is so important!

In the July 1954 issue of that same *Reformation Review*, there is an article "How Heresy Should Be Met" by Francis A. Schaeffer. In this Fran points back to men of the Reformation, and such ones also as Spurgeon, McCheyne, Bonar, as being "men of the burning heart." He urges that Christians have a responsibility to keep in mind that all men are "God's image bearers" in practical matters in dealing with their fellows. Let me quote his conclusion: "And deeper still, there is required a demonstration in our lives, after we have spiritually wrestled the matter through, by God's grace, on the basis of Christ's finished work, that we do love our neighbors as ourselves in all the spheres of life; and for the demonstration to be of such a character as will put Satan's counterfeit to shame, it must be presented in such a manner as the world can understand, that of the 'turned cheek' and the 'extra mile.'"

As we have jumped together from article to article, we've moved ahead five years in our story, but there has had to be a placing of the microscope on the weaving—the weaving of ideas with threads of growing understanding. If the focus had not been on the continuity of that growth in the area of certainty of truth and of desire for more reality in life, you couldn't have the preparation you need in order to recognize what actually took place in the preparation *of* us and *for* us for what was going to take place in 1955.

But although the number of the pages in this book make it necessary to walk more rapidly through the years than one day at a time, yet we must go back to the approaching New Year's Eve of 1949, our first in Champéry. After the candlelight service, a supper around the fireplace, then music and stories, we were to hear our first mountain village ringing-in of the New Year with fifteen minutes of the church bells. The bells of each village are joined by those of other villages, echoing among the mountains. In fact, all the bells of Switzerland ring for the same fifteen minutes! Our memory now includes many, many years of standing on the brink of a New Year, icy air blowing in our faces from open windows and doors, going out after communion together to be alone with the Lord, asking Him for help and strength for whatever is ahead . . . one day at a time.

That was the first year we had started in the mountains. Looking at the blue-white peaks in the starlight and moonlight, we remembered that as we looked we could know our help would not be coming from the majesty of the mountains, but from the Creator of those mountains, who has told us clearly our help is to come from the Maker of the heavens and earth, who is able to do all things. It is with Him that one day at a time becomes possible.

ONE YEAR IN RETROSPECT 15

The village bells had been ringing in the year 1950! Those Swiss bells weren't heard in Korea, nor would they have been appropriate in ushering in the beginning of the first of the Korean War years of 1950–1953. For us 1950 was an introduction to people and places that had been living through the Second World War, although we were starting our first full year in our new home in a neutral country! We were there to speak concerning "the battle for truth" and the need for teaching children the content and wonder of the Bible to equip them against the onslaught of the enemy of God. We also learned much of courage and bravery that many people had shown against physical enemies who at the same time were enemies of freedom.

We had about two and a half months of "normal life" before we left for our first trip to speak and also to start Children for Christ classes in Scandinavia. "Normal life" consisted of our writing Luke Lessons, packaging children's materials and carting them off to the post office to mail to various ones who were starting classes, and answering piles of correspondence. There were also such activities as washing clothes and sheets, Fran's chopping wood daily, caring for the furnace, marketing, having family prayers and reading times with the children, and having Sunday services (morning and evening then) in the chapel which had been "given" (loaned) to us to use for English-speaking church services. Soon there was an evening a week with girls coming for tea and discussion from Le Grand Verger, a finishing school in Champéry for the ski season. We all looked forward to the fascinating variety of girls with eager questions about life, and truth, and purpose. There were Zoroastrists from India, South American Roman Catholics, Swedish, American, Canadian, English girls of various backgrounds, and a German agnostic. Interest in the home-made cakes brought a question: "If we come some afternoon will you teach us to cook?" So a small cooking class was started, which also continued conversation in whatever area had been under discussion on Thursday night.

What were we "starting" as we began these evenings? Nothing. We were simply talking, discussing, answering questions, because an amazing opening had come to extend an invitation to anyone who might be interested in such an evening, and an eager response resulted. Would we ever see them again after they left Switzerland and the years went on? Some, never; a few have kept in touch. It seems to me the practical reality of living in the light of God's admonition to be faithful in little things, means we don't need to organize our talking to people under a heading or title of some kind. We really didn't think of these evenings as our "work," nor did we have any idea they were a shadow of things to come. A loving concern for people cannot extend to twenty-four hours a day, nor to an unending stream, because we are all people too, and have needs; we are all finite and limited. But a loving concern for people can only be shown in a quiet interest—taking some periods of time, and energy, which are *never* really convenient.

Occasional trips to Lausanne were necessary. One day found us hurrying through the dark streets at 6:00 A.M. with a flannel-board, a suitcase of supplies for children's classes, a typewriter to be repaired, the wooden wagon creaking and bumping along beside us, to catch the first train. Two huge pigs were stubbornly refusing to head straight down the village street to the train and kept agitating their master by turning into every side path. It added variety to life to race for a train with pigs going to market. Daylight came as we moved down the mountain and then slid along the lake past Castle Chillon, with four-year-old Debby announcing each thing she was seeing. "I just saw fifty-six fish in the water" was one we couldn't check on! She was going to spend the day with "Mama Turrian" and was radiant when we put her on the tram for La Rosiaz. "I'll say, *'La Rosiaz, s'il vous plait,'* and if there aren't enough punches on my card, I'll ask for another card," she said as she patted the money we had buttoned in the pocket of her snowsuit. Later she reported a safe arrival (we had checked by phone, however), saying, "People probably thought I was silly traveling all alone at my age, but I thought it was fun." Debby at four was most independent, and her pleasure at staying with Mme. Turrian comforted me when we left her there once during one of our trips to other countries.

By mid-March we were on our way for the long Scandinavian trip. Priscilla and Susan stayed this time at Home Eden in Champéry, a small children's pension where Susan was going daily to school. Priscilla boarded there and walked each morning to *École Alpina,* the boys' school which she attended as a day pupil at that time. The Andrés had invited Debby to stay with them, as they had a little girl the same age. Fran's carefully kept schedule shows a daily report of what took place during seven weeks in Sweden, Norway, Finland, and Denmark, and of the beginning of children's classes, the commencement of translation work on lessons, and our promise to send materials. I even wrote in my family letters (written on boats and trains) asking for yards of black flannel for flannelboards, as rationing made material hard to buy, and American missionary societies were glad to help.

To say that we traveled by third-class train and boats, and that the fare came to a total of $600, gives the basic facts, but leaves much to imagination. We had many surprises in travel! The boat was rolling sickeningly in the open stretch of the Baltic Sea, and we stayed on the deck in the fresh air until we were chilled to the bone. Assuring each other that it would soon be quiet in the Finnish archipelago (as it has been in the Swedish archipelago), we went to our tiny cabin to get some sleep. Suddenly . . . cr-a-a-ack . . . c-r-e-e-e-a-k—boom—crash . . . the boat shuddered. What could be happening? I scrambled out of my bunk, fixed my feet on a suitcase which took all the floor space, and leaned over to peer out of the tiny porthole. "Fran, come and look!" "You look and tell me about it," came his sleepy reply from the top bunk. "We're going through *ice!*" I couldn't believe my eyes as huge sheets of ice as big as tennis courts and seemingly five to eight inches thick were divided from each other by black streaks of water as the boat nosed through them.

The night was spent between trying to sleep and scrambling to look out when curiosity about new noises made sleep impossible. When the boat jerked and the ice thundered against its sides, suddenly coming to a full stop, this time Fran came tumbling out of the upper bunk to get to the porthole first. "Edith, there are *people* walking around on the ice!" It sounded unbelievable, but soon I found place for my feet and shared the porthole. I watched while a man with a lantern in his hand slowly approached the boat over uneven ice. After him came another man wheeling a barrowful of canvas bags, followed by a dignified gentleman dressed in a topcoat, felt hat, and carrying a suitcase as if he were in Union Station! The shore was off in the distance. A ladder descended past our window, and the dressed-up man ascended from the ice to the boat. "How," asked Fran, "do you buy a ticket from the middle of the ice to Abo?" We continued to watch as two men descended, mail bags were lifted off and also put on, and four men now walked slowly away, gingerly putting their feet down with great caution on their way to the shore. At the same time the boat moved away with much creaking and cracking of ice.

Morning brought cold sunshine to light the white ice and snow-covered islands with sparkling brilliance. Our arrival at Abo (the Finnish name is Turku, the Swedish is Abo—both languages are used in Finland) was a day early, so no one was there to meet us, and we only had the name of a church, not the pastor we were to be with. The taxi driver drove us through bleak countryside, dotted with boxlike wooden buildings standing in dirty snow, to a very humble wooden church. A woman who was hanging up clothes in the muddy yard spoke only Finnish but obviously was telling the driver where to take us. Not much later we were standing in a crowded little room on the third floor of a concrete apartment building, where a tiny home-made day bed, a piano and bench, and some other furniture left almost no floor space to put our bags, projector, slides, Children for Christ materials, screen, etc. Dismay? Bewilderment? We were wondering where we were to sleep.

It was a half hour later before Miss Anderson, our hostess, arrived to apologize in her halting English for not meeting us, because of course we were a day early. She was so happy to have us, and this was to be our room. She and another woman shared this three-room apartment, but now, she informed us, because of the 450,000 Finns made homeless by the war, it was a bit crowded, as everyone had to share their space. "Now we must rent one bedroom to another woman." So as they themselves shared the only other bedroom, this tiny third room was what they were so generously sharing with us—it was all they had. She proudly showed us that by shoving all the furniture over to one side, space could be made for the piano bench to become a bed. You see, it unfolded. When the top was lifted we discovered a hinged-together folding framework, hidden all day by the bench. With the unrolling of canvas, also stored in the bench, and the hooking together of the hinged pieces of wood—presto, a bed was there. Comfort is another thing, but with a quilt on top of the canvas, there was a place to sleep. One of us had this, the other one the day bed.

The beauty, on the part of many Finns these next ten days, of sharing whatever there was to share filled us with much emotion. Miss Anderson apologized for the fact that since the war most Finns were eating only two meals a day. Breakfast consisted of porridge and milk, bread made with dark rye flour, a bit of cheese, a berry sauce something like jam but with very little sugar, and coffee. The next meal came at 4:00 P.M., with boiled potatoes, a small amount of meat or sausage or fish, and some pudding and coffee. Vegetables were almost nonexistent and too expensive for ordinary people. Beets ground up in vinegar sauce were the only vegetable we had during the ten days. But the Finnish people had nothing different *after* ten days, as they stayed on in the same situation! Fruit was also scarce and expensive. Most families gathered the berries in the woods in the summer and served them for both fruit and vegetable. Coffee and some little cookies were the only extra treats in addition to the two meals. On menus the hot drinks listed were "coffee," "tea," or "silver tea"; we found that "silver tea" was just hot water, with a tiny bit of milk and sugar in it. A brave name invented in the war time when even tea and coffee were almost nonexistent.

Brave and courageous, uncomplaining and hard-working, sacrificing everything for freedom, the Finnish people should be an example to us in a very realistic way as we face question marks about what is worth fighting for in our own countries. Our admiration for these people was to grow as we came to know individuals and heard the history from those who had lived through it at such personal cost and variety of suffering. There is a monument built in the middle of a grassy lawn, right by the quay near the Territet boat dock, near Montreux, which honors General Carl Bon Mannerheim, who led the Finns in two wars, and whose Mannerheim line is known to many. The Swiss have erected this monument near to the place where he died. As we so often have walked along that quay, Fran and I have often stopped there to talk about Finland, our friends there, the history, the indomitable will of this man . . . and we have stood praying for the present Finland, and others in countries where the Iron Curtain or other forces are cutting off every variety of freedom to live and grow as a person.

A few hours after our arrival, we were sitting around a map and having some important bits of history made very real to us by our young interpreter, a pastor who had been a soldier serving in more recent needs of the country. If you can find on your map the section of Finland called Karjala, you will see that it is in the south, right by Russia. It is full of lakes, and we were told it is very beautiful. Many of the Russian nobility had summer homes in this area and fled there to live during and after the Russian Revolution. (We spent time in Finland with the brother of Mrs. Paul Wooley, whose husband Dr. Paul Wooley substituted for my father in "giving me away" at our wedding. She was visiting her brother the Baron, that summer of 1935 in Germany. When they fled Russia to their summer home, it was later totally taken away by the Russians. As we had this personal touch, we listened with even more interest.)

It was the winter of 1939–1940 when the Russians advanced against the Finns. Actually the war started November 30, 1939, and it is called the "winter war," lasting until March 13, 1940. It is an amazing thing, attributed by the Finns to answered prayer and the care of God, that this little nation was able to fight against that mighty and terrible neighboring enemy and win a victory.

During this war Russia took Karjala and Hanko (which you will find on your map between Helsinki and Abo). In 1941 the Finns were faced with a terrible decision. The Germans were advancing and the Russians were coming against the Germans. Russia had been an enemy of Finland for a long time. Finland had known and hated Communism. The Finns knew well the Russian determination for conquering the world, and they had experienced the ruthlessness of Russian soldiers. The whole of Finland had only the number of total inhabitants of the city of Philadelphia—how easily they could have been swallowed up by Russia! Should they join Russia against the Germans? In spite of the fact that at that time America and Russia were allies, our pastor-interpreter said, with strong conviction, "We knew it would be better to have Russia as an enemy than as a friend." They believed that if they allowed the Russians to come in as "friends," they would never leave the country after the war. Many Finns assured us during our time there, "We had only one choice—we know the Russians too well."

They joined the Germans against the Russians on June 24, 1941. The Germans went to the north of Finland, they told us, where there are very few Finns, and fought on that front, and the Finns themselves were fighting the Russians on the southern border. This lasted until August 1944. Picture the years of war for a people only as numerous as the city of Philadephia—with Russia! You have had glimpses of what was happening in St. Louis, and Scarsdale, and other parts of the world on that day the war was over and "the allies" had won. For the Finns it meant that Russia had won. However, by the grace of God they were again given the freedom for which they were fighting. Karjala was kept by the Russians. People lost their homes and almost all the furniture and paintings and other property in them, although at one time there appeared in Helsinki an enormous pile of stuff thrown together from many different houses, and people were allowed to go and search to see if they could find anything of theirs. Hanko was given back, but in its place Russia "rented" a piece of land for fifty years, sixty by sixty kilometers, right on the shore between Hanko and Helsinki—like a bite out of a sandwich.

When we left Abo for Helsinki, we experienced what it was like to travel through this bite of land by train. As our train approached the border of that section, it stopped, and a Russian engine was put on in place of the Finnish one. Then our windows were covered on the outside by iron curtains pushed into grooves made for that purpose, so that the car was pitch black inside. These remained in place while the train went through the Russian territory, with Russian soldiers standing, one at each door, "protecting" the cars! The Finns joked to us about this being "the longest tunnel in the world." The Finns living in that area were given two weeks, and some only two days, to leave their homes and land for fifty years, carrying only what they could take on buses or trains. The rest of the Finns provided space for them in their houses, and also built some housing projects. By the time we were there most of them had been provided with some sort of work too. Russia had imposed heavy war taxes which we had the feeling Finns were working unitedly to pay off, without grumbling.

Although Russia controlled their land and although the sea borders two sides, at their first election after the war, the Finns voted for the very man Russia had told them they could not have as President—General Mannerheim, who had led them in two wars! As we spoke from the platform in churches or halls and as we talked to individuals sharing meager meals and homes, we were looking into the faces of people whose courage had been tested "in the furnace," as well as some who had stepped out "into the fog," trusting the Lord far from any theoretical slogans.

Just what subject, and just what diploma, would cover the scope of lessons *we* were learning in Finland? We have nothing to hang on a wall, but unforgettable realities are tucked away in our memories of what the God of Gideon had been doing in *that* particular spot of His Tapestry among some "threads" that had looked to Him for strength. When you talk about what part Christians should have in revolution and in fighting for freedoms for the generation in which they are living, with hope for the next generation, in spite of their being a terrific minority, don't forget the Finns. I know all this has had an effect on some of what was hidden from us then, and is now past history, in *all* that prefaced the beginning of L'Abri.

Our talks were eagerly received in each place—Fran's lectures and his warm sermon about the need of reaching children, and my explanations about teaching children. We loved their singing, most of it in the minor key, led by violins and mandolins, sounding like the waves of the sea—sad, yet strong. What a diversity of praise goes up to the Lord from truly honest, believing hearts! People begged us to stay longer, and to come back. One old woman with just one tooth (no money for dental care, I'm sure), who had lost her home in that section the Russians took and who had lost her two sons in the war, clung to my hand and kept repeating with a smile, "You come back, you come back," in Finnish, of course.

One often wonders what "another choice" would result in, considering all the things one might choose to do. It would have been so easy for us to decide to stay in one country or another to work with children. I believe the Lord is very gentle to *His* children in leading each of us in our finiteness when He says, "If any one lack wisdom, let him ask. . . ." We are so lacking! We need to ask repeatedly.

We went from place to place, keeping up on our correspondence by taking out the little typewriter and setting it up in the most amazing spots. Every day, along with the office work, a letter also was written, or post cards, for the children. It is bad enough to be separated for a work they understand and care about— but communication must be kept up at any cost. My feeling has been that when all are in the same house together, one takes time to "stand on one foot" and talk, even when there is no time to talk . . . if one wants to stay close in family relationships. The same thing holds for writing a letter or a card when apart, and purchasing some surprises to take back. This is something that needs to be done "when there is no convenient time," or it doesn't get done at all. As I write today, I am refreshing my memory by reading a twelve-page letter (closely typed on legal-length paper) concerning our time in Finland which was written after we got to Denmark for my own mother and dad. Communication from one period of life to another period of life is also important.

One early morning found us being helped by a pastor who had brought a taxi to take us to the train and had presented us with second-class tickets to go to the next place as a special gift from the church. Pink azaleas were being pinned in Fran's buttonhole and on my shoulder by two smiling ladies, while the pastor carried out bags and all our "stuff." Soon we were waved off, sitting in elegance on upholstered seats instead of the wooden third-class ones, in a rusty old train. At a small town where we were to change trains, another pastor, dressed in riding jodhpurs, a shabby tweed jacket, and high-laced boots, with a high black caracul fur hat topping his smiling round face, met us to see that we got on the right train. He told us of tank traps, long lines of sharp natural rocks that we would be passing, "where our men stood holding them back for five months," and "no man's land," where the trees were blackened stumps. We were to watch out for these, because it would be soon after all that that we were to get off.

Finally we came to a jolting stop in an apparent wilderness. "Hurry, get off . . . it's not a regular stop . . . hurry." Out we tumbled, dragging our bags and other things, shoving them to each other. The train started almost before we got the last foot off the step, and we were alone in the wilderness! Then a sleigh came bouncing toward us as a young lad tried without much success to stop a half-broken horse. "Brrr," he said, rolling the r's (this is equivalent to "whoa" in English). But this horse, though Finnish, didn't seem to understand, and reared up. In a brief moment of time the bags were thrown in and I was pushed up beside them. Before the director of the Bible School and Fran could get in—swish—we were off at a gallop! "Take care of the projector and the screen," Fran shouted, and I held on for dear life, one hand and both knees caring for those precious objects, the other hand holding myself *in*. The boy standing on the runners behind me tried to guide the horse on the road, but the horse had his own ideas and tilted the sled as he ran halfway up a bank as if he wanted to dump out the contents. I won, though. I was still there with the baggage intact when he stopped in front of the school which suddenly seemed to appear out of the forest. Fran and the director of the school walked, arriving about a half hour later.

Our welcome was an unforgettable one. Strangely, at that time of history, America didn't have saunas, and I had never heard of a sauna! I can't imagine this now, but it was so. When Fran arrived, the director announced to the small group gathered for tea, "First I take Mr. Schaeffer to sauna, then" (nodding to the lady Bible teachers) "you take Mrs. Schaeffer to sauna." It was all in Finnish, but even when he translated for us, we hadn't a clue what we were being taken to. Supper had been served and I was eating when Fran and the director came in, looking like boiled lobsters. "What is it, Fran?" I whispered anxiously. "Oh, you'll find out" was all he would say to me.

I was helped out of my chair, and three ladies indicated that I should follow them. (Gesticulating was our only form of communication. Finnish has no relationship to any language I know, and they understood no English.) Arriving through the snow at a wooden building that looked like a shed for undressing for swimming, we came into a room with hooks to hang clothing. "What next?" I wondered. I got the idea, but was mystified—totally. One of the women opened a door and motioned me to follow her. The blast of heat hit me almost like something solid! It was the real thing—rocks heated all day by burning wood—all prepared in our honor. Or was it an initiation? I had an old-fashioned sauna—birch sticks, the pail of cold water sloshed on me at the end, and all. Then after a glass of pink lemonade, we began the walk back, going out into the frigid air, exuding heat waves! The door I expected to have lead me back to the supper table, opened instead to take me immediately to the platform where Fran had just finished his lecture on liberal theology, and I was introduced like this: "And here is *Mrs.* Schaeffer . . . coming from her first sauna . . . who will now speak to us!" A roar of laughter greeting me, and I was "on"! I think it was our most unique welcome, anywhere—certainly in a Bible school.

We met a bishop, a leading government official, all sorts of people. And finally, after a tremendously full ten days, we stood on the deck of a boat again, waiting to set forth. A whole group of girls sang hymns as a farewell, and dear Miss Anderson, our first hostess, handed us a special Finnish teddy bear called Nallee, home-made of natural brown sheepskin, for Debby, to say "thank you" for letting her mother help Finnish children. We parted with hearts full and tears close, wondering when we would ever be back. Many years later Debby's husband, Udo, a Worker and Member of L'Abri for so long now, went to speak in Helsinki along with Fran. And a number of Finnish young people have come to L'Abri who weren't even born when we were there. Some of the books have been translated into Finnish now too. But no such ideas of what might be future ever entered our imaginations.

We set forth into a thick fog, and anchors went down that night, and much of the next day. We were thankful for a tiny cabin rented us by one of the crew, with a narrow bench to sleep on, and to use for a desk as we set up office. We were to be thirty hours late . . . and the sister boat *Bore One* struck a rock during the night, necessitating the transfer of its 213 passengers to lifeboats. We were even able to call Stockholm and break our first appointments, as well as to experience a vivid reality of what a break in the fog meant as sun came through and the engines began to throb again. Using our time of waiting to such good advantage and having that sharp contrast of the waiting come to an end, gave us a new impetus to "keep on" until the foggy night of waiting for the Lord is over, when the Son of God will return with all His radiance to bring a rapid ending to all the difficulties that squash us in one way or another.

We had had our time in Sweden before going to Finland, and our Swedish friends cared for us that day in Stockholm before putting us on the night train for Oslo. When is finiteness not something of an agony in the area of making decisions? We had thirty-seven letters that had arrived for us, and Fran needed to dictate some answers that day; a variety of people were wanting "a few minutes of time to talk" and we had just come from two nights in that squashed cabin. But time then—and space on pages of a book now—have a great relationship to each other. All I can say is that in trying to give "One Year in Retrospect" as a part of The Tapestry, the magnifying glass must move rapidly past some of the threads woven into that year. We had had fifteen meetings in ten days in Sweden, most of them for Children for Christ. Now, thirty years later, Staffan and Lisa, who have been Workers in Swiss L'Abri for four years, are soon going back to Sweden. Who knows what interweaving has taken place of "threads" one has lost sight of? The books and films are being used in Sweden too . . . but that also is ahead of the year we are talking about in this chapter.

Just as the casting of fishing nets fascinated us in Stockholm, so the mixture of buildings and boats thrilled us in Oslo. Norway has such a diversity of beauty with its multitude of fjords, lakes, rocks, hills, mountains, and pines. The folks who had met us and were driving us in their car were remembering that just ten years ago that day—April 9, 1940—they had awakened to find that the Germans were entering Norway. As we looked through the trees, over the rocky gardens, and down to the shining waters of the fjord below, they were telling us, "The warships entered right through there. . . ." They shook their heads as they relived the time vividly—planes roaring overhead, boats filling their harbors, and the occupation that followed for five years. Some of their pastors had been imprisoned in Norway, while others were sent to concentration camps or work camps in Germany. In the north of Norway, many whole towns were burned to the ground, and the Free Church had lost some church buildings, a school, and an old folks' home.

As we heard these things, we realized how short a time five years is and how vivid memories are. I thought of the reality of our oneness which cannot be broken by any sudden changes of governments in our mutual citizenship which is in heaven! How amazing to think that all the little children who were in our many audiences in our seventeen days in Norway are all in their thirties or forties by now. Blond hair and red hats, sweaters, or scarves seemed to brighten all the churches full of people. We became very fond of Pastor Engeset in Oslo, who had not only preached there for thirty years by then, but had written many lovely hymns. At Fredrikstad, the pastor and his wife and four children doubled up to give us a place to stay, and then became very enthusiastic about starting Children for Christ work right away.

How can I describe Fran's Easter sermons, the various conferences, the individual conversations, except to say that the warmth of reception and increasing invitations to stay or come again could easily have resulted in a totally different story. Now, in looking back, we have the certainty that the Lord was preparing us to do more for Norway through what He would lead us to do in Switzerland. It is amazing how many Norwegians have been at L'Abri!

My permanent reminder of Norway is a special Norwegian dress that was made for me and presented during this trip as a complete surprise. It seems very appropriate now, since a new branch of L'Abri (moved from California) has been started in Rochester, Minnesota—a town with many Norwegians, and a state with a Norwegian Governor (Al Quie). The wonder of being able to look back over so many ten-year periods is to see the intricacy of the pattern in the threads that are entered to be used later with great richness.

Threads! In the carefully embroidered pocket of that wonderfully embroidered white wool dress is a yellowed bit of paper with a handwritten note. On the evening of January 22, 1981, Fran and I were on our way to the Governor's mansion in St. Paul, Minnesota, for a special dinner in our honor. I pulled my precious envelope out to read the note to Governor and Mrs. Al Quie, and to Bob and Avis Dieseth, as we stood in the hall of the mansion. "Listen to this," I said, "I've worn this Norwegian dress because I think it is so appropriate for you Norwegians." The note explains:

> BUNAD—an original Norwegian dress.
> It gives different "bunads" in Norway—one for every part of the country.
> This one is a VALLSET *bunad*—Vallset is not far away from Oslo—only about 12n miles—near *Hamar*.
> The composer is Miss Olava Ansteinson—a well known artist here in Norway—and abroad too—Mrs. Sophie Lien—her sister—has embroidered it—and made it to the nice and becoming Vallset-*bunad*.
> Inger Margrethe Lien

With this came a card sending best greetings from Oslo. Bob Dieseth exclaimed, "Hamar! Why, that is the village where my father was born!" "Amazing," remarked the governor.

The evening was even more amazing, however. As we began our dinner at the beautifully set table, Governor Quie prayed as one only can who is in constant communication with the Lord. Praying about many things, he also prayed for the new president, Reagan, as he and Gretchen had just come from the inauguration. Then in a time of our hearing something of the background of each of the guests, we were stunned at the Lord's weaving, His detail of design. Almost every one there that night had had some special help from the books, from the films, or from being at L'Abri.

Mr. Arthur Sidner, a tall fine black, Director of State Planning for Minnesota, said he had gone far from believing God existed back in 1963 in Washington University, St. Louis, when someone gave him Francis Schaeffer's books *Escape from Reason* and *The God Who is There*. These had brought him to a place of certainty and belief and changed his life. His wife said, "I've run our home by *Hidden Art* and *What Is a Family* that Edith Schaeffer wrote, so though you didn't know us, we do know you." We were stunned! Paul Marshall, who had been helping in the governor's campaign, had been a Farel House student in Swiss L'Abri before that; Mr. Eggen, a banker in the Twin Cities, had helped enthusiastically with the seminar in Minneapolis for the film *Whatever Happened to the Human Race?* The Dieseths spoke of their time in Swiss L'Abri having turned their lives completely around, and the governor spoke of their son-in-law having been greatly helped in Swiss L'Abri, and also of his own time in Washington as a congressman having brought him into contact with Fran's books through his friend, Representative Jack Kemp. Gretchen Quie had been a member of Joanne Kemp's study group called "The Schaeffer Class," during which about twenty-five congressmen and senators' wives (the number is limited) study our books chapter by chapter, discuss, and pray together.

But in 1950, as our first Scandinavian trip came to an end and we "slid" through the German landscape on our way to Basel on the Scandinavian Express, we were not dreaming of threads being woven into a pattern that might be glimpsed in 1981. Just what human committee could have planned it? With what method?

We had talked with Mme. A. by phone so knew Debby had had bronchitis, but when we saw two little girls, identical straw hats tied under their chins, racing to meet us, we scarcely recognized Debby with her face so white and her hair arranged quite differently. Soon a little pair of arms had given us a strangling hug, and she was perched on her daddy's shoulders hugging the new teddy bear Nallee who had made the trip safely under my arm all the way. We were soon on our way to the Lausanne station with Ninette leading the way, and Mme. A. telling me all about Debby's illness and the doctor's good care (as he lived in the same building).

Waiting for us at the Champéry station were two beaming
jumping-jacks with *le petit char* (the wooden wagon) and Vic, waiting behind them. Unlike Debby, Priscilla and Susan were not
troubled by silence. Both of them tried to talk at once and continuously all the way home, and for the next few days. Everything
that had happened in the seven weeks—both happy and sad—
came tumbling out. Life in Home Eden was described minutely,
with hilariously accurate imitations of the teachers and the mothers who had come to visit. As a surprise for us, the house was
a bower of daffodils, picked by the girls in the fields and filling
every pitcher and vase in the house. Life was not just a sudden
time of uninterrupted joy, however. Fran had picked up a bad
cold in Norway and there was a grippe epidemic in the village,
so we had one form or another among us, along with cold rainy
weather. Packages of Children for Christ materials had to be laboriously wrapped up, and the discouraging moment came when
most of them were returned from the post office to be rewrapped
to meet postal specifications!

We had seven weeks of this "normal life" during which the
excitement of digging up and planting the vegetable garden in
the front yard took place. The seeds had come from Burpee's in
Philadelphia, and nothing could match the wonder of seeing the
variety of green shoots come up in that garden in the Swiss Alps
except the wonder of eating the crop a few months later. A sight
that staggered the villagers more than that of seeing us install
the garden, however, was seeing Priscilla, Susan, Debby walking
with a young goat, scrubbed and fluffed up, a blue satin ribbon
tied around his neck, and a new rope as a leash. After the scrubbing
of his wee kid, which the children had rescued from being someone's Sunday dinner (they had been petting it at the "milk lady's
chalet"), they had perfumed it and were going to make it an
unusual pet. This lasted a few weeks before the chores connected
with keeping the basement room "clean and sweet," assigned
to Priscilla, became too heavy to bear.

Three birthdays were celebrated before we had to leave for
Southern France with all the materials for presenting Children
for Christ there. Debby became five early in May, Susan nine
later in the month, and just the day we were leaving, June 18,
Priscilla had her thirteenth birthday. We celebrated that the day

before with a special dinner topped off by cake. Our meal was shared by a retired officer in the WAVES, Mary N., who had contracted an incurable malady that left her with no feeling in her fingers. Mary N. was to stay with the girls the four days we were away. The mixture of longing to stay home and of being sure we were to fulfill the requests from pastors in southern France produced the type of sighs we were so often to experience. That particular time the briefness of separation helped, and we were soon to be doing a piece of traveling together as a family.

Although it was six o'clock in the evening when we stepped off the train at Nîmes station, the sun was still hot and bright. No one was in sight to meet us, so we carried our bags and all the equipment through the old station until we reached the sidewalk. Now what, we wondered. Suddenly a little car splashing dust turned and came to a stop in front of us. Pastor Samouelian and his fat little three-year-old son had come to pick us up. We drove through the century-old streets past the Colosseum of Nîmes, built by the Romans, crumbling, but still in use as bright yellow placards announced a bullfight that week. We turned down an even narrower street bordered by the typical stucco or yellowish plaster houses. The streets were full of holes and dust was everywhere, with hot sun beating down and not even a tree or a blade of grass in sight.

"Here we are!" We stepped out and almost immediately into the house through the doorway opening directly onto the sidewalk. It was cooler inside the thick walls, where stone floors and closed shutters helped to keep the house cool. The pastor's wife, thin and tired-looking, greeted us and showed us the room where we were to sleep—obviously their living room, with heavy furniture and a pump organ and surprisingly original oil paintings covering the walls. The pastor had done the paintings himself before he got too busy in his work. We were taken to have tea out in a courtyard, which we found was the courtyard for the church and the school as well as for their house.

That night, giving the story of Gideon with the flannel board and following with discussion, we did not get to bed until midnight, and 6:00 A.M. was to be our departure time to drive to the district meeting of the Methodist Church where we were to speak during the day. I wish I could take pages to describe the dipping, jogging, swaying, of our drive through the most interesting hills and ancient villages, past streams where women were beating dirt out of their clothing on rocks and washing them in the running water. We had a fascinating day as Fran discussed what he felt was so essential to these pastors to encourage them in their firm stand for the truth and against liberalism and Barthianism. They wanted to send a representative to Geneva for the I.C.C.C meeting. While we were presenting the Children for Christ material which was being translated into French, the church women listened "around the edges" as they busied themselves cleaning rabbits for the dinner they were getting ready to cook for thirty-five people. Our travel from there on was by bus, except for the final train trip back to Switzerland.

We had one evening at home to read the mail, dash off a few imperative notes, and begin sorting out Bible School material to take to Germany. Then there was one day to weed the garden and cultivate it, adding some fertilizer and other aids for our three weeks away. This time there were suitcases to pack for us all, but by 10:00 P.M. clothing was laid out to jump into in the morning, each child's hair was washed, and their rucksacks were readied with their own personal things. After they were all tucked in we still had Bible School to pack for!—from report cards to colored stars, study books and flannelgraph stories. Not much time to spend in bed; by 5:30 we were all up again, and soon on our way down the village street to the station. The girls had proudly stuffed the hard-boiled eggs and fruit into their red, green and blue rucksacks which we had brought them from Norway and Denmark. We made quite a procession!

Where on earth were we going now? To Dachau, Germany, to fulfill a request from Captain Meyers to have a Bible School for American Army children at the post there. With their parents they lived in the red brick Nazi officers' headquarters, then converted into American officers' homes. "Afraid you'll never hold these children without handwork," was what we were told. Forty-five children came that first morning to see what it would be like—forty-five laughing, pushing, skipping children who shoved open gates in spiked-top walls, and raced over ground that had been walked on by the doomed (even during the lifetime of these tots). There is a bleakness and depression that hits people living in a spot that has so recently been a concentration camp, but children *can* ignore history in the present of their lives. We had a hard time finding teachers for our Bible School, as there weren't many people who were understanding Christians. Priscilla and one of the chaplain's daughters helped teach, and three other women and Fran and myself. Then Fran held a series of evening meetings for adults, with a series of sermons. He gave fifteen messages there in Dachau.

Closing night of Bible School was the climax of the two weeks. All afternoon we had had thundershowers. Would this stop people from coming in response to the invitations the children had held so tightly in their hands as they ran home through rain? The little chapel had been built by prisoners during the war, out of scraps of wood and material, and it was situated inside the stockade, across a stream of water that had been electrified during the war to keep people in the concentration camp. Music floating out of the windows reached both the ears of American soldiers held in the stockade prison for some misdemeanor, and displaced persons in their camp from which we were separated by only a high barbed wire fence. Here hundreds of DPs were living in tiny two-room apartments (if such a name could be applied to drab wooden shacks) which during the war had been occupied by thousands of the Dachau concentration camp inhabitants.

Through the rain people began to come—officers of various ranks, wives and little tots, proud students of the Bible School with their Bibles under their arms, and even some curious G.I.s. "We haven't had this many people since Christmas," the chaplain exclaimed excitedly. Visitors were also coming from other posts to see what kind of a Bible School this had been. One of our teachers leaned over to whisper to me, "There's the head chaplain from the Munich Bible School. All they had were songs like 'I'm a little teakettle, short and stout,' and they made Indian teepees." She couldn't wait for them to hear what our children had learned.

Never have I heard such a fine closing night for such a short school. The books of the Bible came out loud and clear and the choruses were sung with much enthusiasm. The little tots (three and four years old) answered their questions led by one pale little girl with an enormous voice! The five-year-olds were led by Debby, who stood up straight and tall, thrilled to be in a real Bible School with other children. They said the 100th Psalm quite perfectly, the Lord's Prayer, and twenty-five of the children's catechism. On we went through all the classes, sandwiching songs and short object lessons in between the recitations to show what the children had had, but to speak to the parents too. The last class closed with the 90th Psalm and many questions and answers from the geography of Palestine and Bible history.

Two weeks we had had the children—none having been in any Bible School previously—yet what a testimony they were to the worthwhileness of the time spent in having such a school. The parents were really flabbergasted with what their children had learned in nine mornings. The Air Force major got up and spoke of the fact that he imagined many parents and friends had realized how little they had taught their children in all the years of their lives. He went on to say he wanted Fran to come back and give the whole Air Force (four thousand men there) a talk on the moral implications of the Occupation in the light of a Christian viewpoint. Fran said that he felt God would hold our country responsible for signing away so much of Europe to Russia in the peace treaties, and also for the generally un-Christian attitude and actions of those making up our Occupation forces in Germany and Austria.

You have all had descriptions of Munich and Dachau after the war, but we saw them then only five years after the war had ended, in a way that made a lasting impression on us. Not only did we see the gas chambers and gas ovens before they were made into a museum, but Fran met and talked with an artist who had been a survivor of Dachau and bought a sketch from him which he has always kept on his study wall—a forlorn tragic figure of a very thin man standing looking out through barbed wire. We saw the center of Munich with bombed-out apartment houses with the curtains still at stark windows in half-broken walls. A bombed-out department store surrounded by ornamental lamps, twisted and black, with shades still on some of them and filaments sticking out at all angles, seemed to speak so loudly: "What is man? What misery if our only hope is to be in the goodness of mankind!"

Back in Dachau we strolled along a walk, a breeze fluttering the leaves of the trees on either side. Coming to one that looked perfect for a child's swing, we were informed by a sign—here, many were hung. A bleeding heart was growing under the tree. We were taken through the largest building by a Polish survivor of Dachau. "I was just like a skeleton when the Americans came in to free us. I don't go back to Poland, I am no Communist," he said. "Yes, five years ago we were liberated." As we stood in the furnace room where steel stretchers still remained, he played idly with a torture rack, and our minds echoed his words. "Five years ago—not a century ago—not in the dark ages—civilized people, university people, scientists put these charts on the doors telling how long it would take for the gas to kill people—Jews, Polish people, political prisoners, people too weak or old or sick to be of any use to society—five years ago."

As we returned to our temporary home on the post, the radios were blaring forth the news of the War in Korea (as the Communist north moved against the south), and the Air Force in Munich was immediately put on a six-hour alert. What honest and real comfort could we give anyone involved? What comfort can we have in the multiplied agonies and fears of such a wide variety of devastation, viewed or contemplated in such short periods of time? What is ahead of any of us?

The only true and reliable comfort is the comfort the Lord told us to comfort one another with. We are to remind ourselves, and each other, that He is coming again, and we are to meet Him in the clouds. We are going to be like Him, with the same sort of body He had when He rose from the dead. The New International Version of the Bible puts it, "For the Lord himself will come down from heaven with a loud command, with the voice of an archangel and with the trumpet call of God, and the dead in Christ will rise first. After that we who are still alive and are left will be caught up with them in the clouds to meet the Lord in the air. And so we will be with the Lord forever. Therefore encourage each other with these words." What an encouragement to keep on! What an incentive to make the truth known, and to make known the fact that truth exists. Unchangeable truth that cannot be voted out by a committee of people! God's truth.

The final evening, after Fran's last message, one young Army wife from Atlanta, Georgia, sobbed her thanks for his sermon as she came out. "We don't live right over here. We need messages like that but we don't get them!" That, and many other invitations to come back, voiced in a variety of ways, bore heavily upon our emotions and thoughts. How do you know? What constitutes a call? Should we give our time to Americans living under these very unnatural conditions? Where were we meant to be?

Never do you—do we—get past the problem of choice, the mystery of choice and the Lord's plan, the Lord's weaving of threads in His plan, the need to have balance in asking for His will, then courageously making specific choices. We always face the reality that to say "yes" to one set of things we are doing in an hour, a day, a week, a month, or a year is to be saying "no" to another set of things, because we cannot be doing two things at once. This reality applies to saying "yes" to people, and "no" to people too. Finiteness is limiting, and we remain finite. We didn't cease to pray for the Army, Navy, Marines, and Air Force in various parts of the world, in spite of being reassured that we were to keep on, for the time, in exactly what we were doing. We had no idea then that the Lord was laying a foundation for eventually reaching more people in the military forces through books and films than our changing our work and going in person could ever have done!

Years later, Priscilla and I, during our one time of taking a speaking invitation as mother and daughter, were to go to Berchtesgaden in Germany to speak at a conference of leaders in the Protestant Women of the Chapel groups from every military post in Europe. There were over four hundred there. Many of them had read the *L'Abri* story, which was already out, as well as Fran's first books. Priscilla had lecture times and workshops on relationships in marriage and the family, and among other things I gave "The Bird's Eye View of the Bible," which I was soon to be putting into book form in *Christianity Is Jewish*.

It was astounding to be standing at the very lectern where Hitler had spoken (Berchtesgaden was the site of Hitler's headquarters, and also a ski resort for his top people, with a fabulous elevator going up inside a small mountain), in this lodge which is now used by American military people for conferences of all sorts. What a contrast in messages! I began with a "bird's eye view of where relativism had come from," borrowing from my husband's book *The God Who Is There,* as he speaks of Hegel as the doorway. Think of Hegel's effect on Hitler in the realm of his providing a "base" for Hitler's actions. People open doors "down" for following generations—down into depths of despair which they didn't realize would be down those cellar steps, so to speak. The next generation takes things farther in various directions—sometimes better, thank God, and sometimes worse! Hegel lived from 1770 to 1831, Nietzsche from 1844 to 1900, and Hitler from 1889 to 1945. Ideas and philosophies don't end up just in people's heads or on the pages of books, but in the actions of individual lives and nations. To get back to my message from that podium that not so many years before had had its last speech from Hitler—it went on to give the bird's eye view of the Bible as I traced the "lamb" throughout the Scripture. What magnificent continuity the Bible gives us of the door of salvation and communication with God the Father, through the Lamb, His Son.

What Priscilla and I gave in those days of speaking, nights of talking into the wee hours, and listening informally to marvelous singing (with some blacks who really knew how to sing), was to be taken back to various posts and taught to others, via copious notes in notebooks, and books. Just a few weeks ago at a seminar for *Whatever Happened to the Human Race?* in Honolulu, a medical officer and his wife came up to send greetings to Priscilla who had been such a help "back there when. . . ."

In February of 1980, Fran and I, along with two L'Abri couples, Mary Jane and Greg, Jim and Gail, were to have an incredible view of an olive-drab United States military plane come swooping down from a clear blue sky, skimming along parallel to the mountains and making a perfect landing on the Swiss army airfield in Sion. It was incredible not simply because it was beautiful, but because to the best of our knowledge it was the first time an American military plane had ever flown over a part of Switzerland, let alone landed! Because Switzerland is a neutral country, it has no arrangement for air passage for American military planes to fly across; hence the pilots always have to skirt around Switzerland. What on earth was this plane doing?

I need to shorten a long story. Some weeks before this, we had had a phone call from Heidelberg. Chaplain Lieutenant Colonel Richard Perkins wanted Fran to speak at the National Prayer

Breakfast at the Heidelberg headquarters of the U. S. military community. Fran said he was afraid he could not, first, because he had had symptoms of a cancer flare-up and we needed to be going to Mayo Clinic by early February, and second, he simply could not travel and speak at 7:00 A.M. He added, "Perhaps Edith could speak." Permission had to be given by "higher authorities" to have a woman speak at a prayer breakfast with top generals present. Research also was made to see whether a plane could be sent to make the travel easy—a one-hour flight from a nearby spot. Both possibilities seemed impossible!

Several officers, including Lieutenant Colonel Perkins, began not only to work on this project that they felt so important, but to pray earnestly. By earnestly I mean that for a time they made it a special priority to get up at 5:00 A.M. and urgently "pray the impossibilities away." Day by day, things began to happen . . . such as permission being given for me to speak (as some of my books were looked over, and perhaps some bits even read!) and the issuing of "status" for three days for the two of us. Fran was to be a three-star general (in status) and I a two-star general! The U. S. Army issued this flight permission: "From Heidelberg Army Airfield to either Bex or Sion Airport, Switzerland, and return to Heidelberg Army Airfield, 6 February 1980, to transport Dr. Francis A. Schaeffer, GSE-17, and his wife Edith, GSE-16, to speak at the National Prayer Breakfast in Heidelberg." It is a long paper with all the details of arrival and departure times in both directions and so forth. After that, of course, permission still had to be given by the Swiss, and miles of red tape had to be unraveled.

It was a thrilling thought that God can unravel an impossible tangle of red tape, in order to take two threads He wants to weave into The Tapestry in a particular spot at a particular time. Had we no choice? A million times, yes. When we received the news by phone and in impressive documents, although the way things had worked out was startling and a bit breathtaking, we had a choice. We had to say "yes" or "no." What we had been told was that the Swiss had researched all our dossier (that would have gone back over all of our living in Switzerland from 1948 on, a crucial part of which you don't know about yet) and had issued special permission for this plane to fly in to Sion Military

Airport, get us, fly out in a specified route over the mountains to Heidelberg, fly back again the 8th of February, and deposit us once more! Times of arrival and departure were precise. The further step had been taken of sending a document to Moscow to inform whoever keeps track of such things (!) that this flight was to be made for speakers for the National Prayer Breakfast.

We also were given our tentative schedule. I was to speak at the prayer breakfast for precisely twenty minutes, being called for at 6:20 A.M. to get there a bit early. My wake-up call was for 5:20 A.M. (though I was awake when it came). Fran was to speak at a luncheon for chaplains and their wives from Heidelberg and the surrounding communities. Dinner in the evening was to be with a group of colonels, in the home of one of them, and the evening meeting at the Patrick Henry Village Chapel was to show the last episode of *Whatever Happened to the Human Race?*, with Fran giving a short lecture first, and answering questions afterwards.

Remember, this is a flash ahead, thirty years into the future from the year that is the focus of this chapter. We had been concerned for the military communities in 1950, and had not stopped being concerned. L'Abri had been a help to a number of military people of a variety of ranks in the intervening years, and the books had gone to the front to help many in Vietnam, Korea, and various places, including West Point. (We have piles of letters that could be copied here!) This 1980 invitation was coming in the midst of prayer that the new film would be widely used in the various military posts in the world. We could see continuity of our concern as we prayed, and we felt the right answer was "yes."

It was a thrilling experience to fly in a little plane for the first time over the Swiss Alps on a gloriously clear day (sandwiched in by terrible weather both before and after). We were rewarded with a never-to-be-forgotten glimpse of some of God's creation, and, inside the plane, conversation both going and coming back was extremely worthwhile. The Lord very specifically answered prayer for His strength in our weakness in the speaking, and gave us the "words" we had prayed for. As to "results," Chaplain Perkins wrote to us with comments from "generals to those of enlisted men and women telling of what the visit meant." I will give only one out of the many. From a young chaplain: "Last Monday I was ready to resign and get out of the Army and quit the ministry. Now I have been revived. I am going back to my place of ministry and *be* what God has called me to be. My words have been right, but my heart has been so cold. Now my heart is on fire. . . . God has given me new courage and new zeal to be faithful to Him." Chaplain Perkins went on to say in his letter that the next Sunday they had a larger attendance at chapel than he had ever seen in his time. Strangely enough, while I was writing this chapter, a call came from him, saying that now, a year later, the effects of those three days is still bearing fruit.

Before going back to 1950, there are two things I feel I must say in the whole thing of "choice" and finding "God's will." First, in the "escalator look" that Fran and I now have because of having so many years to look back on, we can see an amazing number of ways that we probably have been able to be more help to the military by having L'Abri and writing the books than if we had stayed in Munich in 1950. Certainly it was not cleverness on our part that this is what took place. It was *not* our plan to have anything like L'Abri, nor did we ever expect to write books. All we did was take one stepping stone at a time, live one day at a time, asking God that we might be honest and sincere in wanting His will, and courageous in continuing to do it when it was made known.

The second thing is that *it was not easy to spend those three days in Heidelberg.* The criterion of being in God's will is *not* that things then are made easy. Fran felt more miserable than he had ever felt. His breathing was labored because—we later discovered— he had water in his lungs. At the colonel's dinner he spent most of his time alone in a bedroom eating very lightly, unable to face more than some juice and a bit of the food and feeling he could *not* lecture or give answers to the crowded chapel that night. But, at each moment when he needed to speak—and this was true for me too—an almost visible flow of strength came, like a transfusion from God, in answer to having asked for His strength for the task. All that the audience was aware of was that the messages, or the answers, were clear and were given with some measure of power.

The next couple of days, and our arrival at Mayo Clinic, must come later in the book. We need to finish that "one year in retrospect"—1950—in which we have progressed only as far as June.

We arrived back from Dachau to have almost no time to unpack before three missionaries arrived for the summer—Dot Roberts and Marion MacNiel from Africa and Edna Barter from India. Not only were they going to attend the I.C.C.C. Congress in Geneva, but this was to be a mixture of rest and helping in a variety of ways, from gardening and office work to tutoring the children in English school work. They compared notes as to who had the largest scorpions, the least rainfall, and the worst malaria attacks! In addition Miss Barter offered to give swimming lessons, and daily the girls enthusiastically tore down the hill to the swimming pool, returning for dinner bedraggled but full of stories of progress made. Posters had to be made for the Children for Christ booth we were going to have at the Congress, and I typed and retyped Fran's speech, as he kept needing to shorten it.

Fran kept going to Geneva to make various arrangements, and brought the Hedegards from Sweden up to spend the first weekend. You can imagine the scramble to double up the children, and prepare another guest room. Then came the first of August, and the village was full of Americans from our Congress . . . which made it seem unreal! That summer is a blur of gardening, making jams and jellies, serving meals to as many as twenty-five guests at a time as people came up from the Congress to "see Champéry." Through my limited view from the kitchen window suddenly appeared not only American heads like Phil Clark's and Peter Stam's, which seemed to belong thousands of miles away—but heads of people from the countries we had just been visiting. The Finnish delegation slept in our house one weekend, among them Pastor Salaranto, who had told us the history of the wars, and the Bible school director who had had the sauna prepared for us! There was Mr. Modalsli from Norway who disappeared before breakfast, later to say, pointing to an impossibly distant glacier, "Sorry, I took a little bread and went for a walk . . . up there. . . . Norwegians are incredible hikers!

The Congress itself took a chunk of time, but the stream of people coming early, or staying weeks later, continued until September 11. It would take pages to describe the mixture of all that took place. While Fran, as recording secretary, took minutes in the Theater where the Congress was held, I stayed at a table that was the Children for Christ Booth, explaining the work to people from Singapore, Hong Kong, and Palestine, as well as those who came from Europe and America. The children each "did their own thing:" Susan was heard to remark, "I got *so* much out of it today; I listened all day in Portuguese." The lectures were simultaneously translated and the little "sound boxes" were fun to plug into. Debby listened usually in French, and was seen to vote, both by raising her hand and by saying "aye"! As for Priscilla, her time was spent in helping translate in the office, running errands, and helping in the press office, with an earphone plugged in to hear what was going on at the same time. Mrs. Max Belz taught her to operate the mimeographing machine.

Before Fran's lecture at the Congress, he went to visit Karl Barth. Bad connections resulted in his missing his train, so he had to walk from Aigle but didn't realize how far it was. Fortunately, he finally got a ride with a villager, and as he ate his warmed-up dinner by the fireplace that evening, he told us about his interview. Now he knew his paper for the Congress would be giving a true picture of this school of thought, he told us.

Early in the week Fran's paper was given, and I went into the auditorium to hear it, not because I had not heard it before, but because I wanted to be praying as he was giving it—the wife's part. Among those from Switzerland who had come for that lecture, were Frau Dr. Wasserzug from Beatenberg and Dr. and Mrs. Alexander from Geneva's Le Roc.

As mid-September came and the last visitor left, fatigue overtook us. The doctor said that we must go away for ten days at least, as he feared I might lose the baby. You see, I was three months pregnant. That ten days in Alassio was a special gift of the Lord. Our modest, rather bleak hotel (as to food and room) was beside a wonderful beach where warm sand and salt water brought tremendous relaxation. Fran sat reading stacks of printed matter, but I shut my eyes and did nothing, or else floated on the restful water. We walked through the clean stone streets, narrow between plaster buildings, the walls alive with twittering canaries hung on hooks outside the windows. We were impressed with the antiquity of the place as we followed a road above the town, built in Caesar's time. Man's life is so short compared to

the length of time bricks remain useful . . . and the blue sea
continues . . . and the wind blows through the same pine trees.
But where is Caesar? Where are the myriad people who have
walked this same way? Suddenly eternal life becomes more precious than ever. The myriad are somewhere. There is eternal life,
and for those who have "walked on the way that leads to eternal
life" there will be a fulfillment of God's promises in places which
far surpass the Mediterranean, made by the same Creator! Made
for us to walk in forever and ever. That is the rest He has pointed
to when He tells us, "This is not your rest." No vacation here
is worth comparing to the rest which is ahead.

We came home all full of plans for October. But it was a time
when "Lord willing" had to be looked at full in the face, not as
an expression but as a "bowing before Him." October was to
be a month of physical trouble but personal spiritual blessing.
On October 4 the loss of the baby we had been looking forward
to welcoming was a great disappointment—to each of the family.
While I was still in bed, struggling with emotions and reading
the Bible with much soul-searching, as well as feeling terrifically
weak, Debby came to give me a loving hug, and I discovered
that she was feverish. "My neck hurts, back here," she announced.
The thermometer was brought, and I soon found she had a temperature of 102° . . . but it went to 104° in two hours. This
was the beginning of a variety of grippe, current at that time,
which each one of the family had. When the doctor came a week
later to look at Debby, who had then started an acute dysentery
and vomiting, he left remedies and said he would return the next
week. It was a week of very real nursing care on my part, and
very little food or sleep on Debby's.

Meantime the Lord had supplied—really so, in a specific way—
the secretarial help Fran needed during this time when I couldn't
do his work. It was the cup of tea, so to speak, that gave comfort
that the Lord was caring for us in the midst of the storm.

When the doctor came back to check up on Debby (by then
Pris was in bed with the neck grippe), he decided I had to go
to the hospital for a D & C by the end of the week. So at 8:00
A.M. on the 27th of October, I found myself in that pretty little
building perched halfway down the mountain. Strange, I was to
be coming back into that same place where my thoughts were

sad because of the loss of *this* baby . . . coming to fight for the life (literally by prayer and careful watching) of two-year-old Franky . . . almost literally three years later. In all probability Franky would never have existed, had we not lost this baby. Whoever this dear baby is, now in heaven, I am certain that the Lord wanted Franky for His purpose, to be an important thread in The Tapestry!

This brings us back into the first chapter with "the mystery of being" once again. Never do I cease to marvel, as I thank God for Franky, that He is indeed an all-powerful, all-wise God Whom we can trust with the overall pattern of The Tapestry. Marvel? Yes, marvel, wonder, awe, are words that should really describe our feelings as we contemplate the reality of the mystery that choice is real, not a trick to fool us, and yet that God is God and is not manipulated by chance. The true balance of these two realities is a mystery that should cause us to get on our knees and worship God, not to sit demanding to understand exhaustively nor to pace up and down figuring out a system which squashes out all the mystery so that we feel self-satisfaction, instead of overwhelming worship. How *finite* infiniteness makes us feel! In the contemplation of my own existence following my parents' loss, and then of Franky's existence following, or rather taking place because of, our loss, my sense of worship grows. However, in the hospital *that* day, I wasn't sure I'd ever have another baby.

The next day the doctor stopped to see me and said I might go home if I would stay in bed a couple of more days. Fran was leaving for Rome the next day to be there to observe the official defining of the dogma of the Assumption of Mary, and I needed to be home to be with the children. Susan was the victim during that time, with dysentery, and Debby was in the recovery stage. So we rounded out one month of illness. Yet it was a month with more encouraging mail than we had ever had. Letters came telling of children's classes starting, and urging us to come back to Scandinavia and Holland. Other letters came asking Fran to come and speak on Barthianism, as well as letters from France and from the army camp at Dachau speaking of results and of children's classes and Empire Builders' groups starting. With all the disappointment and illness, mail at that time was like finding a patch of specially fruitful plants in the middle of a garden spoiled by a storm.

I do believe "trust" is given encouragement, although "trust" is a meaningless word if there is *no* "fog" in which to trust! We have a special time and special happenings in space and time, during which trust is our greatest contribution to the battle. Someday, in the face-to-face moment of glory, the kind of trust that wins a victory will not be possible. The story of the succession of days, and years, is a story of increasing situations where trust can be real!

In Rome, Fran stayed up all night to get a place by the rope so that he could get clear pictures of the papal procession. An amazing set of slides resulted which he used many times to illustrate a lecture he gave on this ceremony. It was November 1, 1950, that this amazing event took place in the Roman Catholic Church. The pope had met with the cardinals after a study had been made by "the experts," and he had posed this question: "Is it your good pleasure, venerable brothers, that we proclaim and define, as dogma revealed by God, the bodily assumption of the blessed virgin into heaven [that is, that Mary was taken in her body to heaven]?" After the vote, the pope said, "This shows that with one thought and voice we agree." The official declaration proclaims, in part: "On the first of November, the feast of all saints, the radiant brow of the queen of heaven and the beloved Mother of God will be wreathed with new splendor, when, under divine inspiration and assistance, we shall solemnly define and decree her bodily assumption into heaven."

Fran had gone for the day before, when thousands of pilgrims from many lands were going from basilica to basilica, following instructions in their Holy Year books. They kissed the doorposts, put money in the boxes, said prayers, and confessed to priests, listening to two people at once to accomplish more. It was a sobering preparation to his watching the lavish procession and rituals of the next day.

Fran's article "Rome" described the spectacle and also gave explanation as to the origins of many of the Roman pagan customs that had been adopted into the Roman church. He felt there was no place like Rome to "feel" the history of what happened. This article was published in a number of periodicals in America, South

Africa, Scotland, Ireland, and in Spanish. In this year of "education," certainly Fran's time in Rome was another "course" which prepared him for future discussion. It also filled him with deep compassion for the needs of people who are yearning for absolution or forgiveness of sin and assurance of salvation, while they have no understanding that the free gift of God was His "one and only Son" so that "whoever believes in him may have eternal life." The sadness of misunderstanding "whosoever will, may come"—and worse, the sadness of never having heard that God's invitation is clearly given over and over again—was captured in the faces Fran looked into as people toiled up steps on their knees, earning merit.

Let me quote from Fran's paper: "The crowds are so great people are injured as they are extruded by the crowds behind them, out of the doorways, into the square, out past the Castel Sant'Angelo which was begun in 135 by Hadrian. Tonight it has a tremendous cross of flaming torches upon it. These shiver and move in the rising wind like some live thing. The day is done. We go to the station and enter a compartment on the train. How important is it for us to understand what was done? I will let a Roman Catholic priest who is sharing the train compartment with me, speak. He is earnestly saying to me, 'Today is the most important day for the Catholic Church in the last two hundred years; probably it is the most important day since the resurrection.'" Then, toward the end of the paper, Fran states, "If, after a careful study of the Bible as God's Word, we Bible-believing Christians are sure we are right, then we are in a battle for the souls of men. . . . The Bible is our authority; do we only march under it as a banner, or do its standards control our lives?"

Fran got home from Rome on my thirty-sixth birthday, in time to help celebrate as we cut the sponge cake (made in memory of birthdays of the past with my mother's sponge cakes), and the girls presented their gifts planned for for weeks with many whispered conferences. It was a real party, but the entertainment was Fran's report to us of the jeweled magnificence, the elaborate lighting and decoration, and the pagan aspects of what he had just seen.

Soon after that, we had at our chalet for a few days, a Senegalese, tall, black and so impressive to the village as people peered out of their windows when we walked from the train. He was the first black many had seen. His father was one of thirty-seven children brought up in the religion of sorcery; his mother a Roman Catholic. You can imagine that amid his tales to us, he was exposed to the gospel that week. As we heard of two million people with almost no light to show them the way, a little voice popped up in the quiet, "I could go." It was Susan, with her eyes shining and cheeks flushed as she thought of telling lost ones the truth.

Thirty years later Susan and Ranald Macaulay have been in Africa several times to visit Ran's family, but also spending time with the people. They prayerfully considered their yearning for that continent as their "call." However, as they look back, they are convinced that God clearly led them to what they have done as they review the years in Ealing L'Abri (Great Britain). Now they have had the tenth anniversary celebration of Greatham L'Abri (also Great Britain) which has been and is truly a lighthouse to many on stormy seas who are being blown into dangerous twentieth-century ideas, as well as into the morass of ancient paganism presently being revived. Africans have not only come to Swiss L'Abri, but also to Susan and Ranald in England. The books and films are even now in various parts of Africa. But that is later in The Tapestry, and no blueprint of the Weaver's plans were given to us *that* night!

Two more months of 1950 still remain. We were to go for a few days to Le Roc, the Bible School in Geneva, to talk with Mr. Hugh Alexander and speak to students. By chance, during our Christmas shopping for ice skates for the children in Schaefer's Sport Store, we were to meet Monsieur F. of Le Grand Verger: "Hello, hello . . . can you come to us for dinner; I want to talk with you." An evening's conversation included his telling us how much he apppreciated the time we had given the girls of his school those evenings of discussion. "I can't do that kind of thing for them. Will you do it again this year? . . . And Priscilla could have ski lessons with us, and some classes in exchange." Rather than having to try to get permission to have the girls, we were being asked! Our joy about that was matched by the invitation to keep on with Christmas Eve candlelight services, and a multitude of things that came in mail and people who came to our door.

1950. In sickness and health, in better moments and worse, in excitements and disappointments, in moments of tenderness and in times of impatience and anger, in sudden waves of discouragement and bright certainty of hope, in overwhelming too-muchness of work and astonishment at visible results, in times of being ready to give up and of new surges of determination to endure to the end, in the winds of "what-is-the-use," as adversity would rattle the shutters, and in bright glimpses of the enormity of God's caring to use such cracked vessels as we were for His purposes— in all the ups and downs, the year drew to a close for us in Chalet des Frênes with the usual breathless curiosity as to what another year would bring.

Come to the hotel where we sat for an evening, totally astonished at being invited by the hotel manager and his wife to talk with an Englishman and his wife and sister from Kenya, well-educated, widely traveled. The blond wife of the hotel manager perched on a moroccan stool by the fire blowing smoke curlicues into the air, in between supplying others with refreshments or cigarettes. Conversation centered on skiing, world conditions, war, Russia, who could remain neutral, what will come next; then quite naturally turned to God.

Eyes turned to Fran as he began to speak at 10:30. On and on he went, each pause bringing another question, with interest never wavering. I looked around and no one looked bored as Fran started with Acts and went on through the history of the early church, the perversion of the church of Rome, up through the Reformation, and on to the present day, giving archeological proofs of the Bible's validity in areas of history, finally explaining the way of salvation. The blond, supposedly Protestant, said she had never heard anyone talk before who knew why he believed. "Tell me, why did Jesus have to die? I never understood, and didn't know who to ask." Her Roman Catholic husband, who never went to mass, listened intently. The English District Commissioner, puffing on his pipe, asked about the differences between the Bible and the Koran (he had read the Koran three times), and as Fran answered, his respect and interest seemed to deepen. At 1:30 A.M. no one seemed anxious to go.

As we walked back up the path through a blinding blizzard, we agreed that this had been the most unusual evening since we had been in Europe. We had not one single idea that it was a shadow of things to come. We would have been totally astonished, flabbergasted, and incredulous if anyone had handed us the L'Abri story that night! The blond had ended the evening by saying, "Don't ever leave Champéry; we need you here." It was her husband who would be signing a petition to keep us there when we were being put out. But all that was four years away!

EVENTS 16

C urrent Events" could be listed in brief telegraphic manner like this: "In 1951 the Schaeffer family moved to Chalet Bijou above fields on the lower side of the village. This rambling old chalet had a hayloft and a stone trough of water outside where cattle used to drink or clothes used to be rinsed, and the rooms were heated by wood stoves. Hot water bottles and blankets were the 'added heat,' making typing or school work possible in rooms that froze water in the nights and took hours for the chill to be removed by small wood stoves. The stone stove in the living room held heat longer and made that the place where everyone gathered for special events and for all the daily 'living' that could take place there."

Of course that short paragraph leaves out the part telling of the sale of Chalet des Frênes and the fact that we could not buy it, and all the happenings of the moving.

The hayloft of Chalet Bijou, still full of hay being stored for the peasant owners, was the scene of one of the central "events" of Fran's life. He describes something of his struggles there in the Preface of his book *True Spirituality*. Before we had left Chalet des Frênes he had said to me, "Edith, I really feel torn to pieces by the lack of reality, the lack of seeing the results the Bible talks about, which should be seen in the Lord's people. I'm not talking only about people I'm working with in 'The Movement,' but I'm not satisfied with myself. It seems that the only honest thing to do is to rethink, reexamine the whole matter of Christianity. Is it true? I need to go back to my agnosticism and start at the beginning." After we moved we had a lot of rain, and the hayloft became Fran's retreat. He would pace up and down, inside, or since it also had a long balcony, he would often pace out there, up and down, the length of the house, under the eaves.

Pilgrim's Progress talks of the Slough of Despond, as well as Doubting Castle. Where was Fran? How long? It is impossible to analyze someone else's struggles for honesty and sincerity and uncertainty. It is foolish to try to copy other people, or to repeat another person's experience. Sometimes it is important for someone to walk among thorns and sharp rocks in order to post warnings, or to mark the trail with freshly painted hiking signs, indicating the best path around some hornet's nest of a precipitous cliff. It isn't necessary for everyone to set forth in the wilderness to mark his or her own trail if others have walked that way before!

The advantage of writing thirty years after the fact is that I can see something very startling now as I read hundreds of letters from people helped by the unshakable certainties Fran ended up with as he came out of that struggle to "blaze a trail" for himself, but with markings for others to follow more easily. As he says, "L'Abri would have not been possible without that time." If he hadn't had the "asbestos protection" of the honest answers to his own honest questions, he couldn't have coped with the blast of questions coming at him at times like a surge of heat from a steel furnace. He isn't giving things to other people that he has thought up as clever answers, in an academic way, for theoretical questions. He asked his own questions and discovered—and rediscovered—the answers in the Scriptures. A great deal of prayer is interspersed in his thinking—prayer asking for wisdom.

Was I so wise as to know this would be the result? No, of course not; I was scared. And when a wife or husband, a friend, a brother, sister, mother, father, son, or daughter is scared of the "searching" or the "struggle" or the "rethinking" of the other person, it is hard to know when to talk, and when simply to "intercede"—that is, to intercede by asking for God's help for the other person. It is as important to know when to keep quiet as to know when to speak clearly and courageously. Just keeping quiet can at times be the greatest work or activity of a whole period of time during which an "event" like this is going on! Surely not one of us has wisdom enough to know when to talk, and when to be quiet, without asking God for such wisdom— time after time. I can still hear the cowbells in the field in front of my little office window as I would stop typing, often during those days, open my Bible on the typewriter, and pray.

Fran came to the end of this time with firm conviction that indeed God is there, the Bible is true, the word "truth" applies to the whole scope of life, and that the Christian life can flow on into all areas of creativity, as well as into day-by-day living. I'll quote what Fran himself has said: "In going further, I saw something else which made a profound difference in my life. I searched through what the Bible said concerning reality as a Christian. Gradually I saw that the problem was that with all the teaching I had received as a Christian, I had heard little about what the Bible says about the meaning of the finished work of Christ for our present lives." He began to "feel" songs of praise, as well as to actually sing in his hayloft! One day he said to me, "Edith, I wonder what would happen to most churches and Christian work if we awakened tomorrow, and everything concerning the reality and work of the Holy Spirit, and everything concerning prayer, were removed from the Bible. I don't mean just ignored, but actually cut out—disappeared. I wonder how much difference it would make?"

We concluded it would not make much difference in many board meetings, committee meetings, decisions, and activities. From then on, my own prayer times became more central to each of the day's twenty-four hours! I made a private resolution that each day, whenever the time occurred, I would not read a newspaper, a book, a magazine, until I had first read whatever chapters I was planning to read in the Bible, and interspersed that reading with prayer. I read and prayed as a two-way conversation. Also I began to write to the Lord, simply as one would write a note to emphasize something to another person in a more concrete way than speaking. For me, it was a more vivid way of communicating. Although I had struggled in prayer during Fran's time of search, now, with thanksgiving for his conclusions, my resolve was to have more reality in my life, in behaving (privately, alone with the Lord) as if it mattered, as if it would make a difference in history, if I acted upon the admonitions to pray ". . . on all occasions with all kinds of prayers and requests."

Did Fran then feel he had "all the answers"? Did he even feel he had asked "all the questions"? No, definitely not. He himself had come to a firm place. He had fresh preparation for all that was ahead. But—much more was to come, still completely hidden.

It was soon after this period that he began to write scribbles, somewhat like the "poetry" he had written in college on those calendars and diaries. I'll quote one:

> Lord, keep our feet in the slippery place
>> When friends are gone away.
> When we stand alone in the dark and cold,
>> And all men answer, 'nay.'
>
> Lord, keep our feet in the slippery place
>> When friends all crowd around.
> When men as echoes with smiling face,
>> Give but an echo's sound.
>
> FAS

This was his way of making a request in writing a very central prayer at that time. This whole period was a central *event* in Fran's life.

The phone rang on February 6, 1952, just as we had finished sending off lessons to be translated, sighed with relief, and sat down to lunch, saying, "There, we have two hours before the girls are coming to tea with their questions." It was M. Fonjallaz, Director of Le Grand Verger, announcing the death of King George VI: "Both M. Juat [Director of Juat, another girls' finishing school] and I feel that our English girls would appreciate a special church service because of this." "Why, yes," said Fran, "eight o'clock tonight." Ordinarily, with our news coming via *Newsweek*, it would have been a week before we would have heard of the king's death; now here we were at two o'clock of the same day, calling all the hotels and schools to inform them of a special service. Fran called the Vice-Consul to ask if "God Save The Queen" should be sung and was told not only "Yes, she becomes our queen immediately, the moment the King dies," but also, "My wife and I and a friend from the State Department in London will be coming for your service." Vic ran across the snowy field to find Michel and dispatch him to the chapel with a load of wood from our woodpile. "Make as hot a fire as possible in the chapel stove, and stay by it until eight o'clock to see that it doesn't go out." Fran shut himself up to prepare a message, and one of the girls ran to Mme. Fleishmann concerning the music.

At eight o'clock over sixty people were gathered in the chapel. Not only English people had come, and Swiss directors of the schools, but also Indian girls, Swedish girls, and in fact, everyone who understood English. Who would have dreamed that the death of King George VI would have opened up the way to Fran to preach a strong sermon to people who normally wouldn't be listening to anything from the Bible? He brought them face to face with the fact that if the great of the earth must die and stand before the King of kings, so must we—and we need to be prepared. He used Scripture showing what our relationship should be to kings and rulers, and also what our relationship should be to the King of kings. An *event* that was spread by the media in the world, became an event that was not publicized but changed individual lives when some eyes were opened to The King who died so that whosoever, among kings and peasants, believes, might live!

Just as death is an event, so birth is an event. By this time we were looking forward to a birth later in the year, and in addition to the doctor's shots to keep me from losing "it," the children were shoving me down frequently and ordering, "Put your feet up, mother; we don't want to lose our baby." Susan had made a careful chart as to what I should be eating, embellished with drawings to entice me to be faithful!

The eagerness and attention spent on protection of this growing person within me was matched by concern for a variety of people who were coming close to the "new birth" as they listened and asked questions in Chalet Bijou. Added to the Sunday nights, when Le Grand Verger girls came, were the Thursday nights with the Juat girls, and another time that was fitted in for Florrisant girls. Most of them came from aristocratic families of many countries, and were separated from their way of life and atmosphere for a period of time that gave freedom to really think and consider truth as they heard it presented. Priscilla was teaching children Saturday afternoons in her Children for Christ class in French, and Monsieur Ex. was coming regularly to ask questions as he was systematically reading the Bible daily. Fran would take time and patience to deal with people individually, as I brought tea and orange rolls or nut bread (all homemade of course, and fresh out of the kitchen that used to be a part of the barn, and was kept warm with the wood stove.)

What were these evenings like? How did we see them? Were they a beginning of a new work? Not from our viewpoint. We had no thought of more than our interest in each individual as a person. (By "we" I'm including our children.) We were interested in diverse varieties of individual personalities. The evenings were as different as the people. Questions may fall into the same general categories—but each person is different. It is exciting to contemplate that we are separate, different individuals to God too, and that He deals with us as persons with importance, offering us not only a solution to life and death, but helping us individually along the time zones of our lives. I dislike lumping together the events of new birth in this period—or any period. I wish I could talk about Betty and Gea, about Ush and Shirley, about Helen and the Kay twins.

One evening there was Carla, Priscilla's old roommate, an intellectual agnostic completely disillusioned with the Roman Catholic Church because of her years in a convent school. Carla, the clown of the school, with her short curly hair giving her the look of an impish, newly shorn lamb, was an Italian who knew French well, but had only a half a dozen or so words she understood in English. On this night, she plopped herself on a rug in the center of the room full of girls—on her tummy, with the Italian Testament Pris had given her, in front of her. Those who expected to laugh were rewarded at the beginning. As Fran was answering a question about a philosopher, he started out, "Well, as a thinker he—" Carla's face lit up with delight. "A stinker—a *stinker*"— one of her half-dozen words had been used, she thought. When the laughter died down, Priscilla straightened her out, and Carla began to monopolize the questions. I wish we could go back in

time and space and transport you along with us into that chalet
room, the granite stove sending out heat, Carla's eager face center
stage, so to speak, and the others listening with growing interest
as they drank tea and tasted cake right along with gaining an
appetite for the more basic things in life. Priscilla, with her French
Bible in front of her, translated into French as Carla asked questions from her Italian Bible and from things in her past thinking
that had troubled her, and Fran answered in English.

Carla and two other Italian friends came regularly after that,
and Sunday nights became bilingual affairs. However, as time
went on, it seemed she needed to be alone, without the roomful
of girls listening in. So one morning we were to have translated
to us her whisper . . . "Oh, I want to believe all this more than
anything in all the world—more than anything I have ever wanted.
Must I wait until I understand it all? How much more do I have
to know before I can accept Christ as my Savior?" . . . "Except
ye become as a little child . . ."—Fran made it as clear as he
could. He prayed, asking the Lord to make it clear. Carla prayed
silently in Italian. How could we know what had taken place?
It didn't take long to be "told." Carla's face was wet with un-
ashamed tears as she threw her arms around me and we wept
together for an unexplainably happy moment.

As Debby and Susan came in for lunch, I had slipped out to
explain what we were doing and to ask them to go quietly up
to their rooms. During the minutes of Carla's "birth," we were
together in a sharing of a very natural mutual interest, as prayer
on the part of the younger children was real and *did* have a specific
part in what took place in the living room. So many times in
life, people—whether children or adults, whether "upstairs" is
a place in the same chalet or a place thousands of miles away—
have a definite sharing of a work in prayer which is defeating
the hindrances Satan would be putting in the way, or which is
being answered in the area of "opening eyes of understanding."

If anyone is thinking of "credit" for results . . . we all have
to wait until the astonishing discoveries will one day be made,
and we find out whose faithful prayer in hospitals, prisons, jun-
gles, wheelchairs, crowded city apartments, cabins in the woods,
farms, factories, or concentration camps has been a part of a specific victory in snatching someone from a circle of death, or in

breaking chains so that there seems to be an ease for that one in stepping into a new life. I feel sure that we'll be surprised beyond measure to discover who or how many will receive the rewards for their part in taking literally and with simple faith and trust the responsibility to intercede, to pray, to make requests day in and day out.

In sports, the *event* we were most involved in was the interschool ski meet with eight schools and fifty-nine participants in Chateau d'Oex. The whole family pitched in the night before to prepare our skier, Priscilla. Mommy checked on clothing, extra warm things "in case," and mundane things, while Daddy gave the skis several coats of quick-drying Skiwax to try to improve on the three-year-old cheap skis . . . with twenty minutes to dry between coats. Debby and Susan pranced around giving unwanted advice and wishing they could go too. M. Fonjallaz was to take the girls entering from his school the next morning for a day of practice before "the day." The Junior Champion for Switzerland was one of the fifty-nine contestants, and there were several other outstanding skiers too . . . so when Prisca came in fourteenth with a bronze medal for her downhill race and slalom, it was thrilling. The glories of doing so well soon faded, however, as the director set school exams for two days later, and there was no way of making up the time lost in ski practice. However, Priscilla did extremely well on the exams too.

Events for individuals coming to our chalet to "understand and believe" continued to take place, as girls who discovered that Carla had been able to come alone, asked one after another for a morning or afternoon to come alone too. Before they all left Champéry for that year, this culminated in our having a special communion service for all those who had become Christians as a part of our little church which had a handful of members—The International Church, Presbyterian, *Reformé.* We had formed this little congregation for ourselves, and for the ones who were becoming Christians and had no church home, never dreaming that it would continue to be a church home for our family and for many who would be coming to L'Abri in the years to come. Remember, we did not dream there would be such a thing as L'Abri nor did we expect to leave Champéry. How could we possibly imagine that one day there would be sister congregations in

Milan, Ealing, and Greatham, and a Korean congregation in Wimbledon?

Madame Fleishmann, who played our organ in the chapel, and who taught the children piano, had spent a week with us when her mother died. Fran had taken the funeral and cared for a variety of details for her. She had been brought up in Germany in liberal Lutheran churches, but came to a clear understanding and belief. She wanted to be a member of the church, as did a Czechoslovakian couple, the Cerneys, who taught in one of the schools spending the winter in Champéry. As people were added, it was without any attempt to make the little church grow. We just kept being glad for its existence for people who needed it—including ourselves. We had no idea that for many, many years there would be people becoming Christians in L'Abri who would want to be baptized and declare their belief that God existed and that they had accepted Jesus as their Savior, some of whom would also ask if they could join the church until such a time as they could find a church home somewhere else in the world. This church was not a conscious preparation for a future program; it was that which we felt was right for that time.

It was just before Easter that Debby, in bed with a cold, reported what she was hearing through the floor (the living room was beneath): "I think M. Ex. is getting saved right now. . . ." And her think was right! The book *L'Abri* needs to be read to fill in parts at various places in our lives, but it is important to know that M. Ex., a leading man in the village, did become a Christian at this time, and that without his knowing it, and without our knowing it, this *event* was to be central in an astounding way in changing our lives, our work, his life, and the lives of countless other people!

The mystery involved in our glimpsing enough of God's plan in His weaving of threads in The Tapestry is as brilliantly floodlighted at this point in our history, as is anything that has happened in our lives. That is true also in terms of the reality of the specific historic part our choices have. We rejoiced together as a family because of dear M. Ex.'s choice. We had no idea of what would spring forth from that choice that would affect us, and so many other people. Nor did we have any idea of the cost involved to him in his life in one way, or to us in our lives in another way. None of that was announced to us. There was no handwriting on the wall. We knew M. Ex. had become a believer, that we would be going to Le Roc in Geneva for the Easter services, and that Debby and I would go a day later because of her cold. The day-by-day things were mingled together in that mixture that our minds, emotions, and actions are always full of. Happily, future difficulties and excitements are hidden.

The *event* of my first airplane ride seemed enormous to me. In fact I couldn't sleep the night before! After crossing the fields with a cart, pulling Debby and Susan's suitcases and a box full of birthday party fixings for Debby's seventh, to be celebrated at Home Eden (all this through a pouring rain), I hugged and kissed my good-bys and went off with my suitcase to the train. Fran and I met at midnight in Geneva. The Spanish line—Iberia— was to be my introduction to flying. Our flight was in a DC-3 with eighteen seats, paint off in spots and the upholstery worn. I felt the need of praying for angels to be sent to bear it up! Landing at Barcelona just two and a half hours after leaving Geneva, and stepping out into the hot dry Spanish sun, I felt more as if I had made a map study and a distant city had come to life than as if I had made a journey. Flying didn't seem like travel to me then. The speed of boats and third-class train cars was "normal." In this new experience, time and space seemed to have been lost sight of!

In the lobby of our hotel in Madrid, who should be there to greet us with an armload of pink carnations but Ush and Carla from Priscilla's school. They were taking a bus tour of Spain and were eager to talk about their new-found Christian beliefs. Soon we were standing in front of our first Spanish church audience—looking so different from the blonds dressed in red in Scandinavia. Here we saw black mustaches, black hair, black eyes; black lace mantillas on all the ladies, girls, and tiny little girls; with splashes of magenta and brilliant green jackets.

The contrast was not just in the dark, sparkling eyes and lace mantillas or mustaches, but in the realization that those tall men in uniform, with guns at their sides, were not standing at the back for decoration or effect. They were members of the Civil Guard, standing there to make sure nothing was said or done which this Fascist regime did not allow. In the first place no sign was allowed outside at all to show that the building we were in was a Protestant meeting place. It had to be unmarked. Bibles were not allowed to be sold in Spain at that time, nor sent into the country in quantities. No converts were to be made! Men in military service had to take Mass as part of their duty and were cruelly beaten if they refused for conscience's sake. Mass also was required for everyone who was a patient in a hospital. When Protestants died, there was a problem as to where to bury them, as the cemeteries were refused to them. The list is a very long one, and these things represent only a small portion.

Just what were the Civil Guards listening for in our messages? We had meetings in nine different churches in Barcelona—some for Children for Christ, and some to point out the dangers of modernism, Barthianism, and the ecumenical movement. In most places we both spoke. I had to be very careful not to endanger the folks who lived there, because open children's work is prohibited. If men and women (at that time) came out of Catholicism, they were not permitted by law to bring their own children with them. A child could not leave the Catholic Church, so a Protestant church with over two hundred adults would have a Sunday school of about thirty children. I spoke of what people in *other* countries were doing to reach children, and sang songs and showed the flannelgraph stories as examples of what was happening in Finland and Norway. Pastors said this guarded the message, and people could draw their own conclusions. The Civil Guards simply stood at attention and didn't "charge," anyway.

Fran felt it was a shame to have to speak of the insidious dangers of Barthianism in a country where there was so much persecution, but he found that the World Council had been sending in Barthian speakers, so the confusion and questions were already there. We not only had meetings every night, but appointments after the meetings, for conversation, and for supper! Since supper at our hotel was served at 11:00 P.M., Fran talked to the pastors and other men until the wee hours of the morning.

As Fran always says, in most battles there are "two dragons" to be aware of. In Spain it was first a case of bearing persecution in such blatant forms as a man's being given only a single man's pay, even if he was already married and had several children, simply because records showed he had not been married in the

Roman Catholic Church. Yet at the same time, as he is valiantly living on that meager bit of money to be "true to one's faith," he backs into another "dragon" in the form of a liberalism, or Barthianism, which would take away the very "absolute" which is *worth* suffering for! Fran came to feel that rather than ignoring the dangers of liberalism here, he must do quite the opposite— this was the place where clear warning must be given. The "price" being paid for living on the basis of the milk and strong meat of the Word of God was too great for the "buyers" to be given a watered-down milk, and a contaminated meat. These Spanish believers, of all people, needed the pure unadulterated food and water of the Word of God.

Fran spoke in Valdepeñas and in Seville, while I stayed in Madrid. I was in my seventh month of pregnancy and was trying to "be careful." In Seville, Pastor Molina showed Fran his church, demonstrating the manner in which seven young men had fought him, poured gasoline on the hymn books and Bibles, and set fire to them. He told how the police had "searched" the town for them, but never found them! Fran spent an interesting day talking to Molina, and in the evening four churches came together for the meeting, at which he spoke. It would take chapters to describe adequately our time in Madrid, the art of El Greco that we visited in his own village, the sadness of visiting Montserrat, with its gold-encrusted Black Madonna, and the astounding poverty of the "shanty town" of fifty thousand people living in shacks built out of bits of tin and even cardboard. We were being given as much as we tried to give, however—not just in education, but in a "fire in our bones" to keep on really fighting for the truth, that people might not be confused and then robbed of the wonder of the solid Rock upon which they can stand! We also wanted to fight for it with greater reality in our own lives, having come through the "event" of Fran's own struggle.

Spain to Portugal was my second plane ride. In spite of rain and grey evening skies, our first impression of Lisbon was one of light and color—intensified when the sun came out, but not dimmed by rain. Modern-shaped buildings with circular balconies and windows at the corners are plastered in pale green, pink, yellow, peach, stark white, and pale blue. Green lawns, shaped flower beds, and flowering trees abound all over the city. Trees that border the boulevards are not content to have leaves and flowers, but their trunks are often the supports for rambler roses. Sidewalks of avenues are paved in hand-set, patterned squares of stone, designs in color showing up against basic grey. Along these streets walk the greatest contrasts of society. Women with straight backs and proudly held heads carry enormous flat baskets of fish, or a variety of boxes or wooden containers of fruit or vegetables. Almost touching shoulders, other women pass, wearing the most expensive and chic "creations," with perfectly matched accessories and jewels. The whole scene looks like an overdone stage setting, or a background that *Vogue* magazine would choose for photographing their summer collection.

We were greeted at the hotel by the head clerk at the desk. He was dressed in snappy blue with "tails" and brass buttons, and after speaking to us in English, gave orders in Portuguese to the head waiter and then to "my fellows," as he called his staff, to take good care of us. This gracious gentleman had a story that thrilled us, provided when the *Action Biblique* Swiss missionary who had met us at the airport "took us back to see him as a boy." A ragged, barefoot boy, child of a workman in a fishing village in the south of Portugal, he and his brothers and sisters had never known what it was to be satisfied with food. Twenty years before the day we met him, when he was fourteen, M. Mathey, a Swiss Christian worker, arrived in Faro to live and work. At that time there was not one single Christian there, only Romanism of the most superstitious variety. The first person to come out clearly and courageously and accept Christ as Savior was this fourteen-year-old, who had never had shoes or enough to eat. The man behind the hotel desk, who was that boy, is now every inch a Christian gentleman, earnest, soft-spoken, intelligent, with a dignity and a bearing that is amazing. He first taught himself French by reading the Bible with the help of a French-Portuguese dictionary. He went to Geneva to Le Roc for a year of Bible School. At that time he was teaching himself English with the Bible and dictionary. Now he speaks several languages and handles a responsible position, as well as taking some of his employees to services and talking to them about the Bible.

We had many meetings in Lisbon, feeling a great difference between the usual bored congregations and these people whose

faces showed their eagerness and appreciation so vividly. These
were not people who had generations of Protestant members behind them, but groups that had started twenty-five, twenty, ten
or even five years ago and had paid a price for their faith which
had made it precious to them.

I want to leave Lisbon now and take you to Faro where M.
Mathey had worked for just twenty years. Crossing the bay was
like taking a trip through the pages of a history book with pictures
of old Portuguese sailing vessels. The early morning sun came
streaking through clouds and lighted sails of boats whose bows
curved up in picturesque shapes. There were boats like Chinese
junks, three-masted sailboats, and every variety of sails—for fishing or for carrying freight, not pleasure boats. Our train on the
other side of the bay was an American aluminum streamliner,
the once-a-day *"rápido"* to the tip of Portugal in the south. The
best hotel in Faro is built for Portuguese travelers, not for tourists,
with real Portuguese food flavored with olive oil and vinegar
and shell fish (unknown varieties to us) as the main "treat."

We were taken to Olhão for our first meeting. Here the houses
were the flat-roofed variety with steps up the outside—like the
ones we had read about in the New Testament. In so many ways
this is like Morocco. As we left the car and walked toward the
meeting house, people hurried past us, among them women with
wool shawls wrapped snugly about them, a corner over their
mouths to keep the cold night air out, though it seemed balmy
to us.

It was a crowded meeting hall that night. Was that group of
160 people the fruit of twenty years? No, that was just our first
glimpse. The next night, as we went forty kilometers over a bumpy
road to the other side of a small mountain, we came to the courtyard of a farmhouse. The light of the full moon bounced off a
whitewashed wall around the courtyard, illuminating the way
for the people who were arriving. For ten years now a dear Christian couple have scurried around preparing their kitchen for the
meetings.

No ordinary kitchen this! We stepped in and looked up at a
steeply arched ceiling covered with closely spaced bamboo poles.
The walls were whitewashed and spotless, and the floor was
scrubbed stone. Into a huge chimney place were built a brick stove

and oven, and the light came from just one bright gasoline lantern hung from a great hook in the ceiling. Words can't describe the wonder of the light in those weatherbeaten faces with skin like old wrinkled leather, many framed in grey hair, smiles often toothless, dusty black scarves tied under their chins, black wool shawls falling down below their knees. These are the old women so like all the others you see on the roads—as far as clothing goes— but the shining eyes and happy faces have something of glory in them that must be seen to be believed.

Have they no troubles? Ah—but more than the usual ones. They have sickness and poverty, death and loss of crops—and in addition they have persecution that seems almost too much to bear!

There were no chairs or pews, just a few board benches on which some were sitting back to back while others stood, some on tiptoe, to see their first flannelgraph illustrations, which I was using for my talk. As I sat listening to Fran and watching the faces, I prayed for "whoever the child is kicking away within me . . . please, may he or she make your truth known to many like these who haven't heard." They filed out, wringing our hands, old ladies kissing me, the ones who had been singing lustily, with cracked voices or with strong young voices. We were conscious that here were . . . ? . . . 130 "underprivileged"? . . . No. . . . Here were "hidden plots of good ground" where seed had been planted and had sprung up to bring forth "thirtyfold" or more! Fishermen and peasant farmers, old and young . . . and there were eighteen more groups like this. . . .

Let me take you away from the south of Portugal, up past the cork forests and into the midst of pine forests. Each tree has a cut in its trunk, and a cup to catch the sap which comes to you as turpentine. We are in Leiria, where a fairylike castle on a hill towers over the town. The opposite hill is the site of a Baptist church and seminary where another good work had been done through the years. Sit where I am and you will see a contrast that you will never forget. Remembering the people in the south and remembering also the sermon Fran has just preached to two hundred in the Baptist Church a few minutes ago, now sit on a bench in a little park and watch the pilgrims plod past—dozens of groups of women, dressed in the same kind of black shawls,

huge baskets full of provisions on their heads, extra shawls, umbrellas, and occasionally a pair of shoes on top of it all. Such
tired drawn faces; such dusty, bleeding, blistered feet. Where
could they all be going? Our Baptist friend caught up with us
and answered that question. "These are pilgrims to Fatima. I look
with sorrow that some do not understand. . . . You see, my
mother was once one of them."

We couldn't look without great emotion either. Walking fifty,
sixty, one hundred, even two hundred kilometers with these loads
of food and provisions on their heads, sleeping by the roads at
night, aiming to get to their goal before that Monday night, May
13—why? To worship at the foot of a statue of the Virgin Mary
in a field where three children are supposed to have seen a vision
some years ago. They have been told this trip, especially in bare
feet, will give them great merit; and the right prayer to Mary,
said the right number of times on the right days at that spot,
will open the door of heaven to them. I found, and Fran did
too, that it was impossible to look up at those heavy-burdened
faces, completely devoid of joy, and not weep. To remember the
radiant response in two hundred faces to Fran's message that
morning, and the faces in the other services, especially in the
south, and to know the weary pilgrims would be continuing hour
after hour after we stopped watching—this made a contrast I
will never forget. We went on to Alcobaça, then to Marinha
Grande. In each place we felt fresh joy that what we had to
give, what people were responding to, *is true* . . . and not just
an aspirin pill!

Fran actually went to Fatima for the midnight before the 13th,
and spent part of the 13th there, discovering among other things
that the majority of the barefooted ones walking for merit are
women, that usually men arrive on bicycles, and Americans in
big cars. How can the truth of the Bible become an academic
thing of polemics, words, intellectual games, when human beings—people, not machines—are being affected for the whole of
their short lifetimes and for eternity? How to make truth clear
was becoming a burning necessity to Fran. "Help me make it
clear" was an urgent request.

We came back by boat, trains, and finally up our mountain
to Champéry where we were greeted with hugs from the children

and a satisfying pat of their hands on my growing tummy: "You still have our baby."

Another *event* came toward the end of June when we had seven girls from one school, Juat, for a "weekend conference." This consisted of my fixing seven extra beds (doubling up the family) and cooking what seemed to me to be mountains of homemade rolls, casseroles, fresh salads, etc., while Fran took them, along with our girls, on hikes (talking along the way about many important things), had Bible classes with them, and brought them into our family prayers, discussions, and a "High Tea" and service on Sunday.

On the first of July the *event* was the arrival of Marco (13) and Maurizio (10) from the Island of Sardinia (we called them our Sardines). They were brought by their aunt to spend a month with us. You see, she was the manager of the hotel in Alassio, and had offered to have our three girls "free" for three weeks in exchange for our having her nephews for a month. As our baby was expected in August, we felt this would give the girls a vacation we couldn't afford that year, in a familiar place, and Fran could do his speaking in Italy and then come and join them while I cared for the new baby and the correspondence in Chalet Bijou. Bright boys, years ahead in interests and intellectual questions, they made a fascinating time of our table discussions about many things, including the Bible, as they compared their Italian New Testaments we had given them with Priscilla's French one. We often wonder how they are now, twenty-eight years later. They became such a part of our family then.

I had a Home and Farm Manual (something the U.S. Government sent out) with explanations as to how to have a birth at home, which included sewing up newspapers in pieces of sheeting, and baking them to sterilize them! I had stacks of these toasted papers and sheets in readiness, along with everything else I thought might be needed. This time I had Grantly Dick Read's book *Childbirth Without Fear*, the year being just a bit too early for the Lamaze method of proper breathing, which my own girls have all found works so well in natural childbirth! But I was determined *this* time to have a new and "natural" experience *à la* "relaxing."

The *Great Event* of the year was the birth of Francis August

Schaeffer V at 2:00 A.M. Sunday morning, August 3, 1952. However, there was another event on the first of August—the great annual event of Switzerland, celebrating their Independence with parades, bobbing lanterns, flares set on various mountain peaks (by experienced mountain guides who climb with a certain amount of danger involved to set magnesium flares that can be seen for miles), and fireworks. Earlier the others had gone off to the fireworks, saying, "You mustn't go—the baby might come," after which I had stealthily made my way to a place near the tennis courts, where I could see. Now, about 10:00 P.M., I was returning, a bit guiltily, across the fields from the village "do." Our dentist had a summer chalet right in my path of return, and the dark hid his form as he was putting a Roman candle in a bottle. Suddenly—whoosh—the firework went whizzing past me and burst into a spray of stars high above my head. I must say I jumped a bit uncertainly, not sure that was the best thing at that moment! There had been a first flurry of dismay on the part of my family, who had rushed home to find an empty chalet, but soon we were all happily sitting down to have the coffee milk shakes and sponge cake I had made for the occasion. "We all" consisted of our family, plus the two Sardines, and *sage-femme* (midwife) Helen Waridel.

It was after midnight and I was in bed when the first contraction started. We began timing them immediately. Everyone else was asleep, so Fran and I got up and started to prepare "the hospital room"—a bedroom we had set aside for The Event! "Don't let's waken the *sage-femme*," I said; "she'll have enough work to do later." So we scrubbed the floor with antiseptic, made up the bed with fresh sheets and the sterilized brown-baked sheet-and-paper pads, to simulate a sterile delivery room! By early morning we had moved the boys to a children's pension across the field, I had esconced myself in the bed with my book trying to do all the suggested things, and the doctor had arrived, asking, "Just what page are you on now?" Which wasn't much help at that point. Priscilla supplied the doctor with orange juice, the other children tried to keep quiet . . . and the day went on into another night . . . with contractions getting farther apart.

Actually the doctor thought he might lose both of us! Whereupon there would have been no more story to tell about my life, no L'Abri, no Franky's movies, to say nothing of Franky's three children (and wife Genie!). Once again we have the mystery of "being," the amazing thing of survival. This birth was a face presentation, the hardest sort of position, and with Fran holding a lamp, the nurse putting chloroform on gauze over my nose and mouth, the doctor proceeded to pull with instruments. He did this so forcefully that the bed went the length of the long thin room, Fran trying with all his strength to hold it back.

It was not long after that that I was holding Franky in my arms, with the doctor giving me spoonfuls of coffee and my tears spilling down my face. "What are you crying for? It's a beautiful 9 pound, 6.2 ounce boy." The tears were tears of unbelievable joy after a long two nights and the fearsome uncertainty of the diminishing contractions, in a chalet high in the Alps, far from a hospital! They were tears of thankfulness to the Lord for hearing and answering our calling on Him in that particular moment of need.

How can we know how critical "the Battle" is, and just what Satan is attacking, just what is "cause and effect history," just what is due to the Fall in terms of bringing in the "un-natural" rather than the original perfect "natural"? We can't know, and we don't need to have it all figured out and analyzed, but we can be sure that God is giving us something we are meant to do when He says, "Call upon me in the day of trouble and I will answer you." A perfect answer fitting in with our desires exactly? No, but an answer fitting into the overall Tapestry which one day we will see.

Don't forget, in my mother's case she lost her baby, and her husband. I would never have been born had she not gone to China as a widow. Do we become smug with understanding when we contemplate this fact? Not at all. The mystery remains. Satan has accomplished certain results in events he has influenced—first in the Fall and many times since. Also, God is God, and never must we reduce Him to anything less. God does give victories as we come to Him praying and believing, and those victories are a terrific diversity of "changed events." The answers to prayer are in themselves a victory against Satan who has tried to discourage us from praying at all. The answers to prayer at other times are the fabulous realities of courage given to keep on in the face of adversity, such as mother had—which also results (farther on in the "weaving") in changed events.

In my Family Letter of that time I wrote: "We do praise the Lord for this precious *bijou* (jewel) God has given us and for answered prayer for both of us. Because of the baby's size and poor position it was only Dr. Otten's skill which saved life that might otherwise have ebbed out."

The *event* that stands out in memory for the three girls is their trip to Alassio and the time their dad spent with them carefully showing them Florence, during that time away. Memories of paintings, sculpture, museums, churches, last a lifetime after a concentrated time like that, and those memories color understanding not only of art, but of the history of the periods of time surrounding the artists' lives. Then too, the reproductions seen in art books always bring back the special time of being right there looking at the originals. Somehow time is multiplied in a few days spent digesting art, and the rare wonder of a city like Florence. It has such a continuity with reading and looking at reproductions later, that the memory seems to be of having *lived* there for a time, rather than just visiting. Of course, the same is true of that kind of time spent in Vienna, or Venice, or Paris; suddenly the art belongs to you.

Years later Hurvey and Dorothy Woodson of Italian L'Abri were to persuade Fran to give a lecture series of a different sort, by walking around Florence, in and out of the Accadèmia and museums and churches, explaining what they were seeing to a group of missionaries as he went, and giving supporting lectures in the evenings. "The Florence Lectures," recorded on tape, are listened to still, and people find them helpful as a preparation for going there.

That was the time I was able to go along, but in August of '52 I spent my time taking care of the baby, whom I was just beginning to know! Very much later that baby was going to be making it possible for me to see Florence very thoroughly (as recompense, perhaps, for staying with him) when a section of filming for the series *How Should We Then Live?* was done in Florence. The evening we filmed in the Accadèmia, after closing hours, I was elected to "go out and find food for seventeen to be served here in an hour." With Roseanna, the Italian production manager,

I raced around the little streets until we found a cafeteria where we got huge pots of pasta, Parmesan cheese, and some veal slices. Then we hurried on to a delicatessen to get a variety of olives, etc.; to a fruit store for fruit, a box of candied chestnuts (marrons), and bottles of a variety of drinks; and finally to a five-and-ten-cent type of variety store for plastic plates and glasses and forks and spoons. We made it in time, dished out the meal, and placed the plates on those slanty tables on which postcards are displayed—a feast for the crew, electricians from the town, etc. Meantime, Fran, who was standing on the scaffolding beside Michelangelo's *David,* had had the unique honor before saying his lines up there, of dusting that famous sculpture with a feather duster handed up by one of the museum guards.

As I took care of baby Franky during that 1952 "vacation" I wasn't having, I didn't know that twenty-two years later he would be making it up to me with *plenty* of time to sit and "look" at art all floodlit for filming, seeing it as most people haven't a chance to see it! No—I was feeling a little lonely and left behind, even though I had chosen to stay while they went, and even while I was enjoying the baby whom I didn't know was going to be an artist and film-maker.

Jesus made it very clear that there is an *event* which brings rejoicing in heaven among the angels. He had just told the parables of the lost sheep and of what joy the shepherd feels over finding the one lost one, and of the joy of a woman seeking her lost coin and finding it. Going on, he told us the exciting fact that what takes place on earth is considered an event in heaven. It matters to the angels when "a lost sinner repents" or is "found." That really is a staggering thought—not fanciful, but given us by the Lord as a reassuring fact among the hard pieces of news and the difficult days of life. We may rejoice with our "measure of knowledge" concerning what a person has in the way of eternal life when he or she (as far as we can know) has understood and bowed before God and accepted the death of Christ as having been for the atonement of their sins. But at the same time, with a different measure of knowledge, angels are rejoicing, actually in space and time—right then when it happens. We had many such *events* in Champéry during that time, as many of the finishing school girls continued coming one at a time to ask their final

questions, so to speak, to be sure of understanding, and then to pray with us, thanking God for sending Jesus and stating their acceptance of Him in their own words. (One was Deirdre whom you will read about in *L'Abri* and who was to illustrate the book *L'Abri* many years later.)

New Year's Eve 1953 was to usher in a special time of rejoicing in heaven as well as for us. When the candlelight service ended and people hurried to the hotels for the balls to be held that night, one man and woman and two teenage boys hung behind, and Fran invited them to spend the evening with us. They were Scottish, from Glasgow—Mr. A., Mrs. H., and Ian and Douglas. After Mr. A. got over his flying down the hill as Susan brought him on her sled—"Whee, mother, I went faster than ever and I was steering by memory!" (in the dark)—we ate and talked together as the New Year began. It was one of those evenings that stand out in memory, when understanding grows and questions flow naturally and in wonderful sequence. A base was being given for recognizing the logic of the truth of the Bible, starting with Genesis. There was also a bird's eye view of both the negative things they had been taught in their very liberal instruction (not only in public school but in their church) and the positive teaching of the Bible.

That week, one after another, these four came back to Chalet Bijou earnestly and seriously wanting time alone. Fran talked to the man (who had been a church warden for years) and had the joy of being with him as he was "found." I talked with the lady who expressed such thankfulness in coming to know what she had never been taught, begging us to come to Glasgow. Fran also talked to each of the boys, one at a time, as they came from skating or skiing with faces glowing from the cold and left with a different kind of a glow.

For us it was a time of reassurance and appreciation of the Lord's way of "finding lost people." Each of the four was "found" that week. Method? Simply trying to make the truth clear . . . and helping in the moment of four differing births! Yes, we served tea and hot muffins. Yes, we luxuriously lighted a stove in my cold office for Fran to talk to the man while I, with the baby, used the living room for my conversation. Not a "method"; simply an attempt to be human. But it turned into four *events*. Seven-year-old Debby excitedly voiced the feeling we all had as she exclaimed: "I can't imagine four people all together getting saved in three days—it's so wonderful because most people take so long!"

Priscilla was having the same kind of *events* in her children's class which had not only village children, but boys and girls from pensions for children. Where are they today, twenty-eight years later? It is a good thing to thank God for memories. Where is tousle-haired Stevie who stuffed his mouth with cookies while eagerly telling us, "My dad's professor in ——— University, and he's staying near a library over here for a year reading big books, but I can just ski. My brother Ricky broke his leg so he can't ski but he's a stamp collector so that's all right. —Hey, when is your church service? You see, I have to find out about these things because I have to choose. My folks say we kids can choose whatever we want to be—Protestant, Catholic, or Jewish—whatever." Stevie not only came regularly to Pris's class but came in between times to ask questions, and brought his Jewish friend whose father was in the UN "so he can hear these stories from the Bible, 'cause he doesn't know anything."

Stevie had a sensitivity and understanding of God's love that was overwhelming to us all. His eagerness in "making sure" he had been accepted by the Lord, and then in hauling his dad up (from Geneva) for a talk with Fran, can't be forgotten. He brought his brother Ricky too, " 'cause Rick belongs to a religion a boy started in our town—a god named George that you have to worship by not eating apples with red streaks in them, and rules like that. Ricky needs to hear the truth."

By April 2, 1953, we were on board the S. S. *Liberté,* steaming out of Southampton Harbor. Debby had just had her appendix out, and had had a terrible siege of fever (undiagnosed) in a hospital in England. Fran had had very productive times in Holland, Denmark, Sweden, and Norway, without my going that time. Vaccinations had been given at our last suppertime by Dr. Otten who brought his vaccine to the table! (Americans at that time had to be freshly vaccinated before being allowed back in the country.) Mme. Marclay had hurried up to us just before we left the chalet at the end, "Oh, Mme. Schaeffer, I want to go to the same place as you people when I die. How do I do that? "

Trunks were off ahead of time, but the last suitcases had been packed in the bathroom as I was "steaming" baby Franky for his cough before leaving. An assortment of tearful villagers were at the train to see us off. Halfway down the mountain I discovered I'd left behind the important bag with Franky's formula and orange juice. The conductor jumped off at the next tiny station, phoned back to Champéry, and by the time we got to Monthey a jeep was waiting with a grey bag! "Oh, there isn't any place like Switzerland," I thought. "It's really our home." "Good-by—good-by," we shouted at the airport to the *Action Biblique* group who had come to see us off. And "good-by, good-by," again later in Southampton to English girls who had become Christians and were waving us off.

We sighed as we settled into our cabins and looked at the ship's program. Previously the President's office of the French Line had written Fran; now, here it was on the program. Fran was to preach for a Good Friday service, on board, and for the Easter service, while I was to have an Easter service for children.

Floating now between two continents, there were immediate *events* to be turned to as important. Floating (without knowing it) between two "works," there were also coming events to be turned to, without having any warning as to which event or which time was to be crucial. You see, we were leaving Switzerland without having any inkling that there was going to be an upheaval ahead of us out of which would come a new beginning. We had not yet any idea there was to be a new work, let alone a work called L'Abri. That was as hidden from us as the gorgeous world that exists under the waves we were seeing as we watched the beautiful white wake. All we saw were the surface waves, and occasional breaks where a dolphin surfaced. Everything else of the wonderworld in the sea was hidden. Just as completely was our future hidden from us until "time" would plunge us into a surprising view.

UPHEAVAL— 17
BOULEVERSEMENT

Our time in England had seemed a series of upheavals as Debby's stay in the hospital removed me altogether from the schedule we had planned. Fran went on alone and had Bible classes with girls who had become Christians in Chalet Bijou, and even went to Glasgow to have a time with the four who had been with us New Year's Eve, and their friends. It was embarrassing for me to have to impose upon the hospitality of our hosts, but there seemed no other way to have a base from which I could daily take a thirty-mile bus ride to spend one precious hour with Debby in her ward, and where Franky could be cared for by Priscilla during my absence and by me the rest of the time. Now as we reveled in our togetherness on the boat, having rescued Debby from the hospital ordeal and enjoying her ordering everything on the menu from the surprised steward, we turned our minds to being out of the upheaval and into a new period of a smoother sequence.

The continuity of life seemed emphasized by the familiar Easter service and fine sermon Fran preached on the resurrection, especially as one of the congregation turned out to be a scientist from Canada whom we had talked to five years before when he had been on the Holland American Line boat with us, the *Nieu Amster-*

dam. The quietness of our floating home with all its familiar aspects should have warned us, however, as the beauty and orderliness of the lounge we were in suddenly turned to chaos. We had come into the edge of a hurricane, and chairs and tables slid across the floor, people who had been dancing landed in a heap at the corner of the room, and squeals and little shrieks of dismay drowned out the music. Stewards came rushing to put up rope railings (these were fastened to posts that were suddenly screwed into holes in the floor that had been hidden under brass plaques), while the dining room stewards put sides on the tables for the meal that would soon be served.

We were to have many storms during the next two years, many upheavals that would remind us of that storm at sea. We were many times to be thankful that our God who is so all powerful can be cried out to in every variety of storm. And so often we were to be thankful that His Word reminds us we may talk to Him in the midst of trouble and ask for help on the spot geographically, but in the time of difficulty too.

> Others went out on the sea in ships;
>   they were merchants on the mighty waters.
> They saw the works of the Lord,
>   his wonderful deeds in the deep.
> For he spoke and stirred up a tempest
>   that lifted high the waves.
> They mounted up to the heavens and went down to the depths;
>   in their peril their courage melted away.
> They reeled and staggered like drunken men;
>   they were at their wits' end.
> Then they cried out to the Lord in their trouble,
>   and he brought them out of their distress.
> He stilled the storm to a whisper;
>   the waves of the sea were hushed.
> They were glad when it grew calm,
>   and he guided them to their desired haven.
> Let them give thanks to the Lord for his unfailing love
>   and his wonderful deeds for men.
> Let them exalt him in the assembly of the people
>   and praise him in the council of the elders.
>
>   Psalm 107:23–32, NIV

This whole book is an attempt to exalt Him and to praise Him in showing something of the waves of our own storms in life and of His calming them time after time. Yet a succession of winds has followed the calming of winds, and we recognize there must be more winds and storms to follow, until that magnificent day arrives when instead of shrill winds and slashing waters, there will be a trumpet sound and the final storm and everlasting calm will be ours to live through—the most fabulous "before, during, and after" period of the history of all human life! That will be the final upheaval, with an everlasting stilling of the storms. What a gorgeous "whisper" to look forward to.

What a titanic comfort it must be to you, and to me, that the God of Abraham described in Psalm 148:5–8, NIV . . .

> Let them praise the name of the Lord,
>   for he commanded and they were created
> He set them in place for ever and ever;
>   he gave a decree that will never pass away.
> Praise the Lord from the earth,
>   you great sea creatures and all ocean depths,
> lightning and hail, snow and clouds,
>   stormy winds that do his bidding.

. . . is so recognizable in Matthew 8:23–27, NIV. The disciples were Jews to whom the Psalms were very familiar. They had the Psalms, and then the words and actions of Jesus to compare!

> When he got into the boat, his disciples followed him. Without warning, a furious storm came up on the lake, so that the waves swept over the boat. But Jesus was sleeping. The disciples went and woke him, saying, "Lord, save us! We're going to drown!" He replied, "You of little faith, why are you so afraid?" Then he got up and rebuked the winds and the waves, and it was completely calm. The men were amazed and asked, "What kind of man is this? Even the winds obey him!"

The power of the Lord to still the storms and to hear us cry out in a variety of distresses was going to be trusted in the context of these passages over and over again in our next years.

We were missionaries on furlough—a strange kind of category, we found. Family ties were tied a little tighter again, and conversation took the place of writing. There was no home to move into, however, as my parents were in a small apartment in Faith Theological Seminary's big house in Elkins Park, and Fran's mother was not expecting us there.

Fran's Aunt Mabel had recently died, and his Uncle Harrison was going away for a year, so he offered us his tiny "row" house for the year. It was a narrow house, the width of one small room, and for us to move in with none of Uncle Harrison's family possessions moved out was a very different thing from going into an empty house. Not even a bureau drawer was empty. Franky was going to sleep in a crib directly against my side of the double bed which almost filled the room; Debby and Susan had bunk beds in a room just big enough to put them, next to ours; and Priscilla slept on a couch in what was called "the back room." The first floor consisted of a small living room with a big piano and heavy chairs so that when the playpen was put up, there was no room to walk. Next came a little dining room, then a kitchen and a tiny laundry room that opened onto a pocket-handkerchief-sized plot of grass bordered with narrow flowerbeds. We kept our things in our trunks in the cellar, which also was the storage place for boxes of old papers, etc., for Uncle Harrison.

To contemplate living here for sixteen months with four children, the youngest of whom would be in the growing period of from eight months to two years, filled me with dismay! Yet how could I complain or even sigh too audibly, when Fran felt then (and still feels) that the provision of this house was one of the most vivid provisions of the Lord that he had ever experienced?

Come back to the balcony of Chalet Bijou in Champéry where Fran had taken his long "thinking and praying walks" day after day. When he thought about our being in America for the furlough, and his acceptance of teaching Pastoral Theology in Faith Theological Seminary for a year, he began to pray about where we could live so that our children could have an unbroken year of school. "Aunt" Margaret Walker, then principal of the lower school of Stevens' School for Girls in Chestnut Hill, had offered as a gift to our girls, the last few months of that year, plus a full year, at Stevens. The bus would pick them up anywhere in that general area. This was a wonderful gift indeed, and would tie in as far as continuity went, with the half year they had had before we left for Europe, in 1948.

Up and down the balcony Fran walked, praying, "Where can we live, Lord? Please show us." Only one other time in his life, thus far, has Fran ever heard a voice answer him. Today, in March of 1981, he said, "Edith, I can still hear that voice in memory, as distinctly as I remember any voice I have ever heard." He has told me that the voice was so clear that he felt if another person had been with him perhaps they would have heard it too. It seemed not to be inside his own head. What he heard was nothing startling as far as content went, simply three very practical words: "Uncle Harrison's house."

It was such a direct and startling suggestion that Fran felt impelled to write a letter and ask, "What are you going to do with your house this year, Uncle Harrison?" . . . feeling a bit foolish, as it seemed the answer would naturally be, "Live in it." Instead the answer came back, "I'm going to live with my brother and his wife in Wildwood this year, and I'd like to have you and Edith and the children live in the Lensen Street house as soon as you are home. Only I can't face cleaning it up or emptying out Mabel's drawers or anything like that." Looking at it humanly, it was an impossible and very unlikely answer from a man who had never given us anything before, but who was now saying all we would have to do would be to care for heat and light and incidental expenses.

People who think of Fran as "coldly intellectual" really don't know him at all. He really is a very emotional person, who is moved by people and their needs, as well as by the wonder of the reality of living "in the supernatural now." When he wrote "The Two Chairs" and spoke of the reality of prayer changing history, it was not just an academic possibility to him. He believes God can, and does, answer in a diversity of ways. In this case he believed God chose to speak audibly to him to have him write that letter. Of course He could have put the idea into his head. Of course he, Fran, could have turned away and tried to ignore the voice. But—he is sure he heard the voice of the Lord tell him to consider that house, and he is sure he was obeying when he wrote the letter. This kind of thing has never happened again.

His other experience of hearing a voice was not in response to needing guidance, but was in connection to asking forgiveness for something.

I myself have never heard a voice. I have had many amazing answers to prayer in a diversity of instances, some of which will be told later. Is there any "more spiritual" or "less spiritual" kind of answer to prayer? I think not. Fran thinks not. God is a personal God, a very personal Father dealing with us as individual children. When He answers by *not* healing a tragic illness, by not providing some material thing, by not giving the diploma or the job, and instead gives "grace sufficient" and special courage and strength to continue in the *midst* of disappointment . . . then the "victory" of *that* answer is just as "spiritual" as the provision of whatever has been prayed for, no matter what form that provision took.

Now Fran's answer to prayer and very special experience of hearing the Lord tell him to turn to this house could not be dashed to pieces by my spending the year complaining about the difficulty of living there! Nor, far more important, could I complain against the Lord by failing to be thankful for what He had given in that particular shelter. However, I needed God's special grace, in answer to my pleading, time after time, as I stayed awake patting Franky as he was teething, in order to keep him from crying and disturbing the sleep of the rest of the family, and the neighbors on the other side of a thin wall. I also had to have God's grace and strength in my weakness to live through a variety of other "hardships" such as the hot water heater bursting one midnight hour when Fran was away speaking in another city, so that I had to dash to the cellar and haul trunks to one side out of the flow of hot water. That was the night that resulted in my hernia (in *Affliction* I tell of an answer to prayer for its healing, which God did reply to in the affirmative, four years later.).

Prayer is not a pushbutton in some sort of "vending machine" that connects the earth with the throne of the Living God. We do not put so much faith, or some formula of words, into a proper "connection" or coin slot, putting our finger on a button and then receiving a sudden solution to our health problems, psychological state, or need for a more convenient place to live, nicer food to eat, and a perfect vacation for our fatigue. We are not

promised freedom from hardships on the basis of prayer. We
are promised answers, including comfort in sorrow, sufficient grace
to bear the "thorn in the flesh," and also answers which supply
our needs in a variety of ways, at very different times of life.
Along with a supply of material needs comes a supply of what
we need in our continual growth. Spiritual growth is a centrally
important thing in our lives, and is as important to our Heavenly
Father—we discover in His Word, as well as in constant contact
with Him—as physical and intellectual growth in children is important to a good human parent.

As had been true so many times, I had no idea that year that
we were being prepared for what was ahead. Looking back on
it, the ingenuity, creativity, patience, and tribulation involved
could be seen as a specific school for what was to follow. God's
choice was not for luxury but for "boot training." It's true that
we are in a battle and that Satan has various ways of attacking
as he stalks around like a lion "seeking whom he may devour,"
but it is also true that God gives His people boot training for
the battles ahead. Time after time we suddenly get a glimpse of
what it means to be pressed to our knees and thrown completely
upon the Lord and to see Him working out the impossible in
such a way as to take it completely out of our hands. "The baby
was awake all night. My gentle patting him and bottles of orange
juice kept him from crying or disturbing anyone—but what weariness! But, thank you, Lord, for those hours of undisturbed prayer
I wouldn't have had otherwise and for the discovery that it is
true that 'they that wait upon the Lord shall renew their strength'!
What an assurance of Your power." . . . "That new sweater, in
tissue paper still, eaten by moths in Aunt Mabel's drawer—what
a disappointment. But thank You for the reminder that it is so
easy to transfer affections to earthly things when they aren't worth
it. Thank you for the resultant peace after recognizing this reality."

There were sudden baffling misunderstandings, situations in
the mission board and the denomination as Synod time approached, lack of certainty as to whether we should return to
Switzerland. So often in "big" or "little" things we were so pressed
with urgent need that we felt hours must be spent in prayer.
The surprise is that time after time such fervent prayer, because
there *is* no human "solution" to the problem, brings a new close-

ness to the Lord. There is also an appreciation of him which in turn brings a result of an unexplainable peace—that "peace that passes understanding." That kind of peace is not unbroken! And it so often comes when one is hungrily reading in Psalms or Isaiah or the Epistles and asking the Lord's solutions for the present *needs*.

If I were just writing statistics of the year, I would be telling you that Fran spoke 346 times in 515 days. How do I know? He has methodically written down in a tiny red pocket notebook the titles of his sermons, or talks, and where he gave each one! This was done in addition to his teaching a full course for a year at Seminary. He spoke on "Art," on "The History of Europe," on "The Lord's Work in the Lord's Way." He preached on "Living in the Supernatural Now," or "The Two Chairs," and, "It Is Difficult to Walk in Mud and Not Get Dirty," and "Ash Heap Lives." He showed slides on Rome, and on Spain and Portugal, and told of the situations in these countries. He spoke on the children's work, and told of what was happening in Champéry. However, the burden of his seventeen months was the result of his own struggle in the hayloft. As he was speaking in a Summer Bible Camp in Dakota, he worked into the wee hours of the morning, night after night, preparing one by one a series of talks which, in his little notebook are called "Sanctification I, II, III, IV, V." He gave these July 5 through July 12 at the Camp, along with messages such as "You Must Not Choose" (stressing the need of balance and not of choosing, between demonstrating the Holiness of God and the Love of God). The Sanctification series was one day to be the book *True Spirituality*, but Fran was *not* giving it as a preparation for a book. It was not academic with him at all but a growing understanding which became a growing fire. It started as a "spark" and was fanned into a flame that was igniting other people.

Today, in March of 1981, as I was talking to Fran about this period, he said he couldn't remember preaching that series more than twice during that seventeen months, so I read from his own little notebook the places, dates, and sermon topics, and we both were astonished at what we were suddenly hearing—an account of another aspect of that boot training time, a preparation for what we did not know was ahead! With great earnestness he preached the series that were so basic to him in Willow Grove Presbyterian Church, in Wharton Baptist Church, in Collingswood Church, in Lake Louise at a Miracle Book Club conference, in Tacoma, Washington, and in several places in California. He preached in Atlanta and Valdosta, Georgia, and in Shelton College and Seaside Heights, New Jersey, and many many other places. It was unbelievable to us, had we not had those clear pencil notations, that Fran spoke often three times in a day, and that the "evangelistic fervor" was in the direction of pleading for a balance between fighting for truth, and showing love—and of doing all that we do in the power of the Lord, not our own zip.

This was the period of time in which Fran was wrestling with the things he wrote in some of the articles I've listed already, "The Dangers from Within and the Dangers from Without." When he gave the seminary graduation message, it was "Tongues of Fire," on the need of the necessity of standing for truth, but coupled with the equal necessity of doing this in the power of the Lord. After this message a leader's wife came up to me and said with no smile, "Edith, there's going to be a split in our denomination." This was because the message had been so contrary to what was normally given of the centrality of pointing out the errors of *others.* Objections came to such statements Fran had made as: "There is no source of power for God's people—for preaching or teaching or anything else—except Christ himself. Apart from Christ anything which seems to be spiritual power is actually the power of the flesh."

On Fran's part he felt he would be false to the Lord if he did not speak in the areas of his discoveries. It is not that he had arrived at any state of perfection of constant balance himself at home, with me, or with the children, or in the church; nor did he claim to have arrived. However, he felt that reality lay in this direction, and together we were praying for a greater reality in our lives and work. We didn't know what change would take place in our work, but we began to pray, alone and together, for a reality of drawing on the Lord's strength by prayer hour by hour. The "how" of that reality becoming a part of our history, we did not know. We had no glimmering of an idea yet that L'Abri was ahead. However, no one can really understand what went into "preparation" since we can only see this from a vantage point of looking back—a perspective which we couldn't have had then. This is why we find it so hard to explain to some eager person with a little notebook who comes to Switzerland, or who stops us after a seminar somewhere, and says, "I am going to start a work like L'Abri. Could you please tell me how?" And they expect a fifteen-minute outline of "How to."

The *answer* to the prayer of a person crying out with even a small measure of sincerity, "Please give me a reality of living as You would have me live. . . . Please give me your strength in my weakness to do what you would have me do" . . . is an answer, so often, of a deluge of things for which there is a reality indeed, a reality of *needing* the Lord's strength, courage, and power to keep one's head above the waves! We need to ask for strength to bear or live through the answers to the diversity of prayer that is connected with the theme "Lord, use me; here am I, use me."

During the month of January 1954 Fran was back in Champéry. He and I felt strongly that it was important to continue the New Year's Eve service in the chapel, the regular Sunday services that month of the "high season," and also to have evening discussion groups for the schools. He slept in my office in Chalet Bijou. A cot had been placed there for him by the missionaries who had rented our chalet for the time of our absence. On his way back to America he spent a week in England and gave the series of basic talks to the English girls who gathered daily that week for further teaching. (These were people who had become Christians in Champéry.)

Meantime, the year and a half had been a time of extremely enjoyable school experiences at Stevens for our three girls. Each morning the big school bus, which normally stopped at luxurious homes, made its way down our narrow street and picked up Priscilla, approaching graduation from high school, Susan, in seventh grade, and Debby, who had finished third grade and also completed fourth grade, from in front of our inadequate little row house. Not only were they having a good education, provided so wonderfully through the Lord's giving Margaret Walker the desire to do this for them, but sports and special friends filled out that education.

It was during that time that our Debby became friends with

Dr. and Mrs. Kiesewetter's daughter Connie in her class at school, and that I got to know Grace Kiesewetter. At times she came and swooped up Franky and me and my overflowing basket of dirty wash to spend the "day"—until school was out. We would get my washing done in the big laundry room and then hung out in the sweet air of Chestnut Hill, while Franky upset people by climbing—climbing out of the window in the laundry, running lickety-split across the lawn, climbing up on the slide and whooshing down before anyone could follow him. He didn't act like a "toddler" at all, with his growing vocabulary, and endless ideas as to how to liven up life! Also, the incredible balance he had gained ever since walking at nine months, made him *not* fit into the categories people expected him to, whether at twelve months, or fourteen months, or whatever!

So few months after that, Dr. Kiesewetter was going to get a call, in the Pittsburgh Children's Hospital where he had moved to become surgeon-in-chief, from Chalet Bijou in Champéry, with an urgent plea for advice about Franky who had contracted polio and couldn't walk at all. But that wasn't spread out before us in Philadelphia; neither the Kiesewetters nor we knew that the Lord was giving a preparation for that phone call. Nor did we know that over five years later Franky as a seven-year-old would be having a most important muscle transplant in their Pittsburgh Hospital, by Dr. Fergeson, the leading orthopedic surgeon. Preparations are not labeled for us. But they should be recognized later, and consciously *thanked* for. Our God who cares about details should be thanked with adequate appreciation!

There was a ten-week period during the first few months of being in America, from mid-September until nearly the end of November, in which I accompanied Fran to speak too. Any of you who have had children can imagine that period, perhaps. Debby had had the trauma of being torn from us in England and being taken through a frightening array of medical tests. She begged to go along now, and we felt it was more important to take her, along with schoolbooks and workbooks, than to have her attend school; she needed the reassurance. Franky, of course, was going with us too. So with the two older girls happily cared for (one with my mother and one with the Kiesewetters), we started off. There were suitcases, schoolbooks, a stroller, a folding baby bed with complete mosquito protection—fine mesh sides and a top that zipped on, complete with its own legs and frame— and our slides, projector, and screen, along with a bag of Bib orange juice and the necessities for feeding the baby! We went by train—to Albuquerque, New Mexico; to Southern California, Highland College, Long Beach, etc.; on up to San Francisco, Seattle, Tacoma; on to Denver and Colorado Springs, St. Louis, Alton, and so on, and finally back to our little Lensen Street house.

I still remember trying to fit that bed in by our bunk beds on the train while amusing an active thirteen-month-old, reading to Debby, watching the Grand Canyon go by, and having a "normal life" . . . as a gypsy family! We often would arrive to be met by totally unimaginative people who thought the best treat they could offer would be a steak dinner in a restaurant. "Then we'll go straight to the church, where Mr. Schaeffer will preach first, and then Mrs. Schaeffer will speak after the choir sings." A baby that has been cooped up for hours of night and day on a train—an eight-year-old too—needs a bit of grass and freedom, a big bathtub and a quiet room for the night. Instead a restaurant high chair comes first; then next, undressing and bathing baby for bed in the back of a church with a borrowed bowl of warm water, and towels hung around the traveling bed for privacy, and for later shutting out the light. Debby would valiantly sit there with the baby to "pat him if he wakens" while I spoke; and invariably he would waken when we had to pick him up and transfer the whole *ménage* to someone's home for the night. Short sleep for mama and baby.

This was a portion of the variety of "costs" that went with the fiery messages Fran had to give, being given. There is always a diversity of costs.

At Highland College in Long Beach we had some days in which to settle in, with proper outdoor space for the children. That was the time also that I was able early in the morning to buy "seconds and thirds" of Franciscan Earthenware, Apple pattern, at the factory outlet. I managed to pack a whole barrel of the stuff to send to Champéry from there. With some breakage (!) and some additions (procured by Jenny Guiness much later), we are still using these dishes for guests on Sundays. Also, that barrel was made into a chair (covered in red leather) that Fran sat in all the early years of L'Abri, to discuss by the fireplace, and it is still a part of our living room. So even our gypsy life brought in some pieces of continuity to tie that period together with the future.

The next year, on May 28, 1954, Dr. Robert Rayburn, on the recommendation of the faculty and board of trustees of Highland College, presented Fran with the honorary degree of Doctor of Divinity. Many years later, after L'Abri had helped many hundreds of people, and Fran's lectures had grown into books such as *Escape from Reason* and *The God Who is There*, helping thousands of people to find Christianity to be reasonable and logical truth, Fran was to stand on the platform of Gordon College, Wenham, Massachusetts, and give the commencement address, after which he was given the degree of Doctor of Letters recommended by the Honorary Degrees Committee. The following reasons for his selection were preserved on a plaque: "Francis August Schaeffer IV. Founder and President of L'Abri Fellowship Foundation in Switzerland. A distinguished author and lecturer, he has been among the most dynamic evangelical spokesmen to bring historic Biblical Christianity into contact with the intellectual and cultural problems of the Twentieth Century. He has ardently proclaimed that historic Christianity is a more reasonable alternative to the dilemmas of modern man than the contemporary flight into the non-rational world of religious and philosophical cults. Gordon College recognizes Francis A. Schaeffer as an aggressive apologete for the validity and redemptive power of Christian truth in today's society.

"We honor ourselves this twelfth day of June, nineteen hundred and seventy-one by presenting this degree."

Those two occasions were seventeen years apart—and right now I must take you through the next "piece" of 1954. It is the end of May and if you could follow along for a long drive across the United States, you'd see Bob Rayburn and Francis Schaeffer driving straight ahead, with no stops to eat or sleep except for the minimum basic needs and a bit of food. They are keeping each other awake with conversation, surely about Fran's emphasis on "sanctification," the work of the Holy Spirit in us and through us, the need of doing all that we do in God's strength and not ours, and the need of revival combined with reformation. Bob is interested in Fran's illustrations to the students the day before, of the impossibility of an impersonal universe fulfilling human beings' needs. "Pretend this room is the only universe that is," he had said. "Now imagine this room being full of liquid and solids, with no free gases, no oxygen. There are fish swimming about in this 'universe' and they can be fulfilled. But suppose that suddenly after billions of years one of these fish by chance develops lungs. Is this lower, or higher?" The answer is, of course, lower, because there is no air, no free gas to enable this creature with lungs to live. It would drown. Just so, an impersonal universe which has come forth by chance has no place in it for "personality." If there is no personality to relate to, if "nobody is home" in the universe except chance particles, there is no meaning to existence. Yes, they would have been discussing some of Fran's thinking which had already started, but was not yet developed in these areas as it would be later. And the main thrust of the conversation would have been one of Fran's longing for greater reality in the *living* of that which he believed to be true.

As they arrived at Greenville, North Carolina, the Synod started with a day of prayer. In Fran's little notebook he writes of the word "restore" being related to both reformation and revival, and of the need to pray for the world in darkness. Then he puts down, "Fear not—to you is the future," as an encouragement for living in reality. The evidence of disagreement with Fran's emphasis became clear, on the part of leaders both in the church and the mission board. His pleading for balance and greater reality was taken for an attempt to take over leadership. The disagreement of these things brought a line of division, although the church did not divide for another year. One year later the Synod split, and out of that came Covenant College, Covenant Theological Seminary (with Robert Rayburn as president) and The Evangelical Presbyterian Church.

Where was Fran one year later? Buried as a grain of wheat! Buried on the side of a mountain, in a little old chalet in a village not on most maps. Buried as far as he knew, so completely that he would never have any leadership again. Far from rushing back to try to "lead," he had come to a step of reality in asking that his life and work be a demonstration of the existence of God. This step seemed extremely foolish to any friends looking on.

It was a step into what seemed total disappearance. Who would ever hear of him, or from him, again? He and his family were going to pray for the people of God's choice to come to them? What an idea! Whose idea?

But we are ahead of the story. Here Fran is at the end of May, 1954, and the turmoil his speaking has caused is to be added to by his speaking along the same lines fifty-three times more before we sail on September 1! We were living in uncertainty, as there were rumors that the board would not send us back because of Fran's emphasis on the need of cleansing on the part of Christians, and of being dependent on the Lord's strength and the power of the Holy Spirit, and of standing for truth with love. In fact, this is his emphasis given in the book *True Spirituality* which was written years later.

As the uncertainty as to the board's decision and our prayer and concern for the work in Champéry was talked about and prayed about in our family, Priscilla took the initiative of making a chart—a huge thermometer to stick up on the refrigerator. There were lines showing amounts of money, and at the top was the amount it would take to purchase boat tickets for the family, with some added for trunks and crates, to take us back across the Atlantic. We contemplated sending a letter out to friends making this need known, and then decided against it. "If the Lord wants us to go, He will send it in. We really want to do what the Lord wants and this will be a good way to find out. Let's just keep praying." That was the conclusion in which Priscilla, sixteen, Susan, twelve, and Debby, eight, joined us as we talked about it together. When Fran was back in Switzerland in January he had talked to M. Buchser at Voyages Kuoni and arranged the trip back. We counted up that if we were to make the reservations definite we would have to have a check in the mail on July 29, so we prayed that if the Lord wanted the reservations kept, He would send us enough money by that date.

At the end of June we left Philadelphia and the hot little house, to spend four weeks in a Ventnor missionary furlough cottage, just two blocks from the beach. My mother and dad had been given the cottage next to us. You will remember that, twenty-two years before, this was the place where Fran and I first spent hours and hours talking and walking along the boardwalk as we rapidly approached the realization that we were in love, and that lifelong decisions were "in the next act," so to speak!

Here in the very same location we had again been brought for cataclysmic events. We were to be spending the very last period of time in our lives with my mother. It was to be a beautiful time of being next-door neighbors, so that she could run over and watch me giving Franky his first haircut, as he sat on a stool in the cool breezes coming from the sea and blowing over the porch. I was to be with my father on the beach when suddenly he felt and acted "all queer," and I was to walk home with him as he was having a mild stroke—to make the phone calls to his doctor in Philadelphia, and to help mother through that time. (He recovered and was back teaching in the seminary by the end of September . . . and lived to be 101 years and 2 days!) The girls took down the thermometer and brought it to Ventnor to tack up on the dining room wall of the Janvier Cottage. "Mummy, just four more weeks, and there isn't *anything* in it compared to what we need."

Fran was away speaking in Atlanta and Valdosta and other Southern places then, and that night I couldn't sleep, pleading with the Lord not to let me make a mistake leading the children in this prayer for the boat tickets. I read of Gideon's asking for the "fleece" and of God's patience in giving not only two signs but even more confirmation. "Please, Lord, send me some word from Europe tomorrow that will reassure me in continuing to pray this way with the children." The letter that came in the first post had been sent a long time before, but had followed Fran around, and there were many postmarks on it. It came from a group of missionaries in Italy, postmarked "Pescara," asking Fran to speak at a conference they expected to have starting September 14, and the subject they wanted was his series on true spirituality. "We have heard of your messages in America and do want something on the reality of the work of the Holy Spirit in us and through us." September 14 . . . if we took the *Île de France* reservations, we'd be arriving in Champéry on September 9. The timing and the subject matter seemed to me to be a clear answer to my prayer for reassurance. We had a wonderful time praying at breakfast the next morning, and I couldn't wait to tell Fran of the letter.

However, before Fran came home there was much more to tell. Suddenly gifts had started to arrive, from people who had no idea that we were praying for this ticket money. Two women who lived next door to each other had started a prayer time daily "over a cup of coffee in the mid-morning" for the Schaeffers. Each of the two, independent of the other, had started to save up money to send us "for some special need." The problem was they had *no idea of any address,* and the way they found the address would take more pages to tell. The "timing" of that discovery and the sending of the two envelopes of money brought our first big answer to prayer the very next morning, and Priscilla and Susan raced to the chart with a red pencil to "see the thermometer go up." One day mother had the children for meals while I went to Philadelphia by bus and train and trolley to clean the house, water plants, and do some packing. It was during those few hours that Dr. Koop called and said he wanted to give us a personal gift, "for some need as you approach the time of going back."

"Timing" is what impresses me when the Lord is "pushing," "pulling," "clearing the path," "putting up a signpost"—whatever way you want to look at His guiding your steps to the next stepping stone. It doesn't happen every day. It doesn't happen when we are simply impatient and demanding. It takes place "in time—in the very piece of time that is essential to the pressing choice." Patience involves a period of time of *not* having an answer or solution to some critical problem or difficulty in your life, in mine. Patience is real, over and over again in a diversity of situations, if it is to be a growing quality. Perfect? Never. But gradually we are meant to look back on shorter or longer periods of patience in the midst of "impossibility."

Fran answered the letter to Pescara, along with sending a check to Voyages Kuoni in Lausanne and asking them to get him a train ticket for the 5:55 P.M. train to Southern Italy from Aigle on September 13 and to reserve passage for the family on the *Île de France!*

Exciting answer to prayer? Oh yes. There was jumping and squealing enough to be satisfactory to anyone who loves response rather than a flat, no-reaction, poker-face kind of existence. Doesn't it open a person up to terrible "hurts" if "joy" is allowed to brighten one's face and to bring a surge of feeling of excitement?

Shouldn't you attempt to squash all rejoicing until you find out what dreadful upheaval might follow to spoil everything? Shouldn't you drown out any jubilation because there may be crushing sadness just ahead of you, or others?

Perhaps one always should be aware of praying that one does not have "un-Godly excitement," *but* it seems to me there is to be a reality to actively rejoicing. I don't think we're meant to waste the opportunities we have to rejoice. Philippians 4:4—"Rejoice in the Lord always; I will say it again, rejoice"—does not hint of any such self-protection. That admonition to rejoice comes right before speaking of not being "anxious about anything" but rather bringing all the causes of anxiety to the Lord in making specific requests. The "hint" is that right after, or even during, the special rejoicing, the next cause of "anxiety" can penetrate and bring an urgency of prayer, intercession, petition. A reality of trust is demonstrated to the Lord in our real rejoicing, as well as in our prayer of thanks.

We were nearing the end of our time in America. Priscilla had graduated from high school with twenty-three other girls, making an unforgettable picture in their white frocks with armfuls of red roses. She carried that memory along with her diploma with high honors and the National Honor Society membership as she went back to "cram" for the necessary requirements for entering the University of Lausanne. We had finished our time in Ventnor, and had seen that my father was recovering from his stroke. We had had our "farewell" service in Willow Grove Church, although we hadn't been told until after that that the Board had decided to send us back. "Uncle George" Gilchrist had been in our little house with a pile of lumber, amusing Franky and the girls with his sawing, hammering, and "enclosing" of all the things we were taking, from double-decker bunk bed to an assortment of things that would give continuity. The boxes he made "around" the things were later to become desks and bookshelves that we are still using—so that day's work has *lasted* in a way a "cook's day's work" disappears! We had had a prayer meeting in our cabin, hugged my mother and others good-by (not knowing it would be my last hug of mother until we have our new bodies), then went up on deck to watch the water widen and the dock recede into the distance.

Soon we were sitting on an inside deck so that Franky would have protection from the open rails, reading letters with Betty Carlson, who was returning with us. She had become a Christian in Chalet Bijou when she and Gea had spent ten days there some years before, but now she wanted to live with us for a while "to learn and help." As we read the stack of letters that had been delivered in the cabin, we interspersed this with talking to Betty about our new "fire" to live what we believed to be truth. We were coming back, we told her, to live with more reality on the basis of prayer, asking that the Lord would give us His strength moment by moment, and that we would learn more and more not to depend on our own strength. We were interested to see what would happen.

Fran preached on Revelation 1 at the Sunday service on the *Île de France*, and quite a few people wanted to discuss with him afterwards. Betty, who is a writer, said she thought she'd write a book about "The boy who ran across the ocean," because Franky was so active. While on the boat I wrote a Family Letter and mailed it in the ship's post office before we landed. I'll quote my last three sentences: "Tomorrow we land at Plymouth at 6:00 A.M., then at Le Havre at 4:00 P.M. . . . We'll stay in Paris one day to get our breaths before taking an early morning train to Switzerland. Think of us leaving for Italy on the 13th and pray too for the ease the Lord would have us have in obtaining our permits to live in Champéry again. Lovingly, Edith."

Franky was trying to climb up and help me type as I was finishing that letter. I had to hurry to put the typewriter away and begin the packing before the stewardess appeared with a tray for Debby and Franky and me. I was going to eat and read quietly so that an early sleep would be possible for Debby, who wasn't feeling well. It wasn't long after supper that Franky began to shriek, with violent pain in his stomach, and then to vomit, until he finally fell asleep in my arms. He seemed better in the morning, eating a bit of breakfast and drinking his favorite orange juice while the packing got completed. As we watched the beauty of Le Havre harbor—a study in buff, cream, and tan against a bright blue backdrop of sky—it seemed a natural thing to let Franky run around in the warm sunshine of that top deck, away from the crowds lining up to be checked. It was to be the last time he would run on those perfect legs before polio was to hit one of them.

I was carrying Franky as we emerged from the train station, the Gare St. Lazare. He solemnly looked around and announced, "This is Paris, Mommy; this is Paris," . . . with the air of an explorer making a great discovery. "A day in bed resting and he'll probably be all right. You go sightseeing and I'll stay with him," I said in the morning. Franky was asleep when Fran and the girls all went off to see the museums, so I left the heavy curtains drawn to shut out the light. When I heard a stir in the crib, I pulled curtains to let a streak of sunshine in, then turned to see that, as if in a spotlight, Franky was "performing" his trick of lifting himself up as if on parallel bars with his arms, then over and down on the floor. But soon I saw—and I knew— though I didn't want to acknowledge it even to myself. His leg stuck out strangely from his hips and his cry went up as he fell. "I can't walk. . . I can't walk. . . mommy. . . put on my shoes." Polio—it was an unspoken word in my thoughts. "Please, Lord, not that," I prayed, still silently, while I swooped up Franky in my arms and put him on the bed, saying, "Let's string these beads together" . . . and . . . "Would you like some orange juice?" Happily I had brought a big canvas bag of canned Bib baby orange juice with me in case of sudden need. I hadn't a clue what to do about polio, and kept silently crying to the Lord for help, while playing Franky's favorite games with him on our bed, and reading him his favorite stories.

When the "sightseers" returned, I had to greet them with the sad news, and Fran and I had immediate choices to make. Phone calls to Switzerland brought no response from Dr. Otten (later we found he had had a heart attack that day) and as minutes slipped past, we prayed that if the Lord wanted me to take Franky and Debby (all on one passport) by plane, there would be seats. Established in those three free seats the next day we were soon flying past the train carrying the rest of the family and Betty with the baggage. Franky interchangeably slept, drank juice, and chattered brightly.

As we arrived in Geneva to be met by M. Berthoud, he couldn't believe Franky could be ill, he was so full of questions. The sleepy-looking villages and terraced grape vineyards seemed so calm and peaceful, it didn't seem possible this soft-haired two-year-old could be having an illness that would cause upheaval in his life, and ours. Was this the beginning of our new life of reality? Soon the doctor's pronouncement in Aigle, ". . . just a touch of grippe and a case of rickets," added to the dreamlike quality of the day. I knew he was wrong, but there was nothing to do at that hour but go on up the mountain to the chalet. The girls were delighted to be *home*, but the dark shadows cast by trees and the cliffs, the cold damp mountain air, the wooden walls of the chalet in dim light must have mingled in Franky's baby mind with his sick feeling and inability to walk or even sit up by now. For a month that word stuck in his mind with, "I'm scared of home . . . I'm scared of that noise" (cowbells in the night), . . . as he whimpered with some pain and connected it with the girls' exclamation, "Oh, isn't it great to be *home*!"

"Lord willing, *we'll* be going to Pescara." How important that "Lord willing" was again. It always is. In three days Fran was on his way *alone*, and not long after that a doctor from Monthey was hurriedly called again. He had already come the first day we were home, and had pronounced Franky's illness "polio." . . . He had suggested hot baths, massages, and rest. Dr. Kiesewetter had already been called in Pittsburgh and had consulted a specialist in his hospital who had said to stay there—"Don't travel"— and follow that schedule. But now a second attack had come, and already it seemed Franky's right side was being affected. "Quick, your boy has paralysis on the left side; you must bundle him up and bring him with me to the hospital. I have an invention that can prevent paralysis on the right side. The second attack is more dangerous than the first." Fran couldn't be reached; the decision had to be immediate. "Oh, Father, don't let me make a mistake. Please keep me calm. Help."

Our footsteps echoed through the halls of the night's quiet of a tiny hospital, and a nun all in white with a black cross and beads jangling pulled a lamp nearer to the operating table. "Hold him still," I was told, as an ether mask was put over Franky's perspiring, screaming face. The doctor's daughter said to me, "Father has been working on this injection for years, since his own son died of polio. It stops paralysis. It really does. He has used it on six human beings, and a lot of monkeys." This didn't stop my tongue from clinging to the roof of my mouth . . . and you may be sure that I stayed on my knees by Franky's crib all night, praying, wiping his head with a damp face cloth, giving him a bit of ice to suck on for a moment, and later the inevitable orange juice. I struggled for calm as I prayed for his life and for this second attack to do no damage.

I had my Bible beside me on the floor, and as Franky dropped off for periods of sleep I would read for comfort, in between moments of praying. I was in Proverbs and came to the twenty-first chapter, first verse: "The king's heart is in the hand of the Lord, as the rivers of water; he turneth it whithersoever he will." It was almost time for the doctor to come for the next injection. . . . "Oh Lord, if you can turn a king's heart in the right direction, please now turn this doctor's heart; may he do what is the right thing for Franky. Don't let him gave a second injection if it would be harmful." The nun came in and started to wheel the crib out towards the hall, when the doctor came and said sharply, *"Arrêt . . . ,"* put his hand on the rail, looked at Franky, and said, "I've changed my mind. . . . Put the crib back."

Meantime, at home, Betty was holding the fort with the girls. Priscilla had called her father in Pescara to tell of the second attack, and he had decided to leave immediately for the seventeen-hour train trip back, not knowing what the outcome would be. Was this child who had almost died at birth to die now . . . or to become completely paralyzed? Fran says he had the greatest struggle he had yet had, during that long train trip. This time it was a struggle to really bow before God and trust Him, asking for His will, as well as to pray for Franky's healing. It was a struggle to have a balance between these two things—continuing to love God and to have faith in His power no matter what happened. By the time he came to the hospital, the second night had passed (much as the first) and Franky had shown improvement in the morning and *no* paralysis on the right side. It was still only the left leg that was involved. As we hugged each other, and Franky, it was with such relief. We were to go on together, with Franky.

The girls welcomed their daddy back that night, happy to see him and to rejoice over the answered prayer. A week later the day came when Franky could stand alone, and he and I returned from the hospital to a much happier homecoming. Betty helped with the now two baths a day (an hour each), the exercises, and massage, so that I could get some unpacking done, in between cooking, letter writing, typing for Fran, etc. Priscilla was cramming for her needed studies for University, translating a technical article about the "injection for polio" for Dr. Chouquard, and teaching the children's class. Her excitement was the interest of two little Egyptian girls who came in between the classes with questions, and wanted to have a Bible to read back in Cairo where their dad was an automobile dealer. Betty gave them her French Bible, so Chahiror, twelve, and Rarvya, ten, looking as if they had stepped from an Egyptian frieze, asked if they could also have Fran's 25 Basic Bible Studies mimeographed in French to take along!

This was all taking place in September, but the month isn't over yet. Susan was to come home one day from playing tennis to complain that her knees were swollen and painful. A few days later she came back from a hike and said she was afraid she had done "something funny" to her ankles as they were swollen and hurt. Dr. Otten was now back from his own time in the hospital with the heart attack, and told us that he felt Susan had rheumatic fever and must stay in bed. He consulted with another doctor who confirmed the diagnosis and said, "Yes, no school, just bed for weeks." So, we got out the English school-books, and wrote concerning the Calvert Home Study Course, preparing to make Susan's little room one of "balanced life" by putting a bird feeder outside the window, and installing other things to enlarge her horizons.

Mail brought unhappiness at times during the next weeks as the disapproval of the board was expressed in several ways, including one hundred dollars being removed from our monthly salary, which had always been not quite adequate for basics anyway. As Fran looked down at times, and I wondered how to cheer him up, I took the name he had talked about on the boat, "L'Abri," and sketched a little "folder." He had said one day on deck that the French word for shelter, l'abri, would be a good name for our chalet in Champéry. "We could change it to 'L'Abri' and tell people it is to be a spiritual shelter they can come to for help. You know, people are already coming for coffee in the

mornings and tea in the afternoons—children, as well as the school girls, adults from hotels as well as M. Ex. from the village." As I thought of that I took India ink and art paper and sketched a few pine trees and chalets and a sweep of hill with a few black stick figures skiing. Then I wrote, "L'Abri . . . come for morning coffee, or afternoon tea, with your questions." Fran smiled as I showed it to him. We both thought it might be a good idea. It helped a bit as we began to get evidence from other countries that there were things being written, in letters, against us. We were entering a low time, a dark time—polio, rheumatic fever, and now an unpleasantness that nagged at quietness.

Betty departed on November 2, after the autumn crocuses had faded and the grass had turned brown. As the train wound down the mountainside and we walked back to the chalet, Franky asked, "Where *is* Betty?" and kept asking it as if we were hiding her. There were adjustments for us all. Priscilla took over for a few weeks, taking Franky down to visit the lambs just under our hill, exercising his leg as he climbed back up imitating the "baaaaaaaing," and rubbing Susan's back to break the monotony of her having to be in bed. One evening M. Ex. asked if he could be baptized and have communion with us. In the quiet solemnity of that service, no one would have known that I had Franky soaking in his hot bath, with Susan in a canvas lounge chair in the bathroom to watch him. Nor would they have known that Priscilla slipped out after playing a hymn to quickly dress Franky and pop him in bed with Susan so they could look at books together while she came back to play the next hymn. Debby took communion with us downstairs, and right after the service Fran took communion up to Susan, while I tucked Franky in bed and sang to him. As we said good-by to M. Ex. we were filled with emotion as we thanked God for what He had done. None of us realized what the outcome of that wonderful "oneness" in Christ was going to cost!

The official formation of the International Church took place on Thanksgiving Day when Fran and Priscilla met M. Ex. at the station and rode down the mountain as the sun played its daily drama of changing the view every moment, sliding from one position to another behind the peaks. They were going to Lausanne to Mme. Turrian's pension, to meet with M. and Mme. Cerney (the Czechoslovakian professor who had become a Christian at our chalet, and who now was preparing Priscilla for the University by "setting" her courses for study). It was appropriate that the formal formation of the little church was to take place where Fran had preached so faithfully to us, to Miss Massey, the Irish lady, and a few others, for that whole year. Miss Massey was there, and Mme. Turrian also. M. Ex. and Professor Cerney were very solemn as each accepted the office of elder. I wrote at that time, "Services will be held in Champéry, but also some services will be held down at Pension Riant Mont. Deirdre, at art school in London, is a member now and would come this winter but has to go to Egypt with her family, and Caroline, saved in Chalet Bijou the first New Year's Eve we were there, is coming back here for Christmas holidays. Helen, an American army colonel's daughter, is joining too and hopes to come back for a winter. God alone knows the future of this church."

So we were beginning to be hopeful of a special work continuing there in Champéry, in spite of the children's illness and our uncertainty as to the "silence" about our permits! Our denim curtains and bedspreads were finished, the kitchen had been painted yellow, the children had built-in desks made out of Uncle George's packing-box wood, Franky was learning to ride his tricycle around the house, and Susan was going to be allowed downstairs. Christmas had come, the chapel was again being decorated, and Edward Wooley (Paul Wooley's son) had joined us in decorating a tree and delivering food and flowers to village people. Franky kept us all in good spirits being so appreciative of each gift, and in asking the blessing he enumerated each item of food and each decoration in his thanks. With good food, warmth, and a stream of interesting people coming for afternoons or evenings with questions, it was one of those special moments of life, a period that seemed to be ushering in a "settledness." We had evenings with a dozen or so people coming from hotels or schools, with as widely diverse people as a Cambridge physics professor, a Member of Parliament, a Spanish girl from Mexico City, and a Swiss hotel-keeper's son from the Far East. We thought we saw a pattern unfolding of our "ideas" of what "L'Abri" would be!

We had had good days of snow and sun, fine skiing in Plana-chaux, and were taking Caroline back to the station to leave for

England when rain started. Early the next morning we were awakened to the sounds of muffled talking coming from outside, and excited voices from Priscilla's room. The girls were looking out of her window, watching men dig ditches to carry away the torrent of water coming down and overflowing the banks of the stream. Rachel, Herman, and Robert were soon joined by Fran, and they worked all day trying to direct the water back into the stream bed. That night avalanches began to make their way down the mountainside with frightening rushes. The roar we heard was made up of mud, stones, branches slithering down the mountain, sweeping everything in their path. Upheavals of the seemingly solid material things are such a clear picture of the upheavals of other kinds . . . which are just as unsettling as seeing houses look like matchsticks, or sides of mountains look like a child's sandcastle when a wave hits it! Shifting earth, whether in avalanches, earthquakes, or volcanoes, puts human beings into perspective so far as showing how ineffectual they would be in fighting the Creator of the universe! It is impossible to fight the created things that are involved in floods and unstable conditions. . . . How do people think they will face a battle with the Creator Himself?

I've described the details of the week of avalanches in the Family Letter of that time, and partially in the book *L'Abri*. Not only were Fran and Priscilla involved in battling the elements outdoors, but we were all involved in serving coffee to the workers and in watching the searchlights being played by the Swiss Army soldiers all night on the sides of the mountain above the village to watch for new outbreaks and to ring the church bells as warning. Mud, stones, branches and other debris came through the side windows into our chapel, making a discouraging work not only of shoveling it out, but of repairing the broken and spoiled things. Our own house missed being hit twice when the avalanche came straight at it, and then separated and went around two sides. We did have enough mud to keep us busy cleaning for days, to say nothing of bringing back downstairs everything Susan and Debby had carried upstairs to rescue . . . such as all our dishes, among other things!

I had had a "comforting passage," as I called it, come in my daily Bible reading, right after the soldiers had left the village.

It was Isaiah 2:23, and it read, "And it shall come to pass in the last days that the mountain of the Lord's house shall be established in the top of the mountains, and shall be exalted above the hills; and all nations shall flow unto it. And many people shall go and say, Come ye, and let us go up to the mountain of the Lord, to the house of the God of Jacob; and he will teach us of his ways, and we will walk in his paths . . ." (KJV). I knew very well that this is speaking of a future date in Jerusalem, but I felt comforted, as if it were written for me too. It had the smell of fresh-baked bread, if I could put it that way, and it satisfied my hunger that morning. I put "L'Abri, January 1955" in the margin of my Bible, and my imagination went to the people who had been coming, and I imagined a stream more coming to Chalet Bijou from many nationalities and nations, to inquire about the existence of God, to discover that He did exist, to ask about His ways, and to really come to Him in belief. I imagined people saying to other people, "Come, let's go to that chalet in the mountains and find out about the Word of God." It isn't that I thought that the Bible had been written about my idea of L'Abri, it was simply that I was comforted after all the upheavals, and hugged that comfort to me like a hot-water bottle, keeping out "cold fears"!

Then February 14 arrived. I had planned a celebration for Valentine's Day. Both Susan and Franky seemed better, and the house was clean even if the bridge still consisted of just boards, and the paths and fields were still full of rocks. We were "back to normal" . . . so it seemed a cause for celebration. Susan, who usually made a puppet show for us, had something ready, and the others were making Valentines. It was eleven o'clock in the morning when the phone rang and a message came from the *gendarmerie*, the police: "We have something that will interest you concerning your *permis de séjour*. Please come now." Fran took Priscilla with him to translate, and we felt this must be the five-year permit we had been told was being prepared for us! The cold blast of air that hit us when the kitchen door was open didn't chill us nearly as much as the content of the two pieces of paper Fran held out in his hands—an orange one and a white one! "Mother, you *can't* imagine what it is . . . ," said Pris. I began to read: " 'Monsieur and Madame Schaeffer, Priscilla, Susan and Deborah must leave Champéry and the Canton of Valais by midnight the night of March 31. . . .' Why, that's six weeks from now! Six weeks? We have to *leave!*"

I read on, finding the reason given as this: ". . . having had a religious influence in the village of Champéry." By now the children were exclaiming with excited voices. "Shhhhh . . . let me read the other one, from Berne; the federal government is there. 'Monsieur and Madame Schaeffer, Priscilla, Susan and Deborah must leave all of Switzerland by midnight the night of March 31, not to return for the space of two years.'" And the same reason was given!

"But that isn't possible! That couldn't happen in Switzerland!"

The children—Susan and Franky—weren't well enough to move. Where would we go? What about our hard work fixing up the dining room wall so that the stone shows now? What about our painting the kitchen? What about the hot water boiler we just installed in the bathroom?

"Why, this is our home, and our work."

Upheaval? *Bouleversement?*

"This is worse than the avalanches for instability."

e are standing in the kitchen. Two layers of my brain were occupied with the shock of the news—one with the enormity of the facts; another with lists already forming of how to organize how to pack, how to take care of Franky's therapy since we had now found a Swedish masseuse who came several times a week, how to care for Debby's school wherever we were to be going, what about Priscilla's studies, how would Susan get along at this stage of her illness with a *move?* Although those layers were buzzing with a succession of thoughts, a third layer was remembering that my cake needed to come out, even if it never got iced, and I put the layers of the heart-shaped cake on racks before following Fran into the living room. My second layer kept zooming along as the children found places to sit on the favorite couch behind the stone stove, or on the floor near that warmth, and Eileen (an English girl who was prolonging her ski time by helping us a part of each day and skiing the other part) was an interested onlooker.

What were we going to *do?* My unmanageable brain went on, no one hearing it except myself. . . . "We haven't any money . . . we've put it into reupholstering the furniture that belongs to this chalet with stuff we brought from Philadelphia . . . where will we go? . . . this is our home . . . we haven't any other

. . . the girls' schools are coming three evenings now, and a boys' school is going to begin coming this week . . . this is impossible." But, our new name for this chalet, *L'Abri,* seemed to be so right for people wandering down this path, across this rushing stream, for help. Hadn't the Lord made that verse in Isaiah comfort me? How could all this be happening? How could *this* staggering blow be in line with that "life of reality" we'd been praying for?

Fran spoke to us, as each one had been sitting in stunned silence, although probably their brains had been noisy with a string of thoughts. He spread out his hand, then curled up three fingers, letting two point like a path dividing and going in two different directions. "As I see it," he said, "we have two courses of action open to us. We could hurry and send telegrams to Christian organizations, our senator, any influential person we could think of. . . . Or, rather than trying to get human help, we could simply ask God to help us. We have been saying that we want to have a greater reality of the supernatural power of God in our lives and in our work. It seems to me we are being given an opportunity right now to demonstrate God's power. Do we believe our God is the God of Daniel? Do we believe our God is able to do something in government offices, in this present situation, as He has done in past history?"

He put it to a vote, to choose one or the other of these two possibilities. So, a mother and father, a seventeen-year-old, a thirteen-year old, a nine-year old, and a two-year-old voted to take the path, or course of action, which meant praying rather than frantically calling for human help.

We each knelt, and each one prayed, including Franky. "Please, dear heavenly Father, show us what to do." "Oh God, if it be Thy will, please let us stay." "Dear Lord, guide us." And when we got up from our knees Fran said, "While we were praying, it occurred to me that we must let some Swiss Protestant friend know immediately what has happened, before any twisted rumor starts being spread. I'll call M. André in Lausanne right away." M. André's reaction gave us a clue as to what people would think of such a story. "I'm sorry, you must have made a mistake in the French. . . . You see, this couldn't happen in Switzerland. Send one of the children with the papers to me immediately so I can read them." Susan eagerly offered to be the one to go, and with a promise of her being met with a car and put to bed to rest, we felt it would be all right. The Monivert boys' school was coming that evening, and Priscilla said she had better stay and help me with the two younger children, and with the refreshments.

The chocolate cakes were iced with a seven-minute icing (beaten by hand) which turned out perfectly and formed a thin crust a minute before they had to be cut. The evening had been an especially good one as, instead of being distracted, Fran had evidenced a special power of the Spirit in his teaching, and the questions had been very good. M. Ex. had arrived in time for the ending, and as he stayed on later he told us he was sick about what had happened to us because of his salvation. Although we had only had the papers a few hours ago, the news was around the village via the grapevine. "Some of the men are talking about getting a lawyer to fight this thing here in Valais," he told us, "but they don't realize the power of the church. What has happened is that the Bishop has said you must go . . . and even a liberty-loving lawyer will fold up if enough pressure is brought to bear on him." His fondest hope was that we could live somewhere very close by.

The next morning found us on the first train down the mountain, then speeding past Castle Chillon and on to Lausanne to sign the appeal papers. Susan's "mission" had been a success in that the discovery had been made that not only were the papers indeed putting us out, but they had been pre-dated, so that only thirty-six hours of the ten days for an appeal were left! The appeals had been written for us in proper French legal language, and all we had to do was to sign them, and they were sent Special Delivery to the two offices—one in Berne and one in Sion, where they arrived in the nick of time. This whole sequence seemed to us a very definite answer to prayer. We could not have accomplished it in our own wisdom.

Geneva was our next stop. Upon leaving the train we made our way to the American consulate, where we were obliged to report in person to tell of being "put out." His kindly attitude did not change the consul's statement, "America has no treaty arrangement with Switzerland whereby they are obliged to keep any of our citizens here. However, I urge you to go to Berne to see the consul of the Embassy, in spite of our not being able to help you officially." He handed us a list of train times to Berne and a letter of introduction to the head consul.

Our friends at Le Roc, Mr. Alexander's Bible School, had invited us for the night, so we not only had a place to sleep, but a very real time of prayer with them that night. In the morning we drove through the cold dark of 5:30 A.M. to the train station feeling chilly, depressed, and rejected—a very physical feeling in the pit of the stomach!

Both of us read our Bibles during our hour-and-a-half ride. My reading included Isaiah 30, and as I began, I asked for the Lord's strength and counsel to be vivid and real for us, in the context of the first two verses. As I got to verse 17, I was praying that indeed we might be "left as a beacon upon the top of a mountain" to continue in some way "lighting" people to the path of truth. And as I came to verses 20 and 21, I had a bubbling song inside me that wouldn't be stilled. "This is my God who is *able* to bring us through affliction, dry our tears, and direct us clearly as to which way to turn." As we stepped off the train, Fran and I exchanged the things that had been encouraging us and then walked through the snow to an Embassy still closed!

Our reception in the office of the younger consul was cool. He had no interest in what became of us, or where we lived. However, the letter of introduction brought a shrug of the shoulders and a grudging beckon of his finger: "Follow me." We felt like outcasts as he told us we could have ten minutes with the important top consul. Reading the letter, the top consul asked, "What part of Philadelphia were you born in?" "Germantown," Fran replied. "Why, so was I," exclaimed the consul. "What school did you go to?" "Germantown High," said Fran. "Why, so did I." Then the consul looked carefully at the name in the letter, and Fran turned to look at the name in gold letters on the door, and both exclaimed . . . "Why, Francis Schaeffer!" . . . "Why, Roy Melburne—of all things!" "Francis was the secretary of our class," explained Roy to the surprised younger consul. "It's been twenty-five years since we've met."

What followed was a long conversation, luncheon with Roy and his wife, and an appointment that very afternoon with Madame the Ambassador, Miss Willis, who listened carefully, said she couldn't do anything officially, but would certainly "talk to the Chief of the *Bureau des Étrangers* at a cocktail party that night," saying that it was "strange Switzerland was putting out one of the consul's old school friends."

What did all this accomplish? Nothing, officially. But it was to us clear evidence of what God *can* do. He who put Joseph next to the men in prison whose presence was to mean something in his life later, is still able to move a consul from a distant country to another one for just a three-month period for His own "weaving of The Tapestry." We felt we had an answer to prayer that gave us courage to keep on.

It is impossible to rewrite the whole story, which if completely told would be longer than what has been written before. We continued to have "solid walls" rear up in front of us, "impossibilities" which could have stopped our attempt to make an appeal. Time after time we were helped by people—a lawyer who offered to draw up the official papers, as soon as we could take the next step; villagers in Champéry who wanted to "fight for us"—but each encouraging thing was followed by a discouraging one, and the tale would be a confused jumble if I took you through each briar patch to feel the scratches along the way, while pointing out the sunsets that broke through the trees, so to speak. And each mail brought letters urging us to leave Switzerland and come to "be pastor of a church," or to "teach in a seminary." There were no "sounds of music" ushering in an exciting stage of the drama.

We had been sent a sheaf of green papers to be filled out to apply for a permit to remain in Switzerland. We were completely refused the appeal to stay in Champéry, and the edict from Sion remained the same—"out by midnight of March 31." Days were going on. The green papers had one important blank to be filled in with the name of a house, in a specific village, in a specific canton. We had to have proof that we had made a financial arrangement to rent or buy that house; then the village had to state that it wanted us to live there, and the commune had to agree and apply to the canton for permission to have us stay there, after which the federal government in Berne had to annul the edict against us! This seemed the most impossible string of things yet. Who would want to bother to go to the trouble of keeping this ejected American family in their village and canton? However, by this time we had had, day by day, many things which we felt were direct answers to prayer, and not "chance" or "coincidence."

Pulling out a map, we prepared to take the next step, that of looking for a mountain area in another canton which would give possibilities of having something like Chalet Bijou, in that people would be in the area to walk or ski. Another requirement was that it had to be near Champéry so that train cost would be minimal, and travel time for housëhunting would not take us away from the children for too long. "There . . . Villars and various villages around it are in Canton de Vaud, and a train connects in Bex with one from here." We started off in a blinding snow-storm the next morning, spent a day fruitlessly searching in several villages, with Mrs. Davis being our one bright spot. She was manager of Hotel Marie Louise, and when we told her our story, inquiring about a house, she invited us back for the night. The lovely room and a cold supper, beautifully arranged on a table, was a gift which we felt was like Elijah's supply that the ravens brought him evening and morning!

It was encouragement to keep on looking, although the days had been nothing but one disappointment after another—prices were far higher than in Champéry. Arveyes, Chesières, Gryon, Villars are all familiar surroundings of home now, but then we were tramping around feeling as if we were refugees, not dreaming of our children and grandchildren loving this area, going to these schools, having their photograph albums full of twenty-six years of pictures taken with these mountains, rocks, and trees as a back-ground. No, then we had no idea we would even be able to stay, let alone any idea of a full life springing from being buried on one of these pasture-covered hillsides.

The sheaf of green papers had a date after which we would be "too late." "We have only two more days to look, Edith; then we'll have to give up the search."

Walking past École Beau Soleil, we bumped into Professor Cerney and his wife. "Please, could you talk with us? We have a problem in our lives." We had a problem too, we thought, but we didn't feel we could push them away. Before we went two feet toward the direction of a tearoom, Madame Cerney pulled on my arm and whispered in my ear. She was seven months pregnant—the waters had just burst—my help was an urgent need! After getting her a place to lie down in the school, finding Dr. Méan, calling her clinique in Lausanne, getting a taxi, making a "bed" with sheets and blankets on the back seat . . . we finally got her esconced in her improvised ambulance, and Dr. Méan, standing beside me, pointed to a spot near her feet. "You will sit right there, Madame Schaeffer."

I looked appealingly at Fran and the doctor, not noticing the doctor's house in the background. (It was Chalet le Chardonnet that we were standing in front of.) One day it would be our home—many many years later—and in it some scenes of Franky's film *Whatever Happened to the Human Race?* would be made. I was unaware of being in the midst of "history" that would have a continuity of threads that would take my breath away some day. My breath was gone all right! But—it was with dismay and a feeling of being hopelessly trapped. What about our househunting? What about our time limit? What about our having to leave the country?

The taxi was moving now. "Good-by, Fran. . . . I'll call. . . . What . . . ?" Fran waved forlornly, "Good-by . . . I'm going back to Champéry—now." And I turned my attention to Madame Cerney, who really needed me, then, and through the night. The baby was a boy, but lived only two weeks. The Czechoslovakian grandmother had been given permission in her country to go out to see her grandson, but when he died the permission was taken back. Grief-stricken, the grandmother hung herself from a rafter in the kitchen rather than to go on living in the "regime." The Cerneys' baby's funeral, the shock when the news came from Czechoslovakia, meant that we could very readily see why my time with her was more important than our finding a house that particular day. It took time to make the discovery, however, that we had been brought together so that Fran as pastor could be close to these people as the days went on. After the night in the hospital, I went back up to Villars by train, determined to go on alone to find a house. Fran had given up. He and the girls were packing books, as he was sure the door had shut and we were going to have to leave Switzerland.

"Fran," I was phoning, "if I find something, will you come

back tomorrow to look at it, so that if it is right we can put the name on the green sheets and send them off in time?" "Yes, I will, if you find anything, but—I doubt that you will." My determination received a new rush of adrenalin. I would find something. I would go on trusting. I rushed up and down the streets of Chesières and Villars, and did see one *"À louer"* (for rent) sign on what looked like a nice weatherbeaten old chalet. Stopping at a chalet-type hotel called Gentiana, I asked the little lady who came to the door, "Who owns that chalet for rent?" Now, in 1981, for almost ten years Chalet Gentiana has been lived in by Debby and Udo Middelmann along with their children, our grandchildren, and students coming to L'Abri to study. But then it was still a little hotel, with no L'Abri anywhere in sight for it ever to become a part of. The little hotelkeeper politely told me where to find the owner, a schoolmistress in Arveyes, and off I plodded, planning my story which would "touch her heart" and make her offer me her place for a reasonable rent! I had a "good plan" to succeed.

As I was ushered into the school-chalet living room, tired from the tramp through the snow, my first words were *not* the planned story, but a blurted question, "What is the price of your chalet a month?" and the answer came just as rapidly, "1700 francs a month." 1700 francs was what we paid for Chalet Bijou for a year! I burst into tears, incoherently explaining, "Sorry, I don't usually break down like this but I've been assisting at the birth of a baby during the night, and we have just an hour to find a house, or we'll be put out of the country!" Where was my neat story? The schoolmistress slipped her hand under my elbow and I was halfway across the room as she started to murmur, "I know you need a cup of tea, my dear, but if you'll excuse me—" I was outside. "Bang" went the door behind me. I knew she thought I was mentally deranged and not to be taken seriously!

As I dragged through the snow, I suddenly realized I had been insisting on my own will, *my* determination to find a house. "Oh, Lord," I prayed, "forgive me. I really do want Your will. Please help me to be sincere in this. I am willing to live in the city slums, if it is Your will." Suddenly in the midst of my prayer I felt a surge of faith in the God of Elijah, Daniel, and Joseph, and I continued: "But God, if You want us to stay in Switzerland, if Your word to me concerning L'Abri means our being in these mountains, then I know You are able to find a house, and lead me to it in the next half hour. Nothing is impossible to You. But You will have to do it. I can't even talk to anyone without crying."

As I walked down the street of Villars among the laughing crowd of skiers going into tea rooms for hot drinks, I looked down at the sidewalk to avoid having anyone see my eyes, which were red from weeping. Suddenly I heard my name called. *"Madame Schaeffer, avez-vous trouvé quelque chose?"* ("Have you found anything?") I looked up and saw M. Gabuz, a real estate dealer who had not shown us anything because he said he only had *"deluxe"* chalets we couldn't afford. I was amazed that he remembered my name, or cared whether we found a place. *"Non, Monsieur Gabuz . . . rien."* ("No . . . nothing.")

Within half an hour we were parking in front of snow-covered wooden steps leading up from the twisting main road, partway down the mountain from Villars. "Do you mind living in Huémoz?" M. Gabuz asked. "I have never heard of Huémoz," I said. Now we were walking up the steps to the chalet, walking into a musty dark house and opening the shutters. There were three floors, with small kitchens on each floor—really three apartments. No living room for teas and discussions—but really a big enough place. I was sure God had answered my prayer, and that this was the chalet He was showing us! After arranging to meet in the morning, with my husband, I watched M. Gabuz turn the car around to start up the hill, when I suddenly called, "Oh, M. Gabuz, how much is the *rent?"* "It's not for rent . . . " he called back. "It's for sale." And with that he roared the motor and shot on up the road.

I stood in the fog with snow whirling around me. I couldn't see the fabulous panorama of mountains I had been told were "out there." They were totally hidden in the fog. I couldn't see in my mind how it could possibly make sense to return the next day and look at a chalet for sale, when we had no money at all and anyway we had no permit to stay in Switzerland. Something else I couldn't see as I stood there by the Postal Bus sign and the mail box was "the future." Time is hidden to us by a very thick swirl of fog! Future time, that is.

Had *that* fog lifted for a moment, I wouldn't have been so crushed. I could have seen the long stream of people coming by bus, car, truck, motor bikes, motorcycles, hitchhiking. I could have seen people from the East and West, from Africa and India, from Hong Kong and Malaysia, from Venezuela and Argentina, from Europe and Canada, from Australia and New Zealand. I would have been astounded to see who would be standing where I was standing, and to discover that they would be a part of a family that would have a special bond. I would have been incredulous that hundreds would be coming, and going, and identifying themselves to each other in London or New York simply as "part of the L'Abri family." You see, I didn't know that I was standing at the steps that would lead to L'Abri's central chalet. I didn't even know there was going to be a L'Abri. I thought I had heard a statement that had brought my day to a close with a failure to report.

As the bus came, I climbed wearily up the steps. My sleepless night and varied emotions were catching up with me! But there was time going down the hill, crossing the valley by train, and then on up the other mountain to Champéry to think and pray. As I reviewed all that had happened, it became increasingly clear to me that the Lord had been answering prayer to encourage us to keep putting our feet down, one in front of the other, as we crossed stepping stones. "Dear Heavenly Father, I'm sure You took me there today and that we should return tomorrow."

"Did you find anything? Oh, mommy, did you find anything?" The children jumped up and down, impatient to find out what had happened. The story of the night and day came tumbling out . . . but stopped short of telling that the chalet was for sale. Frankly, I feared Fran would think it no use going to look at a house for sale!

That night I again prayed fervently, telling the Lord in an hour's communication all about my fears concerning my own honesty, as well as bringing my requests. As I struggled for true willingness for His will, and for sincerity, I started to ask for a change in the owner's mind, expecting to ask that he would rent it to us. My sentence changed in the middle as I became overwhelmed with assurance that *nothing* is impossible to God, and I ended my prayer with a specific request which even startled me as I made it, "Please show us Thy will about this house tomorrow, and if we are to *buy* it, send us a sign that will convince Fran as well as me. Send us one thousand dollars before ten o'clock tomorrow morning."

It had snowed more during the night, and as we plowed up toward the village for the first train, the postman came swooshing down on skiis, skillfully pulling his mail and packages on a sled behind him. He handed us three letters, and we opened them on the train as it filled with the sunlight that was just spilling over the rim of the mountains. A warm memory for both of us is of that letter from Mr. and Mrs. Salisbury, who had been reading the Family Letters and praying for us, but had never contributed to our work.

"I have a story to tell you that will interest you," Helen started. "Art came home from work three months ago with a check that was a surprise. The company paid all the insurance premiums for men who had worked a certain length of time, and made it retroactive. We went to look at houses to invest in, and as we looked at the beams in a likely small house I said, 'Art, look at those termites. Doesn't that remind you of the verse in Matthew which says not to lay up treasures on earth where moths and rust corrupt?' Art said yes, it did. And I said, 'Would you be willing to take that literally and invest this money in heaven by giving it to the Lord's work somewhere?' He replied, 'Yes, Helen, I would.'" She went on to tell of their praying for clear certainty as to where to use this money, during *three months*. "Now tonight we are convinced we should send the enclosed to you to buy a house that will always be open to young people." The amount of their check was exactly one thousand dollars.

What a gorgeous answer to prayer! All that I had *not* told Fran spilled out on that ride down the mountain, and he wept with me as we marveled over God's timing. This was actually the last day we had to fill in the papers with information showing that we had made a decision about a house. We needed crystal-clear direction before making an arrangement to do such an outrageously impractical thing as buying a house in a country where we had been put out and where we had no permit to stay on unless an "annulment" was made. One thousand dollars was a fraction of what would be needed as a down payment. Had we not been sure that God had answered my prayer, we would have been stupid to take the next step. "But wait a minute," someone is saying as they read this, "let's figure out the time factor. Wasn't that letter on its way before you called out to God? So . . . ? Huh . . . It was going to arrive anyway. So what about that?"

There is a mystery that must remain in God's understanding. I am satisfied not to be satisfied. There is a necessity to let God be God, and to actively bow before Him time after time in being a creature created by the Creator. The temptation *not* to be willing to be the creature did not only come to Eve, and then to Adam. It is an oft-repeated temptation in insidiously diverse forms.

The Bible gives us something no other religion of man's inventive mind, nor philosophy of man's mind, has given—and that is a *balance*. Someone is constantly trying to tip the balance by putting lead on the seesaw behind us, and we wonder why we can't get off the ground. We're not meant to concentrate on *one* side of the delicate balance until we understand, because instead of understanding, we become twisted.

Yes, God is sovereign. He is the Creator. He is One Who has a will that is perfect, wisdom that is perfect; and in our "picture" He is the Weaver of The Tapestry of history. But also, equally, He has told us that He has created us, human beings, in His image, with both creativity and choice as real. We are not puppets. We are not manipulated. We do not turn out to be computers with cards in our backs to direct us. We have valid choice that affects history so much that that choice affects God, the Trinity. Because of Eve and Adam's choice, and the sin of each of us, God the Father had to be separated from His Son with the experience of suffering an agony we can't imagine. Because of human beings' choice, Jesus died in history that people might live. Human choice is terrifying real as well as marvelously real.

Prayer is a moment-by-moment example of the reality of the validity of choice. God Himself has given us this communication for a diversity of reasons. One is that our calling upon the Father in Jesus' name, and in the power of the Holy Spirit, is time after time a slap in Satan's face, that proves the victory of Christ's death to defeat the primary purpose of Satan's temptation and the resultant separation of Adam and Eve, human beings, people, from communication with God.

It is imperative to understand in one's bones the reality and *result* of the Fall, when Adam and Eve chose to reject God's word. It is also imperative to remember time after time that God did not send the cancer, the polio, the hatred and cruelty of people to other people. The spoiled creation was spoiled in all its parts. We don't know what it would be like to look back on a history that has not been spoiled. We have a mélange of things we can't analyze and explain perfectly, but we have been given enough in the Bible to base our lives on, not just in the realm of ideas, but in practical hour-by-hour life.

Before we call . . . God can prepare the answer, but believing all we are given by God to know, the making requests, asking, calling upon Him, interceding, are historically important if He is to answer. He has given us prayer to have a realistic "work" that can be done in prison, in a wheel chair, in bed in a hospital or a hovel or a palace, on the march, in the midst of battle of a diversity of kinds, out on a Villars street as skiers are pushing and shoving past, or in the dark of a chalet when everyone else is asleep. We can have a practical, realistic part in the battle between God and Satan.

Astonishing? Unbelievable? But true. In Ephesians 6:10–20, the whole point is that the "armor of God" is needed to stand against, to wrestle against the "wiles of the devil." And it is there, in that context, that we are commanded to "pray always with all prayer and supplication in the Spirit." Prayer is not just icing on the cake of a so-called "spiritual life"; prayer is warm, close communication with the living God, and also a matter of doing an active *work* on His side of the battle.

The Salisburys felt so pressed to mail that letter, written after undressing for bed, that they dressed again, drove out through a slashing rainstorm, and mailed the letter at the Hamilton main post office. God was answering my prayer, before I called, but on the basis of being God, He could do it "backwards." I can hear you say, "Isn't she simplistic." Maybe so, but it is a comfort to me often as I plead with God in prayer to say very simply, "I know you can answer this 'backwards' and you can have a beginning of this already accomplished." It in no way cancels out my urgency of prayer and the certainty that it *makes* a difference.

Now Fran and I were looking through Chalet les Mélèzes in Huémoz for the first time together. An old chalet, it had adequate furniture for moving in, and some lovely antiques such as the grandfather's clock in the dining room. We felt as if we were interestedly looking at God's extra surprises in the house He had chosen for us in answer to our pleading for guidance, as well as for provision of a need. It was with the kind of curiosity one has when opening a well-wrapped gift to discover what a loved person in the family has chosen. The view was still wrapped up in fog, with ribbons of snow keeping it for future suprises!

"Yes, we'll buy it" was our firm word that morning, as we left quickly to take the first bus down the hill, and changed at Ollon for the train. We had to get to the lawyer, the police, and the notary to fill in the papers properly, and to be told that we were just in time. The papers had to be sent to the President of Ollon right away. When Fran saw his name, he remembered he was a friend of M. Ex.'s, M. Favré, so in the end it was M. Ex. himself who presented the papers to the commune's president, with explanations given with great feeling as to why we had been "put out" of Champéry. Another prayer answered in a thrilling way of having people threaded together in The Tapestry— in the right place at the right time. M. Favré made the proper presentation to the cantonal authorities.

Did everything go as smoothly as a Swiss train slides along its rails? Were our emotions given a rest now, and did we have a clean crisp blueprint tacked up in front of us? No. Not this time either. We walked through marshes and bogs and almost got caught in quicksand—over and over again. Easy to follow a path when guided in answer to prayer? No. The criterion, test, verification of being in the Lord's will, being where He would have you be, is *not* an unbroken ease of progress, nor a smooth road with the bumps and potholes repaired! We had many things, day after day, which seemed to negate the reality of what had already taken place. We needed to keep on praying, asking, seeking God's help, as well as requesting that His strength be made perfect in our weakness. After all, we had an enemy who is versatile! . . . and we still have that enemy who is continually versatile in his attacks.

With all the impossibilities came new cracks in the wall, big enough to walk through. On top of all the other difficulties the gutted-out paths and roads made it impossible for moving men to keep their promise to come on that fateful date, March 31, 1955. But a M. Schneider of a new moving company in Lausanne, came with a bright idea of ferrying our things across the fields in his Land-Rover to his big truck waiting above. God Who cares about little children and details had sent us a man who not only skillfully got our moving accomplished before the midnight hour when the police had specified we had to be out, but who was sensitive enough to realize that two-year-old Franky was really upset about his room being torn apart and about things being carted out that were his precious stability during that important year, especially when he had polio. So he stood at the foot of Franky's crib the night of the 30th and suggested: "How about riding with me in the jeep tomorrow when we move these things?" A delighted pair of brown eyes responded, and the next day Franky acquired a new swagger as he leaned against the wall drinking his milk in exact imitation of the men drinking their coffee.

Our three girls had different parts. Susan had gone over to Huémoz early with Mme. Fleishmann to "make beds and get stuff ready." Unhappily, this brought her down with a new attack of rheumatic fever because of the cold damp house. Priscilla and Debby helped me with last-minute packing, and with our strange "last entertaining." In that living room that had seen so much during the years, we served tea and food to the moving men and to others who dropped by, using a weird assortment of left-over cups and glasses.

It was just before midnight that the last jeepload was ready, and the truck had gone, and we were crossing the Rhone River, taking us out of Valais and into Vaud. It gave us a strange feeling to look across that river and realize that leaving had not been our choice. We had been ejected, put out, and at that time we couldn't have gone back if we had wanted to. Through the years of L'Abri, as we have had refugees and displaced people come from Hungary, Czechoslovakia, Chad, and many other countries, we can understand just a little of how they feel, not only in our minds but in our stomachs.

We awakened April 1, 1955, to see the view from Chalet

Mélèzes's balcony for the first time. It was one of those magnificent days in the Alps when everything, including the air, is washed clean, and the peaks sparkle as shadows and dark trees and chalet rooftops give a series of angles that would look overdone if completely included in a painting. The view unwrapped! It was a tiny illustration of what awaits us when God unwraps future answers to prayer, or finally the gorgeous solution of the return of Christ.

Breakfast on the balcony, with blue and white cups and plates found in the cupboards, included the six of us, plus Mme. Fleishmann; a German musician; Rachel, a Swiss peasant; and Eileen, an English travel guide and ex-Wren. They were our first guests, and from them came our first questions, as we sat in that sunshine talking about serious things over another cup of tea and one more piece of bread and jam, hating to leave the beauty of the view! In a way this was our first "L'Abri meal" . . . but no one labeled it that way. We didn't have an announcement telling us that we had arrived at a location that would become known around the world by many people as "L'Abri." We were thankful *we* had had a shelter to come to the night before and were praying that we might be able to stay, but we were not at all sure what the outcome would be—not sure enough to start unpacking books!

It is almost exactly twenty-six years later that I am writing this in the same Alpine mountains on a day as clear as that one. My perspective is one of being able to look back at that which was future then. The book *L'Abri* tells something of the first thirteen years, as it was finished in 1968. Now another thirteen years have gone by. It would be impossible to repeat all that is in that first book, and then add a sequel to it in this book. Enough must be told, however, so that you may see that God alone could have done what has been done. You have a background now to recognize that God had demonstrated in our lives that He really does "take the weak things of the world to confound the mighty." In a sense, the scenery has been painted and the stage set, the orchestra is in the pit, the score has been written, the script is in the hands of the Author . . . so that as the play begins you may recognize Who wrote it, Who chose the locations, Who placed the people together to have the major and minor parts, and Who alone could bring about the blend of incidents, the accompanying music, the tragedies and comedies and realities which make up the understanding that is to come forth from listening with "ears of understanding" and watching with "eyes of understanding" and being involved in all that has taken place. Contrary to the illustration, however, a human director of a play or a movie has control of all the elements. Although I visualize God having planned L'Abri, and having brought a stream of the people of His choice, and having moved the people of His choice to give gifts to make it possible day by day for people to eat and have heat and light, and having chosen the stream of "Workers" to carry on though various parts of the years, and having brought about the results in human lives and in a wide circle of events . . . yet, many of the crew God has been working with, have rebelled, or refused, or stepped away from His direction at one time or another. So as with all other works or lives directed by the Lord, L'Abri is not perfect—because of the "imperfect people"! and their imperfect choices! I do not feel L'Abri has perfectly pleased the Lord.

That breakfast took place on Saturday morning. Fran went down to the two ugly bedrooms on the first floor, each with a washbasin, the bigger one with a pot-bellied stove and a hanging light with a moth-eaten fringe around the "plate" shade. By tugging and lifting and much puffing, Fran moved the boxes and trunks, beds and furniture out of one of these rooms. After that he found twelve straight chairs and carried them down, placing them in three rows. At the front he placed a table (a round one that folded into a half-circle). With a wooden screen he happily hid the washbasin, and off he went to prepare "the sermon." The title he wrote in his little red notebook, so we have it! Sunday morning we sat in our prim rows—all nine of us, plus M. Ex., who had come over for the hour's service. Fran had chosen as his title, "Put Your Feet in Jordan" and as a starting scripture, Habakkuk 2:4: "Behold, his soul which is lifted up is not upright in him; but the just shall live by faith." He spoke of the three places where this is quoted in the New Testament and stressed the antithesis between two kinds of people. "On one side," he said, "you have a person who is 'lifted up'—a person of pride— and on the other hand you have the 'man of faith' or the one who lives in the sight of the God Who is there."

I can quote, because I have a copy of that sermon. How? Because, although he did not then know it, years later Fran was to preach this same sermon as the *last* sermon to be preached in Chalet les Mélèzes, the Sunday before we moved into the chapel! That was to be in October of 1964, and L'Abri would then be nine years old. He had no idea on April 2, 1955, that he would be preaching to a stream of people coming to L'Abri, in that funny old room which would be turned into a lovely living room with a fireplace before many months had passed by. He had no idea of the appropriateness of the message to the work that was about to be begun.

But I will quote: "Faith is acting on the invisible, but not an abstract invisible! It is seeing Him, the Creator Who is a person . . . It is not some vague optimism. . . . There is to be a life of faith, a life of faith not only at certain climatic moments, but a life of faith in not forgetting what faith is. . . . It is believing the promises of the Creator of the world, and acting upon them." He went on to tell of Joshua and the priests approaching Jordan and seeing the river groaning and grumbling as it came down in flood. How could they cross? But the promise was that as soon as the feet of the priests touched the water, *then* the change would come. As he completed the story of that wonderful miracle of the waters piling up to let the people pass—*after* the feet of the priests first touched the water—Fran urged us that day to be ready to step in without waiting to see the waters go back first!

That day we were watching floods of troubles of little and big varieties, and had no idea how we could walk across, so to speak. Nine years later when Fran preached this message again— on the last day we had the church service in Mélèzes' living room, before we started to meet in the chapel—he preached it from a perspective of looking back over nine years of L'Abri and the amazing things God *had* done. However, the ending needed to be the same. It is always so for each of us: the future is hidden and if we are to follow the Lord's leading, there is always a moment when, in faith, we must get our feet wet in that immediate Jordan.

We had been calling our chalet in Champéry "L'Abri" in our thinking of it as a shelter for all those who wanted to bring their questions as they came for a morning or an afternoon. Now we, and the children, used the word "L'Abri" for Chalet les Mélèzes, as from that first day we had people coming who wanted to talk to us about their own needs, and desire to be sure of the truth. People like M. Ex. and Rachel, Mme. Fleishmann, and the Marclays came from Champéry and exclaimed over what God had done in choosing a chalet with such a fine garden and fabulous view over the valley, where thirteen towns and villages could be seen from the balconies.

When Priscilla and we prayed about her starting the spring term at the University, we had no idea how with our lowered "salary" we'd be able to pay for her fees! But just before we went down to register and find out all the details, a gift of one hundred dollars came from a Sunday school for the children. The other three (maybe unfairly to Franky!) voted to give their share to Priscilla to "pay for her university" then waited eagerly to hear what proportion that would cover. Priscilla came home to delightedly report that the total amount for the year (at that time when the dollar was worth 4.32 Swiss francs) would come to just under one hundred dollars! An attic room was found in a house opposite Mme. Turrian's pension for fifteen dollars a month, and Mme. Turrian made a special price for meals. Priscilla was to be able to come home Friday afternoon and return by the first bus Monday morning. We all felt it was a special provision that our new home was so conveniently close to Lausanne for Priscilla, but we didn't know yet that it would be convenient for transportation for so many to be coming to L'Abri.

It was the weekend of May 6–9, 1955, that L'Abri was really "born." Priscilla had called to ask if she could bring a girl home for the weekend. "Grace is tall and looks as if she had stepped from a *Vogue* cover, but, mummy, she has so many questions and is studying oriental religions; she needs daddy to talk to." I hesitated. The hot water boiler had broken. The furnace did not work. The wood stoves smoked. I had to do washing in the bathtub as the electricity was of different voltage than we'd had and so the washing machine didn't work, nor the refrigerator, nor the iron. Boxes and trunks were still not unpacked because we had had no word as to the permit being granted. In other words, I felt things were too "messy" to have a society girl who had been described as so beautiful and impeccably dressed. Pride nearly brought a negative answer. Then—compassion and the realization that there might not *be* another weekend made me say, "Of course, just explain our circumstances."

The same weekend Dorothy Jamison from California and her friend Ruth Abrahamson from Minnesota, university graduate students, stopped by. A storm had knocked out the electricity, so candles were the only light. The tablecloth I had quickly dug out of a trunk was a best lace one, so with a flower arrangement and with a good meal cooked—using all three gas stoves on three floors—the atmosphere was conducive to continuing the questions from three very different backgrounds and areas of interest into the wee hours of the morning.

Saturday conversations continued at mealtimes, and a long walk along the Pannex road brought the breathtaking beauty of changing views to accompany further questions and answers. We put a circle of stones on a gravel terrace at the side of the chalet and made a fire for a hot-dog roast. By the light of an oil lantern, Fran read the Bible and had family prayers out there, and then questions started again. Sunday we had our usual church service in that same first floor room. Afterwards we had a chicken dinner, with home-made sponge cake for dessert and coffee to linger over. That is, I washed dishes as silently as possible, and went upstairs to see how Susan was getting along, as of course she was in bed always (with short breaks) with rheumatic fever, and continued to be for three years. It was Fran who answered questions and talked, nonstop, and I gave a sort of appearance of being there, coming in and out, and caring for all the essentials "around the edges."

As they went for a Sunday walk, I began to prepare another kind of meal that would come to be known as "Edith's High Tea." My logic was that I didn't want the smell of cooking Sunday afternoon, and I didn't want dishes to be difficult for Sunday evening. A "High Tea" consisted of a great variety of little sandwiches with imaginative fillings and interesting ways of being cut, all to be eaten with the fingers, by candlelight, while sitting informally, drinking tea, and talking! This was to be L'Abri's general weekend pattern, not planned as a method, but something that was conducive to conversation—and continued to be so.

That weekend, and all the succession of weekends that were to follow until the children grew up, I disappeared to read to Debby and Franky, and later just to Franky, with the door shut and our time alone protected as much as possible. If there was no help for dishwashing, I did all the dishwashing later, but the reading was a "must." I may have made many mistakes in not taking days off, but that time of being alone for reading, talking, personal questions and togetherness at bedtime was precious, and protected from invasion! I could be persuaded easily to "read one more, please; don't stop now" . . . so that an hour easily passed and at times much more than that. You can't imagine how many books and what a variety of classics can be consumed in spending that much time daily. It is fascinating for the reader— an education and relaxation to discover new writers as well as to reacquaint oneself with the familiar old ones of one's own childhood. Reading aloud to a child does *not* make the child grow into a nonreader; it's too much television that does that, not closing the eyes and listening and visualizing in imagination all that is being described. Incidently, Susan got in on the reading aloud too, although it was hard to keep her supplied with books. Naturally both Debby and Susan also read to Franky, especially when they were sick with rheumatic fever, so Franky had a rich base of books! It was an upstairs-downstairs situation—daddy discussing downstairs with a stream of people, and books being devoured upstairs! Then, as time went on, there was a mélange, as I began to read aloud each Sunday night at High Tea, making an enlarged family of the circle of whoever was there with our own children.

By Christmas the two "ugly" bedrooms had been made into one long room with a fireplace at one end and the sagging ceiling repaired, so "church" had more space. Not only that—plaid curtains covering one wall, cushions on the fireplace stone bench, plants flourishing in the copper holder, a piano at one end, built-in bookcases filled with books, and furniture recovered made a homey setting for both conversations and teas. Was this a plan to make L'Abri "homey"? No, it was our home furnished, and then shared with whomever the Lord might send.

A list of facts has to be substituted for story-telling right here. The yo-yo effect of a succession of impossibilities and then answers to prayer continued through the weeks. By May 31 God had brought to us—as we had decided to simply pray for money to make a down payment (if He wanted us to stay in that house)— gifts in varying amounts from 156 scattered people, totaling exactly enough for Fran and Priscilla to take to Aigle to pay at the *notaires'* office. Eight days before that we had had only $4915.69. Yet when the last mail the morning of the thirtieth came, Alice had brought us fifteen letters, with gifts which added up to make $7366. Although we did *not* have a permit to stay in Switzerland even yet, the miracle of that arithmetic and timing gave us assurance that the money should be paid and the papers signed.

Not until June 21 did the permit finally arrive. Arriving also were our passports. In each, the page with its mark putting us on the list of people prohibited entrance to Switzerland was now marked *"annule, annule, annule"!* Excitement! Worship! Thanksgiving! But you see the excitement *now* was being shared by a stream of people coming to be a part of the family, one after another. After that first weekend, we *never* had a time without someone arriving on the doorstep with questions! L'Abri had begun.

Notice *this* date in the list of facts: It was June 5 that Fran said, "Edith, I'm going to dictate a letter to the Board," and I sat down in our "church room" (not yet a living room) and took that cataclysmic letter. We had been asked what we were doing, with strong indication that it would not be acceptable for us to stay there and receive people simply as guests to ask questions. Also we had come to a conclusion that if we were going to set forth to answer honest questions with honest answers, we needed to balance that with continuing to live by faith in some practical fashion. We had been living by prayer in a very vivid way, trusting the Lord to show us literally hour by hour what to do, where to go, and to provide the means. Now we were sure it was not meant to be an experience for a few trial weeks, nor even for a few weeks of trial, but rather that it had been a beginning without our realizing it. We wrote to the mission board that day, resigning as of that date. Fran continued that we wished our salary to stop as of that month. We said we felt led to call our new work "L'Abri Fellowship" and to pray that the Lord would send the people of His choice for us to help, and that He would also send sufficient money for the needs of our family, and the work, from the people of His choice. It was scary to mail it!

A Family Letter written on June 17 stated that my father, Dr.
George H. Seville, had offered to be the Honorary Home Secretary
of L'Abri. He had offered to have receipts printed and to care
for the sending of the Family Letter, the receiving of any gifts,
and the transmitting of any money. Mother was going to help
him in this, and also in promising to pray at least an hour a
day, and half of one day, once a week. One by one, people who
had been in that cabin prayer meeting on the boat, and others
like Dr. Bertha Byram, made a serious promise to the Lord to
take a specific amount of time a day to pray for L'Abri and for
the individuals coming for help. We called them "The Praying
Family" and sent a letter and a prayer list to them once a month,
starting with a Day of Fasting and Prayer July 30, 1955. That
same June 17 letter tells of both Miracle Book Club and Children
for Christ offering to send tax-free receipts for any gifts designated
for L'Abri, until L'Abri might have that designation and be able
to give our own.

All this in twelve days from the writing of the letter to the
board, resigning! Yes, we had made the choice to resign. Yes,
the name "L'Abri" was something that we had been using even
in Champéry as descriptive of our home. But we *couldn't* have
been clever enough to organize all that fell into place so quickly
as we started to pray for God to unfold His will, as well as to
send the people of His choice to us, and to supply the material
needs. We were asking one basic thing, that this work would
be a demonstration of God's existence. We asked, first, that He
would help us to answer honest questions with honest answers,
that people might know of His existence in recognizing the truth
of true truth; and second, that our living by prayer, and His answering in a diversity of areas, might also point lost people to
His existence.

L'Abri had started! What were our "visions" or "expectations"
or "goals"? Simply a desire to demonstrate the existence of God
by our lives and our work. Had Fran become a "perfect" person
now? Had his quick temper been conquered never to rear its
head again? Would he never do anything in his own strength
again, and perfectly live by prayer, moment by moment? Was I
now going to have no faults? Would all my decisions, moment
by moment, be the Lord's decisions? Would I really be "dead

to self" *all* the time, and have no frustrations as I cooked, weeded gardens, and washed dishes for an endless stream of people? Had Fran an "outline" of the answers he was going to give? Did we have a sense of having "arrived"? No, a million times *no.* But, God is very patient and gentle with His children, as in a real measure (only He knows the ingredients of sincerity and honesty) they attempt to live in close communication with Him, asking for help, asking for strength, depending on His wisdom and power rather than on their own cleverness and zip!

We were asking for "reality"; we were to be overwhelmed by "reality"! We continued to live moment by moment, having things to be thankful for, things to rejoice about with excitement, things to regret and ask forgiveness for. We wept, we laughed, we thrilled, we agonized, we squealed with surprise. Reality is not a flat plateau.

I wrote a letter August 9, 1955, describing the first month of L'Abri. How I wish I could just clip it to this page for you! I wish you could read in detail about John Sandri's arrival with Karl Woodson, on the yellow bus—John, nineteen years old, who was to say, "I feel as if I were looking at a new world I never knew existed before. You know, I never ever heard the word 'sin' in my church, though I went every Sunday. I thought Christianity was a rosy glow that didn't make any sense." Karl had been two years in the army and had been in Summer Bible School in St. Louis. Only the Lord's sense of weaving could have brought Hurvey's brother that day, along with John, who was within two years to be marrying Priscilla. There sat Franky waving his hot dog in and out of the fire to inspect it frequently, announcing, "This is the men's place. Only mens can sit here, other people sit somewhere else," moving over on the green bench for his future brother-in-law.

I can't possibly give you the flavor of that weekend, let alone that month. Jackie, a Jewish girl who had been in Champéry three years before with a school, started out aggressively against what we were teaching and then thrilled with hearing of the Lamb all through the Old Testament and of the fact that early Christians were all Jews. It was a Sunday afternoon just as I was getting ready for High Tea that Jackie heard all this, including the part the twelve tribes have in the structure of the heavenly city in the Book of Revelation. The dining room had to be quickly cleared for the Sunday school I had for Debby and Franky, before setting up downstairs for the High Tea. How can I make it clear that the mélange of people took shape right away? That it was during the cutting of Franky's blue cake for his third birthday that Siamese Pookie arrived (she was also one who had been with us three years before, Buddhist in background, sister an atheist now graduated from an American University) . . . and how that same night four boys *walked* up in the night through the woods from Ollon because one of them thought a man in the cafe had said "five minutes" (in French) when he had really said "fifty minutes." How can I help you to see and hear the fireworks, the lanterns bobbing, the blazing bonfire, the village band of twenty (then—no band now), and Debby's sweet voice as the village soloist for the First of August celebration!? How can I help you to see that the questions and answers were spontaneous because we very naturally had family prayers with the children reading verses, and one of us praying, and questions flowing freely—but equally that the questions sprang from Priscilla's enthusiastic descriptions of what her professors, or other students, or a book had been saying. Susan, Debby, Franky took part in discussing and their questions were a part of the whole.

We had only one rule: discussions for our own family and for those who had joined us must revolve around ideas and not organizations or personalities—that is, people. The realm of "ideas" was a wide one, including art, music, books, creativity of a variety of kinds, science, philosophy, medicine, law, world events, religions, and how you can know truth. Of course the Bible was read and discussed, but in a wide spectrum of being "true" and "important"—in the *whole* of life. Discussion was not categorized into subject matters and separated into "disciplines" but invited thinking and recognizing relationships across the board.

How was all this happening? Where? What difference would it ever make? Huémoz was not on the map. We were committed to staying in that chalet and praying for the Lord to bring His choice of people. A trickle that was steady, but not impressive as to numbers, came only to disperse, so far as we could see. Although Dorothy came back to help us, we had no idea anyone else ever would. There was nothing to "join"; we were simply praying that the Lord would bring people to be helped and then take them to the place where He would use them, rather than our trying to hold onto them. As a month went by, the arithmetic of the gifts that had come showed there was sufficient for food, utilities, seeds for the garden, the few bits of clothing the children needed, and our amount to put away for mortgage. That month's total amounted to about three hundred dollars. A special gift also came in for the urgent repairs and electrical work. It was a picture of what would be taking place through the years ahead— God had met the needs (He would), but there was never to be a possibility of stopping praying. We have always needed, and still do need, to pray for the needed funds—for regular expenses, and then for guidance as to any repairs or, later, houses to be added or branches to be added. We found that praying for money for needs accomplishes two things—it repeatedly reminds us that God is able to answer in these areas, and it also opens the way to have assurance that He *has* answered a prayer for guidance by supplying the money for a plane ticket, a boat crossing, a second chalet, a new branch of L'Abri—whatever.

A little old chalet on the side of a mountain, on a winding narrow main road to a ski resort. A family of six—father and mother, an eighteen-year-old in the university nearby, a fourteen-year-old in bed with rheumatic fever, a ten-year-old now deciding to study Calvert Course at home, a three-year-old needing some special help for his leg partially paralyzed by polio. No church, or foundation, or "home board" behind them. No big list of people—just 350 at that time on the Family Letter list, and 27 people committed to the Lord to praying as The Praying Family. Four people made up what other works might call a board or committee; we called this group who were to make decisions, praying for help, "The Members." These first four Members were George Exhenry, George H. Seville, Francis Schaeffer, and Edith Schaeffer. The first Worker of L'Abri to be signed up in the blue Workers' Book (still the same one in use) was written in at the top of the page, July 1, 1955—Priscilla Schaeffer. The second Worker's name was dated July 18, 1955—Dorothy Jamison. The ending of that August 9 Family Letter was this sentence: "Won't you continue to pray that the existence of God may be demonstrated here in every possible way—materially, spiritually, and with His plan bringing the right ones here at the right time for the need of each heart? Nothing is impossible with Him."

What can possibly happen with such a weak beginning? Weak? "But God. . . ."

CHANGING SCENES 19

A detailed account of the answer to "what happened" would take volumes. Perhaps a few "scenes" can help you to visualize some of the answer. Of course, no one but God knows the extent of *all* that has happened, because it is hidden in the minds and hearts of individuals. And anyway, it is *still* happening.

Have you seen the book *The Story of an English Village* by John S. Goodall, detailed painting which starts out in medieval days and, as each page is turned, shows a different period of time, in the same village? This is what I want to do in these scenes—to give you some tiny glimpses of the changes through the years of L'Abri. Families do not remain static, you know. Our family of six, for instance, has changed into a family of twenty-five in these twenty-five years! We go through very different periods in our own history. Fran and I are grandparents now. Each of our children and the ones they married are parents, and our grandchildren are the ages our children were when L'Abri began. We had four of us working together as Workers at the beginning; now in all the branches we have about 55 Workers. Through the years there have been a total of 198 Workers (who have come for shorter or longer times). Each Worker and each couple with children who have been working in L'Abri through the years have changed and grown older, as have the children. It is a "fact of life" that a family sitting by a fireplace and reading together, consisting of four children ranging from two to seventeen, is having a different experience together than that same family twenty-five years later having a reunion which includes people the children have married and fourteen grandchildren plus one grandson-in-law.

If individual families grow and change through the years . . . of *course* the L'Abri Family, which is made up of individuals, changes! The really amazing thing is, however, that with so few resources from the world's way of computing the assets, and with such a small number of people, God has done something which demonstrates very clearly that *He has done something!* Do you remember in the account of Gideon that God said very firmly and clearly that He could not use so many men, because then Israel would boast that their own strength had saved them? The tiny group of three hundred obeying the Lord, made it possible for God to make known, to demonstrate without a doubt, that indeed He had saved Israel. It is the picture of reality that is being given. The reality of God's work is meant to be seen in His giving to us His strength in our weakness in circumstance after circumstance, and in many periods of our own history. We need ourselves to remember that we especially asked that *our* lives would be a demonstration of *His* existence, in some small way, and not of *our* own strength.

CHALET LES SAPINS

Scene 1, Autumn 1955. Bill McColley, eighteen, on leave from the Army, is picking Thomas Laxton peas in the pouring rain, in Mélèzes' garden. Franky, now three, is enjoying poking and carrying around boards and pieces of rough cement from broken walls, and shoveling sand into buckets that workmen have left as they slowly change our two rooms into one and build a fireplace. A man from Ollon shakes the rain from his umbrella and asks if we would like to come to look at Chalet les Sapins, built by his grandfather and grandmother years ago. "It would be perfect for enlarging your work, and they would have liked you to have it."

Donning our raincoats, we go dripping up the back road to see the well-built chalet with its wonderful beamed ceilings, and we marvel at all the bookcases full of books which the man tells us he is *giving* to us. Well-marked Bibles and books of Bonar, McCheyne, Hudson Taylor let us know these Hoffmans were Christians. We lug the "library" back, wondering if the Lord will send the money to buy this chalet, offered with all its furniture for an amazingly low price. We tell the man we will pray. He says they can't wait long!

In spite of the rain, we find Anne Bates and Mary Johnson (American occupational therapists from a Basel hospital) have arrived with three others for the weekend. Dorothy goes upstairs to "move in" with Priscilla, releasing one more bed, but even so we need to put three mattresses on the living room floor after the discussion is over that night. Thinking of Chalet les Sapins, we begin praying earnestly for more space. Finishing the dishes, stuffing the chickens and preparing dessert for Sunday dinner, preparing vegetables, setting the table for breakfast, we find it is nearly 2:00 A.M. and decide to collect the hot chocolate cups from the "discussion" as a hint we'd like to "make up the mattresses" soon! There is no sign of boredom in the living room; people are still avidly asking questions. "Lord, please give us more space," I ask silently as I back out and shut the door.

Scene 2, 1956. The news has reached us on August 15 that Chalet les Sapins has been sold! Money had *not* come to us to buy it, and now we have found it has been sold to the people who had been running a "Vegetarian Pension," combined with Hindu teaching connected with a specific guru, next door to us. Now they have moved to Sapins. Sun is streaming into the cobblestone patio on the west side of Chalet les Mélèzes as Fran sends one of the children to get big pieces of wrapping paper and a measuring tape. Lydia and Debby obligingly hold up the paper cut into "windows," and Fran squints as he says, "A little more to the left . . . no, too much . . . back a bit." Now an idea takes shape. By adding this room as an extension to the first floor, we could add a double-decker bunk bed and, under the window, a narrow shorter cot for narrow short people! . . .

Look into Susan's room and watch her making the list for the weekly day of prayer (this was her idea in the first place that we should divide fourteen hours, and sign up for hour or half-hour periods and have someone always praying one full day a week, nonstop, "watchman on the wall" idea). This day she has chosen a verse to catch our eyes as we put our initials on the chart on the kitchen bulletin board. "Ah Lord God! behold, thou hast made the heaven and earth by thy great power and stretched out arm, and there is nothing too hard for thee" (Jer. 32:17). As we take our turns in the little "prayer room" at the end of the middle floor, one after another we read the page of verses I have prepared and pray about the requests, including this one: "Your answer, Lord, has been 'no' about Sapins right now, but please send us money to have this new room made for this winter, and give warm enough weather for the mason to do the foundations in time."

In the middle of that day of prayer, Alice, the post girl, comes with the mail, and there is a general rush to see what it might contain. Fran calls us all into the dining room and spreads a check before us—$2,000 . . . "to give more space." You would see in this scene all our family, plus Alice, two English boys, Hurvey, and Dot—all feeling a part of the answer as we follow Franky's response to clap in thanksgiving after praying. The person who sent the gift, with a feeling of urgency, was living in Valdosta, Georgia, then, but is in heaven now, along with Art, who with Helen gave the first $1,000, and along with my mother and father and two other former L'Abri Workers, Anne Bates and Hans Rookmaaker. That day M. Brachi and M. Dubi are told, "Go ahead with the job because God has sent the money."

Scene 3, 1965. John and I are going up to the same back road to Chalet les Sapins, in the rain. The only difference in scenery is that it is ten years later. We are answering a call from Mlle. L., the owner of Sapins, who soon asks us, over a cup of tea, if L'Abri would like to buy the chalet. We say we will pray about it; we hear of her plans to take a smaller house; we leave. . . . A week later John is recalled to Mlle. L.'s bedroom where she is evidently very ill. Her voice rises to a scream as she says she has had a "vision" and that the "vision" has told her she is never to have anyone in that chalet who eats meat. Meat, she says, is responsible for all the evil in the world—wars, sexual sin, and cancer. She has never eaten meat. . . .

The scene shifts to the inside of Mélèzes' living room at Sunday High Tea. Seventy-nine people are jammed in and spilling over into the hall as we serve, then stop for prayer. Steve is the first to pray. I catch my breath. Steve has come from a long line stretching back to Abraham, Isaac, and Jacob, literally coming to L'Abri through Egypt where he met Sue. Now he is praying the prayer of a newly born member of the family: "Oh God, please give us Chalet les Sapins so that no one who comes to L'Abri, as I came, need ever be turned away but may be received and made to feel at home, as I was."

Scene 4, three weeks later. In an Aigle hospital room, Mlle. L. is on a bed with drips going into her arms. Nick Cornelisse (a Worker then, now a Member in Dutch L'Abri) has driven me to Aigle "in between a million things." I hardly recognize Mlle. L. as she lies there in her weakened condition, but she turns her head, recognizing me with pleased welcome. She is dying with cancer! I ask her if I may read the Bible to her and she assents. As I read Isaiah 53, John 3, and John 14, she listens eagerly, whispering, "My father used to read that when I was a child." I speak of the mansions in heaven as being really the only important houses. I try to make clear the possibility of assurance of entrance to heaven by accepting the work of Christ for us as He died on the cross—not by presenting our own works. It seems to me she understands. I pray with her, and for her. She smiles as I kiss her good-by, and she gives my hand a slight pressure of response. . . . A week later Mlle. L. dies. My comfort is the "hidden" time alone with her, and the hope that she believed and really trusted the Lord. Now the chalet is put into the hands of the lawyers, to await the reading of the will.

Scene 5, April 1967. On a wonderfully sunny day nearing the end of Franky's Easter vacation, you would "see" several letters and a phone call bringing excitement—five answers to prayer in one day. After coming home from speaking in Holland at the end of March, Fran and I have led a day of fasting and prayer for "more space" for the summer, and for Chalet les Sapins in particular. The "five answers"? Hodder and Stoughton have sent a letter officially accepting Fran's book *The God Who Is There.* A girl sacrificially has sent an "extra tape recorder" to L'Abri so that other people can hear more, with money she would have used to travel to L'Abri. The lawyer has called asking John and me to meet him at Chalet les Sapins on Saturday afternoon at one o'clock to discuss matters pertaining to the sale. I receive good word about my manuscript for *L'Abri,* and a letter has come from Bermuda from a missionary who had worked in Dohnavur Fellowship in India, saying she feels it might be possible for the proceeds from the sale of a property to enable her to buy Sapins and let L'Abri use it! All this in one hour of one day, Monday.

Scene 6, Saturday. John and I sit with the lawyer at the dining room table of Sapins, to hear that there are ten inheritors of the property. We also hear that two other people will be bidding. One is a hotel; the other, a wealthy Swiss family. L'Abri may also put in a bid May 10, and the inheritors will vote on May 20. We walk back to Mélèzes a bit "hit in the head" to read a letter that has just arrived saying that it seems "impossible" that authorities will allow pounds sterling to be sent out of Bermuda to buy a chalet in Switzerland!

Scene 7, in the first week of May. We are having a full day of fasting and prayer for Chalet les Sapins. Everyone has met at the chapel for preparation first, then gone off with Bibles, prayer lists, pencils and papers to find spots alone in the woods and on balconies, even on a rock, to be alone to pray for uninterrupted hours. If you look at a patch of dry grass with spring flowers splashing color in it and ferns curling around a mossy rock at the side, you'll see Fran and me above Chalet les Sapins looking down on the roof, praying during that day for all of the people who would be affected through the years, if we did get the chalet, or if we did not.

As we talk to God, I'm sure He sees each one of you who are to live, eat or talk in Chalet les Sapins. The ones we speak about are Debby and Udo who have applied to come back into L'Abri work in Huémoz, and we pray this might be their home.

That very day a letter has come from behind the Iron Curtain, saying that thirty Africans studying in Sofia University are eager to come during the summer to L'Abri. "Oh Lord," we pray, "please provide space, beds, food enough for all whom You would have come."

Scene 8, Bermuda, in an official's office. Peer in and be amazed at the effect on this man who has power to grant a permission to send money out of the country for purchase of a house. You would see the earnest face of a woman explaining her reasons for wanting a house in Switzerland, and using the need of beds for thirty Africans as her immediate concern for this very summer. You would see a change in the official's face as amazingly, slight boredom turns into keen interest and involvement. The answer changes from "no" to "yes" . . . and the conversation turns to taxes that cannot be wiped out. Impossibility becomes possibility, but not final. Now fly from Bermuda to Cambridge, England, where Fran and I are speaking, but are called to a phone to get the encouragement from Bermuda: "The man with the authority has said 'yes'."

Scene 9, May 20, 1967. The bids are in now and a day of fasting and prayer is again taking place not only in L'Abri in Switzerland, but also in Japan, in St. Louis (where Debby and Udo and others are praying), in London, in Manchester, in California, and everywhere that there are Members of the Praying Family—from a chicken farm in Nova Scotia to little homes in Chester, dorm rooms in Boston, and other scattered towns. We had had a surprise in Cambridge when we found that every Tuesday eight students had breakfast together to pray for L'Abri, and they were praying for Chalet les Sapins. The threads in The Tapestry are blended into a detailed pattern in one area this day!

Fran and I pray as we travel by train to Wales, and again as we arrive in our hotel in Lladdudno. I have ordered tea for three, and Fran is watching out the door for the arrival of Franky from his boarding school, when I am called to the phone in a "call box" down the long hall. "Mother, it's Susan. Pris just told us that the answer is 'yes.' . . . The inheritors voted 'yes' that L'Abri's bid was accepted; L'Abri can have Sapins." The news is immediately shared with Fran and Franky as they came through the revolving door . . . and a High Tea is our celebration!

Scene 10, May 20, 1967, in Huémoz. You must look carefully at the Day of Prayer with everyone scattered on the hillsides praying so earnestly. Then follow the solemn group of men in three-piece suits and ties, walking down to Chalet TziNo with Priscilla suddenly frightened to hear their reply, diving under the bed, and John receiving the "yes" . . . "Yes, we have decided to sell it to L'Abri" . . . and Prisca crawling out again to jump up and down and squeal. The big cow bell is to be the signal to all the others praying, if an affirmative answer has come. The bell clangs out the message, loud and long. A big cake is quickly made and iced and an evening celebration of rejoicing finishes off the day! Thanksgiving!

Scene 11, June, 1967. As the missionary who has bought Chalet les Sapins walks with us and the lawyer around the house and on Sapins's balcony, the clouds rolled away and a burst of sun lights up the view, as if God Himself were setting a scene for an audience. The transaction was made in Aigle where each of the other chalets, before, and since, have been signed for and purchased, each one with an amazing story. As we have supper that evening at Chesalet, the doorbell rings and the lawyer comes in and bows, as if he were in a play, handing a key so large and dramatic in looks that it doesn't seem real. The owner takes it, and then turns to me and says, "For L'Abri."

Scene 12, two days later. Fifty people march around Les Sapins, up to the first terraced level in the field above, as others sit in the doorway playing instruments. It has been Fran's idea to have this march, as he is going to bring us a message from Joshua on the falling down of the walls of Jericho in the dedication message he will be giving in the house.

We crowd into the dining room—people from so many nationalities, one African girl ahead of the twenty-nine others yet to come. And the very dear one who has bought it, who has spent much of her life in India where Hinduism spreads darkness, prays with such understanding as Fran asks for prayer that "all the

darkness might be cleansed from this chalet where Hinduism has been taught for so long." We serve the first meal in Sapins this day, big homemade rolls filled with chicken salad, and a huge cake iced and decorated for Priscilla's birthday which had not been celebrated two days before! This is June 20. With a few cots put in, L'Abri also begins to have people sleep in Sapins the same day!

Scene 13, July 8, 1967. Debby and Udo arrive at the chalet which is full of people. Double-decker bunk beds, cots, sleeping bags fill not only the rooms but the wide balconies. Among the thirty-five people here at this time are not only some of the Africans, but two from India itself. Back in 1955, twelve years before, two missionaries staying in Mlle. Chaudet's pension, which was then in Beau Site, had prayed for L'Abri's future on our first day of fasting and prayer. They had taken prayer lists and given that day to that kind of "work with us." These two Miss Stammerses were to continue praying faithfully for L'Abri, one back in Dohnavur Fellowship, India; the other, in Beirut. How thrilled they have been about the Indians who have come through the years but also that one of their friends has been chosen by the Lord to provide Les Sapins.

The weaving of threads in The Tapestry covers endless miles of geographic space, and blends together so many periods of history. To take one spot of geography such as Chalet les Sapins and to try to keep the microscope in place long enough to catch some small idea of the Lord's amazing blend of continuity and diversity is overwhelming. One becomes dizzy in "looking," let alone in trying to capture it in words.

Scene 14, July 1967. It has been a marvelous answer to prayer for Debby and Udo to have had a chalet to come into when they arrived, and the many others that summer. But . . . look at this scene and see what it is like to have thirty-five people with two bathrooms—twenty people lined up on one floor and fifteen on the other, waiting their turn to shave, brush teeth, etc. That answer to prayer has meant feeling "drowned" not only with people but also with their moment-by-moment needs. For Debby and Udo, having just finished exams and come into their new home and new work, it is overpowering. Udo immediately takes over the doing of the "meal lists" (planning where each one should eat) as the numbers in L'Abri have gone from 90 to 135 in a few days . . . because . . . it is July 10 that the "Arts Festival" begins. This is a truly "wonderful week" of special lectures and concerts, but the meals, dishes, bed-making, washing, gardening, marketing, potato-peeling have to continue . . . and stoves have broken down! Feeding people with one burner for cooking adds a challenge for me that does not always generate a calm response, as I cook while others are at the lectures.

The Sunday night High Tea at Mélèzes that week has all 135 and amid the chattering of the varied languages one hears Rookmaaker's voice and voices of others who have come for the lecture at Arts Week. Not only have lectures been given and music performed, but ideas are being exchanged, creativity encouraged, inspiration to "keep on" has been given to artists, and much discussion—living and very *real* discussion—has been stirred up. Sandwiches disappear so rapidly that we who have prepared them so artistically wonder if the "art" of that cooking is being noticed! We reflect then that the background for an artistic discussion is important! So often my part has been to prepare food, provide candlelight, and create flower arrangements as "background" for diverse discussions.

Scene 15, March 23, 1981, Chalet les Sapins. A lot of pages have had to be turned over to jump fourteen years from the week that Debby and Udo entered into Sapins. Preparing this book, we've turned over the "scenes" of hundreds of arrivals and departures, mealtime discussions and the reading aloud of books. We've skipped the page sketching the moving day in 1972 when Debby and Udo, Natasha and Samantha, moved up the hill to Chesières and into the little old Hotel Gentiana, where so soon after their moving in you would have seen someone knocking at the door—not knowing what would be on the other side. Jorge, caught in the middle of the drug scene of the '60s and looking for a physical shelter, was flabbergasted at being taken down to a candlelight meal where the ongoing conversation drew him in. That scene could be so often repeated as "pages" of the stories of *all* the L'Abri chalets in Switzerland and houses in England, Holland, France, Italy, America, would be turned over. So often you would be astonished, catching your breath to see that the timing of a knock on the door has come just when the Lord has moved in the right person to answer the knock.

When Debby and Udo moved out of Chalet les Sapins, Larry and Nancy moved in. . . . And we are turning the pages over so swiftly you can't peek, as the changes take place while people *keep* knocking. . . . Now in March 1981 snow is still in patches on the ground and clinging to many rooftops. Flurries are falling in between rain showers, as another spring is coming to L'Abri. Les Sapins is still one of the "central" chalets, and students still live and study here. But no longer do thirty-five crowd in here, nor in Beau Site, nor in any of the chalets. Long ago, complaints from a man trying to put a "stop" to L'Abri, brought local police with measuring sticks and tapes who, a bit sheepishly, went around measuring and computing the cubic space of each room. By law we were limited. It was a law which God used in His own way as a protection for growing families through the years.

"Compassion" can be bigger and a more all encompassing emotion within us than we have strength to carry out in action. We are finite. We have one life to live one day at a time. Our children have one childhood. To be parents, whether in L'Abri or elsewhere in the pattern of the Lord's people in space or history, is to be given responsibility for balance in use of time, and space. But to be a single person is also to have responsibility in use of time and space. And no one can apply the pattern of another person's history to make a life that "fits" his or her "calling" in this moment of history.

Ann Brown would be in Sapins instead of preparing to go to Sweden to learn the language if it weren't for the matter of "government regulations" again, this time concerning the impossibility of having permits to stay in Switzerland. Having Sapins as her "open home" for some years is a colorful page we've just turned past. Because, in today's mixture of snowdrops, coming up from their hidden roots as the first spring flowers, and snowflakes drifting down . . . what we see in Sapins is two homes. Mary Jane and Greg with tiny one-week-old baby Fiona are in the apartment on the top floor. They have a few weeks to share the apartment now, before they move to make Beau Site their home. As Rodman and Becky Miller (so short a time ago her name was Sandri) prepare to have that apartment the place where they will serve meals to some students, Fran and I are brought up short with the changes all these "scenes" and others have brought to *one* piece of territory in *one* piece of history. Rodman and Becky are a third generation of L'Abri Workers on the same hillside, and she, our first granddaughter to have a L'Abri home. (Continuity is a precious reality in the midst of changing scenes.) The second "home" is the larger one of the bottom two floors. Bob Jono is furnishing it with a variety of Oriental dishes and candlesticks brought back from his time as L'Abri's missionary to the needs of refugee work in Cambodia. We voted to send him as our representative when he was asked to help the UN efforts there. Now he is back, and as a L'Abri Member, is happy to be at home again.

* * *

Diversity under one overhanging Swiss chalet roof is a very small fraction of the diversity in all of L'Abri. Each home is a home, not an institutional replica of a home. L'Abri Workers are not carbon copies of Fran and myself, and their homes are not carbon copies of ours. L'Abri is made up of human beings who are in the midst of their lives, not going somewhere to work so many hours a day, then leaving that work to "live" somewhere else. For Fran and myself and our family, as we look back over the years now, the important thing to say is that "people ought to be given a chance to change and grow and learn and develop." As husband and wife, we are two separate people and we share the need to realize that the situation of a relationship is not frozen at one moment of history, because we are not static; we change. Our own understanding and sensitivity changes. The "scene" which is you, me, us, is a changing scene. The danger is that people try to approach Fran and myself, and also all the other L'Abri Workers, as some sort of "finished products" who will "dish out" both food and conversation that is never "burned," "too thick," "too salty," "too sweet," "too undercooked," "too indigestible," "too light," "too heavy," "too dull," "too exotic." People expect too much!

The truth of it is we are all imperfect, weak, very human beings in different stages of life. There are times when people are coming down with a cold, or fighting a virus, or having a toothache, or needing new glasses. There are times when people are pregnant with a growing baby inside, or with growing "ideas" for a lecture or a book. There are times when people are having a special struggle with some spiritual thing in their own lives, or are rethinking some phase of their priorities and are starting a new resolve to exercise every day, to diet for health or weight, to take a morning hour before anyone is up to run up to the woods and pray. There are fresh resolves and heavy temptations. There are the moments of wondering, "Is all this intensity worth it?" and of feeling like replying to someone's complaints about their heavy problems, "You ought to hear *my* problems." The scene changes, not just over the periods of history in *places*, but in the combination in families. A family with three teenagers has very different pressures from that same family when it has a baby in diapers, a preschool child having measles, or a first-grader needing to get off to school in time. L'Abri people face changing scenes in their bodies, as legs get broken, teeth need a huge job, operations are undergone, arthritis sets in, a dreaded disease hits, or just plain exhaustion affects the whole outlook.

In writing of The Tapestry's being woven with lives threaded together in patterns, it is excruciatingly important to emphasize for a "weaver" and for the "woven threads" that the threads may be brittle, or break, or get tangled at times . . . and these changing threads affect each other! We are each affecting the warp and woof of the fabric. But—we are too likely to blame someone else.

ENGLISH L'ABRI

Scene 1, April, 1958. A dark-haired, beautiful, vivacious girl, kneeling, being watched only by God, is praying. This physical "child of Abraham" has just become a spiritual "descendant of Abraham," and she is calling out to Abraham's God, through the Lamb, who has recently become her Messiah-Savior as she came to believe, in Chalet les Mélèzes. The place is Basel, Switzerland, where the girl has put aside her concert violin career for a career in occupational therapy. What will action based on this moment of prayer have to do with L'Abri in England?

The plea to the Lord is for His opening eyes of understanding among people of her family, and other friends in England. The action is a resolve to take money saved up for a pleasure trip and send it anonymously to a girl in England to purchase tickets for travel, make hotel reservations, and ask the Schaeffers to go to London for a week. The simple prayer then would be that the Lord would bring the people of His choice to those hotel rooms during that time, as a small handful of people who have become Christians in L'Abri are told the Schaeffers will be there. The letter is sent. Information and tickets are sent to the Schaeffers. An affirmative decision is made that the Lord is leading in this Week's Venture!

Scene 2, June 1, 1958. Deirdre meets us at London's Heathrow Airport and eagerly listens as we tell her of the amazing "send-off" in Geneva Airport. A girl met us right there to ask if she could pray with us and "become a Christian." (This was someone who had been at L'Abri several weekends, studying in Geneva.) We eat together at a Lyons Restaurant for supper and look at Deirdre's empty notebook and spaces marked Morning, Afternoon, and Evening for each of the eight days ahead, praying together as to how God would fill them! The two rooms at the Mount Royal Hotel are "faceless" as we peer in, then enter, wondering what could possibly happen in a week's short time.

When we leave after seven days, we glance back at rooms filled with memories. Over seventy-five different people have come in and out of those rooms, nineteen at a time some evenings, with questions, with problems, with eager welcome. Some are those who were in Priscilla's school in Lutry, some have been in our chalet in Champéry, some are friends of Deirdre's, and others have been at Swiss L'Abri. There are art students, doctors, a Yugoslavian violinist, a Hungarian Jewish professor and his psychiatrist wife, three atheistic Jewish friends of Deirdre's, and Hans Rookmaaker, with five Dutch students who are on tour with him. The phone rings and we are urged to "come, please" to two other places. We promise each place a part of a day.

Scene 3, same week, Cambridge, St. Catherine's College. In a room where a student, Mike Cassidy, is welcoming about a dozen friends, the kettle is puffing forth steam as it boils on a gas ring, and tea, bread and butter, and biscuits are being passed around. Crossing the grass, thrilling over the beauty of the ancient stones and the history of the quadrangle, Fran and I climb up the worn steps to the second floor, to look out the other side of the leaded windows—our first time on the inside of a student's room in an English university. Glimpses of the quiet River Cam and the cows grazing placidly within sight of the walks nearby have already made us long to spend more time here. Fran gives his message on "The Two Chairs," during which first expressions on the dozen faces are aloof and suspicious. "What has this American to say that is worth listening to?" was a question that seemed to be in their eyes.

A red-haired boy comes bursting in late from hockey practice, face flushed, eyes brown and shining. "Wonder who that is?" I ask myself. But my own imagination does not answer, nor does the idea come into my head, "That's who Susan will marry . . . and the one who will be carrying on L'Abri in England for many years." I would have to reject the idea as a time-wasting piece of fiction! The expression on each of the students' faces changes during the answers to questions that continue for "too long." When we say we must "run to catch the train," several eagerly beg us to come back. As the red-haired boy, Ranald Macaulay, and Mike take us to the train, they insist that the time has been all too short. They say that next time they would like to invite others, for individual conversations, as well as more group discussion.

We have no idea what has been started that day. One "beginning" is a special series of discussions which will give Fran some amazing opportunity to develop his own thinking and discover answers in the arena of questions from many different disciplines and bright minds in those disciplines. The other "beginning" is that of a series of "return trips" which will include many universities, not for public meetings but for deep, long discussions. We arrive back at the hotel at 9:00 P.M. after a three-hour trip by train, to find people waiting for us to "begin the evening."

Scene 4. Sunday of the same week. We go for Sunday lunch to visit the parents of Wendy (a recently born-again music student who had come first as an atheist to Chalet les Mélèzes and now wanted us to talk to her parents). The charming old house is set in apple orchards, with a rambling garden, a tiny stream, and a fenced-in field where a storybook horse lived. In retrospect, the outstanding "purpose" of being there is the story I wrote about "a wistful ballet dancer who has had a very difficult life" in *L'Abri*. That was Linette, who was to be very central in the "weaving" in England.

Scene 5. Phone calls keeping coming until the last minute, with Jennifer calling to say that an anonymous gift has come to help with the next trip. "Too late this time, we're on our way out," we have to say, but we promise those who call that we do expect to be back.

There is space in these pages for only a few of all the "scenes" that followed in the English story. Linette came to Swiss L'Abri almost as soon as we arrived back. And came not just to Swiss L'Abri, but to the Good Shepherd who had been so clearly gentle in His "finding" her. She would be the one to have a notebook ready to follow us around as we went on the next English trip and to listen in on all the discussions. Ranald was to be the one to organize the exact time schedule for conversations each day in Cambridge with a variety of students from many backgrounds. Once there were twenty atheists who came to fire questions at Fran during a long evening, and once Fran spoke to the Humanist Society. There was also a debate with a humanist, which ended with the humanist taking such a beating, as far as audience response went, that Fran decided never to debate again. He preferred to "discuss," he said, with the hope of helping the other individual rather than "winning" a debate. Cambridge, Oxford, St. Andrews University, Durham, two universities in Dublin, London School of Economics, Kings College London, Manchester University, Edinburgh University, and other schools were added to the places where he and I visited by invitation of students, to discuss in groups, or at times larger numbers, and often with one or two individuals. As "honest questions" were listened to, thought about, and answered, not only were the people helped who *asked* the questions, but Fran grew excited as to the reality and truth of the answers—answers true to what *is,* and recognized as so by people of many disciplines: science, philosophy, law, literature, etc.

Because there were no books, no tapes, nothing to continue listening to in the area of his answers, there were people—such as Dick Keyes—who came and followed around on these and later English trips counting it as a part of their education.

Scene 6, January 1959. An English taxi with curtains tied back at the windows, full of laughing faces, chugs up to the Mélèzes front garden. It has been announced as arriving at 3:57 P.M. and makes it exactly! Out tumble Mike Cassidy and his sister Olave (from Basutoland, Africa) and Denise, Vicky, Richard, and Tom Barlow of South Africa. Later Ranald comes, and a stream of others, in a sort of "Cambridge comes to L'Abri" event. No one knows this is a preparation of something future in each life, but also in England.

Scene 7, March 1959. We've hugged and kissed Debby and Franky, and I've written a note to be read each evening, along with leaving a small gift to open each night and Prayer Charts to say just what we expect to be doing each day. Now here we are in Linette's London Chelsea flat. The tiny flat has a beige-carpeted living room, brightened by soft yellow satin curtains and an electric log fire with a remarkable resemblance to flaming logs. Linette has made a gift of the use of this place for a L'Abri Center in London. We will use it for our discussion times here, and Hilary will have it as a temporary home and a place in which to talk to people. Later, Ros will oversee it as a "shelter" where people come to listen to tapes and discuss. Now the little room is crowded with a variety of people drinking tea out of an assortment of cups, mugs, glasses, and even a pitcher. Among them are John D., the opera singer from Fran's Milan class, Jane S. S., two English Buddhists, Jewish Nurite, German Walter.

Two very brief added scenes during this time in London will give you further glimpses of Fran's practical meeting of people's needs, and of his lack of being "legalistic and stuffy." You first need to peer into a restaurant where at a round table Linette is sitting with us, answering Fran's questions as to her understanding and belief. This is the moment of her entering into the membership of the International Church, Presbyterian, *Reformé,* since she doesn't want to wait until she might again be in Switzerland.

Next come to a hospital where Deirdre has had operations on her foot. What is happening at this hospital bedside? There stands Deirdre's pastor Francis Schaeffer (you remember Deirdre was one of our charter members in Champéry when she was in school there), reading the Bible, giving a short message, and then asking appropriate questions of Nurite who is answering fervently. With Deirdre and myself as representatives of the congregation, and Walter there as a visitor, Fran then baptizes Nurite with water from a glass, and we pray together, completing our special church baptismal service. I am reminded of Philip and the Ethiopian in the desert. The Bible gives no formula for the "proper surroundings" for the most important declarations to be made before the Lord, and the Lord's people! (At that time we had no idea that there would one day be four congregations of the International Church in England. It was indeed a tiny beginning.)

[This small bracket is simply to say that during this same month I took Franky for our frequent train trip from Lausanne to Frankfurt to get a new brace and check-up for his leg. Pounding on pieces of metal in the brace shop and pretending to make braces himself, interested Franky more than the doctor's report that he thought the good progress and growth could be attributed to Franky's extreme activity—climbing trees, skiing, running, jumping, skating, trying everything with enthusiasm.]

Scene 8, mid-April, 1964. It was the 17th of April that we were going to bed after a push of work, getting gardens ready to leave, and other things in preparation for the "English trip" . . . when I looked down and saw what had happened to my left leg. I had had shooting pains in it all day, and now it was swollen double its normal size. As I awakened Saturday morning, I found that sleeping with it up on a pillow hadn't done anything to help! After getting the dough for the rolls started, clutching the table when the pains would shoot through my leg, I started over to Beau Site to get comfort and advice from Sue and Ran—which resulted in a trip to the doctor. "It's a phlebitis. Go to bed with the leg elevated, hot alcohol compresses every hour; take this medicine. Don't get up even to go to the bathroom . . . stay there a week." "But I can't," I wailed. "We're leaving for England Monday. I have to serve a hot dog roast tonight and cook for many for Sunday and pack . . . and I'm buying Franky's outfit in London for boarding school. We're taking him with us. I *can't* go to bed!" "You are going to bed with your leg up . . . and you are *not* going to England this Monday." The door had slammed in my face.

Everyone pitched in to divide my work, and Susan, Prisca, Debby and even Franky took turns putting on the hot compresses, with my leg slanting upwards on a board propped on a box! As I spent the next hours praying, I realized that this was "guidance" for someone else to go, not me . . . and I asked for two notebooks to do what I could right there on my back. One I labeled "Edith's Brain," jokingly, because the schedule of where we were to speak and stay (in people's homes), and what had to be bought for Franky, were in my brain. I made lists and notes explaining who people were and how we had come to know them. When it became clear that Ran was to take my place, I reassured Fran that he wouldn't have to worry about details; Ran had it all in a notebook . . . my "brain" would be going along! The other notebook was for menus which I carefully made, along with recipes, for not only my time in bed, but for the end of the week when I expected to be well enough to go on to England!

In this "scene" I'm in a single day-bed sort of bed in my tiny office. Our bedroom, in all those eighteen years in Chalet Mélèzes, was also Fran's office. As soon as the bed was made each morning, he put a board and blotter, his books and other desk necessities on the foot of it, hauled his work out of a box from under the bed, and our bed became his desk. It was on *this* "desk" that he wrote all his first books, did all his dictating to whichever secretary was there, and served tea to the people with whom he was talking—discussing deep things of the Bible, philosophy, science, their questions, or helping as much as he could with their varied deep problems. You can't imagine the wide range of people with whom he—and at times we—talked in that "private sitting room" which doubled as our bedroom and also as an office. They ranged all

the way from an American ambassador and his wife, Miss Wethe-
rill Johnson and Miss Hertzler from Bible Fellowship, to Timothy
Leary and many others who had started drugs because of Timothy
Leary. We prayed for the people of God's choice to come. God
brought an astonishing range of people to sit one by one in that
same chair. Our bedroom just didn't have the capacity to be a
"sick room" too, however. And often if I awakened with, "Oh,
I'm afraid I have the flu," Fran would say, "You can't stay in
my desk! . . . You'll have to find another place." Harsh? No,
just practical . . . and realistic, as he would have letters to dictate,
two appointments coming soon, and an emergency that had just
arrived at our doorstep before I could get started settling myself
"some other where" to be ill, or before I had given up because
I had too much to do anyway. Laziness wasn't enticing. There
was no convenient way to be lazy! Also it's good that we both
worked until very late at night so that his "office" or "sitting
room" didn't have to be a "changed scene" until 2:00 or 3:00 A.M.

Scene 9, a week later. Ran has done a good job in the school
clothing supply store with Franky, and Cynthia and Jill Spink
have done the job of sewing on name tags. Ran also has been
present with Fran at meetings in Reigate, Burgess Hill, and Ealing,
at which he has met many people whom we now know the Lord
has meant him to know *before* he and Sue commence to live and
do L'Abri work in England. That is going to take place in the
summer, but we have not a clue as to *where* "the L'Abri House"
will be! Now I have arrived, a week later, my leg done up in
bandages, but ready to go.

Fran, Franky, and I have a time all together at Burgess Hill
before our traumatic moment of having to leave our youngest
child in boarding school and Franky's moment of leaving home
for the first time. He is eleven. Had he not himself wanted to
enter this school, and had we not been convinced that Gordon
Parke and his wife were a great couple in understanding of boys,
as well as of a wide range of cultural things and of Christianity,
we couldn't do it. When the final moment comes, his bags are
standing on the gravel, the Parkes are welcoming him and boys
in grey shorts and bright pink blazers are darting around, Franky
says, "Come with me." We walk together to the beginning of

the woods, where, after entering for a few feet, Franky does an amazingly understanding thing. "This is my good-by hug and kiss, and when I start walking into the woods, stand here until you can't see me any more. I want to leave you, rather than having you leave me." It is a symbolic profound action of choice—choice that has been his, but is now hard to carry out. He wants to be the one to take the decisive hard action.

The big changes of scenes in life should not be lived through endlessly ahead of time, but neither should we stamp out emotion and try to be cold, dead, hard creatures because of fear of feeling our feelings. Fran and I had very big emotions that day, tears at seeing that straight back and head held up high, demonstrating such strength and will power in stepping into the next period of his life with strong determination. We also wept at the emptiness of going back without him.

But let me say here, communication and "togetherness" can go on. So many parents and children, or friends, or couples, fail to write letters or phone, or to send tokens of continued thinking, loving, and concern for each other. I wrote a letter that very day, and kept on writing every day, as well as sending packages for the "tuck box" (an English boarding school custom—each child has a box to keep food for special moments each day, and to store precious possessions). Franky wrote to us every day too, until the headmaster suggested he save postage by writing that often but not mailing the letter more than once or twice a week. Franky spoke very naturally of missing us, of being homesick at times, and of small regrets about being away when "this" or "that" was going on at home. But on the whole his letters were comforting.

Let me quote a snatch from one: ". . . And another thing, guess what, what I have always wanted to do, in science class we are doing—real discetions with the right kind of disceting tools, and not homemade ones. We started with a frog, and are working up to more complicated things and bigger things like rabbits. Also it is so much fun in a real laboratory with a big microscope and all. You know something, somedays I just think . . . am I at Great Walstead, then I think, yes really at Great Walstead, how wonderful, and I can hardley believe it. What with so many things. Well all I can say is I love it here and wouldn't go back

to that other school if you tried to push me with a buldozer."
Then another day, "Just think how fast time has gone. Also I
have found I have a hidden tallent, at the highjump. I am one
of the best highjumpers in the school and I am hoping to really
do something on sports day. Even if I came in 5th it would be
pretty good out of 115 boys in the school. In the running I don't
think I will be able to do much but still it will be fun. I wish
you could come to sports day, still I am happy Jennifer, Tim
and David are coming to see me. I wish I could see you but I
love it here and everyone is so nice. Also there is such a difference
in having Christian masters. Mr. Parke is always fair." His letters
are a vivid picture of life at Great Walstead, interestingly written
although with original spelling!

That English trip ends with Ran taking us to see the house
in Golder's Green that has so amazingly been "found" by him
while we were at St. Andrews in Scotland. The story is a very
special one of "guidance." But—does God lead up a blind alley?
As time goes on it is discovered that this "perfect house for L'Abri"
is a leasehold which would go back to the original owner at the
end of so many years, and that there are restrictions on its use.
What about it? Confusing.

Scene 10, Beau Site living room. A Members' meeting is in progress, with long discussion about the Golder's Green house and
Ran and Sue's approaching need of a place to go (as the decision
has been made that they will be moving to commence a more
permanent English L'Abri work). . . . Decision that one person
needs to go, research the particulars about that house, and look
for another one if need be. One week should do it. Vote taken.
Edith Schaeffer chosen to "go do it." . . . "That's her kind of
thing."

Scene 11, airplane seat with me in it, feeling like Alice in Wonderland dropping down the hole, but praying with a verse I am
clinging to—"They shall not be ashamed that wait upon
thee. . . ." I am on my way to London to "talk to the lawyer,
and see . . . and don't leave a stone unturned." See what? I wonder. What stones? I muse. I have *no* place to sleep, as far as I
know. The flat has been sold and furniture moved out already.

Where am I going, literally, that day? I don't even know if Cynthia has the word that I am coming. She was out when we called. . . . "You go ahead; we'll try to get her." Now I am pulling my typewriter out from under my seat and taking my place in the aisle, waiting to get off the plane. I am halfway down the aisle when a man puts his hand on the typewriter handle and pulls it away from me firmly—"I'll carry this for you." Other people are pushing, and it doesn't seem the place to have a tug-of-war, so I let it go, for the moment. He steps up beside me and walks to the immigration desk and then to the baggage claim, saying, "I've been watching you during the flight, and I wondered if you'd have dinner with me tonight?" "Oh, no, thank you," I hastily reply, "I'm really very busy." "Well, I'll take you to your hotel, or wherever you are going. My chauffeur is coming, and I'll just get a porter for these bags." Off go the bags. "Where are you going?" he asks next as we "flow" with the crowd that is pushing to the outside doors. I don't answer. I don't know. "Oh, Lord, what a predicament I'm in. Where, Lord, *am* I going?"

Just outside the door Cynthia throws herself at me with a squeal of welcome. "Oh, *here* you are, I was so afraid I'd miss you in the crowd." We have to extricate my baggage from the back of a limousine where a chauffeur is tucking it away! "My friend has come for me, thank you very much, but she'll take me where I am going." A card is handed to me, and a phone number, "Call me if you'd like dinner in the next few days." A high-ranking name is there. (I didn't call, and as I thanked God for sending Cynthia and giving me a place to go all in one fell swoop, I prayed that somehow this man might find "truth," which I didn't think it was up to me to give him.) Cynthia is bubbling: "Guess what? You are to go to the David Spinks in Burgess Hill where Franky is for mid-term with his roommate John. You can go to London from there whenever you need to." Later I have a face-to-face account of that sports day, from an extremely happy boy, who keeps saying, "I keep being afraid you are a dream. I never expected to see you until summer vacation." It is Franky who goes along with me to the lawyer's, to Golder's Green, to attempt to meet with the leasehold committee. Things look very dark as to that house being "right." Why? What is "leading" anyway?

Over and over again each of us needs to remember that we

go from stepping stone to stepping stone; we don't get to the other side of a stream in one jump—not if the stream is wide! As I look back, I know I *needed* to be at the Spinks at just that time. I needed to be at the end of the phone when Cynthia rang at eleven o'clock at night. We needed to know how "impossible" the leasehold place was before we could be ready to appreciate what we were going to be shown.

Cynthia said, "Edith, guess what, I went to bed early tonight and I was sound asleep. Then I awakened with a start, and thought I *must* call Mrs. Gilbart-Smith where Ran and Dr. Schaeffer had a discussion evening a couple of weeks ago, and tell her you are here." *She* said, "Why, you don't *mean* that L'Abri wants a house in London? . . . I know a Dr. Bird and his wife who have been praying for over a month that they could sell their house in Ealing to Christians. Cynthia, do tell Mrs. Schaeffer to go quickly tomorrow morning to 52 Cleveland Road, Ealing. Tomorrow night is the time the Birds have promised an atheist he may have it, if God does not send Christian buyers before. Get there in time to speak at the coffee hour."

Scene 12. After losing my way and taking the wrong underground from London, I finally arrive at Ealing Broadway, take the bus, and arrive just as the morning coffee-hour ladies are saying their good-bys! As I wait for Mrs. Bird to finish talking to her ladies, I look around and "feel" the house—the sweep of stairs, the two living rooms looking out on small but lovely gardens, the wonderful greenhouse with its grapevine, entered by a door from the bigger living room. This is a "city house," but with charm and atmosphere that has come from living, not just from wall and window structure. "This is right," I think, even before Mrs. Bird and I have our exciting time talking together over lunch and comparing notes as to the amazing answer to prayer she and I have just had . . . at the time that is "last minute" for us both. How many hundreds of people are going to be sitting in that dining room talking to Ran and Sue, with their children playing at the blackboards where the Birds' boy was that day? How many people think of 52 Cleveland Road as their spiritual birthplace, their "shelter in times of need"? (During the years Ran and Sue were there, and during Dick and Mardi's time there, we came frequently.) Not a hint of this comes to me this day. I have no vision, but I *feel* "at home." It has been love at first sight.

That night I phone Fran in Milan, where he is speaking, and by calling Susan I get in touch with the Members in Huémoz. By the next morning I have word that they are all in agreement— "go ahead." Amounts have come in to pay cash for three-fifths of the total; the Birds have loaned a thousand pounds, interest free, for five years, and the rest has been arranged as a mortgage by a Christian businessman who is interested. It all happens so swiftly that the lawyer is startled, as he has warned it will take at least a year to find a suitable place.

That day Jill Spink accompanies me as I go from office to office and things "fall into place." Finding that I can take seventeen minutes to shop, we zip into Liberty's of London, up to the fabric and pattern department, and are "hit in the eye" by a bolt of green and yellow changeable silk taffeta. I choose patterns and buy enough yards of material for bridemaids' dresses for Debby and Udo's wedding and a tiny one for Lisby (our first grandchild). I pay for it in pounds, American dollars, a few traveler's checks, and Swiss francs—in "no-time-flat"—because of the efficiency of that cosmopolitan store! In a short time Debby will be taking her exams, receiving her diploma from the University of Lausanne, preparing for and having her wedding, while Sue and Ran will be taking *their* next step on the stone that has been made so clear—the house in Ealing. From the seed planted in England, L'Abri is growing roots and bursting forth into a plant.

Scene 13, Spring, 1968. A lovely old English estate, Ashburnham has been turned into a conference grounds where people can wander along paths by a lake or in woods and talk, think, pray, and read in free time between lectures. Here a *L'Abri* "first" is taking place. Just little Xeroxed bits of information had been sent out to people who had come at times to Ealing, and to those who had "heard Schaeffer speak" in various colleges at universities. Only a fraction of the addresses of these people were even known!

The results are being seen as Sue and I watch from an upstairs window. There is a Jaguar pulling smoothly in with a motorcycle behind it; an antique Bentley with its lovely headlights is stopping in front of the steps, and a dignified young Englishman in tweeds steps out to help a well-dressed girl get out. Right behind this prim scene, a dusty, tiny red car with huge canvases of modern oil paintings tied on top comes to a jerking stop, and out jump several "beatniky-looking" young people to undo the ropes holding their "art." Walking across the courtyard is a fellow from Nepal, and we recognize a hitchhiker with a pack on his back as a liberal young theological student from Germany. There are vicars, curates, and a canon. There are university students, lecturers, dons, and professors. There are doctors, lawyers, engineers, artists, writers, actors, nurses, social workers, patients, missionaries, and scientists.

First what? This is the first L'Abri Conference. We had no idea whether 90 or 100 would come . . . but it turns out to be 450!

The diversity in age, background, and interests of the people who have come is matched by the diversity of the lectures and the discussions. Francis Schaeffer lectures on "Art in the Bible," "Is Evangelicalism Evangelical?," and "Ecology from a Christian Viewpoint." He preaches on the two Sundays as well, and also holds general discussions and talks to individuals. Ran lectures on "Verification"; John Sandri, on Sartre; Hurvey Woodson, on changes in modern Roman Catholicism as seen in his experiences in Italy (as he and Dorothy led the Italian L'Abri); and I give the story of L'Abri, a talk on prayer, and one on marriage. Susan teaches daily Bible School to all the children who have come, and during an informal concert they give a recitation of what they have learned. Nigel gives readings at that concert, Rex and Christian give a two-piano selection and Helen Sinclair sings. There are two formal evening concerts too, with Jane Stuart Smith singing, Frances Kramer with her violin and Rex at the piano. And . . . at this conference an Englishman, Mr. Holdsworth, decides to publish the L'Abri Story!

A wonderful "first" of many L'Abri conferences to follow, in Tennessee, Calgary, Copenhagen, and Rochester, Minnesota? Yes, but. . . . But what? But—this really needs a note of "battle" to be a true report. While very exciting things were going on in England, before the Ashburnham Conference was finished a stream of difficulties had started in Swiss L'Abri which were to continue. "Oh, don't be so vague," you may say. "What sort of difficulties?"

There was a "hippy" who was found to be giving "speed" to a girl at one of the chalets. There was a case of theft, and a lot of illness. The first weekend we were home a fellow who was a member of a devil worship group dominated the first half of the Saturday night discussion (though before the evening was over, Fran was sure God had given a victory). Jane's mother had to have a sudden serious operation as soon as she got back to America from the conference. Priscilla was in the hospital for over three weeks with a threatened miscarriage. Fran had recurring attacks of intestinal flu which had never cleared up since they started during the Pike Debate in Chicago in January—which made his work an uphill push. I scalded my right leg badly with boiling hot tea one day and two days later fell and skidded on my right leg, taking all the skin off, while running down the hill to church. (This took weeks to heal, and was a daily hindrance.)

At the yearly Members' meeting, we seemed conscious of a heaviness we had never had before, and we remarked on the reality of being under "attack." When Sue and Ran got back to 52 Cleveland Road, it was to find that the house had been broken into by burglars. Everything had been turned upside down, letters opened, desk in chaos, bureau drawers turned out on the floor; money, a tape (in a box that said "Beatles" but was really "Basic Philosophic Questions and the Christian Answers"—one of Fran's best basic studies!), and Susan's small amount of jewelry were stolen. Larry and Nancy had just moved into Beau Site, and that first evening Nancy fell down the outside steps and hurt her back. And . . . during all that period of time the funds were "low" so food money and personal money were drastically cut.

Both Fran and I, as we walk in the woods, up a mountain, or along the quay, continually discuss the reality of the split-level battle at every period of life. We can't see what is going on in the heavenlies as Satan attacks us and challenges God (as he did concerning Job), hoping that we will fall into despair; but we can have an "inkling" that it is a "raging battle" and that we are in the "thick of it." At that time, as a deluge of troubles hit during, and after, the Ashburnham conference, we remarked at how much we had to be thankful for that Natasha Middelman, Debby and Udo's first child, had been born on February 28, healthy and beautiful, and had been during this time hungrily eating, growing, responding. Quite visibly, the months of trouble for Debby before her birth had been erased! Four little cousins welcomed Natasha as the fifth girl in the family with much rejoicing. Just so, during this time of "hot battle," spiritual births were also taking place as a direct result of the Ashburnham conference.

It is totally unfair to present a picture that when one becomes a Christian everything is going to be "sweetness and light"— and especially that when one is involved in making the truth of God's existence and Word known, one's person, possessions and peace will never be assailed! Yet the "changing scenes" will always be a mixture, a mélange, an interlacing of ingredients, and we need to ask God for sensitivity to the marvel of victories or special answers to prayer in the *midst* of what seems to be a tidal wave against us. It's all too easy to let the noise of attack drown out reassuring sounds of rejoicing. We don't rejoice over the hard things, but there are things that are meant to bring forth a different sound from us, even in the midst of battle. Some of the "scenes" should be accompanied by trumpets!—especially when God is setting a table for us in the very *presence* of our enemies.

Scene 14, January 5, 1971, Greatham Manor, Greatham near Liss. Cynthia and Kim are busily trying to get a stove going in the big old (part of it eighteenth century) manor house which is to be English L'Abri. They are preparing to have supper for Ran and Sue and the children, with a proper pot of tea steaming in time for their arrival. As a succession of houses were looked at, with Fran going to help look this time, this house was recognized as "right" by all unanimously—a lovely old village manor house with horses grazing in nearby fields. The purchase was made with a designated gift by someone who also recognized that—on the spot! Now the "changing scene" consists of Mardi and Dick Keyes moving into the Ealing house and its work, while Ran and Sue are moving to Greatham.

The latter had been a discouraging house to move into, with the top floor thick with the dust of unlived-in-for-years kind of accumulation, drains not functioning, and all the electric wiring "unfit." Before painting, repairing of floors, wiring, digging of drain pipes and sewerage conducts out to the road had been more than started, people had begun to arrive! Needy people being "born again" in the midst of the restoring of the house had meant two kinds of restoration simultaneously! Before there were enough pieces of furniture, cups and saucers, silverware, sheets and blankets, desks and tape recorders, a Farel House had been started, with the "half-day-of-work-and-half-day-of-study" balance tipped a bit to the work side as people had plunged in (pretty literally) to digging drains and "mucking about" in the chaos of urgent need.

Who was one of the first students in Greatham? Someone from Australia. Where had he heard of L'Abri? In India where he had gone to seek answers in Indian philosophy and where an Indian introduced him to . . . "Schaeffer's books!" From India he had come to England to discover Greatham and to become not only one of the first Farel House students there, but one of the first converts. Was it chance that Greatham was "ready on time to receive him?"

It was in February that Fran and I went to Greatham for the dedication, not for a "finished" building, but of this whole property in its state of "need" of changing. Somehow the property was like the people—the stream of them who came to that dedication from all the previous years—some "restored" and beaming, others in stages of breakdown and further need—need of restoration. A picture of what we are all like in one way or another . . . until the final restoration of all things, when we'll have our restored bodies to enjoy the "perfect houses!"

Scene 15, early Spring of 1971, Holland. Members and Workers in Dutch L'Abri have been praying through years and recent months for the right place to start a country L'Abri. Now they have found it in Eck en Weil, a village about an hour and a quarter's drive from Amsterdam, where a farm house stands surrounded by apple orchards and small canals. Some Dutch pastors have formed a committee called "Friends of L'Abri" in order to purchase the property. Now, in March, soon after Greatham L'Abri's dedication, Hans and Joanne Van Seventer have moved into the Eck en Weil house to begin the work, with Dr. and Mrs. Rookmaaker coming weekends for discussion. Hans and Joanne have not only been Workers in Swiss L'Abri, but met and became engaged there. The couple who will follow Hans and Joanne are Wim and Greta Reitkerk, who also met and became engaged at Swiss L'Abri. She had come from Germany, he from Holland, and the Mélèzes gardens were the scene of early conversations! Continuity is maintained when Nick (Dutch-Canadian) and Mina (from Florida) meet at Swiss L'Abri and are married in Vevey, not only because they will become Workers in Switzerland, but they are one day to be leading the work in Eck en Weil!

The continuity of threads being woven in Holland includes a special English thread appearing in a literal way to change the scene. At the time the house is bought, an English art student (part of the wider L'Abri family) wanders around the orchards, and becomes sure that God is putting it into his mind to use an inheritance to buy the orchards too! This fellow, a student under Professor Rookmaaker in the Free University of Amsterdam, has been a constant part of discussion groups which will be changing location from Rookmaaker's home to the country L'Abri. The pattern resulting from this English thread has been adding color to this part of The Tapestry through the years, since the "half day of working" required of Farel House students often takes place in the orchards, where the trees produce not only fabulous fairylike blooms, but apples and pears amounting to 20,000 kilos during a good harvest.

One of the first Farel House students in Dutch L'Abri was a portion of the "harvest" coming from books that had been "planted!" Helen, a New Zealander, naïve, had been drawn into a drug group, foolishly agreeing to go to Europe with three others. In Italy the four had been picked up for selling drugs, and put into jail. Into the jail some American missionaries took books— *The God Who Is There, L'Abri,* and others of Fran's and my books. It was from prison that her correspondence with us started, and *in* prison that this wandering "lamb" was "found" by the Lord in the reading of the books. Starved physically for nourishing food, and spiritually for further help, she arrived first in Switzerland for a period, then moved on to the quiet countryside of Holland! The other three also became Christians, but that is another long and involved "unraveling" of threads, not to be attempted here.

Scene 16, Greatham, 1981. The big old house is buzzing with excited voices and squeals of greetings as long-lost friends hug each other. The scene is the occasion of the tenth anniversary! Changes are spoken about as people talk about "what it used to be like ten years ago." . . . "Remember the stables before they were made into a house?" "And all the agony of work—and re-work—as dry rot made the rebuilding of the village hall into a house for Jerram and Vicky so discouraging for years?" "Now, imagine, the old 'brewery' is being dedicated today as a lecture hall!" "Yes, isn't it exciting? They just lifted up that cupola a day ago!" . . . "And did you know that the room has facilities for showing the films, and it can even be darkened in the daytime?" "That seems so good a choice, since the films are great for giving a 'base' as new people come, and they help open up important and essential questions for the discussion." "Yes, that's logical, since the films, both *Whatever Happened to The Human Race?* and *How Should We Than Live?* are being shown all over England, Ireland and Scotland . . . yes, Wales too, and Ranald, Jerram, and Richard are called on to come and answer questions." "It's incredible what a difference there is in the climate of interest, and in the reading of the books—Susan's children's book *Something Beautiful from God,* as well as all the others." "And as for the tapes . . . the tape program has taken L'Abri discussions, Dr. Schaeffer's lectures, and lectures of L'Abri Workers into homes all over the U.K. as well as into New Zealand, Australia, Canada, and the U.S." "This tenth anniversary really is being properly celebrated with all these festivities—and that big birthday cake too, which looks more like a proper wedding cake, that those dear people made for us."

Ranald writes, "Someone who lives nearby [Greatham] and who has known the work intimately over quite a number of years said recently it was wonderful to see God's work here 'coming to fruition.' " . . . Ranald then changes the metaphor and speaks of the fruit of the Gospel spreading "like a wake behind a boat." One of the greatest indications of the wake, Ranald feels, was the seminar tour of the series of films *Whatever Happened to the*

Human Race? in April and May 1980. Fran and Dr. Koop, along with Dr. Zachary (an English doctor) took part in giving lectures, answering questions, and discussing with people, and I lectured also. It was an amazing experience for Fran and me, for, in addition to our being thrilled (along with the other two speakers) over the enthusiasm and determination to "do something" about abortion on the part of the audiences in London, Birmingham, Manchester, Glasgow, and Brighton, we were filled with awe and wonder at the threads we saw which had first been woven into our first trips to England, back in the "tea and bread and butter in student room days." Now these threads were coming with friends, husband or wife, and children—children of university age themselves now.

Such continuity of the weaving was beautiful and moving to us. In addition to seeing many old friends from every year of twenty-five years of L'Abri, we realized the people were also made up of those who knew us only through our books and who had never been at L'Abri in any country, let alone in England. It was something like seeing the multiplication of bread and fish, and the results of nourished people who had eaten some of the multiplied food. What God had done with the books took shape and form with voices and warm handshakes.

"Changing scenes" were very much in our minds as we stood on the stage in a London theater and looked into faces of those who filled every seat and sat on the steps, stood against the walls, and filled overflow rooms from early morning until late night. I thought back to that figure kneeling in prayer and giving her own form of bread and fish so many years ago. I thought also of the suspicion and wariness in the Cambridge bedroom, and thanked God for all the surprises He prepares for us to enjoy—"in the presence of our enemies"—while the battle is still raging. He gives a variety of "tables" in the midst of changing scenes.

SWIFT GLIMPSES 20

Have you ever gone to Italy on the Simplon line, from Brigue on down toward Milan? Remember the tunnel that runs along the side of a mountain, with arches opening out to sudden views, tantalizingly beautiful glimpses of river, trees, rocks—but so swiftly gone that you wish you could go back and have another look? The arches are like windows, yet the solid stone rushes together, and then it is dark again and the tunnel is just a tunnel. Life is like that so often. It isn't just the changing scenes, with people growing into different stages of their own history, and places losing their familiar look because of what is called "progress" but so often may be destruction; it's that even while important things are taking place, other things crowd in and our attention is turned aside and precious moments whiz by—like those views through the openings. Someone needs to nudge us— you and me—and to say, "Look . . . don't miss that sunset" . . . or, "Hurry before we pass that marvelous waterfall." We need that kind of nudging too in the very midst of relationships, family togetherness, precious moments we need to protect. As I try to focus my microscope on The Tapestry where there is such intricate weaving, I find far too much that demands real concentration in order to discover the detail of what makes up the "whole." Here, then, it becomes necessary simply to get impressions—the

471

kind of impression one gets in going seventy miles an hour past openings to bits of view. There has always been so much "going past" in our lives!

We Schaeffers have been what is called a "close family" with a tremendous continuity. But our most important times have not been hedged in by green bushes shutting out "the world." So often "the work"—which we believe to be important because we believe truth exists, and which our Director has a right to direct in the light of His wisdom and knowledge—makes it necessary to continue when we'd like to take time off, or makes it necessary to shorten times we'd like to prolong together! With that having been said, we do feel, both Fran and I, that beauty is important, and that memories are excruciatingly valuable—even if the times remembered the most vividly are like those brief glimpses of streams. Perhaps our weddings, and the way they fit into L'Abri through the years, along with grandmother's care for seven years, would illustrate some of the reality of weighing priorities, not by other people's standards, but by what we felt fit in with the Creator God, whose idea it was in the first place to create families.

The year is 1957, and L'Abri is just two years old. Thursday of that July week, Fran, Susan, Debby, and I went off to Lausanne on the early morning bus. It was the day for the last Bible discussion class in the Café Vieux Lausanne, which had started when Sandy and Murray and John Sandri had become Christians and wanted more study. Now twenty-two were coming. Priscilla met us at the station, looking white and tired from exam study but excited because she had received her Certificate! Now one more year for the *Diplome* . . . but that year she would be married and she and John would be studying together. As the class was going on, I shopped for food for L'Abri, and for materials, patterns, threads, buttons and so on for sewing her trousseau. Shopping and meeting Mme. Sandri to talk about wedding plans had to be fitted in between classes, as that evening there was a Bible class in Montreux, where friends and relations of Claudie's (a Swiss girl who had recently become a Christian at L'Abri) were gathering in a hotel room.

Now we are looking at another Thursday nearly a month later, right before the wedding day. John is pulling out weeds, and

Lydia and Susan are beginning a cooking spree, when suddenly it is 10:00 A.M., time to get into the taxi for the "civil wedding" (in Switzerland everyone has both a civil and a church wedding). The girls and Franky climbed into the car, all in their ordinary clothes as this is a quick affair in M. Guex's office (he also reads the electric meters when he isn't marrying someone!). We crowded around to see the official booklet that stated that Pris was now Madame Sandri. "Mommy, guess what . . . he said that John is the 'chef de famille' and Pris is the 'chef de ménage' (John is head of family affairs, and Priscilla head of household affairs)!"

The next day Franky was my alarm clock at 6:00 A.M. as he called, "Hey, mom, when is Mme. Marclay coming with my suit she's making? Can I go down and meet the bus?" Mme. Marclay had helped with all the sewing and was now happily coming from Champéry for the wedding. When the bus arrived, she eagerly mounted the stairs, with Franky's suit safe, and offered to press the girls' dresses. The chalet had very little space to hang anything like a wedding dress, so after pressing, it had to be hung from a curtain rod. Mother had sent yards of white organdy, and I had found a lovely piece of Swiss embroidered organdy to make the bodice, with an Elizabethan collar, and tiny white covered buttons. Debby, twelve, and Susan, sixteen, were in simple pink organdy dresses with Peter Pan collars and clouds of gathered skirts. All but the Swiss embroidery had come from Wilmington's Bancroft Mills—a perfect provision not just for a necessity but for beauty . . . at 39 cents a yard.

The church was built in 1100, with fat carved stone pillars holding up the double-arched ceilings. Across the front are the organ pipes, and at the side there hangs a painting of "The Sower," done by a Huémoz man years ago. On the wall opposite is a plaque saying that Farel preached in this church 450 years ago, starting the Reformation in this part of Switzerland. The village of Ollon was full of Swiss soldiers on Prisca's wedding day, having some sort of "tactics," and the only available "dressing room" was on the third floor of the city hall. So down these steps the bride and bridesmaids came . . . out past the grinning soldiers . . . quickly across the courtyard to the low church door. As the organist began to play Bach, the bells began to ring. It is the Swiss custom for the bells to ring for fifteen minutes before a wedding. Then it was time for Jane to sing, ". . . Thy people shall be my people, and thy God my God. . . ." Priscilla said afterwards Jane's beautiful voice and those gorgeous words took away all her nervousness. Little Debby looked so solemn and serious as she walked first, rosebuds in her shiny hair and in the bouquet, with Susan following the right distance behind, looking even more serious as she was trying to hold her dress, three inches too long (Mme. M. had forgotten what "those pins were for"), with the same hand that held the roses!

Then came Priscilla, slim and dainty in billows of organdy and a fairylike veil, hanging onto her daddy's arm, and walking up those same stones Farel had walked. Francis Schaeffer and his first daughter, walking together to the altar where he will hand her to his first son-in-law. It all seemed to fit into the twelfth-century building. John's voice rang out firm and clear as he repeated the lasting vows; Priscilla's was soft and low. Dr. Martyn Lloyd-Jones gave a splendid talk on Christian marriage. He and his wife and daughter had been coming to visit L'Abri, just at this time, and we were so happy they could be a part of the special day. No one knew until afterwards that when John said, "with this ring I thee wed," the ring was his own, and it almost fell off Pris's finger. Dan (the best man) had handed him the wrong ring. Pris fixed it, though, as she slipped it off and substituted it for the one Sue gave her when it came her turn! Such radiant smiles as John and Pris had as they turned to walk down the aisle to the happy "going out music"! (For days five-year-old Franky and Margaret Williams, also five, played "wedding," which consisted of Franky being organist and playing "da-da-da-da" with much gusto on the fence, while Margaret walked around the vegetable garden carrying field flowers.)

Lydia, Patsy, and Anne scurried to get our six pounds of caramels to throw to the village children crowding around the church door (a Swiss custom), when it suddenly became impossible to form a reception line outside as it started to sprinkle! The reception was in Villars, and was given by Mr. and Mrs. Sandri, John's parents. Other members of his family—grandmother, aunts, sister Yolanda—were there, along with the people from Champéry, Lausanne, Huémoz, and all who were at L'Abri at the time. As Mr. Sandri read the telegrams, there were many of them in other

languages—an international set of "greetings" that he could translate, as he knows seven languages.

There had been smiles all day, but when the moment of going away came, Susan threw her arms around Priscilla in the garden and began to weep; then Debby and Franky followed. "Oh . . . I don't want you to go away . . . it will never be the same. . . ." The break had come! So Pris went off with a red nose and streaming eyes and said, "Oh, do be nice to each other when I'm gone . . ." However, forty minutes later she and John reappeared. "Hi, mom—nice trip we had." They had forgotten one suitcase, and something had gone wrong with the taxi so the driver had to come up and get another, he said. That night each of us found a little letter from Priscilla under our pillows. We were delighted at this thoughtfulness. Such moments do pass swiftly like a view through an arch . . . and a piece of paper with communication that can be read and re-read really underlines *reality*.

The "train" didn't stop passing through the tunnel with its arches, so to speak, as that night we sat around the fire and Martyn Lloyd-Jones told us of his leaving his Harley Street medical practice to go into the ministry. The next day we were having a hot dog roast and discussion, and also arranging for all that Greek Anna would need, because we expected to be away on vacation when her baby would be born. Anna had come to us pregnant— a very brilliant philosophy student from Athens, Greece—and was going to have her baby in September. Our niece Lydia was leaving after a year with us as a part of the family and of L'Abri— another hard parting—*just* before we left for the Milan class. Susan, Debby, and Franky went along as the next day we would be putting them on a train for Alassio. They were to stay in an Italian doctor's home in exchange for our having had the doctor's son with us for a month. This would give extra time at the sea before we came to be together for our first vacation without Priscilla. We were to have ten days of catching up on office work, full speed ahead, before going to be with the children in Alassio. Each day was "interrupted" with a constant stream of needy people!

Before we pass the next "swift glimpse," let me tell you that in these early years of L'Abri there was *no* thought at all of ever having a thing called "Farel House"; there was *no* expectation of having tapes made of discussions or sermons; there was *no* plan ever to write a book (except for the twenty-five Basic Bible Studies). If you had asked us what we imagined *might* happen, we would either have said truthfully we didn't know, or we might have guessed that "perhaps the Bible classes and discussion groups will spread into other places." You see, Fran was going every Thursday to Lausanne, to teach and discuss at the café from 11:30 to 2:00 P.M., and often Thursday afternoons to Geneva to a group that had asked for a class. Every other Tuesday he went to Milan where a class had started with Jane, Dino, Lorna, Luciana, and a diversity of others in the Hotel Florida lobby. Every other week he also went to Basel, Zurich, and Montreux, as well as back to Champéry for an evening class. With a glance at a clock and a calendar, you can see that Fran was not "always available"—but also that he had a lot of train time to study and think. Often his best articles were written around the edges of the pages of *Newsweek,* as he used the margins to outline the ideas that were flowing as he was reading, that he was discussing with such diverse minds, and that he was thinking about in the context of current events.

One Thursday in early January of 1958, I was furiously typing away in a hotel room in Lausanne, trying to catch up on 135 letters in one magnificent effort. I made carbon copies (23 at a time!—with airmail paper and thin carbons) and then wrote personal notes. We had prayed for money to take a day in a hotel for me to type while Fran was teaching and doing errands and it had come. In today's standards it was nothing, but then the less than six dollars paid for bed and breakfast and a lovely view of the lake! (The dollar brought 4.32 francs, remember?) The phone rang while I was working, and Susan was on the other end of the line. "A telegram has just come from Grandfather Seville, good news. On January 6, 1958, L'Abri Fellowship Foundation has been granted the right by the United States Government to grant tax-free receipts." What a very special and practical answer to prayer that was to share with Fran. Father had been sending the Family Letters to someone in that department in Washington, who had been reading them and who felt the work was one that deserved tax-free receipts. We hadn't even been aware of my dad's pursuit of this permission.

Now another glimpse, as we speed to August 7, 1958, and you see Priscilla and John laden with luggage, accompanied by the whole family, leaving Ollon Station to take the train, change in Aigle, and go on to Lausanne together. The occasion? The year of studies in Lausanne had come to a very successful end, Priscilla had her *Diplome* with honors—John also—and now they were leaving for St. Louis, Missouri, where John would be studying at Covenant Seminary and Priscilla would be teaching French at Mary Institute for the next three years. We were going to have a "good-by luncheon" at the Lausanne station restaurant. Even then we were not to be alone for the entire time, as José from El Salvador caught sight of us, pulled up a chair, and joined us for coffee. We had prayed that we would see him again soon, as he had not yet become a Christian (José, Mario, and Marco had all three won, in three successive years, El Salvador's top prize for scholarship—a period of study in Switzerland. They had never met in San Salvador, but the story of their coming one at a time, not only to L'Abri but to Christianity with understanding and acceptance, is startlingly "stranger than fiction.") This weekend eight Italians were coming to the chalet from Milan, and as José heard of it he said he'd like to come and translate for them. It had been an important interruption indeed, but as so many in life, not conveniently timed in *our* plan.

Crying and laughing, we said the not-so-important last things to each other—precious all the same—and as the train pulled out Franky led us in running along and waving as long as we could see each other. Ten years before we had arrived at the same station—with Priscilla as an eleven-year-old. Life is such a fast train!

If you had listened as well as looked in Mélèzes dining room on Friday, you would have heard a babble of voices. . . . "How many places shall I set for lunch?" . . . "I forget how many there are. Linette just left, and Pris and John have gone . . . soooo there'll be five Schaeffers, one Alie, one Lucinda, one Alice, one Karl, four from Basel, one Annie, one Marcia, three Macmanuses. Put ten at the big table and four at the other two tables, or shall we put eight outside?" . . . "Say, when is José coming back? Will he be on the bus in time for lunch? Better put another place to be safe." . . . "And when it comes to ordering hot dogs for

Saturday from Grimm the butcher, don't forget all those coming from Milan, and Karl's friends John B. and Tom H. from Princeton, and Claudie's coming because she's going back to Sarah Lawrence so soon." . . . "Oh yes, there's Miss Stephen, the governess of the Sheik of Kuwait's children who came for her vacation from Kuwait to Villars just to be near L'Abri. She'll be down for the hot dog roast, and so will those people who are in a rented chalet with their two children—Vera and Mario from Milan." . . . "Good thing we have lots of lettuce, radishes, and tiny onions in the garden to make our own salad!!"

It was after the Sunday High Tea, during the evening's conversation, that José's questions became the center of the evening's "teaching." An engineering student, he had a mind that seemed to follow along phenomenally with the next question in sequence, with the result that the answers were like a complete course! He asked questions that were most helpful for the other Roman Catholics to hear, which meant that Ezio was also getting all his questions answered as Dino translated into Italian. Finally José said, "My intellectual questions are all answered. I do see it all as truth and accept it as such, but one thing remains before I can accept Christ as my personal Savior. I cannot accept the Substitute until I really feel I am *guilty* and deserve the punishment He took." It was Monday morning that Fran brought José to the room where I was typing. Both were beaming. José told me of how he had gone up into the woods the night before, and had struggled over the reality of his guilt. At 2:00 A.M. he had accepted Christ up there, all alone. "At my first birth I was completely unconscious of what was going on; at this my second birth, I was fully conscious and had the joy of knowing the very moment of my entering life eternal." It was thrilling at the next Bible class to hear José take over at one point and answer, in an amazingly clear way in French, the philosophical questions raised by an atheistic schoolteacher.

It isn't always as clear as it was in this case, but often the interruptions that could so easily be turned from, turn out to have been God's interruptions. Does that say we should never protect family moments? No. The continuity of family life is centrally important for other people to observe, as well as for the family itself. Memories are worth preparing for, and protecting.

It is simply that we need to pray moment by moment for sensitivity to The Tapestry. Threads that are meant to be woven in with us for a part of the pattern are at times in danger of being rejected. Such sensitivity is a careful consideration, however, and not just a careless insensitivity to the family's needs. Broken threads and unraveled threads are all too common a sight in today's view of portions of The Tapestry which were meant to have a beautiful continuity! Choice of hard work is a part of an artist's life. Choice of hard work must be the choice of repairing breaks, or continuing beauty in relationships.

Am I daring to suggest that "we did it right"? No, absolutely not. In today's world it is so important to say that it is worth "trying again" after mistakes have been made when an argument or a downright fight has been had . . . that something too valuable to break is in danger of being smashed for trivial reasons. Someone has to realize that the whole of life, the continuity of generations, is more important than insisting that the other one "be fair." "Whose feet have I washed today?" is a good question in the midst of temptation to be proven "right" in pointing out the other person's drastic "wrong." "Footwashing" is not, in most people's daily walk, symbolically or literally carried out, but it is our pattern given by Jesus. To say, "I'm sorry," or to do something to "clear the air," is a kind of footwashing that is necessary for a parent-child relationship, or child-parent, or husband-wife . . . and when you speak of "family" remember that the whole is made up of the parts, just as "life" is made up of minutes and hours! A weaving is a painstaking thing of concentration on detail.

In the midst of all the "swift glimpses" you are having from the train windows of this chapter, you'd see the "ivy being thrown on the floor" by Fran (see *What Is a Family?*), or my being "difficult" and running up into the woods, fiercely determined to stay up there forever! No, we were not politely bowing to each other, always saying the right thing in sweet tones of voice!

Do all the "glimpses" of thousands of conversations that have taken place through the years end up with people "bowing and believing"? Is there always a happy ending to be glimpsed? Of course, we haven't seen the real ending yet—nor have you! There may be many surprises ahead. We need to be encouraged to keep on, and to keep on praying. But the answer to those questions above is "no." We have heaviness and disappointments, with people's names, faces, and personalities remaining with us and being remembered in prayer as they suddenly come into our heads.

Look . . . the Mélèzes living room has been freshly cleaned and windows polished. There is just one person having tea with me—Peter, who is about to leave. It is June, 1959. "My questions are all answered . . . and I don't think I have any particular doubt left." Peter has been in the Lausanne café class regularly, and on weekends has seemed the most eager to ask questions. "This will be it," I think to myself, and pray for wisdom. Five long minutes go by, Peter looks at the floor, then gravely shakes his fair head and looks up with sober blue eyes. "No . . ." (with an indrawn breath) . . . "It's . . . no . . . I—it would mean a break . . . with everything I have ever known—my family—my friends—the business. . . . No one would understand if God became the center of my life. . . . It . . ." and he just shakes his head. There is no time for more conversation. Fran comes in and we pray with him. Then . . . "Bus, bus, bus, bus! . . . the bus is HERE." Franky pops his head in the door, and Peter goes sorrowfully away. We could only think of the rich young ruler. . . .

It was in August of 1959 that Lok, a brilliant Chinese Malaysian, made his choice—after saying he believed that what Mr. Schaeffer had given in answer to his questions made "the only sense I have heard." But his choice? "I don't want to bow as a creature before a Creator; I prefer to be Lok in a world of chaos." No, all the glimpses are not of fulfilled beauty! Some are of Satan's victories, although we pray always that they will be temporary ones.

Susan was the one to study in Lausanne University after Priscilla left, and also to bring students for the weekend, or to the café class. Then came her time in Oxford, when she attended the School for Occupational Therapy, and also gathered students together for when her dad and I would be in Oxford for times of discussion. It was during that time she led her roommate, Veronica, to the Lord—another thread to be woven later into L'Abri for many years.

Our swift train now is passing an arch in the tunnel that looks into 1961. March finds me rushing around with a list pinned to my cardigan with a safety pin. "Sew for Susan" was one big item, and the "long time" we hoped for got squashed into four days, as Fran left for a time in Milan, and we fixed up a dressmaker's establishment in the living room of Chesalet (the chalet Betty Carlson had now bought and loaned for L'Abri's use). A lovely embroidered organdy with sprays of snowdrops—white on white—came in a gift box for Susan one day, as suddenly as snowdrops pop up in the spring! With a short length of silk taffeta for a bodice, we were on our way making the wedding dress. Mme. Marclay came to help Marry Meester, Linette and myself, and four of us in four days accomplished a lot—cotton and linen dresses for the trip to South Africa and Rhodesia, Ranald's parents' gift in place of their coming to the wedding, so that Ran and Sue might visit the grandmother and other relatives. Susan was teaching at Beau Soleil each morning, so came puffing in from her run down the road to "try on."

Seven days before the wedding, another arch would give you a small view of Fran and myself going to Zurich to talk to the brother of M. Annex, about renting Beau Site for a long period of time. In the twenty-five minutes in Aigle in between trains I managed to get all the wedding flowers ordered, running to a nearby florist. (I didn't need to jog). That night Fran was teaching the Zurich class and they all felt this businessman's willingness to rent us Beau Site for a long period at the same low price we had been paying was the biggest miracle they'd heard yet!

The next clear opening shows you a group sitting in an old chalet in Champéry—yes, almost six years to the *day* from the time we had been put out! This is the chalet where the regular Bible class has been held, but this night there is something special going on. You will see Ranald kneeling, as M. Ex., an elder in our church, and Pastor Francis Schaeffer, put their hands on Ranald Macaulay's head, ordaining him as an elder in the International Church. Votes had come in by mail from many scattered members of the church, and a telegram had come from Milan to let us know they were in prayer at the same time. Fabien, the ski and mountain climbing guide, prayed that night, thanking God for sending Jesus to die for him. "My feet are on a new *chemin* (a new path) tonight," he said.

The wedding day dawned grey and unpromising. I hurried into

old clothes and hastily scooped up white satin ribbons (freshly pressed, but left over from other L'Abri weddings) and buckets full of wild daffodils the Marclays had picked and brought over from the Champéry fields. When Susan was a little girl she had had her picture taken in a field of daffodils in Champéry, and declared, "When I am married I'll have the place full of these flowers." The time of the daffodils is not always the same, and the wedding plans were not made around that possibility! As the taxi arrived in front of the Ollon church, Mme. C., the taxi driver, helped pick up what had been dropped and came in to help us all tie bunches of daffodils to each of the seventeen pews—at both aisles—and to outline the straw carpets on the bumpy stone aisles with daffodils peeping out.

Mme. Marclay puffed in for a moment, "My train just got here, and I'm catching this bus to go up and iron the wedding dress." "Oh, thank you. The ironing board is all ready in the living room with a sheet under it!"

Ten o'clock found us back at the chalet beside Mme. Marclay, bending over the coffee table, wiring white roses and lilies of the valley into a wedding bouquet for Susan, and yellow freesias into a headdress and bouquet for Debby.

The "quick luncheon" for all of L'Abri was for once going to be on special paper plates, which the butcher had happily said he could get for us. They turned out to be 6" × 3" oblongs such as are used for meat!

The taxi took us to the same City Hall of Ollon to dress, and we all missed Priscilla, as she was still in St. Louis, but Dorothy took her place as "big sister" to help in the dressing. No soldiers this time—but the village street was lined with children, waiting for caramels, and with villagers, as the bride came out beautifully flushed and brown eyes smiling, Debby following in yellow taffeta with an overskirt of dotted Swiss, looking like a daffodil herself. Ages by now? Susan was nineteen—to be twenty on her honeymoon. Debby was fifteen, Franky eight. As the bells rang and we looked at the people filing in, we saw what seemed like the collection of people from all our years in Switzerland, and from every place where we had lived, or had classes.

Ran stood straight and splendid, head erect and brown eyes smiling, so Scottish-looking with his dark red hair topping the

Macaulay tartan kilt and tweed hunting jacket, Jeremy Jackson beside him in a similar kilt as best man. Debby walked in first, with Franky following in a kilt identical to Ran's, looking for all the world like Ran's little brother and carrying a taffeta pillow with the rings on it. He had seriously asked Ran, "May I join your clan, please?"—for he felt he would be partly Scottish when Ran became his brother-in-law. Susan came regal as a queen on the arm of her father whom she resembles so much. Continuity?

Let our train back up a bit. We missed an arch. The wedding was on April 7, 1961. A year *before* that . . . you would need to glimpse a sudden number of vistas as they slid by the train. The year started with the sudden arrival of a telegram January 2, 1960, which Susan brought to me as I was dressing for our church service in Mélèzes. My mother had suddenly died of a heart attack just hours after she had finished writing notes on 1300 Family Letters and my father had lugged them to the post office! I had not seen her for six years, as during those years we had not had money or time to go back to the States, but the Family Letters I wrote, had been for her. Then in the summer of 1960 we were given a reasonable price to travel by freighter—to be with my father, and though we did not know it, the Lord had another reason! That was when Dr. Kiesewetter had Franky examined in the Pittsburgh Children's Hospital, and Dr. Ferguson advised an immediate operation to move a muscle from the front to the back of Franky's left leg. The operation was a success, but we couldn't know that until the final examination six weeks later. It meant that had you watched that summer on Long Island you would have seen an eight-year-birthday party for a boy who was using crutches as athletic equipment—scaring us that his cast might get bashed.

During this unexpected summer in America, Ranald Macaulay, Linette Brown, Susan, Elizabeth Hull and Patsy Williams *were* L'Abri! A weak work? A strong work? God has always used His strength in our weakness. A number of people who have gone on to be important in the Lord's "army" became Christians that summer. Please look as we "swoosh" by. Right under those trees beside Beau Site—if you are looking on the right day—you will find Ranald Macaulay talking to a young law student from Germany, Udo Middelmann. This is the moment when Udo has be-

come convinced that what Ranald has made clear to him *is* truth, and when he "steps from death to life" in accepting Christ as Savior.

As the summer draws to a close, you are swiftly passing another titanic "view" of the future, as you pass something that looks quite "nothing." . . . Nothing? You would see two letters being sent to America. One from Ranald Macaulay asking if he may stay and study four hours a day at L'Abri, and work the rest of the day. "Could such a program be worked out?" In the same mail one from England from Deirdre asking if she and her airplane pilot husband, Richard Ducker, could come to L'Abri "and study half the day and work the rest of the time." The two writers of the two letters had not consulted each other.

As Fran and I prayed about these letters in Long Island, the thought came to us, "Why not? And why not call the study arrangement 'Farel House'? . . . bringing the Reformer Farel into a place of special honor in Huémoz, 450 years after he was chased down the mountain by angry village women!"

If the October 1960 Family Letter were held up in one of those places where the past could be seen for a moment, you could read, "Farel House will open this November with three students, in the sunroom of Beau Site, where five desks have been ordered to be made to special measurements by M. Dubi . . . and where a branch library of the Evangelical Library of London will provide the needed books to start. We have no plans for enlarging Farel House nor any desire to see a big thing, but feel that the Lord has opened this as one step more in the same direction. 'Answers' to atheists, Hindus, existentialists, etc., will not be learned academically, but in listening to the constant and very real discussions with the stream of people the Lord brings here." Ran, Richard, and Deirdre were the first Farel House students that fall.

As I was asking . . . continuity?

The continuity of Ran and Sue's wedding, with Jane singing "Thy people shall be my people and thy God my God . . ." and of the bride and groom making the same lasting vows, in the *very* place Farel had preached, was not only a family continuity, but continuity with the people of God who had stood for truth in Farel's footsteps for hundreds of years.

The reception was a gift to Ranald and Susan from the Tchividjian family. They prepared a living room, dining room, and a terrace of a house situated on a hilltop overlooking the lake, Castle Chillon, the Dents du Midi, and the Savoyan Alps—all the way to Lausanne. A fabulous view, especially on that spring day, which had cleared up, so that the flowers and shrubs were ablaze with spring blossoms in the sunshine. Tea, cake, and sandwiches were eaten in a relaxed atmosphere which made it seem like a Sunday High Tea at L'Abri with the eighty-five there. We waved Sue and Ran off, but they returned to stay in this empty house, which had been given them for their three days before leaving by train, then boat, for Africa and three months with various members of Ranald's family.

The three months were almost up, and you must turn to look as I nudge you now. First look at the Fourth of July. Franky has gathered money and persuaded the village grocery to sell him Swiss "First of August" fireworks for the American *fête,* Fourth of July! All day he has been hammering and inventing amazing things, with pinwheels nailed to tree trunks and a frame with a variety of "surprises" fastened ready to go off. He has invited the Bellevue workers and children (the rehabilitation home for cerebral palsy children that Anne and Mary had started next door to us), written notices on various spots on our flagstone—"THIS SPACE RESERVED FOR WHEELCHAIRS"—and then put on the display himself with very little help from his father. My part was to provide homemade cake and ice cream in sufficient quantity to go around!

Quickly look or the next day will be past. . . . The fifth of July was even more exciting for Franky. He had been up very early preparing. The preparations, you see, involved the donning of an old brown fur rug, pinned over one shoulder with a safety pin, and the painting of his face as well as the fixing of an old broom handle with a pointed stick tied on for a "spear end" and the slinging of a "bow" (homemade) over the other shoulder. Now he was properly ready, so he felt, to welcome Susan and Ranald home from Africa! His astonished dad didn't want him to go up to the train platform that way, but when we came to the taxi outside Aigle Station he was standing at attention beside it!—like an African warrior, so he thought.

We had been trying to have the house all ready for Sue and

Ran, and there were many nice surprises in Beau Site, but not all nice. Workmen who were to do electrical work and plumbing had just arrived that day, and the house was full of young men who had come to L'Abri—fourteen waiting to get in the one bathroom to shave the next morning! Speaking of a new bride's "cooking"—Susan had to begin with a bang! And it was not an easy beginning. It was even harder when later on Priscilla and John and baby Lisby came to live and work there for a year. (But that is another "view.") Hard beginning? But possible.

Sue and Ran have been married twenty years now; and Pris and John, twenty-four. Continuity takes time. You can't live twenty years in one, as so many seem to think. Art works are not instantaneous—not those of Michelangelo, Rembrandt, Leonardo da Vinci quality—and relationships take *time* to come into view from dark tunnels, revealing themselves through sudden "windows" of beauty. And even then, there is the swish-swish-swish of darkness interspersed with the beauty you are in danger of missing because your head is turned in the other direction—away from the window!

What do I mean, "The house was full of young men"? What was going on that weekend? We need to quickly look and get an indelible impression of not just the "costliness" of L'Abri in daily life and work, but of what God was doing in bringing the ones of His choice in answer to our prayer, not only on days of prayer, but daily. This was the weekend that there were more than twenty-five young men. Take a quick look at the sixty people crowded into Mélèzes living room as Fran preached on John 10 that Sunday morning. It was a vivid and strong message that carried us to the Sea of Galilee as the disciples folded up their nets for the last time, to follow the Shepherd . . . and the "wind" of the Spirit seemed to leave an effect as He "moved" people, as a breeze moves long grasses on a beach.

Who was there? Chinese Peter, an engineer from Shanghai, formerly, but now of Hong Kong (we found he knew Lok, for whom we were still praying). Chinese David, studying engineering in London, who became a Christian shortly after our last London trip during which Fran spoke to a group of Orientals. David's brother, John Chang, a businessman from Hong Kong, who was so deeply moved during the service that by the time of the singing of the last hymn he had passed from death to life (though we were not to know of the decision until later in the day). Kyung, the Korean theological student who was at L'Abri all the summer before, was sitting beside Peter Pattison, a young doctor "on his way" to working in the Far East who brought eight Orientals that week. In the next row were two fellows with olive skin— Probal, an engineer from Calcutta, and his friend from Bombay whom he brought to "hear why I have left Hinduism to embrace Christianity." Next to the Hindu was Jim Hurley, a teenager from Aiglon College who, with his brother Morris, had been coming regularly to the chalet. It was their last Sunday before going off to America for college years and I prayed, "Oh Lord, thank you that Ran has led these special boys to You; please hold them fast during these difficult years ahead."

(Flash ahead to the present, and you will have passed Jim's Harvard years, his time in Westminster Seminary, his Oxford post-graduate studies, his time back with his wife as a L'Abri Worker, and now you will have to look at him as Dr. J. Hurley, leading a seminary post-graduate school, as well as writing books. That prayer for him was answered!) Susan was hoarse after that service, having translated it phrase by phrase in French for Cecile, as was Trudy, having done the same thing in German (in whispers) for the cerebral palsy patients in their wheel chairs.

Among the twenty-five men were six Cambridge students, and over by the door sat Marika, the Hungarian girl who came as a refugee. Don't forget we are living in the midst of "history"— you, and we, year by year. When the Russians had gone into Hungary, we had been listening to our radio and having special times of prayer for them. Now here was one person who had been described during those terrible hours, for she had been among the ones scrambling under barbed wires, with cruel searchlights making targets for the guns out of any moving object. She had been "missed," and a long series of "events" had brought her to L'Abri.

Among those there for that weekend, were Joe Martin who had just come and four Dutch—Rita, Friedus, Adri, and Marry. "Just names," you say? To any there at that time, faces and personalities spring into view as the names are printed. John Chang's birthday was on Monday, and as he had been "born again" on

Sunday, I made two big cakes, enough to share with everyone, and asked Kyung to write John's name in Chinese characters for me to copy. My pink-tinted icing wrote beautifully on the white boiled icing, and John was astounded to see that the Chinese meal that night was finished off with a birthday cake . . . with his name in pink Chinese characters surrounded by candles! What language, I wondered, is used for writing our names in the Lamb's Book of Life, as they are faithfully recorded when we accept Christ as our Savior? Is there a heavenly language for that recording, or will it have a diversity of languages to demonstrate that some from every tribe and nation and kindred and *language* are there? At any rate, we know our names are important, and He calls us each by name, now, as well as in a "roll call" later.

During this same period, if the train had taken you past one of the chalets, you would have had a glimpse of Udo faithfully listening to the Romans studies on tape. By this time Fran was able to "speak on tirelessly" as without any planning, tapes having been made of some of his discussions, lectures, and Bible teaching. (You'll find out the truth of that phrase "without any planning" in another chapter!) It was also at that time that Debby, who had had a strep throat just before Susan's wedding, dragged at school and in her home life in Lausanne, and came down with rheumatic fever.

Now our train moves at a higher speed through more years of tunnel, and comes suddenly to a few more openings in the summer of 1965. It looked like an "impossible" summer, in so many ways. Debby, who had just had her nineteenth birthday, was preparing for her big *Diplome* exams at the University of Lausanne: "But that is impossible; people take three or four years at least to study for those exams, and Debby has only been there a year and a half." It was an astonishing "feat" and not a "defeat." To this day, so far as I know, Debby is the only one who ever completed both the written and the difficult oral exams in front of the French *Faculté* in such a short time, and the results were . . . "with high honors." Among a string of "impossibilities" came Ran and Sue's decision that they must leave in mid-July for the move into the house and work in Ealing, so that Ran could register in Kings College for further study in theology in London University . . . with the sad factor that they would not be with us on

August 8, 1964. Debby and Udo had chosen this date for the wedding with a stream of "factors" pointing to it.

The wedding preparations were a demonstration of how L'Abri "works," conversation and real working together giving the kind of understanding that listening to lectures and watching "how to" exhibitions couldn't accomplish. Whether it's cooking, or life, there is nothing that equals doing things together. You need to really show which are the weeds, and which are the plants, before a person can be helpful in a garden—whatever sort of a "garden" it is! Susan's being married had freed a back room, which became "the sewing room" at the time. A dozen girls of different nationalities took turns helping Mme. Marclay and me sewing, as we talked together while getting the wedding dress made, and also making those changeable silk bridesmaids' dresses from the stuff I'd bought in Liberty's. Others formed an army of cleaners under Gillian Jackson's generalship, with mops, pails, floor cloths and brushes. Farel House students and helpers went off to a lush woodsy spot on the other side of Gryon to bring back masses of ferns (which we planted in flower pots), sheets of moss, moss-covered logs, and trailing pieces of ivy. We trimmed Farel's old church this time late in the evening and early in the morning, so that it not only looked like a spot in the woods, but smelled of moss, fern, and leaves. Pale yellow dahlias nodded their heads at the end of each pew, finishing the natural woodsetting with a touch of color. A great idea? Yes, but it took Jean with her car and Larry willing to be buried in fern in the back of the car, along with others with knives and energy, to make the idea take shape.

As the traditional bells began to ring, Minna began her organ music, and soon Jane and Frances came to the front, and with violin, organ, and Jane's voice, "Jesu, Joy of Man's desiring" filled ears and minds with beauty of sound and content. Then clear trumpet notes burst forth, with organ and cello sounding the theme of Purcell's "Trumpet Tune and Voluntary." Look carefully as you listen. The organ, in the center, with its pewter pipes, is flanked with trumpeter Joe Commando (from Rome, Italy) and cellist Hugh Bradley (an English Oxford student who had just become a Christian at L'Abri a few days before) on the other side. A triumphant, joyous piece of music, this composition of

Purcell's always makes me think of the future moment when a trumpet will announce a triumphant joyous moment of history. Twelve-year-old Franky, as junior usher, led the men as they stepped into their places. First came Bernd (a German forestry student whom Udo had led to the Lord); then Egon (Udo's brother whom Udo also had brought to Christianity); and then Udo himself. Three tall blond young men, looking not only at the aisle of the church, but with a special reality at the aisle or path— not always to be bordered by fern, and flowers—in the "walk" ahead of them in God's work, Whom they had resolved to serve. Then Allan Baldwin took his place on Franky's other side. Allan, a high school classmate of John Sandri's in Scarsdale, had formerly been a liberal and had studied under leading liberals at Union Theological Seminary. Now he was ready to be pastor at this wedding, to speak with courage and conviction with a completely Bible-believing stand. (With Claudie his wife, he had recently finished his Farel House studies and was beginning his work as a L'Abri Worker.)

What a cross-section of humanity turned their eyes to watch the bridesmaids and bride walk in. There were the eager Bellevue children in their wheelchairs, many of whom Debby had taught for Sunday school. There were again all the "years" of our times in Switzerland represented, with all sorts of people, from taxi drivers to the President of Switzerland's sisters. There were Udo's relatives, and his lovely aristocratic grandmother, looking so dignified and charming, and there were people from at least fourteen nations. My eyes saw this fleetingly—as you would if the "glimpse" sped by you—for suddenly they were riveted on Debby, our last daughter to walk up those uneven stones with her father. She looked like a princess in her satin gown with its short train and lace top. "Oh, may Udo be as faithful to your Word in this generation as Farel was in his," I prayed. One bites one's lips to keep them from trembling. Emotions are not on a "plateau." There are the beauty of vows, the song so full of memories—"Thy people shall be my people . . . thy God my God"— the realization that the moment cannot be "held." Then as time brings the burst of music after the sermon on forgiveness already the wonderful moment is history. The reception was as full of music—violin, cello—as the wedding had been, with after-dinner

coffee served in the hotel garden, by the lake, Castle Chillon in full view.

Happily, Debby and Udo had a quiet week of honeymoon nearby. This was to be a rest before the long bus trip to Beirut to be with his family, but—the careful schedule was to be changed, suddenly! The afternoon of their one-week anniversary, they had an accident going down a mountain road on the motor scooter. I stopped making rolls for the hot dog roast, and listened to a weeping report. ". . . And Udo has stitches above his eye and behind his ear, and I have cut my knees terribly. . . . We're being taken from the hospital by a French couple, to the Swiss border; can you meet us there?" After giving quick instructions as to how to finish making the cinnamon buns, and how to fix up the sewing room as a bedroom for two patients, I scooped up blankets, aspirins, hot water bottles (filled, of course), a jar of orange juice, and Jean M. and I went off to the border at St. Gingolphe. Jean would make a good racing driver!

Painful days of recuperation followed, and the trip to Beirut became impossible. However, both Debby and Udo's reaction to this disappointment and "affliction" in the midst of a honeymoon was helpful to everyone at L'Abri at this time. Again, it "spoke" in a way verbalizing cannot do. Speaking of "stepping stones," it was during that very week that Debby got a letter from a private school in St. Louis, John Burroughs, offering her a position teaching French during Udo's seminary years. It needed an immediate telegram, as time was an important factor in giving the affirmative answer, since travel had to be arranged earlier than would have been possible had they been in Beirut. The timing of this guidance concerning the next three years impressed not only Munnie, Udo's grandmother, but also many of the people at L'Abri. Understanding of the diversity of ways in which guidance can come, or a new stepping stone can suddenly appear in the swirling waters of a stream at flood-time, often breaks upon us as we are watching the happenings in someone else's life.

The Schaeffer family, now diminished to three, went away for the first vacation alone with Franky in Italy. A new custom of my reading mystery and adventure stories at "teatime," lengthening to "sunset time," gave us a companionable new togetherness and helped us not miss Debby as much. Continuing that same reading as we are now just "two" adds a dimension to life as Fran and I make the switch into being ancestors!

Five months after Debby's wedding—January 18, 1965—I was in the midst of washing, ironing, and packing to take Franky to Geneva to fly back for his winter term in England, when a letter arrived informing us that Fran's mother was ill. It was unclear as to how ill, so we called Margaret Walker of Stevens' School and asked her to please visit grandmother, talk to her doctor, and call us back with definite facts and advice. A few hours after Franky was safely back in school, the message came back which turned our small world upside down. Grandmother Schaeffer needed 24-hour-a-day nursing and I was needed immediately to take over from a neighbor who was filling in temporarily.

We had expected to have Fran go to America for ten days of lectures and discussions in the Boston area, at which time I was to have gone to England to be with Sue and Ran to help make curtains, etc., and to be there for Franky's midterm break. Now—suddenly—we were both on our way to America and soon I was in a small apartment in Germantown, nursing Mother Schaeffer twenty-four hours a day. There was just one bedroom, and I put up a canvas cot beside her bed to be near enough to care for all her needs. For seven weeks I worked on careful nursing and nutrition, spoon-feeding her with yogurt, wheat germ and brewer's yeast, and watching her come back from malnutrition to life! The doctor had said she was dying! It was a strange "shut-in" time during which I found that when she slept, I could write letters quietly or make doll clothes (by hand) for Lisby, Becky, and Margaret, our three granddaughters. For anyone else who may be going through that sort of time, I would share that I found it was important to do exercises in my small floor space each day, and to do something creative to make up for not going out at all. Grandmother did recover but could never live alone again, so she chose to go back to Switzerland with us, rather than to go to a nursing home.

Meantime Fran had been traveling and speaking. Twelve days in the Boston area were exhausting but satisfying, he said. He had three main lectures attended by about four hundred students of MIT, Harvard, Wellesley, Radcliffe, Smith, Mount Holyoke, Barrington, etc., and there were many discussion groups, personal conversations, and so on. Fran gave approximately the same lectures in Wilmington for the Philadelphia area in three seminars and one public meeting.

Debby and Udo drove from St. Louis to spend one weekend with us (sleeping at a neighbor's) and to take some of grandmother's things back with them. We had begun to pack trunks of her things to take with us, and to give other things away. Poor grandmother had no idea what to expect, and was at that time in a wheelchair, but her first airplane flight was also to be her last, as she was to live seven years in Switzerland before going to heaven. As we returned to the chalet, the room which had just been turned into my sewing room, became the bedroom, and my "office" across the hall became her sitting room. We hoped that would help her feel she had her own place, in the midst of what remained a confusion to her—L'Abri. "Don't they have homes of their own?" she'd ask at times. The many people coming and going remained a bit of a mystery, although she did begin to enjoy the visits of helpers and students who would come to play checkers with her, or to write letters for her. During the first years she ate her meals with us downstairs, and dried dishes, and came to the services and concerts. It in no way resembled the "nursing home" she had always dreaded!

Don't forget we are on a train, having swift glimpses as we pass arches or windows or "holes" in the tunnel. This is not a chronological account, but "glimpses" of the weddings which speak of our blend of "life" and "work" woven so closely together that threads can't be separated in places. It is important to say, however, that the total mileage of this train—the total countryside through which we are passing—is all part of the abnormal world, and spoiled history, which is a result of the Fall. This is what really exists. This is not a "stuffy theological doctrine"; this is what our own history consists of and this is the world we live in. There isn't any other. We can't take a vacation from reality!

People search for "reality" and often refuse to accept what exists. So often brilliant minds, thinkers who do not know God, come to conclusions that are very near truth—recognizing the futility and stupidity of living as if affluence and a profusion of material things, entertainment and a profusion of distractions, sexual pleasures and a fulfillment of abstracted, noncontinuous relationships, would in the end satisfy the question of "purpose" in life, or even the question "What is life?"

Thinking people who are sensitive often come to the conclusion that there is *nothing* but blackness, and they would say to me, "Aha, aha. . . . You see, that 'beautiful princess' in her satin gown, happily walking over romantically ancient stones with her dear father giving her to her dear husband, is in a week's short time to have not only all the flesh on her knees shattered but all her precious plans changed, so as she lies there hurting physically, she can have time to think of how useless it is to make any plans. Aha, aha. It's as we had said. Life is meaningless. Life is a cruel joke." And of course they are right, if there had been no Fall. They are right if nothing at all affects history except God's creation. They are right if there is no reality to "the battle."

But God has let us know, as He has shown us "behind the curtains" in Job's life, that Satan is using all his ingenuity and intelligence to think up new ways of attacking the relationship between God and human beings whom He created. Not only do we know this in Job, but we are warned that Satan is charging about like a lion—ready to pounce, seeking "whom he may devour" intellectually, emotionally, psychologically, spiritually, as well as physically.

There is a war. We have an enemy. But—also there is "cause and effect" history. There were stones on that mountain road that the motor bike slipped on. There was a cliff at one side— that Debby and Udo did not go over. Was the "cause and effect," plus whatever Satan was trying to do, stopped in their case by an angel who pushed them to the wall side, and not the cliff side? Then—what do you do about David Koop who clung to a rock that came off the mountain, and went to heaven immediately? We can't come up with "pat answers," but we *do* have answers up to the extent that God has made much clear to us, and we can say to the "thinkers," "You are right in being so black—if all you have are the facts you are working with; but you are *wrong*, because God who made all things—which have now been so spoiled—is going to *restore it all.*"

Yes, we are on a train, rushing through glimpses too quickly to concentrate on all that surrounds those glimpses in the geography and history of each spot. But please remember that the glimpses we are having are also the "life" or the "history" or the "reality" of our own growth as persons, and in whatever understanding *we* have gathered through the years. Francis Schaeffer, apologist, as some have described him, never had time to "sit in an ivory tower" thinking up answers to possible questions. When he gave the lecture that so many people have found helpful, and countless numbers have listened to and then literally "bowed twice"—metaphysically and morally—before the God whom they have become convinced really does exist, accepting Christ then and there as having died in space and time and history (not mythologically nor theologically) for them . . . he gave it to real people with whom he had had real discussions, in many different parts of the world, and coming to L'Abri from many parts of the world. He was struggling to think things through honestly in order to be a help, not in order to "develop something new." It was always truth that mattered to him, as well as helping people who do "think" and who do "care" to find that truth to be true. The lecture I am talking about is "Basic Philosophic Questions and the Christian Answers."

One of this sort of searching young person was Bob. A dropout of Harvard, a user of drugs, an intellectual, Bob was looking for a purpose in life. Skiing in Zermatt, he heard Peter Moore preach in the English chapel there. That night in the youth hostel a copy of *L'Abri* was passed around. Bob read it. Others read it. Discussion started. The next day Bob and two others turned up at our door. What background had Bob had? A home with every advantage; a father in government circles; culture, morality, standards stressed . . . but what was the base for all the "values" stressed? Udo, Os Guiness, and Donald Drew spent hours talking to Bob. He asked questions at discussions with Fran, and at all the meal tables. At 10:00 P.M. one night Bob came to my office, and at 2:00 A.M. a "long hard birth" came to a happy conclusion, and I am certain that a new name was written in the Lamb's Book of Life—Bob Kramer. He, with his wife, is working with sixth-grade drug youngsters, and he also pastors a church—so unusual a work that they as a couple were written up in *People* magazine.

Who is his wife? It was the same spring of 1970 that Dianne, a graduate of my old Alma Mater, Beaver College, a friend of Bob's, decided to "drop in" on that "strange place in Switzerland" Bob had told her about. Questions, objections, resistance, more questions. Then one night when Fran was leading a discussion in the chapel, a hippy stood up to proclaim his position. Now this hippy (a true hippy of the '60s, even though the year 1970 had come in) had arrived with his girl, to take possession of our kitchens as it suited them to make bread in our ovens, and to ask for "yang" food! That night as he read his very black poems, Dianne jumped to her feet and thanked him.

On those same feet she tore up the hillside, past Chalet Bourdonette, across the road, and into my ground-floor office (in exchange for the one grandmother now had as her sitting room). "Mrs. Schaeffer," she said in a sort of breathless whisper, "I've just become a Christian. I saw it all while that fellow was reading his black poem. It made it all so clear." Although he had yet to be told, her "thank you" was not what the hippy had thought it to be. His talking had had the opposite effect on her and had brought her to a clarity of contrast, and she believed. Bob and Dianne's engagement and marriage came later, but their "birth" was during the same period of time.

We're passing miles of such possible glimpses . . . but this is *not* a story of L'Abri. It is necessary, however, to have you not think I am being ambiguous in saying that Fran's developing apologetics were in no way academic to him, but extremely practical. Hundreds of examples would be impossible to include, but this suffices to underline what I mean.

Yes, space doesn't "permit," but I must slip in another glimpse here. From the Far East, from a tiny spot among rubber trees, from a long line of Moslems, came a very young boy, through miles of geography—India first—and miles of "answers"—Hinduism taking over from Moslem teaching, then drug "answers" being experimented with. Impossible that a pinpoint on the earth's surface in the Alps should be a final destination. "Impossible" is the *only* word. Impossible thinking of history and geography . . . and impossible thinking of a "chance" meeting on a street corner in Basel with someone who said, "L'Abri" . . . and impossible that two rides, hitching, would deposit Mus at the Mélèzes steps where I had stood in the fog so many years before! The "tiny glimpse" is to include an answer to Mus's prayer, one of his first after he became a Christian: "Please bring others from Malaysia, like me."

Now it is the same spring, the same time I have *just* let you "see" Bob and Dianne. Mok and Dean were the ninth and tenth Malaysians to come. Gini had been praying with the others for their arrival. Members of a pop band in Kuala Lumpur, they had heard that some of their former musicians were in "Mélèzes Switzerland." "This," they thought, "must be a pop band." They were traveling and playing in Rome, Italy, and stopped an Oriental whom they saw. "Hey, we're looking for a guitarist. Have you heard of Mélèzes Switzerland? We think a friend is playing in that band?" "Yes," Kim, the Korean fighter pilot whom they had asked, did indeed know. In fact Kim was a Christian who had been at L'Abri! (To glimpse ten years ahead, Kim today is pastor of the two Korean congregations of our church in London). "Yes, I can direct you. . . . " So Franky and his good friend Mus delightedly welcomed the ninth and tenth Malaysians that spring—who were to discover, and begin playing in, another band together!

Fantastic glimpses of "perfection"? No, "some fell on good ground . . . and other seed was choked out by weeds." But, if I can use my book metaphor, the "weaving of the tapestry" must be noticed. Threads are woven in with reality. Mok today is a printer in Manchester. With his English wife, not only is he involved in Operation Mobilization, but is in a Chinese church where a retired missionary who worked in mother and father's mission is joyously active. History spoiled? "Choice" affecting so much of "what might have been"? Yes, but it is also true that God is all-powerful, the final victory is His, we are on the winning side, and "All hell shall not prevail against Him . . . nor against His people." We are held by the hand of Jesus, and by the hand of the Father covering that hand—two hands firmly around us—and the Holy Spirit remains in us, sealing us as an "earnest," a promise. We do get glimpses of the gorgeous victories of God's weaving appearing in The Tapestry. These are nudges to "look, quickly, look."

The same spring, now March-April 1970, and you are looking at the port of Venice, with a boat sailing out at sunset. It is the *Cristoforo Colombo* of the old Italian Line (weep, that it is a thing of the past), slowly going out that same port past Santa Maria Salute about five hundred years after the original Christopher Columbus, and crossing the ocean in a much shorter time. "Seminar 70" at Buck Hill Falls, Pennsylvania, was where Fran was to speak, and huge wooden crates of paintings and sketches were with us as Franky was to have his first art exhibit in the Edward Frisch Gallery on Third Avenue in New York City (sponsored by The Lady Edward Montagu and by Mrs. James Morrison, who had much interest in Franky's art). The time in New York, on my part, was to be a combination of doing all that needed to be done for the art exhibit; on Fran's, it was to be lecturing in Columbia University, discussing with students, and preaching in Broadway Presbyterian Church. Os Guiness came at the same time and spoke in a number of colleges around New York, in Annapolis, and in Willow Grove and St. Louis. It would take pages to tell of results in the lectures in each place.

It would take much more of a look to "see" the art exhibit, as you would want to divide your time between looking at the paintings and sculpture showing the artist's creativity, and looking at the beauty of Genie in her white lace dress. She and Franky, hand in hand, glowed with the amazing "happening" of that exhibit, combining so many people of L'Abri's history, as well as of some art experts of New York. They were standing on the brink of a future together, hidden behind the same screen as all future is hidden . . . but, without knowing it, beginning a tremendously varied future together, with art and creativity as the area that would be central—but central upon the Base, not floating without a base. Franky and Genie didn't know that night, that what Fran had been *saying* at Columbia, and would later be saying in so many places (some of which was right then in a book called *The God Who Is There*), would be a part of what Franky would have as a "fire in his bones" to put into film form. No, they would have been quite unbelieving of any glimpse of that even if it had been given.

For that time in New York, we had been given an apartment by Mr. and Mrs. Roger Hull. It meant that there was a quiet place for the three of us to sleep and to talk with Franky and Genie before he walked her to the former L'Abri nurses' apartment nearby, to stay for the nights. It meant also that Fran could work every free hour into the early morning hours, checking the proofs of *Pollution and the Death of Man: The Christian View of Ecology*. If during that time you had given Fran a glimpse of the portions of this book to be quoted just ten years later in a secular book by a Jewish writer coming out of the counterculture, Jeremy Rifkin, he couldn't have believed it either. The name of Rifkin's book is *Entrophy*, and the quotations come in part six, in a section called "A second Christian Reformation," pages 234–40. At that time we were praying for wide reading and understanding, but as Fran finished his checking, he hurried down to the boat ticket offices to use his first portion of royalties from *The God Who is There* (*just* enough to give a gift) for the gift of taking Genie with us on the *Leonardo da Vinci*. Your glimpse of that voyage would be of the four of us sitting in the sunshine, my reading aloud. Calm sea and a wake, gorgeous in full moonlight. Such glimpses are of portions of life that are precious gifts, and are impossible to order ahead of time, or to go back and do over. Choices and decisions are swiftly past, if not made in the time given for them. But the results of choices go on, and on, through history.

Franky and Genie were engaged during that period of time. Later we had a family announcement dinner, combining the celebration with John's April birthday and Udo's March birthday, which we had missed. This joyous celebration welcomed Genie into our family. Franky was our fourth child to marry a person who had become a part of the Lord's family in L'Abri. (To keep the records accurate, Ranald had become a Christian in Cambridge in Holy Trinity Church, with the help of Basil Atkinson, but had had his intellectual questions answered in L'Abri.) As Genie showed her ring to the others, I rejoiced in my decision in Porto Fino, where I felt it "beautiful and right" to give that which my mother had left me in her will, to my one son, for his wife-to-be. That diamond engagement ring, for which father had sent to Pittsburgh for sixty-five years before, and which he had kept in his pocket until mother finally said "yes," was now on Genie's finger, and it seemed the right place for it. It still does. Continuity is worth marking with whatever precious mark one has that combines history and memory.

At 1:00 A.M. May 21 I was listening for Udo's car on the back road. Its familiar sound came at that moment, and I ran out to say, "Good-by . . . I'll be praying . . ." as he drove Debby to the hospital, not any too soon! At 3:50 A.M. little Samantha Abigail was born, a lovely little sister for Natasha—seven pounds and three ounces of beauty! While Debby was still in the hospital, Fran left to speak in Milan. It was a Thursday afternoon and I was at the Workers' meeting in Chalet Bourdonette, when Franky came running down the steep road calling, "Come quickly, mother. Grandmother had fallen, and I think she's broken something." He had lifted her into bed, from the hall floor, covered her up, left someone with her and had run to get me. That was May 28. Doctor, ambulance, X-rays, three-hour operation, seven screws and one pin in the hip. Then came days of "interrupted schedule" indeed. Grandmother understood no French and was also confused by the anesthesia. I stayed for three full twenty-four-hour days and then we worked out a schedule of people taking turns, with Ann Sizer and Kathie Cross running a sort of taxi service for the various "shifts." The cooperation and sharing of a burden was a special thing to see. It was true community.

In the midst of all this, there was a wedding to prepare for. Kathie and I cut out the simple Swiss turquoise-and-white-striped cotton for the little cousins who would be attendants: Lisby, eight, (our first grandchild, born in St. Louis, with wonderful pictures and full descriptions by Priscilla keeping us up on details until we could hold her in our arms at eight months when she came back with her parents to live in Beau Site); Margaret, six months younger (our second grandchild, born in Aigle hospital when Sue and Ran were still working in Beau Site); Becky, seven, Lisby's younger sister (born in Vevey, to be brought home to Chalet TziNo where Priscilla and John had moved just a few weeks before her birth); Kirsty, four and a half (born in London, Margaret's little sister, and Sue and Ranald's second, of course). Natasha was two and a half but was proudly now a "big sister"! Kathie stitched these dresses on the sewing machine set up in Mélèzes' dining room in between serving meals, while Veronica cut out and stitched the bridesmaids' dresses from the same material for Pam (Genie's sister) and a friend from California. Grandmother's hospital room was filled with turquoise-and-white-striped cotton as I steadily kept at the handwork—hemming, sewing on eyelet embroidery at neck and waistlines, etc. So often boys at L'Abri during that time remarked what a fantastic thing it was to see people "sewing like that, making clothes for a wedding. . . ." It brought a thoughtful look into their eyes. Creatively combined, necessity and beauty blend together to add something far more than can be captured in words. Barry making tables and benches, and teaching others; Fran landscaping lawn and flower gardens; Susie's garden crew being instructed by her; Birdie knitting as she talks to people; Pris and John's terrace developing out of the careful work of John's "huge stone" being lugged home from the "day-off" hike; Udo and Debby's garden and interior growing more beautiful with each year's additions; Jane and Betty's raspberries climbing over the fence, loading it with beauty as well as food. Yes, this sort of blend can't be "cooked up for atmosphere" in an artificial way, like an "activity" in a school; the important thing is, it is a natural part of life. Real family life. Growing family life.

Early the morning of the wedding I had been driven by Boyd and Nancy down to the same twelfth-century church in Ollon in which our other weddings had taken place. Rob and Tom were helping me with the buckets of wild daisies gathered by people on their day off. So the ends of the pews had daisies this time, as did the flower pots already arranged with ferns. . . . Now as the bells ring, and Jane takes her place to sing, I feel astonishment as well as deep emotion that Franky's desire when he was five and walking up with me at Priscilla's wedding had been fulfilled. "When I am married, it will be in this church too . . . and Jane will sing that same song." This time it had been possible for the whole family to be together—for the first time since Priscilla's wedding. A glance to the front and I saw Fran enter to take his place as pastor this time, with Franky and his best man Os beside him. Now the girls were coming up the aisle, each one on the arm of one of Franky's brothers-in-law. Denise brought in by Ran, Pam coming up with Udo, and then the bride on John Sandri's arm. (Genie's parents had chosen to come later in the year when they could have a visit with Genie and Franky. They were giving the reception *in absentia,* so John substituted for Stan Walsh, and we were later to get to know both Stan and Betty very well.)

Genie looked as fresh and beautiful as the daisies that surrounded her. Her long brown hair had a crown of natural daisies,

and daisies were the flowers in the children's hair, as well as the flowers of the bride's and bridesmaids' bouquets. Franky had designed Genie's dress, and Mme. Marclay had made it as her last wedding dress for our children—promised when they were little. It was white piqué, with a high neck outlined with two rows of delicate eyelet embroidery with turquoise velvet ribbons run through it. The full sleeves had long tight cuffs also threaded with the turquoise velvet. A four-meter cape designed to button on the shoulders, was of piqué lined with turquoise, and as it swooped out behind her, the little girls—four of them—carried it, their dresses matching the lining. All this gave a medieval look which fitted in with the church. Jane's beautiful song brought an echo back to us from other weddings through the years. There was a completeness of the continuity. Ran and Os read the scripture passages. John and Udo prayed. Fran preached a full sermon. For our personal family it was a time of thanking God for our oneness in Him. In a day of the loss of communication, of splitting from Christianity or from each other, of scattering in ideas and philosophy—it was a tremendous "together" time for us.

As we had the reception line, threw the caramels, greeted the tremendous variety of people, looked at the brand-new babies—Samantha and tiny new Fiona who had come with Susan straight from the London maternity hospital—and remarked about how Giandy, eight months old, was growing ("isn't he advanced!"), we were telling the ones who would be serving the reception food for L'Abri people at Sapins just where the two wedding cakes were and "not to forget to heat the vol-au-vents before serving them." We also were arranging the cars for the family to go to the hospital so that Grandmother Schaeffer could be in on the day. Aigle Hospital may never have had such a procession up its hall as when the bride and groom and little attendants paraded up to grandmother's room at the end of the third floor! It is possible not to leave out people if extra effort is made. At least flowers and a piece of wedding cake should be sent to any ill, absent members of the family. The reception for the wedding party—all the family, including Os, Jane and Betty, Gini, Donald Drew and Gracie—was in a restaurant in Caux; its magnificant view was shrouded in fog, but that made the pictures look mysterious even if the view was missing. The L'Abri reception consisted of ninety-five, and even though the rest of us were "missing," they reported a great celebration.

Our next swift glimpse comes a year and a month later. This was a year of many L'Abri weddings . . . glimpses of all them would take a separate book. It was, however, also a year of a new kind of care for grandmother. She came home from the hospital to need very careful care for a year and a month. She was lucid part of the time, then drifted in and out of reality as time went on. Susan was extremely happy to be with her during a few hours when she was very clear . . . and Susan talked to her about her certainty of salvation, making the way simple and clear again and again. Fran had never been sure but now Susan assured us she was satisfied that grandmother had really trusted in the Lord Jesus as her Savior, and that she was His "found lamb." This was to be a comfort in the next difficult weeks.

We rented a hospital bed for the weeks of twenty-four-hour-a-day care. Grandmother had had a second stroke. You know, "family life" is not just made up of new babies, picnics in flower fields, weddings, birthday parties, or even shared hard work in gardens or house. It is not just made up of washing diapers, scrubbing burned milk off of stove tops, picking up the pieces of a broken pie and pie dish, rebuilding a burned barn or house. Family life is also fears, old age, severe illnesses, disagreements . . . and the need of someone to share these with is greater than the need of someone to share joys with. The hedonistic drive to "be happy" makes it definite that people will have no one to share the unhappy moments with.

The sharing of grandmother's care was as much a part of L'Abri life at that time as the sharing of any other portion of life. By being a part of it, people learned as much during that time as at any other time in our history. We also were living out the reality of promises—"in sickness and in health, for better or for worse." The name of all this is: reality. Joy, a Canadian nurse, not only took turns nursing grandmother as her Farel House "helping," but stayed on longer as a "special call" for a time. Diane, a L'Abri guest, also a nurse, took the shift from nine to nine for a week. German twins, Elka and Ellen, took turns along with Wendy and Virginia. Dr. Gandur, grandmother's faithful physician, had had an automobile accident so couldn't come for some time, but three fine doctors "happened" (!) to be in L'Abri when needed—Dr. Garnes, a black New York urologist; Dr. Seer, a missionary surgeon from Korea; and Richard, an English doctor, then a Farel House student.

But with all the wonderful sharing and help, I needed to spend my nights for weeks very near by, and my sleep was sketchy. Family life includes this kind of cost too. Debby came to sing hymn after hymn during the last two weeks, running down from Sapins in between times of caring for her baby and her three-year-old and all the houseful of students. Priscilla came too, and the children took turns bringing flowers.

On Sunday afternoon, July 11, 1971, Franky was sitting with grandmother, Becky was helping me make Sunday tea sandwiches, Natasha had brought some field flowers to grandmother, Priscilla had brought Giandy, in her arms, along with Lisby to see grandmother. Each one in the family had been there that afternoon. I had just said, "Tea is ready," when Elka ran downstairs calling, "Come quickly." Fran and Franky bounded up, I ran after them . . . and we arrived just before grandmother left. She died in Fran's arms. Yes . . . it was clear that she had left. A very ill person, weakening for many days, is extremely different from that same body, out of which the person has gone. It is impossible to think of what someone feels who does not believe in the existence of the soul . . . and the one who thinks there is nowhere to go! Absent from the body . . . present with the Lord. A going from . . . to . . . is so stupendously different from the squashing of a fly.

Birdie and Joy prepared grandmother for the burial. In Switzerland, the "box" is brought by the policeman and the man who sells it. Also, when the third day comes, it is the policeman who puts the body in the casket. There are no funeral parlors, with all the embalming and so on. The funeral was held in our chapel, with the policeman waiting outside to officially take the casket to the cemetery. Udo, John, and Franky read passages of Scripture; Hurvey, who had come from Milan, prayed, and Fran himself preached the sermon. It was a L'Abri family funeral. The grave is near the Hoffmans' (the Christian people who built Chalet les Sapins). The children had brought their flowers while grandmother's body was still in her bed, talking about her resurrection so naturally that one of them asked if her dress would have holes in it when Jesus comes back. Weep, yes. Weep in loneliness. Weep as Jesus wept because of the enemy, death. But look forward to the defeat of that enemy. The defeat that is assured because of Christ's death.

The "swift train" has been flying through a tunnel of about ten years now to give you a recent glimpse! It is October 6, 1980, and another generation is stepping into the continuity of our part of The Tapestry. Fran has just flown in from Edinburgh the night before in time for a wedding practice. I have been with Debby at the hospital, as she has had a difficult time after a miscarriage, while Udo has been in Australia speaking in a series of seminars, television interviews, and so on. Now the family, and the L'Abri family, are gathered together in the Ollon Church . . . with Jane ready to sing again the musical vows of Ruth as she declares, "Thy God shall be my God. . . ." There is a tape machine ready to record what Franky and Genie, now in America, and the Macaulay family in England, will want to hear at the next family reunion. This is the first marriage of one of our grandchildren! Who is getting married? Look quickly—this is just a glimpse!

It didn't seem that long to me, just a "few pages ago," that John was waiting up at the front of the church for Priscilla. Now John is the father in this drama, walking proudly with his lovely young daughter Becky, looking sweet and old-fashioned in a Laura Ashley dress, tucked bodice with cotton lace high at her neck, and full skirt with ruffles, a lovely bow at the back. With roses in her hand, and petals in her hair, she looks like a rosebud herself! Becky Sandri—now to become Mrs. Rodman Miller. Where did she meet him? L'Abri. Probably at a meal in Chalet TziNo kitchen, where Priscilla cooks and serves meals.

Where did Rodman come from? It was when he was in William Jennings Bryan College that Rodman began to read Fran's books, and to have a lot of things "clear up" for him. From a Christian background, Rodman nevertheless had questions and struggles about reality, and that which so many students come to L'Abri with—questions concerning the obvious that is "happening" in many of today's evangelical circles, the possibility of "saying the right words" with a hollow empty void where there should be certainty and conviction. Rodman not only read all Fran's books, he took with him to his Marine assignments a copy of *True Spirituality*. It was as a lieutenant in the Marines in Okinawa, and on the boat during his many "tours of duty" in the West Pacific, Korea, Japan, Taiwan, Hong Kong, etc., that he read and re-read Udo's book *Pro-Existence*.

He would have been flabbergasted if he had known that Udo was going to be his uncle! . . . But he really felt the book was a help in changing his outlook on life, and work. At the Atlanta Seminar of *Whatever Happened to the Human Race?* Rodman was assigned to stand guard outside Fran's door to give him time to pray and prepare for his lecture and discussion times. He would have fainted if someone had told him that before another year was over Francis Schaeffer would be his grandfather-in-law! No, blueprints aren't given to any of us, nor glimpses of the future. But it helps, at times, to take a swift trip through the tunnel of the past to look through any gaps (arches) there are and to gain some understanding of what is being woven into The Tapestry.

Now as the music bursts forth (Becky has asked that the bells be rung after they come out, rather than before, to celebrate the reality of being man and wife) there stands grandfather Fran up front, and Giandy, reminding me so much of Franky years before, solemnly carrying the rings, which wouldn't come off easily when the moment arrived!

The wedding reception in the chapel gave us an opportunity to hear what we had wanted for years to hear: three generations playing a Mozart quartet—Mr. Sandri (now in his eighties), his sister Tante Tita, John, and Becky. Mr. Sandri played first violin; Becky, second violin; Tante Tita, viola; and John, cello. It was beautiful to listen to . . . but also wonderful to watch. Three generations blending together!

How lost are people who have lost their continuity! Fran's sermon had been centered on the responsibility of "passing on the flag" to the next generation. The reception was a low-key and relaxed time, one of being able to meet Rodman's parents, who had come from South Carolina, and some of his family; to watch Lisby and Natasha, and the bride and groom, and others, do an Israeli dance; as well as for us to talk to L'Abri people for the first time after months away. Priscilla was responsible for good planning in that. And she, with each of us, marveled at the transition being so smooth and natural, as we each shifted into a new generation, so to speak!

Swift glimpses . . . of what? Swift glimpses of some of the results of the weaving in The Tapestry's continued pattern. Swift glimpses of some of the breathtaking beauty along the way. But, also, swift glimpses of all the "blood, sweat, and tears" that are involved in continuing continuity. Costly? Surely. But, how cheap is brokenness? What is Jesus talking about when He says, "He that loseth his life shall find it"? It isn't something to write in a notebook, and to be satisfied about in some sort of "Bible class." It is *life* . . . lived.

GOD'S MATHEMATICS! 21

If it were up to the devil . . . he would subtract every one of God's people from history, and would divide all of God's people from each other, setting them at each other's throats, with hate erasing love, and occupation with lesser battles diverting their attention from the Major Battle of God against Satan. The devil's "darts" or "flaming arrows" are real, and we are told we are meant to know they exist, not as a kind of fairy-tale illustration for children, but as a dangerous "happening," assailing us day by day.

We are to quench or put out the fiery darts . . . how? By taking the shield of faith. The shield *is* faith. The sword is the Word of God. Day by day, hour by hour, we are meant to take the protection we are warned we seriously need. We are to read, meditate upon, dwell in the Bible as the true Word of God. We are not meant simply to talk about how much we believe it; we are to use it as a "sword" in our portion of the battle—the portion in which we are involved. We are to have a "shield" in front of us—a bullet-proof vest, so to speak, which is the shield of faith. We are to believe what we have read, to remember that our God is the God of the impossible, that He is greater than our enemy, and that He has promised us that this shield is effec-tive! We have a "tried and tested" shield against the fiery darts

513

that *do* come against us day by day, even if we are not aware of them. We are to pray with faith, staying in communication with God actively.

As I write this, in the midst of history, it is March 31, 1981, and today's *International Herald Tribune* printed in Zurich has come out with screaming headlines. Fran called from Montreux to read it to me: "Reagan Is Shot In Chest By Gunman In Washington, Undergoes Surgery." We stopped to pray for President Reagan, for his family, for the family of William Brady (the President's press secretary, who was also shot and critically injured), and all the others who are personally affected, and for many in Washington who will be making immediate decisions. We prayed for our country, and for other countries in this moment of history. Enemies are of a variety of kinds. The darts, arrows, bullets of enemies have an insidious way of hurtling through the most sophisticated and well-prepared protection of Secret Service men, or well-planned ways of approach or departure. What seems to be the very best protection can be penetrated by the fiery darts of much weaker people. The Devil is weaker than God. The Tapestry of history is full of such examples. "But," you ask, "wasn't Reagan a Christian? So didn't he have the 'shield of faith' to protect him as well as the Secret Service men?"

The answer to that is that the bullet's hitting a person is not a criterion of his or her being a faithful Christian or not! History shows us a long progression of God's choicest servants who have been "hit" by the enemy's arrows, and there are many hidden ones we don't know. But what the enemy doesn't know is that God's arithmetic or mathematics is done differently, and the enemy's subtraction of people, the enemy's "success" many times in wiping people out of history in the period they are badly needed, is not always a success!

Many, many times the enemy oversteps himself in his apparently clever use of subtraction. That would hold for organized human enemies as well as for the master enemy, the devil. Yes, we could name a long line of martyrs who have died in the prime of life. We could name men like Jeremiah or Isaiah, sawed in half, and Stephen in the New Testament, stoned to death. We could speak of the missionaries killed in my mother's time, and Chester Bitterman, the Wycliffe man so recently killed in Colombia. We could speak of the arrows or fiery darts of plane or auto accidents, of cancer, of heart attacks, and a variety of other sorts. True—God's very precious children, whose "hairs are numbered," who are being prepared a marvelous future, and who are promised protection against Satan, if they use that protection, also are targets in which the results of the battle can lodge. In spite of Satan's apparent successes in his attempt to subtract people, Bibles, and other sources of truth in history, we have evidence that God's mathematics have prevailed, time after time. Thousands of Chinese Christians and pastors were killed when Communism came in. We know now that the living witness of truth was not stamped out, as the church in China is alive and strong today. Glimpses of the final victory are noticeable in the lesser victories of history.

During 1958 a man flying across Ohio read one of my Family Letters, given to him by his cousin. He was on his way to a business meeting, but, feeling stirred by that letter, he thought he should immediately send off a well-packaged tape recorder to L'Abri's Chalet les Mélèzes. He had no idea how it might be used, but as this was his business, he gave what was a part of his own interest. When that tape recorder arrived at Mélèzes, Fran remarked, "Leave it in its box, we have no space to put it . . . and anyway, I will *never* speak into a mike, and I don't want our discussions recorded, ever. People must feel free to ask their real questions in privacy." For six months we used that sturdy box as a kind of extra "table space" near my typewriter, to place cups of tea or books and paper that needed to be within reach! One late evening, when I was washing dishes and preparing to cook something for the next day's meals, John Boice, who was a L'Abri Worker at that time, came hurrying into the kitchen. "Mrs. Schaeffer, I'm going to unpack that tape recorder right now, and set it up in the downstairs hall. I'll run an extension cord in and hide the mike in the plants. Could you serve tea to everyone, and make a *lot* of clatter? You see, those Brandeis University girls and the Smith College girls are asking wonderfully intelligent questions, and Dr. Schaeffer is giving fabulous answers. I don't want it to be lost. In fact, I should think the girls would want to have copies of what is being said tonight to listen to again and digest, and perhaps have friends hear. Please?"

I wasn't sure Fran would approve, but it sounded like a good idea, so I did my part, fixing a tray of cookies, popping some corn to nibble, and making a pot of tea. As I brought all this, along with sugar and cream to hand around, I clattered the cups noisily on the saucers, and acted as awkward as I could. Fran told me afterwards that he wondered what had happened to me, and to my coordination! It worked. The mike was hidden and no one noticed what John Boice was doing, although some may have wondered why he didn't help pass tea.

That was the beginning of the tape program. And—let me quickly say—that was before widespread teaching by means of tapes. It was way ahead. But—we didn't recognize that it was the "beginning" of anything. All we knew then was that when the girls discovered the next day that they could have a copy of what had been said the night before, they eagerly exclaimed, "Oh, good! Please, may I buy a copy? I want to listen over again, and to have friends hear it too!"

From time to time in the next two years, a few tapes were made of discussions. It wasn't until November of 1960, after Farel House had started, with three people studying individually in the Beau Site sun room, that the Farel House Luncheons started. Fran would gather clippings from current papers, and at lunch— while I served silently and simply guessed whether someone wanted tea or coffee—he would read various bits concerning the ideas coming forth in films, music, science, art, law, government, etc., and then talk. He called this "The Twentieth Century Climate." This grew into thirteen lectures called "The Development of Modern Thought," or, as it came to be known, "The Basic Farel House Lectures."

Now, in that beginning with the three Farel House students— Ran, Richard, and Deirdre—the idea came, "Why not tape these luncheons, because soon Hansjorg, Roger, and Danielle will be coming as students, and they can catch up on what has already been said." Soon after that Harro (Dutch) and Anne (Swiss-English), a couple who had become Christians at L'Abri, met there, married, and were then in Lausanne, asked Fran to come and teach once a week in their apartment. Since the Farel House students wanted to hear the discussion too, Harro taped these studies. There was an exact ending time, because Fran had to catch the 10:20 P.M. train, the last one in those days from Lausanne to Aigle!

These are the "Romans Tapes," which are so basic that they usually make up the first series of studies people follow in Farel House. People still hear Harro's voice, a clink of teaspoons, and others as they asked questions! These Romans Tapes have been, and are being listened to all over the world.

After John and Priscilla had moved into Chalet TziNo, just before Becky's birth in June of 1963, John quietly began to do something he felt extremely important: he began setting an alarm clock for 2 A.M., 3:30 A.M., etc., so that he could "turn over the tape"! Without the proper equipment, he was copying tapes which he felt were extremely important for people to listen to. When I asked him once if it wasn't too much of a hassle, and too disturbing to his sleep, he said, "Look, I feel the content, the material covered in these tapes is so basic and so essential that I want as many people as possible to be able to hear them—whether they can come to Switzerland or not."

Sermons were taped and copied. Lectures were taped and copied. Bible studies were taped and copied. Discussions were taped and copied. People could borrow tapes or buy tapes. As Bill Wysor (a cousin of Jane S. S.), who became a Christian through Fran, and his wife Jane began to send out the Family Letters after mother died, their home in Virginia also became a L'Abri Tape Lending Library. Bill, who was contributing his time, said he worked harder than he had in the days he was giving full time to his business. (Bill has joined my mother and father in heaven now. I wonder if they discuss their part in the same work? They hadn't met "in the land of the living.") The tapes then went to L'Abri in California, where Claire Olsen first handled them, and later a succession of other Workers. Now they have a new system and a new L'Abri center. Cassettes were first made from the tapes by Bud and Barbara, who called themselves "Chalet Cassettes." After a period of years, the cassettes and their copying were transferred to the Greatham L'Abri in England, where they are still made.

Added to Fran's lectures, sermons, discussions and Bible studies, there grew a large library of tapes that includes the studies, lectures, and sermons given by other L'Abri Workers, both in L'Abri branches and in the L'Abri Conferences. These include, among others, tapes by Ranald Macaulay, Udo Middelmann, Jerram

Barrs, Dick Keyes, Barry Seagren, Edith Schaeffer, Priscilla Sandri, Jane S. Smith, Debby Middelmann, Wim Rietkirk, Richard Winters, Nick Cornelise, Henk Geertsema, Hans Rookmaaker, Hurvey Woodson, Franky Schaeffer, Susan Macaulay, Larry Snyder, Donald Drew, Os Guiness, Bob Jono, Ellis Potter, and others. Why such a long list of names? To make it clear that, out of the 198 L'Abri Workers there have been thus far, and the 55 who are in the work right now, first of all there is a continuity of people, and also a continuity of ideas, but great diversity. Each person is an individual.

The tapes are a picture of God's "multiplication." Fran's physical voice could not reach many miles—if even one! In the days when Jesus and the disciples spoke to thousands on the hillsides, their voices carried to all who could hear. These were strong voices, but the range diminished, and stopped at a certain distance. With microphone and amplification invented, God used such means to reach many more ears with important facts concerning truth, and with the truth itself. Then as at a startling point in history it became possible to capture the sound of voices on records or discs and to reproduce them to be listened to as a needle tracked along in the grooves, another dimension had been reached. Then a succession of things came tumbling one after another—radio, tape ribbons and recorders and cassettes, along with the capturing of people's features and gestures on film! God has used what He enabled men to invent, what He created people for in the first place—to be creative—as means for multiplication. God, in making people to be finite, gave ways in which to circumvent that finiteness.

We were astonished as we heard of tape listening groups beginning in so many places. The astonishment came not because we heard officially but in unexpectedly casual ways. Once when Fran was in the Kennedy Airport in New York, a girl walked over to him and asked, "Are you Dr. Schaeffer?" "Yes, I am." "Oh, I was sure I recognized your voice. I've never seen you, or even a picture of you, but I have listened to hours and hours of your tapes. Oh, thank you for helping me so much in all you have taught me." (Our ancestors, whether in Bach's time, or during the Revolutionary War, would have been quite unbelieving if you had showed them a bit of "ribbon" and told them that ribbon would preserve their words, their music, or the sound of their cannons booming for someone miles away, or years away.)

It was overwhelming as the tapes began to bring the fireside discussions, and the studies in Romans in that Lausanne apartment, into homes in Japan, India, South Africa, Rhodesia, Ghana, many states in America including Hawaii and Alaska (not yet states), Hong Kong, Singapore, Australia, New Zealand, England, Canada, Sweden, Norway, Finland, Italy, Spain, the Philippines . . . and so many other places it made us dizzy. It wasn't just that Fran's teaching, and then later the teaching of other L'Abri people, was being heard as sounds that reached around the world and back again; minds were listening, and ears of understanding were hearing, digesting, and bringing conviction of truth, and a bowing to the God who exists, accepting Christ as Savior. We were getting letters telling us so. People who had always heard, "You must just believe, you can't ask questions" were suddenly finding there were real answers that fit the reality of what is. No one needed to be ashamed of being a Christian.

We had been willing to remain in a chalet on a mountainside and pray for the ones of the Lord's choice to come to us there. The time came when we realized we must open ourselves also to being willing to go wherever the Lord wanted to take us to the people He might want us to speak to. It was another one of those things we all face over and over again in life, a matter of balance. An intertwining of the next multiplication of the Lord's involved division, and addition. We had to face dividing our time among America, Great Britain, and the chalet. And we had to face adding a kind of gypsy life, where we would be speaking in other people's atmosphere, rather than by our own fireside, or along the paths of our own mountains. The other multiplication which took place in the same period of time, or began to take place, involved radio.

The serious speaking at Harvard, at Massachusetts Institute of Technology, and other American universitites, came in 1965 when I was caring for grandmother. Fran was listed in the M.I.T. Calendar of Events as lecturing on February 9 on "Christianity and Existentialism" and on February 11 on "The Intellectual Climate of the New Theology." Chapter 24 tells more of the "where" of his speaking at that time; here the fact simply needs to be injected that, having discussed with Cambridge, Oxford, London University, St. Andrews, Durham, and Manchester students for a long time, now Fran was having questions fired at him on campuses on the other side of the Atlantic. In terms of the growth of the books which were soon to come forth, this was a part of the preparation.

A spiritual struggle on my part, so it seems to me, needs to be exposed here. In the very early part of the 1960s, I had been going through a time that could only be described as one of self-pity. I had begun to look away from "willingness for anything" to a desire for "something for myself," and this filled far too much of my thoughts and prayer times. It was an elusive thing that could be rationalized as something I "deserved"! Now one night when Fran and I were in Zurich, in the very "arty" apartment of an airline hostess for SwissAir, I was sitting in a corner on the floor of a candlelit room, sipping a cup of tea as the room filled up with pilots, doctors, lawyers, businessmen, and a few air hostesses and others. The hostess of the evening was a Christian who wanted her non-Christian friends to "hear some answers." I watched the faces from my almost hidden spot in the corner, and saw scorn, amusement, superiority, scepticism, and cynicism in their changing expressions as questions were asked, rather belligerently, and answers were being given. Then—I saw those expressions change to curiosity, interest, surprise, serious consideration, thoughtfulness, and even admiration. The questions became "real," and they grew into sincere searching.

Before the evening had come to an end, something happened to me. I silently talked to the Lord, "Oh, Lord," I said, "please forgive me if I have been a piece of dirt in the water-pipe. Forgive me if I have hindered the work of Your Spirit in any way. If *You* want Fran to do a much wider work, if You want what happened here in this room tonight to happen on a much larger scale, if You have people in other parts of the world who should hear what Fran has said tonight . . . then I am willing for whatever it takes on my part. Forgive me for my selfish prayers for a different life. I promise I'll go on, as You give me strength, to do whatever my part requires." That struggle, and that victory, came just *before* Fran went to America to speak after having not crossed the ocean for speaking engagements for five years. It came before this first time in the Boston area, and before *any* of his books had been written.

Am I setting myself up to take credit for all that came after that? No. Not that. It is something that has been hard for me to "expose": it was a realization that I could be hindering, in tune with the matter of "finding the speck in my eye" rather than thinking about a piece of board in anyone else's eye. It suddenly became clear to me that I could be a hindrance with selfishness. It is another aspect of "losing" one's life, or being willing to "die to self" or to be "buried as a grain of wheat"— that sort of thing. There is an importance in taking the Lord seriously when He takes the time and trouble to tell us in His instructions to us what *might* be subtracting from the effectiveness of our lives. I have already spoken of the devil's trying to "subtract" God's people, His Word, His influence *out* of history: we need to search our own motives, our sincerity, our "limits" we have built around our love of the Lord, and realize we also can be subtracting something from history. It is a solemn thought.

It was in 1966 that we were away from Switzerland for six weeks in response to this call: "Why can't you come over here? We need help in the effects of the twentieth-century thinking upon our schools, churches, and families." There were several reunions during this period of time, although of course they were not the object of our time. One occurred in Indianapolis. Fran was lecturing and I was speaking at another meeting when I found the Salisburys, who had given that first $1000 to buy Mélèzes, and learned that they had driven many miles to meet us. Then at the University of Michigan, in Ann Arbor, I "found" Lok by telephone, and he and his wife became flesh and blood people too, even as former L'Abri Workers Jim and Joyce came to our Detroit meetings "out of a fog." A time of special reunions, yes, but, more important, of Fran's continuing to develop ideas even as he was in the midst of meeting people's needs.

At Wheaton College Fran gave ten lectures in five days. Even as his 1965 talks had turned into the book *The God Who Is There,* so these lectures became *Death in the City.* Here in Wheaton also I talked to girls in the dorms, who came in their pajamas and robes, with hair in curlers, ready for bed. The idea was for them to be able to hear an intimate, candid talk about marriage, sex, and the career of being creative as a homemaker, whether for a husband and children or for oneself. At my urging, many of the girls interrupted with questions.

We went on to St. Louis for two weeks. Fran for a few years became a visiting lecturer in Covenant Theological Seminary, St. Louis, and in the Theological Academy in Basel, Switzerland. He gave fifteen lectures in Covenant, a concentrated course with an exam at the end. He also had evening meetings with university groups and with groups of medical students, a Christian doctors' banquet, etc., and my time was filled up with ladies' meetings and speaking in girls' schools. It was a delightful treat to be in the same city with Debby and Udo, as this was when Udo was studying at Covenant and Debby was teaching at John Burroughs. Naturally we had many ties in our old church there so this was a homecoming as well.

From St. Louis we went to Los Angeles, where we spent time speaking at Dorothy's father's church and stayed in the home of her parents, the Jamisons. This combined being with old friends and being with parents of our L'Abri Workers, who by that time were in Italy! Our time in Westmont paralleled the time in Wheaton, as Fran gave the same series of lectures and I spoke to girls in the dorms at night. Questions after lectures are essential in providing insights of whose need a lecturer cannot be aware if he leaves the platform with no idea of what his listeners' responses or questions are. And always during this time of lecturing there was the double concern of Fran's preparing for the next book he was to write.

San Francisco and Berkeley gave us a special time with seven former Farel House students—Alma (now Alma Hoyte), Deirdre and Richard Ducker (he was a Pan Am pilot then), Donna and Danny, and Beverly and Roger. This time clearly fulfilled their need for having L'Abri come to them. It was also a time in which the entire Berkeley happening as well as thinking became real to us, and not just as something we had read about. Now we know it as a place we have walked in and eaten in, and as people whom we have walked among and, in some cases, to whom we have talked. Yes, a small stream of people came through the years from Berkeley to L'Abri in Switzerland, but we were there too, to walk up Haight Ashbury. Seattle and Tacoma came next, with a fast succession of meetings, discussion groups, and glimpses of keen interest on the part of students in several colleges.

Returning to Switzerland via London, we had eighty people sitting on the few chairs and floor space in the big room at Ran and Sue's 52 Cleveland Road—with people from many parts of L'Abri's history, as well as of many nationalities. We felt so keenly that, from one part of the world to another, there is no difference in *need.* "The '60s" was taking place on *both* sides of the ocean. We may have observed the vividness of what was taking place on the Berkeley campus as we walked around Berkeley, and ate a meal with our own young people where "druggies" came to finish up leftover scraps of food on people's plates at tables vacated next to us, but the ideas were permeating minds everywhere we went. It *was* the '60s. Questions in London made that clear.

While in London we went to visit Franky. It was Guy Fawkes celebration and we watched Franky cavorting around the fireworks that night. We were able the next afternoon to watch Franky play soccer on the school's first team against another school. In our constant missing of him it was a comfort to find a happy, growing Franky in a school the Lord had obviously chosen for him. Within a month I was back in England, as a mother this time. Susan was expecting a new baby at any minute, and my help was needed with four-year-old Margaret, who had fever, earache and a bronchial cough that kept her awake most of the night Sue was in the hospital! Yes, she did have Kirsteen Merritt Macaulay—at 4:00 A.M. on December 8. Help was really needed, however, as Susan came home in two days with the new little sister. On December 18, Franky was able to come home with me for his Christmas holidays, so we had the treat of traveling together.

It seemed "impossible" to prepare for Christmas in such a short time. But Priscilla stayed home from the Champéry service to prepare the meal for Christmas Eve for everyone. Claudie and Allan had the students for Christmas breakfast, and Peasy and Sandy prepared a buffet lunch so we could be alone for a time of gift-opening as a family. It was during that Christmas season that Inka, a Dutch girl who was in a Swiss finishing school, came to a crystal-clear understanding and accepted Christ as Savior. Since then she and her husband Mike, as IVF workers, have led many other young people in the Seattle area into understanding.

This year the mid-'60s came to an end with a continued awe in watching the Lord work with individuals and in larger groups, at home and abroad—individuals from Eastern thought and Western thought and from '60s attitudes and concerns. The stream of people coming to L'Abri was matching the stream of people going in and out of campuses at that time. History was being made, and we were not in an ivory tower. Fran was especially exposed as he continued to be open to questions and to give answers he felt were true and relevant to what was behind the questions. Books were to grow out of these personal conversations with a diversity of people, and they would meet the needs of a matching diversity among his readers.

By Easter 1967 we were having a thrilling musical feast, because so many who came to L'Abri were musicians, and Franky, home from school, was having his first experience of monitoring guest tapes. In that period of time his dad had a "first" too—Hodder and Stoughton Publishing Company in England accepted for publication *The God Who Is There*. God was preparing the stage to bring out of the wings his next example of multiplication! Books usually take nine months to bring out once they are accepted, and we of course had not a clue as to the fact that this was only the *first* book, nor that English would be only the *first* language the book would be in. The beauty of the music at Easter had been a fitting sound effect, but before we were to "see" the unexpected multiplication, the musicians had scattered and the stage was silent.

On May 3, 1967, Priscilla stopped at my window to say that John and her dad had just left for Lausanne to make the experimental radio broadcasts. As Becky and Lisby played around in the snow flurry, we talked about John and Fran's "trying it again" soon in Monte Carlo at the Trans-World Radio station. Priscilla had recently had a miscarriage, the one that kept her in the hospital three weeks, and told me of how five-year-old Lisby had sighed deeply when she heard her mother was leaving for the hospital and said, "Oh, mommy has to be in the hospital; *I'll* have to do the work lists then!" Among Pris's multitudinous jobs, making the L'Abri "work lists" was one. That involves choosing people for their four hours of work who seemed to have an aptitude to help wash windows or stitch patches for a quilt or chop wood, or whatever. Lisby had the job of handing these papers of assignments out to the chalets day by day.

John and Fran came back saying that Lausanne was too expensive, and that they couldn't go to Monte Carlo each time. But just at that time a woman came from the Boston area to ask what she might do so that what Dr. Schaeffer was saying could spread out into a wider circle. Things fell in place as she bought a proper piece of equipment for recording the broadcasts. The place? John has a tiny office in a tiny *mazot*, which is a chalet with an upper and lower floor, normally built for storing hay. John's office is the top floor. When this was chosen to double for a studio nothing was taken out. All the books and papers for doing the financial work remained, plus John's cello and music, and Priscilla simply added a big green turkish towel to give the proper sound. Strangely enough, this worked better than the expensive studios, and the radio programs began to be made.

Late at night, John and Fran would get themselves ready in that "studio," starting the broadcast just after the village clock chimed either the hour or half-hour. Bong—bong—bong . . . "o.k.?" . . . "o.k." And Fran would start. Somewhere along the way John would break in and ask a question. The whole thing was all very informal, but the tapes covered the material that was in *The God Who Is There* and *Escape from Reason*.

The broadcasts were just about twenty-seven minutes, giving time for the burst of guitar music, and for station announcements. The series was called Euro Club. There were seventy-eight broadcasts, enough for one a week for a year and a half. At first Trans World Radio used them to broadcast behind the Iron Curtain on short wave and medium bands, and this also covered Europe. To reach this audience was the original purpose of these informal chats discussing "the relevance of Christianity today." They were so popular among thinking people, who wrote that they hadn't heard anything like this before, that they were used again for another year and a half—three years on the same Euro Club.Then the series was taken by a station in Cyprus and broadcast into the Near East and Africa. An Israeli girl came to L'Abri once who had heard it regularly in Jerusalem! Later the Far Eastern

Broadcasting system of stations used it to beam into China, and
HCJB, "The Voice of the Andes," used it to broadcast from
Ecuador into South America and all the places this large station
reaches.

Domain Agency, a Christian agency for placing radio broadcasts, normally charges the programs for placing them, but became
interested in airing this series. Speaking of "threads," back in
our St. Louis church, a little girl with initials F. A. used to pride
herself as having the same name as the pastor. Many years later,
F. A., now married to a doctor near Wheaton, and daughter-in-
law to the people who began Domain Agency, worked and prayed
and helped in many ways to get this series of her namesake's
put on American stations. The series has now been on many
many American Christian stations and is still being asked for.

Multiplication? Multiplication of the use of Prisca's towel! Of
the use of John's little *mazot!* Of those midnight hours when both
John and Fran were weary after long days! Of the message that
is still relevant to people's needs, still answering questions, still
bringing understanding. There was no plan on L'Abri's part, on
Fran's part, on John's part, to multiply in that way. Chance? I
believe it is a picture of God's diversity of ways of multiplying.

Our speaking trips were being multiplied now. People who
feel they wish they could have been in L'Abri when we were
always there are picturing something that only existed in the
first six years, and even then, remember, Fran had regular Bible
classes in six or seven places. It was in that same month, May
1967, that I wrote in the Family Letter: "The Lord is answering
prayer in amazing ways . . . but we are often ready to murmur
or cry out, "It's too much . . . we can't go on" . . . as exhaustion
accompanies the physical demands of what has been unfolded
for this year." That was fourteen years ago. Little did I know
what was going to be unfolded.

The same May, after my writing that, we left for England where
Fran spoke in Oxford, in Cambridge, in Durham University, and
in Manchester University. He was a summer lecturer at the London
School of Economics, in connection with London University, and
he spoke at a ministers' meeting of the Evangelical Alliance. He
had a "confrontation" before the faculty and students with the
Dean of King's College Divinity School of London University

(a very liberal school whose theological degree is considered by many to be scholastically the highest in the world). At each of the universities the groups were larger than those reported for former events.

Space simply doesn't permit going on with lists of places and subject matter for lectures. For instance, 1968 was to be the time in America when we went to fourteen cities and the time Harvard Christian students were to prepare for Fran's lectures by wearing white buttons with red letters stating "SCHAEFFER is not a BEER." This brought the question, of course, "What is it then?" A modest little typed paper prepared by a committee of students gave the answer, "Dr. Francis Schaeffer: philosopher-critic-theologian-organizer of a community in Switzerland where scholars and students gather to analyze and discuss topics of major contemporary importance—frequent lecturer at major universities of Europe and Britain. His field is the analysis of contemporary thought and culture from a specifically Christian viewpoint, but directed beyond the Christian community. He is concerned about the world in which we live and is sensitive to the despair which blights our achievements. He argues that only historic Christianity, rightly understood and fearlessly applied, can solve the dilemma of modern man. His answers may not be the ones modern man expects, or even welcomes. But clearly they cannot be ignored." (Times in Lowell Lecture Hall are then given.)

During one of those fourteen or fifteen city periods-of-times, Os Guiness was with us to speak also, and teenage Franky went along, having just had hepatitis and being unable yet to go back to school! In Berkeley that time we not only sat and talked about the problems of the '60s, but after a discussion one night, went to Fillmore West. There we milled around with the hippies and druggies listening to the music highlighted by the Jefferson Airplane, a band whose superiority we recognized. We watched the light show, breathed the heavy air, and sorrowed over not only the glassy-eyed young people, but the tiny toddlers staggering around with their bottles of half-finished milk, dropping the bottles on the dirty floor and picking them up to start sucking again. Our brains whirled not only with the music, which threatened in volume to break the eardrums, and the dizzying effect of the light show, but with the lostness of humanity in search of "peace" where there is no peace. Incidentally, we felt it most important to go with Franky and discuss afterwards with some measure of understanding.

Whatever "the generation gap" consists of, from generation to generation, a time of listening is needed—listening to what the next generation is saying, listening to the words of the music they are listening to, listening to the meaning behind the words. If true communication is to continue, there is a language to be learned—and I don't mean just that the word "gay" doesn't mean "light-hearted" any more! Whatever our need is in order to communicate with our own children, with our pupils in school, with other people we don't understand, we need some time to truly listen and determine what the "search" consists of, and whether there is honesty and sincerity that might be stepped on too easily because of our utterly selfish ignorance.

On March 4, 1973, Fran gave the Sunday morning sermon in Battell Chapel, the Church of Christ, in Yale University. There was a packed church—and real responses. Some of that congregation later appeared at L'Abri, but others were old L'Abri family, excited to hear Fran. The church bulletin announced: "The Reverend Francis Schaeffer and his co-workers from L'Abri Fellowship in Huémoz, Switzerland, will be giving a series of lectures which begin this evening, in 114SSS, at 8:00 P.M. Mr. Schaeffer will speak tonight, Wednesday and Thursday, and Udo Middelmann will lecture on Monday, and Os Guiness on Tuesday." The subject of the series was "Christianity: Cause or Cure?"

Udo and Os also had a busy week speaking at a couple of classes, having spontaneous discussions and talking to students who wanted appointments. Fran felt that whatever the results were, he himself had once more been given, "without plan," an opportunity to listen and to discover how relevant his answers were to current discussion, as well as to the climate of the university thinking and life. After a lecture one day at the Divinity School, Fran was invited by the Reverend William Sloane Coffin, Jr., who had just heard him, to have lunch with the entire staff of the University Chapel. Sitting around a table strewn with books and papers, midst clouds of smoke, people munched on sandwiches, and a most lively discussion ensued as they voiced their disagreements. Perhaps this worthwhile confrontation should be put into a slot with Berkeley under the heading of "keeping in touch with the heart of twentieth-century thinking," as it progressed.

Yes, our trips multiplied—and I do mean journeys by planes and cars, not chemically induced trips (sorry about the confusion of the English language)—and the results overwhelmed us. During a time in America in 1969 we were to be in Washington, D. C., where, among other things, Fran was to speak at a breakfast seminar with a couple of hundred student leaders attending. I will quote a portion of the report from the *United States Congressional Record,* Tuesday, November 25, 1969. This issue is entitled "National Student Leadership Seminar": "The great majority of attendees were students representing colleges and universities in 36 states, stretching from Harvard to the University of California, Berkeley, and from the University of British Columbia, to the University of Mississippi. There were also National Leaders there. . . . Alan Boles, a former editor of *Yale Daily News,* opened the seminar. 'Its purpose,' he said, was twofold, 'to create an atmosphere in which meaningful dialogue between a broad variety of campus and national leaders could take place, and second, to provide an open opportunity for men to discuss the relevance of the person of Jesus Christ in modern times.' . . .

"Friday, October 24, Schaeffer's speech: A personal highlight.

"Senator Mark Hatfield, who assisted the students in sponsoring the seminar, spoke first at the breakfast. He was followed by the principal speaker of the morning, Dr. Francis A. Schaeffer. [The report then explains who Fran is.] Dr. Schaeffer analyzed the major philosophic and historical developments since the time of the early Greeks and then identified the influence of these streams of thought on contemporary life. I found myself taking copious notes on what he said."

The *Record* went on to report quite fully on the speech, but I will include only a few excerpts: "Because people think and act like machines, Dr. Schaeffer said, they have no basis for their values. They only function on the basis of memory." . . . "Schaeffer pointed out, 'In modern theology "God is dead." Reason has no place. All content about God is dead. All we are left with are high motivation words, "God words" without content. Banners without content. . . . What we have then is religion in the modern theological sense being just another kind of trip. And if reason is gone how do you choose between one kind of trip and another? It doesn't matter.' "

The reporter then goes on to say, "I thought this analysis of our present-day situation was both pointed and accurate. But I was even more fascinated with his solution for our current problems: . . . 'My answer is that we need reconciliation on the basis of a different kind of revolution. It must be love. But not love alone, but also a God who is holy and gives categories which can be a basis for reconciliation. It must be a personal God. On this basis man is not dead. . . . He is made in the image of God. On the basis of the substitionary death of Christ there is an answer for man's true moral guilt. On this basis man can be returned to horizontal fellowship with men, as well as fellowship with God.' . . .

"As Doctor Schaeffer concluded, I looked at my watch: he had talked seventy-five minutes. It seemed like fifteen. I began to wonder why he had captivated me so? Why was his talk so meaningful? . . . Schaeffer's convictions do not seem to be defense for ignorance as they are for some people; he clearly understands why he believes what he does."

Reports like this multiplied even as Fran's articles were appearing in more and more journals and papers in many different parts of the world. I sit here today, on the floor, sneezing from dust that may not be seen but has certainly gathered in these papers (kept under the eaves in cardboard banana boxes from Migro's), and I don't know where to pull one out from next. There are so many I feel the way Alice in Wonderland did when she looked up and all the cards were floating down from the ceiling. I dream about being buried under such papers, but they need to be noticed as a part of God's multiplication. I'll grab up a handful, as I did with our letters so many years ago.

At the end of 1959 a well-known reporter came to L'Abri for a day, to thank us for what we had done for his daughter. He was impressed with what he had never heard before, in spite of his wide contacts as a reporter with all sorts of religious people, and sent an official *Time* magazine reporter. We had a most interesting four hours with a United Nations reporter for *Time* from Geneva, who enjoyed the discussion. A photographer was sent who also enjoyed the discussion and took many pictures—some of the best he had ever taken, he said—of our family on the balcony, with the mountains and valley behind us, as well as of students crowded into the living room, and another series in Lausanne at the cafe class. The article written was a long one. But—what appeared was two columns on the religion page, and one picture of Fran, showing our nephew Barney, then thirteen, and Franky, age eight. Not the photographer's best "shot" by any means! The article was entitled "Mission to the Intellectuals": "Each weekend the Schaeffers are overrun by a crowd of young men and women mostly from universities—painters, writers, actors, singers, dancers and beatniks—professing every shade of belief and disbelief. There are existentialists and Catholics, Protestants, Jews, and left-wing atheists. . . . 'These people are not reached by Protestantism today,' Schaeffer said. 'What we need is a presentation of the Bible's historical truth in such a way that it is acceptable to today's intellectuals. Now as before, the Bible can be acted upon, even in the intellectual morass of the twentieth century.' " In all it was fair, and quite amazing.

The Church of England paper in 1968 had a report of the Evangelical Alliance Conference of Ministers held February 12–14, 1968, in Swanwick: "A record number attended last week to hear a small, fast-talking and fast-thinking American by the name of Dr. Francis Schaeffer. From the moment he started his first lecture on 'The Mood of Our Times' by quoting from the *Listener*'s review of the film 'Poor Cow,' to his closing address at the united communion service, his audience was spellbound. His appraisal of present-day culture, his analysis of philosophic concepts, and his assessment of trends in the arts and in theology broke fresh ground for many. Around the world this little man from L'Abri Fellowship in Switzerland is attracting more and more attention. . . . Dr. Schaeffer maintains that the mark of this century is the victory of the Hegelian concept of synthesis, instead of a recognition of truth in the sense of antithesis and absolutes."

Two years later another Church of England newspaper printed a long letter under "Dear Editor," which began with: "One of the most significant comments upon the writings of Dr. Schaeffer is that they arouse strong feelings. This in itself is cause for gratitude at a time when there is a suffocating complacency and mental indolence upon the Christian scene."

In the February 4, 1977, issue of *Christianity Today*, David E. Kucharsky, then senior editor, began an article concerning philosophy by saying: "Next time you say grace or kneel in private devotions, say a word of thanks to God for Francis A. Schaeffer, who has induced many people to think about the presuppositions—conscious or unconscious—that undergird their thought patterns and their actions. Schaeffer's newest work, and his most comprehensive, *How Should We Then Live?* (Revell) promises to carry the self-examination goad even further."

In the June 3, 1977, issue of *Christianity Today*, Kucharsky interviewed The Most Reverend Fulton J. Sheen (since deceased), who had the distinction of being the most eloquent spokesmen for the Roman Catholic Church, on radio, TV, and in his writings.

"Question: Some evangelicals are also concerned with a more rational approach.

"Archbishop Sheen's *Answer:* Francis Schaeffer is taking that approach and doing it extremely well. His summary of philosophical doctrines is one of the best that I have ever read, and I taught philosophy in graduate school for twenty-five years. The world needs philosophy to set up norms outside the self as a watch needs a norm outside itself. Philosophy has become a history of philosophy. If we taught architecture today the way we teach philosophy, no one would ever be able to construct a building."

In *Eternity* magazine of June 1977, an article called "The Rise of Francis Schaeffer" by Stephen Board, which is full of criticism and especially accuses Fran of "oversimplifying," ends with quotes from two men. One of them is Richard Terrell, associate professor of art at Doane College in Nebraska. Here Board is quoting Terrell, who says: " 'Dr. Schaeffer's thoughts on art find points of contact with even secular people like Ayn Rand. For both of them, rational intelligibility is a prime criterion of artistic virtue. This causes Schaeffer (and Rand also) to take a dim view of abstract art, which he claims "alienates" the viewer from the painter. Inasmuch as I work in a direction that is quite abstract, tending toward "non-objectivity," I find Schaeffer's assertions interesting but I think him mistaken on this point. Of more value to me has been Schaeffer's insight that the Christian world view is the only path of a truly integrated approach to learning. I am convinced that the Christian base is the only foundation for a true liberal arts experience in learning. Schaeffer has helped me to see this.' "

Board goes on to say, "If Schaeffer is right that art and culture display religious and philosophical problems—as most intellectuals would agree—*How Should We Then Live?* stands as the most ambitious illustration of that thesis from evangelicals in the century. It is also the most influential among conservative Protestants. In a gathering at Wheaton College in the early '70s, various opinions were being aired on culture in relation to Schaeffer's views. Some said it was simplistic on this, he was glib on that, arbitrary on something else. Then John F. Alexander, of the philosophy faculty at Wheaton, remarked, 'Say what you will, just remember that without Francis Schaeffer, most evangelicals would not even be in a discussion like this.' "

Speaking of multiplying, if people start really thinking and discussing and considering not only the ideas involved but the effect the "truth of what exists" should have on their own lives and actions, then the reality of the *impact* of Christianity ought to begin to be felt among artists, doctors, lawyers, government people; in social questions, in community decisions affecting born and unborn people of the next generation, etc. Then already the mathematical possibilities are endless! People sitting around simply clinging to a lot of trite phrases and rules and regulations without ever seriously caring about truth, and, what is more, falling into not living consistently with even those phrases and rules "if no one is looking," can bring about devastating destruction with great rapidity. Just having people sparked into thinking is already the multiplying of an "honest search"—even if people loudly disagree. It is better to think and consider and disagree, than to sit like an oyster or a clam on the beach with a moronic lack of interest as to whether there is any meaning to life or not . . . or any truth.

Here is another paper I picked up from the banana box, the Dutch equivalent of *Time* or *Newsweek*, named *Elseviers*, March 11, 1978. A long interview with Fran, accompanied by two good clear pictures, came out just at the time of the seminar for *How Should We Then Live?* which had been on Dutch television (put on by the Evangelische Omroep). The seminar was held in the Free University of Amsterdam. This had been Professor Hans Rookmaaker's university before his sudden death, and it was both a joy and a sorrow to sit with Anky (his wife) that day. The full auditorium, with over one thousand there, would have so pleased him. The magazine has a "spread" which when translated is eleven pages long, so I won't attempt to include much of it. Rex Brico, the journalist, came to our chalet for the interview. (Edward B. Fiske, the *New York Times* journalist who wrote an article entitled "Fundamentalist Conducts a Spiritual Haven in Alps," September 10, 1973, also came to the chalet for his interview. Reporters and journalists have come from England, Scandinavian countries, Hong Kong, Australia and New Zealand, and many from Switzerland itself. A great variety of articles have appeared through the years.)

The Dutch news magazine starts out: "Dr. Schaeffer has been very much in the limelight in Holland, owing to the television series inspired by his book *How Should We Then Live?* which was broadcast by the E. O. in ten installments." The reporter goes on: "So it seems we are confronted with a crack in our Christian philosophy. But how did it come about? I put these questions to the aging, bearded clergyman sitting in his simple, but comfortable wooden chalet, some 6000 feet about sea level [actually 3100]. Around the cottage the snow lies almost seven feet deep, but in the living room an open fire is blazing. It seems that Dr. Schaeffer, every detail of whose personality and attitude calls up associations with both the explorer and the mountaineer, has prepared himself to answer this question. . . . 'To discover the cause of this crack we must first of all go back to the Renaissance,' Schaeffer says. 'At that time people showed an increasing tendency to place man—instead of God—in the center of knowledge, truth and cognition. This important change was passed on to later generations by such philosophers as Jean-Jacques Rousseau, Kant, Hegel and others. Finally, to start with in the Protestant churches, but later in the Roman-Catholic church as well, Latitudinarianism has attempted to bring about a kind of link between the rationalistic principles of the Enlightenment and Christian philosophy. I do not think, however, that such a link is feasible.' "

At another season, a *New York Times* journalist wandered around L'Abri talking to people, and started his article with: "Larry Snyder was working in a wine factory in Oslo several years ago when a friend told him about a place in Switzerland where people can find answers to basic questions. He sought it out, was converted to Christianity here, and now, with his wife, spends his time helping others sort out the meaning of their lives." Then he goes on to give a brief history of L'Abri and to report his interview with Fran. Larry, along with other of the L'Abri workers, has a story of the wonder of how God brought him to L'Abri and to Himself that can't be squashed into ten lines of a newspaper column. But the constantly multiplied stories about L'Abri, or the giving of some of Fran's ideas, or the telling about the content of some books or films—these were all unplanned-for, unasked-for multiplication.

William F. Buckley Jr.'s *National Review* had an article by D. Keith Mano about Fran in the March 18, 1977, issue. It ended: "Once Christian culture lost its accreditation, men had to entertain a functional schizophrenia. There could be nothing immanent in nature; and reason, through elitist insolence, had given up citizenship in the spiritual domain. Schaeffer is a powerful and accurate summarizer. Divorce on trumped-up grounds of incompatibility between mind and spirit has been the pre-eminent human misadventure. Christian energy must yet survive and abundantly. After all, it made *How Should We Then Live?* into a best seller. Hopefulness, stern morality, trenchant anti-communism: these we have the evidence here, are qualities that America can respond to. Francis Schaeffer is a sentinel phenomenon. I know you have other things to do. Still, you should read *How Should We Then Live?* It's part of a good education."

More recently, in the *National Review* of October 31, 1980, Dr. Harold O. J. Brown wrote an article entitled "The Road to Theocracy?" In speaking of the strong fact that "over the Constitution there is a God, and attention needs to be paid to His laws and to His will if the nation is to survive," Dr. Brown is specific in telling of what has been taking place recently in the areas of drawing Christians together in "battle." I quote what he has to say with regard to another aspect of the multiplying of Fran's influence: "When the U. S. Supreme Court handed down its epoch-making pro-abortion decision, *Roe v. Wade*, in 1973, Francis Schaeffer, the outstanding spiritual and intellectual leader of conservative evangelicism in the English-speaking world, strode into battle. But the intellectual and spiritual ferment that Schaeffer had stirred would probably have remained limited to the more intellectual circles of evangelicals and fundamentalists—never very large—were it not for the tremendous visibility and financial power that nationwide television has given to preachers such as Jerry Falwell, a Baptist pastor from Lynchburg, Virginia."

There are Fran's books, which have taken what he has said in lectures, discussions, sermons, in a diversity of areas—twenty-one books, which have sold now in the millions and have been translated into twenty-seven languages. The bookcase where he has his books is made of unpainted boards stretching beside his small desk along the wooden wall just under the famous ivy plant that covers the wall. We keep getting books that we are unable to be sure of. "What language is this—and which book?" We find out, but it takes time, and a bit of research. "Who knows this language?" Chinese, Korean, Japanese might look a bit alike? Just today as I was writing this, Fran came in to show me the mail—a Coptic translation of *Escape from Reason,* the Swedish translation of *Whatever Happened to the Human Race?* and the German translation of *The Church Before the Watching World.* We didn't know the Coptic version was being prepared, nor did we know before they arrived about the Arabic, or the Hebrew, or some other translations—surprise! As to the Swedish, that was being done by Staffan, our Swedish Worker, and we prayed for his work, done late at night and early in the morning "in between" his L'Abri work. Multiplication of all twenty-one by twenty-seven? No, some of them in one language, some in another. Some languages have more books, others less. But the multiplication goes on.

Recently Fran was being introduced to a large audience numbering close to five thousand. The Christian leader who was introducing him was a much younger man, who has a wide leadership. "I want to introduce you to someone," he said, "who has been far up in the Swiss Alps, thinking, having ideas, thoughts, understanding, which we never would have had. God has used him in a mighty way to give me, and many others, the teachings, the ideas, the direction of our thinking, which has enabled us to do what we are doing, and preach what we are preaching . . .

in order to fight the battles we are fighting today, for the Bible, for truth, and for life. Many people don't know where this thinking that has influenced them came from."

I sat there remembering. Remembering Saturday night after Saturday night, Sunday night after Sunday night—any night after a discussion with some of those Cambridge men, Harvard men, Brandeis girls, Smith College girls, Wellesley girls, Dutch students, German law students, Italian businessmen, American singers, scientists, inventors; people with searching minds from all over the world, in twos and fives, tens and twenties—when Fran would come upstairs to our bedroom and hit his fist against the wooden wall until his knuckles would get red. "Oh, Edith, I'm *sure* I have true answers. . . . I'm *sure* they are right answers. . . . I know they can help people. People 'saw' tonight! Incredible how the lights came on for so many of them . . . amazing the excitement and the logical sequence of questions and understanding time after time. *But . . . no one is ever going to hear . . . no one . . .* except a handful. A handful of people will understand something, and then . . . forget. What are we doing? What am I doing?"

He was "thinking," as a thinker. He was not piling up degrees as an academic. Some need to do that, and it is important. But this wasn't Fran's place in The Tapestry. What he had to contribute, I believe, God gave him the possibility of contributing. It is always a matter of handing over a titanic variety of small numbers of bread and fish in so many forms, secret to us and to God, before we can see them multiplied in ways we may see now in the land of the living, or may not see until we stand before the Lord!

The banana boxes also have a category labeled "Thesis." No, not a thesis or theses of Fran's, but other people's doctoral dissertations and master's theses written about Fran's work or his apologetics. Not *his* idea; theirs. One is being written in Finnish! And there in front of me is a pile of creative work which has been flowing from creative people who say they have been "set free" at L'Abri, or through Fran's books or mine. There are records of Larry Norman's, and a poetry book titled *Nice and Nasty* by Steve Turner, London, with this written by hand, "To Francis and Edith, with continuing thanks for your work and love and example which became so much a part of me, and I believe, this book. With love, Steve."

The new *His* magazine for March 1981 just arrived. In an article by Noel Becchetti (the promotion manager for *His*), "Where Are All the Christian Men?" he says, "I was delighted to discover the works of Francis Schaeffer, because here was a Christian man who understood where I was coming from! He didn't try to tell me what God can do for me; he argued the case for truth and demanded that I act on that truth. That's what I needed to hear."

Yes, people have heard what was being said in that hidden old chalet on a Swiss Alp twenty-five years ago. It has been multiplied by a living God, who is able to do the impossible. It has been added to, the chalet has been "divided" into a dozen chalets, and branches have been added in other countries. Today Ran and Jerram and Richard are speaking truth and answering questions in a seminar in England, not as parrots repeating formulas, but because they have come to believe that truth exists, and they are acting on it. Today there are not only fifty-five L'Abri Workers adding their own thinking and creative ways of communicating to the ones and twos as well as the multiplied ones and twos, but there are countless people who have "heard" Fran and his thinking in countless parts of the world. Countless, that is, except by God—The Mathematician.

HOUSES—HOMES 22

The global map of the world can whirl around on its pivot and be seen at a glance under a good lamp on a living room table. Whish, swish—that's the world in blues, greens, sand colors. Continents, seas, oceans, and some countries and mountain ranges, recognizable at a glance. A closer, longer look, plus an atlas beside you to give more detail, brings some larger measure of comprehension. A flight around the world (if the pilot flies on a clear day, and not too high) brings more reality of deserts, fertile land, forests, mountains, cities, rivers, and man-made roads. There it is—the world. A helicopter over a smaller section of the map brings individual buildings—castles, high-rise flats, houses, cottages, and huts into focus. Suddenly the world becomes a place where people spend their lifetimes in some sort of a house, tent, shack, mansion, boat-house, tree-hut, or cave—as a dwelling-place, a home, a refuge from storms. Then, in times of disaster, the same kind of flight over people's places of birth, or a lifetime of living—their homes—shows the scattering of refugees, of homeless rushing to get away from floods, earthquakes, hurricanes, famine, drought, volcanos or invasion of enemies, human enemies. The warning "here we have no continuing city" (Heb. 13:14) includes the warning of "no continuing house."

Permanence, completely secure and uninterrupted permanence

in one place, is God's promise for the future. The mansions and dwelling places God is preparing for the people who have come to Him will have no flight of refugees, nor will they ever be inadequate. There is no better way to have an increased understanding of the diversity of hopes, fears, longings, and needs of human beings than to "visit" them in their own homes—if indeed they are still in their homes! Nor is there a better way to come to a fresh recognition of the emphasis God has placed on preparing a *place* for us, as well as the emphasis on His *being* our dwelling place right now! How exciting to know that God cares about people being homeless, without a "continuing city," and that He takes the time in His book to us to tell us He is building one. What a gorgeous city it must be "whose builder and maker is God" (Heb. 11:10).

In time, Fran and I were to have our education increased, not only in being in a tremendous diversity of houses and homes (many of them the homes of people who had been in our home at L'Abri), but in seeing face to face rather than on a map, "displaced refugees" of our moment of history. History has never had more people who have lost their houses, or homes. This is another facet of the "abnormal world," another indication that it is not as God intended it to be—had the Fall not taken place. God made a perfect original home. God meant human beings to understand the centrality of their "dwelling places" in their quietness. He, who is our dwelling place, has made us to enjoy, feel peaceful, feel "at home" when we discover the wonder of that truth, and actually spend time "dwelling" there, thankfully. Our "threads" were woven with others, in The Tapestry of our own history and theirs, in homes other than our own. This gave us a new perspective of the very important truth that just as "some from every tribe, and nation and kindred and tongue" shall be a part of the people of God, these people will come from widely differing homes, houses, dwelling places.

On May 26, 1971, I rushed around the kitchen of Mélèzes preparing lunch for thirty-five people, got it all served except for tea and dessert, and then ran off to Betty Carlson's car. She had offered to drive me to Dr. Méan's chalet, where I was to wait in his waiting room for my cholera shot. How differently I would have looked at the room if I had known then that it would be a part of Franky's home within not too long a time and that later it would be Mary Jane's home, when Franky and Genie moved to their remodeled barn, and after that it would become Gail and Jim's home. You see, we were to move into Chalet Chardonnet, and Dr. Méan's offices would be "the downstairs apartment." Right then, it was just my waiting place. After the needle's prick, and before the shot had time to make me suddenly dizzy, Betty took me on up to Villars where I was to speak to a group of women from Tulsa, Oklahoma, in the lobby of the Parc Hotel. I couldn't linger to shake hands because I needed to get back to Mélèzes to pack my suitcase and get the train from Aigle which would connect with my plane to Africa.

It had been Franky and Os who had persuaded me first: "Sure, go; it would be good for you. We can get along here for five days." The Members and, more important, Fran had also agreed: "Yes, accept the invitation." The women of the Africa Inland Mission had been praying for money to send a ticket to me to fly to Kenya and speak to them for a three-day conference. They had felt God answered wonderfully. A woman many miles away sent money that each of them had added to until there was enough for the round-trip ticket they had sent me. A delayed plane gave me a long wait in the Rome airport, and I called home—collect— to find out if they had managed the supper all right!

That night, flying over the "map" to Kenya, I felt as if I were dreaming. I had never been in Africa. Morning sun was furnacelike when we stepped off in Khartoum. The roof of the low building which was the airport was filled with white-robed men, their black faces swathed in white too. I felt I now had something more than a map to relate to when I read newspapers about trouble in Sudan. Only hours later, as I was being driven by Jackie and Martha through flat lands with scrubby trees, I was met by my first giraffe outside a zoo—coming close to peer in the car as we slowed down. The next morning, speaking to the black students of the Kenyan Bible School and College at Machakos, I was really impressed that it was possible to hold their attention for far longer than I had been told would be so and to make fascinating the things *they* needed to know about twentieth-century thinking, which some would be facing in university not too long from that time.

My first impressions were of the fact that there were no walls around the missionaries' houses and the mission school buildings to separate them from the tiny African village. The latter was a cluster of huts on the other side of a hedge low enough to step over. Contrast of homes? Yes, but the mission houses—one-story cement block houses—were furnished very simply with iron beds and wooden tables and chairs. Only in recent years had they had electricity supplied by a small power plant the men had made themselves, by ingenuity and hard work. Not all mission stations have this much, nor do people shy away from weeks of walking, eating food cooked over small fires, and sleeping on the ground, as they make trips to preach out in the bush. The Bible School girls bring and cook their own food over an open fire, so that there will not a false separation in their school days from the life they will go back to in most cases.

The next day I was driven to Limuru to the conference place. Even more fantastic than seeing wild ostriches and giraffes running in their floating fashion across the fields, was seeing a hand waving as a car stopped on the road on the other side of Nairobi—and discovering that it belonged to Clive Boddington, Ran's friend from Cambridge days, who had thought he had missed me at the conference grounds. He was then the Chaplain of Nairobi University, but later became a L'Abri Worker in Greatham and now is pastor in the Greatham congregation of the International Church. What a place to meet and pray together with Clive and Daphne and the children!

There were 111 women at the conference from many parts of Kenya, and also some students from Nairobi University and some residents of Nairobi. I spoke three times a day for about two hours each time. There was so much to say, and when would we ever be together again? When I say that the Lord gave me strength an hour at a time, I really mean it, because I had left Switzerland exhausted, and had a terrific headache and nausea all those days—but not when I was speaking! Letters still come to me from women who felt those days were very valuable in their lives and work. The day after the conference the Lord put some threads together as in Nairobi I made a search for Duncan, who had been saved in L'Abri when he stayed with Debby and Udo in Chalet les Sapins. I found him in the offices of an oil company, where I had a wonderful talk and prayer time with him and put him in touch with a good church, pastored by a Scotsman, which had Indians, blacks, and whites in it. Also Mike Cassidy (whom we met on our first Cambridge trip) and his wife came to see me in Nairobi.

The next item on my schedule was to go to the missionary school in the hills and speak to the high school students. Early the following morning I was driven over rutted and gullied back roads—by choice, because I wanted to visit the home of a Christian Kenyan. Walking through small cabbage patches and fields, we came to the grass hut. It had an opening like a cave, and inside were dividers made of cardboard from grocery boxes—"walls" which didn't reach higher than my shoulders. One section had two piles of rags—one of which was the parents' bed, and the other a bed for the seven children. We sat, a tiny board holding two of us, while the mother and children settled themselves on the floor around three burning sticks. There was no chimney. As I prayed with this mother, the artist and his wife who had driven me there translated. I thanked God for the true expectation of another home being prepared for her. I thanked Him for the truth of His Word and for the literal truth of Jesus' promise as He said He was going to prepare a place for us. I am so glad she is one of us. No missionary is perfect; no Christian is perfect. But—thank God He uses weak, imperfect people like ourselves to make truth known to people in grass huts "in the middle of nowhere" . . . with no address on a post and no mark on the map.

A few hours after returning from Africa I was taking moss, ivy, logs, wild flowers and cultivated daisies with Udo and some others, to trim the Ollon Church for Os and Jenny's wedding. The bride wanted candles to brighten the dimness of the church, but no candlesticks were available. Then suddenly an idea came to me, and people hurried to find old coke bottles and mineral water bottles. With moss and ivy, we soon had white candles "growing in the woods," as the bottles, wrapped with moss secured by fine wires, disappeared under the woodsy greens. Natasha and Becky were flower girls, and Lisby and Brenda (not our grandchild, but daughter of the Hiskeys who were studying at L'Abri) carried the bride's train, a long veil caught by lilacs in her hair. Their home was going to be as artistic as Jenny's design of lovely appliqued flowers on her wedding dress and veil—a long, far cry from the hut I had just been in. But the destination of the people in both homes is the same, and the oneness of that future community will be something none of us can imagine!

Immediately after this wedding, Fran and I had a flying trip to America for two purposes. The first was for Fran to speak at a Press Club dinner in Washington, D.C. Forest Boyd, at that time the pressman assigned by Mutual Broadcasting Company to do the daily radio newscasting from the White House, hosted the dinner. The interest that was aroused and the questions that followed were "real," not simply superficial. I spoke in two large women's meetings, one a congressional wives' gathering at Fellowship House.

That was also the time I entered another house that was to be used by the Lord in a special way. Joanne Kemp, wife of Congressman Jack Kemp, had invited about twenty-five women—wives of congressman, senators, and some other Washington residents—for morning coffee, and had asked me to speak for an hour. After I had given the story of how four very different kinds of people had come to L'Abri, and of what they had learned after they did come, the guests asked: "Where can we study more of this kind of 'answers'?" Joanne's response was: "Let's start a Schaeffer class, and study all the Schaeffers' books." This was ten years ago. The class had been held to twenty-five, and the members have only been replaced when one or another has left for another part of the states because of a change in her husband's career. Joanne has had each woman buy the current book being studied. They started with *Introduction to Francis Schaeffer*, then did *The God Who Is There* and *He Is There and He Is Not Silent*, *Escape from Reason*, *Joshua and the Flow of Biblical History*, and on through all twenty-one of Fran's books. They also went through all my seven books, starting with *L'Abri* before going on to *What Is a Family*, *Christianity Is Jewish*, *Affliction*, etc. They read a chapter during the week, and then Joanne teaches the chapter, with discussion, remarks, and questions from the others. Sometimes various ones do a paper, researching a portion of a chapter with study in the library. Lots of material is available in the congressional library. This group has also been serious about prayer for their husbands, and for various critical situations in Washington. Intercession for each other is a "support" that cannot be described in words. The hidden connection with the all-powerful God that is available in a "closet" alone, or with others who believe God hears and responds, is a power that committees can't sit and vote down! This is true for those meeting in a home in the capitol city, or in a tiny farmhouse, or in that hut in Africa. A variety of "spiritual children" were born and grew in the Kemp home, as well as Joanne and Jack's four children, who have had reading from *Everybody Can Know* as well as treasure-hunt suppers from *Hidden Art*, when daddy was held up at "The House" until after midnight! That study group still continues, while both kinds of "children" have had ten years of growth.

That was not to be our only time in Washington, nor the only house we would be in. There were a succession of times and a variety of meetings. We often stayed with Verma and Forest Boyd. At one time in Washington Fran was asked by Forest to speak to a gathering of press men and their wives, along with some congressmen, senators, lobbyists, and others. At this dessert and coffee evening, with over ninety-three in Fellowship House, Fran spoke nearly two hours, outlining the central things that were later to be in *How Should We Then Live?* Jack Kemp took copious notes and asked the first three questions with preciseness as sharp as three bullets hitting a target. Ideas were seeded in fertile minds that night, to take root in some, and to grow, put out leaves and buds, and become a fruitful harvest in years to come.

Another time we went "home for dinner" with a couple that had been Farel House students at L'Abri, and wanted us "to meet mother and father." We were staying in a hotel where Fran was speaking to a group of Southern Baptist leaders. (The thing that struck me about the hotel was the ugly thick grey chains fastening all the furniture in the halls to big rings in the floor. Not very homelike.) "Hi, Mike!" . . . "Hi, Gayle!" . . . "It's so great to see you again, and we do appreciate your coming down from Boston." . . . We chattered about L'Abri news—how Franky and Genie and Debby and Udo were, about the children growing— and said we hoped to tell them all about the new project. They told us how they were getting on with their studies, and what a hassle it was to be surrounded by Secret Service men. Equipped with their ever-present guns, and looking extremely efficient, tall, and serious about their job, four of the men were in the elevator with us then, and they both led and followed us to the waiting car. It was strange to realize they were real people.

As we swept up to the White House, one car in front, one behind, the gates magically opened and we soon were getting out and walking through the impressive red-carpeted hall. This was my first time in the White House. The private elevator stopped on the family floor, and in a moment's time we were in that beautiful long yellow and white "Center Hall" sitting room, being warmly greeted by President and Mrs. Ford, Mike's mother and father, and meeting the dog, and other members of the family. Dinner was served in the intimate family dining room, a fire blazing in the lovely fireplace—brass and silver and crystal chandelier gleaming. Home! The White House has been "home" to a diversity of presidents' families over a long period of history, and in many ways has been the "central home" of America. Changes in décor, the stock of antiques and gifts from foreign dignitaries, the bewildering choices in dishes and furnishings—all these possibilities mean that the White House changes according to the taste, personality, and creativity of each First Lady. Yet the White House is not an easy home to fill with a total change of atmosphere. The time is short. And necessary roots are still experiencing the shock of being transplanted, for all presidential families.

That night we had a homey menu, delicious pot roast of beef, with the vegetables blended in flavor with each other and with the roast, hot biscuits, and salad. The ice cream was the president's favorite, butter pecan, and there was coffee. It's hard for young people, who are hoping a "L'Abri discussion" will grow and flower in a short time, to realize that conversation can't be forced, nor become a lecture, but must grow naturally. It was a very special evening, and as we went into the yellow living room again, before Betty had to go to bed with an extreme attack of her neck and shoulder pain, we stood together, in a little circle—the President, Betty, Mike, Gayle, Fran and myself—holding hands as Fran prayed very earnestly for the family, for each one in his or her own need, for our country, for the present and the future. Then with a hug and assurances we'd meet again, Betty went off to bed, while the President kindly took us on a personally conducted tour. Not only did we have his unusual explanations of what we were seeing, but we were seeing the White House all empty—no tourists present. The Christmas tree had just been trimmed with hand-made flowered-cotton shapes—stuffed animal type things made in the South—and we were fascinated by having this quiet look around, guided by the "head of the house"!

Fran and the President had some minutes of good discussion, but at 10:30 the President had papers to sign preparatory to an early flight to an island near France the next morning. It was then that Mike, Gayle and the two of us went to the Lincoln Bedroom to sit down and talk. Quietly tucked away in that historic room, we told them of the plans Franky had for filming his documentary series *How Should We Then Live?* and then prayed together about the project and other things in our lives and theirs. It seemed a bit bizarre to drive back with them and the Secret Service men, to be deposited in our chained-down hotel after having been in that gracious relaxed home in the city. There are so many contrasts in this spoiled world with its spoiled, destroyed human beings—we should all look eagerly forward to the new heaven and new earth where the homes will be peaceful, and without fear.

The next evening I spoke to the White House Christian Fellowship at their Christmas party, so I met people who work in the White House—a few of them, that is, for there are about fifteen hundred altogether. Fran had lunch on the Hill with some men from the Senate and the House that Jack Kemp had invited for discussion.

It was our next time in Washington that Betty invited me to have lunch with her. While we had a "tray lunch" on lovely silver trays, but with simple bacon, lettuce and tomato sandwiches on whole wheat toast, we talked alone about a wide range of subjects. Betty is an extremely human person who has many interests and a variety of friends as well as the ability to make people feel at home. The problem with life, however, is "time." Twenty-four hours slides by for presidents and peasants alike: the busier a person is and the more interrupted and the more full a schedule is, day after day, the less time there is to choose what to do with it. It is a constant danger with each of us to expect more time in the future, or to feel "today is impossible" and to let time for communication slide by. That is true both of horizontal communication with friends and family and of vertical communication with God, our Father.

The last time I spent at the White House was on a hot summer day. In an early morning phone conversation Betty had said, "If you have your bathing suit with you, I'll send a car to pick you up and we can swim and have lunch together." We had ample time that morning for good exercise doing laps in the pool, and then talking. It was after Betty's operation for cancer, and she related the depth of experience she felt had been real for her in becoming a Christian during that time of having such a sharp perspective of life. Before we ate the simple but delightful salad, I ran to get my Bible out of the bag I'd brought for my bathing suit. Alone there as we had our lunch, with the noise outside the hedge of a pavilion and platform being hammered together for a late afternoon reception at which Betty needed to make a speech welcoming some head of state, we quietly read some of Isaiah together. I prayed for the things of that immediate moment of history and in the life of the White House in which she was involved. All too soon her secretary called her to the need of preparation for the next event and a bit wistfully she said, "Oh, I wish . . . I wish there were more time." The echo of that wish floats back—from you, and from me as time after time we long for "more time."

Fran and I were having a short ski vacation during the election time, and I was able to speak to Betty immediately after she had to concede for her husband (who had laryngitis), acknowledging that the White House was no longer "home." The feeling of being displaced comes in a great and titanically differing variety of ways. Many of us know what it is to leave a house and yet take our home with us. In a very real sense, it's not the walls and décor that make a home background in which communication is easier or harder to find *time* for. For each of us, it is using the place and the time of the present moment by pushing something else aside, to write a book, read a book, or "talk a book," in order to communicate something of the reality of life to each other while there is still a matter of years, months, days, hours left to make choices as to what comes next.

Come to Chicago with me for a minute. It is August 1970, and Fran is having the distinction of being the only non-Lutheran to speak at a very important Congress in the history of the Missouri Synod Lutheran Church. This conference had importance in all that followed later in this denomination. His topics, which brought warm and lasting response, were: "Truth Versus the New Humanism and the New Theology" and "A Protestant Evangelical Speaks to His Lutheran Friends in a Day of Theological Crises." I'm sure the men felt that pulpit was the right place and atmosphere to communicate such solemnly important facts.

Just what a group of them were discussing as they sat in a restaurant on Chicago's main street, eating lunch, I'm not sure, but one supposes it was in the same line of communication that Fran had sparked off that day. Glancing out of the window, one pastor called to another, "Look! . . ." Sitting on the sidewalk, oblivious to the men watching him, his back against the wall of the building, was Fran. He was surrounded by a group of what looked to the men like "those hippies"—blacks and whites, in typical clothing and hair-do—listening with intent faces, butting in with arguments or questions. Genuine communication was taking place that had started spontaneously with two and had grown to an interested group. The seriousness and reality of that communication was as important a "handing on of the flag" of *truth* as the formal "proper" lecture had been in its dignified surroundings. For that hour the sidewalk had become a place of hospitality as much as might the most gracious home.

Whatever the pastors had learned from the lecture was underlined or added to by what they saw out of the window, in a way that multiplied its effectiveness a hundredfold. True communication of the true truth comes with an intensity that makes it obvious that the person that matters is the one the Lord brings to you, in answer to prayer for such ones. Or this person may be one He takes you to as you are willing to go, whether to someone who lives on the street, or in a castle. Intensity of response is not turned on and off with a switch, like a TV or radio.

You realize by now that I am not following our lives chronologically. In May 1971, we had left Washington to go to Gordon College, where Fran was to speak, and to be presented with an honorary Doctor of Letters. Flying back to Switzerland immediately following that event, we entered into special days of fasting and prayer, asking for clear direction as to the building of a new

house for L'Abri on the property across from the chapel. The architect's plans were very interesting, with a library and study room, large living and dining rooms with fireplaces, a separate but attached house for Workers, a couple with children, and "efficient" features for making L'Abri life smoother! We had been told we had to get rid of a number of people, *or* have a larger place. As we Members had a long, long prayer meeting, first having had prayer and communion with Workers and others after an early Sunday tea, we were pleading for the money to go ahead and for permits to build.

It is important when attempting to live by prayer, with real faith, that you, we, do not insist that things "go in a straight line." We are all too afraid of losing face if outsiders think we have made a mistake. We had already paid for the architect's plans; we had the land. It would have been easy to be resistant to any change. In the middle of our prayer that night, Fran said, "Why not put these plans aside, and go up and look at that old chalet-hotel for sale in Chesières, Gentiana?" I bit my lip in annoyance or resistance. "Never," I thought. But as we prayed on, my resistance faded, and I spoke . . . "I'd be willing to go look at Gentiana." At 2:00 A.M. we had all agreed to meet in the morning.

Fran and I, Debby with three-year-old Natasha and little Samantha in the "seat" on her back, John with twenty-month-old Giandy, stepped into Gentiana's old wide hall, walked through the big living room with its olive tile stove, and went on into a bedroom with a squeaky board floor. As we looked out the window over vegetable and flower gardens and big trees onto the view of the mountains, and mountains, and mountains, we shared a sigh. "This is *it*. What new building could be really L'Abri?" Built sixty-five years ago, Gentiana would cost half the price of the new building with furniture, sheets, and even dishes; scrubbed and clean and ready to enter by September 1. Repairs to do? Yes, of course, but the vote was unanimous, and by 2:00 P.M., twelve hours after our prayer meeting had ended, John Sandri had made arrangements for signing the promissory papers and had the first payment in hand. Fast? We had prayed for four years for the "new building" and had now "lost" money for architect's plans. But God has His own way of taking His people along His paths in a lot of original ways. We are the ones who "jump the gun" so often in "knowing" what comes next, when we are only guessing.

When I saw the lovely log barn on the corner of the land, my heart leapt, and I thought, "That's Franky's barn I've been praying for." We couldn't see then, of course, that Franky would be having a studio for painting, in that barn, and later a room where Genie and Gayle would help him pour candles on bitter cold nights, and that out of it all would come a beautiful chalet with a room where ideas would multiply for making a film series. But we also couldn't see that we ourselves would be moving from Chalet les Mélèzes to live in Dr. Méan's old chalet, Chardonnet, with our land joining the barn and Gentiana's land. Had our prayer for the new building across from the chapel been "answered," we would never have seen what God had in His knowledge. The Chesières story, with the multiplied homes to house a stream of people, would never have taken place.

But we were to be seeing homes of people in many parts of the world before we were to see our own "new home" or know anything about it, let alone what it would mean in a change in our own lives.

It was February 26, 1972, that Fran and Udo flew to Finland, looking down on the miles we had gone by train and boat twenty-two years before. They were to give a series of lectures in Helsinki University. Now Fran's books, translated into Finnish, were in homes, bringing something of L'Abri discussions there even before he and Udo began answering questions.

The bitter cold temperatures and winter snows couldn't have been a greater contrast to Mexico! A few days after Fran and Udo's return from Finland, Fran and I were on our way to that country for the twenty-second Annual University for Presidents (a Young President's Organization educational program for presidents of companies who fit the exclusive qualifications of the organization). Jerry Lewis, who had been given Fran's books *The God Who Is There, Escape From Reason,* and others by his son Buz, was sports chairman that year. He felt Fran's approach might interest a number of the men and be acceptable to the program committee. So it was that Fran became one of the "Essayists" and was listed to speak on "Post-Christian Visions: Man as a Machine, or Man as Mystic?"

It was an experience of another world for us, in many ways, with some fascinating discussions. For myself I had the experience of George Wald's lecture (Harvard Professor of Biology, Nobel prize-winner) which spun the theory of the origin of the universe in an eloquent and fascinating way, showing that nothing but particles swimming about in chaotic disorder, which formed affinities "by chance," with "chance" happenings continuing, was involved in the wonder of all we see and know as the world, and the universe. A totally impersonal universe was "unfolded". . . and in an hour's time we were being asked to be deeply concerned in working for preservation . . . ecologically, and in "banning the bomb." I was left gasping at the "faith" involved in living on such a basis—faith in faith, with no person at home in the universe to whom to look—no Creator! As Dr. Wald closed, he said he had no place for the supernatural in his scheme of things, but he wanted to quote from the Bible. The quote was, "Therefore choose life that ye and your descendants may live." If you want to see the context, read Deuteronomy 30:11-20. Later in the book I want to tell you what a similar passage in Ezekiel came to mean to Fran, in a special way. But here let me say, I had sudden admiration for my husband in a new way! My reaction in that big lecture room was: "Fran is right. This is what these professors *do* say. It is accurate that they have no place for meaning, purpose, morals, and values because there is no place for personality, for the human being to be different from anything else." That week educated me.

Martha Dell and Jerry had hoped there would be results from the week. Only God can know real results, but I do know of two of the presidents' wives who came to "see and understand and believe" that week, and another couple found their way to L'Abri the next summer. But it was at the seminar of the film *How Should We Then Live?* in Anaheim in 1977 that I discovered one result. A former L'Abri girl from Mexico had brought her parents, a sister, and a girl friend—all of whom had had some involvement in a strongly occult set of "happenings"—to talk with me during lunch at Acapulco. The sun was hot, my lunch was left uneaten, and my face was sunburned as I tried to answer questions, giving a whole "bird's eye view of the Bible." It all seemed to no avail—a disappointment in the eager girl who had felt that now that I was in her home country, all would be clear! Then, five years later, down from the bleachers, across the gymnasium floor, during the intermission, ran this girl. "Oh, Mrs. Schaeffer . . . I want you to know they are all Christians now. . . . They are up there . . . (pointing to the higher bleacher seats) . . . mother and dad, my sister, my friend. Thank you for talking." What a fantastic "homecoming" set of surprises awaits us—some day, in the definite future. We'll discover then how much has been worthwhile that we don't know about now.

We stopped in England on our way back, to be with Dick and Mardi in Ealing for a few days—just in time to help a girl who had come from California with the express purpose of committing suicide in Europe. Chance? We didn't think so. Homeless, and with a tragic tale of horror, this girl had "by chance" met someone from Charlie Manson's "home" in the American Express. The person she met had been helped at L'Abri, and directed her to the Ealing address to "find the Schaeffers." We had arrived only fifteen minutes before. When Mardi opened the door, she could say, "Yes, Schaeffers *are here!*"

When we were in Greatham for a special meeting of the church there the next day, this girl was among those gathered. The twisted "home" she had come from was in sharp contrast to the beauty of the home of Sue and Ran, Margaret, Kirsty, Fiona, and Ranald John. Along with other L'Abri families there, this gave her hope that the words *home* and *family* were not after all just a cruel joke of obsolete symbols for something that has gone out of existence. The word *father*, which had also been destroyed for her, slowly came into focus as having meaning, as she watched children playing with their fathers, and heard the basic wonder of a loving, compassionate Heavenly Father. "House," "home," "father," we were to discover, need careful defining, and example!

For ten months I had been having pain in my left lower jaw, where a deeply imbedded wisdom tooth had been cut out of the gum. A lump had been undiagnosed by a variety of dentists and doctors in various parts of the States. It was May 23 when, blissfully unconscious under anesthesia, I awakened to find I had had a fibrous tumor removed. A *"très délicat"* operation it turned out to be, with a facial nerve involved. Days of waiting for the laboratory report were filled with excruciating pain. Nancy Snyder and other visitors backed out of the room, not recognizing me! For some days I looked somewhat like a prizefighter on "the day after," but the enormous black and blue swelling finally diminished. A branch of the facial nerve had been disturbed, and for many months I had a partially paralyzed lower lip, with a dent where flesh had been cut out. Exhaustion was slow in departing after this ordeal, especially as it was followed by a small gynecological operation a short time later. It took a vacation of ten days on the Island of Elba (a discovery of Debby and Udo's) to "pick me up" again.

The family reunion had been especially precious that year. We have found that, whether in our adult "afflictions" or the children's, it is helpful to be able to have the warm and very genuine sympathy of a caring family, as well as the distraction of hearing everyone's excitements and new hobbies—relaxation exercises, growing plants, building cold frames, dressmaking. We need the lift of each other's positive ideas, as well as deterrent if we "get off the track" in something. Our family doesn't have "carbon copy" houses, or homes, or ideas! The only way to affect each other at all is to take time to communicate.

Communication that is deep and real and not superficial takes *time*. Time, like money, is the "impossibility" that needs choice in using or saving—however you look at it. If families are to have more than a superficial effect on each other as years go on, the time must be set aside carefully, and take precedence over all else, especially as the family grows larger, and becomes three and then four generations. We took that time, in 1972, before the trip that would take us around the world for our second family reunion.

We left October 3, 1972, to fly first to visit my father in Watertown, New York, where he lived with my sister Elsa and her husband, Roger Van Buskirk. Father was ninety-six years old then, and still active enough to take a walk with us so that we could have a milkshake with him on his daily visit to the snack bar. By the evening of October 6, we were in the Princeton Club of New York City, where Bill Jadden hosted a L'Abri Reunion. No one knew how many might come, but then a crowd began streaming in, a cross-section of ages and types. All had been at L'Abri—students from a variety of Eastern colleges, nurses, lawyers, architects. There was a black doctor from Harlem, and a Chinese; there was Lady Edward Montague with her Jewish friend; there was a girl who hurriedly asked if she might be "baptized tonight, please. Udo examined me in Huémoz before I left, and I would like to join the International Church tonight." A brandy glass was found, and I went to the ladies' room and filled it with water. After the discussion, with many questions flowing, the 115 people sitting on the floor as well as all in the chairs shared refreshments together, then had a time of prayer before the baptismal service. An incredible L'Abri atmosphere in the heart of New York City!

The next morning Fran preached in the Princeton University Chapel. The chapel was filled to overflowing, even the balconies. People had driven great distances, from as far north as Maine and as far south as Baltimore and Washington. This was a "reunion" too, and so many old L'Abri people were there, with their families, and some from my old hometowns of Newburgh, West Point, Philadelphia, and Chester. The Lord answered prayer for strength—physical and spiritual—as Fran's message was a powerful one, entitled "Before the Beginning." It stirred up much discussion in the coffee hour afterwards. The next day we went to Geneva College in Beaver Falls, Pennsylvania, for two days of lectures. October 11 we "split" for a few days, as Fran went on to San Francisco to be with the Hoytes and Claire in the L'Abri work there, while I flew to Houston, Texas, to be present at an art show of Franky's paintings which John Graham (who had been at L'Abri) had arranged. What a marathon that was. I stayed at the art show for the two days it was open and spoke at a ladies' meeting at lunchtime on one of those days. Flying then to San Francisco to meet Fran, I changed planes and talked in both San Antonio and Dallas with people who had come to have "lunch" and a kind of "meeting" with me. On October 14 and 15 there was a L'Abri Conference-reunion on the property at Los Gatos. There were 450 there altogether, crowding the chapel and the two little houses, which were wired with loudspeakers. Many people had helped Claire to cook and freeze food, so that if anything there was too much rather than not enough. Too much happened to tell you about, as Fran, Os, and I lectured, and had group and individual conversations and discussion.

In my hand, however, was the first chapter of *Everybody Can Know* which I had written a few days before we left Switzerland. Franky and Fran had agreed I should write this book "by a family for a family," and I had awakened with the first paragraphs writing themselves in my head. So Fran said, "Let Ann and the girls prepare the hot dog roast, and you get that on that paper—now." I was still in my nightgown at 8:00 P.M. when I finished Chapter 1. Now here it was, going around the world with me, to be read aloud to a diversity of people.

Libby was sitting on the floor in the little California house (which she was one day to call home as a L'Abri Worker) while she listened to the chapter. She would have fainted if she'd known the future—at least *then* she would have! After having turned away from Christianity when she was at L'Abri years before, this former French pupil of Debby's, a Jewish girl, was sometime during *this* L'Abri Conference to make up her mind to go back to Switzerland, and later to accept the Messiah as her Lord and Savior.

Who can know what are the important and unimportant days written on a schedule of the year's calendar? A calendar of dates promised and a diary of events lived out form a contrast, but I'm sure it is nothing compared to the contrast of the "notations" that are made in heaven of all that *really* happens each day! Whose prayers were being answered? We can ask that, over and over again, when wonderful things take place. When we find out which threads of The Tapestry were involved in a particularly beautiful spot in the weaving that we hadn't noticed until now, we'll be astonished that their part of the whole was going on in a wheelchair, or in a tiny little home from which they have never traveled anywhere—visibly—although their prayer has affected people and events thousands of miles away. God knows each "who" that has had a part.

The soft air of Honolulu, the pineapple juice at the airport, the leis thrown about our necks, and the Weisenbakers' warm welcome made us feel as if we were entering a vacation! But the weaving there was to be most important—in spite of the tantalizing sunsets to be seen from a supper sail lasting long enough for us to eat while tossing in waves, and the amazing luau prepared for us by Lynne Hudson and her family. The beautiful Hawaiian food, the basket of fresh flower leis for everyone, three apiece for us, the luxury of bare feet, made a never-to-be-forgotten evening. But this was more than a "treat"; Lynne herself was soon to be going to L'Abri. She thought it would be just to study in Farel House, but she became a Worker, then married Harold Schweizer, now teaching in Zurich University. She has been a special thread in L'Abri, and among so many others—thousands of miles from Honolulu!

There were some there in Honolulu who had already been at L'Abri, and one day, years and years later, dear Dick Weisenbaker who had welcomed us, was going to come to L'Abri—a second time, to come to an assurance of his understanding and believing true truth. It would make you dizzy to know how many other lives he is affecting in Texas now, if you had examined his thread back there in that tiny bit of weaving in that Hawaiian home, where soft music, special food, profusion of flower scents and colors, seemed like a great party.

It thrilled me to sit in the University of Honolulu, watching the students pour in. "No one much knows Schaeffer's books out here; this room will be too big," someone had said. After five hundred packed the room, over two hundred were turned away. They sat on the platform, and in the window sills—so many questions from atheists, agnostics, Buddhists—how very agonizing it was to have to fly on. I spoke at a couple of church meetings too, though the schedule had just said "stopover in Hawaii for a *rest.*"

We were to come back again eight years later, in 1980, for a seminar of *Whatever Happened to the Human Race?* in a Honolulu hotel. Tickets had not sold very well. There was panic as to how the hotel and the food that had been ordered would be paid for! Then the day dawned, and early in the morning people began to come. Well over a thousand packed the room, with people standing around the walls—for a fourteen-hour day! It was an exciting thing to me to look into so many Chinese faces, as well as the cross-sections of others there—to hear how the books had made people feel they knew us, to have such enthusiastic and concerned response to the issues in the film, with determination to "do something."

I thought back to five-year-old me, leaning over the railing of our ship *The China* as we came into Honolulu harbor in 1920. I loved the pink tile roofs and green palm trees, and determined to come back some day. I was on my way to that great country, so I fondly believed, where people all knew the true God, and where nobody threw little baby girls in a pagoda to die because they hadn't been boys, as they did in my China. What a fierce desire I had to see that that would stop happening anywhere, to make sure I could speak some day and explain why babies shouldn't be killed. Now, these sixty years later, I was standing in a part of America, a country in which people have come to think it is quite all right to kill their own children, whether boys or girls—the ones of whom they will be the ancestors. How five-year-old me would have screamed in disappointed shock, had I known that people were going to think they were being "liberated" by plunging into the heathen practices of throwing away their sons and daughters. I was old enough to speak now, I thought, as I gave my lecture. The message was tragically needed in the latter part of the same century. What an incredible thing "progress" is. An evolution of evil! . . . or a confusion as to what is bitter and what is sweet, what is food and what is poison, what is life and what is death.

Now back to 1972. We flew out on my birthday, November 3, but passing the date line I lost most of it! The arrival in Tokyo was a great celebration, however, as I love Japanese food, and counted as a birthday our meal with "the two Annes," missionaries we had long prayed for. Don and Martha Hoke spent time with us too, and introduced us not only to a very special restaurant, but to the real Japanese tea ceremony. This took place in a home that was so very peaceful and uncluttered, with its one fine original painting, and its one expensive authentic vase, its perfect flower arrangement, its delicate teacups, its lovely smooth floor covered with fine straw matting, and the sunken stove for the boiling of the proper tea kettle. During the daytime, the bedding and the sleeping mats are all put away in a carved chest so space can be enjoyed without the interruption of "things." Gardens are beautifully balanced, whether with smooth sand and stones, or with wonderful balance of twisted trees and flowers. However, it must be understood that all this—the tea ceremony, the artistically pleasing flower arrangements, the subtle garden designs—all these things are rooted in Buddhism. The philosophic base in Japan is Buddhism, and if you want to understand this better, I'd suggest that you read the book Phil and Laurie sent us, *Zen Way—Jesus Way* by Tucker N. Callaway, which was written after thirty years in Japan of really studying and coming to understand.

Buddhism is not understood, read, believed as a base for life, consciously by most Japanese, but the language itself is rooted in Buddhist concepts, so that many who learn Japanese have not yet learned to communicate Christianity in Japanese. The deeply rooted idea that nothing exists except the mind, and that that doesn't really exist either, makes it hard to make contact in a brief moment of time. The centrality of "group" rather than "individual" makes it hard to say even "you" and "I" and have the concept mean the thing it means to Westerners. The wonderful "working together" of huge companies is incredible to Westerners, but to the Japanese "the company" is the center of life. Identity *is* in that group in a way that fits in with a basic philosophy. "Peaceful countryside" . . . with the gorgeous beauty of the unique patterns of haystacks? "Peaceful gardens" . . . with no clutter? It is another form of "peace, peace, when there is no peace."

In Tokyo the Hokes felt we ought to observe a religion that is drawing many people. We stood sadly watching an enormous crowd, filling every seat in a huge round building, as a service came to a close—a new religion which is a mixture of Buddhism and other things. On the platform was a gigantic table with a shiny gold statue of Buddha behind it. The table had mathematically arranged pyramids of polished fruit—red apples, oranges, green pears. It struck me how like this was Cain's offering of his garden products, brought in place of The Lamb, as people fingered their beads and mumbled their prayers—to whom?

If Christianity were not *true*, if there were no *absolute*, if everything were just relative and truth did not exist, then it would be cruel to change people's way of life. I remember a Jewish psychiatrist in Holland whose patient had been at L'Abri. Fran and he were discussing, and finally he turned to us both and said, "You and I are after all doing the same thing, making people a little happier for this life." "Oh, no," Fran replied, "if that were all there is to it, we couldn't do it." When faced with Moslem Mus and Mok, with Jewish Ros, with Japanese Buddhist Shiro, with atheistic Jim, and with all the others whose families were firmly convinced in another religion, another way of life, it would be cruel, not kind, to introduce them to possible separation from family, and resulting sorrow, for anything less than true truth— true to what really exists. It is *not* for a "better way of life and happiness" that we tell people about the Bible's teaching which God has revealed as the truth about existence and Himself; it is because it is *true*, and therefore matters sufficiently to be *worth suffering to embrace* . . . no matter what. It matters for all eternity, because there is an eternity ahead that is true.

I have spread out the Japanese newspapers, the printed notices, and the programs with Fran's picture on them. I can't write Japanese, nor read it, so I can't copy them for you. But Mike, who is helping me as secretary and "chef" as I write, assures me that Fran's name heads these. Mike is Japanese-American, but has learned enough of the language at home in Los Angeles to pronounce characters and make them turn out to be saying "Schaeffer"! Fran spoke in a Japanese theological seminary (Don Hoke had made sure they had read *The God Who Is There* first, and other of Fran's books in Japanese), and he also spoke for Phil Foxwell. There were several public meetings in Tokyo, Osaka, Yokohama, and also time with some dear L'Abri family, such as Nicky, Shiro, and one of the German twins. In the ladies' room in the club in Yokohama where I was speaking to a women's luncheon of about 125 Americans, Japanese, English, and others, I was washing my hands when a woman came excitedly up to me. "Oh, I'm so glad to speak to you. I was afraid I wouldn't get a chance. My husband is a chaplain in the U. S. Navy, and he was very liberal, from his teaching in a liberal theological seminary. Then—he got your husband's books, *He Is There and He Is Not Silent* and the others, and *now* you should hear him preach! All those people in the chapel are getting true Christian sermons now. Thank Dr. Schaeffer for me."

In Osaka, a Methodist missionary, Bishop Elmer Parsons, and his wife took us into another kind of restaurant, with private rooms surrounded by streams, water lilies, wooden paths and bridges. There were straw mats to squat on as the wonderful

food was cooked at the tables. Here we saw a bit of the kind
of place the Japanese executives eat in with their clients . . .
while their wives wait at home. "Home" for most Japanese is
not where working people eat lunch and supper; it is a part of
a different connotation.

Our flight from Osaka went to Hong Kong. I was surprised
by my emotion as our plane circled the harbor and I knew that
my old home, my birthplace, was not far off. As Mr. Chua met
us, and Hay Him and Kit Chen took us for a "day off" to the
New Territories, it was not only looking over the line of separation
into fields and hills so close to my birthplace (300 miles or so)
that overwhelmed me but the dear familiar smells and sights and
sounds of the crowded streets of Hong Kong. We ate nothing
but Chinese food, with chopsticks, that week. I was thrilled that
Fran loved eating with chopsticks and enjoyed all the food so
much. I must say I do feel *well* when eating rice and Chinese
food!

Our temporary home was the Y.M.C.A. in the center of town.
As we visited others in their homes, we realized the crowded
conditions were often attributable to compassion and hospitality
for those hundreds of refugees who, at the risk of their lives,
were swimming across the water at night from the mainland.
We talked to people who sent packages to their families "back
home" in mainland China, and we heard of the need to send
medicines and other essentials. We stood looking at the boat town
of Aberdeen where a variety of Chinese junks and other small
boats are "home" for crowds of people and swarms of babies
and toddlers. We realized that the sidewalks, where everything
from dressmaking to coffin-making was going on, were also
"home" for some. Rice with vegetables on it was being eaten
directly from newspapers as old men sat where the throngs of
passersby had to step over their legs. There seemed to be *food* in
plenty, however, whether it was being sold in bowls from street
stalls, on newspaper, or in enormous and always crowded tea-
houses or smaller restaurants. With often ten or more living in
one room, "home" is not the place people can cook and eat in,
unless they are more affluent than most.

As I lectured, questions came to me like "Where can I read
my Bible when there are ten in one room . . . and we don't

have a bathroom, just a small toilet?" "What has your *Hidden Art* got to suggest for making a 'beautiful spot' when fourteen are crowded in and the floor space is all slept on?" The questions were real, searching for help, not sarcastic. I learned a great deal about the need to try to be more imaginative in a greater diversity of "impossibilities" as well as to keep thanking God for the wonder of His promises being true, not "religious"—for all who need assurance there is a moving day ahead into an adequate quarters!

Fran lectured at the Chinese University and the Hong Kong University as well as giving an evening series at St. Andrew's Church, which was crowded to overflowing. Hay Him was a marvelous translater, giving the feeling of the lectures as well as the words. His wife, Kit Chen, who herself was a professor in the Hong Kong University, whispered to me that her husband used just the right idioms and was translating so accurately—the meaning, not just dictionary words. Dr. Philip Teng, now President of the China Graduate School of Theology in Hong Kong, had Fran preach in his church on Sunday morning. The congregation were of two different Chinese dialects, so Hay Him amazingly translated in both Mandarin and Cantonese. We remember Hay Him and Kit Chen so frequently as we serve rice in the bowls they later sent to Switzerland to bring a bit of Hong Kong into our Alpine home.

We saw the book store where Fran's books—in Chinese!—sat on shelves and we visited the Inter-Varsity Fellowship headquarters and prayed with them there as the floor below had just been bought by a brothel. As the "booths" were being built, with much hammering going on, a Chinese paper god hung at the open doorway "protecting" the work! But—is that any more incongruous than the porno shops lining the old streets of Amsterdam or other wonderful old "Christian" countries in which beauty has been replaced with ugliness?

Have a last glimpse of Fran sitting on the grass, surrounded by students avidly asking questions with as much understanding and eagerness as they had in Honolulu. Our sadness was once again for lack of *time.* So swiftly our visit was over, so soon we were to be flying out to Singapore, where three hours later we were to be happily welcomed by Berney Adeney and his dear wife, former Farel House students once part of the L'Abri family in Switzerland.

Impressions of Singapore? . . . A park full of both ordinary and rare orchids, amazingly lush hotels and small boxlike houses; a city of very high apartment houses where "displaced" Malaysians who have lived on tiny bits of land with their chickens and maybe another animal and wee gardens of edible things, are squashed into cement with no place to "breathe." A daytime car park turns into an outdoor food bazaar at dusk, stalls suddenly appearing, with vats of bubbling hot oil, french fried bananas sizzling on sticks, and a host of oriental smells and textures tempting the hoards of people—rich and poor, students and executives, tourists and nationals—every night.

Our schedule was full, with Fran speaking and discussing at the University, where there are probably more Christian professors than in any other secular university in the world. Bobby Sung took good care of us, having a supper for us in the little home of one of the professors, where lovely oriental food stimulated a "feast of discussion" as we sat around the tiny dining-living room, and also taking us to visit Chinese temples—all this in between various speaking engagements. Each night Fran spoke in a "Red Room" in a hotel, where he gave a series, attended (by ticket) by a real cross-section of international people, as well as Chinese and Malaysians. After the public discussion was over, we would go with a group of Chinese professors from the university, to sit outside on hotel balconies in the soft midnight air and discuss until the wee hours of the morning, nibbling on all kinds of Chinese and Malaysian delicacies. Fran loved their quick bright minds; he enjoyed these relaxed as well as intensive times as much as anything for years. "If I had ten years to choose what to do with right now—I would like to come and start all over again, right here in Singapore," he said, and meant it.

The "homes" that made us sadder than anything we had ever seen were the paper houses, filled with paper food, paper furniture, paper art, and piles of paper money—all carefully set up near a coffin! This took place next door to our little hotel, out in the street, where a canopy had been set up for a week of mourning before a burial. People sat on chairs and tables in front of the coffin, drinking Coca-Cola—or maybe Pepsi (!)—while professional mourners wailed, and at times some of the family also. The final event was the arrival of a Buddhist monk, in his robes, who burned the paper house and all the paper things that would be so nice for the person to have in the afterlife. Whoosh—up went the flames and smoke, while loud noises came from the living human throats. Bobby Sung told us that this mélange was, of course, not Buddhist, but a religion they call "Chinese religion"—a mixture.

How much I longed to have people know of the "place" and "my Father's house" that Jesus speaks of, which doesn't need preparing and burning on earth . . . as it really exists and is waiting for the people who are themselves prepared. What an injection in our own veins that sight was, an injection to give us new impetus to be speaking truth clearly in our own century, to whomever the Lord would give us to speak. Academic jargon? Theological games? Time wasted splitting hairs? Watch the dolorous procession following the casket with the corpse, now dead a week, whose "heavenly house" was made of tissue paper and has been sent up in flames . . . and weep!

Bobby Sung drove us across the causeway into Malaysia, up and down streets lined with squares of green grass around little square pink or green houses in Johore. "There, oh there," said the Malaysian boy who had stood by a street corner to meet us secretly. He was now in the back seat, pointing out the homes of other boys who had been at Swiss L'Abri. It's not too dramatic to say that our hearts thumped and tears stung our eyes as we actually passed the tiny houses, and saw teenagers standing in groups—so like the teenagers who had found their way to "Mélèzes," which turned out not to be a pop-band after all! The compassionate God can do terrifically astounding things to enable those who "seek Him with all their hearts" to find Him.

Just before we left for the airport, while I finished stuffing into my luggage the growing number of things I was taking home for Christmas, a call came from the lobby. Going down, I watched a stupendous scene. There Lok, who had just discovered we were in town, and who was a visiting professor at the University, was standing, facing Bobby Sung. "Impossible, Bobby!" . . . "It's you, Lok!" Old school friends, they were tied for top place in University days, these two—the brightest of their time. Bobby, a fine surgeon, practices his medicine only a short period each year, to keep his hand in, and is leading Inter-Varsity Fellowship in Singapore. "You are a Christian?" asks Lok. *"You* gave up your bright career?" There was literally only a two-minute time for us to give Lok a hug before leaving for the airport. He promised to read Fran's books, and . . . there was his old friend.

"God," I said to the Father in heaven, "I love your compassion and patience. Thank you for letting me see a little bit behind your 'curtain' as You keep giving people reminders, as we keep praying for them. I don't know how it all works, as we pray and You answer, but I have a huge surge of appreciation and worship today." That was in the car, on our way to the airport, as Bobby told us about the terrible department store fire, *just* the same time I was shopping in another store! . . . And then with almost no time to relax in our airplane seats, we were feeling the wheels go down as we landed in Kuala Lumpur, to be met by Tomas Heng and taken through the hot November weather to a blessedly air-conditioned hotel.

Big orange posters displayed on walls in the university and other places announced "The Christian Impact in an Age of Uncertainty" as the title of a series of lectures to be given "nightly in the Lecture Theater, Faculty of Education, University of Malaya." . . . "Penetrating lectures by the world renowned Christian philosopher, apologist and author Dr. Francis A. Schaeffer." In the university, Malayans would be allowed to come to a lecture as "educational"; in the church where my series of talks was given, my audience was mostly Chinese. You see, Malay Malays are prohibited by law from changing their religion from Moslem to anything else and are regulated by law in such things as observing fast days and feast days, so that a penalty is given both to a restaurant and to the individual if a Malay is sold food on a Moslem fast day. Our time there, my long talk with Miss Cooke at a Chinese tea house, and our visits alone with people in their homes made us marvel more than ever at the historic uniqueness of the few who "find their way," after such barriers and obstacles have been put in the path. Before we were driven to the airport again, we passed a "street of the dead." It had shops that sold the paper houses, paper money, and so forth, but also houses where people take their dying old relatives or others they find "homeless" who are dying. There, with almost no attention, with no one to make the hours bearable through loving care, people come—or are taken—to die. Street of the dead! What a name for a street full of houses! Yet—aren't many of the streets in the world exactly like that, filled with people who know nothing about stepping from death to life . . . and are living only to die, rather than finding the One who died that they might live?

We had added a cheap rayon suitcase by this time to hold my "Christmas shopping" and I was carting Chinese paper umbrellas back to my grandchildren, much to my husband's disgust, so our departure was not such a "neat sight"! Arriving at the Bombay airport, we panted a bit as we walked through the hot dust outside to get to Vigu Abrahamson's car. Vigu's brother Rogu, a doctor, had studied at Farel House in Switzerland and we had much to talk about.

The time in Bombay could take a chapter by itself! A million people living on the streets, lining up by the thousands to get water from one small pipe; washing their saris in a bucket and hanging them on the railroad station fences, or any other place to be found; lying with fevers, on the sidewalks, putting up a few pieces of cardboard for shade, never knowing a home other than a sidewalk or patch of dirt. Taxis shrieking to a stop behind a cow, or an oxcart, or a man sweating with the strain of pulling a two-wheeled cart full of iron "trash." All this is impossible to describe in a condensed way.

How can I tell you the impossibility I found in sleeping, when outside my window I could see a long line of human beings— pregnant women, mothers of small children, young girls, old bent people—carrying baskets of rocks and dirt as *they* were the "buckets" to empty the place being dug by men with picks and shovels for the foundations of a new hotel. A long line of them, like ants, and the ocean's waves so close, which only the men ever felt when work finished in the evening. I stood and wept as they made their tiny fires right there on the dirt where they would be sleeping—fires the size of a candle flame, to cook some mixture wrapped around a little stick, for their supper. The fires kept flickering, and I stood praying and weeping.

Before daylight, the scene was again the same. What a "speck" I felt myself to be in the midst of humanity. Yet, as Vigu drove us to Hindu temples and took us far out into the country to visit the enormous statues of the Jain religion, and we heard the "religious base," the "philosophical base," of this country in a fresh light of seeing the results with our own eyes, we could not forget the Israelites turning to Baal worship. We could not forget that, time after time in history, people have turned away from the true and living God and have turned to false religions of men's own making, pleasing Satan rather than God—always bringing tragic results into the culture.

We had three evening speaking times (not on our schedule), and a precious time in Vigu's home with his mother, a medical doctor, and his wife and baby—all vivid in our memory. We "listened" and "learned" as well as talked, finding that twentieth-century thinking not only penetrates India but drifts back in to merge with what originated there.

It seemed incredible to see Western drug people, hippies, sitting among the poor on the streets, begging that which should be given to the Indians . . . having left their country's affluence to steal food from the mouths of hungry as if this were a virtue! The ashram that Vigu took us to visit was empty that day, so two young Indian novices, studying under the Guru, pranced around showing us where they eat, where they study, "and this is where the idol has her bath"—for all the world as if they were talking about a circus. At the end they seriously asked Fran what he taught. The conversation resulted in an exchange of addresses—"We want to come to L'Abri." We left December 8.

Home again . . . to plunge into two L'Abri Workers' weddings, to prepare for Christmas, to have our last Christmas in Mélèzes, and then for me to be shut away in our little apartment in Veytaux. We had it for one more month.

December 27, Fran said, "No New Year's Eve for you . . . we'll manage. Stay here and write *Everybody Can Know*. Try to finish before we move on January 27. Send the chapters up to me, and I'll read and check them." "Thanks to know," I thought. That useful expression originated with Priscilla, or Debby, but it is a favorite one in the family. "Thanks to know!" I had the first chapter, well read to a variety of people around the world, and I had been reading the Book of Luke in planes, day by day, wherever we were! Now I plunged into writing, trying to weave "Fran's kind of thing" into a form that children, along with their older brothers and sisters, uncles and aunts, parents and grandparents would also find interesting, and that would spark off real discussion around the meal tables of a variety of homes.

I wrote day and night—at times all night—and the book grew, and developed, and was finished at 9:00 P.M. my last day. "Fran, it's done!" "Great, dear . . . wonderful. . . . John and I will arrive at 7:15 tomorrow morning, in time to help with the moving." I was floored. The movers were arriving at 7:15. . . . Who was going to pack the medicine cupboard, the dishes and pots and pans, the food cupboards?? It wasn't our permanent home, but a lot had accumulated. Debby called soon after that. "Who's helping you, mother?" When she discovered what was going on, she said, "I'll be down." Udo drove her, and a half-hour later she was helping me fill boxes. We worked, drank tea, talked and enjoyed working together until 4:00 A.M. in this "once-in-a-life-time" situation. While Debby slept her short hours, my head was keeping me awake with the "Hallelujah Chorus" surging through it. . . . My book was done!

For any of you who have ever had your husband seem to be "unreasonable" (!!!) I'll let you listen to Fran as he and John burst happily in in the morning when Debby and I were folding up sheets and towels and getting last-minute things in boxes. He looked around in dismay and exclaimed, "Aren't you ready YET? What have you been doing, anyway?" It's not usually that bad . . . I must say to this day he doesn't know when he expected me to do "it"!

Where on earth were we moving? Didn't we have a home? As you know, Mélèzes had been our home for eighteen years. Now with a long series of strange "openings of doors," Dr. Méan's house was offered for sale to us, before anyone knew that both he and his wife had only a few months to live. I have written pages, which I won't copy, giving my feelings in moving from Mélèzes—uprooted feelings, strange feelings of coming to an "end" of something. Then there are more pages about the sheer wonder of our finding how the downstairs apartment would be "just perfect" for Franky and Genie's, and Jessica's, home, as they prepared for the new baby in June.

Along with that excitement came our own surprise at feeling

at home in this chalet, built at the same time as Gentiana. From the first, we appreciated being able to see the lights in Debby and Udo's windows, and to stand on our balcony wondering what the barn was going to develop into. We had moved into an old chalet, twenty minutes' walking distance up the hill from Mélèzes . . . what change would there be? Immediately Mélèzes became apartments where single Workers had separate homes (Gary and Cynthia and their baby live on the top floor now, Juanita Ellwood downstairs, as their L'Abri homes). Also, as people were arriving at the front door—often thirty a day—it was becoming impossible for us to "open the door" ourselves.

A change *had* taken place already. We had all kinds of imagination as to "a slower, quieter life" being just around the corner for us in our new home, Chalet le Chardonnet. "No one will be able to find us easily. We'll be a bit away—a bit hidden. We can have people quietly for tea and conversation." We fell in love with the living room and dining room—a home not filled with people sleeping on the floor—"Ah!"

We had no idea of what was coming next! But thank God, it wasn't a surprise for Him, and He had given us a home to share in a new way. That living room was going to "open up" to bring thousands upon thousands to the fireside to look over Fran's shoulder at his Bible, so marked up, so worn, so full of what he wanted to make clear!—as he would be talking "on film" in *Whatever Happened to the Human Race?* Not a very private room.

The first Christmas in Chardonnet, we were sitting in front of that fireplace, just ready to open gifts, when the doorbell rang. I went to find Vic there with a shivering Indian boy, hesitantly waiting for a greeting. I recognized him in his thin suit, even though he had had on white robes when I saw him last. He was one of the two boys from the ashram near Bombay where Vigu had taken us a year before. Fran had been corresponding with both of them during the year. Now all the permits, visas, and tickets had been received—and here he was! We quickly made a place, and found some gifts to wrap so he would be included for the next half-hour. However, it seemed better to check and see when Prisca's family would be eating, as we had finished lunch, and dinner wouldn't be for some hours. Prisca exclaimed that they were just sitting down to eat, so John would come

and get Regu, then bring him back with them when the whole family came for the evening turkey dinner. Lisby, Becky, and Giandy loved it, especially as Regu frankly explained he had never used a fork and John quickly responded, "Oh, we have never learned how to properly eat with our fingers, so please teach us." So the Sandri family had a wonderful lesson of how to eat with just one hand, deftly placing the food in the mouth with a special movement, not getting the fingers soiled beyond the first knuckle, and not touching the lips with the fingers. A specialized art.

On June 17, 1973, Francis August Schaeffer, VI, was born! He was the second Francis Schaeffer to be born in Switzerland, and soon there were three Francis August Schaeffers living under one roof for a period of time. Later this youngest namesake would be following his father and grandfather around the land (with sister Jessica, and cousins Natasha, Samantha, Naomi, and Hannah) as they gardened, chopped wood, and cut the grass, raked leaves, and walked about the "family homestead."

HISTORY: 23
PAST—PRESENT—FUTURE

trange about history—whether you are studying it as a child at school or living through it, the dates get muddled very easily. (Or maybe they don't with you!) If you count the years from birthday to birthday, they contain two sets of "year-dates," or if your mind runs from summer to summer, or from ski season to ski season, it is the same. "Was it '73 or '74 when that happened?" I find myself asking. Do you? History marches on, with "the New Year" sliding in with a new, confusing number to get used to. I suppose it was the same in Caesar's time, Rembrandt's time, or Cromwell's time. "Just when," I can imagine one of them saying, "did I fight that war, or paint that painting, or make that rousing speech?" To follow the threads that have been woven together, are being woven together, or are about to be woven together, is what viewing The Tapestry is all about. Accuracy is important, which is why I am still surrounded with piles of papers arranged by dates, and with stacks of books, family letters, birthday books, guest books, and my Bibles filled with my dated prayers (remember, I often write to the Lord).

My prayer time, after returning from around the world, fervently thanked God for the safe birth of Ranald John Sabiston Macaulay, as I had several "pleas" earlier asking for this before he was born. Susan had been in the hospital seventeen days,

and the "turned around" position of the baby brought a decision
to do a Caesarean operation. Then, at just the last minute, literally,
a natural birth took place! That seventeen days had been an important time in Susan's roommate's life, as when the time came for
her to go back to Greatham L'Abri, Susan went with her own
baby, and her roommate plus her baby to L'Abri. History may
be very different for other people, because of Susan's long stay
in the hospital.

In 1973 when Francis was three months old, he was to have
a baby cousin born who would be walking to school with him
one day! Naomi Katrina Orloff Middelmann was born September
9, 1973. The next family reunion needed more high chairs—and
fleet-footed mothers and cousins to keep little ones in the right
places and rescue them from the dangerous ones! When Naomi
was just a month old, Udo and Fran went to speak in Sweden
at Lund University, and then Fran and John Sandri went to speak
in Paris. In November of the same year, Udo and Fran gave lectures
to young pastors and theological students in German-speaking
Switzerland. It was Fritz and Ina who arranged these meetings.
Fritz, now a Swiss pastor, had come to Chalet Mélèzes from the
Lausanne cafe classes years before, and, convinced that truth existed, had been "born again" after having gone away altogether
from Christianity when studying under Karl Barth. Ina, a German,
had become a Christian the same summer that Udo had, when
Ran and Sue were taking care of L'Abri and we were in Long
Island with Debby and Franky (after Franky's operation), and
John and Pris were visiting us there. Do you wonder why I call
people "threads" and see a "weaving" going on? Threads keep
reappearing together.

You see, 1973 was the year we began our "new life" in Chardonnet, which was to be a beginning of a partial "slowing down"
and "doing less"! In addition to a L'Abri conference in Lookout
Mountain where many L'Abri people went to speak, including
Birdie, Donald Drew, and Ranald and Susan for their first time
(Ran's first time in the U.S., Susan's first for eighteen years!) . . .
when we returned Fran began a weekly seminar for people who
were at L'Abri as guests or were living nearby (because he would
be having more time to take care of people he had not had time
to care for before!). For the same reason, I began a weekly Bible

class for people living in the area, for members of our church, and for guests coming for a short time to L'Abri. This was to use our new "freer time" to do things we hadn't been able to do before. You see, we didn't know we were soon to have less free time than we had ever had. We were blissfully ignorant of that.

In July 1974 the Congress on World Evangelism was held in Lausanne, the first such congress having been held in Berlin eight years before. At the Berlin Congress, Fran had given a talk called "The Practice of Truth." Everyone at the congress had been impressed the day before as the tour guide had pointed out the Berlin Wall, telling us forcefully that it was there because twenty years before some Americans—as well as others—had not understood the enmity of the enemy. Fran said, "We who are here in Berlin in front of this horrible wall must ask a very serious question: Whose fault is it that the wall is there? Whose fault is it that those people are shut away on the other side with the machine guns trained on them as they work near the walls?" As he went on to speak of the tremendous importance of a balanced presentation of truth, he said, "If we do not make clear by word and practice our position for truth as truth and against false doctrine, we are building a wall between the next generation and the Gospel. And twenty years from now, men will point their fingers back and say to us, this is the result in the flow of history." He closed with, "Evangelism that does not lead to purity of life, and purity of doctrine, is just as faulty and incomplete as an orthodoxy which does not lead to a concern for, and communication with, the lost."

Now, eight years later in Lausanne, Fran's message was "Form and Freedom in the Church." He made a plea again for an understanding of the need to stand for truth, and also for a reality of a life that conforms to that truth. He spoke in this speech of the "tragic infiltration of the existential methodology in evangelical circles," that is, the splitting of the Bible into that which can be called "true religiously," or "an authority on religious matters". . ."but *not* an authority where the Bible touches on history and sciences." He spoke of "two contents": one, sound doctrine, and two, honest answers to honest questions; and of "two realities": one, true spirituality, and two, the beauty of human relationships. He ended with this sentence: "And when there are the two contents, and the two realities, we will begin to see something happen in our generation."

That speech in Lausanne brought a standing ovation from the delegates from so very many countries. It was not the standing ovation, however, that brought the greatest measure of joy to Fran, but something that happened with a small group of men, Presbyterian pastors from the Southern part of the United States. "Please, could you come into this room and meet with us for a few minutes?" one of these delegates asked. A division had taken place in the Southern Presbyterian Church a short time before. Some of the men in that room had come out to form a Bible-believing church, while some had not felt that was the action to take. Here they were together, discussing and praying together. "We wanted you here, Francis, because it is your book *The Church Before a Watching World* which has made this meeting together possible. Thank you for what you have done." Fran wept as he told me about it back at the hotel that night. Why? Because, as you know from earlier parts of this book, he had struggled since the '30s for beauty rather than ugliness in relationships, even when there had to be division. Does that mean he felt he, and others, had now "arrived"? No more need for struggle and prayer asking God for help in these areas? No, let me say very seriously that it is a fearful thing to even write about this, because Satan is a mean enemy. The enmity of our enemy is titanic, and he will never be "past history," not until Jesus comes back again, and the final victory is won.

Why was I "back at the hotel" and not with Fran that week? Except for the actual time of his lecture, when I was there listening and praying simultaneously, I sat at a typewriter from early morning until late night, without a break. I was writing *Christianity Is Jewish* that summer, and couldn't take a "day off."

After we had packed to go back up the mountain to the chalet, we had our one meal together in the balcony restaurant—a lunch. (Sandwiches had been my fare, to nibble as I wrote.) As we sat eating, a very vivid-looking lady came across the room to us, with a pile of books under her arms. "Could you please autograph these for me?" she asked. I hadn't met her before, but wrote, "May the Lord fulfill whatever purpose He has brought us together for," in one of the books. He has, and still is, bringing forth much joy in our friendship, as well as a variety of results in history because we met that day—Mary Crowley and I. We had no idea of "His purpose," as we smiled at each other, but we have observed some of the weaving since. Future history only God knows about. It is a bit staggering to think about that, especially at three o'clock in the morning when you have a toothache, or the baby is crying! God does know, but our being "awake" gives us a part in the future by letting us pray when otherwise we would have been sound asleep. We can be in danger of being "sound asleep" about our effect on future history in *many* ways.

It was a Sunday afternoon at the end of July that same year—1974—that Billy Zeoli had a chance talk with Franky, whom he had gone down to see before having tea with us. The tea was forgotten as film-making was discussed and Franky expressed the kind of things he objected to in "mediocre Christian movies and art." That discussion has grown and become a full-fledged book just this year (*Addicted to Mediocrity—20th-Century Christians and the Arts,* by Franky Schaeffer). When the conversation led to the question "What kind of film would you make?" Billy made a decision, "Go, ahead . . . start," and named Franky producer for a ten-episode documentary film. Before Franky's twenty-second birthday on August 3, he had started full speed ahead to work with his dad on ideas in the area of "The Rise and Decline of Western Thought and Culture, covering Philosophy, Art, Science, History, Music, Literature, Films, Law, Government, Theology." On Wednesday night I was serving a hot dog roast in the garden, but Fran had been waylaid. Franky had come, pencil and paper in hand, and perched in his dad's office. "If you were going to do this, just where would you start?" And as Fran began to talk, a rough outline was scribbled by Franky. Trisa Edwards, who had been my helper and had expected to leave to work in Texas, had agreed to work on the project, so by that time she was Franky's secretary and had begun to type. The rough outline was the beginning, followed by many rewritings as the manuscript grew.

Here I'll plunge into one of my famous [brackets].

[Hiking has always been a part of our lives in Switzerland, from the time Fran first hiked with the girls in Champéry, through years of very long hikes to the shorter ones of the present day.

Come for a moment to a day when Franky was a boy climbing up a mountain on the other side of the lake from Villeneuve. Woods filled with ferns, moss, and hidden patches of violets are chilly when the sun is not filtering through the trees, but even then there is the breathtaking appreciation of the delicate perfection of varieties of moss that not many eyes see. Drudgery is a part of all climbs, hard slogging up, up, up, with a branch suddenly flying into one's face, with a slippery rock giving a twist to one's knee, perspiring, wondering if the top will ever be reached. "It's no wonder," one thinks with a puff and a deep breath, "that climbing hills and mountains is used to illustrate the unending difficulties of life, and the sudden disappointments."

This day's climb was a very long one, with its share of aching legs and out-of-breath moments. A good twenty miles of up and down were covered before the day was over. A staggeringly vivid memory of another kind of illustration of the ingredients involved in life's climb remains to this day for Fran and Franky. When they got to the top, having come from the back of the mountain away from the lake, they were at last over the edge ready to look down. Disappointingly heavy clouds blotted out all view! "All that just to see a grey swirling cloud below?" Then suddenly the clouds parted and a hole appeared, as if a giant spoon had separated a mass of whipped eggs. The hole became a larger and larger window, opening a marvelous view of what had been hidden from sight.

There below them was the lake, and sharply in direct focus, as if they had been looking out of the top floor window of a high building, was the dock at the lake village of Bouveret, with a white paddle-wheel boat sliding smoothly in place, the gangplank shoved across by two men, and people beginning to disembark. We never walk along the other side of the lake at Castle Chillon, or ride on a lake boat, without Fran pointing to that spot high on the opposite mountain, and reminiscing about that hike with Franky. "See—up there? Are you looking where I'm pointing? That's where we stood that day looking through the hole in the clouds."

Very often the Lord doesn't give us a "hole in the clouds" . . . we look down into a grey monotony, or we are surrounded by mists. It's a help to remember there is something being hidden from view! The fogs themselves are not all there is to present, past, or future life. The opening, or window, or hole, or the total lifting of the clouds and fogs will reveal what exists—just out of sight.

Fran and I went through a long stretch of years when hiking was a Monday day-off part of each week. He has a stack of maps marked with the hikes he has taken with one of the children or me, and a stack of memories of both hard and dangerous places, and wonderful surprises or rewards that came sometimes at the top, sometimes just around the bend of a path.

Our most memorable hike was a six-day vacation when we took light backpacks with a change of clothing, paperback books to read aloud to each other, Band-aids and aspirins, a Bible, toothbrushes, soap and a non-mussable dress and sandals for me to wear to dinner. We hiked over the Bernese Oberland route, from Gruyères to Spiez, from village to village, through woods, over some trails, but mostly along gentle back roads among fields and rushing streams. We stopped at village stores to get bread and cheese and fruit for lunch to be eaten in a field or by a stream, and stopped for the day when we were tired, by five o'clock or so, at a station hotel or some little place we thought would be interesting. We'd have a bath, dress for dinner, eat a hot meal, read aloud (I usually am the one to read while Fran shuts his eyes; I love to read aloud) . . . and sleep with interest to see what next day's hike would cover. Ninety-five miles were not too difficult divided among six days.

Yes, hiking was exercise, recreation, a time for thinking and communicating, a time when new ideas sprang forth and could be discussed, and a time for understanding an amazing number of things in life—illustrated without any labels attached! Perfect harmony? No. There were so often times when I would have resentment for the first hour or so, thinking I had had enough exercise all week racing up and down stairs, standing long hours in the kitchen. . . . Why couldn't I simply sit on a lake boat and *rest?* There were times when frayed nerves and exhaustion caused disagreements of very foolish kinds to flare up and make conversation nothing but an argument. Vacations are like this so often for all of us. We expect too much, and become disappointed too quickly, and are apt to want to blame someone, the other one! For us, each individual hike had some period of this sort, but it changed and the wonders of the perfection of a tiny fern or flower, the marvel of a distant view, the song of the birds, the quick scurry across our path of a squirrel or rabbit, the sight of a deer or wild chamois in the woods, would chase away the complaining and wishing for something else, and bring instead a window in the clouds of our own feelings through which appreciation would shine through, with the rest of the day bringing the unwinding that had been needed. We need to learn not to "give up too soon," whether in a day off, a week's vacation, or life as a whole.]

On a day off soon after Fran had been considering ideas for the new project, he and I were hiking along a road not far from Chateau d'Oex. Cows were grazing and their bells made a pleasant music for the walking in unison—tramp, tramp, tramp. Fran had been making complaining noises about the impossibility of starting the book ahead of him, when suddenly he said, "Edith—do you have paper and pen with you?" I took my light rucksack off and proudly produced a notebook and pencil. "Write this: 'There is a flow to history and culture. This flow is rooted and has its well-spring in the thoughts of people. People are unique in the inner life of the mind—what they are in their thought world determines how they act. This is true of their value systems and it is true of their creativity. It is true of their corporate actions such as political decisions, and it is true of their personal lives. The results of their thought world flow through their fingers or from their tongues into the external world. This is true of Michelangelo's chisel, and it is true of the dictator's sword.' There . . . that's the beginning."

It was. It was the the beginning of the film and of the book that were going to be "out" two years from then. All it was at that time, however, was a penciled scribble in an old notebook, being shoved back into my rucksack. The conversation from then on was a flow of developing ideas. Meantime Franky was working to line up Dr. Jeremy Jackson as principal researcher, Dr. Hans Rookmaaker as chief art researcher, Jane Stuart Smith as music researcher, John and Sandra Bazlington for cultural researchers, and Udo Middelmann as book researcher. Fleming Revell Company was going to bring out the book and study guide, with

Richard Baltzell giving the editorial touches, and Gospel Films was going to bring out the film. There was a crew to gather, and there were endless details to begin working on as autumn and winter came. While Fran did his first portions of work on the manuscript, I finished *Christianity Is Jewish.*

February and March of 1975 were the months for intensive work on Fran's manuscript. By that time his early writing had been completed, and Tresa had produced many copies, with very wide margins, which had been sent off to the researchers. The "intensive work" consisted of Fran's standing for hours a day, bent over a long line of copies of the manuscript, each with copious suggestions made in those margins in a wide variety of handwritings. You can appreciate that he nearly went crazy and felt he would like to chuck the whole thing out the window into the lake. The ducks might have enjoyed it! "I just can't do it" was his general feeling, along with remarks of nonappreciation of all the handwriting in general, and the writers' suggestions in particular. Frustration. In between these fits of frustration came the times when John Gonser (the director whom Franky had chosen) would come down and sit on the floor with Fran to go over a movie script being made from the book. Complication and further frustration. Then one morning, before breakfast, we were both reading our Bibles, separately, when Fran looked up and said, "Edith, listen to this:

" 'Ezekiel 33. Son of man, speak to the children of thy people and *say* unto them, . . .' What must be done, God says, is to post a watchman to look out for the sword coming against the land, so that he may warn the people. And if he does not warn the people by blowing a trumpet, then if they are killed, their blood is upon *his* head; it has been his fault for not warning them."

He read through in the King James Version until the 10th and 11th verses, which are: "Therefore, O thou son of man, speak unto the house of Israel; Thus ye speak, saying, If our transgressions and our sins be upon us, and we pine away in them, HOW SHOULD WE THEN LIVE? Say unto them, As I live, saith the Lord God, I have no pleasure in the death of the wicked; but that the wicked turn from his way and live: turn ye, turn ye from your evil ways; for why will ye die, O house of Israel?"

"Edith, there it is. I feel certain that God is speaking to me this morning. God willing, I'm not going to complain about making this project—book and film. Don't you see . . . that is the perfect title—How Should We Then Live? It is the answer the humanists need. It is the answer everyone needs. God giving the strength, we *must* go on."

Amazingly enough, this Ezekiel passage fit in perfectly with that partially quoted passage of George Wald, the biologist! "Choose life" is nothing when applied only to ecology and getting rid of bombs. Listen to the rest, Deuteronomy 30:19, 20a, KJV: ". . . I have set before you life, and death, blessing and cursing: therefore choose life, that both thou and thy seed may live: That thou mayest love the Lord thy God, and that thou mayest obey his voice, and that thou mayest cleave unto him: for he is thy life and the length of thy days." Exciting! There is an answer to how we should live—choose life; but that choice involves choosing God who *is* our life! The cutting of the Bible into bits and pieces is like Solomon's suggestion to the mothers, to cut the baby in half and each take half. The very cutting destroys possible life!

I am not saying that from that time on there was no struggle involved, no battle both in the writing and the making of that film and book, but it never was the same. Fran didn't forget the forceful striking view from the "window" that was open to him that morning as to the imperative for making it! He knew he *had* to go on, come wind, come waves! The name of the book and film was far more than a name; to him it came as a directive to "blow the watchman's trumpet" in his way, as one of the "watchmen" on the wall in this moment of history. The bending over the manuscripts didn't get any easier, the work days weren't shorter, the suggestions weren't suddenly slipped into place or discarded without just as much agony; but there was an underlying difference.

Meantime I worked in another room, except when Fran called me to check something with him. I was writing *What Is a Family?* The one day we had decided we should "get out and fill our lungs with air," we were coming back, happily deciding this had been perfect, and now we could get back to work *really* renewed when . . . smash, crash! . . . I had tripped, with the sole of my cross-country ski boot hitting an iron grill in the sidewalk, right in front of our hotel. Ski sticks still clutched in both hands stuck out in the air . . . I did a swan dive to the cement sidewalk, crashing on the cement, knocking all the air out of my lungs, ending up with a concussion of the rib cage. Fran was bending over me calling, "Edith, Edith—" but no sound came! I had fainted, and when I did come to, I couldn't speak. As the doctor examined me and pronounced that I wouldn't be out of bed for four days, I wailed, "but I have to . . . I'm writing a book." "No, you'll see . . . you can't."

He was right; I couldn't breathe without pain, and sleeping was impossible for a time. Moving a few inches in bed was excruciating. My groans had to be silent though, as I was in bed in Fran's workroom, which was our bedroom. You see, my small workroom had no bed! It was during those four days that an urgent Members' meeting was needed, so they piled in about 9:00 P.M.—Barry and Veronica, Jane, Prisca and John, Udo and Debby, Larry and Nancy—and I "attended" on my back! Our urgent business was not finished until 4:00 A.M. Yes, it's important to remember that a clear certainty as to being in the Lord's will and doing the work He has unfolded, is *not* any guarantee that from that moment on, "the work," whatever it consists of, will be smooth sailing with no hurricanes. The first "storm" after the deep assurance usually hits pretty rapidly!

It was August when the filming actually started. A whole book could be written about the filming, the locations, and the incidents, and another one about the filming of the second film series. I dislike condensing, as anyone knows who knows me, as I much prefer telling a story with all the interesting details! But the history of this must only be given in fleeting impressions. First you need to know that no film is made in consecutive order. Scenes from the final episode may be made before the first or third episode; one minute may be followed by a minute that is going to be made weeks later. This is why it is so important to have clothing fit with what has gone before and after. You can't have a person start running down the hill with blue socks and end at the bottom with red and white striped ones! Hair has to be washed every day so that one minute it does not look freshly washed, and a second later, as if it had been washed three days before. The word *continuity* has terrific importance in filming. In fact, one person's sole job is to check for continuity in terms of clothing and hair and the exact second-to-second preciseness of the action of the script, so that each sentence follows the right sentence in the final cutting.

We were to enter a new world, separated from the rest of our life. It was closer to joining a circus than anything else I can think of, though I have never been in a circus! Traveling by car in a kind of caravan of cars with the truck leading, or following, full of all the equipment, cameras, props of a variety of sorts, the precious boxes of the film itself, sound equipment, emergency food or coffee, folding chairs, etc.; waiting sometimes for hours to have the truck inspected at the borders of countries, losing precious hours of sleep, or anxiously watching the light . . . "It's going to be too late . . . the sun is getting too high," etc.; packing and unpacking day after day; arriving at a hotel with Linny Dey (assistant to the producer, in charge of handling the props, the slate for takes, Fran's wardrobe), needing to check to see where the nearest cleaner was or looking for an iron, as the wardrobe needed to be "kept up," and with Anita Benedict, (assistant to the director, responsible for continuity in script, taking Polaroids, notes, etc.) bringing Fran his script to be memorized for the next day. Fran's first job daily was to cut and paste up the script he had to memorize, as he felt he could do it much better if it were cut out and separated from the rest of the manuscript. The hated early morning hair-washing and drying was his waking "bugaboo" daily, in spite of what his immediate "ailment" was that day.

Long hours of takes and retakes took more than a "normal day" with many "dawn shots," as well as "night shots" making the passage of time a new kind of unreality. In this situation the crew becomes, in a sense, the whole community, and the ups and downs, delights and horrendous difficulties, answers to prayer and crushing disappointments, resemble those of a whole city, or at least a village, in miniature. One almost could say it resembles a lifetime in miniature. Then at the end, it falls apart, much like the arrival of an ocean liner. People who have been together—sharing so much, hoping, fearing, loving, hating, feeling excited, feeling depressed, sharing joys, sharing sorrows—become skeptical of the supernatural, or recognizing Satan's attacks. Fran said to me he felt he had never felt the presence of evil in his personal form so thoroughly as during this time. There were not only "attacks" on Fran's health and body, but a stream of tremendously diverse attacks came to hinder the filming. It would be untrue, or unbalanced, to say this, however, without also quickly saying we saw astounding answers to prayer in a great diversity of areas—from "impossible permissions" given to film in "impossible places" to the sun coming out at the right moment, or the truck being protected from theft, or a very near accident averted on an icy road. Time after time we were reassured that this project was the Lord's, and that we were simply following His plan. For Fran it was a time of coming to a fresh understanding of Paul's shipwrecked journey, and of the reality of calling for God's strength to be made perfect in his weakness, recognized in the practical things every day.

In each country there were production assistants who procured permissions, arranged locations and hotels, found props and actors when needed, etc. These people were a part of the "crew" in the several countries: Udo Middelmann for Germany, Claudine Tapernaux for Switzerland and France, Francesco Boesch for Italy, John and Sandra Bazlington for England, Ko Durieux for Holland and Belgium, Jim Buchfuehrer for America. The basic crew consisted of Franky Schaeffer, producer; Billy Zeoli, executive producer, basically responsible for the financing; Wendy Collins, associate producer, handling advance arrangements for filming; John Gonser, script writer and director; with Franky planning and directing some portions. The filming took the better part of six months, with a long period of editing and cutting after that, before it came to be what it is today. In English, German, Spanish, and Japanese, the series is being used in teaching and in churches, in Army camps and seminars, in ways beyond the knowledge of any of us in out-of-the-way corners of the earth as well as in central cities.

Who can say who really is "responsible" for the whole production? There are those who gave money at various times of extreme need, and those who prayed incessantly with seriousness and faithfulness. Certainly the three cameramen were essential— Harry Konig, Dutch; Alan Hall, English; and Earl Miller, American. What was being said couldn't be heard without what the sound man—Werner Walter, Swiss—cared for in his work. Mus Arshad took many of the stills for the book and posters. Skip Collins as "gofor" had charge of all the equipment in the truck and had to go—for many things! Such a demonstration of The Tapestry in a relatively short length of time, with a relatively small number of people, is valuable in seeing that each thread has an effect on other threads, but also an effect on "the production."

Unmentioned, unsung, unknown people have had an effect on every period of history—short periods, and long periods! Whether it is in newspaper reporting, history books, or the Bible itself—the people of any one period of history who have had a part or an effect have not by any means all been mentioned. Finite human beings haven't the capacity for "digesting" the significance of a long, long list of names. That is what finiteness is all about. God has no problem knowing each individual, and his or her part in helping or spoiling a portion of history, and He understands each one.

Noises, the barking of a dog, the sound of a jet, the honking of a truck horn, can "spoil" a shot, as can distracting arrivals of curious people wanting to "look in"—wherever! But soundlessly, and invisibly in a few paragraphs, you can "drop in" without being chased away. Come to Cambridge. It is early morning, and the crew, under John's direction, is setting up lights, sound equipment, etc., in a science laboratory on a small Cambridge street. As Fran is positioned to stand by a window, near an experiment, the "shot" is going to catch church spires visible outside the window, as well as the scientific experiment. Linny is sitting on the floor in a tiny dusty hall looking up the accurate translation for a Latin quote. Fran is away from the window now, in another dusty corner, studying his lines, memorizing them. . . . "Lights, cameras, sound" . . . (as each assents all is ready) . . . then, "Action" . . . and Fran's voice is beginning. "Cut—" Something is adjusted and it all starts over again.

As time goes on, Jill Spink and I give each other a nod, and slip out into the street. "I think I saw a bakery down here." . . . We go into a crowded little bakery with wonderful fragrance of fresh bread and buy two whole wheat loaves still hot from the oven. With other customers looking a bit annoyed, I borrow a knife, and we cut our loaves! Then we run along two more blocks to "The Copper Kettle" where morning coffee is being sipped by students, housewives, professors, all earnestly talking to each other. "Please could I have thirteen cups of coffee, with a pitcher of cream and sugar? . . . I mean, on a tray to carry out? You see, we are a film crew, and there is no time to stop right now. . . . I'd bring the cups back in a half hour at the latest." It takes a bit of persuasion, and a "deposit" for the blue cups and saucers, and then we march proudly off down the streets with a tray of coffee as people look a bit curiously at us. "You go on with coffee, I'll go to the market and get some cheddar cheese and butter for the bread." says Jill. Silently, silently, I open the door, slip my shoes off, and make my way up the narrow stairs to the lab and . . . listen. Yes, filming is still going on, so I don't dare breathe! Suddenly—"Cut." . . . and the signal is clear that the coffee can be taken quickly before the next "take" is arranged. Franky, Anita, Fran, Linny, Skip, John—in fact, everyone is grateful for a bit of a "pick-up"! "Hey, thanks."

After the crew has moved on to the next location, filming along a walk near a college, Jill and I have delivered the cups, and are spreading the bread and making cheese sandwiches in the tiny kitchen of the laboratory! We will be ready for another urgent need of refreshment. As we come to the college where the filming is going on, in between "takes" Linny comes over to Jill and me and says, "I think you'll have to go and cancel the restaurant for lunch, and just bring some sandwiches or something. We aren't going to stop longer than a half hour, because of the light going . . . and we have to get to Nelville's Court in Trinity College as early as possible to get that shot of Dr. Schaeffer's dropping the ball for the echo, when he is talking about Sir Isaac Newton."

It had been a very early morning. "People are really hungry," I think to myself. "I wonder if—" Then I say to Jill, "Come on. Let's go to that restaurant where we reserved the tables and ordered steak dinners to be ready at 1:00 P.M." . . . "I've put the tables in an L like this; do you like it?" Everything had been arranged so prettily with flowers and red napkins. "Look, the director isn't going to give a lunch hour . . . soooo—" Her face fell and she started talking about the steaks they had bought specially. "What I was going to ask was, do you suppose we could fix up thirteen plates, in cardboard boxes, all served, and get the dinner over to where they are? They could eat it in half an hour. I'll come to the kitchen and help you myself." Soon I was helping in the restaurant kitchen, and we had the plates heated, the steaks sizzling away, French fries almost ready. With a hot plate underneath and one on top—twenty-six plates in all— keeping each meal warm, we slipped them into grocery boxes. With napkins, ketchup, olives, and a pot of tomato soup, a ladle and cups, we were tucking everything into the back of the station wagon. "Thanks so much. . . . We'll be back with the plates and silverware. . . . What a surprise this will be!"

You can't imagine how enthusiastically the "kitchen" had been about doing all this—nor how surprised the whole "crew" was, when they had expected only sandwiches. Incidentally, the cheese sandwiches disappeared with the soup, and *then* the dinner! Everyone had been especially hungry. In a very short time they were ready to go on and do a good job on Isaac Newton's brilliant working out of the speed of sound, as they filmed that portion of the science film. Talking together afterwards, we marveled at how far scientists have departed from the early Christian scientists like Newton. Hurried times of eating, short times of sleeping, rushing to go from one place to another—all this did not cut out a certain amount of discussion among ourselves about the content of the whole film series.

It was when we were in London airport that Fran lifted a couple of bags, and pulled his back with some sort of twist. By the time we arrived in Paris and got into our room on the sixth floor of a hotel, he couldn't walk across the room but was lying on the floor with an acute sciatica attack. I asked the hotel man about a doctor, then went to a drug store and asked for a doctor they would recommend. The same name was given, so I decided this must be the answer I had prayed for. The doctor's word was most discouraging, however. As he gave Fran a shot he said, "I recently had a man who couldn't get up from the floor for eight days with a back like that." Thanks to know!

I gave Fran hot compresses, aspirin, and lots of vitamin C and B's, prayed a great deal, and went shopping in a department store fairly near the Louvre and brought home the sort of groceries with which I could make meals without a stove! Meantime the crew took shots of buildings and cathedrals, hoping Fran would get better. I think I prayed more than I slept those nights. "Dad," asked Franky the second day, "if we get an ambulance, would you try going in it, lying down until the shot is prepared, and then just going in and sitting at the table and talking?" So . . . Fran did. Those shots you see at the Cafe Deux Magots where Fran is sitting at Jean-Paul Sartre's table, talking about Sartre and Barth, with all the books on the table, were done as I sat at another table praying and handing him aspirin at intervals! In between times of shooting he spent his days—yes, two of them—in the ambulance outside. That scene was "attacked" in other ways. A dumb waiter . . . pulled up by a dumb waiter . . . cut the special cables and wires for the special lighting! And the Paris electric company had to come to respond to an "emergency," while the filming was held up for two hours.

It's impossible to give you even an impression of the hundreds of incidents involved in this filming, such as Fran's two torn ligaments, making it necessary each morning for me to wrap elastic bandage around his leg, and for him to have to have help in climbing 132 steps to the top of the Campanile in Florence. It was Skip who went up behind him and pushed him up one step at a time, to take weight off the painful leg. You wouldn't guess from the film how many times that chariot and horse and driver charged by Fran as he said his lines in Rome, nor could anyone know what was in the driver's mind as he seemed to be putting Fran to a test by coming closer and closer each time! There were precious moments such as the joy of our granddaughters Margaret and Kirsty in staying in Southampton with us as Franky had brought them along for a treat . . . and of having them sit silently through the filming in the music room for hours, on the floor, out of sight; and the joy of having Susan and Phil Matthews join us for a lunch after that, just before we had to rush off again.

Belgium brought us an unusual four hours with a problem in the Cathedral of St. Bavon in Ghent. Our request to film "the altarpiece" had been granted in writing; but it was the wrong altarpiece! When we made known which one it was, there was great consternation, as Van Eyck's "Adoration of the Lamb" is displayed in a side chapel, and the visitors pay to see it. Anyway, it could not be filmed with *that* permit. Sorry. After hours of "official talking"—and "prayer behind scenes"—the permission was granted, but not until the place was closed to tourists. At 6:00 P.M., after waiting all afternoon, the lighting men began setting up. The camera men followed, along with the sound men. That filming took until after 10:30 P.M., but it meant we had the opportunity to see detail and color under the filming lights that we never would have seen otherwise. This was one of the never-to-be-repeated opportunities we had over and over again, of seeing great art works, whether statues, paintings, or buildings, lighted up in a way that brought out beauty we will never see again!

As you see Fran sitting in front of Picasso's *"Les Demoiselles d'Avignon"* in the Museum of Modern Art in New York City, with John Gonser standing by the camera man, you don't know that on the other side of the room I am sitting on the floor with Dr. and Mrs. Garnes, watching. Dr. Garnes (the same black doctor who helped take care of grandmother when he was in L'Abri as she was dying) did more than "watch"; he was there to give Fran another B-12 shot for his back (they went around into the room next to the one pictured in the film, behind that wall). We were in the museums always at night, after the places were closed, having a totally different "view" from the tourists. When Franky was directing the Galileo scene in Castle Chillon, it was almost an eerie experience being in that dark castle in the night. It seemed as if we were in a different period of history, as if the years had really turned back, rather than that we were just in a place late at night. As Franky came to know the curator, he learned that the curator lived in a part of the castle as his home—a fascinating idea. It would be easy to get the centuries mixed up, I should think—especially since the walls haven't changed, and the lake gulls haven't changed, nor the swans. As I stood by some of the thick stone pillars or leaned against ancient walls and watched the torches or the flames leaping up the fireplace, I had the impression of being transported in time, rather than in space.

Filming a succession of centuries of history and a diversity of fields—such as art, science, philosophy, and law—is scorned by some who would contend that it takes many, many volumes, and many more miles of film, and many more years of life to cover such a breadth of subject matter. Life really is not long enough for anyone to do such a task "thoroughly" nor is it long enough for anyone to read or see the results of such a totally "complete work." In the brief time that any one of us has to learn, in order to have some measure of understanding of the important basic analysis of the key moments of history, we need then to realize we have a responsibility to our children, grandchildren, great-grandchildren. We must leave some help behind us, with the hope that solutions will be worked for, and more readily found. The blast of a warning trumpet is not meant to be an entire symphony, too long and complicated for the "city full of people" to interpret!

In the film, the fascinating portion of the early church scenes was the reality of the actors all being Christians, many of whom had come from as widely differing backgrounds as the people described in Acts, and some facing just as specific persecutions, even if they might not consist of Roman soldiers! Persecution and martyrdom are as much a part of present history as they have ever been of past history. It would seem, that unless changes come, they will be a greater part of future history, until Jesus returns to put a swift stop to them. The "last martyr" will have a quick resurrection. He or she will have a unique experience!

How Should We Then Live? A book, a film, a study guide—for colleges, churches, conferences, camps, military chapels, mission stations—for Christians to get a better grasp of basics, for non-Christians to get a better understanding of what humanism is all about, in contrast to what biblical teaching gives as a base to understanding the universe, and life. Is it just a title? A project to be used for filling a need of programs? The question itself is a never-ending one. Morning by morning—how *should* we then live? . . . How should *we*—you and I—then live? Fran would put into his own words what he struggled with in his personal life, and then in his first books: "To make a reality day by day of the Lordship of Christ in the whole of life, in the area of culture as well as all else." As time went on, in *How Should We Then Live?*, and then further in the next book, he continued "to broaden the reality of honestly exhibiting the lordship of Christ in regard to social issues and political life, law, medicine (human life), and government." It wasn't a matter of making a movie, doing a project, and then turning to life, but of continuing to seek reality in having a consistency in life.

Perfect? No. It must be said over and over again: no. Mistakes, often; sin to confess, much to say we are sorry for in many areas, multiple weaknesses. Often Fran says that what the Lord has done over such a wide geographic area and with such diverse kinds of people, with the books and the films, should bring us to our knees in awe and worship. He *has* made His strength perfect in extreme weakness time after time. To have 5600 voices break out singing "Happy birthday to you, Dr. Schaeffer—happy birthday to you" on his 65th birthday January 30, 1977, in the Oakland auditorium, was pretty overwhelming. It was especially startling since there was no plan—only a sudden discovery that it was his birthday and a spontaneous suggestion to sing to him at the end of the first seminar (of eighteen) for the film and book!

The greatest thrill of that seminar was for us to sit and see that film after all the months of being in the midst of its conception and making. My part had been to pray in the background, work in hidden ways "around the edges"—week after week, in and out of cars, living in suitcases, borrowing typewriters to write my regular column (which I had for three and a half years) for *Christianity Today* to meet my deadline each two weeks wherever we were, to pray with various ones of the crew about private needs as well as the project's needs. Too see it come forth then on the full-sized screen, with the music, for the first time—that was really indescribable. I wasn't the only one to sit in excitement at that "first"; Fran and Franky sat by me with their own emotions, as did other members of the crew. The general feeling that ran through the audience was one of surprise and amazement with all that had been put together—and with the titanic strength with which the *facts* were being illustrated.

Fran was astonished to find, as he sat on a table and questions poured forth from people who filed up to the microphones, that it was much like sitting back in Mélèzes by the fireplace, or in our chapel, perched up on the fireplace ledge. The 5600 were after all simply more people than we had in the chalet . . . but each one was only one! And the grouping of the "ones" didn't cause them to lose their personalness, as they listened together. But there is a problem with finiteness that can be realized easily by using a hand computer or doing mental arithmetic. Having one hand with which to shake hands, one head with which to nod, one voice with which to say, "Oh, Bev . . . it's good to see you," means that it is impossible to *be* personal on a one-to-one basis in "space and time" with that many people in an evening, or day.

People came to the seminars from every year of L'Abri's history, and others came who felt like "old friends" because of the books. Doctors, lawyers, newsmen, businessmen, and others, brought their antagonistic atheistic friends whom they felt they could bring for the first time to something that would cause them to "think," and to be different. People brought their babies born since they had been at L'Abri, and their art works also "born" since they had been at L'Abri. People brought poems to give us, such as this:

Francis Schaeffer

In the forest of men's ideas
   I found a man
     with an axe
He was chopping away industriously
With some helpers
   using his tools
And I joined him
And
   then
saw the Garden
Growing in the Light
   in the clearing.

Dustan Barber

It was a special thing to hear Franky answer questions one day when his father was exhausted, to have father and son working together in a day of split relationships. It was wonderful to have Franky lecturing in the area of "Art Forms and the Christian's World View," while I spoke on "What Is a Family," as my book had come out by that time. Wendy Collins did his best to protect

Fran from too long a time of discussion, and Jim Buchfuehrer introduced the format and day's schedule and so on. The many "emergencies" behind scenes would fill a chapter. Union regulations had to be observed, and that brought all kinds of complications, different in each city. My most remembered moment, however, was a hidden one when Franky drew me to the back of the stage, behind all the curtains, amidst the ropes and pulleys and props for all sorts of productions, and there on the dusty floor among boards, he prayed with me, asking for the Lord's words, His power and strength for all that was ahead of us. I am sure he was thinking of the eighteen seminars that were stretching out over long miles and long weeks ahead. He knew nothing about the drastic pieces of news we would be getting along the way; he knew nothing about a further project; he had no idea that Jim would in future months be his partner and best friend. But the Lord answered in the area of the unknown, as well as in the area of the known portions of that request. I look back to that moment as one of the most valued and precious times of prayer among such moments in a lifetime. People give us a single rose at times, such as Susan has put beside my typewriter today, or a tiny bunch of snowdrops such as Debby brought a few days ago, or the first May flowers such as Priscila has dug up or the first three daffodils Fran brought . . . and the memory singles out such expressions and preserves them far better than pressed flowers can be preserved. Such is the memory of moments . . . to be treasured because they are rare.

The seminars were not carbon copies of each other; each place brought new wonders, and new problems. Film got caught and tore. Heinz F. had to race up when he heard a noise in Chicago and rescue a mistake that soon would have been disastrous. The people, though constantly from a wide cross-section of L'Abri years, or families of L'Abri people, or readers of Os, Donald, Gini, Betty, Jane, Udo, and other L'Abri books as well as ours— all were unique, specific individuals with significance in a significant history. They were all "threads" . . . but we can't even follow all eighteen cities, let alone follow all the threads that were glimpsed!

In Grand Rapids we had a call telling us that Hans Rookmaaker had just had a heart attack and died instantly. We couldn't believe it. The shock was numbing. Franky kept walking back to our room in the hotel to say once again, "I can't believe it. He was so young. He was so alive. He is the only one doing what he has been doing for Christianity and culture. He helped me as a young artist, from the time I was twelve and started painting." When I called Anky in Holland, she told me that he had simply said, "I don't feel well," clutched at his chest . . . and he was gone, out of communication with anyone on earth, present with the Lord . . . as suddenly as that . . . leaving a stunned wife and family and friends. Somehow we felt, more strongly than ever, to use the time we have ahead of us, a minute at a time, for whatever the Lord would have us do. The Lord's strength can be given to go on in the midst of shock, but He weeps with us and knows so vastly more than we do how important the final victory is in this battle in which death is still an enemy assailing God's people.

John Sandri had just had an operation to splice a torn tendon with tissue taken from his calf. He went to the funeral in his cast. Udo went with pain from a torn cartilage in his knee, then straight on to Fort Worth for an operation. We had to go on with the seminars with our hearts torn and spliced, so to speak— Fran's dear friend, out of communication!

Houston was the place we were to get our next shock from a phone call. Fran and I were drawing up our will with a Christian lawyer who, with his family, has been at L'Abri, Tom Berry. We were just in the act of affixing our signatures when the phone rang. It was my sister Elsa telling me of father's death! He was 101 and 3 days so you know it was March 21, 1977. He'd had all those unbelievable years of history since his birth in Pittsburgh. Do you remember I had not been able to go to my mother's funeral, after not seeing her for six years—a fact which gave me recurring waves of hurt? The Lord had been preparing a very direct gift to comfort that hurt and wipe it away, without any earthly person knowing what was being prepared. Some time before the seminars started, Mary Crowley said she felt led to make it possible for the whole family to be together at the final seminar in Dallas. It was an imaginative gift, such as Mary is talented in thinking of . . . but I am certain it was "led."

When people speak about "living by faith" as if one had to

be penniless and pray for funds to do such a thing, they forget
all about the fact that when God answers prayer, He puts it in
the mind or minds of people who do have money, or material
goods, or harvests of one or another sort, dug out of the ground,
cut from trees, grown in gardens, made in lumber mills—whatever—to give certain portions of that harvest to one or another
specific person or groups of people. To carelessly try to get money,
or to carelessly give it without prayer for direction from the Lord,
is an ignoring of "practicing faith" or "living by faith," it seems
to me. But to pray for the Lord's clear guidance, direction, and
help in giving is just as much a demonstration of faith as to
pray for money to do a project, feed poor orphans, give the message of truth to a certain "tribe or nation," or another endeavor.
There are people of great faith throughout history, who have
been the ones the Lord has directed in such ways as to care for
Dohnavur in India, China Inland Mission, college education for
various young people, clothing for others, or vacations or times
of refreshing for weary ones, as well as people of great faith
who have prayed for needs.

Mary, as I was saying, had felt clearly led to provide this togetherness for our family at the last seminar. It was because of that
gift that Kirsty Macaulay, then eleven, had what had been an
urgent prayer in her life answered. "Please, Lord," she had prayed
for some years, "may I see my greatgrandfather before he dies."
There in the hospital room in Watertown, right after Father's
last stroke but while he was still conscious, stood Kirsty, along
with Susan, Ranald, and the others, having her prayer marvelously
answered, because she was on her way to Dallas, her first time
in America. But it wasn't just Kirsty's prayer answered. . . . That
gift meant an exciting joy in our sitting on the floor together at
the front of the auditorium, sharing that film as a *family*. It also
meant that I was able to be at my father's funeral *with* my children,
and with Ranald preaching the sermon. That is the kind of thing
no human being could know about and plan for. It points up
the priceless value of having a Heavenly Father who is all-wise,
who "knows" the future, to consult, and to ask!

There was a tremendous mixture in our being there that evening,
John with his leg in a cast, Udo on crutches, my having just
made father's funeral arrangements by phone, listening as Fran

ended the seminars with a final message which he had said to me before: "Edith, I can't . . . I'm too exhausted. . . . It isn't possible" . . . and then giving it with a power which exceeded all the others! If ever he had preached with the Lord's power, with a "tongue of fire," it was in that night's lecture. The warmth of the response was overwhelming. I remember looking over and seeing John, surrounded by about one hundred-fifty fellows wanting to continue discussion, saying afterwards, "L'Abri must do more in America. Franky's been so right in doing this film." If ever the walls of the chalets and houses of L'Abri seemed pushed out to include many, many more, it was that night with seven thousand there—Trisa's music (classical tapes) filling the place, and conversations continuing nonstop. How right had been the guidance, in spite of all hindrances and attacks, to "endure to the end" with this film and seminars.

We returned to our hotel in a bit of a glow. Within a minute the phone rang and it was Wendy: "I feel terrible, but all commercial flights are full because of colleges getting out for spring vacations. There are *no* flights for six people and a baby to Wilmington for the funeral!" Crash! Six of us were going (Sue giving her place to Ran because she wanted him to preach the service), the rest going to a beach with the children to wait for us for a short family reunion after the funeral. Ned and Sue Walters, who had become Christians through our books, in Wilmington, Delaware, had found out about the funeral, and kindly opened their home to us as "home" during that time. But—how were we going to get there? It had to be the next morning. I sat dejectedly praying: "Please, Lord, show the way."

There was a swift answer in a time of urgency. The phone rang again. This time John Lomax asked, "How are things going?" When I told him of the new blow, he said, "Wait a minute," and hung up. In no more than fifteen minutes he called back. "Dorget and I thought of our friend who has wanted to do us a favor with his private plane. He has said, 'Of course.' It will be ready at Love Field tomorrow morning, with room for six adults, and a half seat for the baby!" Exultation of thanksgiving— to Dorget and John, but really to the Lord, who is able!

But the phone was to ring again immediately. It was Priscilla: "Mother, we've just had a call from Barry Seagren. The chapel is burning in Huémoz. It started sometime in the middle of the night. It was discovered by a man driving his car down the mountain, who honked his horn until he had the village awake. Betty wakened and began calling other chalets. Everyone ran down to help—Workers, students, the village pastor, then finally the village firemen. L'Abri people were carrying out tape recorders and tapes and books, but as it started in the cupboard (a vacuum cleaner had been used to clean out ashes from the fireplace!), all of Dolly Johnson's thirty years of collected music was destroyed. They're having a prayer meeting at Barry and Veronica's now, and Veronica is giving hot chocolate to the ones who have been out fighting the fire."

"Tongues of fire to preach thy word"—that is the prayer, the song, the cry of the heart of each of us who really believe truth is true, and that time slips by quickly. But there is a battle. This seemed so vivid a battle that we were sure Satan was fighting back. Deaths, funerals, operations, illnesses; now a blackened chapel, a ruined organ—beauty exchanged for ashes for a very real period of time. This was not an act in a play that can be watched and then discussed at home, not a page in a book that can be turned to discover something better on the next page. Rather these were realities of "battle scars" that made a difference in history—in the history of Dutch L'Abri, in Anky's life, in my sister's life and our communication with father, in the history of Huémoz L'Abri that very summer and the next two years. Blows in the battle which are made by Satan do not "enter the water and cause no ripple" in history. The blows are real . . . but the victories are real also. This is what it is all about when God tells us to endure to the end! We have some miles to go yet.

We had a precious time of communication flying alone—an incredible time, when most planes were grounded because of storm, that the sky from Dallas to Wilmington was "open"! It was a time of being uninterrupted, shut away from phones and people, with sandwiches to satisfy our hunger. It was a time of seriousness of life that in a way clarified the air of inconsequentials and allowed us to have very important communication we can't often have—not all six people at a time, but two by two. When we reached our destination, the Walterses made us all as much at home as if we had been on our "old family homestead." We had a rare time of being with my sister Elsa and her husband Roger, as well as with nieces and nephews . . . with Barney at the organ, later in the evening giving us a piano recital (he is a concert pianist, John Barnes Van Buskirk, and we hadn't been able to hear him play very often in life).

Strange how at a funeral people from so many parts of life gather. That church was full of people who were in earlier chapters of this book! Vida, father's sister's daughter; people who had known father in China; Betty Schlichter, daughter of a friend in Wenchow, who has done the stencils for my Family Letter all these years; Margaret Walker from Stevens; Allan MacRae from the Biblical Theological Seminary; Paul Wooley from Westminster; people from our Chester church and from father's Wilmington church. Yet there was no time to really talk, not even to the "two Annes" from Japan. Whish—a warm handshake, a feeling of oneness in looking forward to heaven together, a sudden recognition of what "time" really means—and car motors are starting up, people are looking at their watches, someone is remembering a chicken burning (if they really had forgotten to turn the oven down). Amazing, isn't it? Titanically big emotions, and the trivial ones, all mixed, consuming our attention. At the grave it was good to be with the intimate family, and to have my children there—my sister and the cousins—and to see mother's grave too. To read her name, and his, side by side, waiting for the Lord's return, having walked together after the wedding in China brought her up from fifty paces behind to father's side. Their life. An end, but a future.

After a family reunion at the seaside, with long-lasting though not "perfect" memories, because of various illnesses, we were soon back in various parts of L'Abri. Fran and I were not there for long, as first we had to go back to Chicago for his part in the beginning of an Inerrancy Council and for my speaking at Kalamazoo at a conference of Women Alive, after which we both were to speak in York University outside of Toronto. There are a number of "threads" that have been woven from that time (one Jewish family in L'Abri right now, as a direct result), but among them was our long and quiet conversation with Dr. Koop, who was there as a speaker also. He spoke of the possibility of stopping at Swiss L'Abri after a medical convention in Sweden. When we returned, after that and the nonstop list of seminars, we were exhausted. "Why don't you," said each of our family with different suggestions, "take a really long rest? You can't keep up this pace."

Debby and Udo began to look in newspapers for ads of apartments for rent. "You should have a place not far away, where we can come and take you for tea, and walk with you on the quay. You should be near the lake and take lake boat rides, or take a rowboat out, or go by the blue train to Saanen and walk. Be near enough so you don't have to travel, but out of reach of telephone, hidden, so that you can rest a long time."

The search finally brought results. A tiny old house was being renovated, in an alley, out of sight. It seemed to be the right "vacation." We were to move in June 1. Gospel Films had given us a gift for a vacation which enabled us to furnish it, and we had fun browsing in secondhand shops. It seemed *much* better than traveling one more time—anywhere. At first we were so tired, Fran said he thought his heaviness would never get less and that we'd have to take short walks and sit on benches! But as the days went on, the walks were longer, and we were gardening in the patch of ground we shared with a neighbor, and enjoying eating outside, surrounded by the bushes Debby and Udo had had planted. "This is really peaceful," we said. *"Bonjour"*—that was to a neighbor walking by. "This is like starting a retired life in a new neighborhood." *"Bonjour, madame . . . monsieur . . . bonjour."* People were friendly. We could start another life altogether! Interesting thought. I went back to the book I was reading aloud to Fran, after pouring him another cup of tea. This is what people do in Florida! "Oh, Fran, look at the little blue train . . . just above that church spire, on its way to Gstaad. Doesn't it look like a wonderful Lionel train set? What a place this is. . . . Listen to the six o'clock bells."

Yes, it was June 1 when we moved in. It was June 28 that Dr. C. Everett Koop gave his lectures in our chapel in Huémoz. We had seen him the day before, but we were in our "hidden vacation," so the lecture hadn't anything to do with us. Not then. June 29, early in the morning, Franky's green Toyota came to a sudden stop in front of our kitchen-everything-room window, which is right on the alley. *Wonder why he's here so early.* . . . "Hi, Franky." . . . "Dad, I've got to talk to you. Chick Koop gave a wonderful lecture last night on abortion, infanticide, and euthanasia, and then came up to our house and we talked almost all night. Look—we have to *do* something, before it's too late. . . . We have to make a movie, combined with the biblical answers. This is really serious, and people are ignorant of the extent of what is going on." A very long discussion took place, after which Fran was convinced that he should say "yes" to Franky's urgent request that he start working on a new project right away—a project that would lead to a book and film made with Dr. Koop, to speak to the issues that needed defining, and to the alternatives. The *when* was "now," "immediately," "no time to be wasted."

Meantime Franky and Jim Buchfuehrer had been talking on the phone and had reached a certainty that they should start a company to make this film, and also to do whatever God would lead them to do in films or in other ways, to fight the battles that needed to be fought in the twentieth century. They chose the name of Franky Schaeffer V Productions for this nonprofit company in which they would work in partnership. Jim was to be the producer and Franky the director of a series of films which would go with a book and study guide titled *Whatever Happened to the Human Race?* As Fran started to work and collaborate with Chick, Franky took whatever pages were finished so he could begin thinking of visuals and working on a film script, and the "skeleton" soon began to be put together.

As Fran spread out the research material in piles on the floor and set up the big kitchen table in the little living room, I "retreated" into another little room, put blank paper in my typewriter, and wrote a title: "Affliction." A new book began to grow! I read a chapter at a time to Fran, as he liked to have that "break" in which to lie down and listen. I hoped it might encourage him in the new "affliction" of work amidst exhaustion. Neither of us knew how much we were going to need that book ourselves— we and our family—within a year of its being finished!

Each week as time went on, Fran went up to Huémoz for the Saturday night discussion—held in the drab village schoolhouse because of the chapel being a black ruin at that time. We also had Sunday dinner each week for from twenty to twenty-eight people in our Chalet Chardonnet, with Mary Jane and Linny helping me to cook and serve. Conversation, as Fran headed the table, often went on until 6:00 P.M.! We had our special day of fasting and prayer for the rebuilding of the chapel, starting the morning in that same drab schoolroom, with the bedraggled tinsel from the former Christmas still dangling from the lights, earnestly praying for our chapel to be restored, with its clear glass windows overlooking the mountains and the Rhone valley below.

The word of God to Jehoshaphat in the Old Testament comforted us a lot at that time: "Be not afraid nor dismayed by reason of this great multitude, for the battle is not yours but God's." We weren't thinking simply of the succession of "attacks" we had been living through, but of the great multitude the new book and film would be stirring up against us! Abortion, infanticide, euthanasia—the sin and horror of treating the murder of one's own children as something to be compared with having a wart taken off a finger, should be something people would recognize after being told, and say, "Thanks. Never thought of it before." Some would . . . but an "organized multitude" would be fighting back! Far from retiring, in any sense of the word, we were getting ready to do what the next verse speaks of—"Tomorrow go down against them . . ."—in a realistic and exposed way. We were entering a new, but essential, battle for life.

My manuscript "Affliction" was finished on October 2, 1977, and Dick Baltzell (at that time vice-president of Fleming H. Revell Co.) came to pick it up and read it in Villars. As we went over it, neither he nor I knew how much the contents were going to mean to us in the months ahead. So often books mean more to people who work on them than to anyone else who is to read them. As for Fran, his work was completed on his manuscript, as was the work of the researchers and of Dr. Koop, and by the next April the film script was finished and bound, ready for the work to commence. Franky, Jim, and Allan (one of the camera and lighting men) traveled together to "block" in preparation for the timing of the filming, which was to take place in August, September, and October of 1978. No one had any idea what an exact "block" of time that was going to be in Fran's life. Just before we were to leave for filming in Philadelphia, I had to have a cyst removed by my gynecologist, so a time in Samaritain Hospital preceded our annual day of fasting and prayer July 30. Priscilla and I shared the leading of the opening meeting that day, and the next day Fran and I were driven by friends to the airport, where a wheelchair met me to get me to the waiting SwissAir plane. I couldn't walk that much yet.

Philadelphia was hot. One of the first scenes Fran needed to speak for was in the city dump, among the squashed cars and dirty puddles. As we sat for hours, taking and retaking shots here and there, I spent my time inside a car, when the temperature was well over 100°. I had a notebook, to use my time usefully in between praying for the shots and all the difficulties that were presenting themselves! The notebook and pen were for writing an article I wanted to compose and get off for a deadline—to be entitled "Christmas at L'Abri." The snow was a bit difficult to visualize, but it did cool me a bit!

As we spent much time in the Children's Hospital, we could understand how it was that Chick became so strong in his stand against abortion. Right out of the windows of the intensive care unit, where the babies he had operated on were often small premature babies and where nurses and doctors were fighting so faithfully for life, one could look into the windows of another hospital, into the very area where normal babies, premature but with no defects, were being killed by abortion methods. In my Bible I have a picture of a dear baby for whom I pray daily. He could have been aborted, and in his big brown eyes I see all those aborted babies. "Why," I ask, "can people think of them with the same emotion as for a cyst, or a tumor? . . . It seems so ignorant, in a supposedly educated country." The time in that hospital was the beginning of intensive filming in a variety of places, the results of which you will see in *Whatever Happened to the Human Race?* During the filming, as well as during the seminars, I was to receive an education and to gain an intensity about this battle for "life."

I'd love to take you from place to place in the filming—from Dr. Koop's hospital with the children we fell in love with, to the California beach where Craig sat eating our delicious sandwiches in between the episodes of shooting. Tense moments always come in filming, I'm sure, but somehow this film seemed to be a target Satan would want to hit. Each day as the films were sent to the laboratory, we prayed for safe arrival and for chemical solutions which would have no error to mar this film. Human beings, and computers, can make mistakes. For the scenes being shot at the beach, a monument had been made and hauled on a truck out to the sand. To protect it from vandals, Jim ended up staying all night as the hired guard copped out. Fran stood his ground while the helicopter in the scene came close, then flew out to sea, although each time the sand was whirled up around his head until his face and hair felt sand-blasted. He continually held his head high, in case he might "spoil a shot," while the rest of us crouched out of sight behind the monument, bending our heads and covering them with our hands. We hadn't brought food out into the dunes, and the shots took longer than we thought they would, so the few English black currant candies were the only thing I had in my pocketbook to keep us all from "starvation"—well, from dry dusty throats anyway. All this took place near that monument at the end of episode three (the "still picture" taken by Mus is opposite page 118 in the book).

For past, present, and future history, you must come to Israel and have glimpses of a few of the unforgettable moments. Yad Vashem is the monument in Jerusalem to the six million Jews and others killed in the Nazi holocaust. To film in there after midnight, wandering through the dark, sitting in corners out of the way of the cameras, was a chilling experience. At one point, we were taken, Fran and I, through those enormous banks of records—alphabetized files with the names and facts about the individuals who died, a flame burning in memory, kept open for relatives wanting to search for evidence of someone's having been included in the millions, or for a relative bringing evidence to add to the files. A very different kind of cemetery for 6,000,000 people, but a cemetery nevertheless.

Where is the cemetery for the 7,000,000 babies already killed in the United States, with names and records of who they might have been? I sat there wondering about this as Fran stood speaking in front of that glass case with a baby's shoe, with the number of babies killed during the holocaust. It seemed incongruous to eat a dinner in the night, set out on a long table in part of the museum. An Israeli still-photographer who sat next to me said, "I never let my wife or daughters come here. We had people die in our family,

and I think it is too traumatic for them to be reminded so graphically. Why not fill your mind with beauty?"

When we awakened at 4:00 A.M. in the youth hostel in the Sinai desert, Franky and the cameramen had already left to get the very early light, and the rising sun and mists near the mountains. A wobbly old aluminum kettle on a gas ring in the stone courtyard boiled a bit of water, and Genie and I and Jessica and Francis shared a bit of the "liquid"—which is about all you could call the tea—before we went off in our truck. To describe the ride, and the Bedouins we passed, would take a chapter, as the women were going off with animals to graze them on higher pastures, while the men sat down comfortably to a day of smoking and talking. Liberated women! They do all the work. We soon were sharing our cold box breakfast picnics with Bedouin children, as we waited in the stony valley for the helicopter to take the equipment up to the top of Mount Sinai—Fran, Sally, the script and continuity girl, the cameramen and sound man, etc., etc. Genie and the children then went up, and next Franky kindly let me go, along with Judy, Jim's wife, so no one got left behind. What an experience flying over the narrow, tortuous trails going up the rocky mountain, and seeing the surprising bits of fertile patches here and there.

As Fran stood on the rocks at the very top, Franky shouted, "Don't change the position of your feet, Dad." . . . "What do you mean? My feet are so wedged I couldn't move if I tried," answered Fran. His shoes still have the marks of those rock scratches on them! The helicopter hovered near him to get the closeups of his speaking about Moses, and about the fact that the Bible is giving accurate history. Moses said to the people, "You saw, you heard." It is a thrilling scene to watch as the film taken from the helicopter shows you more of the whole of the Sinai desert than we could see from where we were sitting on the rocks. Tim Simonec's music, so majestic and perfect in making vivid the reality of the wonder of that time, was not there as we watched and listened to Fran, over and over, that day. We had only the sound of wind in our ears!

When Franky was filming the last day of the progress of Abraham and Isaac up the mountain to build the altar, the temperature was 114° in the blazing sun. It was a hard job of directing with the ram involved and the stones cutting the sandaled feet of the men, as well as timing the work to have it all done before sundown. I was trying to hide in some of the scrubby bushes at the base, around on a side no one could see. The area was the one where Bishop Pike died—very hard to find one's way, if one were alone. I thought of that as I became violently ill, and dizzier, as the minutes went by, praying I wouldn't die on the spot. As we returned to the kosher hotel in which we were staying, the fine Jewish doctor with his proper yarmulke on his curly dark head, pronounced, "You have a fever of over 103°, and you have a violent food poisoning." "But . . . I've only eaten in this hotel!" "I don't care, you have food poisoning. Take these pills and drink nothing but Coca-Cola." It seemed impossible, but it was 80-year-old Irma Lambie, the widow of Doctor Tom Lambie (Uncle Tom of my childhood), who heard I was ill and came bringing me three bottles of Coca-Cola after she had been at church at the garden tomb! She is a nurse, still running the hospital in Bethlehem which her husband built.

After we filmed that cool, breezy, middle-of-the-night period of time at the garden tomb, we had to go back so that Jim could leave a gift for the mission there. It was the lunch hour, and the gate was locked. We rang the bell, and through a little speaking tube Franky announced it was "Dr. Schaeffer." Suddenly the gate opened and we were welcomed with great enthusiasm by Colonel and Mrs. Dobbs (whose daughter had been helped at L'Abri years before) and by Bishop Goodwin-Hudson, who also had been at L'Abri. To say the least, Franky and Jim, and our Israeli taxi driver who had said, "You can't get in at *lunch* time," were all surprised. That really was an amazing place to find "threads" we didn't expect to be woven into the pattern there at all.

It was September 18, 1978, when we left at dawn to drive to the spot Franky had selected on the shore of Galilee. I know because I have my prayer during that day, written on the back of the menu from the Hotel Tiberias Plaza. We had camp chairs set up, and the children played quietly in the sand as the men set up their cameras and arranged the wood for a fire. Franky inspected the catch of fish and talked a bit to the fishermen. "How do you like the boat? I looked all over the sea for the oldest one I could find," said Franky, as he began pulling at the net and arranging the corks. Somehow that day seemed the one that brought me closest to the feeling of reality of this being ground that Jesus had walked on in space and time and history. Past history . . . with our feet on it in present history. And, once again both Jesus' feet and our feet will walk on it in future history. Fabulous. True. No fantasy about it. The quiet soft breeze in the grasses, the ordinariness of the stones and sand and water emphasized the historicity to me. Our ordinary world, made by our extraordinary God. I sat in the grasses praying.

What did I pray? . . . That this clear presentation of the fire, the boat, the nets, the footprints, the fish, the bread, be well done, and be convincing to many. I prayed that, as Franky directed, the end result might be that men would come to know, with Thomas, that Christ is God indeed. I prayed that Fran would remember his lines, and then give them with real conviction and freshness, with strength and awe and wonder. I also prayed that, as he felt so exhausted, God would for one day more give him His strength with which to do this task. Then suddenly, as the cameramen and sound man and others pulled out the radio, the news of Camp David blared forth—"Carter, Begin, and Sadat announce . . . peace for Israel!" Our Israeli crew went wild with joy, one thinking of his thirteen-year-old son, "Now, no more war." I prayed, "Peace for Israel? Oh Lord, how long? . . . but please give these men the source of real peace, lasting peace."

When the announcement came from Franky, "Cut . . . that's the last shot," we all with one accord, without previous agreement, rushed into the sea and swam in the warm water. Fran had his bathing suit with him, but I dashed in with shorts and jersey. Never has water felt so wonderful, or so exciting. Imagine . . . the water that Jesus walked on, and Peter began to sink in. It all happened near here! Francis, Jessica, Genie, Fran, Franky, Jim, Judy—and I'm sure Sally and all the crew too—will never forget the joy of that moment . . . each in their own way, and for their own reasons.

Fran's tiredness was growing harder to go on with, but we thought it was just the pressure of travel and work—the heat and diversity of "schedule," with early mornings, late nights, and trips like the one to the Dead Sea, where, among other things, Chick performed his part on the salt wastes of the area in which

Sodom and Gomorrah probably stood. Some who have seen the film have said he stood on ice . . . but it was salt, and has been salt since the devastation of what must have been fertile before.

We arrived in Switzerland, to do the rest of the fourth and fifth episodes in our chalet. Night after night, with the windows covered with rice paper and with brilliant banks of light outside, Fran went on with his memorizing and speaking his lines, but with increasing weariness that I kept praying about. Sally remarked to Franky one night, "What's wrong with these jackets? Get one of the others; these are too big for your dad." "But," said Franky, "they're the same ones!" It was that night, on his way to come down for the next shot, that Fran stepped on the scales to weigh himself. He had lost twenty-five pounds! Dr. Gandur had examined him that week and had been worried because his spleen was enlarged. He wanted Fran to go to the hospital for a check-up. But . . . "Not until after the filming," Fran insisted. During the filming by that blazing fire, with Fran's Bible on the table, Debby and Udo, Franky and I had a "break-time" conversation while the crew were eating orange rolls I had made and drinking coffee or hot chocolate. "Mother, why don't you look up that doctor in Mayo Clinic daddy's been writing to and call up right now? He could have something serious." So, with Udo and Debby agreeing, and Prisca and John too (although the filming took place after midnight, into the wee hours, the family had been coming in and out to watch a bit), Udo took me over to his office after I looked up the correspondence, and I dialed Mayo Clinic's number.

Incredible thing, the telephone. Imagine what my mother and father would have felt if they could have called their parents in China in 1900? I twirled those numbers, and soon I was given Dr. Victor Wahby's beeper number 444! In no time flat Victor was on the phone, listening to the symptoms, and urging, "Come as soon as possible. Finish up the film if it's only a couple of days, then come early next week. I'll meet your plane." You see, Victor had read *The God Who Is There* and *Escape from Reason* and others of Fran's books in Cairo and Lebanon when he was a medical student and needed the help of the clear answers to his own questions at that time. He was eager to be of help now.

Fran went on with the filming that night and in the gorgeous sunshine of the next day. We had had rain for a week, causing work for the gaffers as they changed the paper in the storms, but when the mountain shots were needed, the sunrise, and the full sun on the hill as Fran walked up, a stupendous clarity came to air and sky, and the ending of episode four was "in the can." As Fran walked up the hill, he puffed, not his usual way of walking. But the words were clear, and important. "Each man, woman, and child is of great value. . . . We know our origin. . . . As I look at myself in the flow of space-time reality, I see my origin in Adam and Eve, the parents of the whole human race—and in God's creating man in His own image. At this point, words such as *sanctity of life, justice, fulfillment, truth, beauty* and *love* begin to make real sense again." The music came . . . and the beauty of the truth and the green of the fields, the sound of the cowbells in the distance, the mountain peaks glistening with snow stayed in our memories . . . whether that "our" refers to those who watched the filming that day or to those who sit watching the screen time after time.

For Fran, a job had been completed, and the future history of his own life was a question mark. What would be found in the complete examination in Mayo Clinic? His verbalization at that time consisted mostly of, "Well, whatever happens, I've finished this job anyway."

CANCER: AN ENDING? OR A NEW BEGINNING? 24

ood-bys are always hard when there has been a certain never-to-be-repeated time of closeness. Franky had a Swiss fondue party for the crew in an old chalet restaurant farther up in the mountains, and time was spent in thinking back over the weeks we had had together. We laughed, joked, and teased, but conversation became really serious too, as the possibility of being together again seemed remote. Amnon, the photographer, took a book with him to read as his English was pretty good; Buchman, the gaffer, and Etienne we told we would get a copy of *The God Who Is There* given to them after they got back to Israel, as they could read the Hebrew translation, but didn't know enough English. Sally was going back to Hollywood, Jim to Los Gatos, and we were to be on our way to Mayo Clinic. That film-making was now history!

During the last of the voice-over, as Franky worked with Fran and the sound man, I had been making many phone calls—for plane tickets and for the needed new passport, as Fran's had run out. We had help from Len Rogers, who drove us to Zurich himself Monday night and jogged early Tuesday morning to find the quickest route to the Embassy so that we were able to get Fran's new passport in record time. We got to the airport just in time to make it into the already waiting line to board the plane. In

611

Chicago, Jay Kesler (alerted by Len) met us and saw that we had a good meal during our three-hour wait for the flight to Rochester. We were on our way for "a week of tests," we said, with a bit of a gnawing uncertainty as to what those tests might reveal. As we walked into the Rochester airport for the first time in our lives, looking around with curiosity at our first glimpse of Minnesota, there were Victor Wahby, Mary, an anaesthetist in St. Mary's Hospital and Dr. Carl Morlock. And from another side, Avis Dieseth stepped up, surprising us, as she had made the trip especially from Fergus Falls to see that we were cared for and settled in a hotel room. At a time when we didn't yet know we would need it, the Lord had surrounded us with loving welcome that was going to be a comfort. As we prayed together that night in the hotel room, it was with the expectation of probably being a little late for a speaking engagement in Holland. Dr. Wahby had arranged a hospital room in St. Mary's for Fran the next morning. That made us a little apprehensive, although it sounded sensible as he had said all the tests could be made more conveniently and quickly that way.

Our prayer time together the next night, as I sat by Fran's hospital bedside, came after the EKG, blood tests and so on had been taken, and Dr. Wahby had stated firmly, "Tomorrow morning we'll have you upstairs to take one of those glands out of your neck, and have a biopsy." How strong at that moment the reality was of excruciating uncertainty as to what the report would be in the morning. But how strong the reality was also of having the eternal God, Infinite and Personal, as our Father who could stay in the hospital room with Fran, and also go down the hall and out into the street and back to the hotel with me! The truth of God's Word and His promises stood out sharply, as clearly as a landscape in a brilliant flash of lightning. We *can* cry out to Him with our requests, knowing He loves us, and we can *also* tell Him of our trust and appreciate His sovereignty more than ever before. It is not a dichotomy to "ask that the Father may be glorified in the Son," yet also to go on shifting our emphasis minutes later to loving and trusting God "no matter what," realizing that in "the battle" Satan is trying to make us stop trusting God. In the tightrope moments in our walk in life, dusty or heated theological discussions have no place; we need all our concentration and energy to *live* moment by moment in practical ways in the balance of truth which God has put for us in His Word. This is the time it counts, and when we have our opportunity to "run to our Father," with trust.

I went back to the hotel to spend most of the night awake and praying. I could honestly thank God for a list of small comforts—the pleasantness of Fran's hospital room with small panes of glass, brown woodwork, blue and white curtains, and a print of a Dutch painting on the wall; the fact that he had a telephone by his bed from which he could dial out at any time, and that I had one in the hotel room. We prayed together over the phone that night, before he went to sleep.

In the morning as they brought him in a wheelchair from the surgery, sunshine was pouring in through the window that looked out onto the side street. We held hands, looked out at the yellow leaves, lighted as a lantern with the sun, and Fran told me the news. He looked little—as if he'd lost more weight and had been sick a long time—as he spoke the awful words that turned our world upside down. We wept as I leaned into the wheelchair, the arms poking into my ribs . . . and held onto each other. Then a nurse came to help him back into bed, and he dried his tears and said immediately, "The children must hear it in my voice; dial them for me." So, one by one, each in the place they were in Switzerland, and in England, Fran talked to them separately: "The gland is malignant, and the lymph system is involved."

Strange, the sharpness of the words—"malignant," "cancer"—like a sudden change of music that speaks of disaster ahead in the story the music is accompanying. Yet, as Debby remarked, and each of us echoed in our own way, we are always living on the edge of disaster, change, shock, or attack. Peace, and the affluence to enjoy that peace, are always a false separation from the reality of the raging battle. Our perspective gets sadly out of line when things go along too smoothly and comfortably and when all the shocks are someone else's shocks that filter through to us a bit blurred. Not only is our understanding blurred of what the Fall actually consists of, but our understanding of the absolute *marvel* of what God has done for us in making victory certain and complete is dimmed when we can rush on without interruption in our scheduled days, ticking the items neatly off our lists!

Fran talked from his telephone to Birdie in the Samaritan Hospital in Vevey, where she was waiting for an operation—a wonderful connection, not just of voices over sea and land, but of understanding in such a moment in her life and Fran's, as she has cancer very similar to Fran's and had to have her spleen removed. It's rather startling how often we need to share immediately "the comfort wherewith we have been comforted" when we are just beginning to "open the box," so to speak. But the Comforter, the Holy Spirit, has more to replenish what we give to each other out of the supply box when "each other" is in need. Direct comfort? Yes, but we also need horizontal comfort . . . and that is a two-way thing. It is all too easy to be selfish about our sorrows, as well as our joys. Yet we are finite, and we need quiet aloneness with family and friends that is right to protect. Jesus didn't take the crowds into the Garden with Him to pray for his agonizing hour. He who came to die for all who would believe, also understands the small numbers a finite person can be close to.

It was Tuesday the 10th of October when we arrived in Rochester; Wednesday the 11th when Fran entered the hospital; Thursday the 12th when we heard he had cancer; and on Friday the 13th Debby and Franky were on their way over. Billy Zeoli had been bringing someone to L'Abri and was in Switzerland when he heard the news, so quickly made tickets available for our children. Fran had just had the CAT scan and the bone marrow test before they arrived, but the results were not going to be given us until Tuesday afternoon. Fran was allowed out of the hospital Saturday night, so we had a waiting time together before the next news. "Marking time" is never the way to wait, I would say; creative ideas need to begin to take place in one's imagination, whether the waiting involves giving children an interesting time in a dentist's office with a puzzle to do or a book to read, or using time to have orange juice and a worthwhile conversation while waiting for a fog to lift and the plane to take off! Even in times of shock, waiting can be something more than sitting in abject fear. Our days of waiting were filled with a variety of things. Looking back on it, I don't think I'd do anything differently.

First of all, Sunday morning Franky, Debby, Fran, and I had one of those very rare times in life of sharing thoughts in the midst of a sharp perspective that occurs when time and space are not central, and when basic truth and God's Word take the center of thoughts and feelings. For two hours we exchanged thoughts and spoke of things that had helped *us* in the Bible. Fran read the last three chapters of Revelation to us, which filled us with fresh appreciation and expectation of all that is ahead when Jesus comes. Franky gave a report of a fine sermon he had heard on affliction. Debby brought us something from Peter, and I went over some of the Psalm verses and the prayers recorded in the margins of my Bible that had been especially comforting through the last years, ending with the reading of Psalm 71. We all then prayed in the context of verses 17–20 of Psalm 71—a very deep and fervent time of prayer together.

How does one pray at such a time? Does one make it just a begging to have the illness taken away? The perspective needs to be kept straight: the really important spiritual needs come first. In the face of life and death, the balance should be felt even more keenly. The healing of any spiritual needs is so much more of a "miracle" than the words "take up thy bed and walk." Jesus said so.

"Don't let any one of us stop trusting you now, Lord. Please may our love be real for you—solid oak, not a thin veneer. This is the time that counts for your glory; don't let us blow it." The telephone rings and I talk for a while. Then . . . "Please, Father, give us victory in whatever the present battle is in the heavenlies. May Satan be disappointed." It is a time for asking to be able to see and feel things from heaven's perspective rather than using all the time in agonizing. Then can't we pray for our loved husband and father (friend, brother, sister, wife, child, cousin, aunt, uncle, grandfather, grandmother, mother) to get well again? Yes, of course, that is the freedom of choice given us in bringing our requests rather than in worrying. We're not asked to stop making specific requests; the opposite is true. Accepting God's Word as *true* gives freedom which is beyond finite understanding. We are meant to live in the teaching of God's Word, practically—not just to use it as a source of difficult things to argue about! That day we felt real freedom to pray that God would give Fran—

Dad—"time and strength to show forth God's strength and power to the next generation." We were thinking of his own grandchildren, but also of other young people. Both kinds of prayer have to take place in the land of the living, and also in the midst of *real history*—not in the context of religious exercises.

Sunday evening Avis and Bob Dieseth came to have dinner with us. They told us of the househunting they had been doing for us, simply by driving up one street and down another. The "creative idea" I felt imperative was to make a home for Fran as soon as possible, if he were to stay here for treatment—whether he had six weeks or six months to live! By Monday Debby and I had gone to see the little brown townhouse Avis and Bob had found, and Fran and Franky walked there together later in the day. It was a definite possibility. Phone calls continued to come from Susan and Priscilla, keeping us in close communication. You see, one of the doctors had told Franky and Debby that there wasn't much hope of Fran's living—perhaps not more than three weeks.

Why a "home"? I would answer that home is important to a person to help him or her get well, as well as being important for family times together if someone is dying. In either case, beauty and familiar surroundings have an effect on the physical, psychological, and even spiritual state. Of course, it isn't always possible to rent a place, but imagination should be used to do as much as possible with what is available. Figuring out how to make a place beautiful with water-soluble paint to cover the wallpaper, with furniture and plants, etc., not only is going to help the togetherness *in* the place later, but is healthy for active minds. Doing interior decorating inside your head while in a hospital or clinic waiting room is a positive creative activity—as well as a way of planning for demonstrating your love and concern for the person you love.

Franky used Monday to get Heinz on his way with some of the rough footage of the film, so that his father could sit that evening and see it. Fran was filled with rejoicing and tearful thanksgiving for the beauty of what was there in the unedited film. We thanked God over and over again for His timing. We had had to give up a shot in Greece when permission to use a monument was rescinded . . . but that extra week made it possible for Fran's part to be completed a week earlier. Now we knew it was just in time! We watched the shots at Sinai and at Galilee, on the shore where Jesus, in His resurrected body, prepared a fire. "What a gorgeous series of shots . . . it was well done" was a song in Fran's heart, as well as in all of ours. As we considered it in the waiting time of Tuesday's diagnosis, it somehow brought all of life in focus—the importance of doing things *well* for the Lord, as well as for the results of what we are doing, and in spite of the hard things in each day's work.

Tuesday, October 17, brought the second wave of shock when Dr. Petitt kindly spent an hour and a quarter with Fran and me carefully and frankly explaining that Fran had lymphoma, a malignancy of the lymph glands, which had entered the bone marrow with a 30 percent invasion. That is not bone cancer, but a blood system malignancy that cannot be treated with radiation or cobalt, but with chemotherapy. Dr. Petitt suggested a program of twenty-one day cycles, with the formula COPA to be injected intravenously, followed by five days of pills and then sixteen days of rest from the medicine. By this time many suggestions had come by phone, to go elsewhere, stay in homes of friends, to try this or that. We had all been praying for guidance, and before we went to see Dr. Petitt that day Fran said, "This is how I am asking for clarity as to how I should choose. I've told the Lord that if I feel comfortable with Dr. Petitt and like him, I'll say, 'You're my doctor; I am staying here in Rochester.' If not, I'll say, 'Thank you very much.'" When the course of action was laid out, before five minutes were over I heard Fran saying, "Dr. Petitt, you're my doctor. . . ." And within a half-hour Fran was in a bed with an IV drip in his arm, getting his first chemotherapy! "Be careful," the nurse warned; "you may be violently ill before you get back to the hotel." My thought was, "A mild cream of potato soup, his favorite, whole wheat toast and some tea. . . . Then sleep; maybe he won't get nauseated."

The news had been a shock; in fact, it couldn't have been worse. The gathering of glands behind Fran's spleen was the size of a watermelon, and lymphoma was all through his system. However, the first thing to do was to try to get him in bed back at the hotel, with a light lunch as just described, and see if he would sleep. He slept—eighteen hours—waking only to want more soup and tea and toast, then falling off to sleep again. I had started taking steps to arrange for the house, and as Debby and Franky crept in and out of the room, each time they pulled back the covers to make sure he was breathing, as they feared he had died! That good sleep didn't seem possible. He never did vomit, and by the next day he was eating normally again.

By the end of the week the cleaning and painting of the little house was well under way, and curtains and furniture for the living room were too. Chuck Warren had been sent to help Debby and me shop and to get things fixed up. Franky seemed to have disappeared, and as we knew he had to go back to work (there were some other shots to be made for the film, etc.), we wondered where he was this last day. Why not with us? That evening Franky called us into his hotel bedroom: "Dad, I have something to show you." We gasped as we looked around. Fran said, "Franky, *how* did you bring all those over here?" "Look again, dad, *smell!*" The room was filled with turpentine odor, and obviously the paintings were wet! There were four canvases—major paintings, very like ones Franky had done for us at home—and four black and white drawings: one of the mountain view from our windows at home, one of Porto Fino where Genie had been given her ring, one still life, and one mother and child. "Franky, how could you possibly have done all that in one day? It isn't humanly possible!" "Well, dad, I went out and bought the stuff, then came in and prayed: 'Lord, I haven't painted for four years now, but please help me to do these paintings to make dad feel at home. I want to do this for him.' And—well, there they are."

Creativity *is* possible in the midst of a time of shock. That is one of the important things to tuck away in the back of your mind. And also, remember that it is possible to ask the Lord for help in creative projects at any time. Asking for "the impossible" was in its own way *just* as urgent a need to Franky, who had such a short time, as had been our need for the money to buy Mélèzes in 1955 so we could fill in the papers in time. *Time* and special urgency were involved. God cares about the details of our needs.

Susan, who had just crossed the ocean, got there in time to spend a weekend with us in the hotel and to see these paintings and spend time with Franky before he left. She witnessed this amazing diversity of answered prayer, which illustrates something very crucial for artists and creative people struggling with the importance of beauty and works of art, it seems to me: God Who made people in his image to have a capacity to be creative, *cares* about their bringing forth music and landscaped gardens, sculpture and paintings or tapestry, as well as a harvest of corn and grapes, and wood for fires. It is acceptable to pray for help in works of art, as well as for help in fair judgments, or good work in dentistry, surgery, or feeding the hungry. As we live out our attempt to have Christ as the Lord of the whole of life, we also may pray for help *in the whole of life* and *not* just in religious areas. The Bible is God's Word for the whole of life. His communication is for *our* living, not for specialized groups of experts, and our communication with Him is to be taking place in the whole of life, not in rarefied surroundings somewhere away from our work, but in the midst of it.

We had another very wonderful time of worship and communicating with each other that second Sunday, with Susan now there, and Chuck joining in. Such a time can't be planned for in the "schedule of life," but needs to be given time before everything else when a special moment arrives. Shutting the door on the world in order to communicate with each other and together with God is not selfish. In these rare moments when perspective is sharpened, as with a twist of a telescope, one finds that the focus is suddenly revealing things that were in a fog before. However, early that Sunday morning, Susan had scouted around town, finding a church, attending it, meeting some people. She did this the next week too, in another church. A further initiative resulted in her discovering the local library, from which she checked out art books, a history of Rochester, and an armload of classical records. It wasn't long until Susan was introducing us to people who wanted to help, and who became very real friends. But that is getting ahead of the story.

October is the month that Canadian geese fly in beautiful V-formation, swooping into Rochester, Minnesota, above the Mayo Clinic buildings and down to the Silver Lake area. They settle in to waddle around the park, float on the lake, delight people who come to feed them, annoy the farmers whose corn they steal, and give a landmark symbol to the town so that artists sketch them, and postcards and writing paper have them as the motif. The small lake is warmed by water that pours in from an electrical plant, and geese seem to have informed their friends and relatives that they can take a shorter trip for the winter months!

The story of the Mayo brothers, and the way Mayo Clinic became so sought out for medical help by people from all the corners of the earth, is a fascinating one. In many ways it parallels the L'Abri story, in that seemingly no one on earth would choose a small prairie town, so close to Laura Ingalls Wilder's "Little House on the Prairie," to begin a medical clinic that would one day be unique in the world and have respect and honor in medical circles from East to West. Although the town is only about sixty thousand in population, there are about twenty thousand patients to be counted in any one day, and about six hundred fifty consultants, plus one thousand more fellows, researchers, etc. With nurses studying there, and a graduate medical school, one is not exactly "out in the sticks." In fact, Rochester seems a crossroads of the world. Dr. Charles Mayo brought the first geese, not knowing what he was starting as a haven for geese. But I'm sure that as he and his brother also attracted the first people needing medical help, they had no idea what their clinic was going to become.

As we moved into our little brown house, the geese were honking and swooping overhead as if to announce something! There was something to be announced all right—but the geese didn't know it, nor did we. Fran was astonished at stepping into . . . "home." Debby and I in three days had found a combination of furniture, dishes, and curtains, and we had added house plants that had been given as gifts by Ray and Jean Smith and also by others. Dirt-filled wooden boxes on the square of cement outside the living room windows, with pine branches seeming to "grow," gave an instant garden! Franky's paintings, flower arrangements given by dear friends, Debby's gift of a silver-plated teapot and creamer and sugar bowl, ready for our first tea, and other things loaned or given by new and old friends and our children, helped to make home "instant." All these things, along with freshly painted walls, beds all made up with sheets, towels on the racks, and even some books on the coffee table, brought the same exclamation from each of us that day—Debby, Susan,

Fran and me: "Why, *this* seems like a new beginning . . . this is *home.*"

That night as the girls went to bed (there were two bedrooms) and I tucked them in, it was as if we had traveled in time to some period before they were married. It was the first time since they had married that I had had my children "home" to talk to as I sat on the end of the bed at night or to find before breakfast and chat over a cup of tea before getting dressed. Our lives haven't had time for that sort of visiting. Fran felt it too, exclaiming, "Why, we're seeing more of our children than we ever have since they married. This is really a special time." We appreciated it. We allowed ourselves to feel the feelings of appreciation and enjoyment of each other, in spite of the "ax hanging over our heads." We believe the priceless together times in life should be recognized as "rare" at whatever point they take place, without being destroyed by the fearful "what if . . . ?" After all, that is true whether cancer is the threat, or a volcano or hurricane. There are all sorts of "happenings" that can shorten *time,* and the final "happening" will be Jesus' return, or our death. The creativity of "today" will be just as important on "the last day," whatever makes it your, or my, last day. Creativity, beauty, human relationships, and work well done are important for the *now,* just as communication with God is to be a part of each moment, spontaneously and naturally.

But, you may ask, what did you *do?* When Debby left, Susan settled in for her time, helping to market and to grow alfalfa sprouts, bean sprouts, and sunflower seed plants for salads. She went off with her new-found friends Helen Kennedy, Bonnie Rylander, and Jean Smith (who were going to mean so much to us all) to pick apples that had fallen to the ground in Assisi Heights orchards—for free—and she made apple juice for her dad each morning and carrot and celery juice each night. A juicer was given us by Jack and Polly Todd in Pittsburgh, right away, so we started with this regimen immediately. It seemed that tons of books were being sent to us on diet, and piles of suggestions were being made by letter. Masses of vitamins were sent also (one man came from Texas to bring some, and another Texas friend supplied others). I tried to sort through it all and come up with a good balanced diet.

No matter what the weather, Fran walked three miles a day. He got a face mask for the very-below-zero days, but kept on walking. Usually he went along First Street to 15th Avenue S. W. and walked up to "Pill Hill," then down and around through town, back around the Mayo Clinic buildings and home. This was a three-mile circle. Susan walked with him at first; then when Priscilla came, she walked with him. In time Libby came to help— and the walk was a part of that "help," as it was with Linny's time with us, and much later, Ann Brown's. What was the matter with my walking? I developed bursitis in first one knee and then the other, and my walking was very "hindered," to say the least.

Day after day, as the deep snows of that cold winter covered lawns, outlined trees and roof angles, and tipped the window boxes and bushes, Fran would point to one house after another and remark on the beauty. "That one," he often said, as he started up 15th Avenue S.W., "reminds me of a Christmas card. It looks so lovely with those two pine trees against the white color of the house. I like the windows and the door. It's one of my favorites." "Yes, I agree," Prisca would reply, looking up at the lights in the upstairs window. "It's lovely." Both of them would have let out a bit of an unbelieving screech if someone had suddenly said in their ears, "You are looking at the future headquarters of L'Abri. . . . Glad you like it! You're going to see a lot of it some day." No one did. God doesn't usually announce things that way. They would trudge on up the hill, looking at other houses, perhaps stopping at the library for some more classical records. Franky had made sure his dad had a record player for his favorite music, and his first TV set. We joined Americans in a new way as Fran got "addicted" to football and cheered for his favorite teams.

November 13 I flew off to Cambridge, England. Priscilla was there to take care of her dad's juices, sprouts, and meals and to walk and to watch football with him! Hundreds of letters were coming, and I had written a two-page letter which Covenant Church's secretary kindly mimeographed for us, so that Fran and Prisca could answer letters more easily. Phone calls and visits were also numerous; a fair number of these were Christian leaders, but some were artists, football players, lawyers, newsmen. Forest Boyd and Cal Thomas called to have news for the Christian radio broadcasts, and soon literally thousands of people were praying for Fran. Right there in Rochester, however, we were experiencing an America we thought didn't exist any more—friendly Minnesota mailmen, storekeepers, taxi drivers, nurses, artists, plumbers, Mayo Clinic doctors and personnel, and so many other townspeople. We met people who had read our books and felt like old friends, people who offered to take us to go grocery shopping or to meet someone at the airport. It was a refreshing welcome, and we felt roots were beginning to grow. As our children came to be with us, we appreciated the sacrifice on the part of their spouses, doing double work to free them to be away. At such times "family" becomes an amazing sharing of work and burdens—a pulling together in a practical way, a giving of hidden gifts that only God Himself sees. This meant not only practical help but conversation that helped us to get "reacquainted" and be reassured of love that was more than an expression!

While I was away fulfilling promises I had made months before, a lot happened in Rochester. Fran had agreed to have a discussion with medical students after they watched the science episode of *How Should We Then Live?* That night he felt so dizzy he thought he couldn't speak . . . but, after a cup of tea, when the questions started, strength came in a sufficient quantity that he kept on for the full time. The second gathering was one of chaplains from the hospitals, arranged by Chuck (whose brother worked with Udo's brother Egon in Grace and Peace Church in St. Louis). The third meeting was in the auditorium of the Methodist Hospital, where doctors from Mayo Clinic and other staff members gathered to see the science film and ask questions. Just enough energy "was given" to carry on each time. It isn't that Fran felt great. Rather he felt he could ask for the Lord's strength in measure for the needs, and that it wasn't time to "give up" when he could be a help.

Fran had urged me to go to Cambridge, England, even though it was only a month since we had heard he had cancer. "I'll be all right with Priscilla's care, Edith, and it doesn't look like there'll be any change at present. The chemotherapy seems to be right for me, and I'll keep on with all the vitamins and things. You go on; don't break all those engagements. I'll pray for you as you go." Along with the letters I wrote to him to read while I was gone he has kept all the very wonderful letters and cards from our own children and grandchildren during those days. Then I flew out.

Michael Diamond, Vicar of St. Andrews the Less, and his wife, Sylvia, had been former Workers at L'Abri in Chalet Bethany. For a period of three years they had been praying that I would come to speak for three ladies' groups, and each time I had not been able to go because of the filming, or seminars, or other conflicts. Then I had promised that we would be through filming in October, and I could come in November. Meantime the "three meetings" had turned into nine speaking engagements of a most astonishing variety, and they were certain it had all been a tremendous answer to prayer on their part and the part of others there in Cambridge. Susan met me at London Airport and cared for me as we settled in at the Blue Boar, with its tiny old halls and small rooms, each with an electric teakettle—important equipment for the essential beverage! "Mother, you need something new for those three things on Sunday. . . . Let's go shopping." I had a brown skirt, so I was looking for a tailored brown velvet jacket and a matching turtleneck to go with my special brown and beige silk "square." That would look "right," we felt, for what was ahead of me. As we walked past the iron fences of Great St. Mary's, the official University of Cambridge church, we saw posters on the iron fence in various places, announcing "Edith Schaeffer—Prayer Today." "Susan, I don't believe it. It seems to me that it must be a practical joke of Franky's. I just can't believe I am speaking there." I felt like Mary Poppins, floating down on the town with a big black umbrella, an unreal dream. How could it be that relatively few months ago, I was scrambling around Cambridge piling up food on plates for the crew's lunch, carrying thirteen cups of coffee on a tray through the streets . . . and now, all these announcements! "Oh, Lord, please give me the right words, your words, so that I can fearlessly make known whatever you want me to say."

Sunday morning Ranald was sitting at Holy Trinity Church to shepherd me, with Margaret and a friend she had brought with her to "hear Nony," in the very seat he had occupied as a student so many years before when he had come to believe. And there I was, walking down the aisle with the procession, where

Charles Simeon had been vicar in the 18th century, the Reverend Michael Rees, the curate, and the choir singing. In that afternoon, I was to speak in Ridley Hall. The Reverend John Root introduced me and announced my topic, "Marriage and the Ministry," to be followed by a time for questions. The place was filled with seminary students, vicars and their wives, as had been the church in the morning, and I was overwhelmed by the warmth of the response, and the lingering for more questions. I must have spoken for over an hour and a half. Several of the men and women had been at L'Abri, and our books had been read too. Thinking back to Ranald's student time over twenty years before, I couldn't help feeling that it all had an "unreal quality."

Then came the evening. Now I was to speak at the prestigious great St. Mary's Church of England. Ran and I had been invited to the vicarage for tea, but had declined, because of the already tiring day. I wished I could have done that over again, to have had time to talk with the vicar's charming wife, whom I met later, but perhaps it really would have tired me too much. The enormous pillars and vast gothic ceilings seemed to have been there forever, like mountains. Walking up that aisle with the robed vicar and choir, in my little brown jacket, made me feel small indeed. But "Prayer Today" after all is something like giving a tray of coffee and cheese with brown bread, something to refresh a spiritual drop in blood sugar, isn't it? So I went on, and the Lord let me speak where the scholar Erasmus had spoken—Erasmus, who had published a New Testament in Greek, with the accepted version of the church in Latin in parallel columns. This had been put on the "prohibited list" by the Roman church when its "Index" of forbidden works was introduced some years later. But Erasmus walked up these same stones approximately 450 years ago; why was I here?

It was the "men folk" in my family—Ran, my husband, and the rest of them—who insisted that I accept this opening to speak on "Prayer Today," and the other subjects I'd been asked to do that week. "It is an unusual invitation . . . you must, mother" so I was being an obedient wife and mother . . . in a unique situation! Just before the final benediction, Rev. Booth-Cliburn took me back to the dusty room where an impressive and very ancient leather book, an enormous book, has been signed with names, one after another. For *how* many years? I don't know. I didn't see the first page, but I signed for that Sunday evening— "speaker"! People gathered around in the entry hall afterwards, and there were questions and answers. The Vicar is now the Bishop of Manchester, as in a few weeks from that time he was to be consecrated. Somehow the *timing* of the Tapestry's weaving struck me again. He would soon not be there.

Before the week was over, I had spoken in St. Andrew's the Less, at a women's conference, at Bedford for an annual dinner meeting, and at several other things, ending with an evening with professors' wives from Cambridge University. It was at that evening that my voice "departed" with a strangling kind of closed throat right in the middle of speaking. I thought I was choking to death. It really was frightening and someone finished the evening by reading a chapter of *L'Abri*. It had been raining all week, and I had developed a bronchitis, but hadn't stopped talking! As I flew back to Minnesota, I couldn't tell the stewardess whether I wanted tea or coffee; not even a whisper would come out by that time. But Sylvia and Michael at St. Andrew's were delighted with their answer to prayer and the subsequent results. Later, openings came for the film *How Should We Then Live?* to be shown in Cambridge, and Ranald and Jerram went at various times to answer questions.

Loving friends made it possible for us to go home to Switzerland for Christmas. The grandchildren, who had been afraid they might not see "Av" again in this life, were thrilled with that answer to their prayers for that year! When January 1979 arrived, Fran was still alive, and a new year was beginning. The chemotherapy was still following the twenty-one day cycle. It had been only three months since treatment had begun, but it seemed much longer. We couldn't see what improvement was going on inside— but then, we couldn't "see" the cancer that was racing through his body when he was doing all the difficult filming. "One-day-at-a-time" became an important measure to be constantly met. Strength of a variety of sorts was needed for a variety of kinds of days.

Don't picture Fran as having a smooth, easy time. There were ups and downs. The chemicals did affect him, and there were days when depression hit for a few hours. On the whole, I would say, having lived with him for so many years, that the way he went on in the midst of cancer, trusting the Lord, and continuing to care about other people—whether nurses and doctors, or others who came to him—was one of the greatest evidences I have had that the Lord *is* able to give His strength. Just naturally, Fran has always been impatient about illness and has not found even flu easy. The "sufficient grace" spoken of as being given to Paul with his thorn in the flesh I really could observe being given to Fran. I'm not glad he has cancer, but I am glad to have observed this reality. Fran himself has said frequently that, looking back over the time, he feels there are more pluses than minuses that he himself has observed in the way his life and work has gone during this time. There is more to life than being "comfortable" and "happy"; there is growth going on that the Bible points out is important and that we can recognize as very special.

That January the Zumbro Valley Medical Association and the Rochester Ministerial Association together rented the entire film series of *How Should We Then Live?* and hired the local John Marshall High School Auditorium for five consecutive Sunday nights. . . . "We know you are having chemotherapy, but would you mind coming and answering questions, if possible?" Fran wasn't sure he could, but said he'd try. Everyone thought about three hundred might turn up, but the first Sunday night there was a blizzard and the temperature dropped to 27° below zero. Who would come? To everyone's amazement fifteen hundred came . . . and each week there were more. After the film, Fran sat in a metal arm chair and asked, "Is there a question?" People lined up at the microphones that had been placed in the aisles, and questions never stopped until Dr. Chuck Kennedy, who chaired the meeting, stopped them. Questions came from a cross-section of ages; students, doctors, lawyers, pastors, engineers, musicians, artists, businessmen, women of varied professions, mothers . . . and when the weeks were over, people wanted "more, please."

Mary Lou Sather and her Mayo consultant husband Dr. Howard Sather invited a group of interested people to their home one evening in early March, and Dr. John Woods chaired the meeting to ask what further might take place. The conclusion of the evening, with about fifty there, was the formation of a L'Abri Conference Committee to look into the planning of a L'Abri Conference in Rochester, to be about ten days long, within another year. We were seeing a "beginning."

It was May when Fran and I sat waiting for his name to be called in the waiting room on the fifteenth floor of Mayo Clinic. We were praying for the news we would get, but also praying for all the others waiting—some of whom might be getting a major shock. We were so conscious of the fact that it is selfish and unkind to forget the importance of reports for others waiting too. Suddenly, "Dr. Francis Shaeffer" was called, along with two or three other names, and we walked to the hall which would take us to Dr. Pettit's office. I didn't exactly "walk"; I humbly hobbled along on crutches, because of my bursitis. I had not "sailed along" through all this strongly, but had an exhaustion, accompanied by bursitis, and had to "keep weight off" for a time.

Our news? . . . was fantastic at that time. All the details were there in scientific language, but one sentence stood out: "No lymphoma present"! The CAT scan showed the "watermelon" was no longer there; everything was normal. "We'll put the poison back in our pockets, in case it is needed again, but no more now," the doctor said. Fran's "word" for the radio audience was on this order, "Many whose faith is just as great as ours who have been praying for me for this longer time to make truth known, have been praying also for someone else as precious in the sight of the Lord . . . and their answer has been an opposite one. Stephen was being prayed for by the early church as he was being stoned, and he died. It was not a matter of 'small faith.' "

It is not denying God's answer to prayer to notice "the ravens that brought the bread and meat"! God weaves the threads of our lives with other lives, events, circumstances in space and time and history, for a variety of results. The weaving is complicated and marvelous. To deny the medical help of chemotherapy, the benefit of vitamins and juices, sprouts and good food; to deny the multiple wonder of a "new beginning" taking place in our own lives, and in the work of L'Abri even in those few months in Rochester—is to demand to know *exactly* how God works, and to deny the marvel of His doing many, *many* things at one time. Yes, we do believe God answered prayer, but we do also believe we cannot know the balance of all that went on. Rochester was meaning a great deal to us, and we did not believe it was a chance happening. Also we discovered that there were people, now very dear to us, in Rochester who had specifically prayed that we would come there, not knowing that it would take cancer to bring us. Who can know, until we can ask God face to face, all that is involved in The Tapestry?

At Easter Fran gave a strong sunrise message at Key Biscayne. It was not the usual sort of Easter message, not a romantic sunrise sweet prelude to Easter breakfast, and many hearts were stirred to *do* the will of the Lord in the whole of life, including fighting for the right of unborn people to be born rather than to be killed. It was a kind of prelude to the seminars coming in the autumn— a stirring battle cry to fight for truth and life and justice! People who expected Fran to be feeble and half-dead with chemotherapy were surprised. The Lord of life had given him life to speak that day.

A new step was taken in the lives of two who came to have Easter lunch with us, Anne and Jim Price, and once again only the Lord knows the extent of the weaving that took place that day. After a week's vacation in the sun and sea, we went back for the next check in Rochester, and to welcome Lisby, our first grandchild, who was coming to have a complicated tooth and jaw operation. Braces put on in childhood had done the wrong thing to her jaw, and Dr. Sather was to do repair surgery. It was a rare treat to have Lisby with us during a preparatory time, again one of those times deeply appreciated in spite of the circumstances. Lisby was not the only one with us from the Swiss L'Abri family at the time of the meeting about the L'Abri Conference. Also with us were John and Marie Claire Orting, who are now in Minnesota. John was one who came directly to L'Abri after Fran's Harvard lectures. The Tapestry was to have a pattern in Minnesota that had been started a long, long time before. A microscope brings out astonishing new detail that would be missed with the naked eye, and the swift glimpses we get of those details are minimal compared to what we will discover in the future.

Back in Switzerland we had a "normal" busy L'Abri summer. During one Workers' meeting on July 24 Jane Wysor phoned from Virginia to ask us to pray for Bill as he lay in a coma from which he would never recover. That evening of prayer, she felt, brought a miracle of the shortening of his agony and his rapid entrance into heaven—another one who had sent out the Family Letter now to join mother and dad. People are gathering. It is a real gathering taking place!

We left at the end of August to go back and have Fran's next checkup, in preparation for the seminars for the new film, *Whatever Happened to the Human Race?* Flying SwissAir into Boston gave us a chance to stop at Southborough where a new branch of L'Abri had been started. That is another story of prayer and answers and direction—with Barry and Veronica who had been in the work fourteen years in Huémoz, and Dick and Mardi Keyes who had been in Huémoz, then Ealing, then Greatham, covering about eight years. They were beginning the constantly "attacked" and not smooth physical and spiritual preparation for a Farel House there in Massachusetts. Ours was a brief glimpse, but long enough to feel something of their struggles in pioneering, and to pray with them.

It was long enough also to cause us to marvel as we looked back to 1936 when we had worked in the boys' camp in New Hampshire and prayed so earnestly for New England. At that time we had pictured ourselves opening closed churches and living "forever" in some New England town with a "lot of history." Now we had no idea at all that there was to be a "full circle" take place, within another year—that Franky and his family would be settling in an historic area, very close to the road we had driven in our Model A Ford car on our way to our summer job. As we looked out at the towns and villages in 1936, we would have loved to have gone to see our "son's home"—if we had known he was going to be there; if we had had any idea we were even going to have a son; if we could have seen him lugging his furniture out of a van container, forty-four years later. And if we had known that our fourteenth grandchild was going to be born nearby, forty-four years later also—John Lewis Schaeffer—we'd have stopped to have lunch to celebrate! (Our first grandchild, and our fourteenth, are the only two to have been born in America—one in St. Louis, one in Massachusetts.) But in 1936 we were still looking at the map of the world with curiosity, and we had very little to look back on and no child. And in 1979 we were being guided around the new L'Abri property, peering into the pond and exclaiming over the lawn, talking about the coming seminars with trepidation. "Sufficient unto the day is the trouble thereof" . . . as well as the surprises thereof. Any more would be too much.

The surprise to come next was that Fran developed a bad case of shingles just before the seminars started. Priscilla and Lisby were just about to leave the little brown house in Rochester, which the Sandris had been able to enjoy as a home during the summer of Lisby's ordeal. This had been partly vacation for them and partly L'Abri work, as a stream of people came to them there, and also as they came to know many of our Rochester friends. When Prisca left, Debby felt she should come to help in her dad's new misery. We bathed the spots gently with a solution of vitamin C, and gave him lots of vitamin C to take each day, *à la* the theory that it helps . . . and it very well may have. He had a miserable time, but when the seminar date arrived, he was able to travel in a jumpsuit, soft cotton that zipped up like a child's all-in-one overall, and only put on his other clothing for the seminar.

By the way—the *reason* Fran wears Swiss hiking knickers and knee socks all the time is simply that he found them so comfortable for hiking and cross-country skiing; as an adult, he felt he could wear what he pleased, and they are his favorite clothes that he feels most at home in. People who have been at L'Abri are accustomed to seeing him in gardens, hiking on trails, or sitting up on the fireplace discussing in the same clothing, so he simply didn't don dress-up clothing for filming such as he would wear for preaching or a dinner engagement. As a matter of fact, he hates new clothes, and shopping, so is hard to persuade, on the part of wife or daughters, to wear a gift jacket or shirt, though he does do it to please us. (There—that is a frequent question I've cared for.)

Poor Debby was to have a very sad affliction in Rochester that time, as she had a painful and difficult miscarriage, losing a very desired baby, with the added sorrow of having to be away from her husband during a time they would have chosen to be together. So, mother and daughter comforting each other in a difficult time, we went off together to Philadelphia for the premiere of the film, and the first seminar.

September 7–8, 1979. The Academy of Music was where Fran

and I had heard our first major concert together, sitting up in the "peanut gallery" in the cheapest seats to hear Stokowski conduct the Philadelphia Orchestra in 1933. It had been thrilling to have the gorgeous music surge through one's chest as well as to hear it with one's ears. But as Leopold Stokowski had young students stand up and sing with gusto the communist "International," we had kept our mouths firmly closed in resistance. (There are different kinds of resistance.) Now here were Debby and I, forty-six years later, with Genie in the box with us and old friends all around us waving from the audience, coming to put a hand on our shoulders—Lucinda (my niece) with her baby in her arms, L'Abri people from every year of L'Abri, friends from childhood days. It was an unmatched thrill of reunion. Our old hometown . . . and also Dr. Koop's hometown.

What a physical tingle of excitement ran through us as the film came on that huge screen, and the music poured forth. When Caruso sang here, he had commented on the marvel of the acoustics in the auditorium, among the best anywhere in the world. We were told that the special quality of sound results from the auditorium having been built directly above a natural cave. What a place to first see *Whatever Happened to the Human Race?*—with the Philadephia Children's hospital so close; with some of Dr. Koop's patients from episode two of the film sitting in the audience excitedly, with their parents and friends. We had with us Margaret Macaulay representing our other grandchildren, as well as Francis and Jessica, Debby and Genie. We had thought that glimpse of the uncut film might have been Fran's *only* view of it And now . . . he was not only to see it, but to speak and answer questions. What a blending of "threads" from all stages of our history, in one place, and for a purpose, not for a pleasure!

The pleasure was incidental. We were here again, in this same hall, not to sit with our mouths shut now in resistance, but to open our mouths in resistance. We were to open our mouths, to resist the treating of human beings as bits of disposable machine parts, whether unborn human beings, human beings born with a physical or mental defect, or old sick human beings who can no longer "contribute." We were to resist—not on the basis of a different political outlook or party, but on the basis of believing that truth exists, that an absolute exists, and that God who exists has spoken. Not only Dr. Koop and Fran and Dr. Jefferson were to speak and answer questions, but Franky was to speak, and I was to speak. Not only were the local coordinators to have an effective part of "the resistance" in their preparation, but Wendy and others who had arranged the auditoriums. Not only was Jim to line up the "timing" of each portion of the schedule to have precisely smooth programs without waste of time, but Barbara and individuals in each city were to affect what happened in sales of the books and study guides. The film was to speak, however, with its original music by Tim Simonec, and the original songs by Dallas Graham, as well as the visuals, including the animation by Ray Cioni. Margaret whispered in my ear, as the music crashed with the waves, or sang a lullaby to the hospital babies in intensive care, "Oh, Nony, I'll never forget Franky taking Kirsty and me to watch Tim direct the London Philharmonic Orchestra, as he watched the film and fit his own composition *exactly* to it. It was so exciting to watch it happen."

A combined "resistance" to twentieth-century "brain-washing" had been put together. Now we were to have the reality of clutching at each other's hands with wonder as we first saw and heard it all. When it came my time to speak, I looked up at that peanut gallery and imagined nineteen-year-old me, looking down at the orchestra, never dreaming there would be a moment to resist the tide of humanistic ideas in such a far-reaching way!

At the end of the second evening the audience rose unanimously. It was not just a standing ovation to the film, and to each one who had spoken, nor to what had just been said. It was far more than that—it was a rise in determination, far stronger and more determinedly being expressed, than the standing of the young people in 1933 to sing the ideals of communism. This crowd stood in a determined affirmation of resolve to *do something*— locally and nationally, with ones and twos, groups and cities, counties and states—about aborting people, whose ancestors some of us may be . . . or aborting our grandchildren's ancestors, who may be us. It was a determination to recognize the preciousness of human life. How thankful I am, I thought to myself that night, that Fran is still alive to help in this battle for life for others, and that although he made the film with cancer raging inside him, that at the moment it *is* arrested so that he *can* speak in twenty cities, and, with Dr. Koop and Dr. Jefferson, answer questions from people who never asked such questions before—let alone thought about the answers. This is taking what Fran has been saying for years into a further step of social action based on absolutes.

There were twenty seminars in auditoriums made to hold far more people than came. This means that the money to pay for the auditoriums was often not covered by the ticket sales. Some papers have reported that "Schaeffers were disappointed" in the seminars. Both Fran and I felt quite the opposite as to what took place among the people who did come. Fran wrote to a Texas law professor, John Whitehead, a friend of his: "I'm so glad you found 'Whatever Happened to the Human Race' helpful. Two things about the seminars: Edith and I have never seen meetings that ended with such intensity. Secondly, the low numbers clearly indicated a general apathy among Christians, but even more serious, an attitude among leaders to keep people away from the seminars so that their own acceptance by the surrounding culture would not be disturbed. Increasingly I feel that if we let this time and issue go, that the time may be past for any real changes for the country, society, or law."

We often remarked to each other that in our forty-five years of being involved together in camps, conferences, churches, meetings, L'Abri, etc., we had never had such an enthusiastic response by entire audiences, expressed in a variety of ways that meant people expected to go forth and *do* something. In Isaiah 58; 5, 6, 7, God speaks with distaste of fasting that is selfish, and indicates that sharing food with the hungry and clothing the naked is the kind of fasting that pleases Him. But in that same context the end of verse 7 speaks of not turning away from one's own flesh and blood. What more drastic and definite "turning away" can be done than to kill your own flesh and blood before it is born?

God's Word speaks not in easy platitudes, but with a penetrating power. That power, it seems to me, penetrated the audiences in these twenty cities, and people *have* gone forth to do much. There have been obstetricians who no longer do abortions, there have been congressmen and senators who have voted differently, there have been churches, colleges, high schools, army camps, etc., etc., who are showing the series and discussing it. People have affected the presidential and other elections. A spark fell into dry grass and began to burn!

In addition to having great expectations as to an ongoing set of results, in each seminar I had a pair of binoculars, so to speak, to see in the audiences "threads" that had formerly been woven into L'Abri. Here something was being added to the hundreds of letters Fran had been getting since his cancer, and we were finding out small bits of information as to the amazing "patterns" in other parts of The Tapestry; or, to change the figure, we were seeing some extent of the harvest. This privilege that was being given us, both in the letters, and in each city, some people have to wait for until they get to heaven. It was overwhelming to find where the L'Abri tapes were being listened to, as Iowa farmers told us of having their tractors equipped with good sound systems, and listening and praying as they drove around the fields, and doctors told of listening to L'Abri cassettes in their cars on the way to the hospital. One couple wrote, and also came to us, telling of how destroyed they had been in the '60s and then how, as atheists, they had gone out of curiosity to see *How Should We Then Live?* and had had one thing after another of their resistance to truth "knocked out." Now they wanted to greet us as "part of the family." "The Schaeffers disappointed"? We would have liked to have had more people involved at the time. But first, "the time" was a pure gift of the Lord in being allowed to "see more of The Tapestry" . . . and secondly, more, and more, and more, and more, and more people *are* being involved continuously. I firmly believe that God kept Fran alive to be involved in the making of this film in spite of cancer, and then gave him strength once again for the twenty seminars.

In February 1980 Fran's cancer came back full force again. The light maintenance dose of medication and the continuation of all the juices and vitamins did not maintain his excellent remission. Dr. Andre Gandur was troubled about his spleen and reappearance of glands. His breathing was labored, and speaking sounded as if he had just run uphill. We left for Mayo Clinic immediately after we had a time with Bill Buckley at our chalet—the next day, in fact. The CAT scan showed another collection of glands, half the size of what there had been before. There was water on the lungs. . . . The situation was grave. The very wonderful news was that a new heart test had been perfected for determining the heart's ability to tolerate more of the adriamycin in the COPA. Only a certain amount can be taken in a lifetime, and Fran had had almost the limit—unless his heart proved to be especially strong. The isotonic tin solution which had been injected into his veins was followed through its course by the scanner, and a kind of x-ray picture was thrown on the screen giving the doctors who could read it the answer they needed. Fran's heart was great— stronger than that of most healthy men of his age: "Go ahead with COPA again." Back in the familiar chemotherapy department of the clinic, lying on a bed in the cubicle, Fran soon had the intravenous drip in his arm. We were proceeding on the same route—with one big exception. Fran had declared, "If I feel well enough, I am going to keep my schedule." The schedule was a full one of travel and speaking, and chemotherapy was to be given in the veins every twenty-one days.

In a couple of days Fran said excitedly, "I had forgotten how it felt to breathe . . . it's wonderful." In two days' time we were in Pittsburgh, where we stayed with the Todds. They supplied him with juice and proper food, and he spoke at a Presbyterian Ministers' Conference, giving a rousing lecture, urging a firm stand on the truth of the Bible but also urging courageous action on the issues of the day. Right after that we left for Washington, D.C. There we stayed with the McDonalds whom we had known in Switzerland. We had met when he had come to Geneva as Ambassador Alonzo L. McDonald, Deputy Special Trade Representative and head of the U.S. delegation to the Tokyo round of multilateral trade negotiations. As they had a home in Villars, his wife, Suzie, had often come to L'Abri for chapel, or Saturday night discussions, and we had come to know them personally, having some good discussion. Now they had invited us to stay with them in Washington where President Carter had named him Assistant to the President and Director of the White House Staff.

Our reason for being in Washington was a dinner for congressmen and senators and their wives and some from the White House at which *Whatever Happened to the Human Race?* was being shown, with Fran speaking and leading a discusssion. Given in the Gold Room in the Rayburn Building, the evening was hosted by Senator and Mrs. William Armstrong, the Honorable and Mrs. Don

Bonker, and the Honorable and Mrs. Jack Kemp. There were over a hundred there, and people were very impressed by the film as a production of high quality and a thing of beauty, but also as an overwhelming "window" through which to see what is actually going on. Discussion was extremely encouraging, with well-formulated and pointed questions. Various people felt the film and book should be widely distributed. It was as if a realization had come to some as to how blinded they had been by "words," by terminology used as a soft cloak over a skeleton. That same feeling we had had in each seminar was there also: certainly some people meant to really *do something,* not just to discuss doing something.

The next day as I went to speak to Joanne Kemp's "Schaeffer Class," who were having a luncheon in her home, Fran went with Alonzo to his office at the White House for lunch with a number of invited people. McDonald's office was just one away from the Oval Office, and that noon he had also invited Susan Clough (Administrative Aide to the President), Esther Peterson (Special Assistant to the President of Consumer Affairs), Cecil Andrus (Secretary of the Interior), Bob Maddox (Special White House Assistant for Religious Liaison), and Linda Tarr-Whelan (Deputy Assistant to the President for Women's Concerns).

Lunch was brought into the office, beautifully served, and after Fran had been answering questions for some time, McDonald told him that he ought to take time to eat. McDonald himself would give a résumé of the book *How Should We Then Live?* which, Fran told me later, was a brilliant summary. It seemed a most worthwhile private discussion, with individuals. People are people; individuals have their own needs, wherever their talents have taken them in their careers. Future destination is what counts, not just "next job" but whether there is "an ending" ahead or "a new beginning."

Not only did I have a very warm and interesting time with Joanne's class but an evening of questions and answers with high school age young people and a few college ones—sons and daughters of our hosts and of the Kemps and other Washington friends. Lunch at the Congressional dining room, a quick view of the space museum and . . . swooooosh . . . our time in Washington was over. I trundled off a bit like Cinderella after midnight, looking for my gate to fly to Boston, while Fran went in another direction to Rochester—he to have the next chemotherapy, I to speak at Gordon College's Spring Banquet.

Time, when you begin to say, "And then . . . and then . . . and then . . ." can sound like a boring stream flowing by that never changes its speed or direction! Yet day follows day and year follows year, and we are coming to Easter again, 1980. When you are supposed to die in a short period of time, the dates are more appreciated; the "and thens" take on a bit of sparkle! "I guess the Lord has something more for me to do" makes the doing of it more crucial.

When cancer returns, does that cancel the answer to prayer, and the factors God used in giving that answer a year before, or months before? Do you say, "Oh well . . . see . . ." and shrug your shoulders? It seems to me that the whole idea of God's healing various physical ailments in this life has been twisted. The answers to prayer for physical needs in illness or depression, or whatever, are not judged by the length of time the person is in perfect health. It is false to judge the reality of what God has done by its "permanence." When we pray for food, the Lord doesn't indicate we are to pray for a five-year supply. "Give us this day our daily bread" is an indication of the frequency with which we are meant to ask. We are all to die sometime, unless Jesus comes back first, and there is no special "spiritual way to die" outlined in the Bible! Asking for a longer time to live is not wrong, but we do believe it is wrong to judge people's faith by whether a baby dies, or a ninety-year-old dies. That is another element of what "trust" is all about . . . and letting God be God.

Easter with a family dinner at Debby and Udo's (an unusual occasion, as we're not usually able to have that time as a family) was an unexpected "new beginning" as Franky whipped out a *Herald-Tribune*. Showing us an ad in it for an historic house for sale on the East Coast, he dropped a bomb! "What would you all think if we moved to America? . . . Listen to this—" Full of immediate imagination as we are in our family, we began to invite ourselves to pick apples and what not, but nobody really felt this was serious. One somehow doesn't expect changes to be "soon"—always a bit farther away. We'd been neighbors for a long time!

However, Franky was serious. He had been considering and

praying about his future work with books and films and his feeling that in this day and age being with one's wife and children as often as possible is a "must." Marriages and relationships need to be constantly worked on, and time together should be as constant as possible. He felt that much of his work would be on the American side of the Atlantic, so a move made sense. The Lord made very clear His direction, in one type of thing after another. Now our family is based in three countries, but with our working together as closely as ever. We didn't yet know how thoroughly Fran and I were to "have a foot on each side of the Atlantic," however, nor what amazing "new beginning" was on the horizon.

The English seminars for *Whatever Happened to the Human Race?* surprised us all. Dr. Koop and Fran felt there would be the same kind of lethargy as in America about attending. Not a bit of it! The auditoriums were full to overflowing, the questions were extremely sharp and to the point, and what has followed has been a continued stream of showings of the film in all parts of Great Britain, with results tabulated by the Lord! Who can tell what is going on inside heads, hearts, and bodies? We do have letters from women who have told us how much they "love that baby" they decided not to abort, so in that way we have glimpses of what went on inside!

For Fran and me England became a new country, as for the very first time Ranald was able to drive us from place to place for our speaking. It was comfortable in a borrowed car made available to Ran for us, and springtime in Yorkshire made James Herriot's books come to life. Susan came along for a few days . . . and we found we were given a totally new experience as compared to any we had ever had traveling by train. Tea in little cottages along the road and a meal in a house lived in by Christopher Wren took us back into the stream of history.

In London Fran went to a hospital for his chemotherapy injection by a doctor recommended by Dr. Petitt. Strange feeling, living with a battle against cancer cells while fighting another battle against people who want to kill people, and against ideas that breed a cold-chill attitude about any reason to live. While rigged up to an intravenous needle and tubes, Fran turned to greet a man the doctor brought to meet him. "Sorry; can't use this hand to shake. . . . Glad to meet you, Arthur Koestler." And under these strange circumstances Fran met a humanist he had quoted in *How Should We Then Live?* as one who had suggested a tranquilizing ingredient be placed in drinking water to stop aggressiveness. They had a short talk together and hoped to meet again! It's impossible to pick the time and place of the people the Lord thrusts into contact with us who may be the most important ones to talk to. The "being ready" aspect of Christianity means being ready to talk in the hospital, in a hut, on the street corner, sitting on a sidewalk, or in a fish market—not with a memorized spiel, but *to* the person who is there, with words that have some possibility of being understood—and listening with a desire to understand the other person, with compassion.

The L'Abri Conference Committee was made up of a cross section of Rochester people who had no organizational connection at all. They had meetings, divided up the preparation, and worked together to prepare for a ten-day period they weren't sure of. It was quite an amazing phenomenon. The local newspaper took an interest, and some of the best reporting we've ever had about L'Abri came out in it. Lovely posters appeared, as did ads in various papers and church magazines—all without any "direction" from L'Abri, except our attending committee meetings when we were there. It was a startling thing to find that people were writing to "L'Abri, Rochester," when at that time all we knew of was a ten-day conference, to happen once! The letters reached Mary Lou Sather, who became the secretary for the Conference, received endless amazing phone calls at all hours of the day (and, at times, night) and signed up people wanting to register.

People from points east, west, north, south converged on Rochester when the time actually came. John Marshall High School campus in this cold-in-winter prairie town suddenly bursts into green lawns, bushes, formal flower gardens and trees in the summer, as horticultural classes proudly produce a park rather than the expected school-yard look. The site of the meetings, it was blossoming now as the conference started, a bevy of chattering people sitting in groups of twos and threes, walking up the paths, perching on walls and grass in between lectures. Mary Lou and some others on the committee were faithfully sitting at a registration table, eventually recording 1987 names from 47 states, as well as a few from Venezuela, New Zealand, and Canada. These represented people of all ages, with diverse backgrounds, from almost every year of L'Abri's existence. The two film series were shown, and there were lectures by many of the L'Abri members, with six discussions taking place simultaneously in different rooms each evening. What was going on?

L'Abri seemed to be taking root in our new home. But—did we have a permanent home? Wasn't that time at the beginning of Fran's cancer just an interlude? Quickly walk up 15th Avenue S.W. as we are house-hunting one day and find that two houses next door to each other are for sale—the white one and a small green one, with back yards joining. The room at St. Mary's Hospital where Fran had told me he had cancer is within the view of windows from these houses, and they had been on the route of Fran's favorite walk. Could it be true, or a daydream of some too-imaginative person, that we were considering these two houses as a part of L'Abri?

The work in California L'Abri consisted mainly of sending out the Family Letters, sending receipts for gifts given to L'Abri, answering inquiries, sending out tapes, and having some discussion evenings. A new possibility brought a unanimous decision, as seventeen of our members at the L'Abri conference came to look at the two houses, to sit and pray *in* one of them. Unanimous? Yes, Francis and Edith Schaeffer, Dick and Mardi Keyes, Debby and Udo Middelmann, Barry and Veronica Seagren, Jerram Barrs, Ranald Macaulay, Larry and Nancy Snyder, Greta and Wim Reitkirk, Nick and Minna Cornelisse, Jane S. Smith, and Bob Jono— all voted "yes" to the motion to put the California property up for sale and to purchase these two houses in the shadow of St. Mary's Hospital; to transfer the Workers from California; to carry on the financial work and the other office work in Rochester. To make Rochester the headquarters of L'Abri in America, in other words, as far as *business* goes, but also to have an "open door" for tape listening, Bible studies, and discussions for "the people of the Lord's choice," as we would pray for Him to send the ones in need of help—patients, doctors, families waiting for news of patients . . . whomever the Lord might send.

The Lord made very clear the steps this time. They followed

like very evenly placed stepping stones, and soon after we left the conference, our furniture was being carted there by a man and his family from another Minnesota town. They had been at the conference and wanted to "help." With his truck they and other local friends, placed our belongings in the little house which was to be home when we are in Rochester, shared with Diane Gothrup, a single L'Abri Worker, who will live there all the time. The other house is now lived in by Libby and Lloyd Davies and baby Aaron, who was born in Rochester. Libby and Lloyd moved from the work in California too, and all three are carrying on the same work they had been doing there—plus! (Only God knows what the "plus" includes for any of us.)

Now when we go for Fran's checkup, we go home. Our home in America is Rochester, but it is not separated from L'Abri; it is L'Abri. The Lord has arranged it so that we are in our work there as much as we are in Switzerland. The cold windy night when we arrived, with chilled uncertainty, we had no idea in the most remote corners of our imagination that we were coming to as much a new beginning, as when we had endured the cold shiver of being outcasts from Champéry! The way God turns things for our good and the good of His work, and His glory, does not mean He has sent disaster, or cancer . . . but that the possibilities of what He can do *in* us and *for* us are breathtakingly *endless*—endless, that is, in this life with the limits of time; endless when we get our new bodies and make the discoveries we will have forever to make!

Rochester became a place of memories for the L'Abri family in both beautiful and terrible ways. Gail and Jim Ingram were married there by Udo Middelmann in Covenant Church, with both Gail's and Jim's families present. Jim is a L'Abri Worker in Mélèzes, talking to new arrivals and also lecturing, and Gail is Fran's secretary. As they live in the apartment in our chalet in Chesières and think of Rochester as their special memory, it gives us ties in a good way. Rochester was also the place where, during the conference, dear little one-year-old Sarah Snyder had an operation and in a few days' time died. She entered heaven the same day as Dick and Mardi Keyes' niece Lisa, who died in Philadelphia Children's hospital of cancer at five years old, but while the Keyeses were still close to Rochester in memory. Then,

Aaron Davies was born there in October, but during the conference there were those who were born into the Lord's family.
With our own both difficult and wonderful memories, somehow
L'Abri life as a family has been rooted there, as a transplant is
cut off a larger plant and stuck in the damp fertile ground.

My office in Chalet Chardonnet is what used to be a balcony.
On one side, windows take me out to the mountains; a tree wraps
me in on the other, its leaves pressed against the panes. The
mountains, the distance, and the enormous variety of rock forma-
tions, the snow, the trees growing to a certain altitude, the clouds
drifting past—can all be put into one short sentence. To describe
details of the leaves and twigs endlessly, would take more sentences, and end up shutting you "in." Papers and books, trophies
and plaques are covering the floor of the next room, so that it
is like crossing broken ice on a melting pond to get through them!
Each time I go in and out I kick something, and think guiltily
. . . "Oh dear . . . I'm telling about Fran's life, and they need
to know more of some of the things here." I just kicked two
cups by mistake, and the handle broke on one of them: ". . .
ooops . . . where's the glue . . . Gail?" They are souvenirs from
the "KUP" show in Chicago, a talk show Fran was on twice,
once with the economist Milton Friedman, with whom he still
has a good correspondence.

Like leaves, the papers cover the floor. I stop to read . . . *that's
Dutch, that's Finnish, that's Japanese, that's Spanish . . . oh, here's the
Eternity Magazine from 1969, I can copy this bit, it's English!*—Schaeffer's
The God Who Is There (Inter-Varsity Press), relating biblical Christianity to secular culture of our day, won the top prize and became
the 1969 Book of the Year by the largest margin in the contest's
nine-year history. His *Death in the City* (also Inter-Varsity) won
fourth place. It was the first time since 1962 that two books by
the same author ranked among the first six books. In 1971 *Eternity*
picked *The Church at the End of the Twentieth Century* (Inter-Varsity)
to tie for second place as the most significant book of the year.
It tied with Mark Hatfield's *Conflict and Conscience*.

In 1972 Fran had three books on the *Eternity* list: *He Is There
and He Is Not Silent* (Tyndale) took seventh place, *True Spirituality*
(Tyndale) took eighth place, and *Genesis in Space and Time* (Inter-

Varsity) tied for twelfth place. In 1977, *How Should We Then Live?* (Revell) tied for first place and received the *Eternity* brass plaque for the Book of the Year. And in 1979 *Whatever Happened to the Human Race?* by Schaeffer and Koop (Revell) tied for third place.

But—don't you see how boring it would be if I went on and described each "leaf" on that floor? There are three enormous volumes—*Who's Who In America,* for instance, has had Fran in it each year since 1978; *Contemporary Authors* has had both of us in it from 1977 onward; and *Men of Achievement,* an English production from Cambridge, England, has had Fran in it from 1980. There is a silver bowl that was presented to Covenant Theological Seminary by the student body in 1974. Each year there is inscribed on it the name of someone who has contributed greatly to the spiritual and academic life of the school during that year. It is called "The Francis August Schaeffer Award," and Fran was given a small replica of the larger bowl. There are special editions of books presented when one hundred thousand and two hundred thousand copies have sold, and there are the amazing translations. I have a wooden plaque with a medal on it—the Gold Medallion Book Award for my book *Affliction.*

But, like the leaves, they could go on and on, and a person's life is not made up of banana boxes kept under the eaves, of clippings of one kind or another, or awards of a variety of sorts. Can you imagine struggling to take them along with you to heaven? No, the reality does not come in earthly awards, but in the fulfillment of what the Lord has "required" day by day, hour by hour; in what He has "threaded us into the loom" to do in a lasting, *lasting* work, which brings a lasting treasure which doesn't gather dust and which grows more beautiful as time goes on because the Master Artist has had something to do both with the work (giving His strength with which to do it) and with the reward which is being kept as a surprise.

"All those books sold? What about the films? Aren't there royalties?" This questions comes to some people's minds, and other people's lips. Fair enough. When we wrote our first books, we honestly knew so little about publishing that the first royalties came as a surprise. We have always given all our honorariums to L'Abri. Naturally, when we speak, the travel expenses and hotel are cared for by the place that has asked us to speak. When

I tell of crossing the ocean, almost always a speaking engagement has cared for that travel. But the honorarium we do not keep.

When royalties came to us, we turned them over to L'Abri also. At first the Members voted we should have half of them back, and we gave a quarter to the Workers, to be divided among them. As time went on, we felt a "struggle"—akin to the struggle all human beings seem to have, in one way or another, when they begin to have "more." When Paul said he "learned to be content," it was something he learned by knowing what it was to be in need and what it was to have plenty. We felt there was a very real victory in our struggle and an advance in what we were learning when we had our contracts written so that royalties all go to L'Abri and we receive a salary. The temptation had been to put our own "aside."

Now, you may ask, "Does L'Abri have enough from royalties to care for it?" No—with ours, and those from the other L'Abri writers combined—not at all. Way back in the beginning of this story when we first started to pray for our needs, we were praying for a total of about 350 dollars a month. Remember that the dollar brought 4.34 francs in those days. Now, with the dollar down to 1.85 as of this writing (it went once to 1.35, but has recently begun to come "up") and with inflation, plus the growth of L'Abri to a chapel and Farel House and ten chalets in Switzerland (with other chalets rented by married students with families), plus branches in Holland (Eck en Weil), England (Greatham), America (Southborough and Rochester), and now Sweden (still connected to Swiss L'Abri)—the total monthly need we are praying for amounts to between 65,000 and 70,000 dollars! We are still relying on the Lord to supply by putting the needs on the minds of the people of His choice, and we honestly consider the writing of the books, and the sale of them, the making of the films and the percentage that comes from them, as the Lord's way of making up for the "low dollar," or His way of making the "total" come out right. It is His arithmetic.

We have learned to have less and to have more . . . but the thing all Christians should remember is that this can go in both directions, and we can have very much less suddenly and still "learn to be content." Trust can only be practiced when there is a *danger* of fear or shaky lack of trust. It is when we turn to the Lord and say, "I trust You; forgive my lack of trust and help me to trust You more," that we take a tiny step forward in a reality of love, the kind of love that brings joy to the Lord. There are a lot of areas in which we can exhibit trust, but one clear human area is both in praying to whom to give and what to give, and in praying that the Lord will supply our need, whatever that might be. Yes—in all four areas, L'Abri still lives by prayer, with the basic reason or purpose being that we would continue to have our lives and the work be a demonstration of God's existence in a world that has so largely turned away from Him.

It is spring 1981, time for the family reunion again. We will all gather on the quay, with roller skates, tricycles, bicycles, scooters, and a rope I bought near that village in Kenya . . . and go "together" and "apart," converging and spreading out, standing at times beside Castle Chillon. It has been two years and a half since Fran found he had cancer, and the children have been praying for "Av" faithfully. We are thinking and talking, wondering, musing . . . marveling and being thankful. What we have seen, lived through, watched happen, been a part of together through the years, has no human explanation. We are conscious of each other's weaknesses, and each of our own weaknesses. We know there is nothing about ourselves that brought about L'Abri or the books we have written among us, or the films; nothing that would explain the results that have taken place. We know that the resources—whether material, spiritual, intellectual, emotional, or the diversity of talents and the strength to do gigantic amounts of work in the midst of fatigue and frailness of one kind or another—have been resources given by the Lord. Other people might have their theories, but we stand shaking our heads. There is so little we really know, isn't there?

We watch the young brown swans and the mature white ones sailing along together—a family reunion too, sailing past the lapping water of the castle's foundations. A group of tourists pass us. What do they know about François Bonivard's feelings and thoughts when he was chained in the dungeon of the castle they are about to enter? What do they care? But—what do they know about the three generations of Francis A. Schaeffers they are looking at as they pass us? What do they care about the grandfather with cancer, the son with decisions before him about his next

piece of work, the grandson skipping stones in the lake? We could touch each other, but we know nothing about the tourists' hopes or fears, their purpose in life, or their base for making decisions or choices. Do we really care? We've now been in one family a long time, differing lengths of time. There's John Lewis, now six months old, in Switzerland for his first time. He hasn't been in the family so long! There's Hannah Emily Middelmann, born on our forty-first wedding anniversary at 3:45 P.M. so her daddy could come to our party! She hasn't many years to remember. In the Sandri family, there's Lisby, nineteen . . . but we've been in Switzerland thirty-three years! There's Becky, seventeen, and Rodman, twenty-five, and Giandy, eleven. Here are the English cousins—Margaret, eighteen; Kirsty, fifteen; Fiona, eleven; Ranald John, eight . . . Then the other Middelmanns—Natasha, thirteen; Samantha, eleven; and Naomi, seven. The Schaeffers have Jessica, ten, as well as the two boys. We make twenty-five people altogether! Do people think we are a "school"? Many of them don't really know what a family is—nor are they conscious of what three generations look like when all enjoying each other! This is a rarity—like seeing a herd of giraffes or something.

We're a family. A close family. But it doesn't come just by having children. There has been work. There has been agony. Mistakes have been made, and times of "spoiling" have taken place in relationships . . . but glue has been sought for the broken cup handles of our relationships, and ivy has been repotted time after time in our misunderstandings. But—our family isn't a finished product like a Rembrandt hanging in the museum, or a piece of Bach that doesn't change. We aren't "finished"; we haven't "arrived." We're a mobile. We are changing. We are shifting generations gradually. One day Fran and I will be ancestors to another generation, perhaps while we are still living, but another day we will join the family in heaven to await our bodies, and we'll be "put of sight," as the Prisoner is now!

The art work, the career, the symphony of a "family" is *never* finished. But death doesn't break it, nor does death put a hole or a tear in The Tapestry. We as threads are important for the time we've been woven in, during our present history, and we have had significance in affecting past history. We know nothing about the future, but whether we are to be here longer, or whether we are to go to be in heaven earlier than anyone expects, we will be affecting future history. We cause ripples that never end, just like the ripples being caused as all the boys and men now skip stones in the lake. Our ripples go on and on.

The end of this book is the middle of The Tapesty. It's still on the loom. But one thing we know . . . whether the "ending" of our thread in the pattern is sooner or later, we approach a new beginning, and not an ending. Our new beginning is a promise made by the true living God who never breaks His promises. The work of His hands—all of His creation, we are told—will be folded up and put away, and He will create a new heaven and a new earth for that new beginning ahead of us.

Wait a minute . . . aren't we part of His creation? Yes—we are a portion that lasts longer than the rest of creation. We've already been given a new beginning that will never have an ending, and the possibility of strength to live forever, because we've been given eternal life!

LIST OF PHOTOGRAPHS

About the Schaeffers:

Edith Schaeffer's gifts of creative energy, intellectual verve, and warm hospitality helped create the international Christian community known as *L'Abri* (The Shelter). To this spiritual retreat have traveled thousands of questioning men and women from many cultures. At *L'Abri* they have examined the basic Christian truths that God exists, that He is both infinite and personal, and that He may be known by us. Centered in Huemoz, Switzerland, *L'Abri* now operates also in Greatham, England; Eck en Weil, the Netherlands; Southborough, Massachusetts; and Rochester, Minnesota. Edith Schaeffer's nine other books, including *Commonsense Christian Living, Lifelines, L'Abri, Affliction, Hidden Art, Christianity Is Jewish,* and *What Is a Family?,* have sold well over 1,000,000 copies in the United States alone, and have been translated into twelve languages.

Francis A. Schaeffer achieved world renown as advocate and defender of biblical Christianity. His writings and the films in which he appeared made him known to millions as an authority on modern culture from the perspective of biblical Christianity. Dr. Schaeffer was the author of twenty-three books that have sold more than 3,000,000 copies in the United States and have been translated into twenty-seven languages. His last book, *The Great Evangelical Disaster,* was finished in the hospital only a few weeks before his death on May 15, 1984. Among his other books are *A Christian Manifesto, True Spirituality, Escape from Reason, The God Who Is There,* and *He Is There and He Is Not Silent.* Two other books (written with Dr. C. Everett Koop) have become highly acclaimed films on Christianity and the crisis in human values—*How Should We Then Live?* and *Whatever Happened to the Human Race?* Both films were produced and directed by the Schaeffers' son, Franky A. Schaeffer V.

About *The Tapestry:*

To some, the name Schaeffer recalls *Time* magazine's phrase "the missionary to the intellectuals." To others, the name means *L'Abri* and brings to mind the spiritual center in the Swiss Alps that welcomes searching people from all over the world.

In recent years, millions have come to know about the work of Francis and Edith Schaeffer. Through the Schaeffers' own writings, and through films, radio and TV interviews, and countless magazine and newspaper articles, this remarkable partnership has attracted international attention.

Who, really, are these two memorable figures? In *The Tapestry*, we come to know the Schaeffers through their personal recollections, brought to life in Edith's perceptive, warmly detailed writing. We accompany them not only in the events of their lives—both ordinary and extraordinary—but, most important, in the development of their thinking. We experience with them their constant awareness of and total dependence on God's presence and working in their lives.

Here are the Schaeffers . . . .

• As children growing up in strikingly contrasting homes: Francis in a hard-working but religiously indifferent family, rooted in a German neighborhood on the outskirts of Philadelphia; and Edith, born in China to missionary parents, growing up to experience the validity of Christianity in diverse cultures.

• In their college years, as idealistic students, discovering their dreams and their love for each other, intimately shared through letters excerpted in this book.

• As committed students of the Bible who rely on its perspective to understand all of life, including the arts, philosophy, science, and political issues.

• In their struggles and triumphs within the setting of denominational conflicts.

• As a loving family (parents of four, grandparents of fourteen) who champion true and fulfilling Christian values of marriage and family life.

But it is not necessary to know the Schaeffers' identity to become caught up in reading *The Tapestry*. By any standard, Edith Schaeffer is a topflight writer. The story she tells spans several generations, a fascinating family saga with broad sweep and riveting power.

For Edith Schaeffer, each person who appears in *The Tapestry* is a colorful thread, adding to the fabric already begun in the total tapestry of history. In their actions and interactions, each person helps to weave the pattern that eventually emerges. As the family story progresses, Edith Schaeffer compels us to focus our attention upon the effect that individual choices—even seemingly unimportant ones—have in the total fabric. Above all, she demonstrates vividly and unforgettably that all things in believers' lives—frustrations as well as fulfillments, sorrows as well as successes—work together for good, for truth, for beauty, to those "who love Him, and who have been called according to His purpose."